DIXIE REDUX

DIXIE REDUX

Essays in Honor of
Sheldon Hackney

Edited by

Raymond Arsenault
and Orville Vernon Burton

NewSouth Books

Montgomery

NewSouth Books
105 S. Court Street
Montgomery, AL 36104

Copyright © 2013 by NewSouth Books.
Individual essays are copyright © 2013
by the respective authors unless otherwise noted.

Library of Congress Cataloging-in-Publication Data

Dixie redux : essays in honor of Sheldon Hackney /
edited by Raymond Arsenault and Orville Vernon Burton.
p. cm.
Includes bibliographical references and index.

ISBN: 978-1-58838-297-9 (hardcover)
ISBN: 978-1-60306-275-6 (ebook)

1. Southern States—History. 2. Confederate States of America—History.
3. United States—History—Civil War, 1861-1865. 4. Southern States—Race
relations—History. 5. Southern States—Politics and government—1865–1950.
6. African Americans—Civil rights—Southern States—History. 7. Civil rights
movements—Southern States—History—20th century. I. Arsenault, Raymond,
author, editor of compilation. II. Burton, Orville Vernon, author, editor of
compilation. III. Hackney, Sheldon, 1933– honoree.
F209.D594 2013
305.800975—dc23

2013034903

Edited and designed by Randall Williams

Printed in the United States of America

To Francis Sheldon Hackney
(1933–2013)

and his loving family:
Lucy Durr Hackney
Virginia Hackney (1958–2007)
Fain Hackney
Elizabeth Hackney McBride
Alexander "Z" Hackney
Annabelle Hackney
Lucy Hackney
Samantha Hackney
Declan McBride
Jackson McBride
Larkin McBride
Madison McBride

Contents

Sheldon Hackney and Southern History

Raymond Arsenault and Orville Vernon Burton

D*ixie Redux: Essays in Honor of Sheldon Hackney* is a book born of respect, admiration, and affection. All of the contributors to this volume are deeply indebted to Sheldon Hackney—many as colleagues, some as former students, and others as intellectual collaborators. The eighteen authors of the essays in this volume represent but a small fraction of the thousands of individuals who have benefited from his long and distinguished career as a historian, professor, university administrator, and public intellectual. Mentor, teacher, friend—he has fulfilled all of these roles with integrity, grace, and a rare intelligence leavened by wit, humility, and compassion.

Sheldon Hackney's strength of character—why he has meant so much to so many of us—undoubtedly is rooted in both nurture and nature. But it is also firmly grounded in a lifelong inquiry related to issues of race, regional culture, civil rights, social justice, national identity, and democracy. While Sheldon was destined to spend most of his life north of the Mason-Dixon line, the American South—his native region—has always been the focal point of his search for a "usable past." Fascinated by the ironies and complexities of Southern history, and keenly aware of the region's shortcomings—especially on matters of race, class, and gender—he has pursued historical understanding of Southern myths and mores not only for the sake of scholarship but also as a means of promoting social change and humanistic values. His determination to replace self-serving mythology with truth-telling history has taken him from the darkest recesses of the region's archives to the open debates of the academy and the national public arena. Yet in many ways he has remained a son of the South, affirming and sustaining his regional ties through vigilant criticism and concern.

It is in this spirit that we offer the essays of *Dixie Redux* as a reprise of the themes and questions that have propelled Sheldon Hackney through a lifetime of scholarly engagement. In *Rabbit Redux*—the inspiration for our title and the first of three sequels to the bestselling 1960 novel, *Rabbit Run*—the writer John Updike gives us a second look at the life of his harried, suburban protagonist, Harry "Rabbit" Angstrom.[1] Updike's revealing continuation of the Angstrom saga represents the literary equivalent of what we are trying to accomplish in this book. By reexamining Sheldon's South, we hope to bring fresh insight and added nuance to our understanding of regional history and culture.

While the individual essays in *Dixie Redux* take us down varied pathways—history and biography, analysis and narrative, humanities and social science—our common goal is to extend Sheldon's legacy, to pay tribute to him through the practice of imaginative historical research and writing. By relating personal stories and experiences to the larger saga of regional history and by "asking large questions in small places," to use a phrase popularized by the noted historian and folklorist Charles Joyner, we aim to expand the explorations initiated by Sheldon's generation of historians.[2]

As the first cohort of regional scholars to take advantage of the interdisciplinary opportunities and methodological innovations of the 1960s, Sheldon and his peers brought enhanced explanatory power to the sub-field of Southern history. At times, these "new political and social historians," as they liked to call themselves, may have strayed a bit too far from the rich tradition of storytelling that had made Southern history so compelling to the reading public. But the best among them—Sheldon included—never lost sight of the human and contingent dimensions of historical change.

Connecting the local to the universal in Faulknerian fashion, he and others mounted a broad-based and largely successful challenge to the confining dogmas of regional historiography. While some interpreters of the Southern experience remained mired in the romantic illusions of patriarchal, elitist, and white supremacist mythology, most moved towards a more inclusive and open-minded approach to historical study. By the end of the 20th century, many of the South's most hallowed historical shibboleths had lost most of their authority among professional scholars. Relegated either to the manifestoes of reactionary politicians or to the margins of popular culture, the once-dominant interpretations of slavery, Civil War, Reconstruction, Solid South politics, and a host of other topics mercifully had fallen by the wayside.

Thanks to the prodigious efforts of Sheldon and other insurgent historians, the neo-Confederate meta-narrative is now all but gone from the academy. Yet, as the essays in this volume tacitly acknowledge, there is still much to do. The South, like all regions of the nation, still presents us with important historical puzzles to solve and many important and intriguing stories to tell. With this in mind, we begin with the story of the man who inspired us to write this book.

Born in Birmingham, Alabama, on December 5, 1933, Francis Sheldon Hackney was the third son of Cecil Fain and Elizabeth Morris Hackney.[3] Though a child of the Great Depression, Sheldon—as he was known from early childhood—escaped the worst ravages of hard times. Throughout the 1930s, his father found steady work as a newspaper reporter and editor for the *Birmingham Age-Herald*, while his mother stayed at home to raise three young sons—Fain, Morris, and Sheldon (two more sons, John and Rob, were born in the 1940s). Like most of their neighbors in the Mountain Brook section of the city, the Hackneys were white, middle-class, Protestant, and solidly Democratic in their politics. Their ethnic roots were predominantly English and Welsh, and both parents could trace their regional lineage back to the antebellum South, Cecil to Georgia and Elizabeth to southern Alabama.

Though only one generation removed from the farm, Sheldon's parents had grown comfortable with the pace of city life, developing strong ties to local institutions such as the Highland Methodist Church. The Hackneys were devout Methodists, and as a teenager Sheldon came under the influence of a liberal young preacher. This early exposure to the social gospel, he would later insist, represented one of the major formative episodes of his moral and intellectual development. As he grew to maturity, responsibility for the welfare of others and a restless questioning of orthodoxy became key elements of his character, and the spiritual basis of both remained with him throughout his life.[4]

The trajectory of that life was also greatly affected by World War II, most obviously by his father's enlistment in the U.S. Navy following America's entry into the war. For a time, Cecil Hackney's duties as a political information officer took him and his family to the vibrant city of New Orleans, to which Sheldon would return many years later as president of Tulane University. But the Hackneys spent the majority of the war in Nashville, Tennessee. At the close of the war, Cecil returned to Birmingham and civilian life, but the family's connection to Naval service was far from over. Three of the five Hackney brothers eventually joined the Navy, with Morris attending the Naval Academy at Annapolis and Fain serving in the Navy and dying in a military plane crash in 1954. Sheldon followed with five years of national service later in the 1950s.

In the immediate post-World War II years, Sheldon attended the Jefferson County public schools, where he earned a reputation as a gifted student and an outstanding athlete. At Ramsay High School, he played varsity tennis, launched a brief political career with an unsuccessful run for student body president, and graduated near the top of his class in 1951. After completing the required credits for graduation in December, he took several spring-semester classes at nearby Birmingham-Southern College before enrolling at Vanderbilt University in the fall of 1952.

One of the South's most prestigious universities, Vanderbilt proved to be a good fit for an inquisitive but ingenuous 18-year-old boy who was not quite sure what he wanted to do with his life. Supported by a Naval Reserve Officer Training Course (NROTC) scholarship, he gained confidence, direction, and a solid general education during his four years in Nashville. Majoring in history, he took several courses from Dewey Grantham, a prominent scholar of post-Reconstruction Southern politics, and developed a parallel interest in political science.[5] Along the way he became a voracious reader and a budding writer with an appreciation for the literary arts, especially after he took a series of English courses in which he encountered vestiges of the Regionalist persuasion that had dominated the Vanderbilt humanities scene in the 1920s and 1930s. John Crowe Ransom, Allen Tate, Robert Penn Warren, and their fellow Fugitive-Agrarians were no longer in Nashville, but the notion that regional history and culture should be taken seriously was still very much alive during Sheldon's years at Vanderbilt.[6]

His intellectual engagement with the "Old South vs. New South" issues posed by the Regionalists would stand him in good stead in later years. Yet, for Sheldon, there would be no easy resolution of these issues, no dependable balance sheet of the costs and benefits of modernization. Indeed, how could it have been otherwise for a young man coming of age in the midst of massive and often bewildering change? By the time he graduated in the spring of 1955, in the wake of the "with all deliberate speed" dictum of the second *Brown* decision, there was no longer any doubt that the South had entered a critical period of political, social, and racial realignment. With the acceleration of urbanization and industrialization, Eisenhower Republicanism's emerging challenge to Solid South politics, the deepening of Cold War anxieties, the recent quickening of the civil rights movement, and the looming specter of a Second Reconstruction, the proverbial center simply could not hold. Although the Korean War was over, the redemptive struggle for the soul of the South was just beginning.

Fear of impending desegregation was almost universal in the white South during these years, and college classrooms were among the few places where even a quasi-rational discussion of race could take place. In Sheldon's case, college life reinforced his doubts about the wisdom and morality of Jim Crow institutions. Even though there were no black students at Vanderbilt, his occasional crosstown visits to the Fisk University campus gave him his first glimpses of a restive black youth culture yearning for respect. These experiences fostered a growing awareness that something important was stirring in the black South, something beyond the self-serving stereotypes perpetuated in the white community.[7]

Sheldon's openness to racial iconoclasm and liberal ideas became even more apparent in late 1955 and early 1956, during a fateful postgraduate year at Vanderbilt. While completing the NROTC requirements for his commission as a junior naval officer, he also took an array of graduate-level history courses, several of which explored important aspects of the Southern past. This was also the year that he fell in love with like-minded Lucy Judkins Durr, a bright and precocious Radcliffe student from Montgomery, Alabama. Based in part on shared values of tolerance and social responsibility, their courtship and subsequent marriage would lead to more than a half-century of commitment and creative striving. As an admiring friend later put it, their relationship "was a deeply loving one, companionate in all ways. . . . Lucy and Sheldon's visibly abiding affection for each other, their kindred commitments, and their devoted parenting put Lucy at the very center of Sheldon's life and vice versa."

The Vanderbilt years also laid the foundations for Sheldon's eventual absorption with matters of race and region. However, his first direct experience with racial integration did not come until 1956, when he entered the United States Navy. The desegregation of the armed services had begun in 1948 and was not yet complete. Still, Sheldon's five years as a junior officer took him well beyond the boundaries and cultural constraints of Alabama and Tennessee, widening his vision of the world and further opening his heart and mind to racial justice and democratic values.

He spent most of these years at sea, cruising the Atlantic, the Caribbean, and the Mediterranean on a destroyer, the U.S.S. *James C. Owens*. But in 1957 he came ashore long enough to marry Lucy Durr. The couple's June wedding took place in Lucy's hometown of Montgomery, a mere seven months after the city's year-long bus boycott had ended in triumph for Rosa Parks, Martin Luther King Jr., and the pro-desegregation Montgomery Improvement Association (MIA). The city was still reeling from the shock of change, and much of the white community was under the spell of reactionary politicians counseling massive resistance. Among the few local whites applauding the desegregation of Montgomery's buses were Lucy's notoriously liberal parents, Clifford and Virginia Foster Durr.[8]

Staunch advocates of civil rights and civil liberties, the Durrs had been involved in struggles for economic, political, and social justice since the early years of the New Deal. Closely identified with Virginia's brother-in-law, Alabama's stalwart New Dealer—Senator and later U.S. Supreme Court Justice Hugo Black—they became one of Washington's most visible and controversial political couples by the late 1930s. When Cliff's work with the Reconstruction Finance Corporation ended with a principled resignation in 1941—he objected to federal contracts favoring war profiteers—President Franklin Roosevelt promptly appointed him to the Federal Communications Commission. Seven years later he resigned again, this time after refusing to sign a loyalty oath recently imposed by the Truman administration. Returning to private law practice, he specialized for a time in defending the constitutional rights of government employees accused of disloyalty or subversion. But after discovering that he could not support his family with this kind of work, he abandoned the political hothouse of Washington, moving briefly to Colorado to assume a position with the National Farmers Union before relocating to Montgomery in 1951.[9]

Cliff had hoped to find a more peaceful style of life back home in Alabama.

Yet the rising notoriety of his highly political wife foiled his escape from Cold War controversies. Full of vinegar and righteous indignation, Virginia had devoted more than a decade to a full-scale assault on racial discrimination and disfranchisement, mobilizing a circle of Washington-based Southern liberals and organizing a movement to repeal the poll tax. In the process, she had moved to the left, eventually allying herself with Henry Wallace and running unsuccessfully for a Virginia U.S. Senate seat on the Progressive Party ticket in 1948.

After their relocation to Montgomery, the Durrs remained true to their progressive principles, despite being labeled as dangerous subversives by Senate investigators and other conservative Cold Warriors. Defying regional convention, Cliff's law practice often involved representation of black clients, including Rosa Parks, who did occasional seamstress work for the Durr household. When Parks was arrested in December 1955 for refusing to give up her bus seat to a white rider, Cliff, along with local NAACP leader E. D. Nixon, arranged for her bail.[10]

Sheldon's marriage into the activist Durr family changed his life beyond recognition. As a boy growing up in Birmingham, and even as a college student, he had never met people with such iconoclastic convictions, people willing to speak out forcefully against injustice and intolerant orthodoxy whatever the cost. With its bracing vision of interracial democracy and cultural liberation, their worldview was new to him. It was also inspiring, and before long he, too, embraced the tradition of dissent that the historian Carl Degler would later call "The Other South."[11]

Sheldon's in-laws introduced him to a wide variety of activists and intellectuals, especially after he and Lucy moved to Annapolis and the greater Washington area in 1959. Assigned to the Naval Academy for the last two years of his enlistment, he began to think seriously about the possibility of additional graduate work and a career as a professional historian. Fortunately, the Durrs' circle of friends included C. Vann Woodward, the dean of Southern historians and a professor at nearby Johns Hopkins University in Baltimore. When Sheldon first met him in 1961, Woodward had just published *The Burden of Southern History*, a major collection of essays on the search for Southern identity. Already familiar with Woodward's classic works, *Tom Watson: Agrarian Rebel, Origins of the New South, 1877–1913*, and *The Strange Career of Jim Crow*, Sheldon was drawn to the idea of studying under someone who had dedicated his life to the exploration of race, class, and the paradoxes of regional politics.[12]

Sheldon's original intention was to apply to Johns Hopkins, but when Woodward left for a position at Yale in the fall of 1961 the student followed the teacher to New Haven. The next four years in Connecticut brought a whirlwind of activity as Sheldon faced the challenges of a rigorous graduate program while he and Lucy raised a family of three small children—Virginia, Fain, and Elizabeth. Exposure to several of the nation's best historians, including Woodward, Edmund Morgan, and John Morton Blum, sharpened his skills and deepened his interest in political history, especially the often picaresque and dysfunctional politics of his native South.[13] Intrigued by the political traditions and peculiarities of his home state, he decided to write a dissertation that examined ideological and electoral continuity between Populism and progressivism in post-Reconstruction Alabama. This dissection of sequential reform traditions led him into uncharted areas of social theory and quantitative methods, necessitating long hours in the computer lab and extended research trips to the state archives in Montgomery.

Set against the backdrop of an intensifying struggle over civil rights, Sheldon's periodic visits to Alabama reinforced his sense of the social and political relevance of historical research. During the turbulent early 1960s, Alabamians and other Southerners seemed to be burdened with many of the same problems—most notably disfranchisement, racial bigotry, and political demagoguery—that had plagued the Populists and progressives at the turn of the 20th century. As his mentors at Yale had predicted, the task of uncovering the roots of the region's continuing dilemmas was a worthy enterprise that would allow him to combine his dual interests in historical scholarship and social change.

In 1965, just as the voting rights struggle in Alabama and Washington was coming to a climax, Sheldon accepted an instructorship in history at Princeton. With his dissertation largely completed, he packed up his family and moved 130 miles closer to the South and a career as a professional historian. At Princeton he joined a talented cadre of historians, several of whom—Wesley Frank Craven, Arthur S. Link, James M. McPherson, Martin B. Duberman, and James M. Banner Jr.—shared his interest in Southern and regional history.[14] As a junior faculty member, he quickly gained a reputation as a dedicated and inspiring teacher, especially among the students in his popular undergraduate course on the history of the South. From his opening statements on the colonial origins of slavery to his tantalizing closing lecture—"Taps for the Southern Mystique?"—he held Southerners and Northerners alike in rapt attention. Every aspect of his professorial life, from mentoring graduate students and training research assistants to organizing a campus American Civil Liberties Union chapter and chairing a special task force on black life at Princeton, was conducted with genuine enthusiasm and careful attention to detail. He also taught in a special Upward Bound program, collaborated with colleagues Dorothy Ross and James Banner in the creation of an innovative team-taught course on American social history, and helped found the university's Afro-American Studies Program in 1969.[15] And, to the amazement of friends and colleagues, he somehow managed to fit it all in without any noticeable lapses in quality or commitment. With his understated Southern manner and disarmingly unpretentious competence, Sheldon was, as one former student later put it, the "quintessence of cool."

Only the members of his immediate family had any real sense of the difficulty of balancing the demands of professional and personal life, of attending to the needs of students while raising a young family that included a developmentally challenged daughter. Despite these stresses and strains, he finished his thesis with a flourish during his first year on the faculty and with hardly a break began the long process of turning the completed manuscript into a book. Three years later, in 1969, Princeton University Press published *Populism to Progressivism in Alabama*, a gracefully written 390-page exposition of the complexity of Southern politics in the decades following Reconstruction.

Several reviewers marveled at the book's innovative blend of traditional narrative and quantitative voting analysis and praised its highly nuanced treatment of the relationship between agrarian radicalism and progressive reform. The Progressives of the early 20th-century South, Sheldon concluded, were not neo-Populists, as John D. Hicks and several other historians had argued.[16] While they sometimes borrowed specific programs from the angry farmers who had challenged the ruling Bourbon Democrats of the 1880s and 1890s, they were actually harbingers of a new reform tradition, an urbanized and essentially forward-looking, Main Street version that would come to fruition during the New Deal. This argument was consistent with the "Woodwardian" view that discontinuity has been an essential element of Southern history.[17] But in other ways, particularly in its reliance on quantitative data, Sheldon's book represented a new departure in Southern political historiography. Both the American Historical Association and the Southern Historical Association duly recognized and applauded its originality by awarding the book the prestigious Albert J. Beveridge and Charles S. Sydnor prizes, respectively.

This spectacular debut between hard covers confirmed Sheldon's reputation as a pioneering practitioner of quantitative history. Earlier in the year, he had already published a landmark quantitative article in the *American Historical Review.* "Southern Violence," which appeared in February 1969, also demonstrated his skills as an essayist, a forte that connected him to his mentor, Woodward, an acknowledged master of the essay form. Not even Woodward, however, had accepted the truly daunting task of melding hard data with lucid exposition and soaring prose. Relying on logic as well as multiple regression analysis, Sheldon set about to explain why Southerners have maimed and murdered one another with more regularity than have other Americans. Comparing state-level data on homicide and suicide, he measured the relative importance of the factors generally associated with the high level of violence in the South.

This led to the striking conclusion that, while a significant portion of the South's proclivity for violence could be explained by these various measurable factors, the most important determinant of Southern violence—an insecure regional culture linked to a "siege mentality"—could not be measured statistically.[18] In effect, the very nature of Southern history, with its long string of peculiar institutions and lost causes, had inspired a violence-prone social psychology. As he put it so elegantly in the essay's final paragraph, "Being Southern, then, inevitably involves a feeling of persecution at times and a sense of being a passive, insignificant object of alien or impersonal forces. Such a historical experience has fostered a worldview that supports the denial of responsibility and locates threats to the region outside the region and threats to the person outside the self. From the Southern past arise the symbiosis and intense hostility toward strangers and the paradox is at the same time one of grace and violence."[19]

Sheldon's exploration of violence below the "Smith and Wesson line," a phrase he gleefully borrowed from the sociologist H. C. Brearly, earned him kudos from the historical profession and a pile of angry letters from his fellow Southerners.[20] One unreconstructed graduate student from Arkansas even wrote a letter of protest to the editors of the *American Historical Review* dismissing Sheldon's essay as Yankee propaganda.[21] The young historian from Birmingham accepted this bit of irony with his usual grace and good humor and pressed on with his studies of the South's paradoxical past. In 1971, during a year-long sabbatical leave, he returned to the subject of his dissertation and edited *Populism: The Critical Issues*, an anthology of articles that extended the debate over the causes and consequences of the Populist revolt and its relationship to traditions of reform and regional and national political culture. [22]

A year later, Sheldon followed up with *"Origins of the New South* in Retrospect," a *Journal of Southern History* article that surveyed an important part of his mentor's legacy. In the article's opening paragraphs, he offered a brilliant synopsis of Woodward's interpretation of the post-Reconstruction South. "Of one thing we may be certain at the outset," he insisted. "The durability of *Origins of the New South* is not a result of its ennobling and uplifting message. It is the story of the decay and decline of the aristocracy, the suffering and betrayal of the poor white, and the rise and transformation of a middle class. It is not a happy story. The Redeemers are revealed to be as venal as the carpetbaggers. The declining aristocracy are ineffectual and money hungry, and in the last analysis they subordinated the values of the political and social heritage in order to maintain control over the black population. The poor whites suffered from strange malignancies of racism and conspiracy-mindedness, and the rising middle class was timid and self-interested even in its reform movement. The most sympathetic characters in the whole sordid affair are simply those who are too powerless to be blamed for their actions."[23] The insights and elegant prose continued for more than 20 pages, closing with one of the most memorable passages in all of Southern historical writing. "Woodward is certainly a humanizing historian," the former student wrote of his teacher, "one who recognizes both the likelihood of failure and the necessity of struggle. It is the profound ambiguity that makes his work so interesting. Like the myth of Sisyphus, *Origins of the New South* still speaks to our condition. And who knows? Perhaps some day we will get that rock to the top of the hill. But, having learned my skepticism at the master's knee, I doubt it."[24]

In 1973 Sheldon demonstrated his intellectual versatility by producing two strikingly different publications. The first was *Understanding the American Experience: Recent Interpretations*, co-edited with James M. Banner Jr. and Barton J. Bernstein, two volumes that took a comprehensive look at modern

American historiography, and the second was a brief but provocative essay published in *The American Scholar*.[25] In the essay, "The South as a Counterculture," he explored the theme of regional identity through the lens of 1960sstyle popular culture. With wide-ranging allusions to New Left radicals, the pop sociologists Theodore Roszak and Charles Reich, the novelists Donald Barthelme and Jerzy Kozinski, the Scottish psychiatrist R. D. Laing, and even the Holocaust memoirist Elie Wiesel, he arrived at the conclusion that "the key to the Southern past is that Southerners are Americans who have taken on an additional identity through conflict with the North." Extending the argument first developed in "Southern Violence," he declared that "the Southern sense of separateness has been constructed on many layers of defensiveness, particularism, isolation, guilt, defeat, and the reactions to changes initiated from without: abolitionism, the Civil War, Reconstruction, poverty, depressions, industrialization and lately the civil rights movement."[26]

The last of these was an intensely personal matter for Sheldon, and he did what he could to maintain his ties to the ongoing civil rights struggle and related movements for peace and social justice, including the movement to end the war in Vietnam. While he believed that a measure of detachment is essential to good scholarship, he did not hesitate to speak out on public issues or to become involved in the broader Princeton community during the turbulent early 1970s. Indeed, beginning in 1971, he chaired the American Historical Association's special committee on Academic Freedom and oversaw the preparation of its highly influential report, "On the Rights of Historians."[27]

By this time, Sheldon had safely cleared the tenure hurdle and had actually moved on to the challenging and sometimes baffling world of academic administration. After cutting his administrative eye teeth by serving as associate chairman of the history department and by helping the distinguished British historian Lawrence Stone oversee the Shelby Cullom Davis Center, in 1972, at the academically tender age of 39, he accepted an appointment as Princeton's provost. As the university's chief academic officer, he was entrusted with the maintenance of high educational and scholarly standards, not to mention the well-being of students, staff, and faculty, including young colleagues who, like him, had been at Princeton for less than a decade. Indeed, his rise to academic leadership was so rapid that, during much of his tenure as provost, he and Lucy were still trying to pay off the balance of his graduate student loans.

Sheldon served as provost for three fruitful years, working closely with

President William Bowen, a distinguished economist who happened to share Sheldon's love of competitive tennis. A good team on and off the court, they steadily advanced the university's interests during a time of bewildering flux in higher education. Combined with his calm and reasoned manner, Sheldon's perspective as a professional historian served him well during this period of deep change, as he dealt with significant shifts in everything from student rights and faculty expectations to federal regulations and financial exigencies. Of course, the greatest challenge was to oversee Princeton's long-delayed transition to coeducation, to integrate women into the life of the university and to make them feel welcome. Once again Sheldon's sensibilities as a scholar and a Southerner—as someone who had devoted a great deal of attention to the process of social integration—came in handy on more than one occasion, especially when he had to deal with unreconstructed male alumni.

Sheldon's administrative success at Princeton quickly led to other opportunities, and in 1975 he left ivy-covered Nassau Hall to assume the presidency of Tulane University in New Orleans. A century-old private university sometimes known as the "Princeton of the South," Tulane nonetheless faced severe economic and administrative challenges that tested Sheldon's stamina and ingenuity. During his six years in Louisiana, while Lucy earned a Tulane law degree, he worked tirelessly to place the university on a solid economic and academic footing, in part through a series of innovative partnerships with private corporations. In 1983, his creative approach to academic funding was highlighted in an edited volume, *Partners in the Research Enterprise: University-Corporate Relations in Science and Technology.*[28]

The Tulane years were rewarding, both professionally and culturally, as Sheldon and Lucy experienced the social whirl and culinary adventures of the Big Easy and the presidential residence at Audubon Place. Nevertheless, in 1980 they began to entertain thoughts of moving on to new challenges. Sheldon's rising profile in the upper echelons of higher education brought new options, and in 1981 he accepted an offer to succeed Martin Meyerson as the president of the University of Pennsylvania. Leaving New Orleans was difficult, but he could not resist the dual lure of simultaneously leading one of the nation's premier universities and joining a truly distinguished history and American Civilization faculty.[29]

Unfortunately, Sheldon did not begin his tenure in Philadelphia under the best of circumstances. Selected from a list of finalists that included a popular internal candidate, Provost Vartan Gregorian, he had to win over a somewhat recalcitrant faculty. Even more daunting was the challenge of reversing Penn's declining overall condition. Despite its Ivy League status, the university was severely burdened by an aging campus infrastructure in need of restoration and by the deteriorating condition of West Philadelphia, the crime-infested neighborhood that surrounded the university.

No one, not even Sheldon, could fix all of these problems at once. But over the next twelve years, he gradually and painstakingly turned the university and its environs around. Drawing upon his knowledge of urban sociology and African American history, he recast the town-gown relationship in West Philadelphia by reaching out to local leaders and partnering with local agencies and businesses. The results were dramatic, with a positive spillover into all aspects of campus life. At the same time, he conducted an ambitious fundraising campaign—unprecedented in the university's history—that generated more than a billion dollars in four years. This infusion of funds facilitated a makeover of everything from dormitories to research labs, and a notable expansion of Penn's general education, hiring, and recruiting initiatives. He also allocated considerable time and money to controversial but highly successful efforts to bring gender equity and multi-cultural diversity to the university's faculty, student body, and curriculum. Under his leadership, the proportion of women on campus and in positions of administrative authority reached historic levels, minority enrollment rose from 13 to 30 percent, and international student enrollment jumped from 1.2 to more than 10 percent. At the same time, admission standards became significantly more competitive, the amount of sponsored research doubled, and the size of the university's endowment quintupled. Thus, by the time he stepped down in the summer of 1993, the struggling institution of the early 1980s had been transformed into a school on a definite upswing.

During his years at Penn, Sheldon developed a national reputation for creative and effective academic leadership and was in constant demand as a speaker and advisor on a wide range of issues related to higher education. He also served on national boards and committees including the NCAA President's Commission and the boards of the Educational Testing Service, the Rockefeller Commission on the Humanities, the American Council on Education, the Association of American Universities, and the NAACP Legal Defense Fund. At one time or another during the 1980s and 1990s, he chaired the Consortium on Financing Higher Education, the Carnegie Endowment for the Advancement of Teaching, and the Council of Ivy Group Presidents.

Sheldon found this whirl of activity to be fulfilling. But, at the age of 59—with the university he had grown to love on a secure footing—he left Philadelphia and the Penn presidency for Washington and the chairmanship of the National Endowment for the Humanities (NEH), an agency much in need of strong academic leadership after a decade of thinly veiled politicization. Retaining his tenured faculty status at Penn, he took an indefinite leave to become part of the new Clinton administration. Bill Clinton, the first Southern-born president since Jimmy Carter, had selected Sheldon, whom he had met on several occasions over the years, as the best choice to replace NEH chairperson Lynne Cheney, the wife of Republican insider and future vice president Dick Cheney. But during the confirmation process, several ultra-conservative Republicans, including Senator Jesse Helms of North Carolina, used Sheldon's nomination as a convenient symbol of what they viewed as a misguided and dangerous turn toward secular humanism and multiculturalism. All of the nominee's past actions and statements, including several recent decisions involving Penn students and free speech issues, were examined in the light of a Republican orthodoxy that all but rejected the core values of the humanities.

In a series of hearings reminiscent of the investigations led by Senator Joseph McCarthy during the 1950s, Sheldon suddenly became a whipping boy for essentially the same forces of reaction that he had often written about in his essays on Southern politics and culture. In the end, he received enough Senatorial support to sustain his nomination, but the experience of encountering the "siege mentality" at such a personal level was sobering to say the least. In 2002, he responded to his right-wing critics in a book-length chronicle, *The Politics of Presidential Appointment: A Memoir of the Culture War*.[30] During his four-year tenure as NEH chairman, he did his best to calm the waters of political controversy with a judicious and even-handed approach to the agency's activities. Unfortunately, no amount of restraint or reasoned dialogue could deter the repeated attempts by Senator Helms and others to defund the NEH. Forced into a holding action, Sheldon was able to save the Endowment from extinction. But many of the bold humanities initiatives that he had hoped to bring to the fore died for lack of funding. His greatest success was an extensive series of public programs that generated a

"National Conversation on American Pluralism and Identity." Sheldon him-self contributed greatly to the conversation with a number of speeches and essays, many of which became part of his 1997 book *One America Indivisible*. Weaving together sectional and national themes, he advanced the dialogue on American identity to a new plane of sophistication and involvement with the humanities.[31]

All of this was worthwhile, and the years in Washington provided Lucy with the opportunity to work with Marian Wright Edelman at the Children's Defense Fund. Eventually, however, Sheldon decided it was time to leave the Washington scene to return to teaching. On August 1, 1997, he resigned from the NEH and in September returned to Penn as a full-time member of the history faculty. To his delight, the university and the department welcomed him back with open arms and in 2003 honored him with an appointment as the inaugural David Boies Professor of History. Returning to his first loves of teaching and scholarship at an age when many others would have chosen retirement, he set out to disprove the old adage that there are no second acts in American life. While he studiously avoided any involvement in the affairs of central administration—he did not want to undercut his succes-sor's authority—he embraced his professorial duties with the alacrity of an untenured rookie. Determined to do his fair share, he took on a large number of advisees, willingly taught new courses requiring considerable preparation and planning, and even served a term as departmental chair. According to Drew Gilpin Faust, who co-taught a course with him, the former president "did everything but sweep the floor." In 2001, he won the university-wide Lindback Award for distinguished teaching, a degree of honor conferred on precious few ex-presidents at Penn or anywhere else.

Sheldon also returned to the world of academic research and writing, re-engaging with the discipline of history at conferences and on the printed page. In 1999, he published an essay on "Little Rock and the Promise of America," originally delivered as a paper at a conference marking the fortieth anniversary of the 1957 Central High School desegregation crisis, and a year later, following C. Vann Woodward's recent death, the *Journal of Southern History* published Sheldon's moving tribute to his cherished mentor, "C. Vann Woodward, 1908–1999: In Memoriam." In 2001, he contributed a lively essay titled "The Contradictory South," to the winter issue of *Southern Cultures*. Revisiting and refining some of themes in his 1972 essay, "The South as a

Counterculture," he concluded: "The South is full of exemplary Americans and of alternative Americans at the same time. The American identity is multifaceted, and it changes over time, but whatever it is at any one time, the South is both American and its opposite, both endorser and critic. In short, Southerners, both black and white, live with paradox."[32]

Woodward was no longer around to take part in the dialogue that he had inspired so many years before, but Sheldon carried on as best he could with a 2003 essay "*Origins of the New South* in Retrospect: Thirty Years Later." In 2004, he went on to explore the contemporary implications of persistent regional distinctiveness in "Identity Politics, Southern Style," one of several hard-hitting think pieces to appear in *Where We Stand: Voices of Southern Dissent*, a volume of opinion edited by Anthony Dunbar, the son of Leslie Dunbar, the long-time executive director of the Southern Regional Council and close friend of the Durrs. In the dispiriting Age of Bush, it seemed, the Age of Roosevelt was mercifully still relevant—as was the work of a senior scholar at the top of his game.

In 2005, most of Sheldon's historical essays, new and old, were collected and published under the title *Magnolias Without Moonlight: The American South from Regional Confederacy to National Integration*. The consistently eloquent and insightful quality of the collection alerted his fellow Southern historians to just how much he and the profession had sacrificed during his years as an administrator. Paul Gaston of the University of Virginia spoke for many when he offered an admiring but bittersweet blurb for the back cover: "These wise and elegant essays on what it means and has meant to be both Southern and American should remind us of how fortunate we are to have Sheldon Hackney back among us, instructing us as historian and writer, after his long sojourn as university president and NEH chairman. He unravels ironies and complexities, reveals the bright moon that sometimes has shone on us, but always keeps his eye on the defeat, failure, and downright meanness that has been part of our history. These essays may help us to lighten the burdens."[33]

Fortunately, the bright moon of Sheldon's scholarship, to borrow Gaston's apt phrase, continued to shine during his final years at Penn. Moving into his seventies with no letup, he undertook the ambitious new project of writing an intellectual biography of Woodward. Thinking that this effort to comprehend and explain the special genius of his mentor might close the circle, personally as well as professionally, he revisited many of the probing and unsettling questions that he had first encountered in Woodward's seminars 40 years earlier. When Sheldon finally retired from Penn in 2010, at the age of 76, he was still hard at work unraveling the complexities and paradoxes of "the outsider as insider," as he came to describe Woodward's distinctive perspective.[34]

Sheldon's retirement years, if they can be called that, have been spent on the island of Martha's Vineyard, where he and his family have been summer residents since the mid-1960s. The early purchase of a seaside house in the village of Vineyard Haven led to a web of close friendships and inclusion in a community of writers and artists, several of whom have strong ties to the South. Next-door neighbors Bill and Rose Styron, in particular, were at the center of a lively group of Southern expatriates that gave (and continue to give) the Hackney family's summers a twist of regional familiarity (offset only by Sheldon's deepening involvement in "Yankee" history as a volunteer at the Martha's Vineyard Historical Society). This nurturing "southern" Massachusetts enclave has become home, not only for Sheldon and Lucy, but also for their children and grandchildren.[35] As with the real South, their sense of place on the Vineyard carries elements of joy and sorrow, and in 2007 Sheldon and Lucy suffered the loss of their beloved eldest daughter, Virginia, who had spent most of her life on the island. But not even pain of this magnitude could break the spirit of a man of uncommon character who has blessed us all with his wisdom and fortitude. This strength of character, above all else, surely will be his greatest legacy.[36]

☙

IN RECOGNITION OF SHELDON's long life as a gentleman and a scholar, and of his wise counsel and innumerable kindnesses, we offer this volume as an expression of our gratitude and respect. Each of us enjoys a close connection with Sheldon, and taken together the individual essays below demonstrate the breadth and depth of his influence.

The intellectual historian MICHAEL O'BRIEN and Sheldon share an interest in the life and thought of C. Vann Woodward, and O'Brien has recently edited a selection of Woodward's letters. In "The Proslavery Argument and Nazi Ideology," he revisits a theme often hazarded but seldom analyzed in depth, the question of whether the antebellum white South and the National Socialist regime of Adolf Hitler had much in common. On the whole, O'Brien concludes that they did not, a conclusion that aligns him, at least for this purpose, with Hannah Arendt.

After **RANDALL KENNEDY** completed an undergraduate lecture course on the American South with Sheldon at Princeton, the teacher and former student remained in contact and Sheldon became an encouraging cheerleader for the emerging legal scholar and public intellectual. In "On Judging Nat Turner," Kennedy returns to a challenging undergraduate assignment—exploring the ethical and moral implications of the Nat Turner rebellion by examining issues raised by William Styron's controversial 1968 novel, *The Confessions of Nat Turner*. Asking whether Nat Turner should be viewed as a hero, Kennedy concludes that anyone who deploys violence excessively should not be deemed heroic. Even slaves, he argues, must be held to fundamental ethical norms.

JAMES M. McPHERSON, like Sheldon, was a student of Woodward's, but at Johns Hopkins. In 1965, McPherson welcomed Hackney as a colleague at Princeton, where as intellectuals, tennis players, and co-teachers, they became a remarkable team. At Princeton the students sometimes got a special treat when the two professors held joint sessions of their respective graduate seminars on the history of African Americans, the Civil War and Reconstruction, or the South. In a fitting tribute to Sheldon's years in the navy, the McPherson essay below deals with "American Navies and British Neutrality during the Civil War." Because the Civil War spilled over onto the high seas and involved serious interruptions to foreign trade by both the Union navy and Confederate commerce raiders, these naval actions threatened to bring foreign intervention. McPherson discusses the reasons why that intervention did not happen.

When Sheldon became president at the University of Pennsylvania, he found a kindred spirit in the talented, young historian, **DREW FAUST**. Their friendship and a shared love of Southern history found expression in a graduate course they co-taught on "Gender and Southern History" after Sheldon returned to Penn from the NEH in 1997. In "The True Picture as It Really Was: Seeing the Civil War in Art and Experience," Faust explores the challenge of how participants and creative artists struggled in parallel ways to represent the Civil War and its horrors. The difficulty of capturing war's experience in existing verbal or visual forms led to innovations in artistic genres—and in human expression and understanding, as soldiers and artists alike strove to develop, in the words of one Confederate, "the true picture as it really was" of the horrific realities of war.

Sheldon was chair of the University of Pennsylvania history department when **STEPHANIE McCURRY** became a new member of the history faculty. From the outset, he took great pride in her accomplishments and later worked to keep her at Penn when other schools called. Prompted by an implicit challenge from historians of other civil wars in Europe, the Middle East, and Africa, McCurry's "Civil War—Ours and Theirs" reflects on what is exceptional about the U.S. Civil War and what is not. Her comparative perspective throws into relief some discernible patterns (secessionist origins and state centralizing tendencies, for example) and challenges the romantic and exceptionalist assumptions that underlie so many histories of the American Civil War. Ultimately, she suggests, it is the postwar history—particularly the flourishing of a commercial culture of remembering, Union and Confederate—that makes our Civil War different.

As a Princeton undergraduate during the mid-1960s, **J. MILLS THORNTON III** studied and wrote his senior thesis under Sheldon's direction and then followed his mentor's path to Yale to study for his PhD under Woodward. Also sharing Sheldon's Alabama roots—and Lucy Hackney's hometown of Montgomery—he used his home state as a laboratory to understand the American South. In "Alabama Emancipates," he explains that the timing of the emancipation of Alabama's slaves was a matter of heated debate, initially at the state's constitutional convention of 1865, and subsequently within the state Supreme Court, during both Presidential and Radical Reconstructions. These debates cast a revealing light on the efforts of Alabama's whites to understand the meaning of emancipation.

STEVEN HAHN joined the History Department of the University of Pennsylvania when Sheldon, a fellow student of Southern Populism, was departmental chairman. Colleagues and close friends, they co-taught a seminar on the American South. In "Did the Civil War Matter?" Hahn notes that in recent sesquicentennial-related discussions there has been surprisingly little interest in the war's legacy. Examining the West as well as the South, Hahn shows the impact the war had on the course of American development, especially in the composition of class power. Looking at the ways in which the world, and the United States, would have been different if the Civil War had not occurred, Hahn concludes with a set of counterfactuals to emphasize his exciting points and suggestions.

When trying to decide which graduate school to attend, **ORVILLE VERNON BURTON** received a long and encouraging personal letter from Sheldon Hackney at Princeton. In one of the best decisions he ever made, Burton chose to study Southern history at Princeton with Sheldon, who became the co-advisor (with James McPherson) of his dissertation. In "Revisiting the Black Matriarchy," Burton returns to that dissertation and earlier work to explore why scholars and the public have argued that there was a matriarchy. Burton finds the answer in how scholars went about doing their research—how their methodology often led to confusion and an inability to discern the difference between the social dynamics and demographic realities of rural towns and the countryside.

After **DAVID MOLTKE-HANSEN** moved to Philadelphia to become president of the Historical Society of Pennsylvania in August 1999, he and Sheldon became friends and collaborators. The two Southern historians worked together on the planning and organization of two important conferences, the 2003 annual meeting of Southern Intellectual History Circle held in Philadelphia and the 2006 meeting of the Saint George Tucker Society held in Augusta and Thomson, Georgia. In his essay, "Turn Signals: Shifts in Values in Southern Life Writing," Moltke-Hansen begins with that 2006 conference, which had facilitated an extended discussion of Tom Watson and his biographer C. Vann Woodward, both of whom saw the South as a place of conflict—although they understood those conflicts very differently. Reflecting on a subject that has yet to receive its due from the scholarly community—the complex interplay between biographers and their subjects—Moltke-Hansen examines the often deep personal, ideological commitments of "life-writers." Ranging across the broad sweep of Southern history and biography, he offers provocative and thought-provoking commentary on several related genres.

Woodward introduced his student Sheldon Hackney to **CHARLES JOYNER** after a history conference panel in the early 1970s, and nearly a quarter century later, in 1993, Sheldon, as NEH chairman, presented Joyner with the South Carolina Humanities Council's Governor's Award for Lifetime Achievement in the Humanities. Joyner's "A Southern Radical and his Songs," follows the career of the Arkansas-born singer and songwriter Lee Hays from his youthful experiences organizing a biracial labor union in the 1930s, through his performing as part of the Almanac Singers with Pete Seeger and Woody Guthrie in the 1940s, to the Weavers' popular stardom and blacklisting in the 1950s. Hays's communal living and communal composition, and his complex relationship with the Communist Party, are explored with candor and compassion.

In 1978, while researching her PhD dissertation, **PATRICIA SULLIVAN** met Lucy Hackney's mother, Virginia, an encounter that would turn into a friendship and ultimately lead to the edited volume, *Freedom Writer: Virginia Foster Durr, Letters from the Civil Rights Years*. Virginia Durr spent the summers on Martha's Vineyard with Lucy and Sheldon, and after a number of visits to the Vineyard to work on *Freedom Writer* with Virginia, Pat bought a house on the island, becoming part of the local Durr-Hackney circle. In "Lessons Along the Color Line: Radicals, New Dealers and *Tom Watson: Agrarian Rebel*," Sullivan considers how Woodward's 1938 book on the Populist movement influenced a generation of Southerners as they worked to organize a cross-racial movement for economic justice and civil rights. In exploring how these Southerners viewed the struggles of the 1930s through their understanding of the fleeting experiment in interracial alliance of the 1890s, Sullivan offers a fresh look at the efforts to advance economic and political democracy in the South during the New Deal.

LANI GUINIER began teaching in the law school at the University of Pennsylvania in 1988, when Sheldon was president. In 1993, the same year that Sheldon was subjected to the grueling but ultimately successful confirmation hearings on his appointment as NEH chairman, Guinier had an even tougher time as an unsuccessful nominee for Assistant Attorney General for Civil Rights. Nonetheless, five years later, she became the first tenured black female professor at Harvard Law School. In "From Racial Liberalism to Racial

Literacy: *Brown v. Board of Education* and the Interest-Divergence Dilemma," an essay previously published in the *Journal of American History* in 2004, she argues that the cause of racial discrimination in America was not segregation per se, but rather the important role that race played (and still plays) in diverting attention away from the economic burdens suffered by poor and working class whites. Instead of linking racial prejudice to class injustice, the authors of the *Brown* decision focused on the centrality of race alone in the formulation of prejudice among working-class whites. Guinier proposes a paradigm shift away from the racial liberalism that has dominated political thought since *Brown*; in the interests of true equity, she would substitute a new way of thinking that recognizes race's interplay with class and geography.

For more than a decade, TOM SUGRUE was a colleague of Sheldon's in the History Department at the University of Pennsylvania where both taught the history of America in the 1960s and shared personal and scholarly interests in civil rights history. Sugrue currently holds the David Boies Professorship of History and Sociology, formerly held by Sheldon. A specialist in the history of the civil rights struggle north of the Mason-Dixon line, Sugrue examines a little-known aspect of this struggle in "'The Goddamn Boss': Cecil B. Moore, Philadelphia, and the Reshaping of Black Urban Politics." Exploring the transformation of black urban politics through the controversial career of Cecil B. Moore, Sugrue follows Moore's life from his service in the segregated Marine Corps during World War II, to his shift from Republican to Democratic Party affiliation, to his insurgency in the local NAACP, to his embrace of the rhetoric of black self-determination and militancy, and to his belated career as an elected official. Moore's trajectory, Sugrue suggests, underscores the improvisational nature of the black freedom struggle, highlighting both the gains and limitations of grassroots black activism in the 1960s and 1970s.

RAYMOND ARSENAULT studied Southern history with Sheldon as a Princeton undergraduate. From 1967 to 1969, he served as Sheldon's research assistant, and he also wrote his senior honors thesis on Southern Populism and progressivism under Sheldon's direction. One of his first tasks as a research assistant was to compile a book of documents dealing with the Montgomery Bus Boycott of 1955–56, so it is fitting that his contribution to the present volume is "The Montgomery Bus Boycott and American Politics." Arsenault addresses the local politics of white segregationists and the political activism of the Montgomery Improvement Association, but his primary focus is the broader regional and national political context of the boycott. Public opinion, the role of the press, and the responses—or in some cases the lack of responses—to the boycott by Southern Democrats and the leaders of the Republican Eisenhower Administration are viewed as important elements of the Montgomery story.

Sheldon and **PAUL GASTON** have enjoyed a long friendship based on mutual respect and common intellectual and political interests. Since the 1960s, Sheldon has admired Gaston's engaged scholarship and the dedication to racial justice expressed in his long-time association with the NAACP and the Southern Regional Council. In "The Double Death of Martin Luther King, Jr.," Gaston displays a keen analytical eye in examining how conservatives and the "New Right" in politics have manipulated King's story and legacy. Gaston warns of the counterproductive ways in which some Americans have reacted to the thrust for freedom that King and the civil rights movement represented.

WILLIAM R. FERRIS, who succeeded Sheldon as chairman of the National Endowment for the Humanities in 1997, offers a multi-media contribution in "Birmingham, 1978: A Photographic Homage to Sheldon Hackney." In the text, Ferris discusses his associations with Sheldon and offers some insights on what Sheldon has meant to education in the United States. He then turns to a series of photographs that he took in 1978 while visiting Sheldon's hometown of Birmingham. Through these powerful images, he speaks to the power of place in one of the South most hidebound communities.

PEYTON MCCRARY was a history graduate student at Princeton in the 1960s, and Sheldon served on his PhD dissertation committee, which was chaired by James McPherson. McCrary's "Minority Representation in Alabama: The Pivotal Case of *Dillard County v. Crenshaw County*" explores the key role played by historical evidence of racially discriminatory intent in a significant voting rights case. This case ended the use of discriminatory at-large elections in 176 counties, municipalities, and school boards in Sheldon's home state of Alabama in the 1980s. By the end of the decade African American voters in Alabama were represented on local governing bodies by their preferred candidates at a rate approximating their proportion of the voting-age population in their community. McCrary thus views the case as one of the signal achievements of the 1965 Voting Rights Act.

J. MORGAN KOUSSER was a Princeton undergraduate in the 1960s, and like Sheldon, he wrote his PhD dissertation at Yale under the supervision of Woodward. Both Woodward students were pioneers in quantitative history, applying this new methodology to the study of Southern politics and disfranchisement. In "Strange Career and the Need for a Second Reconstruction of Race Relations," Kousser shows that Woodward's *The Strange Career of Jim Crow* was not only an effort to rewrite the history of segregation in broad strokes, emphasizing the importance of laws in maintaining white supremacy; it was also an attempt to launch a history of race relations that would help to bring about a more egalitarian society. In recent years, Kousser believes, historians enthralled with cultural approaches to history have largely dismissed the relevance of history to public policy debates. More specifically, they have misread and wrongfully criticized Woodward's history of Jim Crow, all but abandoning his larger projects. Discussing trends in different aspects of race relations research and in various historians' approaches to the subject since the 1955 publication of *The Strange Career of Jim Crow*, Kousser calls for a revival of "the Woodward thesis" and a rededication to Woodward's public policy orientation.

In the volume's final essay, SHELDON HACKNEY himself offers a brief intellectual biography of his mentor. In this overview of Woodward's life, "C. Vann Woodward: The Outsider as Insider," Sheldon gives us a glimpse of the full intellectual biography that he has been working on for the better part of a decade. This tantalizing essay concentrates on Woodward's youth in Arkansas and Georgia, searching for and identifying clues that might help to explain the apparent inconsistencies in some of Woodward's public stands on politically controversial issues such as academic freedom and the limitations of scholarly detachment. Woodward claimed that he had always been a rebel, particularly against his father, who was a respected but wholly conventional school teacher and principal. Sheldon agrees, finding a certain consistency, and perhaps even a bit of irony, in the supposed inconsistencies of Woodward's liberalism. For a full exposition of "the outsider as insider," we will have to wait for the publication of the book-length biography. But surely, if the Woodward book is anything like the other fruits of Sheldon's remarkably fertile life and career, it will be well worth the wait.

NOTES

1   See John Updike's novels, *Rabbit Run, Rabbit Redux, Rabbit Is Rich*, and *Rabbit at Rest*, and a novella, *Licks of Love: Short Stories and a Sequel "Rabbit Remembered"* (New York: Alfred A. Knopf, 1960, 1971, 1981, 1990, and 2000, respectively).

2   Charles Joyner, *Shared Traditions: Southern History and Folk Culture* (Urbana: University of Illinois Press, 1999), 1.

3   In the Southern tradition, he was named after family. Francis was the name of his mother's brother, and Sheldon was the maiden name of his maternal grandmother.

4   Sheldon's interest in the social gospel and related spiritual and religious matters would become especially apparent in his later years. See Sheldon Hackney, "Social Justice, the Church, and the Counterculture, 1963–1979," Chapter 9 in David R. Contosta, ed., *This Far by Faith: Tradition and Change in the Episcopal Diocese of Pennsylvania* (University Park: Pennsylvania State University Press, 2012).

5   On Vanderbilt, see Paul Conkin, Henry Lee Swint, and Patricia Miletich, *Gone with the Ivy: A Biography of Vanderbilt University* (Knoxville: University of Tennessee Press, 1985). For examples of Grantham's work, see Dewey Grantham, *Hoke Smith and the Politics of the New South* (Baton Rouge: Louisiana State University Press, 1958)*;* Grantham, *The Democratic South* (Athens: University of Georgia Press, 1963); and Grantham, *Southern Progressivism: The Reconciliation of Progress and Tradition* (Knoxville: University of Tennessee Press, 1983).

6   For an insightful survey of Regionalist intellectuals, see Robert Dorman, *Revolt of the Provinces: The Regionalist Movement in America, 1920-1945* (Chapel Hill: University of North Carolina Press, 1993). On the Fugitive-Agrarians, see *Twelve Southerners, I'll Take My Stand: The South and the Agrarian Tradition* (New York: Harper and Row, 1930); John L. Stewart, *The Burden of Time: The Fugitives and Agrarians* (Princeton: Princeton University Press, 1965); Paul Conkin, *The Southern Agrarians* (Nashville: Vanderbilt University Press, 2001); and Paul V. Murphy, *The Rebuke of History: The Southern Agrarians and American Conservative Thought* (Chapel Hill: University of North Carolina Press, 2000). John Crowe Ransom taught at Kenyon College, in Gambier, Ohio, from 1937 to 1959. Allen Tate was teaching at the University of Minnesota during the 1950s, but he eventually returned to Nashville, where he died in 1979. Robert Penn Warren spent the 1950s in Connecticut and Vermont, where he died in 1989.

7   A love of jazz was another important influence on Sheldon's evolving attitudes on race. For him, as for a select few other white Southerners of his generation, jazz served as an interracial bridge that often carried powerful cultural messages of respect and inclusion.

8   James M. Banner Jr., to Raymond Arsenault and Orville Vernon Burton, September 13, 2013 (quotation). See John A. Salmond, *The Conscience of a Lawyer: Clifford J. Durr and American Civil Liberties, 1899–1975* (Tuscaloosa: University of Alabama Press, 1990); Patricia Sullivan, *Freedom Writer: Virginia Foster Durr, Letters from the Civil Rights Years* (New York: Routledge, 2003); and Hollinger F. Barnard, ed., *Outside the Magic Circle: The*

Autobiography of Virginia Foster Durr (Tuscaloosa: University of Alabama Press, 1985).

9   Salmond, *The Conscience of a Lawyer,* 47–153.

10   Ibid., 154–95.

11   Carl Degler, *The Other South: Southern Dissenters in the Nineteenth Century* (New York: Harper and Row, 1974).

12   On Woodward, see John Herbert Roper, *C. Vann Woodward, Southerner* (Athens: University of Georgia Press, 1987); C. Vann Woodward, *Thinking Back: The Perils of Writing History* (Baton Rouge: Louisiana State University Press, 1986); J. Morgan Kousser and James M. McPherson, eds., *Region, Race, and Reconstruction: Essays in Honor of C. Vann Woodward* (New York: Oxford University Press, 1982), xiii-xxxvii; and Michael O'Brien, ed., *The Letters of C. Vann Woodward* (New Haven: Yale University Press, 2013). See also the various essays on Woodward written by Sheldon Hackney, referenced in the bibliography that appears at the end of this volume.

13   On Morgan, who taught at Yale from 1955 to 1986, see *New York Times,* July 10, 2013 (obituary). On Blum, who taught at Yale from 1957 to 1991, see *New York Times*, October 21, 2011 (obituary), and Blum, *A Life with History* (Lawrence: University Press of Kansas, 2004).

14   On Link, see William A. Link, *Links: My Family in American History* (Gainesville: University Press of Florida, 2012). On McPherson, see Orville Vernon Burton, Jerald Podair, and Jennifer L. Weber, eds., *The Struggle for Equality: Essays on Sectional Conflict, the Civil War, and the Long Reconstruction* (Charlottesville: University of Virginia Press, 2011). See also Arthur S. Link, "The Progressive Movement in the South, 1870–1914," *North Carolina Historical Review* 23 (April 1946): 172–95; James M. McPherson, *Battle Cry of Freedom* (New York: Oxford University Press, 1988); Wesley Frank Craven, *The Southern Colonies in the Seventeenth Century, 1607-1689* (Baton Rouge: Louisiana State University Press, 1949); Martin B. Duberman, *Paul Robeson, A Biography* (New York: Random House, 1989); Duberman, *Black Mountain: An Exploration in Community* (Philadelphia: E. P. Dutton, 1972); James M. Banner Jr., *To the Hartford Convention: The Federalists and the Origins of Party Politics in Massachusetts, 1789–1815* (New York: Alfred A. Knopf, 1970)*;* Banner, "The Problem of South Carolina," in Stanley Elkins and Eric McKitrick, eds., *The Hofstadter Aegis: A Memorial* (New York: Alfred A. Knopf, 1974); and Banner, *Being a Historian: An Introduction to the World of Professional History* (Cambridge: Cambridge University Press, 2012).

15   The Afro-American Studies Program later became the Program in African American Studies, and in 2006 the Center for African American Studies.

16   See John D. Hicks, *The Populist Revolt: A History of the Farmers' Allliance and the People's Party* (Minneapolis: University of Minnesota Press, 1931).

17   On Woodward's views on the continuity question, see Woodward, *Thinking Back*, 59–79.

18   Sheldon Hackney, *Magnolias Without Moonlight: The American South from Regional Confederacy to National Integration* (New Brunswick: Transaction Publishers, 2005), 18.

19   Ibid., 18–19.

20   Ibid., 1.

21   See the letter to the editor from Albro Martin, *American Historical Review* 75 (October 1969): 325–326. Martin quipped: "The wit that creates such barbs as 'the Smith and

Wesson line' needs to be corrected with the observation that from the South it looks more like the Sado-Masochism line." Sheldon Hackney's response concluded with the memorable passage: "Nevertheless, I did not intend my article to be a demonstration that quantitative analysis can explain everything. My major conclusion, in fact, is that southern violence cannot be explained by such quantifiable factors as economic development (or weather), but that the answer might be found in the overly defensive and hostile nature of the southern world view. I am pleased that Mr. Martin's letter supports my thesis."

22   Sheldon Hackney, ed., *Populism: The Critical Issues* (Boston: Little, Brown, 1971).

23   Sheldon Hackney, "*Origins of the New South* in Retrospect," *Journal of Southern History* 38 (May 1972), 191–216, reprinted in Hackney, *Magnolias Without Moonlight*, 23–48. The quotation is from p. 23.

24   Hackney, *Magnolias Without Moonlight*, 43–4.

25   *Understanding the American Experience* was published by Harcourt Brace Jovanovich, Inc.

26   Hackney, *Magnolias Without Moonlight*, 61–62.

27   See the AHA website for the text of Sheldon Hackney, Elizabeth Brown, Winton U. Solberg, George V. Taylor, and Alfred Young, *Report of the American Historical Association Committee on the Rights of Historians*, March 5, 1974, last updated on May 22, 2007.

28   *Partners in the Research Enterprise: University-Corporate Relations in Science and Technology* was published by the University of Pennsylvania Press in 1983.

29   The move to Penn also brought Sheldon and Lucy physically closer to their eldest daughter, Virginia, who was enrolled in a special boarding school in Philadelphia.

30   Sheldon Hackney, *The Politics of Presidential Appointment: A Memoir of the Culture War* (Montgomery: NewSouth Books, 2002.

31   Sheldon Hackney, *One America Indivisible: A National Conversation on Pluralism and Identity* (Washington: Government Printing Office, 1997).

32   Hackney, *Magnolias Without Moonlight*, 105. This essay, originally delivered as the keynote address at a Southern history conference held at The Citadel, in Charleston, South Carolina, was published in *Southern Cultures*, Vol. 7, Winter 2001, and in a slightly different form in Winifred B. Moore, Kyle S. Sinisi, and David H. White Jr., eds., *Warm Ashes* (Columbia: University of South Carolina Press, 2003).

33   Hackney, *Magnolias Without Moonlight*, dust jacket, back cover.

34   See Chapter 19 below.

35   All eight of Sheldon and Lucy's grandchildren—Declan, Jackson, Larkin, and Madison McBride, and Alexander ("Z"), Annabelle, Lucy, and Samantha Hackney, live all or part of the year on Martha's Vineyard. On the Styrons and the Southern circle of writers and other intellectuals in the village of Vineyard Haven, see Alexandra Styron, *Reading My Father* (New York: Scribner, 2011); and Rose Styron and W. Blakeslee Griffin, eds., *Selected Letters of William Styron* (New York: Random House, 2012).

36   During Virginia's illness, Sheldon kept friends and family informed about her comings and goings, and other aspects of her remarkable life, with periodic e-mails. Collectively, these often eloquent and moving letters stand as a testament to a father's love and devotion. See Sheldon Hackney, *Following Virginia, 1958–2007* (Raleigh: Lulu, 2009).

DIXIE REDUX

The Proslavery Argument and Nazi Ideology

MICHAEL O'BRIEN

There are several ways of approaching this topic: defining direct influences, establishing the degree of cousinhood among these reactionary ideologies, and comparative analysis.[1] These approaches are not mutually exclusive, but, for the purposes of exposition, it might be best to consider them separately.

Least promising is establishing direct links between the proslavery argument and Nazi ideology. My knowledge of the latter is far from exhaustive, but there would seem to be little evidence that Adolf Hitler and his followers were knowledgeable about George Fitzhugh, William Harper, and the other proslavery writers of the American South before the Civil War. The best that can be said is American racial ideologists, including the likes of Josiah Nott, the ethnologist who was one of the few Southerners whose writings were known in Europe in the mid and late 19th century, formed part of that immense body of racial theory—from Johann Blumenbach to Arthur de Gobineau to Houston Stewart Chamberlain—which was an indispensable influence on the Nazis. But this influence was very oblique, a matter of a European thinker who read an American (or a European paraphrasing an American) and was, in turn, read by a National Socialist.[2]

More promising is the question of what these two social and cultural moments say about responses to modernity. For, if one were cataloguing those societies since the 18th century which have tried, with no little ruthlessness, to use modern technology while resisting what were often claimed to be its progressive social and political implications, the antebellum South and Nazi Germany would be conspicuous on the list, though it is a very long list. Indeed, it would be hard to find societies not on that list, to one degree or another. I will try to come back to this issue at the end, because it does seem to raise the most profound issues. But it is an issue difficult to discuss without first undertaking the comparative analysis which might help us to gain our bearings.

The first thing which needs to be said is that we are not really comparing like with like. For good or ill, Nazi ideology claimed to be comprehensive. It was not merely a vision of politics and economic organization, but a vision of history, human nature, the family, and art and science. It had opinions about music; famously, it celebrated Richard Wagner, while proscribing jazz as the expression of a degenerate race.[3] There came to be an official architectural style, which evolved from Hitler's early liking for "the neobaroque style of Vienna's Ringstrasse" to the cleaner lines of a monumental neoclassicism that Albert Speer persuaded the Führer to admire.[4] Even ballet was choreographed by a Ministry of Popular Entertainment and Propaganda, though it has been made clear that dancers and directors were pleased to cooperate.[5] In short, National Socialism's ambition to control was exorbitant. Although there are historians who think that slavery was so fundamental to the antebellum South that it comprehensively explains everything that Southerners did and thought—I am not one of those historians—nonetheless, even Eugene Genovese would have conceded that the proslavery argument never claimed to offer a comprehensive social and aesthetic program. It offered ideas about history and human nature, and it had firm views on economics and politics, but it coexisted with and did not seek to dominate an eclectic body of other ideas, common in Southern and American society—religion, laissez-faire economics, aesthetics, and so forth—so much as to have a conversation with them. Indeed the proslavery argument was more remarkable for presuming the validity of these other ideas and finding ways to make slavery compatible with them, than for presuming that slavery made those ideas moot. So no Southerner was told that being a slaveholder mandated a preference for Stephen Foster over Mozart. And, popular legend to the contrary, it was not even necessary to prefer Ionic columns to Gothic flying buttresses.

Secondly, the Nazis were impresarios of modern techniques of communication, media, and propaganda, but antebellum Southerners were not. The proslavery argument was, on the whole, a dry and even scholarly enterprise, inferior as propaganda even to that offered by American abolitionists, who understood the usages of the popular press and even the utility of melodrama.

The proslavery argument did occasionally reach a broad audience, usually when it took the form of oratory—sermons, political speeches—and *belles lettres*, but the former, at least, usually had small, local audiences and it is doubtful that William J. Grayson's poem, "The Hireling and the Slave," had too many readers, though a proslavery novel like Caroline Lee Hentz's *The Planter's Northern Bride* did better.[6] For the most part, the proslavery argument was made in print, in books with very limited print runs, in periodicals with small readerships, in pamphlets with smaller readerships which reprinted speeches to philosophical societies. It was a fairly elitist business. I suspect that if you had pulled aside an ordinary Southerner in 1850 and asked him or her to name a proslavery theorist, John C. Calhoun might have been mentioned, but hardly anyone else, and Calhoun's popular identity was as far more than a proslavery thinker. The proslavery argument had no uniforms, no charismatic public rituals, no Nuremberg rallies, and not even American marches and brass bands, even the sort of rituals invented by the Ku Klux Klan in the 20th century. In a culture that threw off many partisan artifacts—party political banners about Tippecanoe and Tyler Too, pottery with slogans about Oregon, clothing buttons enthusiastic about Andrew Jackson, pins with images of Henry Clay—proslavery artifacts are rare, if not nonexistent, although derogatory visual representations of African Americans are commonplace. Partly this absence of populist propaganda was a function of this being an earlier moment in the technologies of communication and the fact that the Old South was not a mass society. It would be pleasant to think that this absence was a proof of weakness. But, to the contrary, I suspect the unimaginative lassitude of the proslavery argument was evidence of its strength, the fact that what it said was what most white Southerners took for granted, anyway. On whether the reverse is true, that the relentless inventiveness of Nazi propaganda was a measure of its weakness, is unclear. The response to Daniel Goldhagen's *Hitler's Willing Executioners* suggests that the degree to which the German public accepted or was skeptical of Nazi ideology is much contested among historians.[7]

Thirdly, Nazism was preeminently a theory of the authoritarian state and of how individuals belong to a collectivity; it flourished on an idea of service and sacrifice. The proslavery argument was, almost invariably, an anti-statist theory, which counterposed the domestic against the public realm. Calhoun spoke of the South as "an aggregate . . . of communities, not of individuals. Every plantation is a little community, with the master at its head, who concentrates in himself the united interests of capital and labor, of which he is the common representative."[8] To be sure, slaveholders were anxious to use the law and, in that sense, to use the state as a bulwark and grounding for the institution, but they mistrusted strong government, had a remarkable faith in individualism (whatever Calhoun may have said), and were very averse to the idea of sacrifice—comfort and safety were their ideas of how a society might work well.[9] The slaveholder was supposed to sit on his own front porch, with his feet up and smoking a pipe, as was portrayed neatly in Frank Blackwell Mayer's 1858 painting of *Independence, Squire Jack Porter*.[10]

The only proslavery thinker who came close to the Nazi authoritarian vision was Henry Hughes of Mississippi in the 1850s. In fact, he came surprisingly close; he knew the romantic thrill of the leadership principle and wrote of "the supreme hero," he was militarist, he presumed men were driven by desire and fear, he suspected that anarchy was imminent but for his own intervention, he demanded that the state control education, religion, and aesthetics, he believed in racial purity, and he had very odd ideas about personal hygiene.[11] However, most people in the South who knew anything about Hughes believed he was more or less crazy, for he broke almost every ideological rule in the Southern book. That book was inscribed with commitments to republicanism, democracy, the rule of law, laissez-faire economics, party politics, all things that Nazism was later to regard as irrelevancies. Like Hughes, a Nazi ideologist would presumably say to an antebellum Southerner that these commitments were incompatible with slavery and racial hierarchy, which to survive would need a different politics. But a proslavery Southerner would reply that the whole point of Southern culture was the compatibility of slavery and racial hierarchy with republicanism, democracy, and the rest.

Obviously, the thing that Nazis had most in common with antebellum Southerners was racial theory. For the Nazi, as for the Southerner, the Negro was an inferior degenerate. However, racial theory takes many forms and there were great differences between these two cultures on the score of race. Technically, Southerners knew little or nothing of the historical construct of Aryanism, which became current after 1865, though they certainly knew about Caucasians and the types of mankind. However, while blacks were central to the Southern imagination, they were marginal for the Nazis.[12] What was crucially missing from the South's racial theory was anti-Semitism, the heart and corrupt soul of National Socialism. It is not that anti-Semitism was un-known to the Old South. Jews had some legal disabilities in some Southern states until well into the mid 19th century. There were moments of anti-Semitism in private letters and diaries, though very rarely in printed texts. But I can think of no instance when there was a formal anti-Semitic movement in Southern culture or society before the Civil War. (The Civil War itself is another matter, because the fiscal and military strains upon the Confederacy did elicit various forms of paranoia, including suspicion of imagined Jewish speculators, and certainly the late 19th and early 20th centuries did not lack for anti-Semites like Tom Watson.)[13] In the lexicon of antebellum Southern racial theory, Jews were white, which was not how some racialists elsewhere saw the matter. Josiah Nott and George Gliddon in their *Types of Mankind* of the 1850s, when summarizing the various theorists who divided mankind into differing numbers of racial types, opted for the typology of Honoré Jac-quinot, who in 1846 had defined three races (Caucasian, Mongol, Negro), and had subdivided the Caucasian into the Germanic, Celtic, Semitic, and Hindu. Nott's chapter on the "Physical History of the Jews" speaks of the "noble moral precepts bequeathed us by the kings and prophets of Judea" and is, for the most part, anxious to praise the Jews and, in line with his usual hostility towards hybridity, anxious to expel from Judaism any who tended to weaken its racial purity.[14] The evidence from the Old South is that Jews were accepted, worshipped freely, and intermarried freely with Gentiles, to the point that it became a worry to the orthodox.[15] Further, Jews were slavehold-ers like everyone else. Indeed, several rabbis (Isaac Wise, Isaac Leeser) wrote proslavery tracts.[16] The history of ancient Israel as recorded in the Bible was, of course, a fundamental element in the wider proslavery argument, whether it was making a point about God's purposes for man or making a point about secular history. And this alone points to a crucial difference. For the Nazis, the Jew was the incarnation of modernity, because he was supposed to direct the conspiracy that was the economic institutions of capitalist modernity. For Southerners, insofar as they had a coherent view, the Jew was the incarna-tion of antiquity, was associated not with banks in Frankfurt but with flocks peacefully grazing in the Holy Land.

There was, perhaps, more sympathy between Nazis and Southerners on the score of paranoia, though I think the Nazis were incomparably more paranoid than the Southerners. Fifty years ago, most American historians would not have agreed with this observation, for it was presumed then that the Old South was a deeply paranoid society, for it was inconceivable that rational people might wish to cease to be Americans and hence must be more-or-less unhinged.[17] Perhaps a few American historians still think this, but I do not. If I am right, we need to make a distinction. The worldwide Jewish conspiracy was a fetid Nazi fiction, but it was not irrational for a Charlestonian to think that the world was planning, with some fixity of purpose, to extinguish slavery from the South Carolinian world or that eventually the black Republicans might move against them. Still, there was, to a limited degree, a cast of mind shared between proslavery Southerners and Nazis: each felt obliged to be aggressive by way of preempting dangers threatened by enemies: for the Nazis, these were preeminently the Jews, secondarily the Bolsheviks; for the Southerners, preeminently the abolitionists, secondarily the slaves themselves, inspired by Haitian dreams of freedom and slaughter. I would add that one reason for the difference, the intensity of Nazi paranoia compared to the episodic anxiety of Southerners, has to do with a differing sense of time. Hitler's world and imagination had a breakneck pace, a dizzy sense of urgency about dynamic weeks and months. By comparison, Southerners lived in slow motion and reasoned about decades, even centuries.

As to the status of slavery itself in the two systems, one can hazard a few suggestions and one observation. The observation is the obvious one that the use of slave labor by the Nazis is, arguably, the strongest single argument against the pleasant fiction that slavery and modernity are intrinsically incompatible. However, the Nazis did not think systematically about slavery, they improvised their slave system, and were much torn between the impulse to use the labor of those they considered inferiors (which was the Southern custom) and the desire to murder those they considered inferiors (which was not the Southern custom). Adam Tooze's economic history of the Third Reich is insistent on this point, that Nazi ideology demanded extirpation, the removal of inferior races from land which could then be colonized by Aryans, and they variously pursued this policy through starvation and extermination. But the reality of economics, that there were not enough Germans to go around for the purposes of running a war and an economy, made the case for keeping these people alive and establishing labor camps.[18] By comparison, Southern thought about slavery is very systematic and not improvised, at all, but long considered. While the Nazis never got to the point of planning what a permanent, peacetime slave system would look like, Southerners well knew that permanence required an intricate body of law, ideology, and social custom which needed to be articulated to masters and slaves alike. Indeed, Southern slavery was founded on the idea of permanence and inheritance. Though they were habitually, even casually cruel, Southerners had a cynical understanding that slaves had to be kept alive and were there to be used. Genocide, insofar as it existed in the Southern imagination, was a thing reserved for Native Americans.

One would be tempted, therefore, to say that Nazi slavery was the child of war, and Southern slavery the child of peace, but that would be to overstate the case. As Adam Tooze has also suggested, Hitler was conscious of American imperialism as a model for his vision of German expansion, especially the advantages of a contiguous continental empire, and one infers that he knew that slave labor was a significant element in the American seizure of land, and so the American South was a precedent for the use of slave labor in facilitating the search for *lebensraum*.[19] The difference, of course, is that until 1861 American imperialism and slavery were able to coexist; forced African labor helped to make that imperialism possible. But this was partly a function of the weakness of American opponents in the southern half of North America. When Southern slavery faced a serious military opponent in 1861, that coexistence disintegrated. Nazi slavery faced still more stringent enemies.

Still, points of sympathy also need emphasis. The proslavery argument and Nazism were both imperialist ideologies, they both presumed that inferior peoples could rightly be pushed aside or enslaved, and they were both committed to the value of colonization, of what we now call settler societies. However, one needs to observe that the Americans, as the heirs of the British, understood that settler societies were most practical in thinly peopled lands. India, with its millions of people and its ancient cultures, required a different technique of empire. The United States prudently refused to annex all of Mexico in the late 1840s, though it might have done so, and contented itself with Mexico's thinly peopled northern provinces, because this fitted the familiar logic of American expansion, which could only deal with extirpations on a small scale, done half in denial. Hitler, by comparison, was incomparably more ruthless and this ruthlessness made it seem possible to do, what a British or American imperialist would have thought a folly, the establishment of a settler society in a densely peopled land, as though one might deal with Poland or the Ukraine as though it were Australia. And, of course, the British and American imperialists would have been right; it was a folly.

For all that, because of the imperialist commitment, the Southerners and the Nazis both had a romantic commitment to agrarianism, to the possession of land, and a propensity for self-regarding myths about family life and kinship, about the *Volk* and about folks. They roughly shared a culture of blood and place, sanctified by history and war, though this was and is a common enough aspect of Western culture, sometimes of non-Western culture. That the preeminent American text for such a culture of national sanctification by the shedding of blood is Abraham Lincoln's *Gettysburg Address* shows that there is little exclusivity here, but a common-or-garden propensity for the messianic. A pessimist cannot fail to observe a sad abundance of last, best hopes in the modern world.

In conclusion, let me turn to the difficult matter, postponed earlier, of what these two social and cultural moments say about responses to modernity. This is what we might loosely call the Hannah Arendt problem, for it is the issue she was among the first to raise in *The Origins of Totalitarianism* in 1951. Was National Socialism merely an intensification of familiar tendencies in German and Western culture and, as such, a first cousin to the slave South? Or was totalitarianism, as Arendt argued, something radically new and peculiarly evil, hence something radically different from anything John C. Calhoun might have advocated or understood? On the whole, the argument in recent years has run against Arendt; the construct of totalitarianism has been deconstructed, and more people incline to George Mosse's view that Nazism did, indeed, have deep taproots in German history, though there may be more disagreement over Mosse's insistence that the German case was *sui generis* and not an instance of the wider European case.[20]

As I understand her critics, Arendt is held to have overestimated the efficacy of totalitarianism. No system, whatever its purposes, can be total. I do not wish to quarrel with that criticism, but, if we retreat to the lesser ground of ideological logics and intentions, it does seem that National Socialism, in contradistinction to the proslavery argument, was a remarkably comprehensive and, by its own lights, internally-consistent ideology. To be sure, both thought the modern liberal vision of modernity's meaning was inadequate, both meditated on how industry and urban life were affecting rural life and virtue, both grasped that domestic life and the larger economy were intimately connected. However, by comparison with the Nazis, the proslavery thinkers look muddled and at odds. For the most part, the latter did not mind cities, at least on small scale; they were not greatly averse to factories; they believed in free trade, elections, and progress; they were amelorists, ill-disposed towards abrupt innovation, but liking incremental change—a new sewing machine here, a steam engine there, an annexed or purchased province somewhere else. At the heart of the muddle was an indecision about whether slavery was the systematic grounding of their culture, as Fitzhugh claimed, or just a way to make money, as Thomas Dew mostly thought.[21] Was it the final solution to modernity's uncertain evolution and unwise experiment with free labor, as Fitzhugh claimed in the 1850s, or just a historical stage, valuable but destined for supersession, as Edward Brown had said in the 1820s?[22] Few agreed. In so decentralized and fragmentary a society, in which many were not slaveholders or slaves, no one was in a position to compel agreement, although there were any number of people in a position to compel enslavement. Here is a paradox: The Nazis believed in modernity less, but used its techniques with extraordinary sophistication and violence, so the contradiction for them was intense, however denied. The Southerners believed in modernity more, but used its techniques less, and so for them the tension was modest, though enough to make them walk away from the United States and its differing version of modernity in 1861.[23]

Such issues are close to the heart of Arendt's analysis. Hers was an argument about the relationship between ideology and power, imagination and coercion. Her commitment was to classical republicanism, latterly embodied in the ideology of the American Revolution, and she most distrusted totalitarian ideologies for their erasure of the distinction between public and private life. Indeed, she may be said to have stood with Thomas Jefferson against Adolf Hitler and Karl Marx, and she did not fail to notice, if glancingly, that she was thereby standing with a slaveholder.[24] What I am calling muddle, she praised as moral, for she claimed that American society in the 18th and 19th centuries, like other Western cultures, lacked a systematic social theory, hence had little to impose, and hence permitted freedom and human dignity. She observed in *The Origins of Totalitarianism*, "In the light of recent events it is possible to say that even slaves still belonged to some sort of human community; their labor was needed, used, and exploited, and this kept them within the pale of humanity." By comparison, those in Nazi labor camps were expelled from humanity, were the victims of something new in human history, something unprecedentedly drastic. "All parallels create confusion and distract attention from what is essential," Arendt observed. "Forced labor in prisons and penal colonies, banishment, slavery, all seem for a moment to offer helpful comparisons, but on closer examination lead nowhere. . . . slaves were not, like concentration-camp inmates, withdrawn from the sight and hence the protection of their fellow men; as instruments of labor they had a definite price and as property a definite value. The concentration-camp inmate has no price, because he can always be replaced; nobody knows to whom he belongs, because he is never seen. From the point of view of normal society he is absolutely superfluous, although in times of acute labor shortage, as in Russia and in Germany during the war, he is used for work."[25] There is much here with which one might quarrel, but the basic contention is suggestive. On the whole, it is plausible to believe that, when passing from the Old South to Nazi Germany, the passage is from a fairly-ordinary historical culture, with the usual mix of virtue and vice, dignity and cruelty, to an extraordinary historical culture with few or no precedents and, one hopes, few or no successors.

NOTES

1   This essay was first written for a meeting about "Racial Ideologies: A Comparative Panel Discussion on 19th-Century American Pro-Slavery Arguments and 20th-Century Nazi Propaganda," held in September 2006 at the Gilder Lehrman Center for the Study of Slavery, Resistance and Abolition at Yale University; it has been revised and extended.

2   On Gobineau and Nott, see Michael Denis Biddiss, *Father of Racist Ideology: the Social and Political Thought of Count Gobineau* (New York: Weybright and Talley, 1970), 146–47. Nott was elected an Honorary Fellow of the Anthropological Society of London in the early 1860s and Pierre Broca praised him as "one of the most eminent anthropologists of America": see Paul Broca, *On the Phenomena of Hybridity in the Genus Homo*, ed. Charles Carter Blake (London: Longman, Green, Longman, & Roberts, 1864), 2.

3   See Erik Levi, *Music in the Third Reich* (New York: St. Martin's Press, 1994).

4   Albert Speer, *Inside the Third Reich: Memoirs* (New York: Macmillan, 1970), 75.

5   On this, see Lilian Karina and Marion Kant, *Hitler's Dancers: German Modern Dance and the Third Reich* (New York: Bergahn Books, 2003).

6   William J. Grayson, *The Hireling and Slave* (Charleston: John Russell, 1854); Caroline Lee Hentz, *The Planter's Northern Bride: a Novel* (Philadelphia: Parry & M'Millan, 1854).

7   Daniel Jonah Goldhagen, *Hitler's Willing Executioners: Ordinary Germans and the Holocaust* (New York: Knopf:, 1996); on the controversy, see Robert R. Shandley, ed., *Unwilling Germans?: the Goldhagen Debate* (Minneapolis: University of Minnesota Press, 1998).

8   "Further Remarks in Debate on His Fifth Resolution," in Clyde N. Wilson, ed., *The Papers of John C. Calhoun: Volume XIV: 1837–1839* (Columbia: University of South Carolina Press, 1981), 84.

9   On using the state, see Don E. Fehrenbacher, *The Slaveholding Republic: an Account of the United States Government's Relations to Slavery* (New York: Oxford University Press, 2001).

10 It is now in the Smithsonian American Art Museum and can be viewed online at: http://americanart.si.edu/collections/search/artwork/?id=16618 [accessed July 8, 2013].

11 Henry Hughes, *Treatise on Sociology, Theoretical and Practical* (Philadelphia: Lippincott, Grambo, 1854); the phrase "supreme hero" occurs in his diary: see entry for 7 June 1852, Henry Hughes Diary, Henry Hughes Papers. Mississippi Department of Archives and History, Jackson, Mississippi.

12 See Clarence Lusane, *Hitler's Black Victims: the Historical Experiences of Afro-Germans, European Blacks, Africans, and African Americans in the Nazi Era* (New York: Routledge, 2003).

13 See, for example, the anti-Semitism of Basil Gildersleeve, evident in his wartime writings: on this, see Ward W. Briggs Jr., ed., *Soldier and Scholar: Basil Lanneau Gildersleeve and the Civil War*, Publications of the Southern Texts Society (Charlottesville: University Press of Virginia, 1998).

14 Josiah C. Nott and George Gliddon, *Types of Mankind: or, Ethnological Researches, Based Upon the Ancient Monuments, Paintings, Sculptures, and Crania of Races, and Upon Their Natural, Geographical, Philological and Biblical History* (Philadelphia: Lippincott, Grambo, 1854), 116.

15 A good case study is Emily Bingham, *Mordecai: an Early American Family* (New York: Hill and Wang, 2003).

16 Larry E. Tise, *Proslavery: a History of the Defense of Slavery in America, 1701–1840* (Athens: University of Georgia Press, 1987), 163.

17 This was a theme of the various writings of Clement Eaton; see, for example, Clement Eaton, *Freedom of Thought in the Old South* (Durham: Duke University Press, 1940), but also Steven A. Channing, *Crisis of Fear: Secession in South Carolina* (New York: W. W. Norton, 1970).

18 See Adam Tooze, *The Wages of Destruction: the Making and Breaking of the Nazi Economy* (London: Allen Lane, 2006), 513–51.

19 Tooze, *Wages of Destruction*, 9–12, 175, 462. For Hitler's views on the American and British empires, see Adolf Hitler, *Mein Kampf* (London: Hurst and Blackett, 1939), 17, 132, 240, 463, 536.

20 George L. Mosse, *The Crisis of German Ideology; Intellectual Origins of the Third Reich* (New York: Grosset & Dunlap, 1964).

21 Cf. George Fitzhugh, *Cannibals All!: or, Slaves Without Masters* (Richmond: A. Morris, 1857) with Thomas R. Dew, *Review of the Debate in the Virginia Legislature of 1831 and 1832* (Richmond: T. W. White, 1832).

22 Edward Brown, *Notes on the Origin and Necessity of Slavery* (Charleston: A. E. Miller, 1826).

23 A recent book would, perhaps, quarrel with this standpoint, since it argues that antebellum Southerners freely used the techniques of modernity: see L. Diane Barnes, Brian Schoen, and Frank Towers, eds., *The Old South's Modern Worlds: Slavery, Region, and Nation in the Age of Progress* (New York: Oxford University Press, 2011).

24   On slavery, see especially Hannah Arendt, *On Revolution* (New York: Viking Press, 1963), 65–66: this book contains her most considered discussion of American political ideology; on the public and private, see Hannah Arendt, *The Human Condition* (Chicago: University of Chicago Press, 1958), 22–78.

25   Hannah Arendt, *The Origins of Totalitarianism*, 2d ed. (New York: Meridian, 1958), 297, 444.

2

On Judging Nat Turner[1]

RANDALL KENNEDY

How should one view Nat Turner? Should he be lauded as a hero, dismissed as a lunatic, condemned as a criminal, or categorized in some other fashion? These and related questions are the subject of this essay in honor of Sheldon Hackney. It was he who introduced me to the controversy that continues to surround Nat Turner, the leader of the bloodiest and most consequential insurrection of slaves in antebellum America. Professor Hackney did so in his course in Southern history at Princeton University in the spring semester of the 1973–74 school year by assigning William Styron's *The Confessions of Nat Turner* (1967). The assignment prompted strong dissent from a cadre of students who, taking their cue from John Henrik Clarke and like-minded commentators,[2] assailed the assignment. They asserted that the novel wrongly vilified Turner, thereby contributing to an insidious, hurtful, and influential force in American culture: the stigmatization of blacks, particularly African American men.

Professor Hackney addressed the students respectfully, devoting a class to a discussion of their protest. He did not disavow his assignment but said that the dissidents raised valuable issues. I got the impression that he derived satisfaction from seeing that the reading had provoked an uncommon amount of extracurricular research and spirited debate.

Decades later, I revisited the Nat Turner controversy. I did so in the context of a course I teach at Harvard Law School on race relations law between the founding of the United States and the end of Reconstruction. I do not assign Styron's novel. Instead, I assign *The Confessions of Nat Turner, The Leader of the Late Insurrection in Southampton, Virginia, As Fully and Voluntarily Made to Thomas R. Gray* (1831). This is a document in which a white lawyer, Thomas R. Gray, claims to set forth in writing a statement conveyed verbally by the jailed Nat Turner as he awaited trial—a statement in which Turner describes his upbringing, religious visions, relations with owners and fellow slaves, and the planning and execution of the uprising. Nothing in the course gives rise to as much unease as that pamphlet and the discussion generated by the questions with which I began.

Turner was born enslaved in 1800 (the same year as John Brown[3]) in Southampton County, Virginia, where he resided for his entire short life. In August 1831 he initiated an uprising eventually joined by 60 to 80 enslaved and free blacks. The rebellion lasted less than 48 hours before it was repressed. Though brief, it was bloody. Turner and his followers marched from house to house in a corner of Southampton, shooting, stabbing, slicing, and bludgeoning as they went. They killed 55 white men, women, and children. The killing began with an assault on the household in which Turner lived as a slave. According to *The Confessions of Nat Turner . . . As Fully and Voluntarily Made to Thomas R. Gray*, "[t]he murder of this family . . . was the work of a moment, not one of them awoke; there was a little infant sleeping in a cradle, that was forgotten, until we had left the house and gone some distance, when Henry and Will [fellow rebels] returned and killed it."[4]

In *The Confessions*, Turner purportedly described other acts of the rebellion:

> We started . . . for Mrs. Reese's maintaining the most perfect silence on our march, where finding the door unlocked, we entered, and murdered Mrs. Reese in her bed, while sleeping; her son awoke, but it was only to sleep the sleep of death, he had only time to say who is that, and he was no more. From Mrs. Reese's went to Mrs. Turner's . . . . Will immediately killed Mrs. Turner, with one blow of his axe. I took Mrs. Newsome by the hand, and with the sword I had . . . I struck her several blows over the head, but not being able to kill her, as the sword was dull. Will turning around and discovering it, dispatched her also.[5]

Turner continued the narration:

> 'twas my object to carry terror and devastation wherever we went, I placed fifteen or twenty of the best armed and most to be relied on, in front, who generally approached the house as fast as their horses could run; this was for two purposes, to prevent their escape and strike terror to the inhabitants.

Having murdered Mrs. Waller and ten children, we started for Mr. William Williams'. . . . Mrs. Williams fled and got some distance from the house, but she was pursued, overtaken, and compelled to get up behind one of the company, who brought her back and after showing her the mangled body of her lifeless husband, she was told to get down and lay by his side, where she was shot dead.[6]

Turner and his followers do not seem to have had a plan for escape. They appear to have wanted to reach the capital of the county, the village of Jerusalem. But before they could do so they were overwhelmed by militiamen. While many of the rebels were apprehended quickly, Turner eluded capture for two months.

The aftermath of the rebellion saw an escalation of bloodletting, with a turnabout in the racial demographics of death. Frightened and enraged, whites summarily killed scores of blacks, whether or not evidence tied them to complicity in the rebellion. A cavalry company decapitated as many as 15 suspected rebels and put their heads on poles for display.[7] One militiaman told a newspaper that he had seen "the slaughter of many blacks without trial, and under circumstances of great barbarity."[8] Another witness related the following regarding the fate of a slave captured by state authorities: "They burnt him with red hot irons—cut off his ears and nose—stabbed him, cut his hamstrings, stuck him like a hog, and at last cut off his head."[9]

Opinion regarding Turner varies widely. Some see him as a base criminal. That was the view of the court that convicted him of "making insurrection, and plotting to take away the lives of divers free white persons."[10] That court told Turner:

You have been convicted of plotting in cold blood, the indiscriminate destruction of men, of helpless women, and of infant children. The evidence before us leaves not a shadow of a doubt, but that your hands were often embrued with the blood of the innocent . . . . [You deprived] us of many of our most valuable citizens; and this was done when they were asleep, and defenceless; under circumstances shocking to humanity.[11]

Appalled by what it deemed a barbaric, inexcusable crime, the court imposed upon Turner its harshest sentence: "The judgment of the court is, that you

be taken hence to the jail from whence you came, thence to the place of execution, and . . . be hung by the neck until you are dead! dead! dead . . . ."[12]
On November 11, 1831, Turner was hanged, his body dissected, his remains
scattered.

Many observers over the years have concurred in condemning Turner as,
in the words of the *Norfolk Herald*, a "wretched culprit."[13] T. R. Gray, Turner's
collaborator in the writing of his *Confessions*, says of the rebels:

> No cry for mercy penetrated the flinty bosoms. No acts of remembered
> kindness made the least impression upon these remorseless murderers . . . .
> Never did a band of savages do their work of death more unsparingly.
> Apprehension for their own personal safety seems to have been the only
> principle of restraint in the whole course of their bloody proceeding.[14]

The editors of the *Richmond Enquirer* condemned the "horrible atrocity of these
monsters. They remind one of a parcel of blood-thirsty wolves . . . or, rather,
like a former incursion of the Indians upon the white settlements. Nothing
is spared; neither age nor sex is respected—the helplessness of women and
children pleads in vain for mercy."[15] Even the destructiveness and cruelty of
the Civil War failed to dim the special indignation with which some observers
recalled Turner's uprising. Writing soon after the war's end, the editors of the
Richmond Dispatch averred:

> Nat Turner's massacre was the most barbarous and brutal of all the human
> butcheries of the century . . . . It was a horror of horrors, a brutal and
> phrensied shedding of human blood, such as has never been exceeded in
> its unprovoked and brutal character.[16]

There are several problems with the perspective that sees Turner's rebellion
as a baleful undertaking that is easy to repudiate unequivocally. Damning
Turner simply for rebelling—putting aside for a moment the method of his
uprising—is preposterous. Slavery was an evil institution which one could
rightly oppose using various methods, including flight, sabotage, and certain
sorts of violence. Some have berated Turner because his master was relatively
benevolent. Gray quotes Turner himself acknowledging that he had "a kind
master" who "placed the greatest confidence in me; in fact, I had no cause

to complain at his treatment . . ."[17] But even with a "good" master, slavery was monstrous, a relationship of legalized despotism. Some argue, moreover, that Turner's rebelliousness, despite his relative privilege, puts him in an even more attractive light. They posit that his resistance was not merely a reflexive, self-interested rejection of his own oppression but a broader rejection of the oppression visited upon his people. "By keeping his mouth shut and saying yes at the right time," Lerone Bennett Jr. asserted, "Nat Turner could have become a driver or perhaps an overseer. . . . He could have become a slave-in-charge. . . . But Nat had too much integrity for that trap."[18]

Some of Turner's harshest detractors complain that his revolt was futile, that he should have known that he could not prevail, and that to proceed in the face of certain defeat was deplorable, a waste of the lives of those he killed as well as a waste of the lives of those he led. The *New York Journal of Commerce* expressed this view. Calling the uprising "a savage atrocity," "one of the most distressing occurrences which has ever taken place in this country," the *Journal* exclaimed: "We cannot imagine what infatuation could have seized the minds of these negroes, that they should even dream of success in attempting to recover their freedom by violence and bloodshed. Do they not know that in addition to the forces of the white population among whom they are placed, the whole strength of the General Government is pledged to put down such insurrection?"[19] The *Journal* went on to declare, "much as we abhor slavery . . . there is not a man of us who would not run to the relief of our friends in the South, when surrounded by the horrors of servile insurrection."[20]

The *Journal's* critique is premised on the assumption that the aim of the rebels was to gain freedom on a long-term basis. From this predicate the *Journal* judges the rebels to have been criminally stupid since the odds of securing their goal was so miniscule. But we don't know for sure what the aim or aims of the rebels were. It is plausible, indeed likely, that the aims of some of them did not include freedom in the long term and that these aims were, in fact, accomplished by the actions they took. According to *The Confessions* transcribed by Thomas Gray, Nat Turner believed that a divine force was instructing him to pursue a holy mission.

> I heard a loud noise in the heavens, and the Spirit instantly appeared to me and said the Serpent was loosened, and Christ had laid down the yoke he had borne for the sins of men, and that I should take it on and fight

against the Serpent, for the time was fast approaching when the first should be last and the last should be first.[21]

If Turner believed that the Holy Spirit was directing him and his comrades to kill slaveholding whites and their kin, he *succeeded* in carrying out what he saw as a religious duty. Pre-Civil War America was awash in the rhetoric and sentiments of apocalypticism, particularly as it pertained to slavery. Thomas Jefferson wrote of trembling for his country when he reflected on how God is just.[22] Abraham Lincoln spoke of God making it so that every drop of blood drawn with the lash would be paid by another drawn with the sword.[23] Perhaps Nat Turner saw himself as God's messenger and his death-dealing rebellion as God's message. That motivation would fit with the impression of Turner that Gray conveys:

> He is a complete fanatic, or plays his part most admirably. . . . The calm, deliberate composure with which he spoke of his late deeds and intentions, the expression of his fiend-like face when excited by enthusiasm, still bearing the stains of helpless innocence about him; clothed with rags and covered with chains; yet daring to raise his manacled hands to heaven, with a spirit soaring above the attributes of man; I looked on him and my blood curdled in my veins.[24]

The *Journal* scoffs at what it portrays as the rebels' *unthinking* martyrdom. But perhaps Turner and his comrades courted martyrdom *thoughtfully*, preferring to end their lives with a dramatic and instructive flourish. History is full of examples of collective martyrdom in which people chose a course leading to certain and early death with the hope that their conduct will nourish a better future. Some maintain that Turner's rebellion hurt the cause of Virginia slaves in that it prompted the slaughter of many during the repression of the uprising and then led Virginia authorities to tighten the policing of enslaved and free blacks subsequently. It should also be remembered, however, that the Turner rebellion helped to prompt a serious debate in Virginia over the wisdom of perpetuating slavery. Virginia, in fact, eschewed emancipation. But it is not beyond the pale of plausibility to imagine a different course created, in part, by Turner's revolt.

There are additional ambitions that may well have been realized in the

course of Turner's rebellion notwithstanding its foreseeable and brutal suppression. One is revenge. Take the case of Thomas Barrow, a slaveowner. Prior
to the rebellion, Barrow refused to allow an enslaved man to marry one of
his enslaved women. During the rebellion that man impaled Barrow upon a
spit. If revenge is sweet, that man may well have enjoyed a delicious moment
(though the ethical propriety of his conduct is a separate matter entirely).[25]
Another ambition might have been the modest aim of simply enjoying, albeit
briefly, certain pleasures—drinking liquor, obtaining money, luxuriating in
liberty—impossible to savor under normal circumstances as a slave. Nat Turner's
uprising, Patrick Breen observes, "offered the Southampton slaves who joined
the rebellion a unique opportunity to act as they pleased."[26]

A second strand of commentary lauds Turner and his comrades. According to T. Thomas Fortune, Turner was "a black hero. He preferred death to
slavery."[27] Subsequently, Fortune expanded on this theme. Turner, he wrote,
"exhibited in the most abject conditions the heroism and race devotion which
have illustrated in all times the sort of men who are worthy to be free."[28]

Marking the centennial of Turner's execution, *The Liberator*—a publication
of the League of Struggle for Negro Rights, a black communist organization—asserted that

> Nat Turner, in deeds, was a revolutionary leader of the enslaved Negroes.
> With the utmost courage and determination he led the slaves of Virginia
> with sword and musket against the slaveowners. . . . He fought for free-
> dom. . . . He lost . . . but his revolt added new strength to the revolutionary
> traditions of the Negro people.[29]

Around the same time, the black activist-intellectual Rayford Logan declared
that African Americans should take pride in Turner because he "kept his
'Rendezvous with Death' rather than live a bondsman. His simple courage
surpassed the comprehension of his executioners . . ."[30]

The most concerted praising of Turner occurred in the 1960s. This
stemmed, in part, from the heightened interest in black history and culture
that was an outgrowth of the civil rights movement.[31] The insistent depiction
of Turner as a hero also stemmed from opposition to the portrayal of Turner
in William Styron's novel. Many arbiters of American culture admired Styron's crafting of an angst-ridden, self-doubting rebel who loved and loathed

his fellow enslaved blacks and who hated and lusted after the whites who surrounded him.[32] Styron's novel won critical acclaim—it was awarded the Pulitzer Prize—and won popular approval as well, attaining bestseller status. Styron's novel, however, also galvanized those who perceived Styron to be desecrating Nat Turner's memory. "No event in recent years," John Henrik Clarke observed, "has touched and stirred the black intellectual community more than this book."[33] "[T]he Nat Turner created by William Styron," Clarke complained, "has little resemblance to the Virginia slave insurrectionist who is a hero to his people."[34]

A group of black intellectuals responded by repudiating various aspects of Styron's novel and, more pertinent to our concerns, rallying to the side of Nat Turner. According to Lerone Bennett Jr., "[T]he real Nat Turner was a virile, commanding, courageous figure."[35] According to Ernest Kaiser, Turner "led a heroic rebellion against the dehumanization of chattel slavery."[36] According to Charles V. Hamilton,

> Nat Turner is our hero, unequivocally understood. He is a man who had profound respect and love for his fellow blacks. . . . Nat Turner *was a success* because he perpetuated the *idea* of freedom—freedom at all cost. He will not be denied his place in the revolutionary annals of black people by white people who—through the guise of art or otherwise—feel a conscious or subconscious need to belittle him.[37]

The fight over Styron's depiction has contributed to a popularization and elevation of Nat Turner. In many settings he is now accepted as an uncontroversial hero by people who know little about the particulars of his rebellion or debates about its morality. In 2009, when Newark, New Jersey, unveiled its largest municipal public park, the Nat Turner Park, all sorts of political dignitaries joined in the celebration, none of whom evinced any awareness that the naming of the park might be problematic.[38]

I am principally concerned, however, not with admirers who are ignorant of the specifics of Turner's rebellion but with admirers who are knowledgeable and praise him in light of that awareness. I should like to make explicit an element of their case for Turner that is often only implicit: they applaud Turner assuming that his motivation had something to do with opposing slavery. *Their* Nat Turner is the figure of black oral tradition, the man who waged war against slavery, the "martyred soldier of slave liberation who broke his chains and murdered whites because slavery had murdered Negroes."[39] It is useful to highlight this matter of motivation because, as noted previously, opinions differ regarding Turner's aims. Those who admire him as a militant proponent of black liberation reject the hypothesis that he was a religious fanatic, though, as noted above, in Gray's *The Confessions*, Turner says quite clearly that he believed himself to be following the revelations of what he took to be the Holy Spirit. Turner's most vocal champions today much prefer to frame his conduct in secular garb. His champions similarly reject the hypothesis that Turner was insane. A notable example of the claim that Turner was mad is the statement by the former slave William Wells Brown that "Nat Turner's strike for liberty was the outburst of feelings of an insane man—made so by slavery."[40] The theory that Turner was insane rescues him from criminal culpability; the insane are not held responsible for their conduct. But that theory also robs Turner of any claim to heroism insofar as it would attribute his conduct to craziness rather than courage.

Admirers of Nat Turner dispute the historical accuracy of certain renditions of his life. They complain of Styron's omission of the fact that he was married to a black enslaved woman. They complain that in the absence of any historical substantiation Styron depicted Turner as yearning for sexual satisfaction with white women and engaged on one occasion in homosexuality with a fellow slave. They complain that without any corroborating evidence, Styron portrays Turner as having considerable contempt for his fellow captives.

Turner's admirers, however, do not dispute the accuracy of even the most gruesome depictions of rebel violence related by Gray or Styron. They are keenly aware of the need to handle these two sets of "confessions" carefully since neither embody Turner's voice directly and both are the handiwork of authors pursuing their own entrepreneurial, ideological, and professional imperatives. Styron's *The Confessions* is a concoction of the author's own imagination, a created version of Nat Turner's consciousness. Whether or not it offers useful insight, it does not even purport to be an "accurate" documentary rendition of its subject. It is, after all, *fiction*, a novel.

Gray's *The Confessions* is a document whose author claims that it represents a written translation of Nat Turner's spoken autobiography. Finding that Nat Turner was willing to make a full and free confession, Gray writes,

I determined for the gratification of public curiosity to commit his statements to writing, and publish them, with little nor not variation, from his
own words. That this is a faithful record of his confessions, the annexed
certificate of the County Court of Southampton will attest. They certainly
bear one stamp of truth and sincerity. He makes not attempt . . . to ex-
culpate himself, but frankly acknowledges his full participation in all the
guilt of the transaction.[41]

Notwithstanding Gray's endorsement of his own handiwork, there is
reason to be careful in mining it. Turner had incentive to misportray his own
situation. For example, he never mentions his wife. Perhaps he was trying to
protect her. Gray, too, had incentives that might have prompted him to omit
important facts or to exaggerate others. A former slaveowner, he sympathized
with the whites killed in the rebellion and detested the black slaves who did
the killing. As a failed lawyer in desperate need of money, moreover, Gray
may well have embellished *The Confessions* to make it more salable.[42]

The big problem with Turner's admirers is that they have been all too
indulgent in their attitude towards Turner's resort to violence. The lengths
to which some will go in defending their hero is vividly illustrated in a paper
written by a student in my race relations course.[44] In this student's view, "Nat
Turner risked his life to free slaves from bondage and . . . should be considered
a hero for his brave efforts." Forthrightly confronting those disturbed by the
killing of children, the student posits two responses. First, "if Nat Turner did
not kill the children, [they] would have been left to die anyway. To spare the
lives of the babies was to subject them to a torturous death by starvation and
neglect." Far from being a reason for disparagement, the student seems to imply,
the killing of the children was an instance of farsighted charity! There is no
evidence, however, suggesting that starvation would have been the childrens'
fate or that that was on the minds of the rebels. Turner could have spared
the children and left them to be cared for by the few poor, non-slaveowning
whites he declined to kill and the blacks in the county who remained where
they were as Turner's insurrectionists moved about.

The student's second response is that it was reasonable for Turner to target
white children since they stood to inherit their parents' property and power
"which meant inheriting the right to subject blacks to involuntary servitude."[45]
White children, the student maintained, "were the future of the slave regime."

That juveniles in slaveholding families would, unless killed, mature into adult slaveholders is inadequate as a justifiable basis for executing infants. The children that Turner's rebels killed were in no position to harm them immediately and directly. Under these circumstances, killing the children was unnecessary, therefore excessive, therefore wrong. The predicament into which Turner and his followers were consigned was hellish, to be sure. But surely that cannot mean that with moral impunity they could do *anything* such as kill *all* of the white children then living in the South.

Although racial pride is a major motif in the writings of Turner's champions, racial shame shadows their commentary. For many of his admirers, his rebellion has become an antidote for that humiliation. A key reason the fight over the reputation of Nat Turner pinches a nerve in the African American psyche even in the 21st century, is that many black Americans still feel tainted by enslavement. Alongside anger, hurt, and defiance, they feel mortification. They are deeply ashamed that their forbearers were slaves and thus enslaveable, that their ancestors were deprived of legally recognized marriage, that mothers and fathers, sisters and brothers were torn asunder by sale, that black ancestral daughters and nieces were commonly victims of sexual depredation by white men who acted with virtual impunity, that slaves could be named anything by their white owners with no recourse, and that their predecessors were made to be wholly dependent on white overlords who exploited them incessantly.

Close observers of the American racial trauma in the early national period anticipated that blacks as well as whites would recall continuously the degradations of Negro slavery. Thomas Jefferson and Alexis de Tocqueville agreed that racial reconciliation would forever be impossible in the United States precisely because of poisonous memories. In his *Notes on the State of Virginia*, Jefferson concluded that among the impediments that would prevent blacks and whites from sharing the country as equal neighbors were "[d]eep rooted prejudices entertained by the whites" and "ten thousand recollections, by the blacks, of the injuries they have sustained."[46] Similarly pessimistic was de Tocqueville who asserted in *Democracy in America* that whites would never forget their historical superiority to blacks and that blacks would never forget their historical subordination to whites. "Memories of slavery disgrace the race," de Tocqueville observed, "and race perpetuates memories of slavery."[47]

In addition to the actual horrors of enslavement and the re-creation of that trauma through collective memory is yet another burden with which blacks must grapple: proponents of slavery argued that Negroes preferred enslavement to freedom because blacks were natural slaves as indicated by, among other things, their accommodation to bondage. In his famous "Mud-Sill" Speech of March 1858, the United States Senator from South Carolina, James Henry Hammond, defended slavery stating that

> In all social systems there must be a class to do the menial duties, to perform the drudgery of life. . . . Its requisites are vigor, docility, fidelity. . . . It constitutes the very mud-sill of society. . . . Fortunately for the South she found a race adapted to that purpose. . . . A race inferior to her own but eminently qualified in temper, in vigor, in docility.[48]

The image of the docile Negro slave was a staple of pro-slavery apologists. Writing in the aftermath of Turner's rebellion, a pro-slavery politician in Virginia dismissed it as an anomaly. "Our slave population," he observed, "is not only a happy one, but it is contented, peaceful and harmless . . . . During all this time [the last sixty years] we have had one insurrection."[49] Writing decades later in his pro-slavery legal treatise, Thomas R. R. Cobb remarked that "the negro race" is peculiarly fitted to be a servile, laboring class because, among other things, their "moral character renders them happy, peaceful, contented, and cheerful in a status that would break the spirit and destroy the energies of the Caucasian and the native American."[50] Born during the age of slavery, the idea of the docile Negro lived on after slavery's end. In an important text published in 1927, E. B. Reuter states that blacks "are patiently tolerant under abuse and oppression and little inclined to struggle against difficulties. These facts of racial temperament and disposition make the Negroes more amenable to the condition of slavery than perhaps any other racial group."[51]

The image of the submissive Negro slave remains influential. When Quentin Tarantino unveiled his film *Django Unchained* (2012) one of the complaints voiced against it was that the movie made exceptional the slave who rebelled, consigning the mass of slaves to the familiar imagery of accommodation—sullen acquiescence perhaps, but acquiescence nonetheless. The exceptionality of the rebellious protagonist and the intensity of the reaction to it indicate that the notion of the submissive Negro remains alive and continues to rankle.[52]

The idea of slavery as a dishonorable fate worse than death runs deep in American culture. "Is life so dear," Patrick Henry asked, "as to be purchased at the price of chains and slavery?" His famous response was unequivocal: "Give me liberty or give me death!"[53] The black abolitionist David Walker voiced this same sentiment: "Now, I ask you, had you not rather be killed than to be a slave to a tyrant, who takes the life of your mother, wife, and dear little children?"[54] Behind the question is the insinuation that to live as a slave is to live without any claim to respect.

Hints that some, probably many, blacks continue to be profoundly ashamed that their ancestors accommodated themselves to bondage is found in songs and writings produced by activist partisans of black advancement. Consider the anthem "Oh, Freedom."

> Oh freedom, Oh freedom, Oh freedom over me
> And before I'd be a slave, I'll be buried in my grave
> And go home to my Lord and be free.

These lyrics suggest that death is preferable to slavery, a belief which is only a step away from the judgment that those who choose to live as slaves did something dishonorable. Or consider the title of a recent memoir by the civil rights activist Dorothy Cotton: *If Your Back's Not Bent: The Role of the Citizenship Education Program in the Civil Rights Movement* (2012). The phrase "if your back's not bent" alludes to the assertion that no one can ride you if you do not cooperate, that no one can oppress you if you resist sufficiently. That statement is probably true so long as one is willing to resist unto death. But faced with overwhelming force most people will bend their backs in submission, submit to the rapist, relinquish their land, surrender what they thought to be their rights. The sentimental talk about preferring death to slavery victimizes victims by making it seem that their choice to seek survival is somehow cowardly. There is, however, nothing shameful in seeking to survive under oppressive circumstances, even if survival entails enslavement. The counsel to eschew submission, even at the price of death, is easy to offer now on this side of abolition. Prior to 1865, however, the question posed a real dilemma. Those who decided to live as slaves rather than perish in rebellion are not properly subject to rebuke. Their decision made possible the better days enjoyed by their descendants.

My main point, though, is not to defend the choice made by the great mass of those who were caught in the grip of enslavement. My main point is merely descriptive: many blacks in modern America feel ashamed at some level of consciousness by the choice of their ancestors to *live* as slaves. That shame fuels the exhilaration felt upon contemplating Nat Turner and other rebels who made a radically different choice.

The idea of the submissive Negro was, of course, a device used to rationalize depriving African Americans of their natural right to freedom. After all, the evil of enslavement would be much mitigated if bondage was imposed on beings who did not much mind it. Indeed, some pro-slavery propagandists maintained that blacks actually *flourished* under bondage, and actually preferred it to freedom. Such arguments have no purchase on modern observers, especially those inclined to praise Nat Turner. More problematic, however, is the historical record that provides some ballast to the idea of the submissive Negro. The key feature of that record is the relative paucity of violent mass uprisings among slaves in the United States of America. There were some conspiracies to be sure—Gabriel Prosser's planned uprising in Richmond in 1800 and Denmark Vesey's planned uprising in Charleston in 1822. There were also rebellions that actually erupted, some of which were hushed up to deprive the enslaved of role models.[55] There was also an ongoing stream of low visibility, day-to-day resistance—the broken plow, the "accidental" fire, the spit in the soup, the stolen animals, the withheld labor, the feigned sickness, and all manner of other ways in which slaves deployed the weapons of the weak.[56] But with all due respect to Herbert Aptheker and others who have mined antebellum history for any and every hint of resistance, the fact remains that there were notably few instances in which enslaved blacks rose violently en masse to challenge the slave regime.[57] That is why Nat Turner stands out so strikingly. What he did was rare. And because it is rightly perceived as rare, those who applaud his conduct often rally around it with vehemence.

In his contribution to an anthology of critical responses to Styron, Loyle Hairston asks, "can a man commit a crime against *slavery?*"[58] He seems to have asked his question rhetorically, believing that the obvious answer is in the negative: no, a rebel cannot commit a crime fighting for his freedom, the emancipation of his people, or the destruction of the slave regime. This view is close, if not identical, to the position articulated by Addison Gayle when he declared, in defense of Turner, "[n]o victim has a moral responsibility to recognize the laws of the oppressor. And, in the same way, he owes no allegiance to a moral code which he did not help to construct, about which he was not consulted, and which operates continuously to keep him in his oppressed status."[59] Michael Walzer gave voice to a similar sentiment when he posited that "[t]here is a sense in which oppression makes men free, the more radical the oppression the more radical the freedom. Thus slaves have a right to kill their masters . . . . They are set loose from the normal restraints of social life, because any violence they commit against masters . . . can plausibly be called defensive."[60]

I agree that slaves have no obligation to observe the moral code of their masters.[61] That does not mean, however, that a slave has no moral obligations. Slaves, like all beings, have *some* moral obligations. They have a moral obligation, for example, to refrain from informing on other slaves even if by doing so they could attain their freedom or some other valuable status or opportunity.[62] I would also posit that slaves have a moral obligation to forego inflicting *excessive* injury in fighting for freedom. They can rightly resist enslavement. They can rightly resist violently. The can rightly resist violently even if that entails causing unavoidable injury to bystanders (e.g., fellow slaves hurt in the fighting), not to mention masters. But can slaves rightly do *anything* without fear of moral condemnation while acting to obtain freedom? Did slaveholders have no rights that slaves were bound to respect?[63] Unless we assume that the slaves were amoral animals the answer to that question must be no.

Some who praise Turner proceed as if the suffering imposed upon him and his followers insulate them from moral censure for anything they did to whites. But as a student in my course observed, "the evils of slavery do not mean that the ends of emancipation justify any and all means."[64] Both detractors and supporters of Nat Turner have noted that he and his followers committed no rapes during their insurrection—a noteworthy fact given the prevalence of sexual violence in struggles such as these. Thomas Wentworth Higginson wrote tellingly about this matter:

> These negroes had been systematically brutalized from childhood; they had been allowed no legalized or permanent marriage; they had beheld around them an habitual licentiousness, such as can easily exist under slavery; some of them had seen their wives and sisters habitually polluted by the husbands and brothers of these fair women who were now absolutely in their power. Yet I have looked through the Virginia newspapers of that time in vain for

one charge of an indecent outrage on a woman against these triumphant and terrible slaves.[65]

But just suppose Turner and his men had committed rapes and explained that they did so to terrorize and demoralize the slaveowners? Would *that* conduct be properly immunized against moral censure? I hope not, at least in the absence of some absolutely extraordinary justification that I cannot now imagine. That is because slaves are accountable to some moral code. At a minimum, such a code should require even the most oppressed person to forego inflicting gratuitous injury. On the assumption that rape of the sort described above would indeed inflict merely gratuitous injury, slaves doing it would be morally culpable. By the same logic, any gratuitous killings perpetrated by Turner and his followers make them morally culpable. Repairing to the facts of the case, it seems hard to conclude that killing the forgotten infant or the fleeing wife was somehow necessary to the achievement of an acceptable mission. If the mission was simply to kill as many whites as possible regardless of the circumstances, regardless of the threat they posed, regardless of any foreseeable consequences, then killing the infant and fleeing wife would be "necessary." But the undisciplined character of that homicidal mission would make it morally objectionable. It would be different if the pursuit of a morally acceptable mission entailed killings. Hence, if one could persuasively argue that sparing the infant or fleeing wife would have seriously threatened the rebellion, I would view their killings as tragic but excusable. But that argument is implausible. Turner and his rebels seem to have mainly been concerned with performing deadly gestures fueled by pent-up defiance, anger, and retribution. Satisfying hunger unloosed by such sentiments cannot justify the taking of lives.

The terrible suffering of Turner and the other rebels cannot appropriately serve as a predicate for extinguishing the lives of persons only tenuously associated with the slaves' predicament and apparently in no position to harm the rebels immediately. In my class, diehard admirers of Turner invoked an analogy to war. They argued that his conduct should be assessed in a similar fashion as soldiers involved in combat. Warfare is brutal and ugly and occasions actions that would otherwise be unacceptable. All of that is true—war is hell. But even warfare against the most dastardly of foes should have rules. The specter of mass rape probably did demoralize and intimidate Nazi soldiers and civilians on the Eastern Front in Germany near the end of World War II. And the Soviet soldiers on hand to commit those rapes had certainly suffered terribly. Yet still we properly abjure their conduct, despite the extremity in which it unfolded.[66]

How should one view Nat Turner? He warrants our sympathy but not our praise. He ought not be celebrated as a hero. He and his comrades rightly sought freedom and the demise of the slave regime even if those aims required a resort to violence. In pursuing those aims, however, Turner was obligated to minimize injury. The historical record suggests that he took no such care; indeed, to the contrary, the record suggests a willingness, even eagerness, to inflict homicidal injury in an indiscriminate fashion. Empathy for the rebels, abhorrence of slavery, and dedication to struggles for justice do not require praising Nat Turner despite the moral deficits of his insurrection. Withholding such praise is a useful discipline that has been modeled previously. An example is found in an article published September 22, 1831, in the Albany (New York) *African Sentinel and Journal of Liberty*, an antislavery newspaper. Reflecting on the Turner rebellion, the *Sentinel* observed that "[t]he slaves have a perfect right derived from God Almighty to their freedom."[67] But it then stated that Turner and his followers "have done vastly wrong in the late insurrection, in killing women and children." Affirming the legitimacy of the slaves' strivings, the *Sentinel* maintained that "[t]heir struggle for freedom is the same in principle as the struggle of our [founding] fathers in '76." It hoped that the slaves would be able to achieve their liberty eventually by "fair and honorable means." But the *Sentinel* insisted, in any event, that the slaves "refrain from assailing women and children" and conduct themselves "on the true principles of heroism."[68]

Demanding exacting standards is difficult in a political culture that routinely valorizes figures guilty of horrifying moral crimes. One egregious example is President Andrew Jackson, a much-honored slaveowner and slave seller who ruthlessly dispossessed Native Americans, pursuing a policy of "Indian removal" that would now be called "ethnic cleansing." Those championing Turner might well argue that if America can overlook the bad Jackson did in order to appreciate his good, then America should also overlook the bad Turner did in order to appreciate his good. They are justifiably angry at the biases that allow for the canonization of an Andrew Jackson alongside the minimization or demonization of a Nat Turner. The proper response, however, is not to become less attentive to Turner's failings but to become more attentive to Jackson's. Given the blood on their hands, neither should be offered as objects of emulation.

Seeking to reach an appropriate assessment of Turner, the great abolitionist William Lloyd Garrison refused to praise him. A pacifist, Garrison objected to deploying violence even against slavery, a practice he loathed. Yet Garrison also found himself unable to denounce Turner. Instead he denounced as hypocrites those who condemned Turner but praised other purveyors of revolutionary violence. According to Garrison, Turner and the other rebels "deserve no more censure than the Greeks in destroying the Turks, or the Poles in exterminating the Russians, or our Fathers in slaughtering the British. Dreadful, indeed, is the standard erected by worldly patriotism."[69]

I agree with Garrison that Turner deserves no more scrutiny than a George Washington, a Thomas Jefferson, a James Madison, or an Andrew Jackson. But he also deserves no less. One's ultimate judgment may vary given the different contexts these figures occupied: white statesmen had access to far greater resources, and thus more choice, than black slaves. For that reason the statesmen might appropriately be judged more harshly. But slaves ought not be allowed to escape ethical examination. By demanding that Turner and his fellow insurrectionists meet high standards of conduct, we morally elevate slaves who are all too often unwittingly demeaned by their champions.

NOTES

1   For useful comments on an earlier draft of this essay I would like to thank Tomiko Brown-Nagin, Paul Finkleman, Eric Foner, Kenneth Mack, Martha Minow, David Moltke-Hansen, Sanford Levinson, James McPherson, Mona Simpson, John Stauffer.

2   See John Henrik Clarke, ed., *William Styron's Nat Turner: Ten Black Writers Respond* (Boston: Beacon Press,1968). See especially Charles V. Hamilton, "Our Nat Turner and William Styron's Creation" at 73 ("Black youth on college campuses . . . can never and should never accept the portrayal (or is the word 'betrayal'?) of Nat Turner as set forth by Styron").

3   John Brown's resort to extreme violence poses ethical dilemmas similar to some of those triggered by Nat Turner's rebellion. See, e.g., John Stauffer and Zoe Trodd, eds., *The Tribunal: Responses to John Brown and the Harpers Ferry Raid* (Cambridge: Belknap Press of Harvard University Press, 2012); Peggy A. Russo and Paul Finkelman, eds., *Terrible Swift Sword: The Legacy of John Brown* (Athens: Ohio University Press, 2005); Paul Finkelman, ed., *His Soul Goes Marching On: Responses to John Brown and the Harpers Ferry Raid* (Charlottesville: University of Virginia Press, 1995); Benjamin Quarles, *Allies for Freedom and Blacks on John Brown* (New York: Oxford University Press, 1974).

4   Quoted in Kenneth S. Greenberg, ed., *The Confessions of Nat Turner and Related Documents* (Boston: Bedford Books of St. Martin's Press, 1996) at 49.

5   Ibid.

6   Ibid. at 50–51.

7   Ibid. at 19.

8   Quoted in Tony Horowitz, "Untrue Confessions," *New Yorker*, December 13, 1999.

9   Ibid.

10 Quoted in Henry Irving Tragle, *The Southampton Slave Revolt of 1831: A Compilation of Source Material* (Amherst: University of Massachusetts Press, 1971) at 318.

11 Ibid. at 319.

12 Ibid.

13 Quoted in Greenberg, supra note 5, at 90.

14 Ibid. at 41.

15 Ibid. at 67.

16 Quoted in Scot French, *The Rebellious Slave: Nat Turner in American Memory* (Boston: Houghton Mifflin, 2004)

17 Quoted in Greenberg, supra note 5, at 48.

18 Lerone Bennett Jr., *Pioneers in Protest* (Chicago: Johnson Publishing Company, 1969) at 88–89. See also Hamilton, supra note 3, at 76–77.

19 The *Journal* is probably referring here to Article IV, Section 4 of the United States Constitution which declares that "The United States shall . . . protect [each state] against invasion; and an application of the legislature, or of the executive (when the legislature cannot be convened) against domestic violence."

20 Quoted in Eric Foner, ed., *Nat Turner: Great Lives Observed* (Englewood Cliffs: Prentice-Hall, 1971) at 75.

21 Quoted in Greenberg, supra note 5, at 47–48.

22 Thomas Jefferson, *Notes on the State of Virginia*, Frank Shuffleton, ed. (New York:

Penguin Books, 1785, 1999) at 169.

23 Abraham Lincoln, Second Inaugural Address, March 4, 1865.

24 Quoted in Greenberg, supra note 5, at 54–55.

25 See Patrick H. Breen, "A Prophet in His Own Land: Support for Nat Turner and His Rebellion within Southampton's Black Community" in Kenneth S. Greenberg, ed., *Nat Turner: A Slave Rebellion in History and Memory*, 116 (New York: Oxford University Press, 2003) ("Nothing was a more potent recruiting tool for Nat Turner's army than some slaves' desire for revenge. For a brief moment . . . blacks had a chance to redress some of the wrongs they had endured").

26 Ibid. at 115.

27 *Washington National Leader*, Jan. 19, 1889. Quoted in Foner, supra note 21, at 148.

28 John Brown and Nat Turner, *New York Age*, Jan. 26, 1889. Quoted in Foner, supra note 21, at 149–150.

29 "Nat Turner Marches On," *The Liberator*, Nov. 7, 1831. Quoted in Foner, supra note 21, at 160.

30 "Nat Turner, Friend or Martyr?" *Opportunity*, Nov. 1931. Quoted in Foner, supra note 21, at163.

31 See French, supra note 17, at 233 ("The stature of the rebellious slave rose dramatically in the years between 1960 and 1965 as the civil rights movement, energized by student participation and leadership, took to the streets.").

32 See Albert E. Stone, *The Return of Nat Turner: History, Liberation, and Cultural Politics in Sixties America* (Athens: University of Georgia Press,1992).

33 Clarke, supra note 3, at vii.

34 Ibid.

35 Ibid. at 5.

36 Ibid. at 57.

37 Ibid. at 78.

38 See "Newark Opens Nat Turner Park in Central Ward After 30 Years," *NJ Com*, July 28, 2009. Though this news account makes no mention of conflict over Turner's reputation, some of the online responses are clearly aware of the controversy and take sides with respect to it. One correspondent writes: "North Bergen needs to name a park for Hal Turner, a Turner who didn't enter a home and decapitate 10 children. This is all you need to know about Newark and its feral population." By contrast, another correspondent writes: "Unlike these folks who kill for nothing nowadays . . . Mr. Turner had a cause. . . . [P]ut yourself in his shoes."

39 Stephen B. Oates, *The Fires of Jubilee: Nat Turner's Fierce Rebellion* 145 (New York: Harper Perennial, 1975). 3

40 *My Southern Home; Or, The South and Its People* (Boston: A. G. Brown, 1880) at 243–244. On a previous occasion Brown had asserted that Turner's "acts and his heroism live in the hearts of his race." Even then, however, he remarked that Turner was "a victim of his own fanaticism." *The Black Man: His Antecedent, His Genius, and His Achievements* (Boston: J. Redpath, 1863) at 59–75. See also Foner, supra note 21, at 141–145.

41 Quoted in Greenberg, supra note 5, at 40–41.

42 See Patrick H. Breen, "A Prophet in His Own Land: Support for Nat Turner and His

Rebellion within Southampton's Black Community" in Greenberg, *Nat Turner*, supra note 25, at 105.

43 Lerone Bennett, supra note 19, at 83 (1969).

44 See paper by KA, on file at Harvard Law School Library.

45 As it happens, Turner was himself owned by a child who had inherited him. See Greenberg, supra note 5, at 2.

46 Jefferson, supra note 23, at 145.

47 Alexis de Tocqueville, *Democracy in America*, J. P. Meyer, ed. (Garden City: Double-day, 1835, 1969) at 341.

48 Quoted in Paul Finkelman, ed., *Defending Slavery: Proslavery Thought in the Old South—A Brief History with Documents* (Boston: Bedford Books of St. Martin's Press, 2003) 86–87.

49 Quoted in George M. Frederickson, *The Black Image in the White Mind: The Debate on Afro-American Character and Destiny, 1817–1914* (New York: Harper & Row, 1971, 1972) at 57.

50 Thomas R.R. Cobb, *The Inquiry Into the Law of Negro Slavery* (Philadelphia: T. & J. W. Johnson, 1858) at 46. Abused throughout the history of the United States, native Americans have enjoyed one advantage over blacks: their reputation as unenslaveable. That native Americans would perish rather than survive in bondage added to the dubious allure of the "noble savage."

51 E.B. Reuter, *The American Race Problem* 7 (New York: Thomas Y. Crowell, 1927). See also Ulrich B. Phillips, *The Slave Economy of the Old South: Selected Essays in Economic and Social History*, Eugene Genoverse, ed., (Baton Rouge: Louisiana State University Press, 1968).

52 See A. O. Scott, "The Black, the White, and the Angry," *New York Times*, December 24, 2012; Dexter Gabriel, "Hollywood's Slavery Films Tell Us More About the Present Than the Past," *Colorlines*, January 9, 2013.

53 Speech by Patrick Henry before the Virginia House of Delegates, Richmond, Virginia (March 23, 1775), quoted in John Bartlett, *Familiar Quotations* 270 (Boston: Little Brown and Compant, 1937).

54 David Wilkins's *Appeal to the Coloured Citizens of the World*, Peter P. Hinks, ed. (University Park: Pennsylvania Srate University Press, 1820, 2000) at 28.

55 See, e.g., Daniel Rasmussen, *American Uprising: The United States of America's Largest Slave Revolt* (New York: Harper, 2011).

56 Lampooning the notion of the docile Negro, John Oliver Killens writes: "The slaves were so 'contented' the slavemasters could not afford the astronomical cost of fire insurance. Dear old Dixieland was in a constant state of insurrection. Thousands of rapturous slaves killed their mistresses and masters, put spiders in the Big House soup, broke their farming implements accidentally-on-purpose, set fire to the cotton patches, and, all in all, demonstrated their contentedness in most peculiar ways." Clarke, supra note 3, at 42. See also Raymond A. Bauer and Alice H. Bauer, "Day to Day Resistance to Slavery," 27 *Journal of Negro History* 388 (1942); James C. Scott, *Weapons of the Weak: Everyday Forms of Peasant Resistance* (1987).

57 I refer to Herbert C. Aptheker's scholarship with deep respect and gratitude. See especially *American Negro Slave Revolts* (New York: Columbia University Press, 1943). See

also Eugene D. Genovese, *From Rebellion to Revolution: Afro-American Slave Revolts in the Making of the Modern World* (Baton Rogue: Louisiana State University Press, 1979).

58   Loyle Hairston, "William Styron's Nat Turner—Rogue Nigger," in Clarke, supra note 3, at 72.

59   Addison Gayle, *The Black Situation* (New York: Horizon Press, 1970) at 68–70.

60   Michael Walzer, *Obligations: Essays on Disobedience, War, and Citizenship* (Cambridge: Harvard University Press, 1970) at 62.

61   The Commonwealth of Virginia itself recognized this to some extent when it dismissed an indictment for treason against a slave rebel who took part in Turner's insurrection. The reasoning seems to be that a slave, as a total alienated outsider, cannot betray a polity that is not his in any meaningful sense.

62   See Randall Kennedy, *Sellout: The Politics of Racial Betrayal* (New York: Pantheon, 2008).

63   This is an inversion, of course, of Chief Justice Roger B. Taney's observation that in antebellum America, blacks had no rights that whites were bound to respect. *Dred Scott v. Sandford*, 60 U.S.393 (1857). Ralph Waldo Emerson maintained during the Civil War that the Confederate rebel "has no rights which the Negro . . . is bound to respect." Quoted in David S. McReynolds, *John Brown Abolitionist* (2005) at 483.

64   Student paper from LB, on file at Harvard Law School Library.

65   Quoted in French, supra note 17, at 118–119.

66   Cf. Anonymous (Marta Hillers), *A Woman in Berlin: Eight Weeks in a Conquered City: A Diary* (New York: Metropolitan Books/Henry Holt, 2005).

67   Quoted in Foner, supra note 21, at 84.

68   Ibid.

69   Quoted in Foner, supra note 21, at 82.

3

American Navies and British Neutrality During the Civil War

James M. McPherson

Most civil wars in nation states through history have attracted foreign intervention of some kind, often military support for the faction rebelling against an established government. A very real possibility for such intervention existed during the American Civil War. The French Emperor Louis Napoleon sympathized with the Confederacy and the French economy was hurt by the sharp decline in the availability of Southern cotton. Several times during the war Napoleon pressed the British government to join France in an effort to mediate peace negotiations between the warring parties in America on the basis of Confederate independence. The British economy was harmed even more than France's by the loss of cotton from the South. Large numbers of Englishmen also sympathized with the Confederacy. But while Britain came dangerously close to intervention on two occasions, the ministry of Viscount Henry Palmerston ultimately backed off. Napoleon did not want to act without British cooperation. So in the end the Union and Confederacy fought it out among themselves without official intervention by any foreign power. But it was a very near thing.

Several factors shaped British policy toward the American Civil War, including pressures both for and against intervention: the "cotton famine," as it was known especially in 1862, which caused massive unemployment and suffering among Lancashire textile workers; divisions between pro-Union and pro-Confederate elements of British public opinion; the importance to the British economy of foreign trade with the United States as well as desire for cotton from the Confederate states; the Palmerston ministry's fears that a rupture with the United States would jeopardize Britain's hold on its Canadian colonies; the slavery issue, especially after Abraham Lincoln's Emancipation Proclamation made it a war of freedom against slavery that strongly swayed British opinion toward the Union side; and international crises in Europe that diverted French as well as British attention from the war in America by 1863 and after. But the single most important factor that directly or indirectly shaped Anglo-American and Anglo-Confederate relations, especially from 1861 to 1863, was the actions of the Union and Confederate navies. Three such actions or proceedings played a crucial role in the international dimensions of the American Civil War and the potential for Anglo-American conflict: the so-called "*Trent* Affair" in November– December 1861; the legal as well as economic aspects of the Union naval blockade of Confederate ports; and efforts by the Confederate navy to have warships built in private British shipyards.

FIRST, THE *Trent* AFFAIR. On November 8, 1861, the U.S. warship *San Jacinto*, patrolling the Old Bahama Channel off the northern coast of Cuba, fired a shot across the bow of the British packet steamer *Trent* and forced her to heave to in international waters. At the order of the *San Jacinto*'s captain, Charles Wilkes, the executive officer led armed sailors aboard the *Trent* and seized James Mason and John Slidell, who had escaped from Charleston aboard a blockade runner and were on their way to Europe as Confederate envoys to Britain and France.

Wilkes was something of a loose cannon in the American navy. He had a bullying personality that demanded quick obedience from subordinates but often defied the orders of superiors. As a lieutenant twenty years earlier he had commanded an exploring expedition in the South Pacific that had produced much valuable information, including confirmation of Antarctica's continental status. But his violent disciplinary measures had earned the hatred of sailors and officers alike. He faced a court-martial upon his return to the United States in 1842, but escaped conviction.

For the next two decades Wilkes remained unpopular in the navy, and his career languished. But the need for experienced naval officers when the Civil War broke out caused Secretary of the Navy Gideon Welles to give him command of the *San Jacinto*. He was in the Caribbean hunting for the Confederate commerce raider CSS *Sumter*, which had captured and destroyed several American merchant ships, when he learned from the American consul in Havana that Mason and Slidell were about to embark on the *Trent*. Here, thought Wilkes, was an even greater prize than the *Sumter*. He lay in wait for the *Trent* in the Old Bahama Channel. On November 8 the *Trent* steamed into sight, and Wilkes pounced.

Although the *Trent* was a ship of a neutral nation on its way from one neutral port to another, Wilkes informed Gideon Welles that he had consulted the books on international and maritime law on board the *San Jacinto* and learned that he had the right to capture enemy dispatches on a neutral ship. As diplomats, he wrote, Mason and Slidell were "the embodiment of dispatches." Whether this novel interpretation of international law would have stood up in a prize court is impossible to know, because Wilkes did not send the *Trent* to a port with a prize court. He initially intended to do so but uncharacteristically allowed his executive officer to talk him out of it. He was already shorthand, Wilkes explained to Welles, and to have put a prize crew on the *Trent* would have made him more so. The *Trent* was also carrying many passengers to England who would have been seriously inconvenienced by diversion to Key West or another American port. So he seized the Confederate diplomats and let the *Trent* go. Ironically, much of the angry British reaction would have been defused if he had sent her to a prize court.[1]

The Northern press lionized Wilkes as a hero. He was feted in Boston and lauded in Congress. Secretary of the Navy Welles, in words he later regretted, congratulated Wilkes "on the great public service you have rendered. Your conduct in seizing these public enemies was marked by intelligence, ability, decision, and firmness." Even Lincoln at first seemed to share the public mood of euphoria.[2]

But the president and other Cabinet members soon had second thoughts. Even before the furious reaction from across the Atlantic reached American shores, Lincoln remarked to Attorney General Edward Bates: "I am not much of a prize lawyer, but it seems to me that if Wilkes saw fit to make that capture on the high seas he had no right to turn his quarter-deck into a prize court."[3] Charles Sumner, chairman of the Senate Foreign Relations Committee, reminded Lincoln that the United States had declared war on Britain in 1812 for behavior similar to Wilkes's seizure of Mason and Slidell. The American minister to Britain, Charles Francis Adams, made the same point to Secretary of State William H. Seward.

The jingo press in England clamored for revenge for this insult to the Union Jack. The Royal Navy strengthened its fleet in the western Atlantic and convoyed army reinforcements to Canada. The risk of war caused the American stock market to swoon. Government bonds found no buyers. Southern newspapers speculated about the happy prospect of an Anglo-American war that would assure Confederate independence. The British Cabinet drafted an ultimatum demanding an apology and the release of Mason and Slidell. Queen Victoria's consort, Prince Albert, ill and soon to die, suggested language that softened the ultimatum, which Foreign Secretary Lord Russell accepted. Russell even suggested to Lord Lyons, the British minister to the United States, that if the Americans released the two Confederates the British could be "rather easy about the apology."[4]

By mid-December the Lincoln administration recognized that it must give in. Attorney General Bates, who had initially supported Wilkes, acknowledged that "to go to war with England now is to abandon all hope of suppressing the rebellion." While Lincoln also recognized that he must not have "two wars on his hands at a time, " he also wanted to avoid the humiliation and political danger of appearing to give in to John Bull. Seward took a hint from Prince Albert's revision of the ultimatum. At Cabinet meetings on Christmas day and the following day, Seward presented a memorandum stating that Wilkes had acted without instructions (which was true) and had erred by failing to bring the *Trent* into port for adjudication by a prize court. As a face-saving gesture, Seward added that the United States was gratified by Britain's recognition of the neutral rights for which America had always contended.[5]

The Cabinet endorsed this document, and the Confederate envoys made their ways to London and Paris where they spent three futile years trying to win the foreign recognition and intervention that might have occurred if they had remained imprisoned at Fort Warren in Boston Harbor. The Lincoln administration suffered less political damage than the president had feared, for most of the Northern public had come to the same "one war at a time" conclusion as Lincoln. And the reaction in Britain was surprisingly pro-American. Charles Francis Adams reported from the American legation in January 1862 that "the current which ran against us with such extreme violence six weeks ago now seems to be going with equal fury in our direction."[6] That favorable current had crucial significance for the United States Navy, for the question of the blockade's legitimacy under international law was coming to a head.

ONE OF LINCOLN'S FIRST actions as commander in chief after the Confederate attack on Fort Sumter was to declare a blockade of the Confederate coast, which eventually extended 3,500 miles from Virginia to Texas, including 189 harbors and coves where cargo could be landed. To block all of these holes was an impossible task. Only a dozen of these harbors had railroad connections to the interior, but imposing an effective blockade on just these ports would require large numbers of ships to cover the multiple channels and rivers and inland waterways radiating from or connecting several of them. Although the Navy Department purchased, chartered, and began to build vessels at a feverish pace in 1861 to create a large blockade fleet, the cordon was at first as leaky as a sieve. Most blockade runners leaving or entering Confederate ports got through, as indeed they did throughout the entire war. But as time went on, the blockade became ever tighter and those runners that did get through were built for speed and low visibility with limited carrying capacity, which much diminished Confederate seaborne trade at a time when the Southern ability to wage war required the importation of large amounts of war material and the export of cotton to pay for it. The blockade became an increasingly effective Union strategy by 1862, helping to cause shortages of almost everything in the South and a dizzying inflationary spiral that eventually ruined the Confederate economy.

The blockade had important diplomatic implications. In 1856 the leading maritime powers of Europe had adopted the Declaration of Paris defining the international law of warfare at sea. A key part of this Declaration stated: "Blockades, in order to be binding [on neutral powers] must be effective; that is to say, maintained by a force sufficient really to prevent access to the coast of the enemy."[7] The United States had not signed the Declaration because it also outlawed privateering, which had been a potent American naval weapon in the Revolution and the War of 1812. Now that the United states was the victim of Confederate privateers in the early months of the Civil War, Secretary of State Seward was eager to sign.

But the complications of doing so in the middle of a civil war postponed the question until some future time. Nevertheless, the provisions of the Declaration of Paris remained in force for European powers. Confederate envoys (including Mason and Slidell when they finally reached Europe) presented long lists of ships they claimed had evaded the blockade to prove that it was a mere "paper blockade" and therefore illegal under international law. Jefferson

Davis condemned the North's so-called blockade as a "monstrous pretension."[8]

Their contention that many vessels breached the blockade was quite true. But they neglected to note that most of them were small coasting vessels traveling often on the inland waterways from one Southern port to another, not ocean-going ships or blockade runners going to or from foreign ports. Nor did the Confederates help their cause by imposing an informal embargo on cotton exports in 1861 as a way to put pressure on Britain and France to intervene in the war to get cotton. By the time Confederate leaders realized that the embargo was counterproductive, the blockade had tightened and efforts to get cotton through it had become difficult.

Some did get through, however, and in November 1861 Foreign Secretary Lord Russell asked Lord Lyons for his opinion of Confederate claims about a paper blockade. Lyons confessed that he was "a good deal puzzled" about how to respond to Russell. He wrote that the blockade "is literally by no means strict or vigorous along the immense extent of coast to which it is supposed to apply. On the other hand it is very far from being a mere Paper Blockade. A great many vessels are captured; it is a most serious interruption of trade; and if it were as ineffective as Mr. Jefferson Davis says in his message, he would not be so very anxious to get rid of it." When John Slidell presented French officials with yet another list of vessels that had run the blockade, they asked him "how it was that so little cotton had reached neutral ports. Slidell answered that most of the successful runners had small cargo capacity, and "the risk of capture was sufficiently great to deter those who had not an adventurous spirit from attempting it."[9]

Fatal admission! The true measure of the blockade's effectiveness was not how many ships got through or even how many were captured, but how many never tried. Lord Russell said as much in a statement on February 2, 1862, when in effect he announced to Parliament a corollary to the Declaration of Paris: "Assuming . . . that a number of ships is stationed and remains at the entrance to a port, sufficiently really to prevent access to it *or to create an evident danger of entering or leaving it* . . . the fact that various ships may have successfully escaped through it . . . will not of itself prevent the blockade from being an effective one by international law."[10]

The Russell corollary drove a stake through the heart of Confederate efforts to convince European governments of the blockade's illegitimacy. But to the extent that the blockade was a practical as well as legal success, it ironically heightened the potential danger to the Union cause. Confederate diplomacy in 1862 switched its focus from discrediting the blockade to seeking diplomatic recognition of Confederate nationhood. The Southern nation was a going concern that had successfully defended its independence for a year. Recognition of this reality by foreign powers, argued Confederate leaders, could be the first step toward commercial treaties that could reopen the cotton trade and overcome the blockade-imposed famine.

A good many Europeans shared this conviction. They viewed diplomatic recognition as part of a package that would include peace negotiations between the warring parties brokered by the British and French governments. Confederate military success in 1861 sustained a widespread belief in Europe that the Union cause was hopeless; Union armies could never reestablish control over 750,000 square miles of territory defended by a determined and courageous people. Northern leaders greatly feared the possibility of European recognition of the Confederacy if Union arms did not do something to convince foreign nations of their ability to crush the rebellion. As Lord Robert Cecil told a Northern acquaintance in 1861: "Well, there is one way to convert us all—win the battles, and we shall come round at once."[11]

In February 1862, Union forces did begin winning battles: Forts Henry and Donelson in Tennessee; Roanoke Island and a series of other victories in North Carolina, Pea Ridge in Arkansas, Shiloh in Tennessee; the capture of Nashville, New Orleans, and Memphis; and a massive invasion of Virginia that brought the Army of the Potomac to Richmond's doorstep by May. The Union navy played a key role in most of these victories, especially the capture of New Orleans. Although Confederate envoys continued to press for recognition, they now found a cold reception. In June 1862 British Prime Minister Palmerston observed that "this seems an odd moment to Chuse for acknowledging the Separate Independence of the South when all the Seaboard, and the principal internal Rivers are in the hands of the North. . . . We ought to know that their Separate Independence is a Truth and a fact before we declare it to be so."[12]

But even as Palmerston wrote these words , the pendulum of victory swung over to the Confederacy again. General Robert E. Lee's Army of Northern Virginia drove General George B. McClellan's Army of the Potomac back from Richmond in the Seven Days Battles and then inflicted a humiliating defeat on Union arms only 25 miles from Washington in the Second Battle of Bull Run. Confederate armies in Tennessee launched counteroffensives and invaded Kentucky in September while Lee invaded Maryland.

This startling reversal of momentum revived the possibility of European intervention, especially since the cotton famine had devastated the British and French textile industries. Louis Napoleon pressed the British government to join France in an offer to mediate peace negotiations on the basis of Confederate independence. Palmerston and Foreign Secretary Russell now seemed almost ready for such an overture. Palmerston observed that at Second Bull Run the Federals "got a very complete smashing, and it seems not altogether unlikely that still greater disasters await them, and that even Washington or Baltimore might fall into the hands of the Confederates." If something like that happened, he asked Russell, "would it not be time for us to consider whether England and France might not address the contending parties and recommend an arrangement on the basis of separation?" Russell needed little persuasion. He concurred, and added that if the Lincoln administration rejected an offer of mediation, "we ought ourselves to recognize the Southern States as an independent state."[13]

Palmerston and Russell planned to hold a Cabinet meeting in October 1862 when they would vote on a proposal to the Union and Confederate governments of "an Armistice and Cessation of Blockades with a view to Negotiation on the Basis of Separation" to be followed by diplomatic recognition of the Confederacy. They also agreed to take no action until the outcome of the Confederate invasions of Maryland and Kentucky were more clear. "If the Federals sustain a great defeat . . . Cause will be manifestly hopeless and the iron should be struck while it is hot," declared Palmerston. "If, on the other hand," he added, the Federals "should have the best of it, we may wait a while and see what may follow."[15]

What followed were the battles of Antietam in Maryland and Perryville in Kentucky, which turned back the dual invasions and forced the Confederates to retreat. These were not tactically decisive Union victories, but they did have important strategic consequences, especially on the diplomatic front. Charles Francis Adams reported from London that most Englishmen had expected the Confederates to capture Washington, and "the surprise" in London at their retreat instead "has been quite in proportion . . ." As a consequence, "less and less seems to be thought of meditation and intervention."[16]

Palmerston did indeed back away from the idea of intervention. The only favorable condition for mediation would have been "the great success of the South against the North," he commented to Russell in October. "That state of things seemed ten days ago to be approaching," but at Antietam "its advance has been lately checked. . . . I am therefore inclined to change the opinion I wrote you when the Confederates seemed to be carrying all before them, and I am convinced that we must continue merely to be lookers-on till the war shall have taken a more decided turn."[17]

It never did take a decided enough turn toward the Confederates as far as Britain was concerned, especially because of another consequence of the battle of Antietam: it gave Lincoln the Union victory he had been waiting for to issue the preliminary Emancipation Proclamation on September 22, followed by the final Proclamation on New Year's Day 1863. Young Henry Adams, who served as private secretary for his father at the legation in London, wrote on January 23 that "the Emancipation Proclamation has done more for us here than all our former victories and all our diplomacy. It is creating an almost convulsive reaction in our favor all over this country." Richard Cobden, a pro-Union member of the British Parliament, declared that the Proclamation "has had a powerful effect on our newspapers and politicians. It has closed the mouths of those who have been advocating the side of the South. Recognition of the South, by England, whilst it bases itself on Negro slavery, is an impossibility."[18]

COBDEN'S ASSERTION WAS UNDOUBTEDLY accurate. But that did not end the danger of a rupture in Anglo-American relations that might redound to the benefit of the Confederacy. In the early months of the war, Confederate Naval Secretary Stephen Mallory had sent agents to Europe to purchase and contract for the building of warships to prey on American commerce and to attack Union blockade ships. The most successful of these agents was James D. Bulloch, a Georgia native and former officer in the U.S. Navy, who in 1861 contracted for two fast and powerful commerce raiders that became the CSS *Florida* and CSS *Alabama* when they were launched in 1862.

The building of these ships in Liverpool was an egregious violation of British neutrality. Britain's Foreign Enlistment Act prohibited the construction and arming of warships for a belligerent power. But Bulloch was a master of misdirection. The Confederate government itself was not named as a party to the contracts he negotiated. The ship that became the *Florida* was suppos-

edly being built for a merchant in Palermo, Sicily. The American consul in
Liverpool, Thomas H. Dudley, uncovered a great deal of evidence that the
ship was in fact destined for the Confederacy. But the British government
did not stop her from going to sea in March 1862 as an ostensible merchant
vessel without any guns or other warlike equipment. In August she took on
her armament, ammunition, and supplies that had been separately shipped
to an uninhabited cay in the Bahamas. Soon afterward she sailed forth on a
career that destroyed 38 American merchant ships.

Even more deadly was the *Alabama*, which Bulloch managed to get out of
Britain in July 1862 owing to the laxness of British enforcement of the Foreign
Enlistment Act. In a contest of lawyers, spies, and double agents that would
furnish material for an espionage thriller, Thomas Dudley amassed evidence
of the ship's illegal purpose, and Bulloch struggled to slip through the legal
net surrounding him. Once again bureaucratic negligence, legal pettifoggery,
and the Confederate sympathies of the British customs collector in Liverpool
gave Bulloch time to ready the ship for sea. When an agent informed him
of the government's belated intention to seize the ship, Bulloch took her out
for a "trial cruise" from which she never returned. She rendezvoused at the
Azores with a tender carrying guns and ammunition sent separately from
Britain. Under her redoubtable Confederate commander Raphael Semmes, she
roamed the seas for the next two years capturing and destroying 64 American
merchant vessels and one naval ship before being sunk by the USS *Kearsarge*
in a dramatic action near Cherbourg, France, in June 1864.

Encouraged by British negligence, which he interpreted as sympathy for
the Confederacy, Bulloch aimed even higher. In 1862 he contracted with the
same Liverpool firm that had built the *Alabama*, the Laird Brothers, for the
construction of two powerful ironclad rams intended to raise havoc with the
Union blockading fleets. Designed with two gun turrets and a lethal under-
water ram, the warlike purpose of these formidable "Laird rams was difficult
to disguise."[21] As they were nearing completion in 1863, another Confederate
agent, Matthew Fontaine Maury, purchased a British steamer suitable for
conversion into a commerce raider to be named the CSS *Georgia*. In March
1863 she was ready to sail from the obscure port of White Haven. Maury sent
coded messages to various Confederate officers in Britain, to rendezvous there.
The British Foreign Office woke up and tried to stop the ship's departure,
but the telegram to White Haven sat in an outbox in London on March 31

until the port's telegraph office closed for the day. After midnight the *Georgia* sailed, took on her armament off Ushant, and began her career as a raider.

The embarrassment caused by the *Georgia's* escape made the Foreign Office determined to prevent any more such occurrences. Also in March 1863 a Parliamentary Committee issued a report condemning the British government for its failure to prevent the escape of the *Florida* and *Alabama*. And Charles Francis Adams continued to flood the Foreign Office with evidence of the Laird rams' Confederate provenance. Adams also pressed Foreign Secretary Russell to seize the *Alexandra*, a small steamer just completed in Liverpool as a commerce raider.

In April 1863, the government did seize the *Alexandra*, but the Court of Exchequer ruled the seizure illegal on the grounds that there was no proof of Confederate ownership or of the arming or fitting out of the vessel in England. That was technically true—it had been built for Fraser, Trenholm, and Company, a British firm that just happened to be the Confederacy's financial agent in London. The government appealed the Exchequer's decision and continued to detain the *Alexandra*. The officer slated to command the ship, one of several Southern naval officers in Britain waiting assignment, complained that "it is clear that the English Government never intends to permit anything in the way of a man-of-war to leave its shores. I know Mr. Adams is accurately informed of the whereabouts and employment of everyone of us, and that Yankee spies are aided by English Government detectives. With the other vessels the same plan will be instituted as with the *Alexandra*. They will be exchequered, and thus put into a court where the Government has superior opportunities for instituting delays"[23]

Despite the obstacles this precedent posed to getting the Laird rams into Confederate possession, Bulloch did not give up. He arranged for the dummy purchase of them by the French firm of Bravay and Company ostensibly acting as agents for "his Serene Highness the Pasha of Egypt." This subterfuge fooled no one, but clear proof of Confederate ownership was elusive despite the mounting circumstantial evidence piled up by American consul Thomas Dudley. Charles Francis Adams sent a series of increasingly ominous warnings to Foreign Secretary Russell against allowing the rams to escape, culminating in a dispatch on September 5, 1863, concluding that "It would be superfluous in me to point out to your Lordship that this is war."

Despite the stark nature of Adams's words, his phraseology was actually ambiguous. Did he mean that the United States would respond to the escape of the rams with a declaration of war against Britain? Or that it would be seen as an act of war against the United States? Or was it a warning that it would make England complicit in the Confederate war against the United States? Whatever meaning Adams intended to convey, the matter was already moot when he wrote these words. Russell had given orders two days earlier for the detention of the ships, and they were subsequently purchased by the Royal Navy. [24]

A disappointed and angry Bulloch moved his efforts to the friendlier environment of France, where he had reason to believe that Louis Napoleon's government would look the other way as he contracted with French shipbuilding companies for the construction of two ironclad warships and four corvettes as commerce raiders. After a promising beginning, however , Bulloch was dumbfounded in 1864 by the French government's decision to seize these vessels rather than risk rupture with the United States. Bulloch lamented this "most remarkable and astounding circumstance that has yet occurred in reference to our operations in Europe, "which" had caused him "greater pain and regret than I ever confederated it possible to feel." The Confederate envoy in Paris, John Slidell, confessed that this failure was "a most lame and impotent, conclusion to all our efforts to create a Navy."[25]

IN THE END THE American Civil War proved an exception to the rule that civil wars tend to attract foreign intervention. Neither the United States nor foreign powers, especially Britain, considered it in their self-interest to provoke or undertake such intervention and acted rationally to prevent it. The Lincoln administration determined in 1861 that it could only carry on "one war at a time" and let Mason and Slidell go. The British government decided in 1862 to recognize the legality of the Union blockade, in considerable part because Britain relied heavily on naval blockades in its own wars and did not want to create a precedent that might undermine the legitimacy of such a weapon in a future war. Later in 1862, the Palmerston ministry resolved that Confederate strategic defeats in the battles of Antietam and Perryville raised sufficient doubts about the ability of the Southern nation to sustain itself as to make it in British self-interest not to risk a break with the United States by recognizing the Confederacy. And for the same reason, Britain and France decided to clamp down on Confederate efforts to build warships in the shipyards of those nations. These decisions prevented the American Civil War from becoming an international war. Perhaps we can learn something from a study of those events.

NOTES

1   Wilkes to Welles, Nov. 15, 16, 1861, Official Records of the Union and Confederate Navies (hereinafter, ORN), Series I, 1:124–31, Craig L. Symonds, *Lincoln and His Admirals* (New York: Oxford University Press, 2008), 75–78.

2   Welles to Wilkes, Nov. 30, 1861, ORN, I, 1:148; Symonds, *Lincoln and His Admirals*, 80–82.

3   Quoted in Symonds, *Lincoln and His Admirals*, 82.

4   Russell quoted in Symonds, *Lincoln and His Admirals*, 86. For the most recent accounts of the much-studied "*Trent* Affair," see Howard Jones, *Blue and Gray Diplomacy* (Chapel Hill: University of North Carolina Press, 2010), 83–111, and Amanda Foreman, *A World on Fire: Britain's Crucial Role in the American Civil War* (New York: Random House, 2010), 172–98.

5   Symonds, *Lincoln and His Admirals*, 92–94; David Herbert Donald, *Lincoln* (New York: Simon & Schuster, 1995), 323; Seward to Lord Lyons, Dec. 26, 1861, ORN, Series I, 1:177–87.

6   Adams to Charles Francis Adams, Jr., Jan. 10, 1862, in Worthington Chauncey Ford, ed., *A Cycle of Adams Letters, 1861–1865*, 2 vols. (Boston: Houghton Mifflin, 1920), 1:99.

7   Ephraim D. Adams, *Great Britain and the American Civil War*, 2 vols. (New York: Longmans, Green, 1925), 1:140.

8   ORN, Series II, 3:271, 299, 331; Dunbar Rowland, ed., *Jefferson Davis, Constitutionalist: His Letters, Papers, and Speeches*, 10 vols. (Jackson: Mississippi Dept. of Archives and History, 1923), 5:401, 403.

9   Lyons to Russell, Nov. 29, 1861, in Adams, *Great Britain and the American Civil War*, I: 254; ORN, II, 3:340.

10 Parliamentary Papers, 1862, vol. 62, North America, no. 8, papers Relating to the Blockade of the Ports of the Confederate States," 119–20, in John D. Hayes, ed, *Samuel Francis Du Pont: A Selection from His Civil War Letters*, 3 vols. (Ithaca: Cornell University Press, 1969), 1:326n. Italics added.

11 Quoted in Henry Donaldson Jordan and Edwin J. Pratt, *Europe and the American Civil War* (Boston: Octagon Books, 1931), 17

12 Palmerston to Austen H. Layard, June 19, 1862, in Hubert Du Brulle, "A War of Wonders: The Battle in Britain over Americanization and the American Civil War" (PhD dissertation, University of California at Santa Barbara, 1999), 210n.

13 This exchange is conveniently reprinted in James V. Murfin, *The Gleam of Bayonets: The Battle of Antietam and Robert E. Lee's Maryland Campaign, September 1862* (Baton Rouge: Louisiana State University Press, 1965), 394, 396–97, from the Russell Papers, Public Record Office, London.

14 Palmerston to Gladstone, Sept. 24, 1862, in Phillip Guedella, ed., *Gladstone and Palmerston, Being the Correspondence of Lord Palmerston with Mr. Gladstone, 1861–1865* (Covent Garden: Victor Gollancz, 1928), 232–33.

15 Russell to Henry R. C. Wellesley, Earl of Cowley; (British ambassador to France), Sept. 26, 1862, in Frank Merli and Theodore A. Wilson, "The British Cabinet and the Confederacy: Autumn, 1862," *Maryland Historical Magazine* 65 (1970), 247n.; Palmerston to Russell, Sept. 23, 1862, Russell Papers, reprinted in Murfin, *Gleam of Bayonets*, 400; Palmerston to Gladstone, Sept. 24, 1862, in Guedella, *Gladstone and Palmerston*, 233 .

16 Charles Francis Adams to Charles Francis Adams, Jr., Oct. 17, 1862, in Ford, *A Cycle of Adams Letters, 1861–1865*, 1:192; .Charles Francis Adams to William H. Seward, Oct. 3, 1862, in *Papers Relating to Foreign Affairs, 1861–1862*, Part I (Washington: U.S. State Department, 1862), 205 .

17 Adams, Great Britain and the American Civil War, 2: 43–44, 54–55.

18 Henry Adams to Charles Francis Adams, Jr., Jan. 23, 1863, in J. C. Levenson, ed., *The Letters of Henry Adams*, Vol. 1:1858–1868 (Cambridge: Belknap Press of Harvard University Press, 1982), 327; Richard Cobden to Charles Sumner, Feb. 13, 1863, in Belle Becker Sideman and Lilliam Friedman, eds., *Europe Looks at the Civil War* (New York: Orion Press, 1960), 222.

19 ORN, I, 1:363, 364, 397–98, 399–400. See also David Hepburn Milton, *Lincoln's Spymaster: Thomas Haines Dudley and the Liverpool Network* (Mechanicsburg: Stackpole Books, 2003), 34–37.

20 Bulloch to Stephen Mallory, Aug. 3, Sept. 10, 1862, Raphael Semmes to Mallory, Jan. 24, 1863, ORN, I, 1 : 775–80. See also Jones, *Blue and Gray Diplomacy*, 192–99, and Milton, *Lincoln's Spymaster*, 39–46 .

21 Mallory to Bulloch, April 30, 1862, Bulloch to Mallory, July 4, 1862, -, II, 2:186–87, 222–26.

22 Foreman, *A World on Fire*, 409–10 .

23 John R. Hamilton to James North, April 23, 1863, ORN, II:409; Merli, *Great Britain and the Confederate Navy, 1861–1865* (Bloomington: Indiana University Press, 2005), 160–77.

24 Merli, *Great Britain and the Confederate Navy*, 178–217; Bulloch to Mallory, Dec. 2, 1862, June 30, Sept. 1, Oct. 20, 1863, ORN, II, 2:307, 445–46, 488, 507–11.

25 Bulloch to Mallory, Feb. 17, June 10, 1864, John Slidell to Judah P. Benjamin, June 2, Aug. 8, 1864, ORN, II, 2:585, 665–68, 1139, 1187.

'The True Picture as It Really Was'

Seeing the Civil War in Art and Experience

Drew Gilpin Faust

Although I am far from an art historian or critic, I have for some time wanted to explore a set of thoughts that have been on my mind during the years I have worked on the subject of death and the Civil War—research I began in the mid 1990s that became *This Republic of Suffering* and then *Death and the Civil War*, the Ric Burns film based upon my book that aired in the fall of 2012 on PBS. I would like to reflect in this essay upon "seeing" the Civil War and the challenge this posed to those who lived through it. How did Americans North and South struggle to apprehend and comprehend the upheaval of long-taken-for-granted lives and customs? How did they grapple with change and trauma in their representations of the new world that war made? How were war's challenges to "seeing" addressed by ordinary men and women seeking to understand, describe, and explain their own lives as well as by those dedicated to more formal rendering of their perceptions in works of art?[1]

For two decades now I have been pondering the meaning of the Civil War's terrible slaughter—a death rate of 2½ percent of the population if we rely on most recent estimates—the equivalent today of seven million people lost. Battles of a scale unimagined and unprecedented left the living struggling to care for the wounded and bury the dead. The Mexican War saw approximately 2,000 battle deaths. After three days at Gettysburg in 1863—a single battle—7,000 lay dead and 50,000 wounded. There were no regular burial details to handle the bodies, no dog tags to identify the slain, no formal procedures for notifying next of kin. The suffering in the aftermath of any such a battle—Gettysburg, Shiloh, Antietam, Spotsylvania, the Wilderness—was unfathomable and, for those who witnessed it, often indescribable.[2] As I read the letters and diaries of Civil War participants, I found again and again their acknowledgment and articulation of the failure of words in face of the horror of battle's aftermath.

Contemplating the scene at the end of his first battle, Union soldier Henry Taylor wrote to his parents in Wisconsin in 1863, "I never want to see such a sight again. I cannot give such a description as I wish I could. My head is so full that it is all jumbled up together and I can't get it into any kind of shape." Oliver Wendell Holmes Jr. called the experience of war "incommunicable." John Caster of the Stonewall Brigade confessed to his parents, "I have not power to describe the scene. It beggars all description." Relief worker and nurse Cordelia Harvey wrote from Tennessee, "There are times when the meaning of words seem to fade away; so entirely does our language fail to express the reality." Words cannot explain; language does not exist: again and again letter writers describe not battle but their inability to describe battle. "None can narrate that strife," Herman Melville noted, himself abandoning the linear form of fiction for the illusions and allusions of poetry in his effort to portray the war. For Emily Dickinson even poetry faced inadequacy and required upheaval:

> The thought behind, I strove to join
> Unto the thought before—
> But sequence raveled out of sound
> Like balls upon a floor[3]

The failures of words represented at their heart a failure of comprehension—the absence of a logic and sequence to link events or observations into a coherent narrative. A story contains a direction, an explanation, a purpose. The trauma of this war seemed to erase these. Heroic tales of glory, courage, triumph, and sacrifice became hollow in face of this war's devastation. This was a crisis of meaning and understanding; the war's "untellability" was the product of its unintelligibility. But this crisis was rooted in the war's challenges to perception and description—Confederate Reuben Allen Pierson wrote his father after Gaines Mill in 1862, "Language would in no way express the true picture as it really was." How then to find "a true picture" in the face of such untellability and unintelligibility? How was it possible to see and speak in the face of the unspeakable?[4]

Even as battle's participants—soldiers, doctors, nurses, relief workers—wrote from the front lines of their inability to explain or describe, they frequently offered instead a report of their experience derived more from the senses than from intellect or reason—sharing, transmitting the stimuli directly rather than fashioning them into a coherent description or narrative. Rather, they offered fragments, vignettes, verbal images almost like snapshots with little claim to comprehensiveness or significance beyond their own subjective moment. Yet some of these images, these snapshots, appeared so frequently in so many individuals' writings and descriptions that I believe them to have had broader significance—to represent what we might regard, to borrow a phrase from T. S. Eliot, as shared fragments against the ruins, embodying a kind of proto-modernist consciousness confronting disillusion and despair in a manner we more often associate with the First World War than the mid-19th century. [5]

Civil War Americans often spoke and wrote of their inability to "realize" the loss and suffering of war, using that word with now-antiquated precision to mean to render it real in their own minds. As Sarah Palmer of South Carolina remarked after her brother's death at Second Bull Run, "I can't realize that I am never to see that dear boy again . . . it is too hard to realize." The concreteness of images or word pictures served as a means of making the ineffability of trauma real, embodying it in an image of the physical.[6]

This search for Confederate Pierson's "true picture" yielded at least some *common* pictures—rendered in words but not as stories or explanations. Instead these were images intended to be shared even if not interpreted or understood. Let me give just two examples of images that I have come across again and again in participants' efforts to convey a "true picture" of war. These became what we might in the language of our own time call "memes"—units for carrying cultural notions, transmitted from one individual to another. The concept of meme originated with Richard Dawkins in 1976 as an explanation for the spread of cultural phenomena. But others have seized on his notion in ways he never anticipated and often did not approve. Malcolm Gladwell has described a meme as "an idea that behaves like a virus." But in the age of the internet, memes have become omnipresent and less likely to be abstract ideas than images in which powerful meanings reside. Visuality was central in the Civil War context as well. Language and ideas had failed—but perhaps the eyes could grapple with what reason could not. Word pictures that spread like viruses enabled Civil War Americans to in some measure collectively communicate the realities of war. [7]

THE FIRST RECURRENT IMAGE I want to describe was that of a field of battle so covered with the slain as to render it impossible to walk without trampling the dead. "They paved the earth," a soldier wrote after the Battle of Williamsburg in 1862. With grim precision a Confederate described a two-acre area at Fredericksburg containing some 1,300 dead Yankees; others estimated stretches of a mile or more at Shiloh—and again at Antietam where every step had to be planted on a dead body. Ulysses Grant himself invoked the image in his description of Shiloh. "I saw an open field . . . so covered with dead that it would have been possible to walk across the clearing, in any direction, stepping only on dead bodies without a foot touching the ground." After Gettysburg, the bodies lay so thick, one witness explained, "I was compelled to walk on top of them to get by." [8]

A curious variant of the meme underscores its power to organize thought and perception. In 1862 after the Battle of Second Manassas, a soldier wrote of the slaughter of a unit of Zouaves, all dressed in their flamboyant red and blue uniforms. "An acre of ground, " he reported in a letter home, "was literally covered with the dead, dying and wounded . . ., the variegated colors of whose peculiar uniform gave the scene the appearance of a Texas hillside in spring, painted with wild flowers of every hue and color." For this soldier from rural Texas, the image brought to mind was a carpet of blossoms rather than a city pavement, a representation that emphasized the disjuncture and disruption of death by juxtaposing it with a natural beauty it seemed horribly to emulate. Another observer at the same scene saw it in much the same way, reporting that the field of battle offered the appearance of an immense flower garden, "the prevailing blue thickly dotted with red. . . . I could have walked," he continued, "a quarter of a mile in almost a straight line on their dead bodies without putting a foot on the ground."[9]

This recurrent image, this meme, embedded its viewer in the sensory—in the horror of so many bodies, of the ground beneath his feet replaced by a carpet of death. The vignette exerted powerful visual impact, conveying scale and horror with no appeal to reason or explanation. This was certainly an example of "show don't tell." But it was also more than visual; it evoked more than just the sense of sight. This meme is tactile as well in its invitation to imagine walking on these bodies. Men turned into carpet or pavement are men dishonored; the living are revolted and dehumanized by the notion of touching and trampling the mangled and bloated remains of soldiers not so very different from themselves. A Sanitary Commission official affirmed after Antietam that "no words can convey . . . the utter devastation and ruin" but urged his colleagues at home who sought to understand: "Visit a battlefield and *see* what a victory costs." For many who did see, the image was enduring—even inescapable. As George Metcalf of the 136th New York described, the picture of the dead and dying on the field at Gettysburg on the night of July 3 remained with him through the rest of his life, transcending any sensory input: "I see them now when my eyes are shut."[10]

For Clara Barton, the horrible images had become so fixed by 1864 that "the coming scenes paint themselves more vividly on my imagination. Having seen and known, I cannot shut my senses. They will perceive even in advance of the reality." The picture had taken on a life of its own. Arising in the immediacy of sensory experience, it became independent of its origins, now a creation of the mind, a representation of reality, in that way curiously like a work of art.[11]

THE SECOND FREEZE-FRAME THAT appears repeatedly—close to universally—in Civil War writings is that of the grotesque and in the language of the day "promiscuous" piles of amputated limbs associated with the aftermath of every battle. They were, as many witnesses put it, "a spectacle." Walt Whitman was perhaps the most renowned recorder of this horrifying sight, which he encountered on his first excursion into war in his search for his wounded brother George after Fredericksburg. In front of a Union hospital he found a "heap of feet, legs, arms and human fragments, a full load for a one-horse cart." He was deeply affected. After such a sight "Nothing we call trouble," he wrote, "seems worth talking about." This meme has such power and longevity it persists into our own time as we continue to grapple with the meaning of the Civil War. In Steven Spielberg's *Lincoln,* the president's son Robert contemplates his obligations of service and sacrifice as he waits outside a military hospital where his father is visiting the wounded. A cart appears, wheeled by soldiers and dripping blood. Robert follows and comes upon a mass grave for amputated limbs. Sickened, he flees in horror. For screenwriter Tony Kushner, who was seeking a visual means of representing the confrontation with the cost and terror of war, a pile of amputated limbs functions as effectively as it did for Walt Whitman 150 years earlier.[12]

Hundreds of observers described hospitals established in churches or schools where surgeons simply threw limbs out the window, sometimes until the pile grew so large it blocked the light—five feet or more in height one nurse reported. Men would then be detailed to haul or shovel the debris away. Josiah Murphy, describing such a scene after Fredericksburg, reported it was the practice to bury all the lost limbs at one time. When I was at the Museum of the Confederacy reading the manuscript "Burial Register of Richmond's Oakwood Cemetery," I found among the names of the dead and their gravesites an entry for a "Box of Limbs," which had been interred in the cemetery rows alongside war's other casualties.[13]

An estimated 50,000 amputations took place during the war, representing a far higher frequency than in other American conflicts. In World War I, for example, amputations occurred at a rate of approximately 1 per 1,000 American servicemen; in World War II, it was 1.5. In the Civil War, 17 of every 1,000 soldiers North and South lost limbs. The rifled musket and minie ball, the source of the preponderance of the war's wounds, fissured and splintered bone, destroying arms and legs. The introduction of ether and chloroform into medical practice in the years just before the war made amputation less agonizing and thus more widely undertaken. But numbers of Civil War amputations took place when anesthesia was not available, and some doctors believed patients were more likely to survive if it was not used. Battlefield surgeons worked swiftly to remove damaged limbs, certain that speed enhanced healing. Often they undertook procedure after procedure on makeshift operating tables for uninterrupted hours on end. After Gettysburg, for example, William Watson performed 14 amputations without leaving the table; he would never even have thought to wash his instruments or hands. This was an era that preceded understanding of the germ theory, of sepsis and antisepsis. As a result, post-operative infection was almost routine and mortality rates very high.[14]

Although records are both inadequate and incomplete, it seems likely that at least 25 percent of those who underwent such surgery ultimately died of related complications. Mortality varied significantly depending in large part on the limb that was removed: in procedures close to the trunk, death was far more likely; only 17 percent of soldiers survived amputations at the hip joint.[15]

Why was the image of the surgeon, the operating table, the pile, or cart or wheelbarrow of severed limbs so compelling to Civil War Americans? Mary Fisher, who confronted the wide range of war's horrors in the days she nursed the wounded on the field after Gettysburg, confessed that only once did she become "utterly unnerved." It was not as she stood on the brink of trenches filled with blackened and rotting corpses or as she found her skirts drenched in blood. Instead it was when she happened one evening as she left the hospital upon an amputation table and "a ghastly pile of several limbs" beside it. "It was so dreadful, so revolting," she wrote, "that my feet seemed paralyzed and I stood rooted to the spot with a horrible fascination." What was the "horrible fascination" of this sight? What did it represent? What did it say to and for those trying to communicate a "true picture as it really was" of the war?

For Fisher, the very casualness of casting parts of humans into piles "none knowing or caring to whom they once belonged" rested at the heart of her revulsion. More than the suffering such a scene embodied, it was the inhumanity—the carelessness—of the appointed healers that troubled her most.[16]

In a memoir composed well after the war, Charles Veil described a similar scene as one he had never forgotten—"a sight I often think of"—an image, a picture that had endured: the lines of men awaiting their own surgery, the surgeon at his operating table, the arms and legs thrown out of a schoolhouse window, the soldiers hauling them away in a wheelbarrow. "It had the appearance," he wrote, "of a human slaughterhouse." Men reduced to animals—or still worse, meat. Humans had become the victims, as another soldier described yet another nearly identical scene, "of scientific butchery."[17]

This was what modern war meant; this was what the much vaunted scientific and industrial progress of the age had brought: the mass production not just of weapons and uniforms and shoes and tinned rations and tents but the mass production of severed arms, legs, and feet. And the contradiction in such violence and harm being inflicted by those intending to heal turned assumptions of care and cure upside down. "If this don't demoralize our men," one Union officer remarked as he encountered limbs stacked "like cord wood," "nothing on earth will do it."[18]

What was a human being? How many parts could be lost before identity and manhood and humanity disappeared altogether? How did parts removed from a body relate to what remained? How did the body or its pieces relate to the soul? How could a war fought for democracy, dignity, and individual freedom so cruelly and wantonly destroy the foundations of humanity, identity, and selfhood? And how could those who regarded themselves as human do such things to one another? These were fundamental, deeply unsettling questions posed by the war. Nothing could embody them more fully than the image of the operating table and the adjacent pile of limbs.[19]

I HAVE BEEN EXPLORING how the imperatives of "seeing" in the changed context of Civil War were expressed in the lives of ordinary men and women. But these imperatives exerted their pressures as well—and in strikingly similar ways—upon those seeking to create the representational forms we know as art. The inability to communicate war's horror in accustomed forms and genres confounded artists as it did ordinary men and women grappling for language commensurate with their experience of violence and loss. In an exhibit and accompanying book entitled *The Civil War and American Art,* curator Eleanor Harvey demonstrates how the traditions of history painting designed to portray glorious and heroic actions for a righteous cause failed in the face of the war's devastation. As historian Steven Conn has written, "the Civil War underscored the inability of history painting to make sense of the world as it once had, yet how else but through grand manner history painting could one even try?"[20]

Conn's statement suggests two questions: first, if history painting couldn't make sense of the world as it once had, was there another direction it could take? And second, what genre or representation other than history painting might capture the meaning of this war for the visual arts?

If the old war story of glory and heroism—the age-old tale that undergirded grand historical canvasses like Benjamin West's *Death of Wolfe* or Emmanuel Leutze's *Washington Crossing the Delaware*—if that story could not be told in the face of the Civil War's destructiveness, its challenge to the narrative of human progress, could painting tell a different story? Could there be a revised narrative to enable history painting? Could a different sort of history painting offer its viewers a "true picture of the war as it really was?" Perhaps this suggests a contradiction at the outset: the desire, the need to see Civil War as it really was, to grapple with its all but unspeakable horror, challenged the

William D. Washington, The Burial of Latané *(1864).*

romantic assumptions of grand history painting from the start.

But let's look for a minute at one example of what we might regard as an attempt to create a new and improved history painting updated for changing times. I refer to a work that has intrigued me for many years: *The Burial of Latané*. Painted in 1864 by Virginian William D. Washington, the 36-by-46-inch canvas first hung in a small Richmond studio where it attracted such "throngs of visitors" that it was moved to the Confederate capitol, where a bucket was placed beneath it for contributions to the Confederate cause. It told a story—a true story, in the most literal sense—so that it might be considered a picture of the war as it really was. The painting portrays the funeral of a young lieutenant, killed during the legendary ride by Jeb Stuart's cavalry around McClellan's army prior to the Seven Days Campaign in June 1862. William Latané, the only Confederate casualty of the expedition, was left among strangers, Southern civilians surrounded by enemy forces and thus unable to summon either his family or a minister to perform his last rites. Slaves built his coffin and dug his grave; a white Virginia matron read the burial service. A Richmond author and editor published a poem based on the incident and began the transformation of Latané's death into romantic and nationalist legend.[21]

A resident of Richmond, artist William Washington had also been a student of Emmanuel Leutze's, so he was thoroughly educated in the idioms of grand history painting. He was almost certainly consciously invoking the images of Wolfe in Quebec and Washington in Trenton, both seeking to guarantee national triumph, when he undertook to memorialize Latané's sacrifice on behalf of Southern independence.

But this genre piece challenges the very foundations of its genre. The hero of *The Burial of Latané* is both dead and invisible. War's terror is rendered not as suffering and mangled bodies, but as Christian sacrifice; a heroism assumed and already complete and not the actual focus of interest here. *The Burial of Latané* depicts women and slaves, hardly imagined as subjects of either history or painting in this way before. They are the actors in this drama; they are performing a ritual at once religious and political that affirms the righteousness of the Confederate cause; their loyalty designates them the heroes of a new and improved history painting appropriate to a modern war engulfing not just armies but societies and populations.

Of course, by 1864, when Washington created his work, its portrait of women and slaves represented less a model *of* than a model *for* the Confederate homefront. The myth of the faithful slave had been shown to be just that as black Southerners fled by the thousands to Union lines and freedom. Many Confederate women had begun to question the purposes of death and sacrifice. As one woman tellingly put it, "What do I care for patriotism? My husband is my country. What is country to me if he is killed?" And white women of the lower classes had demonstrated striking dissent from the ideals of loyalty the *Burial of Latané* enshrined, responding to food shortages by taking to the streets in Richmond and other towns across the South in what came to be known as "bread riots."[22]

The factually true story of Latané—of his burial behind the lines—was rendered as a work of propaganda that sat uneasily with the emerging realities of war and Confederate fortunes. It was not "the true picture of the war as it really was" sought by the Confederate soldier Reuben Pierson. But the new narrative *The Burial of Latané* represented garnered attention and popularity among those seeking a justification and explanation for Southern nationalism. After Appomattox, engravings of the painting were widely distributed and became a standard decorative item in postwar Southern homes. These served as a compensatory narrative of defeat. What has been called by Frank Vandiver the "fantastic popularity" of this engraving derived from its depiction of what became the myth of the Lost Cause, a version of the war in which blacks and whites, homefront and battlefront, work happily together in support of a heroic South, a version in which death is bloodless, and the light of God shines down on the martyred South. Fantastic popularity because a fantasy, very far from true.[23]

IF WE REGARD THE *Burial of Latané* as an effort to provide a new kind of history painting to make sense of the changed world of the Civil War, we must conclude that it was unable to do so, that Eleanor Harvey's argument for the failure of grand history painting is supported, not overturned, by Washington's effort at innovation. Which brings us to a final question: if grand manner history painting had failed, what other sort of representation or genre might capture the meaning of this war? In *The Civil War and American Art*, Harvey offers a number of answers to that question in the exploration of the significance of landscapes in conveying war's impact through metaphor, in the presentation of genre painting as offering a focus on the particular at the individual human scale, rejecting the sweep and claims of preceding depictions of war. But the most powerful visualization of war's meaning proved to be photography. And it is here that I find a very close connection to the challenges of "seeing," the search for a "true picture as it really was" that I have described. In fact, I have used the language of photography—of the snapshot, of the freeze-frame—to capture the way the minds of many ordinary individuals grappled with the trauma and horror that confronted them in their experience of war. The two memes that I described at some length might be seen not just as mental or verbal pictures, but actual photographs as well. Alexander Gardner's "Slaughter Pen. Battle of Gettysburg," a plate from his *Photographic Sketchbook*, first published in 1866, is described in the facing descriptive page in the volume as, "A portion of the field of Gettysburg, located in front of Little Round Top, is known as the Slaughter Pen. Upon the conclusion of that engagement, the ground was found in many places to be almost covered with the dead and wounded. This sketch only represents a few of the dead, the wounded having been removed to hospitals." Or perhaps Gardner's photograph of "Bloody Lane at Antietam," taken two days after the battle in 1862, better approximates the

Alexander Gardner. Slaughter Pen, *Battle of Gettysburg.*

image of bodies paving the earth—or at least this road.[24]

Gardner himself understood his photographs as a direct assault on romantic notions of war. Of his iconic "Harvest of Death, Gettysburg, July 1863," he wrote, "Such a picture . . . shows the blank horror and reality of war, in opposition to its pageantry. Here are the dreadful details! Let them aid in preventing such another calamity falling upon the nation." Gardner sought to link his photographs into a narrative that could go beyond the fragmentary and partial view of any single image. But his *Photographic Sketchbook*, even with pictures enhanced by quite lengthy captions, does not succeed in creating a coherent story or narrative of the war. The partialistic vision of photography prevails in a manner not dissimilar to its impact on human comprehension and perception of the war.[25]

The fragmentation of amputation was an ideal expression for such a fragmentary vision. Not just understanding, but human beings themselves had been disarticulated. The powerful and omnipresent meme of severed limbs

Alexander Gardner, Bloody Lane at Antietam.

found its photographic expression in one of a collection of medical portraits by Army physician Reed Brockway Bontecou. In service of a more scientific and complete accounting of their treatment, he photographed wounded soldiers with a carte-de-visite camera when they arrived from the field at Washington's Harewood Hospital, often recorded them again after their surgeries, and as their cases progressed. His work also included a number of images of single amputated limbs, sometimes posed on a chair or shelf to enable the clearest view. Perhaps the most striking representation of amputation in his collection is a photograph that presents a vivid rendering of the pile of limbs that made such a powerful impression on Whitman and many other Civil War Americans.

The image has been given two different titles; both encapsulate the muted horror of what is on display. "A Morning's Work" conveys the bitter irony noted by so many observers of a world in which maiming and curing have become synonymous, in which humans must inflict pain and disfigurement in the effort to heal. This morning's work, undertaken by a skilled and devoted

Alexander Gardner, Harvest of Death, *Gettysburg.*

physician, is measured and presented in this grotesque heap of dehumanized fragments. Production has become a horrifying kind of destruction. How could it be, as one battlefield nurse noted, that a civilized nation had made "a business of maiming men?" The second title often attached to the image is "Field Day," a phrase used in the 18th century to describe a military review or exercise where men worked, in the words of the time, to "improve their Valour." By the 19th century it had come to mean a day of celebration or triumph. This photograph represents an image of the field of battle seared into the mind of the thousands of Civil War Americans who witnessed something very much like it. It is certainly a rendering of a terrible kind of valor, but one far removed from triumph.[26]

Amputees became a fascination for photography after the war as well, as science and medicine sought to document the realities of wounds and of surgical interventions and innovations. Bontecou himself made significant contributions to this effort, offering prints of his work to the Army Medical Museum, which endeavored to create a visual record of wounds and their treat-

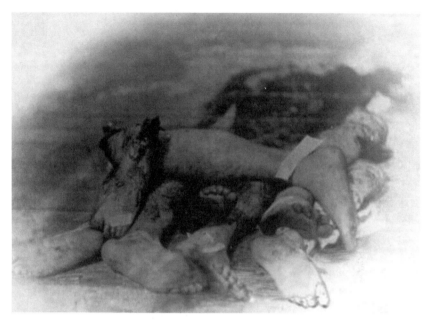

Reed Brockway Bontecou, A Morning's Work *or* Field Day.

ment. In addition many wounded veterans had themselves photographed and sold cartes de visite as a means of support. One can only speculate about what would motivate a postwar American to purchase such an image. Certainly it would provide an unforgettable and "true picture as it really was" of the war.

Dozens, perhaps even hundreds of photographs of amputees survive, recording, analyzing and even commercializing the dismemberment that was a distinctive aspect of the horror of this war. Below is an example of one such photograph. It is an embodiment of the new bureaucracy of record-keeping created by the war; it represents science, data collection, a wound, a therapy, and a process of documentation all made possible by modern technology and modern society. We almost forget it also represents a man. He has become not so much Private Alfred Stratton as a specimen, a thing.[27]

I have juxtaposed it—in a suggestion of before and after—with another photograph, this one not intended to be a datum but a portrait—a portrayal of a human being, not a scientific fact. The two faces are to my eyes eerily similar, but they are not in fact the same man. On the left is John Ryan of

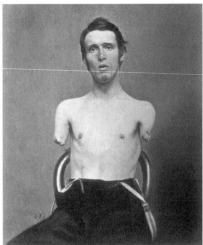

John Ryan, Company H, 2nd Rhode Island Infantry (left); Private Alfred Stratton, Company G, 147th New York Infantry.

Rhode Island, photographed, like so many others going off to war, in his dress uniform. The picture is encased in an elaborate frame to be displayed and cherished by loved ones at home. This is the heroic vision with which the war began. Amputation became a meme that could represent the shattering of men and illusions that proved to be the war's reality. And photography could show this in a manner no other medium could approach.[28]

THERE ARE STRIKING PARALLELS between what the "seeing" I have described in the first section of this essay demanded and what the photograph provided: the seeming accuracy and unassailable truth of the photographic representation, its realism, its erasure of cant and pretense, its existence as vignette outside and apart from explanation or narrative or justification. Photographs were fragmentary, disjointed, just as understanding and insight had proved to be.

Had photography influenced the way so many Civil War Americans described their experiences and their lives? Or had the nature of their lives and changing consciousness made photography the essential visual expression of the human condition? Perhaps some of both. But in any case we can see emerging in the context of civil war, in the face of its trauma and dehumanization, the need for a new way of seeing the world. This need challenged individuals to grapple with circumstances too terrible to explain and challenged art to turn to new technologies and new and renewed genres in the effort to create visual representations of meaning in a world that seemed beyond comprehension or control.

NOTES

1   This essay originated as a talk at the Smithsonian American Art Museum in conjunction with the exhibition *The Civil War and American Art* in February 2013. I am deeply grateful to Robin Kelsey for his thoughts and suggestions as I worked on this project.

2   See Drew Gilpin Faust, *This Republic of Suffering: Death and the Civil War* (New York: Alfred A. Knopf, 2008); *Death and the Civil War*, directed by Ric Burns, Steeplechase Films, 2012; James David Hacker, "A Census-Based Count of the Civil War Dead," *Civil War History* 57 (December 2011) 306–347.

3   Henry C. Taylor to Father and Mother, October 1863, Henry C. Taylor Papers, Wisconsin Historical Society; Oliver Wendell Holmes, *Occasional Speeches,* comp. Mark DeWolfe Howe (Cambridge: Harvard University Press, 1962), 82; John O. Casler, *Four Years in the Stonewall Brigade* (1906; rpt. Columbia: University of South Carolina Press, 2005), 37; Cordelia Harvey letter from Memphis, dated December 1862, published in *Wisconsin Daily State Journal*, December 30, 1862, Cordelia Harvey Papers, Wisconsin Historical Society; Herman Melville, "The Armies of the Wilderness," in *Battle-Pieces and Aspects of the War: Civil War Poems* (1866, rpt. New York: DaCapo Press, 1995), 103; Emily Dickinson, "I felt a Cleaving in my Mind," #937, in *The Complete Poems of Emily Dickinson* (Boston: Little, Brown and Company, 1960).

4   Reuben Allen Pierson, in Thomas Cutrer and T. Michael Parrish, eds., *Brothers in Gray: Civil War Letters of the Pierson Family* (Baton Rouge: Louisiana State University, 1997), 101.

5   T. S. Eliot, *The Waste Land* (1922) http://www.gutenberg.org/ebooks/1321.

6   Palmer in Louis P. Towles, ed., *A World Turned Upside Down: The Palmers of South Santee, 1818–1881* (Columbia: University of South Carolina Press, 1996) 341.

7   Richard Dawkins, *The Selfish Gene,* (New York: Oxford University Press, 1976); Malcolm Gladwell, *http://www.gladwell.com/tippingpoint.*

8   *Frank Leslie's Illustrated Weekly Newspaper,* May 24, 1862, 98; Ulysses S. Grant, *Personal Memoirs* (1885, rpt. New York: Library of America, 1990), 238; L. Minor Blackford, *Mine Eyes Have Seen the Glory: The Story of a Virginia Lady* (Cambridge: Harvard University Press, 1954), 213. On stepping on bodies, see also *Christian Recorder*, July 18, 1863; L. S. Bobo to A. Bobo, July 7, 1862, Bobo Papers, Museum of the Confederacy; Mary A. Newcomb, *Four Years of Personal Reminiscences of the War* (Chicago: H. S. Mills, 1893), 43; John Driscoll to Adelaide, April 18, 1862, Gould Family papers, Wisconsin Historical Society; Alexander G. Downing, *Downing's Civil War Diary* (Des Moines: Historical Department of Iowa, 1916), 325.

9   Quoted in Eleanor Jones Harvey, *The Civil War and American Art* (Smithsonian American Art Museum, Washington, D.C., in Association with New Haven: Yale University Press, 2012), 155–6.

10   Sanitary Commission official quoted in James M. McPherson, *Antietam: The Battle that Changed the Course of the Civil War* (New York: Oxford University Press, 2002) 4–5; George R. Metcalf quoted in Earl Hess, *The Union Soldier in Battle: Enduring the Ordeal of Combat* (Lawrence: University Press of Kansas, 1997), 22.

11   Clara Barton to My dear Mrs. Gage, Winter 1864, Clara Barton Papers, Library of Congress.

12   Rev. J. Wm. Jones, *Christ in the Camp; or Religion in Lee's Army* (Richmond: B. F. Johnson and Co., 1887), 572; Cornelia Hancock, *South After Gettysburg: Letters of Cornelia Hancock from the Army of the Potomac, 1863–1865,* ed. Henrietta Jacquette (Stratford, N.H.: Ayer Publishing Company, 1937), 5; Walt Whitman, *Memoranda During the War* (1875; rpt. Bedford: Applewood Books, 1993), 5; Edward Haviland Miller, ed., *Walt Whitman: The Correspondence* (New York: New York University Press, 1961), vol. I, 59; *Lincoln* a film directed by Steven Spielberg, written by Tony Kushner. I am very grateful to Tony Kushner for his thoughts on amputation in a personal conversation, February 2013.

13   Josiah F. Murphey, quoted in Richard F. Miller and Robert E. Mooney, *The Civil War: The Nantucket Experience* (Nantucket: Wesco Publishing, 1994), 93; Oakwood Cemetery Burial Register, June 28, 1862, Museum of the Confederacy.

14   Julian E. Kuz and Bradley P. Bengston, *Orthopaedic Injuries of the Civil War* (Kennesaw: Kennesaw Mountain press, 1996) 62. See Frances M. Clarke, Honorable Scars," in War Stories: Suffering and Sacrifice in the Civil War North Chicago: University of Chicago Press, 2011), 144–74, and Lisa Marie Herschbach, Fragmentation and Reunion: Medicine, Memory and the Body in the American Civil War, unpublished PhD thesis, Harvard University, 1997; William Watson, July 7, 1863, quoted in Paul Fatout, ed., *Letters of a Civil War Surgeon* (West Lafayette: Purdue University Press, 1996), 108.

15   See War Department, Surgeon General's Office, *A Report on Amputations at the Hip-Joint in Military Surgery* (Washington: Government Printing Office, 1867).

16   Mary C. Fisher, "A Week on Gettysburg Field," quoted in Gregory Coco, *A Strange and Blighted Land: Gettysburg, the Aftermath of a Battle* (Gettysburg: Thomas Publications, 1995), 176–7.

17   "Sergeant Charles Veil's Memoir: On the Death of Reynolds," ed. Robert D. Hoffsommer, *Civil War Times Illustrated* 21(1982), 17; Francis Dawson, June 26, 1862, Museum of the Confederacy.

18   James Eldred Phillips Memoir, 42, Virginia Historical Society.

19   See S. Weir Mitchell, "The Case of George Dedlow," *Atlantic Monthly* 18 (July 1866) 1–11.

20   Harvey, *The Civil War and American Art*, 5–6; Steven Conn, "Narrative Trauma and Civil War History Painting, or Why Are These Pictures so Terrible?," *History and Theory* 41 (December 2002), 22.

21   See Drew Gilpin Faust, "Race, Gender and Confederate Nationalism: William D. Washington's *Burial of Latané,*" in *Southern Stories: Slaveholders in Peace and War* (Columbia: University of Missouri Press, 1992) 148–59, Vandiver quote is on 149; see also Faust, *This Republic of Suffering*, 84–5.

22   Margaret Crawford, "Tales of a Grandmother," in *South Carolina Women in the Confederacy,* eds. Mrs. A. T. Smyth, Miss M. B. Poppenheim, and Mrs. Thomas Taylor, 2 vols. (Columbia: The State Company, 1903) vol. I, 210.

23   Vandiver, quoted in Faust, "Race, Gender and Confederate Nationalism," 149.

24   Alexander Gardner, *Gardner's Photographic Sketch Book of the War* (Washington: Philip
     & Solomons, 1866), Plate 44; Alexander Gardner, Bloody Lane at Antietam, Library of
     Congress. See Anthony Lee and Elizabeth Young, *On Alexander Gardner's Photographic
     Sketch Book of the Civil War* (Berkeley: University of California Press, 2008); Keith
     Davis, "A Terrible Distinctness: Photography of the Civil War Era," in *Photography in
     Nineteenth-Century America*, ed. Martha Sandweiss (New York: Harry N. Abrams, 1991).

25   Gardner, "Harvest of Death," *Gardner's Photographic Sketch Book*, Plate 36.

26   Jeff L. Rosenheim, "Collecting the Wounded," in *Photography and the American Civil
     War*, published by Metropolitan Museum of Art, (New Haven: Yale University Press,
     2013), 178–9; Cornelia Hancock, *South After Gettysburg,* 74.

27   Private Alfred Stratton, National Museum of Health and Medicine, Washington, D.C.
     See Stanley Burns, "Early Medical Photography in America (1839–83)," *New York State
     Journal of Medicine* (August 1980), 1444–69. Guy R. Hasegawa, *Mending Broken Soldiers:
     The Union and Confederate Programs to Supply Artificial Limbs* (Carbondale: Southern
     Illinois University Press, 2012).

28   John Ryan, Company H, 2nd Rhode Island Infantry, ambrotype, Liljenquist Family
     Collection, Prints and Photographs Division, Library of Congress.

5

Civil Wars—Ours and Theirs

STEPHANIE MCCURRY

W hen we Americans talk about "the" Civil War, we know which war we mean: the brutal four-year fight between the U.S.A. and the C.S.A. that settled the question of secession and Union and defeated the Southern bid for national independence. As early as 1861 the idea that we "are in the midst of a revolution unparalleled in the histories of nations" took hold and it never let go its grip on the American imagination.[1] It is a truism of U.S. history: "the" Civil War we call it, a claim to distinctiveness distilled in an article of grammar.

But was ours the unique experience implied by that singular title? After all, there are many cases of civil war in the 19th and 20th centuries to which the one in the U.S. might be compared. Civil war is not in itself a peculiarly American experience. In that sense our reflexively national focus allows us to forget how common the experience of civil war was and is, and it lulls us into a false sense of the distinctiveness of "our" war. It is surely ironic that only a broader, more global perspective would allow us to appreciate what really was unique about the American Civil War.

Put in any, even cursory comparison, the value of that global perspective becomes abundantly clear. To historians of civil wars in Africa, the Middle East, and Europe, our love for the Civil War—and our scholarly assumptions about its uniqueness—seems odd, misplaced. Why, scholars of those conflicts ask, are Americans so unreservedly romantic about their Civil War?[2] Why do they not only commemorate it but celebrate it? In most countries civil wars were such brutally horrific and divisive events that no one wants to remember them. But in the United States the Civil War is not only forever and lovingly remembered but reenacted. Is that, as we tend to assume, because our civil war was so different? What is, in fact, exceptional about the American case of Civil War and what is not?

FIRST THERE IS THE matter of definition and scope. What is a civil war and how many have there been? The list of civil wars waged in the modern world is staggeringly long and difficult to contemplate—as many as 146 by one count.[3] Sad to say civil war has been a commonplace counterpart of the age of nationalism all over the world because claims of sovereignty over people and territory are the sine qua non conditions of nations.[4] Abraham Lincoln was hardly alone in thinking that, as president, he incurred the obligation to maintain the authority of the government and territorial integrity of the country he was elected to lead. And, in fact, it was Lincoln's appointee, Francis Lieber, who would first offer the definition of civil war subsequently adopted by the Geneva and Hague Conventions. In 1863 Lieber was called on to write a code of conduct for the armies in the field—"the Lieber Code," as it is now known—essentially setting down the rules of war that the Union army would observe. "A Civil War," he explained, "is war between two or more portions of a country or state, each contending for mastery of the whole, and each claiming to be the legitimate government." Here we think of classic examples like the English Civil War of the 1640s or the Spanish Civil War of the 1930s. But that definition hardly fit the American case, so Lieber improvised, adding this: "The term is also sometimes applied to war of rebellion, when the rebellious provinces or portions of the state are contiguous to those containing the seat of government."[5] The American Civil War was clearly the second kind. It was, as Lieber defined it, a rebellion and a civil war.

Lieber's definition proved valuable and enduring. In political scientists' sweeping typologies, civil wars come in two basic types: separatist conflicts—like that instigated by the C.S.A.—fought over the integrity of boundaries; and statist conflicts fought for control of the state or the center. There have been plenty of both in the modern world, but broadly speaking there were far more secessionist wars in the 20th century than the 19th.[6] A great number of those wars were fought immediately after decolonization in the 1950s and 1960s, as newly independent African nations struggled to resolve conflicts within territorial boundaries artificially set by European colonial powers.[7] The example of Biafra comes to mind. Indeed Biafra was the bloodiest conflict over secession in modern history and the only one in which the death toll topped that of the American Civil War. That struggle to secede from Nigeria failed only after the conflict took one million lives.[8]

As the example of Biafra suggests, even a cursory consideration of matters of definition cracks open the window on the American case and sheds valuable light on what turn out to be patterns of events discernible in and common to many civil wars. Looking across the historical landscape we learn a number of things. First, it is not uncommon for civil wars to be provoked by secessionist movements.[9] In the 19th century, there were more anti-colonial wars of independence (Latin America) and wars of national unification (Italy and Germany) than civil wars, and in that sense the U.S. was unusual for a time.[10] But by the 20th century, there were secessionist civil wars all over the post-colonial and post-Cold War world. Second, most secessionist movements are defeated. The Confederate States of America was not alone in that bitter fruit of civil war. As it turns out, Texas was the only secessionist movement in the western hemisphere that succeeded. And third, what these cases show is that a stronger national government is usually the outcome of wars for control of the state.[11]

This was certainly true of the reunited United States of America, where ex-Confederates were subject to a set of federal initiatives—the massive expropriation of property by the federal government in its program of slave emancipation, military occupation and rule, and a series of postwar constitutional amendments—that literally remade the U.S. government and its people.[12] This tectonic shift of power from the states to the center turns out to be a classic consequence of civil wars. Indeed, it seems to be the case whether the victorious forces are the progressives or the reactionaries—all move to consolidate power in the center. As in Franco's Spain, so in the United States: victor states typically move to make structural changes designed to strengthen territorial integrity by weakening the regional parts, destroying autonomist movements, and concentrating authority.[13] When historians of the United States talk of the Civil War as the birth of the modern American state they are describing a process common to civil wars almost everywhere.[14] In a strictly structural sense, then, it seems safe to conclude that there is little distinctive or exceptional about "the" Civil War but much that was characteristic of civil wars in general.

BUT THE QUESTION OF American exceptionalism obviously goes far beyond strictly structural matters to touch profoundly on the conduct and meaning of the Civil War. Here the assumptions of distinctiveness go deep in historical memory, in fact, all the way back to the war itself when men like General Robert E. Lee, President Jefferson Davis, and President Abraham Lincoln fused the human cost of war to the value of the political principles contested in it. The duration of the war (four unimaginably long years); the toll of war (as many as 750,000 dead); the level of mobilization for it (75–85 percent of military-age white men in the South), the ferocity with which it was waged (guerilla warfare in the border states); the hard war policy against civilians (Sherman's March)—surely other wars were not like this in the price honorable men were prepared to pay for their political principles. Few assumptions are more important in Civil War history and memory than the belief that this was a war fought by heroic men for honorable causes: political liberty, self-determination, the preservation of the Union, the defense of democracy, the abolition of slavery. Take your pick. It was Lee's point, was it not, in his Farewell Speech at Appomattox Court House in April 1865, that his soldiers, no less than their Yankee opponents, were valiant men dedicated to their country; that the Confederate loss was not a failure of principle or will but an exhaustion of resources in the face of a relentless enemy; that his troops were honorable men, as he put it, "compelled to yield to overwhelming numbers and resources."[15] It is what makes our War different, worth celebrating, worth the horrifying toll in blood and treasure.

And surely there is some truth in this. Few if any wars in the modern world reached the levels of mobilization of the Confederacy, few civil wars exacted a comparable death toll, or could claim such a clearly redemptive purpose as the new birth of liberty that Lincoln spoke of so powerfully at Gettysburg. But other, less elevated views of the American Civil War were offered at the time, and drowned out later, that compared it less favorably to other wars of national independence. Edward Pollard, the Richmond editor and diehard Confederate nationalist, judged his own countrymen's commitment to independence and found it wanting. In 1865, as things collapsed in the Confederacy, he complained that "a large portion of our people have fallen below the standards of history, and hold no honorable comparison with other nations that have fought for and struggled for independence."[16] Perhaps he was thinking of the American War of Independence, or the Dutch in the

United Provinces in the 17th century, who fought for 80 years for national independence from the Spanish, and to whom Confederates have been unflatteringly compared. Reflecting on the Dutch case, a nationalist movement that succeeded despite imbalances of population and resources far exceeding those faced by the Confederacy, one historian has said that clearly "'war weariness' alone cannot provide a convincing explanation for the South's loss of their war for national independence in a mere four years."[17] To these historians, what is striking is that the Civil War did not last far longer, that Confederates were not willing to fight harder and sacrifice more.

And indeed other civil wars put the toll of ours in perspective. Civil wars are often protracted and inconclusive because neither rival force has enough military power to establish full control over a large area. "The big country, small army problem," as a military attache put it.[18] But this was obviously not the case in the American Civil War with its two mammoth military forces. Four years, as it turns out, is not so long, as these things go. And while one can hardly diminish the significance of the death toll on Union and Confederate soldiers—the American Civil War was the bloodiest conflict in the western world between the Napoleonic Wars and World War I—the American Civil War is *not* regarded as a particularly barbaric war, in large measure because, unlike most civil wars, it was fought by conventional means. Where violence did reach egregious levels—in the guerilla warfare of the border states for example—it simply confirms another time-tested pattern of civil war: violence is always greatest in zones of irregular warfare.[19] The American Civil War was one of the few fought primarily by conventional warfare, which explains the comparatively low level of atrocities reported.

But the level of barbarity and violence reached in the American Civil War seems to pale even in comparison to the other example of a major civil war fought by conventional means: the Spanish Civil War (1936–39). There, in addition to 300,000 battlefield deaths, there were at least 200,000 extrajudicial killings of civilians, including the purposeful killing of large numbers of women and children behind the lines. Three-quarters of them were killed by Franco's rebel forces in mass executions which followed the capture of cities like Barcelona, by firing squads in bull rings and prison camps in occupied territory, by starvation, death and mutilation in his massive archipelago of concentration, slave labor, and prisoner of war camps, in bombing attacks on columns of refugees, in the siege of Madrid, and by what is called the

"Column of Death," which was Franco's army on the move from Seville to Madrid. More than half a million refugees were forced into exile and many died in French concentration camps.

A program of terror and extermination was fundamental to the rebels' military strategy during the war. It included the widespread use of sexual violence—gang rape, branding, mutilation, public humiliation—for punishment and revenge. It certainly puts Major General Benjamin Butler's "infamous" New Orleans order in perspective. Historians of the Spanish Civil War are still struggling to come to terms with the evidence, but recent events in Yugoslavia and in the human rights community more generally make us acutely aware of the use of rape as a systematic tool of war and political repression. The level of savagery against civilians reached in the Spanish Civil War has led one historian of the conflict to call it a holocaust.[20] The truth about the Spanish Civil War is still coming to light as Spanish citizens excavate mass graves, begin to confront the ghosts of Franco's regime, and pursue the task of recovering, reburying, and, yes, still counting the dead.[21] There is little in the American Civil War record to compare to this systematic targeting, terrorizing, and extermination of civilians for purposes not of military advantage but political repression.

It is a sad truth of the late 20th and 21st centuries that the civil wars of our own time constantly force "the" Civil War into new perspective. Those familiar with the recent genocidal wars in Africa or in Yugoslavia hardly seem impressed with the violence and barbarity of the American Civil War. To the contrary, what strikes them most is the level of restraint—order—observed by U.S. troops in their treatment of enemy soldiers and civilians in the path of war. What other country, they ask, adopted rules of war in the midst of war? Indeed. It is without a doubt one of the most striking, impressive, and, yes, unique features of the American Civil War: that the Lincoln administration was willing to bind itself to a set of regulations that limited the latitude of the Union army in its military operations, including in occupied territory and guerilla warfare. If the rules were sometimes observed in the breach it is no less striking in its singularity and it says something profound about the American case of civil war.[22]

There are real limits to this view, more I think, than we are yet aware. For the Civil War record holds abundant evidence of one kind of violence to which we have yet to do justice: the torture, rape, and murder of enslaved men, women, and children by both armies, but especially the Confederates. For if the Spanish have undertaken a belated but shocking accounting, in the U.S. there has been no such effort, even by scholars, to estimate the extra-judicial dead. We know of Fort Pillow and the other massacres of black prisoners of war.[23] But shocking as those atrocities were, the death toll must pale in comparison to the number of non-combatant slaves killed in the course of the war. The official and personal records of the Civil War are littered with casual references: to slaves—including children—beaten to death on plantations, runaways hanged as a public example, slave men executed following "drumhead court-martials," insurrections repressed by mass execution, slave rebels hunted down and hanged, and to the torture, mutilation, and murder of men and women by Confederate "scouts," including after the surrender.[24] In Pineville, South Carolina, in late March and April 1865 Confederate scouts waged war against a "slave rebel band." They hunted down and shot Pringle (and 28 others), hanged his brother Harry, and then killed Rosa—the reputed ringleader and the mother of Pringle and Harry—leaving her body unburied on the field to which she had "been tied, dragged, and killed."[25] For this war dead there has been no accounting.

VIEWED BROADLY, THEN, THERE is much about the American Civil War that is not as peculiar or particular to that conflict as we might think, but also a few, arguably critical, features that mark it as unique. The conclusive military outcome; the adoption of rules of war in the heat of war; but, above all, the belief on both sides, victor and vanquished, Union and Confederate, that this war—this massive loss of life—had redemptive purpose. To this day the pattern holds and helps explain the romantic aura that surrounds our memory of the American Civil War. Liberals and progressives have their new birth of liberty. The Civil War they celebrate, remember, and reenact not only defended the Union, it accomplished the emancipation of four million men, women, and children and vindicated the principle of democracy not just in the U.S. but in the world. Confederate ancestors and conservatives of a variety of types have their redemptive fight for political liberty. The Civil War they celebrate, remember, and reenact was waged for the principle of states' rights, defended the original intent of the Constitution, and resisted the tyranny of the federal government.[26] These are enduring principles in American political life, even into the 21st century.

It is not uncommon for victors to valorize their cause, purge the archives of incriminating material, write national history textbooks that inscribe their view, and build monuments to their military heroes, even as they dig mass graves and build prison camps for their now-defeated enemies. Certainly that was what Franco did, pursuing in the aftermath of the war a political purge of vast proportions—as many as 500,000 executed, imprisoned, exiled—to consolidate his regime and its truth about that civil war.[27] But that is not what happened in the American Civil War. There was no political purge, no mass trials for treason, no systematic effort at political repression by the Union victors in the defeated Confederate states. President Davis served two years and was released. President Johnson issued blanket amnesties. Opposition political parties reformed. Confederate memory flourished. Everyone was free to tell their story of the war and they did, sustaining a commercial culture of Civil War remembering that 150 years later shows no sign of flagging.[28] Even African Americans who long viewed Civil War memorializing with suspicion and distaste are now being urged to claim the war as their "own."[29]

In thinking about civil wars broadly compared, the main difference between ours and theirs, it seems, is not so much the war but the postwar. Americans love their Civil War as no other people do. This fondness for the war, as Drew Gilpin Faust has recently reminded us, is a peculiar but essential part of American culture.[30] For better or worse we have a political culture that not only permits but encourages divergent—indeed profoundly divergent—rememberings of the war's causes, principles, and consequences. That is why we can all love it, and why Americans today want to reenact it. And that in the end is what sets us apart from every other people with this bloody past.

NOTES

1   H. W. R. (Henry W. R.) Jackson, *Confederate Monitor and Patriot's Friend: Containing Sketches of Numerous Important and Thrilling Events of the Present Revolution, Together with Several Interesting Chapters of History Concerning Gen. Stonewall Jackson, Gen. Morgan, and Other Great Men of a New Nation, Her Armor and Salvation* (Atlanta: Franklin Steam Printing House, J. J. Toon & Co., 1862), 6.

2   When a group of historians of the U.S. Civil War was invited to a conference at Hebrew University in June 2011 and each paired with a scholar of civil war in another part of the world, this question immediately arose. "Civil Wars and The Civil War," June 10, 2011, Hebrew University of Jerusalem.

3   Stathis N. Kalyvas, "Civil Wars," in *The Oxford Handbook of Comparative Politics*, ed.

Carles Boix and Susan C. Stokes (Oxford University Press, 2009).

4   Anthony Giddens, *A Contemporary Critique of Historical Materialism: The Nation-state and Violence*. Vol. 2 (Berkeley: University of California Press, 1985).

5   United States War Department, Francis Lieber, and United States Adjutant-General's Office, *Instructions for the Government of Armies of the United States, in the Field* (D. Van Nostrand, 1863), 34. On Lieber, see John Fabian Witt, *Lincoln's Code: The Laws of War in American History* (New York: Simon and Schuster, 2012).

6   This was the distinction the political scientist Naomi Chazan introduced at the conference at Hebrew University. For published work see Chazan, *The Precarious Balance: State and Society in Africa* (1988) and *Civil Society and the State in Africa,* edited with John Harbeson and Donald Rothchild (1996). See also the introduction by Don Doyle in *Secession as an International Phenomenon: From America's Civil War to Contemporary Separatist Movements,* Don H. Doyle, ed. (Athens: 2010).

7   Raphael Chijioke Njoku, "Nationalism, Separatism, and Neoliberal Globalism: A Review of Africa and the Quest for Self-Determination since the 1940s," in *Secession as an International Phenomenon*, 338.

8   Aleksandar Pavković, "By the Force of Arms: Violence and Morality in Secessionist Conflicts," in *Secession as an International Phenomenon,* 264.

9   David Armitage, "Secession and Civil War," in *Secession as an International Phenomenon,* 37–38.

10   See, for example, Eric Hobsbawm, *Nations and Nationalism since 1780: Programme, Myth, Reality;* Robin Blackburn, *The Overthrow of Colonial Slavery: 1776–1848;* Paul Quigley, *"Secessionists in an Age of Secession,"* in *Secession as an International Phenomenon, 152–153;.*

11   Don Doyle, ed., *Secession as an International Phenomenon,* 14

12   Eric Foner, *Reconstruction: America's Unfinished Revolution, 1863–1877* (New York: Harper & Row, 1988); Richard Bensel, *Yankee Leviathan: The Origins of Central State Authority, 1859–1877* (New York: Cambridge University Press, 1990); Stephen Skowronek, *Building a New American State: The Expansion of National Administrative Capacities, 1877–1920* (New York: Cambridge University Press, 1982); Theda Skocpol, *Protecting Soldiers and Mothers: The Political Origins of Social Policy in the United States* (Cambridge: Belknap Press of Harvard University Press, 1992); Steven Hahn, "Class and State in Postemancipation Societies: Southern Planters in Comparative Perspective," *The American Historical Review* 95, no. 1 (Feb., 1990): 75–98.

13   Paul Preston, *The Spanish Civil War: Reaction, Revolution and Revenge* (New York: W. W. Norton & Co., 2007).

14   See, for example, Richard Bensel, *Yankee Leviathan: The Origins of Central State Authority, 1859–1877* (New York: Cambridge University Press, 1990).

15   Robert E. Lee, "Farewell Address to the Army of Northern Virginia," Smithsonian Institution, www.civilwar.si.edu/appomattox_lee_farewell.html, accessed 25 July 2013.

16   Quoted in Michael Bernath, *Confederate Minds: The Struggle for Intellectual Independence in the Civil War South* (Chapel Hill: University of North Carolina Press, 2010), 284.

17   Armstead L. Robinson, *Bitter Fruits of Bondage: The Demise of Slavery and the Collapse of The Confederacy, 1861–1865* (University of Virginia Press, 2005), 8.

18   Stathis N. Kalyvas, *The Logic of Violence in Civil* War (Cambridge University Press, 2006), 138–39. See also Andrew Mack, "Why big nations lose small wars: The politics of asymmetric conflict," *World Politics* 27, no. 2 (1975): 175–200.

19   Kalyvas, *The Logic of Violence in Civil War*, 84; Michael Fellman, *Inside War: The Guerilla Conflict in Missouri During the American Civil War* (New York, 1989).

20   Paul Preston, *The Spanish Holocaust: Inquisition and Extermination in Twentieth-century Spain* (New York: W. W. Norton & Co., 2012). For Butler's Order see Benjamin F. Butler, *Butler's Book: Autobiography and Personal Reminiscences of Major General Benjamin Butler* (Boston, 1892), 418.

21   "Rally to Demand Unearthing Of Mass Graves of Franco Era," *New York Times*, June 25, 2004, http://www.nytimes.com/2004/06/25/world/rally-to-demand-unearthing-of-mass-graves-of-franco-era.html, accessed June 25, 2013.

22   John Fabian Witt, *Lincoln's Code: The Laws of War in American History* (New York: Simon and Schuster, 2012); Drew Gilpin Faust, *This Republic of Suffering: Death and the American Civil War* (New York: Vintage Books, 2009).

23   Faust, *This Republic of Suffering*, 53–55; *Freedom's Soldiers: The Black Military Experience in the Civil War,* eds. Ira Berlin, Joseph Patrick Reidy, Leslie S. Rowland (Cambridge: Cambridge University Press, 1988); Richard Slotkin, *No Quarter: The Battle of the Crater, 1864* (New York: Random House, 2009); John David Smith, *Black Soldiers in Blue: African American Troops in the Civil War Era* (Chapel Hill: University of North Carolina Press, 2002); *Black Flag over Dixie: Racial Atrocities And Reprisals in the Civil War*, ed. Gregory J. W. Urwin (Carbondale: Southern Illinois University Press, 2005).

24   On this subject the key scholarship is work in progress by the historian Thavolia Glymph. For one example see the comments delivered at the Annenberg Seminar, University of Pennsylvania, April 14, 2011.

25   The events can be reconstructed from primary sources including *Two Diaries From Middle St. John's Berkeley, S.C., February–May 1865* (St. John's Hunting Society, 1921) and *A World Turned Upside Down: The Palmers of South Santee* (Columbia, S.C., 1996, 429–63). Also see Stephanie McCurry, "Ends and Beginnings: Gender and Emancipation in the Civil War Era," Keynote Session, Society of Civil War Historians, Lexington, KY, June 14, 2012.

26   David W. Blight explores the "emancipationist vision" of the Civil War and the "Lost Cause" ideology in *Race and Reunion: The Civil War in American Memory* (Cambridge: Belknap Press of Harvard University Press, 2001).

27   Preston, *The Spanish Holocaust*.

28   Blight, *Race and Reunion*; Tony Horwitz, *Confederates in the Attic: Dispatches from the Unfinished Civil War* (New York: Vintage, 1999); Tara McPherson, *Reconstructing Dixie: Race, Gender, and Nostalgia in the Imagined South* (Durham: Duke University Press, 2003.

29   "Why Do So Few Blacks Study the Civil War?," *The Atlantic*, November 30, 2011, http://www.theatlantic.com/magazine/archive/2012/02/why-do-so-few-blacks-study-the-civil-war/308831.

30   Drew Gilpin Faust, "Telling War Stories: Reflections of a Civil War Historian," National Endowment for the Humanities Jefferson Lecture, May 2, 2011, http://www.neh.gov/about/awards/jefferson-lecture/drew-gilpin-faust-lecture, accessed 25 July 2013.

6

Alabama Emancipates

J. MILLS THORNTON III

There could not have been much suspense about the action that Alabama's Constitutional Convention of 1865 would take as to emancipation. Everyone who registered to vote in the August 31 election of the Convention's delegates had been required to swear to "abide by and faithfully support all laws and proclamations which have been made during the existing rebellion with reference to the emancipation of slaves." And when the convention met on September 12, Provisional Governor Lewis E. Parsons came into the chamber, all the delegates rose, and Parsons administered the same oath to all of them again.[1]

Moreover, the delegates overwhelmingly had been enemies of secession. In the election of the members of the Secession Convention in December, 1860, only 18 of the 99 delegates had voted for the secessionist candidates. And in the presidential election the preceding month, just 24 of the 99 had voted for John C. Breckinridge, though Breckinridge had received 54 per cent of the state's vote; 45 of the delegates had voted for John Bell and 30 for Stephen A. Douglas.[2]

On the other hand, the Convention's members had been deeply involved with the institution of slavery. Just 16 of the 99 delegates had been non-slaveholders. Forty had been planters (owners of 20 or more slaves) and 19 were large planters (owners of 50 or more slaves). Indeed, six of the delegates had owned more than 100 slaves, including the Convention's president, former Governor and Senator Benjamin Fitzpatrick of Autauga, who had held 118 slaves in 1860, and his almost equally prominent colleagues, former Governor John A. Winston of Sumter, who had owned 112, and future Governor Robert M. Patton of Lauderdale, who had owned 117. The majority of the delegates, however, had been smaller slaveholders. Fifty-nine of the 99 were

80

outside the planter class; 29 had owned fewer than five slaves (including the 16 non-slaveholders) and 30 had owned between five and 19. The median slaveholding among all the delegates was 13.[3] Given the delegates' extensive personal experience with slavery, it is hardly surprising that, despite their oath, they approached emancipation with some ambivalence.

Convention President Fitzpatrick immediately appointed a committee on the restoration of Alabama to the Union, chaired by Circuit Judge William S. Mudd of Jefferson County, who was one of the 21 delegates who would become Republicans. The committee debated the question of emancipation for several days and issued majority and minority reports, revealing that the committee had been deeply divided over the legitimacy of the Emancipation Proclamation that the delegates had just sworn to "abide by and faithfully support." Judge Mudd, for the majority, proposed a resolution that attempted to finesse the question by acknowledging that "the institution of slavery had been destroyed in the state of Alabama," but without specifying how that destruction had happened. The resolution then went on, in a version of the words of the 13th Amendment then pending for ratification before the states, to declare that "hereafter there shall be neither slavery nor involuntary servitude in the state, otherwise than for the punishment of crime whereof the party shall be duly convicted."

The minority report was offered by Alexander White of Talladega, a law partner and close friend of Provisional Governor Parsons. White, like Mudd, would become a leader of the state's Republican party, and the Republicans would elect him to Congress in 1872. But now, in common with a great many attorneys, he was unable to get beyond his conviction that the Emancipation Proclamation was in violation of the Fifth Amendment. He proposed a resolution that specifically attributed emancipation to the Proclamation and the acts of Congress flowing from it and pledged the state to obey them "unless and until the same shall have been declared invalid by the Supreme Court of the United States." White expected that the Supreme Court would eventually declare the Proclamation unconstitutional, and he did not want to write into the state's fundamental laws any provision that would then prevent Alabama from re-establishing slavery if it wished to do so.[4]

The question divided the Convention just as it had the committee. The committee reported on September 16 and the Convention voted to make its reports the special order for September 18. It then postponed consideration of the reports from day to day, each day from September 18 to September 22. During that time the delegates apparently argued the issue among themselves in private conversation. Finally, on September 22, the convention agreed to take the matter up. White made his case, in a speech filled with antebellum prejudice. "I wish to see the experiment of immediate emancipation tried," he assured the delegates, "and if it shall prove a failure, injurious to the North, ruinous to the South, and destructive to the negro race, I wish to keep open the only door by which we can escape such an accumulation of calamities." That it would prove a failure, however, White had no doubt. "The man who was born a slave, and has arrived at years of maturity as a slave, cannot be made a freeman. . . . The negro's idea of freedom is exemption from labor, and being accustomed to compulsion to make him work, when that compulsion is withdrawn, he will not work. . . . Now, sir, contemplate the future of four millions of human beings, idle, improvident and thievish, suddenly thrown upon their own responsibilities and their own guidance, and tell me, if you can, the fate of that people? Misery and want and vice, degradation, prostitution, disease and death." Eventually "the calm, collected judgment of the Northern mind upon this great question, when it is enlightened by experience and can be guided by its teachings," would come to see "that it is the Anglo-Saxon who is suffering here, and that it is their own blood and race whom the radicals North would subordinate, or at least bring down to a level with the negro." At that point the majority of Northerners will accept re-enslavement; or if not, "the political problem whether the negro and his confreres shall rule the United States will sharpen and intensify, until it will culminate in a war of races, and the extermination of the negro or the white man."

But this argument was overwhelmed by pragmatic considerations. As a practical matter, the freedmen could never now be re-enslaved, proponents of the majority report maintained; and without a clear commitment to abolition, the Congress would certainly not permit Alabama's readmission to the Union. And as to the constitutionality of the Proclamation, they observed that emancipation had been in fact accomplished by military force, whatever might be the legal right involved. The minority report was rejected 79–17, and the majority report was then adopted.[5]

The identity of the 17 delegates who voted for the minority report holds some surprises. Probably unsurprisingly, 10 of the 17 had been planters, a fourth of the planters in the Convention. One might well expect that this group would have been especially reluctant to accept abolition. More portentously for the future of Reconstruction, four of the 17 would become Republicans, or a fifth of the future Republicans in the Convention. In addition to Alexander White himself, this group included future Attorney General Joshua Morse of Choctaw, Dr. John G. Moore of Coffee, and Toliver Towles of Chambers. It is clear that for these men, as for a significant number of the state's native white Republicans, it was their commitment to unionism rather than their doubts about slavery that drew them to Republicanism.

And so, on September 22, 1865, slavery became unconstitutional in Alabama. But the delegates' acceptance of emancipation most certainly did not represent an acceptance of racial equality, or even of black citizenship. The state's antebellum Constitution of 1819 had proudly proclaimed "that all freemen, when they form a social compact, are equal in rights." But at the urging of David H. Thrasher, a Tallapoosa County farmer and schoolteacher, the delegates unanimously struck this statement from the new Constitution, lest some court think it applied to the former slaves. And when a conference of freedmen meeting in Mobile petitioned the Convention to consider granting black suffrage, the delegates tabled the memorial by voice vote, without debate.[6]

Indeed, these racial fears and the Convention's acceptance of emancipation came together to generate the legislative opposition to the ratification of the 13th Amendment. When the legislature elected under the new Constitution convened in November, Provisional Governor Parsons at once laid before them the amendment that had been proposed to the states by the Congress the preceding February, abolishing slavery throughout the United States. The state senate's committee on federal relations, chaired by the future Radical leader Adam C. Felder of Montgomery, quickly reported a resolution of ratification. But Senator John N. Drake, a Madison County farmer who had owned eighteen slaves in 1860, launched a fierce attack on the resolution. Drake had also been a delegate to the Constitutional Convention, and there he had opposed Alexander White's suggestion that the state adopt only a conditional emancipation. Slavery had already been "destroyed by the laws of Congress and the sword, which is superior to the Constitution," he had said. But now he argued that, since slavery had been abolished by the new Southern state constitutions, emancipation could not have been Congress's real goal in submitting the 13th Amendment. The actual intention of the sponsors of the amendment, he claimed, was to gain for the Congress, through the amendment's enforcement clause, the power to enact legislation according the freedmen civil rights. The result, he concluded, would be to "establish the black race on a firmer and broader basis than will be allowed to the white race."

Despite Drake's determined opposition, ratification cleared the senate, 23–5. In the house of representatives, however, it encountered a larger group of racial irredentists, led by future U.S. Senator John H. Bankhead of Marion County, at the time only 23 years old and just out of the Confederate Army. These opponents echoed Senator Drake's warnings, and to deal with them the sponsors of the ratification resolution amended it to add a reservation emphasizing that in ratifying, Alabama did not intend to confer on Congress the power to legislate on the political status of the former slaves. Fifteen representatives who evidently did indeed want to give Congress such power voted against the reservation. But with it the opposition to the resolution was successfully broken, and the house accepted ratification, 75–17.

An analysis of these votes produces further insights into the state's political and social cleavages. Just as the proposal for conditional emancipation at the Constitutional Convention had drawn strong support from delegates who had been planters, so the 15 representatives who voted for an unqualified ratification of the 13th Amendment without the reservation were generally poorer members from north Alabama. Twelve were from the hill counties and only three from plantation areas. No large planters and only two small planters were in the group, while seven had been non-slaveholders. Three were among the nine representatives who would become Republicans. The 18 legislators who were intransigently opposed to the 13th Amendment, on the other hand, were a considerably more diverse group. The 18 (13 representatives and five senators) included six planters, four of them—including Bankhead—large planters. But four had been non-slaveholders and an additional six had owned fewer than 10 slaves. Among them was Dr. John G. Moore of Coffee, the future Republican legislator who had also been one of the four future Republicans who had supported only a conditional emancipation at the Constitutional Convention. The diversity of this group underscores the extent to which racial fears transcended class divisions among white Alabamians. [7]

Alabama completed its ratification on December 2, and North Carolina and Georgia followed later that same week, bringing the number of states ratifying to three-fourths, and thus making the amendment a part of the Constitution. With the receipt of these three states' certificates of ratification,

Secretary of State William H. Seward proclaimed the amendment's adoption on December 18, and with it the final eradication of American slavery. Alabama thus could claim an honored place in this epochal achievement. But anyone who had paid close attention to the process through which Alabama had backed into this position would have been aware that the state in fact remained thoroughly blind to the true requirements of the new age.

II.

In the next stage of the stumbling efforts by Alabama's authorities to adjust their state to emancipation, the questions left unresolved by the Constitutional Convention almost immediately moved into the courts. At the same time the legislature was debating the ratification of the 13th Amendment, it was also electing a new state Supreme Court. The incumbent Chief Justice Abram J. Walker sought re-election, and the legislature unanimously obliged. Walker, a native of Tennessee, had been a Jacksonian state representative and senator in the antebellum years, representing Calhoun County in the state's hill country. In 1853 the legislature had elected him a chancellor of the state's equity courts and in 1856 had elevated him to the Supreme Court. He became chief justice in 1859. Incumbent Justice George W. Stone also sought re-election, but he was not so fortunate. Stone was defeated by Selma attorney William M. Byrd. Byrd, an antebellum Whig, had practiced law in Linden and had been a state representative from Marengo County, in the western Black Belt. In 1863 the Confederate legislature had elected him a chancellor and he had moved to Selma to take up the post. The third justiceship was vacant and drew five candidates. But Thomas J. Judge, a former state representative and senator from the Black Belt county of Lowndes, was elected after three ballots. Judge like Byrd had been a Whig, but in the 1850s he, along with the famed humorist and newspaper editor Johnson J. Hooper, had become the leader of the extremist Southern Rights Opposition that demanded secession and denounced even Yanceyite Democrats as compromisers. During these years Judge practiced law in partnership with future Confederate Attorney General and Civil War Governor Thomas H. Watts. All three of the justices had been slaveholders. Walker and Byrd each had held eight slaves in 1860, but Judge owned an extensive plantation and 67 slaves.[8]

The Constitutional Convention had, as we have seen, intentionally finessed the issue of precisely when and how emancipation had been accomplished.

But the January Term of 1866 presented the new Supreme Court with a large number of criminal appeals that required a clearer answer. Ferdinand had for more than 20 years been a slave in Mobile, the property of a firm of cotton factors. On April 12, 1865, "the military and naval forces of the United States took" the city and Ferdinand "left their service on that day, without their consent, and never returned to them," though the cotton factors "never in any wise admitted his right to freedom" until the adoption of the emancipation ordinance by the Constitutional Convention on September 22. On September 16 Ferdinand was arrested for obtaining goods under false pretenses. Defended by one of Alabama's most distinguished attorneys, former Chief Justice Edmund S. Dargan, Ferdinand interposed the defense that on September 16 he was legally a slave and hence could not be tried under the statute under which he was indicted, which applied only to free persons. Justice Judge made short work of this contention. "It is not denied that slavery has had no existence in this State since the . . . day the State convention . . . acted on the subject; but it is argued that it did exist in law, if not in fact, until that action was had. This position amounts to a denial of the legality of the destruction of slavery by the act of war, a question it would be utterly vain and useless to discuss. It is a historical fact that the consummation was effected by the act of war, anterior to the action of the State convention; and whether justly or unjustly, legally or illegally, are not now practical questions." The Constitutional Convention, he added, "was not guilty of the absurdity of abolishing slavery which did not then exist; but it gave a high and solemn sanction to the truth of the fact, before well known, that the institution of slavery had 'been destroyed in the State of Alabama,' by expressly so declaring and prohibiting the existence of slavery in the State in the future . . ."[9]

At the same term the court rejected the argument, offered in defense of a Tuscaloosa freedwoman by former Congressman William Russell Smith, that trying a former slave under a statute that had applied only to free persons at the time of the offense violated the prohibition against ex post facto laws. But here, as in similar cases, Chief Justice Walker "dissents from any expression in the opinion which may be regarded as intimating that slavery was abolished in the State otherwise than by the action of the convention" on September 22.[10] Walker never filed an opinion making a legal argument for denying the existence of an earlier emancipation. But his practical reason for doing so is apparent in his decision in the case of *Burt v. State.*

Burt, alias Burton, was a Marengo County slave who had been indicted in 1863 for killing Christopher Toomey, a white man, which was a capital offense. Because of the dislocations of war, Burt was not brought to trial until September 27, 1865, by which time he was a freedman. Judge James Cobbs instructed the jury that if they found the defendant guilty of murder in the first degree, they had the option of sentencing him either to death or to life in prison, and the jury then ordered him hanged. But this was not the statute under which Burt had been indicted, the Chief Justice objected; this was rather the statute that had applied to free persons. When slaves killed white persons, under antebellum law they could only be executed because, as the Chief Justice explained, a sentence of life in prison constituted no deterrence for a slave; slaves were already bound to service for life, and therefore life in prison would have represented nothing more than a change in the location of their labor. Besides, the antebellum statute had required that in the trial of a slave, at least two-thirds of the jury had to be slaveholders. But since there were now no slaveholders in Alabama, no statutory jury could be impaneled. Clearly, then, the statute that Burt had been indicted for violating had been rendered void by emancipation. But since the general murder statute, under which Judge Cobbs had instructed the jury, had applied only to free persons, and Burt had been a slave at the time of the offense, it followed that in killing Christopher Toomey, Burt had violated no law. The Supreme Court ordered that Burt be released.

Justice Byrd filed a lengthy dissent arguing that when the statute that Burt had offended had become void, the effect had been to revive the common law offense of murder, for which the punishment also had been death. But to this contention the Chief Justice replied, "The punishment may be the same under the statute as at common law; but the offense, in this State, is not identical with murder at common law," because the common law "certainly knew nothing of the crime of murder by a slave, as distinct from all other homicides by all other persons, and subject to distinct punishment."

Under the *Burt* decision the Supreme Court proceeded to bar the prosecution of any freedman for an offense specific to a slave. But it is clear that this was an outcome with which neither Chief Justice Walker nor Justice Byrd was happy. In his dissent in *Burt*, Byrd had written, "If the prisoner is to be discharged, the anomaly will be presented that a white man may still be convicted and punished with death for the murder of a slave; and the slave for the same offense, on a white man or slave, be discharged; and even a white man and a slave may have participated in the crime, and the former be convicted while the latter is acquitted, although both are guilty. Against so singular a result I would labor hard before I would be instrumental in producing it." There can be little doubt that it was precisely in order to limit the effect of his *Burt* decision that Chief Justice Walker had wanted to delay the date of emancipation to the Constitutional Convention's action on September 22. Only Justice Judge was willing to accept the full implications of *Burt*. He had written the *Ferdinand* opinion in which Byrd had concurred. And now in concurring with Walker in the *Burt* decision, he wrote, "It is to be regretted that in cases like the present, offenders escape merited punishment. But if such be the law, courts cannot help it—they must expound the law as it is. The discharge of the prisoner is one of the evils resulting from the war, and is not by any means the greatest that has been brought about by that calamity."[11]

The precise dating of emancipation was no mere academic question, then. A series of three cases forced the court to confront the question more directly. The first of these was decided at the same term as *Ferdinand* and *Burt*. In October 1864, the Confederate legislature had adopted a statute imposing the death penalty for stealing a mule, and under it two Greene County freedmen, Washington and Lafayette Jeffries, were indicted for stealing two mules on August 28, 1865. Justice Byrd—joined by Justice Judge, but over the dissent of Chief Justice Walker—held that this and other Confederate statutes had been suspended by martial law during the summer of 1865, and so the indictment was void. Byrd noted that the federal War Department had issued General Order 100 on April 24, 1863, declaring that any district occupied by the Union Army was immediately under martial law, and no formal declaration of the Union commander was necessary. "Under the provisions of this order, the act of the 7th October, 1864, was suspended by the occupation of the State by the United States army, and the surrender of General [Richard] Taylor in May, 1865" following the Battle of Blakely. The occupation and surrender "thereby subjected the State and the citizens thereof to the status of a conquered country, in which the will of the conqueror becomes the law of the land, regulated and restrained by the principles and institutes of international law."[12]

This decision clearly accepted federal authority, but at the next term the court imposed a sharp limit on the recognition. In January 1865, in the western Black Belt county of Wilcox, John W. Leslie leased a slave named William from his owner L. L. Langham for the coming calendar year, and gave Langham a promissory note to cover the cost of the lease. When the note matured, Leslie refused to pay. He was represented by Selma attorney N. H. R. Dawson, Abraham Lincoln's brother-in-law, and Dawson interposed his brother-in-law's Emancipation Proclamation as a defense, arguing that the lease was void because under the terms of the Proclamation, William had ceased to be Langham's property on January 1, 1863. Justice Byrd, now writing for a unanimous court, would have none of this. "Whether the State was in or out of the Union at the issuance of the proclamation of President Lincoln in January, 1863, makes no distinction or difference. If in the Union, he had no constitutional authority, nor had congress any to confer on him, to issue and enforce it at that time; and if out of the Union, in either case, it could have no force or validity until the Federal government was enabled by conquest or the power of arms to enforce it." Therefore, "slavery in this State was destroyed in May, 1865," when the state fell under martial law.[13]

At the June Term of 1868—the Presidential Reconstruction court's last session—the court again returned to this question, and again at the insistence of N. H. R. Dawson. On February 1, 1865, Leroy G. Weaver had purchased two slaves, Eliza and Caroline, from Selma attorney John W. Lapsley, and had given a promissory note for the purchase price. The note having matured, Lapsley sued Weaver to collect. Weaver's attorney Dawson again raised the question of the Emancipation Proclamation, arguing that the sale was void. But again writing for a unanimous court, Justice Judge replied, "As to the proclamation of President Lincoln, issued by him as 'President of the United States and Commander-in-chief of the Army and Navy thereof,' declaring the universal manumission of all persons held as slaves within any of the seceded States, we have to say that it was manifestly nought but a war-measure, and of no operative effect until carried into execution by force of arms. Such is believed to be the opinion of enlightened jurists and publicists in all sections of the Union. This proclamation, therefore, can bring no aid to appellant."[14]

Thus, despite the initial doubts of Chief Justice Walker, by the end of Presidential Reconstruction the state Supreme Court had come to a clear decision about the dating and means of emancipation. It did not proceed from the action of the state's Constitutional Convention, nor did it proceed from the Emancipation Proclamation. It was a product of martial law, and therefore dated from Confederate surrender—in Alabama, from the surrender of General Richard Taylor on May 5, 1865. The conclusion had important implications for both criminal and contract law, as we have seen. But it had equally significant implications in a third area. The state constitution, like the federal one, contained a prohibition against the taking of private property without just compensation, and the state's single most radical secessionist was eager to invoke the provision. George W. Gayle of Cahaba had just been released from jail, where he had been thrown following Abraham Lincoln's assassination because earlier that spring he had placed an advertisement in his local newspaper offering a reward to anyone who would murder the president. As soon as Gayle was released, he took up the cause of Mrs. Frances L. Logan, a Dallas County widow who sought to be paid by the state for her emancipated slaves. Gayle contended that the action of the Constitutional Convention in adopting the ordinance of emancipation had constituted a taking for which compensation was required. But Justice Judge replied that the *Ferdinand* decision had already held that the Convention had not emancipated the slaves, but had merely recognized an emancipation that had already taken place. "The counsel for appellant earnestly and ably contends for a decision in this case which would be in direct hostility to the conclusion attained upon the same question" in *Ferdinand*. "We decline to disturb the decision in that case; and upon its authority, the judgment of the court below in this case must be affirmed."[15] And although it did not arise in this suit, the decisions of the court holding that the Emancipation Proclamation also was not the source of emancipation meant that there had been no violation of the federal Constitution's takings clause either. As Justice Byrd had said in *Jeffries and Jeffries*, martial law had "subjected the State and the citizens thereof to the status of a conquered country, in which the will of the conqueror becomes the law of the land, regulated and restrained [only] by the principles and institutes of international law." Thus, because emancipation had been a result solely of martial law, Mrs. Logan and her fellow slaveholders were out of luck. A contrary decision would, of course, have bankrupted the state and enraged the entire Northern populace; and it seems quite likely that the justices' knowledge of that fact may have shaped their decisions in all these cases from the outset.

III.

The Constitution of 1867 and the new state Supreme Court that it created, however, allowed for a re-examination of these questions. The three justices who took office with the June Term of 1869 were all Republicans, and legal observers waited expectantly to see what the change portended.

Chief Justice E. Wolsey Peck of Tuscaloosa had been one of the state's most prominent attorneys in the antebellum period. The legislature had chosen him as one of Alabama's initial chancellors at the time of the creation of the separate equity courts in 1839, but he had soon returned to his successful private practice. A devoted Whig, he had nevertheless generally held aloof from party politics. But with secession Peck, a native of New York, became the leader of an anti-Confederate cabal in Tuscaloosa that actively supplied intelligence to the Union army. And at the advent of Reconstruction he embraced the Republican party, and served as the president of the 1867 Constitutional Convention. Thomas M. Peters of Moulton had been a state senator from Lawrence County in the antebellum period. Initially a Whig, he had gone over to the Democrats because of his enthusiasm for manifest destiny; Henry Clay's "Alabama Letters" in the 1844 presidential campaign were addressed to him. He supported Stephen A. Douglas in 1860, bitterly opposed secession, and with the outbreak of fighting, crossed into Union lines. Benjamin F. Saffold of Selma, a son of antebellum Supreme Court Justice Reuben Saffold, was a Democrat before the war. Like Peters, he supported Douglas in 1860, and crossed into Union lines with the commencement of fighting. On his return, he served as a circuit judge during Presidential Reconstruction. Both he and his brother Milton enthusiastically espoused the Republican party as soon as it was created in Alabama.

All three of the new justices served as delegates to the 1867 Constitutional Convention. Professors Richard L. Hume and Jerry B. Gough, in their careful analysis of the Convention's roll-call votes, rank both Peck and Saffold as moderate swing voters. But Peters they rate as one of the Convention's most radical members. All three had been slaveholders in the antebellum years. Peters had owned seven slaves in 1860, Saffold 12 and Peck 19.[16]

As soon as the Republican court took office, it was presented with the opportunity to reconsider its Presidential Reconstruction predecessors' dismissal of the significance of the Emancipation Proclamation, through the case of *Morgan v. Nelson*. Hamlin J. Smith of Dallas County had died in 1859, and

his father-in-law L. B. Vasser was appointed administrator of his estate, including 21 slaves. Vasser himself died in 1867, with the administration of the
Smith estate still open. Richard M. Nelson was then appointed administrator
of Smith's estate as successor to Vasser, and future U.S. Senator John Tyler
Morgan was appointed administrator of Vasser's own estate. Nelson thereupon
sued Morgan , asserting that Vasser had wasted Smith's estate, especially by
taking possession of Smith's slaves and working them for Vasser's own benefit.
Morgan had been an ardent secessionist, but the policies of the Lincoln administration were now suddenly revealed to him in a more alluring light. The
slaves had actually ceased to be a part of Smith's estate on January 1, 1863,
with the issuance of the Emancipation Proclamation, Morgan argued, and so
Vasser's estate should not be charged with any income from them after that
date. Former Justice Byrd, now off the bench and back in Selma, represented
Nelson, and Byrd relied on his own ruling in *Langham's Executors* to refute
this contention. The Proclamation, if constitutional at all, had had no effect
in Alabama until Union victory in May 1865, Byrd had held in that opinion.
But Thomas M. Peters's understanding of recent history was very different
from William M. Byrd's.

Slavery, Peters passionately observed, "was an institution which depended
upon force, and not right, for its preservation. No human being was ever created a slave. Slavery was the creature of force or fraud. . . . The great national
decree which laid slavery prostrate in the dust forever upon this continent,
was the proclamation of President Lincoln issued on the 1st day of January,
1863. . . . The nation fixed the day for its termination, and after that day, it was
simply a struggle of the former masters of the slaves to prevent the decree of
the nation from being carried into effect." It was, he said, "an actual absurdity,
as well as a legal impossibility, that the courts of our country cannot ascertain
the precise day on and from which this great event, of such recent occurrence,
should in legal contemplation be now deemed to have become operative. But
no such day can be ascertained, if the first day of January, 1863, is not that
day." And he added, "The Alabama convention of 1865 and its ordinance
had as little to do with emancipation as they will have with the coming day
of final wrath, when the grave will give up its dead. It would have been all
the same had that convention never met."

If slavery had ended at the beginning of 1863, however, how would one
describe the relationship of slaves and masters in the following years? Peters

explained, ". . . if the freedmen remained on the farms and plantations or at the homes of their former masters, or elsewhere in the care and under the control of said former masters, and there was no actual force used to compel them to do so, it was a consent on their part still to acquiesce in the usages of the old system of servitude on the former terms, without pay except simply their support and lodgment, until the new relation was regulated by law and the rights and duties of each were properly defined. . . . But to the lasting honor of the new citizen, he has thus far shown himself worthy of his new estate. He has parted with his old master in peace and good will, and has shown himself too noble-hearted to quibble with him about pennies, when he has received in reward for his patience and his toil a boon that money could not buy."[17]

In this opinion Justice Peters spoke for a unanimous court, and it initially appeared that the conclusions of the Presidential Reconstruction jurists as to the legal origins of emancipation had been thoroughly repudiated. But only six months later, it became clear that Chief Justice Peck and Justice Saffold had not understood the matter in the same terms that Peters's soaring rhetoric had implied. The case of *McElvain v. Mudd* was the Alabama Supreme Court's final effort to deal with the question of emancipation, and it revealed that the Republican justices were quite as perplexed about it as the spokesmen of Presidential Reconstruction had been.

On February 1, 1864, Wallace S. McElvain had purchased three slaves from Judge William S. Mudd, the Jefferson County circuit judge and Republican who had been the sponsor of the emancipation ordinance that had been adopted by the Constitutional Convention of 1865. McElvain gave Mudd a promissory note for the purchase price, and when the note matured three years later, the judge sued to collect. McElvain was represented by Alexander White, the Republican leader who had opposed Mudd at the 1865 Convention and had urged only a conditional emancipation, under the conviction that the Emancipation Proclamation would eventually be found unconstitutional. But now, relying on Justice Peters's decision in the *Morgan* case, White argued that the Proclamation, issued in 1863, rendered a contract for the sale of slaves concluded in 1864 void, and the promissory note with it. Chief Justice Peck, however, was not convinced.

The question, Peck wrote, was "what influence and effect had the proclamation of the president on the institution of slavery in the rebel slaveholding States, and upon the contracts of the citizens of said States with each other, made in good faith, with reference to that sort of property, between the date of said proclamation and the final suppression of the rebellion, a period of nearly two years and six months? . . . At the time the said proclamation was dated, all the power of the United States could not enforce it within the territory of the rebel States; . . . and more, it was never, until the rebellion was suppressed, officially promulgated in said States, nor could it be. It would seem, therefore, if there were no other reasons, these people should not be permitted to resist a performance of their contracts made with each other in good faith, with a full and equal knowledge of all the facts relating to the subject-matter of their contracts, and each party assuming and taking upon himself all the risks attendant upon them."

Moreover, Peck continued, the text of the Proclamation itself ordered the armed forces of the Union not to repress the slaves "in any efforts they may make for their actual freedom," an explicit acknowledgment "that, notwithstanding said proclamation, the slaves , the subjects of it, were not then, by the mere force of the same, actually free . . ." And the text was equally clear that it was issued as a war measure, to assist in winning the war, with the inescapable implication that it could have been revoked if subsequent military necessity had required the action. "Who can reasonably doubt but that, at the conference at Fortress Monroe, the president might not then have withdrawn the said proclamation if he had thought proper to do so, upon the rebel government and people stipulating to abandon their resistance to the government and authority of the Union and renewing their allegiance to the constitution and government of the United States? If this had been done, would not slavery have been continued under the same guarantees and protection that it had before the rebellion began?" And so he concluded, "We see, therefore that this proclamation, though positive in its language, depended upon a contingency—an uncertain event—the real end of which no one could then foresee, and no one could then know whether its purpose would ever be realized."

But if these were the Chief Justice's views, why had he concurred with Justice Peters in *Morgan v. Nelson*? "We remain satisfied with the decision in that case, and are persuaded, rightly understood, it was decided upon correct principles," the Chief Justice said, implying that Justice Peters did not correctly understand his own opinion. Peters in *Morgan* had concluded that, "notwithstanding the event of emancipation is fixed by the act of the nation at the first day of January, 1863; yet if an administrator used the slaves of his intestate for his own profits after that date, he should be charged with such profits up to the date of the discharge of the slaves from his control by the result of the war." "This," Peck said, "is unquestionably correct. It is common doctrine that a trustee is not permitted to profit by his use of trust property, but is bound to account for any profits he may make by such use to the beneficiaries. But in that case," Peck observed incisively, "if the proclamation by its own vigor so utterly and absolutely abolished slavery from its date that no interest or property remained in them whatever from that date, then it follows that from that date the slaves not only ceased to be trust property, but also ceased to be property at all; consequently, it would seem upon every principle of equity that the profits derived from the use of the slaves did not belong to the estate, but should have gone to those who earned them," the former slaves. But that had not been Peters's holding. "The plain inference from all this is that, notwithstanding the proclamation, there continued an uncertain, contingent interest and property in slaves until the proclamation became effectual by the suppression of the rebellion . . ."

It is hardly surprising that Peters entirely disagreed, and he filed a lengthy dissent. The Emancipation Proclamation, he wrote, "proclaimed the absolute and unconditional emancipation of the slaves in certain portions of the United States, of which the State of Alabama was a part." After January 1, 1863, "it became the policy of the nation to enforce this proclamation; and it was persisted in until it was finally successful. . . . The nation achieved, in the end, what it had proclaimed. In such cases, it is a rule almost without exception that the effect of such measures must be referred to the beginning, or to the first proclamation of the purpose intended to be accomplished." Thus, for instance, treaties are held to take effect from the date of their signing, not the date of their ratification by the Senate. Moreover, the "proclamation was but the culmination of the policy of the several acts of congress which had preceded it, and which had the same tendency and purpose." Clearly, therefore, following the issuance of the Proclamation, the sale of slaves was "against the public policy of the nation, and for that reason also they were illegal and void." And finally, "Slaves were held in their unhappy condition by a regulation founded in force on the one hand and weakness on the other. . . . Slavery violated a great natural law, that is, that man is of necessity, for his own support, entitled to the proceeds of his own labor." To understand that the sale of slaves was a violation of natural law, we have only to imagine a contract "based upon the sale of our more favored fellow-citizens whose good fortune had colored their faces white instead of black . . ." In that case, "very few would be found to stand up for the enforcement of the sales of the sons and daughters of the commonwealth, how long so ever they might have suffered in slavery. Yet this is the question now under discussion; and possibly an old, familiar and carefully cherished prejudice may interpose to prevent us from feeling its enormity." Peters explicitly added that former Justice Byrd's opinion in *Leslie v. Langham's Executors* "ought to be over ruled."

In addition, Peters continued, the principles of contract law also required voiding the contract at issue. The contract was founded upon a warranty deed for the sale of slaves for life. "If the consideration fails, the contract fails. Here the character of the person sold was of the very essence of the consideration of the contract. The sale was that of a slave for life. This was the main and sole condition of sale. It was the cause and purpose of the sale, and it constituted the entire consideration of the promise to pay the purchase-money by the vendee. . . . Emancipation was an assault by the law upon the consideration of the contract of sale which destroyed it." And yet the court's majority "suffers the plaintiff to be released on his part, and then to turn round on the defendant and compel him to perform his part of the agreement of sale! There is, I apprehend, no admitted principle of law that sustains this result. It is radically wrong and unjust. . . . The seeming injustice of an affirmance of the judgment below appears from the fact that the appellant will be made to pay quite eight thousand dollars in legal funds to the appellee for property in persons now citizens of the State, who had been declared enfranchised by the nation and whose emancipation the nation was most solemnly pledged to make good; and yet, get comparatively nothing of any value for his money."[18]

The debate between Chief Justice Peck and Justice Peters in part turned upon this question of the sanctity of contract. Peters thought that McElvain was being forced to pay for non-existent property, founded on a false warranty. Peck thought that both parties had entered the contract equally aware of the risk posed by Union victory, and so each party was obliged to live up to his undertaking. But the difference between them went much deeper, to the meaning of the Civil War. Peters understood the war as a crusade against slavery. The act of August 1, 1861, freeing any slaves used by the Confederate armed forces, the act of July 17, 1862, barring the return of fugitive slaves and President Lincoln's preliminary emancipation proclamation of September 22, 1862, all demonstrated the Union's hostility to slavery long before the Emancipation Proclamation itself, he said, and both Lincoln's amnesty proclamation of December 8, 1863, and Andrew Johnson's of May 29, 1865, made the acceptance of emancipation a condition of the restoration of citizenship. "This important system of measures from the year 1861 to the year 1865, shows that it was the purpose and policy of the government of the United States to abolish slavery in the insurgent States . . ." For Peck, however, the war was about the preservation of the union. The Emancipation Proclamation "being a mere war measure, the president, if it failed to accomplish the object intended and desired, by the same powers and authority by which he had issued it, by his powers and authority as commander-in-chief, might . . . if he had believed it best, [have] withdrawn the proclamation altogether, and have issued any other proclamation or adopted any other war measure that he might have thought would better accomplish the end desired—that is, the suppression of the rebellion and the preservation of the Union and government of the United States," Peck wrote.

This distinction was a portentous one. It divided the scalawags from the very outset. There were 57 native white Republicans among the delegates to the 1867 Constitutional Convention. Hume and Gough classify 23 of them (including Peters), or 40.4 per cent, as Radicals, 15 (including Peck and Saffold), or 26.3 per cent, as moderate swing voters, and 18, or 31.6 per cent, as conservatives. (One of the delegates cast too few votes to be classified.) The differences between Peck and Peters that the *McElvain* decision revealed reflect an important element in determining these insistent internal scalawag divisions, separating as they did those native whites who had been drawn to Republicanism primarily by their hostility to slavery from those who had been drawn to it primarily by unionism and patriotism.

To the thoughtful and arresting debate between Peck and Peters in their *McElvain* opinions was added a discordant note in Justice Saffold's brief concurrence with the Chief Justice. "If it should ever become important to determine the precise time when the abolition of slavery was effected by law in this State," he wrote, "I am satisfied it will be referred to the date of the adoption of the 13th amendment to the Federal constitution." Thus Saffold joined with Abram J. Walker in believing that the legal end of slavery substantially postdated the end of the war, and indeed went even further than

Walker's date of the 1865 Convention's emancipation ordinance on September 22, pushing the date back to December 6, the completion of the ratification of the 13th Amendment. Apparently Saffold agreed with Peters in regarding emancipation as an act of the nation rather than of the states, but since he rejected Peters's belief that the Emancipation Proclamation was its source, he was left only with the 13th Amendment as his authority. Saffold offered no rationale for his assertion, however, and so we are simply left to speculate on what his argument might have been.

Thus, the six justices who considered the question have bequeathed us a range of answers as to the date of emancipation. Chief Justice Walker and Justice Saffold placed it substantially after the end of the war, Walker on September 22 and Saffold on December 6—even though, as a practical matter, everyone knew that the slaves had actually been free for months by then. And Justice Peters believed that it had occurred in the midst of the war, on January 1, 1863—even though, as a practical matter, everyone knew that slaves continued to be worked, and bought and sold, for years after that date. These three justices reached legal conclusions so at odds with common knowledge because each of them sought an official document on which to hang the event—for Peters the Emancipation Proclamation, for Walker the 1865 Constitutional Convention's ordinance of emancipation, for Saffold the 13th Amendment. Chief Justice Peck and Justices Byrd and Judge all joined in attributing emancipation not to legal action but to military force. Byrd went so far as to call the Emancipation Proclamation unconstitutional. Peck clearly agreed with Peters in regarding it as a legitimate exercise of the president's war powers, inherent in his being commander-in-chief of the armed forces. But Peck agreed with Judge in considering it "a mere war measure," without effect until given it by military victory. Judge and Byrd fixed Union victory, and consequent martial law, at the surrender of General Taylor on May 5. Peck, more flexibly, seems to have thought of emancipation as a sort of rolling event, accompanying the progress of Union arms. This conclusion was truer to historical reality, for emancipation in fact came earlier to the Tennessee Valley counties, which fell to Union forces substantially before most of the state. Nevertheless, for almost all of Alabama south of the Tennessee Valley—and hence for most Alabama slaves, and their masters—the date picked by Judge and Byrd would have coincided with Peck's standard as well. These justices therefore retrieve from obscurity a date condemned to the footnotes in even the most detailed histories of the Civil War—the surrender of General Richard Taylor to General Edward R. S. Canby in Citronelle, Alabama, on May 5, 1865—and make it perhaps the single most significant date in all of Alabama history.

NOTES

1 *Journal of the Proceedings of the Constitutional Convention of the State of Alabama Held in the City of Montgomery September 12, 1865* (Montgomery: Gibson and Whitfield, 1865), 7, 12–13; Malcolm C. McMillan, *Constitutional Development in Alabama, 1798–1901: A Study in Politics, the Negro and Sectionalism* (Chapel Hill: University of North Carolina Press, 1955), 90, 93.

2 McMillan, *Constitutional Development*, 92–3; J. Mills Thornton, *Politics and Power in a Slave Society: Alabama, 1800–1860* (Baton Rouge: Louisiana State University Press, 1978), 409–13.

3 I have developed these figures from the manuscript census returns of 1860.

4 *Journal of the Constitutional Convention of 1865*, 19–20, 29; McMillan, *Constitutional Development*, 94–5.

5 Journal of the Constitutional Convention of 1865, 48–9; Alexander White, "Speech to the Constitutional Convention of 1865" (Pamphlet Collection, Alabama Department of Archives and History); McMillan, *Constitutional Development*, 95–7. The prohibition of slavery was an ordinance adopted by the Convention, not a provision of the state constitution. The ordinance also amended the Constitution of 1819 "by striking out all provisions in relation to slaves and slavery" and ordered the legislature at its next session "to pass such laws as will protect the Freedmen of this State in the full enjoyment of all their rights of person and property, and to guard them and the State against any evils that may arise from their sudden emancipation."

6 *Journal of the Constitutional Convention of 1865*, 33, 48, 79; McMillan, *Constitutional Development*, 103, 106.

7 On these events, see my "Alabama's Presidential Reconstruction Legislature," in Gary W. Gallagher and Rachel A. Shelden, eds., *A Political Nation: New Directions in Mid-Nineteenth Century American Political History* (Charlottesville: University of Virginia Press, 2012), 173–4, from which this latter discussion is largely drawn. McMillan, *Constitutional Development*, 96; *Senate Journal, Session of 1865–66*, 77, 79–80, 83–4; *House Journal, Session of 1865–66*, 85–8; *Acts of Alabama, Session of 1865–66*, 597–8.

8 *House Journal, Session of 1865–66*, 76–9; Thomas M. Owen, *History of Alabama and Dictionary of Alabama Biography* (Chicago: S. J. Clarke, 1921), vol. III, 277, 951, vol. IV, 1714.

9 *Ferdinand v. State*, 39 Ala. 706. The title of this case reflects the state of transition that the freedmen were in at this time. The Reporter of Decisions, using the antebellum pattern, referred to the defendant only by his first name. But after his self-emancipation, Ferdinand had adopted the name Ferdinand Smith, and in later years the justices themselves sometimes cited the precedent as *Smith v. State*.

10 *Eliza v. State*, 39 Ala. 693.

11 *Burt v. State*, 39 Ala. 617; see also *George v. State*, 39 Ala. 675, *Nelson v. State*, 39 Ala.

667, *Witherby v. State*, 39 Ala. 702.

12   *Jeffries and Jeffries v. State*, 39 Ala. 655; cf. *Aaron and Ely v. State*, 39 Ala. 684.

13   *Leslie v. Langham's Executors*, 40 Ala. 524.

14   *Weaver v. Lapsley*, 42 Ala. 601.

15   *Logan v. State*, 40 Ala. 733; on Gayle, see Thornton, *Politics and Power*, 190–4, 203, 243–5.

16   Owen, *Dictionary of Alabama Biography*, vol. IV, 1335, 1349, 1486; Glenda McWhirter Todd, *First Alabama Cavalry, USA: Homage to Patriotism* (Bowie, Md.: Heritage Books, 1999), 238; Richard L. Hume and Jerry B. Gough, *Blacks, Carpetbaggers and Scalawags: The Constitutional Conventions of Radical Reconstruction* (Baton Rouge: Louisiana State University Press, 2008), 282, 284, 312; Joel D. Kitchens, "E. W. Peck: Alabama's First Scalawag Chief Justice," *Alabama Review*, vol. 54, no. 1 (January 2001), 3–32; Paul Horton, "Lightning Rod Scalawag: The Unlikely Political Career of Thomas Minott Peters," *Alabama Review*, vol. 64, no. 2 (April 2011), 116–42. Saffold had been a fire-eater in 1850, but had moved in a more conservative direction over the coming decade (Thornton, *Politics and Power*, 241, 243, 455). The new Constitution of 1867 had taken the election of Supreme Court justices from the legislature and given it to the people.

17   *Morgan v. Nelson*, 43 Ala. 586.

18   *McElvain v. Mudd*, 44 Ala. 48. The 1867 Constitutional Convention had adopted an ordinance voiding all debts contracted for the sale of slaves, and in this decision Peck and Saffold joined also to declare the ordinance in violation of the U.S. Constitution's prohibition of laws impairing the obligation of contract.

7

Did the Civil War Matter?

Steven Hahn

T he sesquicentennial of the American Civil War has raised some discussion (though far less than one might have expected) about the
War's causes and its political and military course, but remarkably
little about its consequences and legacies. This is all the more surprising, since
the War has long been understood as one of the country's great turning points,
if not *the* great turning point, and we often use rather powerful, dramatic,
and occasionally extravagant language to describe what happened during and
immediately after it. The quantity of blood spilled—epic even on an international stage[1]—is the most common measure of the war's impact, but to this
may be added the abolition of slavery, new forms of centralized power, the
decisive defeat of the Confederate rebellion, and the ability of the victorious
Union to impose martial law and all manner of conditions attendant upon
securing a peace. If the war and what we call "Reconstruction" are regarded
as inextricably connected, then students of the event often invoke the term
"revolution" to characterize what went on: whether they were appalled by what
the Republican Party did to a defeated South (the Dunningites),[2] sanguine
or critical about the transformations that were effected (the progressives and
revisionists),[3] or ultimately disappointed that the engine of change too quickly
ran out of steam (the post-revisionists).[4]

Yet, if we take a longer view, the picture—at least the picture constructed
and argued over by scholars—is much less clear. At the turn of the 20th
century the United States appeared to be a far different place than it was 40
years earlier. A sprawling, de-centered, and overwhelmingly agricultural and
small-town society had become an urban and industrial power, and a force
in international relations. But how much of all this change owed explicitly
to the Civil War and Reconstruction? It's easy to forget the historiographi-

cal traditions that either emphasize fundamental continuities over the Civil War era, or fail to take direct stock of how what did happen influenced the longer term. Economic historians have debated for years whether the Civil War advanced the course of industrialization, and a good many of them believe the data says "no." A few claim that the war may in fact have retarded industrialization.[5] C. Vann Woodward made a strong case for the Civil War's revolutionary consequences for the South, but the centerpiece of his argument—the destruction of the old ruling class and the rise of a new one—has been forcefully challenged by social historians who have demonstrated, with intensive quantitative studies, that in most places planter families held onto their land and reclaimed the reins of local power, not to mention control of the freed labor force.[6]

And historians who write about the postwar system of tenancy and sharecropping often puzzle over how different it was than the slavery that came before. Indeed, what I see as the general scholarly consensus (which I don't happen to share) that slavery was just another form of capitalism makes one wonder what the destruction of slavery and the transition to different forms of labor exploitation mean in conceptual terms—and scholars who assume that slavery was a form of capitalism rarely confront the question of the transition themselves.[7] Those who also see the main theme of the period between 1865 and 1914 as the reconstruction and redeployment of white supremacy—as Ulrich B. Phillips did in his day—have good reason to wonder if the South "lost the war" but ultimately "won the peace."[8]

Then, of course, there is the question of how wide an impact the Civil War might have had and how big a "world" it might have made. We have become well-accustomed to viewing the Civil War and Reconstruction in international and comparative perspective, but mostly as it concerns a better understanding of what happened here.[9] We know next to nothing—other than conjecturally—about the international, global repercussions of the war, and there's not much help in the world-history literature. C. A. Bayley's recent world synthesis of the 19th century, *The Birth of the Modern World*, devotes only a few pages to the American Civil War and makes relatively little of its international consequences outside the changing technology of warfare. Neither does Eric Hobsbawm's multi-volume history of the 19th century, including the one—*The Age of Capital, 1848–1875*—that directly covers the Civil War era. Nor does any other overview of the era of which I'm aware.[10]

Although American historians have often claimed that the outcome of the Civil War effectively doomed slavery in Cuba and Brazil, the last places in the hemisphere where it still survived, neither the Cuban nor the Brazilian historical literature makes such connections (or at least do not make much of such connections). Even Rebecca Scott's highly regarded study of race and emancipation in Cuba and Louisiana devotes all of one paragraph to the Civil War's meaning in Cuba. The war that concerns Cubanists is the Ten Year's War in their own territory; the one that concerns Brazilianists is the Paraguayan War on their border.[11]

Significantly, the American Civil War does not much register in the historiography of either Latin America more generally or Mexico in particular (consumed as it was during the period with the French invasion, the installation of Maximillian as emperor, and the construction of the Porfiriato). In Mexican eyes there is more of a continuity of American imperial aggressiveness across the 19th century, even though the distraction of the War likely played a role in France's decision to invade.[12]

Compare this to the literatures on the French Revolution, its Haitian component, the abolition of slavery in the British West Indies, or the Revolutions of 1848, for which the international ripple effects figure centrally in scholarly appraisals of their importance. If anything, United States scholars have taken much more account of these events in the coming of the Civil War than of the Civil War's impact on international developments that followed. It's reasonable for us to ask why this is so.[13]

MY INTENTION HERE IS not to dismiss deeply laid understandings and argue that they make much ado about nothing. My intention is rather to suggest the wide-ranging and challenging conceptual and empirical work that we still have before us. If anything, I should like to argue that the Civil War very directly made for a different—in some instances, far different—world, both domestically and internationally, than what had prevailed before it, and in the arenas that mattered most: that is to say, the War and its specific outcome dramatically reoriented the axes of power and the formation of social classes in the United States, redefined the nature and boundaries of governance, redirected the course of economic development, reconstituted the body politic and extended the international revolutionary dynamic that appeared to have ended with the Revolutions of 1848, and reconfigured the platform of international relations, especially as regards the Pacific (we make a mistake if we view the war and its impact chiefly as an Atlantic event).

That is to say, what began as a slaveholders' rebellion in the context of an intense struggle for federal power turned into a bourgeois social and political revolution that simultaneously made for an imperial nation-state for the first time on the North American continent and for a massive capitalist transformation "from above."[14] The main work of Reconstruction, in other words, was reorganizing the political economy of the United States and setting the course for what became the next reconstruction—not in the 1950s and 1960s and associated with civil rights as the case is often made—but in the 1890s and the first decade and a half of the 20th century, when what Martin Sklar calls the "corporate reconstruction of American capitalism" began to take place.[15]

Making this case in its fullness would require many pages. But I will summarize some claims and offer some ways of thinking about their viability. And this will require both a brief return to the world before the Civil War and a brief counterfactual excursion into a world in which the Civil War had not occurred or had turned out differently.

Part of the challenge in more clearly understanding the War's impact is to get a firm handle on the nature of power and the trajectories of development in the antebellum United States. Historians often work off a number of ideas that, in my view, are dubious: that the Revolution and Constitution produced a "nation"; that slavery quickly became organized along "sectional" lines"; that the main axes of conflict were "North/South" and that the power of slaveholders was steadily declining; that the United States was well along the road of industrialization by the 1840s and that it moved down the industrial road with an enfranchised working class; and, of course, that capitalism was running rampant.

There are good reasons to question these ideas. We might like to think of our national origins story commencing in the late 18th century with perhaps a highly embattled march to fruition being completed with Reconstruction. But the structure of governance created by the Articles of Confederation and then the Constitution scarcely made for a national state—a nation-state—in its most basic of terms: as a political entity that could claim sovereign authority over the people and places within its presumed borders. After all, the majority of the voting public in the United States embraced some form of states' rights, and the territory of the country was replete with competing forms of sovereignty, not only built around states and localities and spiritual movements but also around households, slavery being the most politically consequential though hardly the most common. We might, in fact, think about a raft of "counter-sovereignties,"some patriarchal, which not only limited the hold of the center but also threatened, at various points, to dismember the entire Union (not entirely unlike Mexico in this period). Secession in 1860–61 was only one of a number of what turned into rebellious challenges.[16]

FOR ITS PART, SLAVERY was anything but "sectional." The states of the Northeast and Middle Atlantic abolished slavery very gradually, and the legal basis of emancipation in them was often so muddled that many of the states had to do so twice, New Hampshire as late as 1857. Slave hiring and transit made a mockery of any dividing line between "free" and "slave" states—as did the persistence of servitude and lifetime indentures for the "liberated"—and the courts effectively privileged the demands of slaveholders to take their slaves wherever they saw fit and to recover slaves who tried to escape their captivity.[17]

Outside of New England and the Middle Atlantic coast, moreover, industrial activity and the spread of wage labor was quite limited. The rural sector was still organized (North and South) around patriarchal landownership and personal domination (whether of household members or slaves), and manufacturing was chiefly the business of small shops and outworking of various sorts, including the garment trades. Wage labor was most densely in evidence in seaports and on infrastructure projects (most of it foreign-born), and in some places was used in close conjunction with slaves and other coerced workers. In truth, much of the antebellum working class was excluded from the franchise by race, gender, geographical mobility, and (during the 1850s in the heart of industrialism) by place of birth.[18] Not incidentally, the workers in the leading economic sectors of the United States—the production and processing of the cotton staple—had few or no civil and political rights. What was happening during the era of the so-called "market revolution," at least in my own judgment, was an intensification of existing exchange relations, of the circulation of goods and people, rather than a transformation in how goods were produced and people deployed. Merchants and large landowners remained the dominant economic actors they had been since European settlement.[19]

To be sure, paths of capitalist development and nation-state formation were being carved in the Northeast and sections of the Midwest owing to networks of finance, capital accumulation, immigration, transportation, and state activism at several levels. Yet alternative paths were being pursued—and alternative centers of power being developed—not only in the lower South but even more significantly in the Mississippi Valley. There, from at least the early 19th century, entrepreneurs, settlers, slaveholders, and policymakers who would find a political home in the Democratic Party imagined a massive agro-commercial empire stretching out from the riverine (and then rail) corridor linking Chicago and New Orleans, both to other parts of North America and into the Caribbean basin (mainly by way of Havana). Although the slaveholding imperialists of the Gulf Coast may have been the best known, mid-continent allies to the North, like Stephen Douglas (who thought Lincoln's "house divided" idea was ludicrous), were equally important.[20]

Indeed, I'd argue that the main developmental conflict in the first half of the 19th century did not set the "North" against the "South"; it set the Northeast against the Mississippi Valley. The disintegration of the Valley political coalition in the face of slaveholding militants was crucial to the coming of the Civil War and then to the impact the war would have on the American political economy. Significantly, one plank that the platforms of Northern and Southern Democrats had in common in 1860, even as they nominated separate candidates and differed over popular sovereignty, was the call for the annexation of Cuba.[21]

The War, then, would not award victory to the "North" over the "South," or to the "Union" over the "so-called Confederacy" (I prefer the "so-called Confederacy" as Lincoln had it, recognizing its rogue character rather than dignifying it as a state), but rather to the Northeast developmental project over its various competitors. Yet this was hardly preordained. It came in the process of waging war, not in initiating war; and it was decisively influenced by the course of reconstructing the South and especially the West.

WE ARE, OF COURSE, familiar with a constellation of federal measures, designed principally to fund the war and defeat the rebellion, that clearly tipped (or would tip) the balances of political economy in new directions (so long as the war was won): toward cities at the expense of the countryside, toward industry at the expense of agriculture, and toward the Northeast and national state at the expense of every place else. These included the Morrill tariff (and Anti-Bigamy Act), the National Banking Acts, immediate and uncompensated emancipation of the slave labor force by the federal (as opposed to a state's) government, military conscription and the enlistment of African Americans, and the imposition of martial law over much of the South once the rebels began to surrender (though the War and the Rebellion would not be over for some time still).[22]

Yet especially important was the creation and dramatic empowerment of a new class of finance capitalists through the marketing of government bonds and securities, and their close alliance with the national state mediated chiefly by the railroads. This was the developmental wedge that transformed the trans-Mississippi West and, in the process, decisively marked the nature and trajectory of American capitalism, domestically and internationally.

Now, I recognize that, thanks to Richard White, we may no longer see the economic wisdom in the transcontinental railroads that had their birth during the Civil War with the Pacific Railway Act. But the truth is that the transcontinentals were initially governed by a political rather than an economic logic (though the economic followed the political). Lincoln very nearly lost California and Oregon in the election of 1860 (Democrats and Southern sympathizers were the powers there); the New Mexico Territory had enacted a slave code; and rebel troops had quickly moved westward out of Texas with an eye on both Colorado and possibly California (and the precious metals to be found there—the Confederate treasury was effectively bare). Transcontinental railroads had long been favorites of Lincoln's (he wanted to build three), and their authorization must be seen, alongside the creation of new military departments and territories in the West, as a means of extending federal authority over the American territory: as a means of turning a shaky Union into a nation-state. What 19th-century nation-state didn't seek to build some version of a transcontinental railroad as one of its first moves?[23]

The transcontinentals could have been left under public control as some in Congress had hoped, but in effect the federal government socialized most of the costs not only by means of land giveaways and generous financing but also by deploying the Army to facilitate construction through potentially hostile territory. Indeed, the Army—with its top officers being veterans of the Civil War and Southern Reconstruction—embodied the developmental alliance by destroying and marginalizing Native populations who, in their land use, social organization, subsistence strategies, and forms of surplus extraction, were the last significant pre- or non-capitalist societies west of the Mississippi. General

William T. Sherman, who placed particularly high value on his career in the West, was not alone in seeing his goals as the promotion of railroad construction, white settlement, and regional economic expansion; in the early treaties that he supervised, Sherman was careful to have Indian signatories surrender rights-of-way to the railroads. Then, of course, in one of the lesser-known acts of nation-state building during Reconstruction, the entire treaty system, and the status of Indians as "domestic dependent" nations, was abrogated.[24]

THE ALLIANCE BETWEEN NEW finance capital and the new nation-state proved of considerable developmental importance because it favored creditors over debtors, stabilized the formal political system in their general interests (those who opposed the money regime were left to cobble together their own coalitions and mostly fly-by-night political parties), and laid the groundwork for the next reconstruction in a variety of ways.[25] Equally important, the alliance helped establish the framework for the subsequent industrialization of the West, directly providing the capital and other resources for the many extractive industries—mining, chiefly—that would be the hallmarks of the post-Civil War Western economy. Unquestionably, a slower process of railroad building that followed rather than preceded settlement would have made for less of a financial roller coaster during the last three decades of the 19th century and surely would have created more breathing room for Native Americans and small producers alike. But that would have been the result of a different Civil War and Reconstruction than the one the country actually experienced.[26]

The abolition of slavery and soon thereafter debt peonage (at least in theory) as well as the consecration of birthright citizenship did make new popular struggles possible and may have advanced the political prospects of working people in parts of Europe. If nothing else, they help us understand why the United States had the most vibrant and violent labor/political history in the world during the last third of the 19th century. And the most brutal showdowns were clearly in the South and West. We tend to think of Radical Reconstruction in racial and political terms, but we must not forget that emancipation created a new working class chiefly in the rural districts of the South and one that carried out the most impressive political mobilization of any section of the working class in all of the 19th century, if not in all of American history.[27]

For a time, the federal government was an enabler in this regard as it was in early agitation for the eight-hour day. Yet, not by accident did the governing Republican Party almost simultaneously allow the last Reconstruction regimes, whose political base was overwhelmingly working class, to fall while sending its troops (for the first time) to suppress the Great Railroad Strikes of 1877. Jim Crow involved many different things, but it surely involved a counter-revolution by landed capital and its allies principally through the vehicle of the state governments: new lien laws, fence laws, game laws, and vagrancy laws for the agricultural sector, together with the beginnings of a massive attack on the bases of black—read working-class—power.[28]

For the remainder of the century, the United States was convulsed by conflicts of various sorts between labor and capital, and many of the most intense and militarized were in the South and, especially, in the West (I don't think we can understand lynching aside from the reinvigoration of black labor mobility and activism during the 1880s and 1890s, especially in the cotton districts). Here the Knights of Labor helped organize massive strikes against robber baron Jay Gould's railroad system in 1885 and 1886, as they did in the sugar districts of lower Louisiana; here the Colored Farmers' Alliance launched a widespread and bloody cotton pickers' strike; here the People's Party mobilized thousands of small landowners and tenants in the rural areas while finding a working-class base mainly among silver miners in the Rocky Mountains; here the Western Federation of Miners engaged in some of the most militant actions in the country; and here the IWW found support among a wide array of the new western working class, many highly mobile laborers who moved between the agricultural, lumbering, and mining sectors (as well as connections with radicals in northern Mexico).[29] Here, too, territorial governments, closely tied to the interests of the railroads and other finance capitalists, along with the courts, played absolutely crucial roles in tilting the balances of conflict in favor of capital, indeed, in making it almost impossible for labor and its community-based allies to achieve sustained victories either through industrial organization or electoral politics.[30] In its forms of accumulation, deployment of a multi-ethnic and multi-cultural labor force, hyper-exploitation of workers, and close alliance between capital and the state, the trans-Mississippi West became something of a proving ground and crucible for the American form of capitalism.

So, too, for American nation-state building. In many respects, the postbellum West (at least the interior West), even more than the postbellum South, became a political and economic colony of both the Northeast and the federal government: not only because northeastern capital was the great beneficiary of western economic development or because federal policy was so critical in promoting economic activity, but also because the federal government—during the Civil War—effectively territorialized most of the region and, with minor exception, blocked these territories from moving to statehood for a very long time (territorialization, we must not forget, was a central part of the discourse of reconstructing the South). The Dakotas, Idaho, Montana, and Wyoming remained territories for 38, 27, 25, and 22 years respectively. Utah remained a territory for 46 years and Arizona for 49. And New Mexico was a territory for 62 years (territories east of the Mississippi, created before the Civil War, made far more rapid moves to statehood). "There may be no difference between the form of government of a territory and that of a colony," intoned a member of Congress who questioned whether the populations in some of them, on ethnic and cultural grounds, were politically assimilable: whether, that is, the Constitution would follow the flag there.[31]

Not surprisingly, these issues would soon resurface in the Philippines; and not surprisingly, the experience of the territorial West would be regarded as foundational. Senator Henry Dawes, sponsor of the Dawes Severalty Act, thought that efforts spent to manage Indians should guide dealings with "other alien races whose future has been put in our keeping" owing to the Spanish-American War. The directors of the new Bureau of Insular Affairs had military experience in the West; the military governors of the Philippines between 1898 and 1902 had been in Indian service; almost all of the top military officers in the Philippines had formative involvements with western Indians; and most of the American troops there came from the western states and territories.[32]

THE INTERNATIONAL REPERCUSSIONS OF the Civil War are not always easy to measure and, in part, owing to odd periodizations in the organization and writing of American history, they have been inadequately measured. But let me suggest a few areas where we might look. As the invocation of the Philippines intimates, the Civil War and its outcome simultaneously secured American hegemony in the Caribbean basin and in much of the Western Hemisphere—especially in the face of possible British interference—and had an enormously consequential effect on the advance of American influence and power in the Pacific. From the purchase of Alaska to the annexation of Hawaii to the proclamation of the Open Door to the intervention in the Philippines, the reconstruction of the political economy that the Civil War made possible proved decisive (Southerners, we should not forget, were the main part of the anti-imperialist bloc at the end of the 19th century).[33]

At the same time, the new resources and bravado claimed by finance capital fueled growing foreign investments, most immediately in Mexico where the Diaz regime, embarking on its own course of nation-building, allowed American companies a major hand in constructing railroads and in other areas of the Mexican economy, most notably in the mines of the northwest provinces. Indeed, American economic activity in Mexico began to develop during and immediately after the Civil War, partly at the behest of Mexican liberals looking to defeat the French and move toward the commodification of land and labor (or, as they might prefer, the "modernization" of the peasant sector). Which is to say that the Civil War not only dramatically advanced the development of capitalism in the United States; it also facilitated the expansion of capitalist relations of production and forms of resource exploitation well beyond American borders.[34]

Ironically, this happened too in the international spread of the cotton plant. We all know that cotton was truly king in the antebellum United States. It made the fortunes of a powerful slaveholding class, accounted for 60 percent of the value of all American exports at the time of the Civil War, and created developmental linkages between the South and the Northeast. It also limited what the victorious federal government was prepared to do to slaveholding rebels and do for liberated slaves, because the protection and reinvigoration of cotton production in the rebellious states became a central policy objective. But the Union blockade of Southern ports encouraged the advance of cotton cultivation in places where it had been organized chiefly on a small scale, sometimes on the basis of peasant production, and both made for new competitors for the United States and a new labor process in the agricultural sectors of south Asia, parts of the Middle East, Africa, and Brazil. The Civil War, that is, may have contributed to the expansion of, and then the crisis of, new global capitalism during the last third of the 19th century.[35]

What often confounds a compelling assessment of the Civil War's impact is some sense of what the world might have looked like if the American Civil War had not taken place or if the Civil War had ended up differently: without the unconditional defeat of the Confederate rebellion. Most scholars who even approach the issue appear to think of a course of American development and American influence merely devoid of the military elements of the war: devoid of the disruptions, the casualties, and the necessary reconfigurations of trade. But they also generally fail to consider the social, political, and institutional transformations that the War ushered in, and what these have meant.

WITHOUT QUESTION, IT IS difficult and dangerous to imagine a world, here or elsewhere, without the Civil War as we have come to know it. But there are some things that we can reasonably and safely say as a way of evaluating the difference that the War made.

Had the Civil War not taken place (because Buchanan decided to seek a second term, because the Republicans agreed to compromise a bit on the territorial issue during secession winter, because Lincoln abandoned Fort Sumter and bought more time) or had the War, far more likely, ended up with something short of a Union victory, say an armistice, there are a number of possible, and in some cases probable, scenarios. Most extreme would have been a steady disintegration of the country in which the "Confederate" states may eventually have been joined in secession by other regions, led perhaps by a Pacific Coast republic, something in the manner of the Spanish-American colonies-turned-countries. Other separatist interests would undoubtedly have been encouraged and the borders we have come to recognize both in the Southwest and Northwest could easily have shifted.[36]

More conceivable would have been a reunification in which power was eventually shared between big landed interests in the South and West and big industrial and financial interests in the Northeast and Midwest: an American version of the German marriage of "iron and rye" which linked Prussia and the Ruhr, though probably with a weaker center and with persisting limits to the federal government's ability to establish its sovereign authority.[37] At all events, slavery would have been abolished at some point, likely sooner rather than later, but this would have happened gradually under the authority of the states—though the federal government, if it survived, would have had to contribute at least some of its resources to stabilizing the transition: something of a slaveholders' bureau instead of a Freedmen's Bureau.[38] Obviously there would have been no 13th Amendment abolishing slavery without compensation to slaveholders, or any other Reconstruction amendments or related rights legislation: no 14th Amendment or Civil Rights bills granting birthright citizenship and spelling out what some of those citizenship rights were; no Reconstruction Acts enfranchising black men in the South or 15th Amendment enfranchising black men in the North and West. *Dred Scott* would have remained the law of the land, and the conservative political impulses of the 1850s, which defeated black and women's suffrage and looked to disfranchise the immigrant working class, may well have continued unabated, with serious consequences for popular politics in the second half of the 19th century.[39] For its part, the Republican Party would have faced a severe crisis, especially if the country became reunified, since it had little or no basis in the Southern states and, without black enfranchisement, was unlikely to build any in the near term. A new, or multi-party, political system may well have taken shape, as Andrew Johnson and some Liberal Republicans had hoped.[40]

In all probability, the financiers of the Union war would not have come out in nearly as strong a position as they in fact did, and some of the important wartime legislation that reshaped the political economy would have been revised, weakened, or repealed—tariffs, banking, and homestead legislation most conspicuously. The agro-commercial sectors would probably have remained on a stronger footing and the industrial capitalist sectors on a shakier one. Landed interests would have been in a better position to weather the decline of commodity prices beginning in the 1870s and could have expected more direct legislative help from the federal state: which is to say that a Populist movement of the sort that raged in the South and Plains would not have gained much traction.

Internationally, Britain may well have been able to reassert itself as a major power in the Western Hemisphere (it was still an important economic power)—after all, the British were sure that the Union would fail to defeat the rebellion and hoped to mediate a peace—and France may have fared better in Mexico. At the very least, it is hard to imagine the United States, or any substantial part of it being in a position, for a while at minimum, to throw its weight around quite as it did either in the Hemisphere or in the Pacific basin. This would have been an advantage for many international political actors, large and small, not least perhaps for Japanese imperialists.

As for the trans-Mississippi West, the future patterns of development would have depended either on the reunification settlement that was reached as to the viability of slavery and other forms of coerced labor, or on which of the break-away regions was in the best position to exert its authority. At all events, there would have been continuing conflict and political struggle. For the counter-sovereignties there, the Mormons and the Indian peoples chief among them, there may consequently have been more room for their ways of life (the Indians could hardly have fared worse than they did); and for the Canadian West and especially for Mexico, there may have been different social and political experiences, including a rather different dynamic to the revolution that erupted there in the 1910s.

Needless to say, these irreverent conjectures raise many more questions than they provide satisfying answers—and they may raise some readers' hackles as well. Yet they do suggest a very different world than the one that came into being after the Civil War, and thus they demonstrate how very different a world the Civil War indeed made.

Notes

1   Of all 19th-century wars and civil conflicts, only the Taiping Rebellion in China (1851–1864) had greater casualties than the American Civil War. The most recent study estimates that the struggle of the Taiping Heavenly Kingdom against the Qing dynasty resulted in 20 million casualties owing to warfare and related disease and famine. See Stephen R. Platt, *Autumn in the Heavenly Kingdom: China, the West, and the Epic Story of the Taiping Civil War* (New York: Knopf, 2012).

2   See, for example, William A. Dunning, *Reconstruction, Political and Economic: 1865–1877* (New York: Columbia University Press, 1907); Walter L. Fleming, *Civil War and Reconstruction in Alabama* (New York, 1905); Claude G. Bowers, *The Tragic Era* (Cambridge: Houghton Mifflin, 1929); E. Merton Coulter, *The South During Reconstruction, 1865–1877* (Baton Rouge, 1947).

3   Charles A. Beard and Mary R. Beard, *The Rise of American Civilization* (New York, 1933); Kenneth M. Stampp, *The Era of Reconstruction, 1865–1877* (New York: Vintage, 1965); Willie Lee Rose, *Rehearsal for Reconstruction: The Port Royal Experiment* (Indianapolis: Bobbs Merrill, 1964); James M. McPherson, *The Struggle for Equality: Abolitionists and the Negro in the Civil War and Reconstruction* (Princeton: Princeton University Press, 1964).

4   Eric Foner, *Reconstruction: America's Unfinished Revolution, 1863–1877* (New York, 1988); Leon F. Litwack, *Been in the Storm So Long: The Aftermath of Slavery* (New York: Knopf, 1979); Lawrence Powell, *New Masters: Northern Planters in the Civil War and Reconstruction* (New Haven: Yale University Press, 1980); Barbara J. Fields, *Slavery and Freedom on the Middle Ground: Maryland During the Nineteenth Century* (New Haven: Yale University Press, 1985); Ira Berlin, et al., eds., Freedom: A Documentary History of Emancipation, 1861–1865 (5 vols.; New York: Cambridge University Press, 1982). Orville Vernon Burton, *The Age of Lincoln* (New York, 2008). The most powerful influence on all of these studies is W. E. B. Du Bois, *Black Reconstruction in America, 1860–1880* (1935; New York: Free Press, 1992).

5   See, for example, the essays collected in Ralph Andreano, ed., *The Economic Impact of the Civil War* (Boston: Schenckman Publishing Co.,)," and David T. Gilchrist and W. David Lewis, eds., *Economic Change In the Civil War Era* (Greenville, DE: Eleutherian Mills Hagley Foundation, 1965). Also see, Thomas C. Cochran, "Did the Civil War Retard Industrialization," *Mississippi Valley Historical Review*, 48 (September, 1961): 197–210.

6   C. Vann Woodward, *Origins of the New South, 1877–1913* (Baton Rouge: Louisiana State University Press, 1951). Woodward's critics on this account include, Jonathan M. Wiener, *Social Origins of the New South: Alabama, 1860–1885* (Baton Rouge: Louisiana State University Press, 1978); Michael S. Wayne, *The Reshaping of Plantation Society: The Natchez District, 1860–1880* (Baton Rouge: Louisiana State University Press, 1983); Crandall A. Shiflett, *Patronage and Poverty in the Tobacco South: Louisa County, Virginia, 1860–1900* (Knoxville: University of Tennessee Press, 1982); Randolph B. Campbell, *A Southern Community in Crisis: Harrison County, Texas, 1850–1880* (Austin: University of Texax Press, 1983); Stephen V. Ash, *Middle Tennessee Society Transformed, 1860–1870: War and Peace in the Upper South* (Baton Rouge: Louisiana State University Press, 1982). Orville Vernon Burton, *In My Father's House Are Many Mansions: Family and Community in Edgefield County, South Carolina* (Chapel Hill: University of North Carolina Press, 1985).

7   The literature portraying the slave South as capitalist and slavery as a form of capitalism include Walter Johnson, *Soul by Soul: Life Inside the Antebellum Slave Market* (Cambridge: Harvard University Press, 1999); James Oakes, *The Ruling Race: A History of American Slaveholders* (New York, Knopf, 1982); Robert Fogel and Stanley Engerman, *Time on the Cross: The Economics of American Negro Slavery* (Boston: Little Brown, 1974); Lacy K. Ford Jr., *The Origins of Southern Radicalism: The South Carolina Upcountry, 1800–1860* (New York, Oxford University Press, 1988). The major dissenter has been Eugene D. Genovese, especially in *The Political Economy of Slavery: Studies in the Society and Economy of the Slave South* (New York: Pantheon, 1965), but also see Fields, *Slavery and Freedom on the Middle Ground*; Julie Saville, *The Work of Reconstruction: From Slave to Wage Laborer in South Carolina, 1860–1870* (New York: Cambridge University Press, 1994); Steven Hahn, *The Roots of Southern Populism: Yeoman Farmers and the Transformation of the Georgia Upcountry, 1850–1890* (New York: Oxford University Press, 1983).

8   See, for example, Glenda Gilmore, *Gender and Jim Crow: Women and the Politics of White Supremacy in North Carolina, 1896–1920* (Chapel Hill: University of North Caroline Press, 1996); Stephen Kantrowitz, *Ben Tillman and the Reconstruction of White Supremacy* (Chapel Hill: University of North Caroline Press, 2000); David Blight, *Race and Reunion: The Civil War in American Memory* (Cambridge, Harvard University Press, 2001). For Phillips see, "The Central Theme of Southern History," *American Historical Review*, 34 (October 1928): 30–43.

9   Think of Eric Foner, *Nothing But Freedom: Emancipation and Its Legacy* (Baton Rouge: Louisians State University Press, 1982); Peter Kolchin, *A Sphinx on the Land: The Nineteenth Century South in Comparative Perspective* (Baton Rouge: Louisisna State University Press, 2003); Eugene D. Genovese, *The World the Slaveholders Made: Two Essays in Interpretation* (New York: Pantheon, 1969), 3–113; C. Vann Woodward, "The Price of Freedom," in David G. Sansing, ed., *What Was Freedom's Price?* (University: University of Mississippi Press, 1978), 93–113.

10   C.A. Bayley, *The Birth of the Modern World, 1780–1914* (Oxford, UK: Blackwell Publish-

ing, 2004); Eric J. Hobsbawm, *The Age of Capital, 1848–1875* (New York: Pantheon, 1975).

11 Rebecca Scott, *Degrees of Freedom: Louisiana and Cuba after Slavery* (Cambridge: Harvard University Press, 2005), 29. On the Cuban literature, see Ada Ferrer, *Insurgent Cuba: Race, Nation, and Revolution, 1868–1898* (Chapel Hill: University of North Caroline Press, 1999); Rebecca Scott, *Slave Emancipation in Cuba: The Transition to Free Labor, 1860–1899* (Princeton: Princeton University Press, 1985); Ramiro Guerra y Sanchez, La guerra de dos diaz anos, 1868–1878 (2 vols.; Havana, 1950–52); Arthur Corwin, *Spain and the Abolition of Slavery in Cuba, 1817–1886* (Austin: University of Texas Press, 1967). On the Brazilian literature see, Emilia Viotti da Costa, *Da senzala a colonia* (Sao Paulo: Editoria Brasiliense, 1964); Robert Brent Toplin, *The Abolition of Slavery in Brazil* (New York: Antheneum, 1972); Rebecca Scott et al., *The Abolition of Slavery and the Aftermath of Emancipation in Brazil* (Durham: Duke University Press, 1988); Robert Conrad, *The Destruction of Slavery in Brazil, 1850–1888* (Berkeley: University of California Press, 1972).

12 See, for example, Benjamin Keen and Keith Haynes, *A History of Latin America* (9th edition; New York, 2012); Marshall C. Eakin, *The History of Latin America: A Collision of Cultures* (New York, 2007); Edwin Williamson, *The Penguin History of Latin America* (New York, 2010); Michael C. Meyer and William L. Sherman, *The Course of Mexican History* (New York: Oxford University Press, 1987).

13 Most recently, Edward Rugemer, *The Problem of Emancipation: The Caribbean Roots of the American Civil War* (Baton Rouge: Louisiana State University Press, 2009); Matthew J. Clavin, *Toussaint Louverture and the American Civil War: The Promise and Perils of a Second Haitian Revolution* (Philadelphia: University of Pennsylvania Press, 2011); Bruce Levine, *The Spirit of Forty-Eight: German Immigrants, Labor Conflict, and the Coming of the Civil War* (Urbana: University of Illinois Press, 1992).

14 Here I simultaneously embrace and part company with Barrington Moore, Jr's. powerful interpretation of the *American Civil War in Social Origins of Dictatorship and Democracy: Lord and Peasant in the Making of the Modern World* (Boston: Beacon, 1965), chap. III.

15 Martin J. Sklar, *The Corporate Reconstruction of American Capitalism* (New York: Cambridge University Press, 1988).

16 Think, for example, of secessionist stirrings in New England and the Lower Mississippi Valley during the early years of the 19th century, of the Nullification crisis, various filibustering operations of the 1840s and 1850s, the Mormon "War" of the late 1850s, and disunion sentiment on the West Coast, in the Midwest, and in New York City during the winter of 1860–61.

17 See, Don E. Fehrenbacher, *The Slaveholding Republic* (New York: Oxford University Press, 2001); Arthur Zilversmit, *The First Emancipation: The Abolition of Slavery in the North* (Chicago: University of Chicago Press, 1967); Joanne Pope Melish, *Disowning Slavery: Gradual Emancipation and "Race" in New England, 1780–1860* (Ithaca: Cornell University Press, 1998); James Oliver Horton and Lois E. Horton, *In Hope of Liberty: Culture, Community, and Protest among Northern Free Blacks, 1700–1860* (New York: Oxford University Press, 1997); Graham Russell Hodges, *Slavery and Freedom in the Rural North* (Madison: Madison House, 1997); Christopher M. Osborne, "Invisible Hands: Slaves, Bound Laborers, and the Development of Western Pennsylvania, 1780–1820," *Pennsylvania History*, 72 (January 2005): 77–99.

18 See, Christopher Clark, *The Roots of Rural Capitalism: Western Massachusetts, 1780–1860* (Ithaca: Cornell University Press, 1990); Alan Kullikoff, *Agrarian Origins of American Capitalism* (Charlottesville: University of Virginia Press, 1992), 34–59; Seth Rockman, *Scraping By: Wage Labor, Slavery, and Survival in Early Baltimore* (Baltimore: John Hopkins University Press, 2009); Peter Way, *Common Labor: Workers and the Digging of North American Canals, 1780–1860* (Baltimore: John Hopkins University Press, 1993); Alexander Keyssar, *The Right to Vote: The Contested History of Democracy in the United States* (New York: Basic Books, 2000), 26–116.

19 Sven Beckert, "Merchants and Manufacturers in the Antebellum North," and Adam Rothman, "The Slave Power in the United States, 1783–1865," both in Steve Fraser and Gary Gerstle, eds., *Ruling America: A History of Wealth and Power in a Democracy* (Cambridge: Harvard University Press, 2005), 64–122.

20 Robert May, *The Southern Dream of a Caribbean Empire, 1854–1861* (Baton Rouge: Louisiana State University Press, 1973); Thomas R. Hietala, *Manifest Design: Anxious Aggrandizement in Late Jacksonian America* (Ithaca: Cornell University Press, 1985); Robert Johannsen, *Stephan A. Douglass* (New York: Oxford University Press, 1973), 206–680; Walter Johnson, *River of Dark Dreams: Slavery and Empire in the Cotton Kingdom* (Cambridge: Harvard University Press, 2013).

21 Joel H. Silbey, *A Respectable Minority: The Democratic Party in the Civil War Era, 1860–1868* (New York: W.W. Norton, 1977), 27.

22 Richard Franklin Bensel, *Yankee Leviathan: The Origins of Central State Authority in America, 1859–1877* (New York: Cambridge University Press, 1990); Heather Cox Richardson, *The Greatest Nation of the Earth: Republican Economic Policies during the Civil War* (Cambridge: Harvard University Press, 1997). On the war's complex ending see the forthcoming book by Gregory Downs, *The Ends of War: Fighting the Civil War after Appomattox* (Cambridge: Harvard University Press, in preparation).

23 Richard White, *Railroaded: The Transcontinentals and the Making of Modern America* (New York: W.W. Norton, 2011); Christian Womar, *Blood, Iron, and Gold: How the Railroads Transformed the World* (New York: Public Affairs, 2009), 45–190.

24 Robert G. Athearn, *William Tecumseh Sherman and the Settlement of the West* (Norman: Oklahoma University Press, 1956); Francis Prucha, *The Great Father: The United States Government and the Indians* (2 vols.; Lincoln: University of Nebraska Press, 1984), 527–33.

25 Richard Franklin Bensel, *The Political Economy of American Industrialization, 1877–1900* (New York: Cambridge University Press, 2000); Irwin Unger, *The Greenback Era: A Social and Political History of American Finance, 1865–1879* (Princeton: Princeton University Press, 1964); Robert Sharkey, *Money, Class, and Party: An Economic Study of the Civil War and Reconstruction* (Baltimore: John Hopkins University Press, 1959).

26 Richard White concludes his important book with an interesting but I think misconceived counterfactual. See, *Railroaded*, 455–505.

27 See, Steven Hahn, *A Nation under Our Feet: Black Political Struggles in the Rural South from Slavery to the Great Migration* (Cambridge: Harvard University Press, 2003), 163–313; Foner, *Reconstruction*, 228–343; David Montgomery, *Citizen Worker: The Experience of Workers in the United States with Democracy and the Free Market during the Nineteenth Century* (New York: Cambridge University Press, 1993), 115–62.

28 Hahn, *Nation under Our Feet*, 412–64; Harold D. Woodman, *New South-New Law:*

The Legal Foundations of Credit and Labor Relations in the Postbellum Agricultural South (Baton Rouge: Louisiana State University Press, 1995).

29   Terrence Finnegan, *Lynching in Mississippi and South Carolina, 1881–1949* (Charlottesville: University of Virginia Press, 2013); Theresa A. Case, *The Great Southwest Railroad Strike and Free Labor* (College Station: Texas A&M Press, 2010); Richard E. Lingenfelter, *The Hardrock Miners: A History of the Mining Labor Movement in the American West, 1863–1893* (Berkeley: University of California Press, 1974); John P. Enyeart, *The Quest for 'Just and Pure Law': Rocky Mountain Workers and American Social Democracy, 1870–1924* (Stanford: Stanford University Press, 2009); James E. Wright, *The Politics of Populism: Dissent in Colorado* (New Haven: Yale University Press, 1974; Robert W. Larson, *Populism in the rocky Mountain West* (Albuquerque: University of New Mexico Press, 1986); Frank Tobias Higbie, *Indispensable Outcasts: Hobo Workers and Community in the American Midwest, 1880–1930* (Urbana: University of Illinois Press, 2003), 98–204.

30   See, especially, William E. Forbath, *Law and the Shaping of the American Labor Movement* (Cambridge: Harvard University Press, 1991).

31   Walter L. Williams, "U.S. Indian Policy and the Debate over Philippine Annexation: Implications for the Origins of American Imperialism," *Journal of American History*, 66 (March 1980): 810–31; Howard R. Lamar, *The Far Southwest, 1846–1912: A Territorial History* (New Haven: Yale University Press, 1970); Earl S. Pomeroy, T*he Territories and the United States, 1861–1890: Studies in Colonial Administration* (Philadelphia, PA, 1947). Arizona and New Mexico gained admission once the demographic balances assured Anglo political control; Utah was admitted once Mormon leaders there publicly renounced polygamy.

32   Williams, "U.S. Indian Policy and Debate over Philippine Annexation," 810–31.

33   See Walter LaFeber, *The New Empire: An Interpretation of American Expansion, 1860–1898* (Ithaca: Cornell University Press, 1963); Walter Nugent, *Habits of Empire: A History of American Expansion* (New York: Knopf, 2008), 237–317.

34   John Mason Hart, *Empire and Revolution: The Americans in Mexico Since the Civil War* (Berkeley: University of California Press, 2002); Gilbert M. Joseph, *Revolution from Without: Yucatan, Mexico, and the United States, 1880–1924* (New York: Cambridge University Press,1982); Julie Greene, *The Canal Builders: Making America's Empire at the Panama Canal* (New York: Penguin, 2009).

35   See Sven Beckert, *The Empire of Cotton: A Global History* (New York: Knopf, 2013).

36   Lincoln, in deciding to supply the troops at Fort Sumter clearly worried about whether weakness on the part of the federal center would strengthen centripetal forces across the country. One can't help but think, in this connection, of Iraq and Syria today.

37   See the discussion of unifications in Steven Hahn, "Class and State in Post-Emancipation Societies: Southern Planters in Comparative Perspective," *American Historical Review*, 95 (February 1990): 75–98.

38   We might think, in this connection, of the stipendiary magistrates appointed by the British government to oversee the transition out of slavery in the British West Indies

39   Keyssar, *The Right to Vote*, 81–116.

40   See, Eric L. McKitrick, *Andrew Johnson and Reconstruction* (Chicago: University of Chicago Press, 1960), 364–420; John Sproat, *The Best Men: Liberal Reformers in the Gilded Age* (New York: Oxford University Press, 1971).

8

Revisiting the Black Matriarchy

ORVILLE VERNON BURTON

With the 2013 controversy over the Trayvon Martin trial and the acquittal of George Zimmerman, news programs again focused attention on race in America. Bill O'Reilly, for example, did a series he called "Race Relations in America," but the series instead focused on the perceived "problems" in the black community, especially the disintegration of the African American family.[1] O'Reilly was perpetuating an image decried by W. E. B. Du Bois in *The Souls of Black Folk* in 1903. According to Du Bois, the African American presence was defined by the white majority as a problem to be dealt with. The problem, managed by whites who were in various degrees sympathetic or mean-spirited, held no real "solution."[2]

It is déjà vu all over again, and reminds me of my early days as a graduate student. On the advice of C. Vann Woodward, Sheldon Hackney's thesis advisor, I elected to go to Princeton University to study the history of the American South with Dr. Hackney. I had begun my PhD dissertation as a study working with the manuscript census returns to discover the origins of Southern tenantry and Populism. I was then pulled into the controversies surrounding the black family that had been set off by Daniel Patrick Moynihan's "report."[3] Like other academics of my generation, I entered the fray to argue that the then emerging "problems" of the African American family in the late 1960s and early 1970s could not be linked to an absence of black family life during slavery or in the immediate aftermath of the Civil War.

When I first began studying the "Black Matriarchy" in the 1970s, I assumed that this terminology was a continuation of the Old South ideology perpetuated by white scholars to show somehow that the African American family was not "normal" and not able to survive in modern society. The thesis of a black matriarchy implies an unstable and dysfunctional African American family where fathers feel no responsibility for their children and where mothers are less capable of transmitting cultural values. I soon discovered, however, that the scholarly basis for the concept was laid by two African American sociology giants, W. E. B. Du Bois and E. Franklin Frazier.

This article on the black matriarchy adds to a debate that has gone on for more than a century. The debate is still lively because of its implications for the current-day family and issues such as single motherhood and welfare, as reiterated in the O'Reilly series. Ironically, it has been those sympathetic to African Americans, from the abolitionists to scholars like W. E. B. Du Bois, Daniel Patrick Moynihan, and Orlando Patterson, who have provided a basis for the development and misuse of the idea of a historical black matriarchy by those less sympathetic. For example, abolitionists such as Theodore Dwight Weld and Harriet Beecher Stowe originated the matriarchy myth to publicize the horrors of slavery.[4] Southern and Northern whites unsympathetic to racial equality transmuted this abolitionist attack on slavery into an argument that freed African American people were unable to function as full participants in a modern society. Scholars and the white public generally accepted the notion of the "weak" African American home, and this in turn has influenced society's attitudes toward black people in general. The confusion of scholars with "matriarchy" comes from a conceptual leap from counting female-headed households to equating that counting with a complex cultural model.

This confusion has a long historiography. In 1908, Du Bois, in his classic *The Negro American Family*, never used the term "matriarchy," but he stressed the lack of family structure under slavery. Although acknowledging the commitment of African Americans to male-headed nuclear families, Du Bois began a scholarly tradition that ignored or missed the persistence of two-parent black families.[5]

At about the same time, the white Southerner Howard W. Odum published his first book, *Social and Mental Traits of the Negro* (1910), and reflected views of racially prejudiced Southern whites defending a caste system. Odum pronounced, "The negro woman is not unfrequently the head of the negro family." In his study he found 10 percent of the families with a woman at the head. In other words, although he found a male-headed family 90 percent of the time, he chose to emphasize families that were female-headed.[6]

Nearly thirty years after Du Bois and Odum, E. Franklin Frazier studied the African American family. Among other issues, Frazier discussed the question of male-headed vs. female-headed households as an indicant of the stability and quality of family life. Frazier held that the dominant tendency in the black community was toward a matriarchal household, and he explained that this "matriarchy" had carried over from slavery. Frazier did find within the African American community a number of two-parent families, but noted that this "normal family pattern" had developed among the landowners and other elite of the antebellum free blacks.[7]

Frazier joined others who credited tenancy and sharecropping as fostering a matriarchal family organization. He concluded that although at emancipation blacks had had "high hopes that their freedom would rest upon a secure foundation of landownership, the masses of illiterate and property-less Negroes were forced to become croppers and tenants under a modified plantation system. . . . *Consequently, the maternal-family organization, a heritage from slavery, has continued on a fairly large scale.*"[8] [emphasis mine]

Among historians, Ulrich B. Phillips began the modern historiography on slavery, and his racist portrayal of childlike, overly sentimental slave families ironically depicts family life as both overly close and too tender. He wrote of unrefined natures of enslaved barbaric Africans; he reflected the fantasy sexual projections of whites and asserted that blacks had overly sexual natures that led to promiscuity, carelessness toward familial duties, a live-for-today spirit, and shiftlessness. As eternal children, African Americans failed to govern as effective parents, deferring to the rule of "paternalistic" masters and mistresses. Phillips excused white slave owners entirely and transformed them into teachers and heroes. White rape of African American women and miscegenation he explained as mostly the consequence of black lasciviousness. For Phillips, slavery was a "school house of civilization" that provided enslaved peoples with an education in family life. The logical consequence of Phillips's racist interpretation was that after 1865, without white paternalistic guidance black families would fall apart.[9]

Phillips's paternalistic interpretation of slavery dominated for more than a third of the 20th century until challenged in 1956 by Kenneth Stampp. In as much detail as the careful scholarship done by Phillips, but in repudiation of Phillips's white-supremacist interpretation, Stampp changed the way historians looked at slavery. Stampp discussed slave fathers and loving relationships (as well as promiscuity and abuse). Stampp's conclusion, however, was that "Indeed, the typical slave family was matriarchal in form, for the mother's role was far more important than the father's."[10]

In 1959 Stanley Elkins extended Stampp's harsh interpretation of slavery and wrote that slavery was so devastating that enslaved African Americans were not even able to develop independent personalities. He agreed that the white culture was patriarchal, quoting Governor and Senator James Henry Hammond of South Carolina about the "patriarchal scheme of domestic servitude," but did not allow that the enslaved adopted anything from that culture. In a comparison with slavery in Latin America, Elkins found that the American South did not allow an enslaved man to be a husband, father, artisan, or member of a black religious organization. He admitted that such roles, had they existed, would have offered "a diversity of channels for the development of personality."[11] Further studies have shown, of course, that these channels were available in the communities that the enslaved carved out for themselves in the slave states of the American South.

In response to Elkins and Stampp and work that presented slavery as a complete degradation and deculturation, revisionist literature in the 1970s began to question whether a black matriarchy during slavery was more myth than reality. A number of influential scholars, loosely classified as the Slave Community School, asserted that despite the power of the master class, slaves were able to find space for themselves and create a syncretic African American culture and community rooted in religion, a folk culture of resistance, and most especially in a strong slave family with a male head.[12] John Blassingame, Eugene Genovese, and others wrote about family and community life in late-antebellum slavery and of strong family commitments as the Civil War ended.[13] In 1976, Herbert Gutman published the work most associated with the revisionist perspective, *The Black Family in Slavery and Freedom, 1750–1925*. Gutman presented two basic arguments: first, that a male-headed, two-parent family was the typical domestic arrangement for African Americans during and after slavery, and, second, that African American family traditions developed out of the black community's own historical experience and patterns of decisions rather than through imitation of white culture or from planter-imposed arrangements.[14]

Other scholars who examined African American households and found "female-headed" families argued that these families "emerged, not as a legacy of slavery, but as a result of the destructive conditions of Northern urban life."[15] Scholars have shown how differences in the structures of urban and rural families resulted somewhat from the problem of adaptation to a lower-class urban existence, the process of alienation, and the destruction of rural norms and folkways in an urban industrial economy. Sociologist Stewart Tolnay, who found that Southern African American farm families were quite stable, concurs that they became progressively less so the longer they stayed in Northern cities.[16]

Meanwhile, also in the 1970s, at about the time that a number of male scholars were arguing there was no black matriarchy, feminists were turning to African American women as exemplars of strength. They accepted a black matriarchy, but they argued that matriarchy, far from implying cultural inferiority, was a good thing. *MS* magazine, for example, had a special issue celebrating African American women and the Black Matriarchy.[17] This literature, however, refers to strong women in the culture, not in a matriarchal system. A feminist perspective has enriched the debate on African American families, adding levels of complexity to the debate on female-headed families and power relationships within families and communities. Emily West has written an affirmation of the support between slave spouses. Suzanne Lebsock found that antebellum Petersburg, Virginia, had very high rates of female-headed households partly because free women, both black and white, elected not to marry (note that this was a study of an urban area). Tera Hunter looks at the 1881 Atlanta (again urban) washerwomen's strike as a way to explore African American urban women working as all kinds of domestic workers.[18] The new gender and cultural history has shifted the debate somewhat so that now mostly scholars of women's history are investigating in depth the important role and contribution of African American mothers and women, and the role of children.[19] No one much is looking at the society and culture itself or the other gendered dimension, that of the African American male, husband, and father.[20] So far, I have not noticed that any of the studies of women or children during slavery or during the early postbellum years have used the term *matriarchy*.

Following the work of so many revisionist scholars, many would like to agree with Jacqueline Jones that they had "laid to rest once and for all the myth of the slave matriarchy."[21] But sooner or later, scholars were bound to revise the revisionists. Peter Kolchin has led the revision of the Slave Community School.[22] Post-revisionist social science historian Steven Ruggles has marshaled the considerable weight of the Integrated Public Use Microdata Series (IPUMS) for 1850, 1880, 1910, 1940, 1960, and 1980 to confirm "recent findings that the high incidence among African-Americans of single parenthood and children residing without their parents is not a recent phenomenon." (The matriarchy myth does not address children residing without their parents, but suffice it to say here that landowners used debt peonage and apprenticeship laws to force African American children into labor arrangements in the postbellum South.) Ruggles concludes that single-parent families were slightly more numerous for African Americans than for whites over the long run for the entire United States. In 1880, for example, Ruggles's data shows a noticeable similarity between whites and African Americans: 8.2 percent white and 11.7 percent black households had single parents. If IPUMS data could be controlled for urban/town/village/rural differences, these figures would probably show more similarity across the countryside.[23]

In 1998, African American sociologist Orlando Patterson revisited the black family, warning of its sorry state and again looking to slavery as the origin of the black matriarchy. Patterson asserted that revisionist arguments about slavery, such as mine, are "an intellectual disgrace, the single greatest disservice that the American historical profession has ever done to those who turn to it for guidance about the past and the etiology of present problems. Indeed, in many ways this denial of the consequences of slavery is worse than the more than two centuries of racist historiography that preceded it."[24] Patterson did not define *matriarchy* but seems to be referring to the number of female-headed families. According to Patterson, "Sixty percent of Afro-American children are now being brought up without the emotional or material support of a father. This is so because the great majority of Afro-American mothers have been seduced, deceived, betrayed, and abandoned by the men to whom they gave their love and trust."[25] (While not an exact comparison, as the statistic does not indicate how many unmarried white mothers were cohabiting with or receiving support from their children's fathers, it is noteworthy that a quarter of white children were being born to unmarried mothers at about the time Patterson wrote.[26]) Patterson accepts the reality of a black matriarchy and credits its existence as a hold-over from slavery, identifying "the origin of the problem in the socio-cultural depredations of slavery, contra the prevailing school of revisionist historians of slavery." He also "traces its continuation and consolidation through the Jim Crow era."[27]

Patterson's arguments about the role of the slave father are pertinent to any discussion of the black matriarchy. He asserts that African American males were shattered by the slave system: "it was most virulent in its devastation of the roles of father and husband." He agrees that slave fathers had children "whom they loved and by whom they were loved" (a point, I believe, brought out in the 1970s and 1980s by the same revisionists he vilifies), but he finds this incidental to the point that slave fathers had no legal or civic rights and responsibilities for their families.[28] In fact, both points are true, and neither point is incidental in a discussion of the family and a matriarchy. Of course, we cannot deny that slavery wrought consequences, but the legacy of slavery does not stretch linearly to the present; its legacy is more complex than that.

The final analysis on all this historiography is that the white public generally accepts the notion of the "weak" African American home, and this in turn has influenced society's attitudes toward blacks in general. Daryl Michael Scott, in *Contempt and Pity*, analyzed the twists and turns of these debates and how varying connotations affect policy decisions. He examined "damage imagery" and how arguments over the years, and still today, revolve around image rather than reality.[29] Politics may involve image rather than reality, but should not history grapple with both?

Although awkward for me as a white Southern male who came of age with the civil rights movement to challenge the idea of a black matriarchy, I still believe the data argue otherwise. These data involve a demographic phenomenon hidden from scholars until the manuscript census returns were available. Without that quantitative data, good scholars such as Du Bois, Frazier, and other earlier sociologists located female-headed households, which they found to be numerous. Unfortunately, their samples were skewed; and, most important, these skewed samples were then used as the basis to formulate and perpetuate the black matriarchy thesis.

This essay looks at some of the definitions of matriarchy and patriarchy, but within a cultural context. There has been vast confusion about these terms and about how they relate to female-headed households. By not defining matriarchy, scholars have left the impression that matriarchy is simply a matter of counting household heads. If a sociologist found too many (in that person's opinion) female-headed households, that was considered enough to warrant the term *matriarchy*. One of the problems with merely counting families with female heads is the confusion over how many female-headed households are necessary to constitute a matriarchy. Moynihan in his 1965 study of African American families in New York City found 21 percent of the city's African American families headed by females and concluded that there was a matriarchy. In contrast, Gutman looked back at New York City black families of 1925, found that only 23 percent were female-headed, and denounced the black matriarchy theory as a fraud.[30]

This highlights a serious problem. Scholars use terms such as *matriarchy* and *patriarchy* as moving targets to buttress differing arguments. Maybe instead of holding matriarchy and patriarchy as diametrical opposites, we should treat them in dynamic tension with each other, in which, for instance, persons who live in a female-headed household attempt to square that reality with the ideology of patriarchy.[31] However defined, characterizing a matriarchy by the number of female heads ignores the more important cultural basis for relations of power, the central basis for defining a matriarchy or patriarchy.

In my research on a postbellum community in South Carolina, I investigated the role of male domination in the development of tenantry and sharecropping, and I looked at how definitions of matriarchy also apply or do not apply to enslaved families. My own conclusion is that Southern society, antebellum and postbellum, was patriarchal and that enslaved African American men and women participated in the dominant male culture. This essay also ponders why the Matriarchy Myth endures. Although other scholars have attacked the matriarchy thesis, no one has provided a full explanation of the origins and endurance of the myth of the black matriarchy.

Arguments about the black family are engulfed with explosive subtexts. Scholars both sympathetic and not sympathetic to African Americans have argued that African Americans in the South lived lives dominated by fear, deception, and animosity, which tended to warp and inhibit their lives and families. When Howard Odum, U. B. Phillips, and a popularizer such as Bill O'Reilly make these claims, they argue that the amorphous notion of "black culture" is at fault, which lets whites off the hook. Other scholars, like Du Bois, Frazier, and Patterson, can see the ebb and flow of institution-building in the black community. Times of celebratory institution-building in black intellectual and social life occurred especially during Reconstruction and later with Booker T. Washington's emphasis on education. But Du Bois, Frazier, and Patterson also represent another tradition, a pushback against black institutions which they believed were too complacent and confining, and too often seen as legitimating segregation (though Du Bois and Frazier largely lived their lived within them). But a major difference exists between the black scholars and those who excuse whites from responsibility: African American scholars saw a way out—to demand full citizenship and equality in American society.

CULTURE OF PATRIARCHY/DEFINITION OF MATRIARCHY

Terms such as matriarchy and patriarchy are supposed to clarify, but often they have obfuscated our study of the family. We need to see the definitions in the context of the culture. Many scholars agree that patriarchy, and not matriarchy, characterized 19th-century white Southern society. My work supports these assessments; I have found that all sectors, rich and poor, male and female, shared patriarchal values and emphasized the patriarchal tradition. For the most part, in the 19th century the white man's place was leadership in society, and the white woman's role was supporting his endeavors, whether at home, in the workforce, or at church. White women were Sunday school teachers and could form missionary societies but were not generally on church committees until well after the Civil War.[32] Economics, politics, society, religion, culture, law—all reinforced the patriarchal society.

In the 1800s males had extensive authority over the family, and males dominated Southern culture. Bertram Wyatt-Brown's ideal typology of Southern antebellum culture suggests an exaltation of husband and father, masculinity, and bravado as social mores in a patriarchal system.[33] In 1876 the influential Reverend Benjamin Morgan Palmer expounded his views on the family and pervasiveness of patriarchy: the family underlay every other institution, and all such institutions were to be "strictly patriarchal." He declared that the power of God "attaches itself to the husband and father."[34]

Michael Grossberg's study of family life as a legal construct in the 19th century finds a patriarchal system. He writes, "The law assumed the interests of the family to be inseparable and best represented by its patriarch." More than paternal supremacy within the home, patriarchy was "an organizing model for the state, based on the control of all major forms of economic and political power by white, male heads of household."[35] Laura Edwards wrote about the antebellum white family patriarch: "Household heads—master, husbands, and fathers—oversaw these many operations [life on the plantation] and presided over a range of dependents, who included African American slaves as well as white women and children."[36] This was true even as the white family was evolving in the 19th century, as more concern was given to mutual feelings among family members and to the mother's nurturing role, especially regarding very young children.

While planters set themselves up as quintessential patriarchs who exercised "all the high functions of unlimited monarchs," poor whites in the South shared the same patriarchal culture.[37] Working families often received a family wage, which meant the father got it all. The church also supported patriarchy; all leadership roles fell to the men.

Contrary to general assumption, this patriarchal tradition also encompassed the African American family, even under slavery. Patriarchal ideology pervaded class, gender, and race.[38] The dominant culture was patriarchal, and the African American family was part and parcel of that culture. As careful observers, the enslaved saw both the good and the bad within free white families. Not only were loving and protective husbands and fathers modeled under patriarchy, but also male privilege and dominance, cruelty, alcoholism, infidelity, and spousal abuse. On the Sea Islands in the midst of the Civil War near enemy lines where freedom had come suddenly, Northern missionaries and others noted that the formerly enslaved men now abused their spouses. When establishing Penn School on St. Helena Island, South Carolina, in 1862, Laura Towne complained that African American men believed that freedom gave them the right to physically punish their wives; another observer commented, "the colored men whip their wives."[39] The point is that, while other influences such as African culture and the dynamics of African American life on the plantation were at work, one of the pervasive social and cultural models available to African Americans was the family and family values of whites with whom they were in contact. Because masters were generally resident, and because overseers were whites who lived near and interacted with the enslaved, even field hands on large plantations generally had at least some contact with whites. When the most famous African American of the 19th century, Frederick Douglass (1818–1895), freed himself, he recreated himself as a Victorian gentleman. Another famous African American of the late 19th and early 20th century, also born a slave, was Booker T. Washington (1856–1915), who as a free man personified Victorian values of hard work and honest living.[40] According to Sheldon Hackney in a lecture on Southern history at Princeton in 1969, this modeling is very different from saying that African Americans mimicked white culture. But examples do suggest that some African Americans understood family and family responsibilities and actions to be similar to how they saw whites behave.

For the most part, slaves lived in families with two parents. Gutman's study of the black family (samples from North Carolina, Mississippi, and Virginia) showed that most African American marriages, as confirmed by the Freedmen's Bureau, had existed for at least ten years, a pattern holding true across states and various-sized plantations. Stable African American families existed under slavery and were highly valued, and saying such by no means should imply that slavery was in any way beneficial, except to the slaveholders.[41]

Slave censuses show listings that seem to be families. There is also evidence that whites viewed family units of slaves as the normal situation. Although marriages between slaves were not recognized as legal in the South, planters did allow marriage as a social institution, and slaves themselves chose to live in couples and family units. U.S. Senator James H. Hammond, a prominent landowner in Edgefield District, South Carolina, wrote that "Marriage is to be encouraged as it adds to the comfort, happiness & health of those who enter upon it, besides insuring a greater increase."[42] Other evidence that slaves (and later freedmen) had a strong sense of family is their recorded genealogies.[43] Furthermore, newspapers wrote about African American families. Diaries included mentions of African American families, and slaveowners often organized lists entitled "Slaves by families." Speeches of local landowners and Sunday sermons spoke of black families. Church records are replete with stories of slave families.

I am in agreement with many scholars who put to rest the stereotype that African American slaves had neither family life nor culture. I and others have found the two-parent family was a common form of slave family in a variety of locations, size, or economy of a plantation and that unions between husbands and wives and parents and children often endured for many years.[44] Post-revisionist critics like Peter Kolchin, though less severe than Orlando Patterson, believe that our corrective leans too much at times toward a romantic quality that stresses African American autonomy under slavery.[45] Still, our work usefully reminds that slavery was an evolving, organic system.[46] Yet, it is important to remember that within any potential autonomy, slaves' relationships had no legal standing and could be broken up for sale at any time; the black family under slavery was still a controlled enterprise. But a study of structure, along with a historical examination of the cultural context, shows that families served some important functions for the participants. Couples derived happiness from the arrangement. People fell in love. Courting was an important part of the culture, including the slave culture. Men wanted wives and children, and women wanted husbands and children. Families were important. African American parents headed these families; they loved and cared for their children and each other. As articulated by Brenda Stevenson, "Slave parents were the most important authority figures in the lives of young slave children." She adds, however, that as they grew older, "they increasingly realized the limited authority and power their parents held."[47]

While many scholars agree that some slaves lived in families, the extent of such family life remains a cause of debate. Studies of slave communities have shown a wide variety of family structures and dynamics, and we need many more of these local studies.[48] More recent literature has found a variety of forms of family. For example, Anthony Kaye and Donald Schaffer used pension records to argue that African Americans had a range of commonly understood versions of relationships, from "sweethearting" and "taking up" to formal marriage.[49] Nancy Bercaw and Susan O'Donovan in studies of Mississippi and South Georgia find extended, augmented families and adult-male-absent households.[50] In her examination of lowcountry rice plantations in South Carolina, Leslie Schwalm found a predominance of extended families and "extrafamilial relationships" rather than male-headed nuclear families.[51] And in her study of slavery in colonial and antebellum Virginia, Stevenson has concluded "neither monogamous marriages nor nuclear families dominated slave family forms."[52]

However, my own work in the upcountry, cotton-producing community of Edgefield, South Carolina, verifies that in that district most slaves lived in families with mothers and fathers.[53] Looking at the many families that did have two parents, I ask if, aside from the white owner, there was a "head" of the slave family? Revisionist scholars, including me, have noted the father's role. I have found that, although society demanded the subjugation of slaves, the African American male was still viewed as the dominant figure in the black family. Family food allotments were given to the father. Slave fathers hunted and fished to supplement their families' diets. Slave passes were given to men, rarely to women. A slave father would be the one to intercede on behalf of his child with the white master. Although in slave families all authority resided with the slave owner, within these restricting confinements and when white people were not around, the slave father was the person in charge. I have found that the white male culture at the time looked to the enslaved father as the head. Supervisory positions in the fields and many of the skilled oc-cupations were held by men. Men were in charge of work gangs, no matter how capable were the women.[54]

Patterson has asserted that since the slave father could not protect his wife and children from abuse, rape, being sold, or anything else, the role of father did not exist.[55] Although neither an enslaved father nor mother could stop the beatings or the selling of their children or themselves, parents played a role in protecting or trying to protect their family members from lashing, sexual assault, or being sold away. Husbands and fathers intervened on behalf of their spouses and children, and sometimes a man prevailed or redirected white anger away from the woman or child and onto himself. Married women were less subject to sexual abuse. Moreover, the very culture of the Southern slave society, at least by the late antebellum period, was one in which the Christian religion helped limit the worst cases of abuse. Although never actually living up to those ideals, slave owners understood that the "good Christian master" was to recognize the "rights" of their slaves to have families and to encourage among the slaves the same values of Christian piety and family relations that whites were supposed to live up to. Until emancipation, slaves and whites often listened to the same preachers in the same church at the same time.[56]

The patriarchal context was not only how the slaveholder perceived the situation, but also that slave fathers acted as the heads of their families and were considered as such by their wives and children and by the slave com-munity. As Jacqueline Jones put it, "But at home, men and women worked together to support the father's role as provider and protector."[57] Women, who worked as hard in the fields as the men, then continued working into the night on domestic chores. Men did not do domestic chores, even when crucial to family survival; food preparation, cleaning, laundering, making cloth and clothing were women's work. Leslie Schwalm has found that even if a woman slave used a specialized talent for her job (seamstress, cook), the white plantation owner did not call her "skilled." Only men (blacksmiths, carpenters, etc.) were considered skilled: "Instead, rice planters encouraged a social hierarchy on plantations in which overseers, (male) slave drivers, and (male) slave artisans, ranked in that order, enjoyed a privileged status."[58]

Studies such as Schwalm's and Jones's have helped to broaden the picture of enslaved women and of family life. If fathers brought in extra protein from hunting and fishing, mothers brought in extra vitamins from family garden plots. Contrary to my finding in upcountry South Carolina, Schwalm also found that on the lowcountry South Carolina rice plantations, food and clothing allotments were given to the mothers and not to the fathers. In another contrast, Schwalm found that communication between the planter and the slave family was "nearly exclusively" through slave mothers and not fathers.[59]

Thus, even within the group of scholars who deny the matriarchate, the degree of male domination is up for debate. In an important article in 1983 and later in her 1985 book, Deborah Gray White argued that slavery was qualitatively different for women and an over-reliance on patriarchy in the context of the slave community is a mistake. Nevertheless, White concurred with revisionists that the two-parent household predominated in slavery and that males dominated in the public sphere. Patricia Collins disagrees with the patriarchy thesis because the "conceptual assumption of the matriarchy thesis is that someone must 'rule' the household in order for it to function effectively. Neither Black men or Black women ruled." She found instead "African-Americans' relationship to the slave political economy made it unlikely that either patriarch or matriarchal domination could take root."[60]

On the other hand, in both upcountry and lowcountry South Carolina, African American religion reinforced patriarchy, and leadership roles in the slave community usually went to men. Slave mothers imparted moral instruction, but in the slaves' brush-arbors men were the exhorters, deacons, and sextons. Preachers, especially, held a high rank of respect among slaves, presiding over slave baptisms, funerals, weddings, as well as discipline matters. Preachers were always male. Church doctrine put everyone equal before the throne of God, but on Earth the church accepted that men, as the leaders of their families and households, had the right to govern their children and women.[61] Other scholars disagree. White has shown that leadership in the community did not always go to the males; certain women were considered leaders.[62] Schwalm also found that women held a "highly regarded status" in slave families on rice plantations in lowcountry South Carolina because of their role in supervising and training the children. Although never the preachers, women sometimes were leaders in organizing praise meetings called "shouts." Moreover, these slave communities often looked to a "spiritual mother" as a leader in the community.[63] Only once in her diary (December 18, 1864), Towne wrote of a "spiritual mother," who had "tremendous influence over her spiritual children."

Maum Katie had worshiped "her own gods in Africa," though she had lived in the United States for a century. By contrast, Towne referred to "spiritual" fathers in the plural: "they call their elders in the church—or the particular one who converted and received them in—their spiritual father, and he has the most absolute power over them. These fathers are addressed with fear and awe as 'Pa Marcus,' 'Pa Dema,' etc."[64] As far as I can tell, scholars agree that even on the coastal Sea Islands leadership within the organized church, such as preachers and deacons, was reserved for men.

So, was the African American family patriarchal? In previous work, I have made the point that the slave family was patriarchal, but I may have overstepped myself.[65] If patriarchy means "a form of social organization in which the father is the supreme authority in the family, clan, or tribe,"[66] that may apply to Southern white families in the 19th century, but it does not explain family dynamics, neither for whites nor for African Americans. Supreme authority seems to overstate what I consider to be male dominance. Some say a patriarchal family is "a monogamous family in which the oldest male has extensive authority over the other members of the family or the household."[67] I think "extensive authority" is better than "supreme author-ity," but in the families I have studied, it was the father, and not the oldest male, who had the authority. I find more helpful the definition by Gerda Lerner: "the manifestation and institutionalization of male dominance over women and children in the family and the extension of male dominance over women in society in general." Peter W. Bardaglio, in his legal analysis of the family in the 19th century, prefers Lerner's finding that paternalism is a form of patriarchy defined by "the relationship of a dominant group, considered superior, to a subordinate group, considered inferior, in which the dominance is mitigated by mutual obligations and reciprocal."[68] In legal matters, then, the white father was the head of the household; he could demand obedience from his wife, using force if need be, and even the children belonged to the father. When a white woman married, her legal identity became that of her husband's, a doctrine known as coverture. According to a South Carolina judge in 1858, the law, "looking to the peace and happiness of families and to the best interests of society, places the husband and father at the head of the household."[69]

Using this definition of patriarchy, by law the slave father was not the legal head; the slave owner was, a situation impossible to compare to the white

family. Also different from the white situation, the law gave the slave mother
rather than the slave father the determining role in ascribing the status of
the children. In the mid 1600s when so many of the fathers were free and
white, various colonies decided that "all children born in this country shall
be held bond or free only according to the condition of the mother."[70] This
goes against the patriarchal notion that fathers owned the children, but the
legal ownership usually was still that of a male, only it was the white male
owner of the mother.

So, by legal definition, slave families were not patriarchal. What about
economically? Many scholars agree with Jones's assessment, "In denying
slaves the right to own property, make a living for themselves, participate in
public life, or protect their children, the institution of bondage deprived black
men of access to the patriarchy in the larger economic and political sense."
She also concluded that "black males and females were equal in the sense
that neither sex wielded economic power over the other."[71] Towne explained
that on the coastal Sea Islands: "the wife is looked upon as a help" and was
expected to labor on behalf of the family.[72] White finds that, since neither
men nor women controlled their labor, this equality "may have encouraged"
egalitarianism.[73] In other words, the economic system did not credit male
slaves as the patriarchs of their families.

In slave society there were also situations, more often on smaller plantations, in which some of the two-parent slave families were living apart. The
father lived on one plantation, the mother lived on another, and the children
resided with the mother. A weekly visit or two from the father would be very
nice, but without a father present on a day-to-day basis, the children would
look to the mother as the family head. And the slave owners would give the
family food allotment to the mother. Jones has called this family structure
matrilocal, "that is, children more often remained with their mother than
with their father."[74] Some call this situation matrifocal, "of, pertaining to, or
designating a family unit or structure headed by the mother and lacking a father
permanently or for extended periods."[75] In her use of the term *matrifocality,*
White clarifies that the term does not mean that fathers are absent, nor that
women hold the power. "The most important factor is the supremacy of the
mother-child bond over all other relationships." (Others might say that this
mother-child bond was primary in the white culture also.) White also finds
matrifocal families in "many West African tribes."[76] Some excellent recent

literature has tended to focus more on the mother-child relationship than on the issue of the black family per se.[77]

But this essay is looking at "Black Matriarchy." If a woman, or even many women, acted as heads of their families, does that make a matriarchy? Matrifocal families can exist in a patriarchal society, but can patriarchy be the rule if many families are matrifocal? Men cannot be in charge if they are not present. By one definition, a matriarchy is "a family, society, community, or state governed by women"[78]—clearly not the case under slavery. In another definition, a matriarchal family is "a family group in which the wife has the highest status, controls the other family members, and makes the important decisions affecting the family group."[79] In some families, both white and African American, the father is not there, and the mother is in charge of the children and makes the important decisions. According to this definition, would this constitute a matriarchal family? Pondering this question requires an examination of status and control within the larger cultural context.

The debate between patriarchy or matriarchy has set up a false dichotomy. In answer to the accusation (and it has been used as an accusation rather than a description) that the African American family is matriarchal, I have described the family as patriarchal. Yet, rather than being a dichotomy, these concepts are on a continuum. Between the two extremes are multitudinous examples, some closer to matriarchy and some—many more in my opinion—closer to patriarchy. The white culture, while evolving from a stricter patriarchy where the father was the governing authority to one where the mother had much more influence over the children, especially during their "tender years," was still very much male-dominated. I have found in the slave community similar aspects of male partiality in the culture, although not the same degree of male domination. Aspects of African American and white community and family life were similar. If patriarchy is too strong a word, the culture was nevertheless more dominated by men than by women. In no way did a matriarchy exist in the slave family and community.

Of course, scholars cannot ignore the atrocities of slavery, and of course we need to look at the various legacies that slavery has wrought. But the exigencies and cruelties of slavery varied. General assessments ignore differences of region, of size of plantation, of the temperament of the slave owner, and of the crop grown, whether cotton, rice, indigo, or tobacco. In upcountry, cotton-producing South Carolina, for instance, I found that slave communities had an easier time surviving on a large plantation with more than twenty slaves. I found that a single slave in a household was less likely to be abused, and that the worst abuses occurred on middle-sized plantations.[80] Slavery also differed across time. By the time of the Civil War, when many white men were away from the plantation, some plantations were actually run by the slave community, with little or no white supervision.[81]

Patterson has censured revisionist scholars for pointing out that some slaves could make a decent life for themselves. In numerous instances, slaves could marry without interference and remain married without being sold or rented away. Some slave families could work their own garden plots, even earn a little money on the side. Admitting this does not deny the massive ravages of slavery, the oppression of being owned and forced to work for someone else, the inability to prevent rape upon your own person, the terror of having your family sold away, the monstrous knowledge that your posterity would also be enslaved, the realization that a "good" slaveholder could die and leave you to a cruel one. And no one should dispute that within the overall cultural context of patriarchy, some masters were cruel dictators, and even the supposedly "good masters" resorted to violence or the threat of violence to keep other human beings in bondage. Slavery rested on violence or the threat of violence; slavery could not exist without coercion. Nor could it exist without white and black interaction; whites had to force African Americans to be slaves. Even a slaveholder known for his kindness, such as Thomas Fripp on St. Helena Island, had a whipping post close to his house.[82] Nevertheless, although slaves faced oppression and cruelties, slavery did not leave a lasting heritage of weakness upon the black family. Slave families were strong despite horrific oppression, and under the circumstances their devotion to the family ideal was heroic.

RECONSTRUCTION AND AFRICAN AMERICAN FAMILIES

There can be no stronger evidence of a male-headed family structure in slavery than the fact that five years after slavery had ended, the overwhelming majority of African American families were headed by males. It seems quite unreasonable to suppose that a slave system which had little notion of male-headed family units could have reversed itself so quickly after emancipation. African American men and white men headed households in almost the same proportions (yet one never hears about the "White Matriarchy"). While it is true that an analysis of family structure implies little of family function, such an analysis does show that whites and blacks had similar family structures.

Many of us revisionist scholars have looked at the early postbellum years and remarked that one of the first places African Americans looked to celebrate their freedom was in reuniting their families. During Reconstruction, freed African Americans made every effort to find family members who had been taken away from them, and black families went about creating or preserving the concept of stable, loving families. And there are tragic stories of having to adapt to the historical circumstances that whites did not have to face: such as a spouse sold away years before, returning to find the other spouse remarried. Many scholars have pointed out that freedmen and freedwomen showed considerable respect for the institution of marriage and made great efforts to legalize their unions immediately after the war.[83] If nothing else, now they were free from being sold away from loved ones. Getting together as a family, legally marrying, finding lost family members, often took priority. As in the Euro-American culture, a legal marriage meant the children were legitimate, and also that family members of soldiers could qualify for pensions.[84] And who would be head of this legal entity? The legal structure at the time put the male as the household head. According to Bardaglio, changes "modified but did not eliminate patriarchal authority."[85] Moreover, churches, African American volunteer associations, the Freedmen's Bureau, white landowners who hired family workers, all called the father the head of the household. The census takers, simply if the father lived with the family, recorded him as the head of family and head of household. Until very recently, scholars fell into that categorization also, not looking at power relationships within the family, but accepting the census taker's listing of family head and household head.

Thus, the Civil War did not change the patriarchal nature of Southern society and culture. Evidence shows that in the post-War South, this large rural agricultural region was populated overwhelmingly by male-headed households, characterized by the allocation of precedence and power to the males in the family. Although stereotypes present women as heads of the majority of black households, this pattern was not the case. In Southern agrarian society husbands and fathers were responsible for their families' economic well-being, and planters hiring workers recognized the male as the head of the African American family. After the war, almost all labor contracts throughout the South were made between white and black males, the African American man signing his name, or making his mark, as the head of his family.[86] After emancipation, the African American church stressed education, family responsibilities, and male leadership. Postbellum leadership positions in the churches continued to be all-male. Pastors and superintendents, leaders charged with the welfare of their fellow worshipers as well as their spiritual guidance, were always men. Black church and religious leaders went on to become the political leaders who spread their particular concern for the traditional family structure and morality to the entire community. Other organizations also reinforced patriarchal values. Black militias during Reconstruction, in particular, reflected the adherence to a patriarchal arrangement of society; almost every militia leader was head of a family. Fraternal organizations and emigration societies reinforced the patriarchal nature of rural society: Masonic lodges, the Sons of Zion, the Mutual Aid and Burial Societies, and secret orders such as the Knights of Pythias restricted membership to males with a reputation of virtue.

DATA

My work on the postbellum African American family structure verifies that male-headed households were the rule after the Civil War. I used a local study of a large Piedmont area, South Carolina's Edgefield District (after 1868, "districts" became "counties"; five counties now make up what was the Edgefield District), to determine whether postbellum free African Americans had more female-headed households than did whites. Complex patterns of race relations can best be studied on a local level where processes and changes over time can be closely analyzed, and local history becomes a means of seeing and isolating historical problems.[87] My Edgefield database is not a sample; it consists of every slave and free person, household, and farm recorded in the manuscript census returns from 1850 to 1880. My work with this Edgefield database clearly demonstrates that a numerical black matriarchy did not exist in rural Edgefield. The census provides a snapshot picture, but reality is more complex. Using other sources such as former slave narratives and, most important, church records, I have also tried to say something about the *quality* of family relationships. This includes such things as the fidelity of husband and wife, the civility of intrafamily relations, and the values and standards of behavior transmitted by parents to their children. Quantitative historians have been labeled in the past as simple "number crunchers." How ironic that now historians using statistics from an official government census are being accused of "romanticism."

Statistical evidence supports the conclusion that African American males were the heads of their families in the postwar South. Table 1 compares the number of black male heads of households with the number of white for both 1870 and 1880 in the Edgefield database. African American and white percentages of male household heads are nearly identical for both census years. Even before Civil War deaths that might have caused fewer white males in 1870, white males headed 83.6 and 85.4 percent respectively of the 1850 and 1860 white households in Edgefield District, a proportion similar for black and white households in postbellum Edgefield.

TABLE I.
SELECTED FAMILY CHARACTERISTICS OF HOUSEHOLDS, 1870 AND 1880

(percentages shown with selected characteristics)

	1870		1880	
	African American	*White*	*African American*	*White*
	(N=4,873)	*(N=3,419)*	*(N=5,969)*	*(N=3,301)*
Male-headed	83.7	82.0	86.4	86.7
Spouse present	73.8	70.8	75.1	76.2
Children present	76.4	75.1	75.5	76.7
Children/both parents present	59.5	57.7	62.0	64.4

Note: Table excludes African Americans in white households and whites in African American households. For a discussion of these mixed households, see Burton, *In My Father's House Are Many Mansions*, 328–29.

My analysis of male- and female-headed families has uncovered a key element in comparing and contrasting African American and white families: *wealth*. Five years after slavery, the great majority of African American households are recorded as having no wealth whatsoever. About three hundred African American families had some wealth, but much less than whites. Yet, for the African Americans who had some land and some personal property, that was a decisive variable. Because my data includes every household in this large rural region, Table 2 is unambiguous. When compared by the simple categories of wealth (landed or personal property only) versus no wealth, in each category the African American family is more likely to be male-headed, and families with children are more likely to have two parents than are white families.[88] There is no denying that poverty created difficult circumstances for families, both black and white; pension records of African American Civil War veterans and their surviving spouses clearly indicate the strains that poverty imposed.[89] The point here is a simple one: Controlling for wealth, black families were more often headed by males than were white families.

TABLE 2.
SELECTED FAMILY CHARACTERISTICS OF HOUSEHOLDS BY WEALTH AND COLOR IN 1870

(percentages shown with selected characteristics)

Households	Landed		Pers. Property Only		No Property	
	White	A-A	White	A-A	White	A-A
N=	1,861	81	388	187	1,171	4,607
Male-headed	85.3	93.8	94.3	98.9	72.4	82.9
Spouse present	73.8	86.4	82.0	93.6	62.3	72.8
Children present	76.5	81.5	74.5	86.6	73.5	75.9
Children and both parents present	61.2	75.3	66.2	81.8	49.4	58.4
Only those households with children that have both parents	80.0	92.4	88.9	94.4	67.1	76.8

Source: Edgefield Database.

Not accepting that female-headed households define a matriarchy, I nevertheless have looked at all the female-headed households in my Edgefield database in 1870 and 1880. Combining all the African American households in Edgefield District whose families were headed by single women with children, divorced women, and women where a husband might have deserted, they constituted only 4.6 percent of all black households—hardly enough to warrant the term *matriarchy*.[90] Nevertheless, since the 1880 census recorded civil status, single, married, widowed, or divorced, I could examine these female-headed households in 1880 very closely. Table 3 highlights the key differences between the otherwise similar rates of female-headed households by race: proportionately twice as many African American household heads were married (10.1 percent versus 4.8 for whites). Significantly more white women household heads had previously been married, 54.1 percent for African Americans versus 81 percent for whites (this includes widowed and divorced).

TABLE 3.

FEMALE HOUSEHOLD AND FAMILY HEADS
BY MARITAL STATUS, 1880

	Female Household Heads [a]		Female Family Heads [b]	
	White	A-A	White	A-A
	(N=441)	(N=811)	(N=529)	(N=1,007)
Married	4.8	10.1	4.9	9.4
Divorced	3.9	1.6	3.6	1.6
Widowed	77.1	52.5	73.9	48.9
Single without children	9.1	11.2	9.6	12.3
Single with Children	3.6	20.0	5.3	22.6
Unknown	1.6	4.6	2.6	5.2

a. Households headed by females but with a spouse present have been excluded.
b. Includes household heads and family heads in a household of another.
Source: Edgefield Database.

Many of the women running their own households in 1880 were widows. A goodly number of both white and black women were widows in Edgefield, but white widows were a significantly higher proportion. Substantially fewer than widows, women who were divorced were also family heads. The divorce rate clearly differed between white and black families. Ultimately the right to gain a divorce, coupled with a living wage (if she could get it), gave women tools to manage their own households and spelled the beginning of the end of the patriarchal society, though not the end of female deference to men. Proportionately more than twice as many divorced white women were heading households than were divorced African American women. But these figures do not tell the whole story. Divorce was illegal in South Carolina for whites until 1872, when the new African American Republican majority in the Reconstruction state legislature legalized it. (When white male Democratic elites retook political control, they again outlawed divorce in 1878. Divorce was then not permitted until 1948 when South Carolina was the last state to legalize it.)

African Americans under slavery, on the other hand, had divorce as an option, though some owners made it harder than others. "When sufficient cause can be shown on either side, a marriage may be annulled, but the offending party must be severely punished," wrote James Henry Hammond in his Edgefield plantation rule book. "Where both are in wrong, both must be punished, & if they insist on separating must have 100 lashes apiece. After such a separation neither can marry again for 3 years. For first marriage a bounty of $5.00, to be invested in household articles, or an equivalent of articles, shall be given. If either has been married before, the bounty shall be $3.50. A third marriage shall not be allowed but in extreme cases, & in such cases, or where both have been married before, no bounty will be given."[91] As early as 1819 Big Stevens Creek Baptist Church in Edgefield, South Carolina, agreed that when slaves had to separate from spouses because of the master, "the slaves are at liberty to take other mates." Slaves were able to obtain church-sanctioned separations, whereas whites could not. After emancipation African American couples continued to use the church instead of the court system. Legal proceedings were costly and intimidating. Table 3 shows the number of women who reported to the census enumerator that they were divorced. Part of the 10.1 percent of African American women household heads who are listed as married in the 1880 census, but have no spouse present, had followed the pattern of consensual divorce recognized by the church and the African American community even before emancipation.[92]

Proportionately, twice as many African American married women reported that they headed households as did whites. Of the former, two had husbands in the household, possibly disabled. Two who recorded their civil status as married had husbands who were inmates in the local jail.[93] Other husbands had left to find work elsewhere before sending for their families, a common occurrence in 1880.

An examination of the data that many consider the basis of the problem with a "matriarchy" shows that the African American community had a much higher proportion of unwed mothers. Of the unmarried women who headed households in 1880, only 14 white women had children in their households, whereas 166 single black women had children (according to the census, their illegitimate offspring) in their households. These households accounted for less than 2.8 percent of all African American households, but they were a fifth of all female-headed black households. A majority of unmarried black and white women who were household heads with children had more than one child; in this group black women predominated. Among unmarried women with children who were not household heads, but lived in the household of someone else, more white women than African American women had more than one child.

SINGLE SLAVE WOMEN WITH CHILDREN

The African American community had been denied the legal (though not the cultural) sanctity of marriage before emancipation. While the majority of slaves listed by slaveowners for Edgefield plantations were in male-headed nuclear families, a minority of female slaves were listed only with children. Some of these slave women had married off the plantation, but some of the women were not married. Sometimes the children of these women could be identified as having had white fathers. Unwed mothers often went on to marry without apparent prejudice and had normal, stable, two-parent families. It is not surprising that a minority of African American women after the war also had children outside of marriage and that, compared with whites, black women were significantly more likely to have illegitimate children. Among these apparently fatherless African American children were some indications of pride in a paternal heritage. In contrast to unmarried white women who typically gave children the woman's surname, many unmarried African American women gave their children the fathers' surnames.[94]

The community acknowledged a certain legitimacy to these unions. For the most part, the African American community did not condemn but accepted and absolved its members. An "illegitimate" former slave explained his personal predicament and how he had satisfactorily resolved the situation. "Some colored churches 'sinuate a child born out of wedlock can't enter de kingdom of heaven. Our church say he can if he ain't a drunkard, and is de husband of one wife and to believe on, and trust in de Lord as your Savior, and live a right kind of life dat he proves of. Dat seem reason to me, and I jine and find peace as long as I done right."[95] African American culture in the postbellum South, including black churches, was more tolerant of unmarried women with children. The majority white community did not share this tolerance.

CULTURE OF TENANTRY AND SHARECROPPING

Agrarian culture has historically been a family affair with men and women and children all pitching in. This culture did not change with the postbellum development of farm tenantry and sharecropping. These systems have come to mean the lowest of agricultural careers, ridden by debt almost to the point of peonage. Yet, tenantry, including rent for a share of the crop, developed as a compromise between white landowners and newly freed African American workers. Tenantry also changed in nature over the years. During Reconstruction, when African Americans had a meaningful vote and influenced politics, laws favored the tenant. That altered when whites recaptured political control and passed lien laws to favor landowners and merchants.[96]

With emancipation, a family-owned farm was the goal of newly freed African Americans. Whites, however, totally opposed such economic independence. Whites wanted to set up a system of gang labor similar to slavery, while African American families wished for autonomy after the ordeal of slavery. Farm tenancy was part of a compromise over politics and labor arrangements. Most black household heads were not fortunate enough to be tenants or even sharecroppers. Yet historians and economists have portrayed Reconstruction-era African Americans as tenant farmers.[97] Even by 1880 less than half of Edgefield black households were either tenants or sharecroppers; the majority were day laborers. Tenancy was a move *up* the social and occupational ladder, a move made possible by a stable family structure, male-headed. My finding in this regard contradicts the opinion put forth by E. Franklin Frazier. Tenancy helped a family live and work together as a unit. This is simply a quantitative statement on family structure: in spite of economic dependence and severe debt problems, far from contributing to the breakdown of the African American family, tenantry actually helped preserve it.

In 1870 every black tenant-farming household in Edgefield was headed by a man, and in 1880 almost 97 percent were male-headed. These statistics reflect the patriarchal culture and the reluctance of white landowners to rent to a female household head unless she had sons old enough to help farm. Women, black or white, found it difficult if not impossible to run a farm without the help of an adult male or at least a teenage boy. Male household heads predominated on farms because the culture expected men to do heavy, physical work such as plowing. Married men with families were more likely to run farms, since farmers' wives and children helped with the work. While caring for husband and children, women worked full-time laboring in the fields when necessary, and putting up foodstuff. Farming was a family affair. White landowners also preferred to hire men for permanent work as farm laborers.

Contracts recorded by the Freedmen's Bureau in the first few years after the war show that very few women made contracts with white landowners.[98]

There was no black matriarchy in rural Edgefield, nor was there a trend toward families without husbands and fathers. An agrarian society and the predominance of the Christian religion among African Americans fostered strong family ties. In the years after slavery, black and white family structures were remarkable in their similarities. Male-headed, two-parent households predominated for both groups, and they shared similarities in size, occurrence, and structure of nuclear, extended, and augmented families.[99]

Although the postbellum African American farm family was male-headed to an overwhelming degree, within black and white male-headed households after the Civil War there was a major difference. Far more black than white wives in Edgefield worked outside the home, 43 percent as against 2 percent for white families in 1880. African American wives found jobs as agricultural day laborers or as domestics, cooks, washwomen, and nursemaids to whites.[100]

While my work on family structure disputes the theory that distinctive slave or African traditions shaped the development of the African American family in the post-emancipation era, some slave patterns persisted. The continued pattern of more African American than white female involvement in the work force outside the home illustrates the complexity and ambiguity of this and other cultural issues. Working wives do not mean a matriarchy, but, similar to female household heads, working wives have more power, including some economic independence, and that does weaken a husband's autocratic control.[101] Although the regularly employed working wife usually did not see any reduction in the responsibility she bore as caretaker of her own children and husband, she did spend much of the day away from home and gained some autonomy.[102] Whereas African American families on the plantations and tenant farms worked together, those in the towns and cities might be together only after the workday was over. Also, at the same time that more black than white women worked, a substantial number of African American women withdrew from the labor force. Many worked out of necessity, but some working wives had a choice, and many chose not to work outside the home, a source of frustration to whites. In 1871, the Edgefield *Advertiser* claimed that African American women's refusal to work "was so unreasonable" that it was for whites "nothing short of absolute torment." As one white planter put it in 1901, "It has not been a month since I lost my cook. She just went off to a place she never had known or heard of before, on account of no fault with us, but to follow her husband."[103]

Whether or not wives worked outside the home, the essential point to consider is that the typical family, both black and white, in this agrarian community was overwhelmingly male-headed. No matriarchal system of social organization of women heading families existed in the South, black or white.

WOMEN IN TOWNS

The crux of the matriarchy debate over the years, however, has pivoted on the number of female-headed households. Within this group of single parents are the widowed, the divorced, and the unwed. Even though they constitute a minority of households, this group shows a clear difference between white and African American unmarried women with children. One of the points of analysis is the decision of single mothers to live in a town rather than in the countryside. Because female-headed households concentrated in town rather than dispersed throughout the countryside, the number of such families was exaggerated in studies that failed to employ representational samples inclusive of rural areas.

Another aspect of the matriarchal debate is the role of politics. Simply put, political power had a strong impact on family life because it either effected or denied economic opportunity. When African Americans had political power under Republican Reconstruction, African American men could find jobs in rural towns; when conservative white Democrats recaptured political control, they excluded any African American men from such jobs, relegating them again to work only in agricultural fields. This racism significantly transformed African American family structure in town. Family structure, although never the only factor in the debate of whether a black matriarchy exists, was, nonetheless, a significant component. Image is also a component because whites took note of the single African American women living in town.

Both African American and white women heading households, whether they were widowed, divorced, or single, needed to find work and needed safe places to live. Violence during Reconstruction was a fact of life after the end of the war. White vigilantes and terrorist groups like the Ku Klux Klan committed murder and arson with impunity.[104] Freedmen felt a little safer in town than in the isolated countryside. This was true for men and women, but women were more vulnerable to rape and sexual harassment and felt more secure in town. In town also were jobs. African American women could find work as domestics, nursemaids, or laundresses in the home of whites.

TABLE 4.

SELECTED CHARACTERISTICS OF HOUSEHOLDS
BY TOWN AND HINTERLAND, 1870 AND 1880

(percentages shown with selected characteristics except for average number in household and average age household head)

| Households | INCORPORATED TOWNS | | | | HINTERLAND | | | |
| | 1870 | | 1880 | | 1870 | | 1880 | |
	A-A	W	A-A	W	A-A	W	A-A	W
N =	267	119	201	75	4,608	3,301	5,766	3,128
MH	83.9	82.0	63.2	82.9	84.1	82.2	87.2	86.9
CBPP	50.9	48.7	37.8	51.4	60.0	58.0	63.2	65.3
SPF	44.1	57.8	70.1	33.1	39.3	39.7	24.2	22.0
SPF/%	28.7	41.4	65.8	30.0	27.3	29.9	20.1	18.5
WW	13.0	2.8	55.2	0	36.2	1.1	62.4	3.4
WSAC	21.3	53.4	12.6	45.3	5.7	25.5	9.4	30.2

MH = Male-headed

CBPP = Children and both parents present

SPF = Single-parent families

SPF/% = Single-parent households as % of two-parent households

WW = Working wives

WSAC = With school-age children attending school

Notes: Table excludes seven families headed by Indians. Percentages subject to rounding.
a. Includes households.
Source: Edgefield Database.

Although most households, town and country, were male-headed, families in town had a much larger minority that were female-headed. (See Table 4) This trend of more women heading households in town increased between the 1870s and the 1880s. In 1870 white and black women headed households in about the same proportion. By 1880, however, while the number of white females heading households remained about the same, 36.8 percent of African American families in towns were headed by women. This sizable minority was in contrast to a rural norm of around 13 percent of female household heads in 1880.

The significant difference between 1870 and 1880 in terms of town-dwelling African American families with a working female head who had children in the home was due to the developing political situation and deteriorating race relations during the 1870s. The character of race relations in Edgefield changed because of social and political struggles. With the advent of emancipation, African Americans quickly emerged as a threat to white supremacy. The political rise of African Americans challenged the white-dominated society in all areas of social, political, and economic life. This challenge was felt most strongly in the towns. In towns, African American men, supported in their economic and social advance by Republican political control, had professional, managerial, and skilled jobs during Reconstruction. They were postmasters, superintendents, clerks, sheriffs, census takers, attorneys, judges, etc.

Then, too, white reaction to the competition with the freed African American population was most virulent in the towns where the threat was strong and where the black militia was bold. White Democrats in South Carolina determined to seize back political control, and, through fraud and murder, they did so. Once back in charge, whites closed the towns, and the mobility and freedom associated with them, to African American men and reasserted the idea that lower-level farm occupations were the allowable limits of African American male ambition. The end of Reconstruction and the resumption of white Democratic control brought about the immediate expulsion of black men from occupations other than stereotyped agricultural roles.

Consequently, the African American men who most threatened white society were systematically driven out of the towns. When these men and their families were forced to move back to the countryside, the African American families left in these small towns took on a distinctly female-headed image. This was not just the result of the general economic depression of the 1870s, since African American men were not excluded from higher-status nonagricultural positions until after the 1876 white Democrat political restoration. For African American males, Republican Reconstruction political control mitigated the effects of racism in 1870, and the majority of households were headed by males. But the reinstitution of the system of racial discrimination after Reconstruction, along with the job opportunities that attracted African American women, brought a tremendous decrease in the proportion of black male-headed households in the towns.[105] For 1870 and 1880 the selective migration of white and African American women to small towns for employment and safety is not enough to explain the image of the black family as female-headed, or, as generally but incorrectly interpreted, as "matriarchal." It was the discriminatory system existing even in small rural villages and towns that excluded African American men from nonagricultural occupations while providing job opportunities for women.

The living patterns for whites in town and country did not change during this time, but, without the political backing of Republican Reconstruction, most African American men (except for the very few members of the elite who had purchased land in the towns during Reconstruction) were forced to the countryside. In the countryside African American men were less of a threat than when they controlled the political networks in the towns, and, thus dispersed, they found it difficult to mobilize politically or militarily. Racism wrought the exclusion of African American men from town-urban economies. The culture of racism may not be measurable, but it produced measurable results in towns and cities: significantly more African American women headed families and households in town after Reconstruction.

Many may conclude that factors such as industrialization, urban city life, illiteracy, mortality, and the development of the ghetto (rather than slavery) were decisive for shaping the current African American family. I have found, however, that the beginning of the decline of the male-headed black family occurred much closer to the traditional homeland of slavery than to Northern industrial cities. Small towns and villages showed the first signs of the disruption that became characteristic of their counterparts in the great cities of industrial America. Edgefield towns and villages in the 1880s, with their populations measured in no more than hundreds and their relatively slow-changing, nonindustrial economic base, could hardly be classified with the massive industrial cities of the North. Moreover, the community and church and family ties that regulated African American rural society also existed in the small towns of Edgefield County. Yet traces of the same destructive impact on African American families found in Northern urban ghettoes were present in these small 19th-century Edgefield towns and villages. The "destructive conditions" in Edgefield were as sinister as those in cities, but it was not the absence of social control mechanisms that explain a higher proportion of female-headed households and illegitimacy in these rural towns. Instead it was an unquantifiable cultural component: racism and racial discrimination in jobs. Racism existed in town and country and in both settings African American men were economically disadvantaged compared to whites, but racial discrimination against black men in cities and small towns was more hostile than in rural settings. Racism prevented black men from integrating town and city economies. As seen in post-Reconstruction Edgefield, in Southern towns and villages whites insisted on the virtual exclusion of African American men from all but agricultural jobs. As sociologist William Julius Wilson has argued with respect to the current familial problems besetting the black community, the key factor in the cities is the "disappearance of work."[106]

URBAN BIAS OF SCHOLARS STUDYING MATRIARCHY

I believe that scholars betray a distinct, urban bias in their analyses of rural culture. Misunderstanding agrarian society and rural life distorts their scholarly findings. In addition to incorrectly conceptualizing rural life, scholars have gone on to err in another way. Their samples showing a preponderance of female-headed households are not representative; their counts of the number of families and households headed by females are incorrect.

For 60 years scholars believed that black men were not heading African American families, but careful study of the different patterns of families in the countryside, small hinterland towns, and cities shows that in the countryside black families were overwhelmingly headed by men. In cities as well as towns, female-headed families were never in the majority. Yet, since the African American women who did act as family heads were working in the homes of whites and in continuous contact with them, their cases loomed large in the white imagination. They were more visible to those whites and African Americans most likely to write about them. This may have served to "verify" the black matriarchy for many well-intentioned whites, as well as African American scholars such as Du Bois and Frazier. Too often scholars' own prejudices and personal experiences have led to denials of the patriarchal reality of the African American family. Yet it may be an urban bias rather than a racial bias that has distorted the real picture. Almost all scholars live in urban areas and use urban sources. Rare are scholars like the theologian Benjamin E. Mays, who grew up during the Jim Crow era near rural Ninety Six, South Carolina. This son of tenant farmers, both of whom were born enslaved in Edgefield District, understood the strength of the agrarian black family and the patriarchal nature of that African American rural culture.[107] Sociologists Du Bois, Frazier, Moynihan, Patterson, and social science historian Ruggles have urban backgrounds and urban academic experiences.[108] Unfamiliar with the agrarian patriarchal culture of the South, they equated urban and small town data as the African American experience. When discussing the usefulness of the manuscript census, for example, Patterson falls into a typical pattern of citing the numbers from studies of urban areas only. Moynihan extracted his data from New York City. Frazier used Chicago after the great migration as his laboratory. And it is no coincidence that when Du Bois wrote in *Souls of Black Folk* about his experiences of teaching in a rural Tennessee school, he talks about strong African American families with male heads.[109]

Scholars who investigated matriarchy used urban sources and, living in cities themselves, supplemented their sources with their own urban experiences. Scholars conducted their research in towns and cities where a survey of houses was quick and convenient. They did not conduct research in the countryside, which would have required traveling miles on inadequate roads to find tenant homes. The fact that the African American male-headed family survived slavery, Reconstruction, and post-Reconstruction in the rural South escaped those intellectuals who counted numbers in the cities and towns, not the countryside.

Knowledge of agrarian society is also essential to understanding the matriarchy misconception and why rural Southern society was patriarchal. A selected sample of town families gives a definite picture of female-headed households, but it is an inaccurate picture of the postbellum agrarian South. Scholars have mistaken small-town Southern society for rural, when in fact town/country differences were notable. Writing in 1910, Odum noted the problem of generalizing about African Americans, "The problem, in its immediate and practical aspects is different in the cities from that in the town; that in the towns differs from that in the country; conditions in rural districts themselves vary widely." Robert Smalls, African American Civil War hero, wrote in 1863, "The country people regard their relations more than the city people; they often walk fifteen miles on a Saturday night to see a cousin." A Northern newspaper correspondent traveling through South Carolina at the end of the Civil War commented, "The city negro and the country negro are as much unlike as two races."[110] These observations apply to the demographic patterns of male-headed households as well.

Conclusion

Many scholars have documented and lamented the problems of inner-city African American family life and have tried to relate those problems to a preponderance of female-headed households. Yet, although female-headed families tend to be poorer, families that suffer from poverty, violence and abuse, alcoholism, drugs, and gang influence may have a male head as readily as a female. This essay has not addressed the benefits of two parents nor how women in the absence of husbands have been raising good sons and daughters for a long time. This essay has addressed the myth that the postbellum African American family was matriarchal and the myth that the majority of African American families were ever female-headed. I have shown that, in actuality, African American families were almost identical to white families in structure, and this was especially true when controlled for wealth.

If scholars agree that the inner-city family is in trouble, there is, nevertheless, much disagreement on the origins of these problems. That these problems are not directly traceable to the heritage of slavery is shown, first, by the earlier steady strengthening of the African American family in the immediate post-emancipation period and, second, by the continuing strength of former slave families in the countryside. One can not deny that the monstrous injustice of slavery is related to the problems of African American families today, but not in a single, linear way. Slavery had an influence, but not the predominant influence, on family structure. Instead, current problems are caused by the interrelated and lasting influence of racism that, although intertwined with slavery, has survived slavery in American institutions, society, and culture. It is right to put the blame for slavery on white slave owners and white businessmen in the slave trade, but African Americans should not be saddled with some notion of failure on their part to maintain family in slavery. Every indication is that they did maintain family life, despite the horrific experiences of being held in bondage by others. Enslaved people's efforts to provide, protect, and maintain their families under the barbarities of slavery is nothing less than a great story of heroism.

The Civil War did not abruptly end patriarchy. No black matriarchy emerged from slavery. Neither did a black matriarchy emerge from postbellum tenantry and sharecropping. Evidence is overwhelming that postbellum agricultural regions were populated by families with male heads of household, and men held the dominant status in jobs, churches, and also in the family. The typical family, both African American and white, was overwhelmingly two-parent, as opposed to female-headed. Within these families the father was considered the head. White employers concurred, as did white and African American census takers, and the families themselves. The African American community put an emphasis on family values within a patriarchal society where stable marriages, nuclear and extended families, and male dominance were institutionalized in a Christian cultural tradition and were preserved by the nature of rural Southern economics and society (as formed by both African Americans and whites). Nor did a black matriarchy emerge from Northern urban migration and its accompanying dislocation and alienation; the issue of female-headed households originated in small towns and villages, much closer to the traditional rural setting.

Although African American female-headed households were more numerous in the towns than in the country, these differences were neither the cause nor the effect of a black matriarchy. Black female family heads—widowed, divorced, and unwed mothers—moved to the hamlets, small towns, and urban areas because that was where they found jobs and a modicum of safety. African American families with male heads found jobs as rural tenants or agricultural workers in the countryside. The town-country dichotomy developed with the failure of Reconstruction and the end of political power for African Americans. Without the black militia, whites grew more violent toward black men in town. Moreover, they instituted total job discrimination for African American men after Reconstruction. Job opportunities for women and the complete lack of job opportunities for men brought about a tremendous decrease in the number of male-headed families living in town, though not in the number living in the countryside. Scholars counting female-headed households in these towns mistakenly took this for the whole picture of the community and announced that females headed a disproportionate number of families and households. Yet, most people still lived in the countryside, and these families were headed by males. Scholars who identify a black matriarchy in the postbellum South are simply wrong. For one thing, they have erred in their definition of a matriarchy, which is not merely a preponderance of female-headed families and households. Nevertheless, within the group of female-headed households living in the towns, there was a much higher proportion of single African American women with children. This phenomenon is of much interest to society today as the number of families without a father present has grown for black and white families. I do not know the reason, but we cannot ignore that in the post-Reconstruction South it was racism and lack of job opportunities for African American males that brought about this problem.

Reliance on quantifiable evidence is essential in discussing the myth of the black matriarchy. Truth, however, requires more than counting with the correct samples. To that end, Sheldon Hackney often used novels and literature in his teaching and scholarship. To understand the trauma of slavery, perhaps there are truths that we historians cannot adequately express and that are best left to fiction. Toni Morrison in *The Bluest Eye* explores the subject of black family life and racism. She suggests that African Americans are unable to create a sanctuary apart from white racism, and for Morrison that failure is catastrophic. Blacks worked hard to cherish and protect those they love, and yet racism crept in everywhere and corrupted everything; down to the present day, no one escapes unscarred, unwounded, without disappointment.[111]

And yet, against all odds, despite pervasive racism encountered in different forms and in different geographies over time, most African American families have hung together. Even when life in general has been darkest, African Americans have found ways to persevere and even triumph, and one of those ways has been through the strength of the black family.

• • •

The author wants to thank especially the editors of *Change and Continuity* who had accepted this article for publication and allowed me to withdraw it so it could appear in this volume instead. The comments and suggestions of the late editor Richard Wall and anonymous readers were especially useful.

Notes

1   See for example, Bill O'Reilly on Fox News, July 23, 2013, and the series, "Race in America," http://video.foxnews.com/v/2560422134001/president-obama-and-the-race-problem-/; and a response, Sharpton Delivers Searing Open Letter to O'Reilly: Expressing 'Grievances' Is' Not an Industry'–It's a Right; see the various articles grouped under "After Trayvon," *Time* 182 (July 29, 2013), 3–35.

2   W. E. B. Du Bois, *The Souls of Black Folk* (Chicago: A. C. McClurg & Co., 1903).

3   Daniel Patrick Moynihan, *The Negro Family: The Case for National Action* (Washington: Office of Policy Planning and Research, United States Department of Labor, March 1965). See James T. Patterson, Freedom Is Not Enough: The Moynihan Report and America's Struggle over Black Family Life—from LBJ to Obama (New York: Basic Books, 2010).

4   Harriet Beecher Stowe, *Uncle Tom's Cabin: Or Life Among the Lowly* (First published as a serial in the National Era, 1851–1852, (New York: Washington Square Press, 1963); Theodore D. Weld, *American Slavery as It Is: Testimony of a Thousand Witnesses* (New York: American Anti-Slavery Society, 1839) and especially, *Slavery and the Internal Slave Trade in the United States* (1841), Reprint (New York: Arno Press, 1969).

5   W. E. B. Du Bois, *The Negro American Family*, the Atlanta University Publications, No. 13 (Atlanta: Atlanta University Press, 1908), 31. Du Bois defined the slave master relationship before the cotton gin as a "Patriarchal Group" (46–47); in his "A Study of Thirteen Families" 134–148, all but one (a widow with daughters) consist of father/mother, children and sometimes extended family, all with traditional gender roles.

6   Howard W. Odum, *Social and Mental Traits of the Negro* (New York: Columbia University Press, 1910), 156, 153; Odum was to become the center of the great school of sociology at the University of North Carolina in the 1930s and 1940s, but at 26 he was not the scholarly giant who produced *Southern Regions of the United States*. In this more racially tolerant work of 1936, Odum did not again mention, let alone disclaim, his theory of black matriarchal society set out in his earlier study. Howard W. Odum, *Southern Regions of the United States* (Chapel Hill: University of North Carolina Press, 1936), 479, 485.

7   E. Franklin Frazier, *The Negro Family in the United States* (Chicago: University of Chicago Press, 1939), viii, ix, 102, 113, 151–152, 201–202, 362. This paper is not going into a discussion of what is "normal," because it differs among cultures. In parts of Africa, for instance, polygyny is normal. See Phillip Kilbride, Collette Suda, and Enos Njeru, *Street Children in Kenya: Voices of Children in Search of a Childhood* (Westport: Praeger Publishers, 2001), 30–33.

8   Frazier, *The Negro Family in the United States*, viii, ix, 102, 113, 151–152, 201–202, 362.

9   Ulrich Bonnell Phillips, *American Negro Slavery: A Survey of the Supply, Employment and Control of Negro Labor as Described by the Plantation Regime* (New York: Appleton, 1918);

10 Kenneth Stampp, *The Peculiar Institution: Slavery in the Ante-Bellum South* (New York: Random House, 1956), 344;

11 Stanley Elkins, *Slavery: A Problem in American Institutional and Intellectual Life* (Chicago: University of Chicago Press, 1959), 219, 133, 136.

12 The slave community school is large, and only a few of the works are discussed in this paper. The best introduction to the literature on slavery is Peter J. Parish, *Slavery: History and Historians* (New York: Harper & Row, 1989). See also the insightful review essay by James W. Loewen, "Slave Narratives and Sociology," *Contemporary Sociology* 11:4 (July 1982): 380–384.

13 John W. Blassingame, *The Slave Community* (New York: Oxford University Press, 1972), 77–103; Robert William Fogel and Stanley L. Engerman, *Time on the Cross: The Economics of American Negro Slavery* (Boston: Little, Brown, 1974), 5–52, 84–85, 127, 128, 139, 142–144; Eugene D. Genovese, *Roll, Jordan, Roll: The World the Slaves Made* (New York: Pantheon, 1974), 451–453, 482–494; Herbert G. Gutman, *Slavery and the Numbers Game: A Critique of Time on the Cross* (Urbana: University of Illinois Press, 1975), 9–10, 88–94, 98, 100–124, 126, 129, 137–140, 162–164, 176 and Herbert Gutman, *The Black Family in Slavery and Freedom, 1750–1925* (New York: Pantheon, 1976).

14   Gutman, *Black Family in Slavery and Freedom.*

15   Quotation from the Philadelphia Social History Project, Frank F. Furstenberg, Jr., Theo-
      dore Hershberg, and John Modell, "Origins of the Female Black Headed Family: The
      Origins of the Urban Experience," *Journal of Interdisciplinary History* 6 (Autumn 1975),
      211–34, quotation 232. Although there have been no other studies which distinguish
      small Southern towns from the hinterlands, other studies of 19th- and 20th-century
      urban and rural areas confirm the Edgefield patterns: in Northern and Southern cities sex
      ratios were higher for women, and more females and mothers headed households than
      they did in rural areas. John W. Blassingame, *Black New Orleans, 1860–1880* (Chicago:
      University of Chicago Press, 1973), 100, 102 noted that "geographical propinquity to
      the center of the city was one of the most important causal factors in the stability or
      instability of the Negro family." Herbert Gutman, "Persistent Myths," Table 1, 195 and
      Black Family, esp. 442–50, 485–530, 624–25, also indicates a significant difference in
      male headed households between rural and urban black families. Crandall A. Shifflett,
      "The Household Composition of Rural Black Families: Louisa County, Virginia, 1880,"
      Journal of Interdisciplinary History 6 (Autumn 1975): 235–60 and *Patronage and Poverty
      in the Tobacco South: Louisa County, Virginia, 1860–1900* (Knoxville: University of
      Tennessee Press, 1982), 236, found few black or white male-absent households in rural
      Louisa County, Virginia. Peter Kolchin, *First Freedom: The Responses of Alabama's Blacks
      to Emancipation and Reconstruction* (Westport: Greenwood Press, 1972), 69, discovered
      that Alabama urban areas had the highest incidence of black and white unmarried adults.
      After studying seven cities in the Ohio Valley, Paul J. Lammermeier, "The Urban Black
      Family of the Nineteenth Century: A Study of Black Family Structure in the Ohio
      Valley, 1850–1880," *Journal of Marriage and the Family* 35 (Autumn 1975): 440–56,
      suggested reappraising E. Franklin Frazier's studies of the black family in Northern cit-
      ies "in light not of a cultural holdover from slavery . . . but as the results of urban life
      caused by poverty and discrimination" (505). And Elizabeth Hafkin Pleck, "The Two-
      Parent Household, Black Family Structure in Late Nineteenth Boston," *Journal of Social
      History* 6 (Fall 1972), tables 4, 5, 5–6 18–19 and *Black Migration and Poverty: Boston,
      1865–1900* (New York: Academic Press, 1979), 175, 182–84, Table 6, both seminal
      studies of Boston and the African American family, show that female-headed households
      were a product of the urban economic structure rather than a "breakdown" resulting
      from a rural-urban move. Thomas Dublin, *Women at Work: The Transformation of Work
      and Community in Lowell, Massachusetts, 1826–1860* (New York: Columbia University
      Press, 1979), 170–71, speculated that the structure of job opportunities accounted for
      the high proportion of female-headed households among 19th-century Irish millhands
      at Lowell, Massachusetts.

16   Stewart E. Tolnay, *The Bottom Rung: African American Family Life on Southern Farms*
      (Urbana: University of Illinois Press, 1999); see also, Tolnay, "The Living Arrangements
      of African and Immigrant Children, 1880–2000," *Journal of Family History,* v 29, No.
      4 (October, 2004), 421–445.

17   *MS,* 3:2 (August 1974), especially the essay by Yvonne, "The Importance of Cicely
      Tyson," 45–47, 76–79.

18   Susanne Lebsock; *The Free Women of Petersburg: Status and Culture in a Southern Town,
      1784–1860* (New York: Norton, 1984); Emily West, *Chains of Love: The Lives of and
      Relationships Between Male and Female Slaves in Antebellum South Carolina* (Urbana:

University of Illinois Press, 2004) and Emily West, *Family or Freedom: People of Color in the Antebellum South* (Lexington: University of Kentucky Press, 2012); Tera W. Hunter, *To 'Joy My Freedom: Southern Black Women's Lives and Labors after the Civil War* (Cambridge: Harvard University Press, 1997).

19   Dorothy Sterling, ed. *We Are Your Sisters: Black Women in the Nineteenth Century* (New York: W. W. Norton & Co, 1984); Jacqueline Jones, *Labor of Love, Labor of Sorrow* (New York: Basic Books, Inc., 1985); Leslie A. Schwalm, *A Hard Fight for We: Women's Transition from Slavery to Freedom in South Carolina* (Urbana: University of Illinois Press, 1997); Deborah Gray White, *Ar'n't I a Woman? Female Slaves in the Plantation South* (New York: W. W. Norton, 1999); Laura F. Edwards, *Scarlett Doesn't Live Here Anymore: Southern Women in the Civil War Era* (Urbana: University of Illinois Press, 2000); Julie Saville, *The Work of Reconstruction: From Slave to Wage Laborer in South Carolina, 1860–1870* (New York: Cambridge University Press, 1994). On black children: Karin Zipf, *Labor of Innocents: Forced Apprenticeship in North Carolina, 1715–1919* (Baton Rouge: Louisiana State University Press, 2005); Mary Niall Mitchell, *Raising Freedom's Child: Black Children and Visions of the Future after Slavery* (New York: New York University Press, 2008), 143–87; Anya Jabour, *Topsy-Turvy: How the Civil War Turned the World Upside Down for Southern Children* (Chicago: University of Chicago Press, 2010); Catherine Jones, "Ties that Bind, Bonds That Break: Children in the Reorganization of Households in Postemancipation Virginia," *Journal of Southern History* 76 (Feb. 2010), 71–106; and her dissertation, "Intimate Reconstructions: Children in Postemancipation Virginia" (PhD diss., Johns Hopkins University, 2007); Wilma King, *Stolen Childhood: Slave Youth in Nineteenth Century America* (Bloomington: Indiana University Press, 1995).

20   See the insightful and excellent review essay by Jane Turner Censer, "Finding the Southern Family in the Civil War," *Journal of Social History* 46:1 (2012), 219–230, on black family see esp 219–23.

21   Jones, *Labor of Love, Labor of Sorrow*, 41.

22   Peter Kolchin, "Re-Evaluating the Antebellum Slave Community: A Comparative Perspective," *Journal of American History* 70:(Dec.1983): 579–601; *Unfree Labor: American Labor and Russian Serfdom* (Cambridge: Harvard University Press, 1987); and *American Slavery* (New York: Hill and Wang, 1993).

23   Steven Ruggles, "The Origins of African-American Family Structure," *American Sociological Review* 59 (February 1994): 136–151. For single parents (not differentiated between male and female parents), Ruggles's own data suggest very little difference for whites and African Americans. For single parents, in 1880, there is only a 3.5 percentage difference in white and African American proportion of single parent families and decreases in 1910 to only a 2.3 percent difference, and is only a 1.6 percent difference in 1940. Then in 1960 there is a nearly a 5 percentage difference, and in 1980 a significant jump to more than a 13 percentage difference (From Table 1. Percentage Distribution of Household Composition by Race, United States 1880–1980, 138). The increased differences reflect the migration of African Americans from the rural South into urban areas, both North and South. On the usage of peonage and apprenticeship of African American children in the South see Miller K. Karnes, "Law, Labor, and Land in the Postbellum Cotton South: The Federal Government and Oglethorpe County, 1865–1940 (PhD dissertation, University of Illinois at Urbana-Champaign, 2000).

24   Orlando Patterson, *Rituals of Blood: Consequences of Slavery in Two American Centuries*

(Washington, DC: Civitas/Counterpoint, 1998), xiii. See Eric Foner, "The Crisis is Within," review of Patterson, *Rituals of Blood*, the *New York Times* February 14, 1999, 12. For a listing of what Orlando Patterson believes is the "best of the counterrevisionists," see note 34 on 286–87. Note he cites women scholars—he relies especially on White, *Ar'n't I A Woman?*; Wilma King, *Stolen Childhood: Slave Youth in Nineteenth-Century America* (Bloomington: Indiana University Press, 1995), and Brenda Stevenson, "Distress and Discord in Virginia Slave Families, 1830–1860," in Carol Bleser , ed. *In Joy and Sorrow: Women, Family, and Marriage in the Victorian South, 1830-1900* (New York: Oxford University Press, 1991), 103–124. Stevenson's book is now published, *Life in Black and White: Family and Community in the Slave South* (New York: Oxford University Press, 1996).

25   Patterson, *Rituals of Blood*, 4. This argument may be oversimplified, but at least it is refreshing to hear men rather than only women called upon to bear the onus for unwed motherhood.

26   Larry L. Bumpass, "The Declining Significance of Marriage: Changing Family Life in the United States," NSFH Working Paper No. 66 (Madison: University of Wisconsin Center for Demography and Ecology, 1995): 14. Bumpass also notes that definitions of "family" based on observable marriage patterns are increasingly inaccurate due to the increase in cohabitation and divorce.

27   Patterson, *Rituals of Blood*, 7.

28   Ibid, 27.

29   Daryl Michael Scott, *Contempt and Pity: Social Policy and the Image of the Damaged Black Psyche, 1880–1996* (Chapel Hill: University of North Carolina Press, 1997). For this article, chapter 3 is most relevant. Patricia Hill Collins also explores images and stereotypes of black women in *Black Feminist Thought: Knowledge, Consciousness, and the Politics of Empowerment* (New York, Routledge, 1991). Chapter 4, "Mammies, Matriarchs, and Other Controlling Images," is especially relevant to this argument, esp. her analysis on 73–76; and, more recently Nell Irvin Painter, *Creating Black Americans: African American History and Its Meanings, 1619–Present* (New York: Oxford University Press, 2006), 94–95, 348, discusses primarily black artists and depictions of African Americans over time and argues that the "trauma" of slavery influenced African Americans culturally and strengthened black community bonds.

30   Moynihan, *The Negro Family*; Gutman and Glasco, "The Negro Family, Household, and Occupational Structure, 1855–1925, with Special Emphasis on Buffalo, New York, but Including comparative Data from New York, New York, Brooklyn, New York, Mobile, Alabama and Adams County, Mississippi," (unpublished tables presented at the Yale Conference on Nineteenth Century Cities, Nov., 1968; Gutman, "Persistent Myths about the Afro-American Family," 181–210; and Gutman, *The Black Family in Slavery and Freedom*. See also; Ira Berlin, "Introduction: Herbert G. Gutman and the American Working Class," in *Power and Culture: Essays on the American Working Class* by Herbert G. Gutman, edited by Ira Berlin (New York: Pantheon Books, 1987): 3–69, especially 40–45; and Gutman, "The Black Family in Slavery and Freedom: A Revised Perspective," 357–379.

31   For example, Nora Lee Frankel found from her study of Mississippi that black families were male-headed, but not truly patriarchal; see Frankel, *Freedom's Women: Black Women and Families in Civil War Era Mississippi* (Bloomington: Indiana University Press, 1999).

Actual definitions of patriarchy, matriarchy, and matrifocal tend to be anthropological; see for example Thomas Barfield, *The Dictionary of Anthropology* (Oxford: Blackwell Publishers, 1997), 312, 313, 350, and Alan Barnard and Jonathan Spencer, eds., *Encyclopedia of Social and Cultural Anthropology*, (London: Routledge, 1996), 226–28. See also Julius Gould and William L. Kolb, eds., *A Dictionary of the Social Sciences* (New York: Free Press, 1964), 416–7 (matriarchy) and 468 (patriarchy) which cites A. R. Radcliffe-Brown, *Structure and Function in Primitive Society* (London: Cohen and West, 1952), 22; John T. Zadrozny, *Dictionary of Social Science* (Washington: Public Affairs Press, 1959), 201, 243–4; Joan and Stephen Baratz, "Black Culture on Black Terms: A Rejection of the Social Pathology Model," esp. 11–13 in *Rappin' and Sylin' Out: Communication in Urban Black America*, edited by Thomas Kochman (Urbana: University of Illinois Press, 1972); also see *The Oxford English Dictionary*, 2nd ed., (Oxford: Clarendon Press, 1989), XI: 347, IX: 473, 475.

32   Orville Vernon Burton, *In My Father's House Are Many Mansions: Family and Community in Edgefield, South Carolina* (Chapel Hill: University of North Carolina Press, 1985).

33   Bertram Wyatt-Brown, "The Ideal Typology and Antebellum Southern History: A Testing of a New Approach," *Societas* 5 (Winter 1975), 1–29, and *Southern Honor: Ethics and Behavior in the Old South* (New York: Oxford University Press, 1982).

34   Benjamin Morgan Palmer, "The Family, in Its Civil and Churchly Aspects: An Essay in Two Parts" (Richmond: Presbyterian Committee of Publication, 1876), 9–10. See also, Eugene Genovese "'Our Family, White and Black': Family and Household in the Southern Slaveholders' World View," in Bleser, *In Joy and in Sorrow, Women, Family, and Marriage in the Victorian South, 1830–1900*, 69–70.

35   Michael Grossberg, *Governing the Hearth: Law and the Family in Nineteenth-Century America* (Chapel Hill: The University of North Carolina Press, 1985), 25.

36   Laura F. Edwards, *Scarlett Doesn't Live Here Anymore*, 2–3; see also her *Gendered Strife and Confusion: The Political Culture of Reconstruction* (Urbana: University of Illinois Press, 1997).

37   Whitemarsh B. Seabrook, *Essay on Management of Slaves* (Charleston: Miller and Brown, 1844), 15.

38   Stephanie McCurry, *Masters of Small Worlds: Yeoman Households, Gender Relations, and the Political Culture of the Antebellum South Carolina Low Country* (New York: Oxford University Press, 1995); Burton, *In My Father's House*.

39   *The Letters and Diary of Laura M. Towne, Written from the Sea Islands of South Carolina, 1862–1884*, ed. Rupert Sargent Holland (Salem: Higginson Book Company, 1912), 184; Testimony of Elbridge Gerry Dudley before the AFIC, [1863] O–328 1863, Letters Received, Ser. 12, RG 94 [K-77] in the Freedmen's Bureau Papers, National Archives; Leslie A. Schwalm, *A Hard Fight for We: Women's Transition from Slavery to Freedom in South Carolina*, (Urbana: University of Illinois Press, 1997), 262.

40   Frederick Douglass, *Life and Times of Frederick Douglass* (New York: Collier Books, 1962 [orig.1881, rev. 1892]). Waldo E. Martin, Jr., *The Mind of Frederick Douglass* (Chapel Hill: University of North Carolina Press, 1983); William S. McFeely, *Frederick Douglass* (New York: Norton, 1991); Nathan Huggins and Oscar Handlin, *Slave and Citizen: The Life of Frederick Douglass* (Boston: Little, Brown, 1980); Booker T. Washington, *Up From Slavery: An Autobiography* (New York: Doubleday, 1901); Louis R. Harlan, *Booker*

T. Washington (2 vols.): *The Making of a Black Leader, 1856–1901* and *The Wizard of Tuskegee 1901–1915* (New York: Oxford University Press, 1983, 1986); Robert J. Norrell, *Up from History: The Life of Booker T. Washington* (Cambridge: Harvard University Press, 2009).

41 Gutman, *The Black Family in Slavery and Freedom.*

42 James Henry Hammond, Silver Bluff Plantation Stock and Crop Book, in the Papers of James Henry Hammond and Hammond in Beech Island Farmer's Club, 36, in Records of the ABC Farmers Club, both collections in the South Caroliniana Library, University of South Carolina, Columbia.

43 For example, see Alfred W. Nicholson, *Brief Sketch of the Life and Labors of Rev. Alexander Bettis . . .* (Trenton, S.C.: Published by the author, 1913), 6–7.

44 Burton, *In My Father's House*; Blassingame, *Slave Community*; Genovese, *Roll Jordan Roll*; Gutman, *Black Family*; Fogel and Stanley Engerman, *Time on the Cross.*

45 Peter Kolchin, "Re-Evaluating the Antebellum Slave Community: A Comparative Perspective," *Journal of American History* 70:(Dec.1983): 579–601; *Unfree Labor: American Labor and Russian Serfdom* (Cambridge: Harvard University Press, 1987); and *American Slavery* (New York: Hill and Wang, 1993); see also Larry McDonnell, "Money Knows No Master: Market Relations and the American Slave Community," in Winifred B. Moore, Jr., Joseph F. Tripp, and Lyon G. Tyler, eds., *Developing Dixie: Modernization in a Traditional Culture* (Westport: Greenwood Press, 1988), 31–44, and Jeffry Forrett, *Race Relations at the Margins: Slaves and Poor Whites in the Antebellum Southern Countryside* (Baton Rouge: Louisiana State University Press, 2006).

46 See especially Lacy Ford, *Deliver Us From Evil* (New York: Oxford University Press, 2009) on the changing nature of slavery toward paternalism and the regional distinctions.

47 Brenda E. Stevenson, "Slavery," in *Black Women in America: An Historical Encyclopedia* ed. Darlene Clark Hine (New York: Carlson Publishing, 1993), 1064.

48 Censer, "Finding the Southern Family in the Civil War," 219–23.

49 Anthony E. Kaye, *Joining Places: Slave Neighborhoods in the Old South* (Chapel Hill: University of North Carolina Press, 2007); Donald R. Shaffer, *After the Glory: The Struggles of Black Civil War Veterans* (Lawrence: University of Kansas Press, 2004); see also Elizabeth Regosin, *Freedom's Promise, Ex-Slave Families and Citizenship in the Age of Emancipation* (Charlottesville: University of Virginia Press, 2002); Dylan C. Penningroth, *The Claims of Kinfolk: African American Property and Community in the Nineteenth-Century South* (Chapel Hill: University of North Carolina Press, 2002), esp, Chapter 6, "Remaking Kinship and Community."

50 Susan Eva O'Donovan, *Becoming Free in the Cotton South* (Cambridge, MA, 2007) and Nancy Bercaw, *Gendered Freedoms: Race, Rights, and the Politics of Household in the Delta, 1861–1875* (Gainesville: University of Florida Press, 2003).

51 Schwalm, *A Hard Fight For We*, 66.

52 Brenda E. Stevenson, "Black Family Structure in Colonial and Antebellum Virginia: Amending the Revisionist Perspective," in *The Decline in Marriage Among African Americans: Causes, Consequences, and Policy Implications*, ed. M. Belinda Tucker and Claudia Mitchell-Kernan (New York: Russell Sage Foundation, 1995), 52. In addition, see various regional and state studies such as Damian Alan Pargas, *The Quarters and the Fields: Slave Families in the Non-Cotton South* (Gainesville: University Press of Florida,

2010); Ann Patton Malone, *Sweet Chariot: Slave Family and Household Structure in Nineteenth-Century Louisiana* (Chapel Hill: University of North Carolina Press, 1992); Wilma A. Dunaway, *The African-American Family in Slavery and Emancipation* (New York: Cambridge University Press, 2003); W. J. Megginson, *African American Life in South Carolina's Upper Piedmont, 1780–1900* (Columbia: University of South Carolina Press, 2006); Larry E. Hudson, Jr., *To Have and To Hold: Slave Work and Family Life in Antebellum South Carolina* (Athens: University of Georgia Press, 1997).

53 Naming patterns also reflected the patriarchal culture. Many more children were named after fathers, grandfather, uncles, than after mothers, grandmothers, aunts. Burton, *In My Father's House*, 166; Drew Gilpin Faust, *James Henry Hammond and the Old South: A Design for Mastery* (Baton Rouge: Louisiana State University Press, 1982), 83–84.

54 Susan Eva O'Donovan, *Becoming Free in the Cotton South* and Nancy Bercaw, *Gendered Freedoms,* in studies of Mississippi (Memphis area) and South Georgia, found as I did that planters were trying to strengthen black patriarchy because they preferred to deal with man who could contract labor of whole family (but also probably because they considered that the "right" structure); Burton, *In My Father's House*; Laura F. Edwards, *Gendered Strife and Confusion*, 145–83.

55 Patterson, *Rituals of Blood*, 27.

56 Penningroth, *The Claims of Kinfolk*; Burton, *In My Father's House*; Ford, *Deliver Us From Evil* chronicles the development of a paternalistic ethos that complements the classic account by Genovese, *Roll Jordon Roll.*

57 Jones, *Labor of Love*, 36.

58 Schwalm, *A Hard Fight For We*, 21.

59 Ibid., 54.

60 Patricia Hill Collins, *Black Feminist Thought*, 52.

61 Burton, *In My Father's House*, chapter 4.

62 Deborah G. White, "Female Slaves: Sex Roles and Status in the Antebellum Plantation South," in *Journal of Family History*, 8 (3) (Fall, 1983), 254.

63 Schwalm, *A Hard Fight for We,* 68–70.

64 *The Letters and Diary of Laura M. Towne, Written from the Sea Islands of South Carolina, 1862–1884*, ed. Rupert Sargent Holland (Salem: Higginson Book Company, 1912), Dec 18, 1864, 144, April 29, 1865, 161–62.

65 See esp., Burton, *In My Father's House,* "The Rise and Fall of Afro-American Town Life: Town and Country in Reconstruction Edgefield County, South Carolina," 152–92, Orville Vernon Burton and Robert C. McMath, Jr., eds, *Toward a New South? Studies in Post-Civil War Southern Communities* (Westport: Greenwood Press, 1982).

66 *Random House Compact Unabridged Dictionary*, special second edition (New York: Random House, 1996), 1422.

67 John T. Zadrozny, *Dictionary of Social Science* (Washington, S.C.: Public Affairs Press, 1959), 243.

68 Lerner, Gerda, *The Creation of Patriarchy* (New York: Oxford University Press, 1987), 238–9; Peter Bardaglio, *Reconstructing the Household: Families, Sex, & the Law in the Nineteenth-Century South* (Chapel Hill: University of North Carolina Press, 1995), 241, n 70.

69 *Ex parte Hewitt*, 11 Rich, 326 (S.C. 1858) 329; Bardaglio, *Reconstructing the Household*, 40.

70 Brenda Stevenson, "Slavery," in *Black Women in America: An Historical Encyclopedia* editor Darlene Clark Hine (New York: Carlson Publishing, 1993), 1045.

71 Jones, *Labor of Love*, 36, 13–14; on slave ownership of property, see Penningroth, *The Claims of Kinfolk.*

72 Testimony of Laura M. Towne [1863], filed with O-328 1863, Letters Received, Ser. 12, RG 94 [K-73], Papers of the Abandoned Lands and Freeman's Bureau, National Archives; see also Schwalm, 57.

73 White, "Female Slaves: Sex Roles and Status in the Antebellum Plantation South," 251.

74 Jones, *Labor of Love*, 32; On enslaved people owning property see Dylan C. Penningroth, *The Claims of Kinfolk: African American Property and Community in the Nineteenth-Century South* (Chapel Hill: University of North Carolina Press, 2002).

75 *Random House Compact Unabridged Dictionary*, 1186.

76 White, *Ar'n't I a Woman?* and "Female Slaves," 248–261. A short discussion of matrifocal families is in Kilbride, et al., *Street Children*, 5.

77 Daina Ramey Berry, *Swing the Sickle for the Harvest is Ripe: Gender and Slavery in Antebellum Georgia* (Urbana: University of Illinois Press, 2007), 52–59. V. Lynn Kennedy, *Born Southern: Childbirth, Motherhood, and Social Networks in the Old South* (Baltimore: The Johns Hopkins Press, 2010), Marie Schwartz, *Birthing a Slave: Motherhood and Medicine in the Antebellum South* (Cambridge: Cambridge University Press, 2006).

78 *Random House Compact Unabridged Dictionary*, 1186.

79 John T. Zadrozny, *Dictionary of Social Science* (Washington: Public Affairs Press, 1959), 201.

80 Burton, *In My Father's House*, 183–84; Paul D. Escott, *Slavery Remembered: A Record of Twentieth-Century Slave Narratives* (Chapel Hill: University of North Carolina Press, 1979), Tables 2.10 and 2.12, 56–57.

81 Judith N. McArthur and Orville Vernon Burton, *"A Gentleman and an Officer": A Social and Military History of James B. Griffin's Civil War* (New York: Oxford University Press, 1996), 278–79; see also Clarence Mohr, *On the Threshold of Freedom: Masters and Slaves in Civil War Georgia* (Baton Rouge: Louisiana State University Press, 2001).

82 Willie Lee Rose, *Rehearsal for Reconstruction: The Port Royal Experiment* (New York: Oxford University Press, 1964), 115, 105. This owner of Coffin Point on St. Helena Island, South Carolina, a 2000-acre plantation, was a Union sympathizer who advised his enslaved workers to remain on his abandoned land and grow food for themselves and not cotton for others.

83 Rose, *Rehearsal for Reconstruction*, 236, 265; Joel R. Williamson, *After Slavery: The Negro in South Carolina during Reconstruction, 1861–1877* (Chapel Hill: University of North Carolina Press, 1965) , 306–312; William S. McFeely, *Yankee Stepfather: General O.O. Howard and the Freedmen* (New Haven: Yale University Press, 1968), 131.

84 Bardaglio, *Reconstructing the Household*, 133.

85 Ibid, 148.

86 Mary Farmer-Kaiser, *Freedwomen and the Freedmen's Bureau: Race, Gender and Public*

Policy in the Age of Emancipation (New York: Fordham University Press, 2010); Edwards, *Gendered Strife and Confusion*, 145-83.

87   Of course, no one area, however large, is typical, even Edgefield, which was at least statistically representative of the piedmont. For discussion of whether Edgefield or any local study can be considered representative, see Orville Vernon Burton, "In My Father's House Are Many Leaders: Can the Extreme Be Typical?" *The Proceedings of the South Carolina Historical Association, 1987* (Aiken: The South Carolina Historical Association, 1988): 23–32. Also see the Introduction, esp. 4–7, to Burton, *In My Father's House.*

88   The 1870 manuscript census was the last to include the values of land ownership and personal property wealth.

89   See Megan J. McClintock, "Civil War Pensions and the Reconstruction of Union Families," *The Journal of American History* 83 (September 1996): 456–80, on African Americans, 472–75.

90   The values and living arrangements of African Americans in the United States need to be studied in a comparative context. For example, scholars suggest that blacks in the Caribbean and the West Indies, particularly Barbados, were much more matriarchal and tended to have significantly more illegitimate children than in the United States. Anthropologists conclude that in Jamaica, Barbados, and other West Indian societies illegitimacy, matrifocal families, concubinage, and cohabitation are socially approved. Thus, the comparative relative disapproval of these by black Americans suggests how much whites and African Americans in the United States share values. Edith Clarke, *My Mother Who Fathered Me* (London: Allen and Unwin, 1957), has an excellent although dated bibliographical guide. The comparison is confused by the argument in Gilbert Osofsky, *Harlem—the Making of A Ghetto: New York, 1890–1930* (New York: Harper and Row, 1966), 134, that whereas the native-born United States African American family in New York City was matriarchal and unstable, the black family of West Indian immigrants to New York was stable and decidedly patriarchal. It could be that immigration restrictions allowed only the wealthiest of West Indians to immigrate and hence, as in Edgefield, the wealthiest were most often male headed.

91   Silver Bluff Plantation Stock and Crop Book, in the Papers of James Henry Hammond, South Caroliniana Library, University of South Carolina, Columbia, S.C.

92   Big Stevens Creek Baptist Church Records, October 1819 in the Baptist Historical Collection, Furman University, Greenville, S.C. For divorce in South Carolina see Burton, *In My Father's House*, 11, 136–7, 157, 160, 166–67, 293–9, 316–17.

93   Currently, the incarceration of African American males influences the available marriageable pool. David Cole, *No Equal Justice: Race and Class in the American Criminal Justice System* (New York: The New Press, 1999). In 1995, one in three young black men between the ages of twenty and twenty-nine was incarcerated or on parole or probation (4); that rate is even higher today, see also Michelle Alexander, *The New Jim Crow: Mass Incarceration in the Age of Colorblindness* (New York: The New Press, 2010). Of the 2.3 million imprisoned today, 1 million are African American. "After Trayvon," *Time* (July 29, 2013), 33.

94   Gutman, *Black Family*, 73–79, 114–15, 117–18, 388–89, 556–57, explained the acceptance of slave illegitimacy. See Burton, *In My Father's House*, 148–190 for examples; Faust, *James Hammond*, 83–86.

95 George P. Rawick, ed. *The American Slave: A Composite Autobiography*, vol. 3: *South Carolina* (Westport, CT: Greenwood Press, 1972), pt. 3, 41.

96 For changing legal definitions of who controlled the crop and the meanings of tenantry, see Harold D. Woodman, *New South, New Law: The Legal Foundations of Credit and Labor Relations in the Postbellum Agricultural South* (Baton Rouge : Louisiana State University Press,1995); for South Carolina see Burton, "Race and Reconstruction," 31–56.

97 Roger Ransom and Richard Sutch, *One Kind of Freedom: The Economic Consequences of Emancipation* (Cambridge: Cambridge University Press, 1977). The definitive historical study of the era also assumes most African Americans became tenants, Eric Foner, *Reconstruction: America's Unfinished Revolution, 1863–1877* (New York: Harper and Row, 1988). For studies revising this idea see Burton, *In My Father's House* and "African American Status and Identity in a Postbellum Community: An Analysis of the Manuscript Census Returns," *Agricultural History* 72:2 (Spring 1998): 213–240; James R. Irwin, "Farmers and Laborers: A Note on Black Occupations in the Postbellum South," *Agricultural History* 64 (Winter 1990), and Irwin and Anthony Patrick O'Brien, "Where Have All the Sharecroppers Gone? Black Occupations in Postbellum Mississippi," *Agricultural History* 72:2 (Spring 1988):280–297; Robert Tracy McKenzie, *One South or Many? Plantation Belt and Upcountry in Civil War-Era Tennessee* (Cambridge: Cambridge University Press, 1994).

98 Mary Farmer-Kaiser, *Freedwomen and the Freedmen's Bureau: Race, Gender and Public Policy in the Age of Emancipation*; Edwards, *Gendered Strife and Confusion*, 145–83.

99 Burton, *In My Father's House*, chapter 7, esp. 262.

100 White wives were able to work in the segregated cotton mills. In 1870, nine white wives worked in the mills; in 1880, 158 did. Depression and hard times made a difference, as illustrated by wealth as a variable in Table 2. Poorer white women had to work far more than their wealthy peers.

101 Donna Franklin notes in *Ensuring Inequality: The Structural Transformation of the African-American Family* (New York: Oxford University Press, 1997) that it was the transition to Northern urban life that both made female labor more valuable and contributed to the apparent "chaos" of African American family life. See also Frank F. Furstenberg, Jr., Theodore Hershberg, and John Modell, "The Origins of the Female-Headed Black Family."

102 There were real differences between men's and women's work and responsibilities, but there were also areas of shared work and responsibilities. Evelyn Higginbotham, *Righteous Disconduct: The Women's Movement in the Black Baptist Church, 1880–1920* (Cambridge: Harvard University Press, 1993); Glenda Gilmore, *Gender and Jim Crow: Women and the Politics of White Supremacy in North Carolina, 1896–1920* (Chapel Hill: University of North Carolina, 1996); Elsa B. Brown, "Negotiating and Transforming the Public Sphere: African American Political Life in the Transition from Slavery to Freedom," *Public Culture* 7:1 (1994), 107–146.

103 *Edgefield Advertiser*, 12 January 1871; Harry Hammond, in U.S. Congress, House, *Report of the Industrial Commission on Agriculture and Agricultural Labor*, Document no. 179, 57th Cong., 2d Sess. (Washington: Government Printing Office, 1901), 816, 820; Ransom and Sutch, *One Kind of Freedom*.

104 Lou Falkner Williams, *The Great South Carolina Ku Klux Klan Trials, 1871–1872* (Ath-

ens: University of Georgia Press, 1996); for violence in Edgefield during this period see, Burton, "Race and Reconstruction."

105 Orville Vernon Burton, "The Rise and Fall of Afro-American Town Life: Town and Country in Reconstruction Edgefield County, South Carolina, " 152–92 in *Toward a New South? Studies in Post-Civil War Southern Communities*, edited by Orville Vernon Burton and Robert C. McMath, Jr. and Burton, *In My Father's House*, esp. 295–323.

106 William Julius Wilson, *When Work Disappears: The World of the New Urban Poor* (New York: Alfred A. Knopf, 1996), xiii. See also Wilson, *The Truly Disadvantaged: The Inner City, the Underclass, and Public Policy* (Chicago: University of Chicago Press, 1987).

107 Benjamin E. Mays, *Born to Rebel: An Autobiography*. "Foreword" by Orville Vernon Burton. (Athens: University of Georgia Press, rev. ed. 2003).

108 Despite Du Bois's pride in his black consciousness, he nevertheless had some elitist views of the African American family. Du Bois was born in Great Barrington, Massachusetts. Du Bois's own father had deserted the family when Du Bois was young; this was no doubt partly responsible for Du Bois's attitudes toward the African American family. Du Bois studied at Fisk University in Nashville, Harvard in Cambridge (where he received a BA, MA, and the PhD), and the University of Berlin and spent most of his academic career in large cities. Frazier was from Baltimore and had a strong father figure who died when the young Franklin was thirteen, after which his mother worked as a domestic. He attended Howard University in Washington and earned his PhD at the University of Chicago. Patterson "grew up in the market towns of Lionel town and May Pen, in Clarendon parish, Jamaica." *Rituals of Blood*, 288, note 55. Patterson received his BA at the University of West Indies and his PhD at the London School of Economics. He teaches at Harvard. Elliott M. Rudwick, *W. E. B. Du Bois: Propagandist of the Negro Protest* [orig 1968] (New York: Antheneum, 1969), 15; Rayford W. Logan and Michael R. Winston, eds., *Dictionary of American Negro Biography* (New York: W.W. Norton, 1982), 193–99, 241–44; Jack Salzman, et al., eds., *Encyclopedia of African-American Culture and History*, vol. 2 (New York: Simon and Schuster Macmillan, 1996), 807–9; Barbara C. Bigelow, ed., *Contemporary Black Biography*, (Detroit: Gale Research Inc., 1993), vol. 3 52–57 and vol. 4, 191–94; Jessie Carney Smith, ed., *Notable Black American Men* (Detroit: Gale Research Inc., 1999), 336–41, 428–31; L. M. Mabunda, ed., *Contemporary Black Biography*, vol. 10 (Detroit: Gale Research Inc., 1996), 63–67; Shirelle Phelps, ed., *Who's Who Among African Americans* 11th ed. (Detroit: Gale Research Inc., 1998), 1008.

109 W. E. B. Du Bois, *The Souls of Black Folk* (Chicago: A. C. McClurg & Co., 1903), chapter 4, "Of the Meaning of Progress," 60–74 (esp. 62–67).

110 Odum, *Social Traits*, 16; Testimony of Robert Smalls, 1863, American Freedmen's Inquiry Commission, Office of the Adjutant General, Letters Received, Main Series, 1861–1870, file 3, 108–109, Reel 200, National Archives; Sidney Andrews, *The South Since the War: As Shown by Fourteen Weeks of Travel and Observation in Georgia and the Carolinas* (Boston: Ticknor and Fields, 1866), 21–22.

111 Toni Morrison, *The Bluest Eye* (New York: Holt, Rinehart and Winston, 1970).

9

Turn Signals

Shifts in Values in Southern Life Writing

David Moltke-Hansen

In 1990, noted Southern historians Eugene Genovese and Elizabeth Fox-Genovese led in the creation of the St. George Tucker Society, a small, interdisciplinary Southern Studies group. The Society's founding principle was to foster frank but civil discourse across the spectrum of disciplinary and ideological perspectives that Southernists bring to bear on their work. In 2006 this organization gave its early August annual meeting over to a conference co-chaired by Sheldon Hackney. The topic was the relationship of two Souths—those of Tom Watson, the Georgia Populist leader, and C. Vann Woodward, Watson's most famous biographer and Hackney's dissertation director.[1]

The conference had taken a dozen years to arrange. At first, it was planned for 1998, in honor of the 60th anniversary of the publication of the Watson biography. Because Woodward initially welcomed the idea, Watson's great-grandson, Tom Watson Brown, personally gave the necessary funding. But then Woodward decided that he was too uncomfortable with the focus on a man whose memory still angered him immensely. "You'll have to wait until I am dead," he said. Brown was willing to wait, but it was not until seven years after Woodward's death that the meeting finally took place.[2]

About the same time as the conference idea first came up, Woodward and Genovese had an exchange at another Tucker meeting that is famous in the annals of the Society. The vigorous expression of views and the interaction of personalities were memorable, although the points of contention are now lost to view. Watson, of course, was also a slashing exponent of his views.

And, like Woodward and Genovese, as well as Fox-Genovese and Hackney, he used biography to frame or probe issues important to him. One way to consider these writers in relation to each other, therefore, is to see them in the context of the history of Southern life writing.

LIVES WITH A PURPOSE

That history begins in the century after Columbus first made landfall in the Caribbean. It was at the end of that period that William Shakespeare indelibly stamped the character of King Richard III, the last of the Plantagenet monarchs. One of his early history plays fixed the king's later interpretation even among those who understood that Shakespeare of necessity wrote with *malice prepense* on behalf of courtiers serving the successor royal house of Tudor.[3] The distance is great between Richard, King of England, and Tom Watson, the American Populist Party leader who first rose to prominence three centuries after Shakespeare wrote *Richard III*. Yet the two had something important in common. In each case, a single author defined what his subject's life would mean for generations. Shakespeare did it to Richard. Woodward wrote the defining work on Watson. He did so despite the fact that he disliked his subject intensely. "I hate the son-of-a-bitch," Woodward said in a private conversation almost sixty years after the book's publication. The reasons why, in effect, structured the life he wrote—a life told to a purpose.[4]

The telling of lives to a purpose has a long tradition in Watson's and Woodward's American South, although naturally not only there. In the centuries since Shakespeare, different patterns and priorities have shaped those purposes. This is true across genres, including autobiography, biography, diary, and memoir. Journalists, eulogists, oral historians, and others also have rendered lives. The history of purposeful life-telling antedates European conquest, of course. In published form, however, it stretches in the region eventually called the South from the explorations and conflicts of European conquerors and colonizers of the 16th century and runs up through the civil rights struggles of the 1960s to the more recent experiences of new immigrants and survivors of Hurricane Katrina.

The earliest written life narratives with a Southern setting were composed by European explorers and missionaries. They bore the imprint of the Wars of Religion, imperial conflicts, and the pursuit of gold, fame, and Christian converts. Richard Hakluyt—Shakespeare's younger contemporary—translated

René de Laudonnière's *A Notable Historie Containing Foure Voyages Made by Certayne French Captaynes into Florida* (1587) and Ferdinando de Soto's *Virginia Richly Valued, by the Description of the Maine Land of Florida, Her Next Neighbour* (1609). He also compiled accounts of *Divers Voyages Touching the Discoveries of America* (1582) and of *The Principal Navigations, Voyages, Traffiques and Discoveries of the English Nation* (1598–1600). John Smith's *A True Relation of Such Occurrences and Accidents of Note as Hapned in Virginia Since the First Planting of that Colony . . .* appeared in 1608. The lives of the men in such narratives were conducted, conveyed, and cut short very differently than those of colonials who later participated in more settled conditions, while nevertheless ritually invoking the horrors of Indian captivity, the depredations of pirates, or the wild rudeness of the colonies. Since its publication in 1841, no colonial Southern accounts have been better known than those found in William Byrd II's *Westover Manuscripts*, which included *The History of the Dividing Line Betwixt Virginia and North Carolina.*[5]

The American War for Independence gave rise to a new kind of life and life writing—that of supporters or resisters of the Revolution from Britain. In the war's wake, those lives became sites where writers could explore the implications of patriotism, progress, and civic engagement. The American Civil War posed anew the question of the consequences of wartime commitments and conditions. Different answers eventually shaped the narratives of former Confederates' and freedmen's lives. In the interval, Reconstruction rewrote the meaning of citizenship, race, and civil rights.

Thereafter, new or newly charged struggles emerged, resulting in divergent, sometimes conflicting, reform impulses and leaders. In the midst of this welter of ideological and emotional confrontation, writers turned to the lives of precursors and movement figures—different sorts of warriors in different sorts of revolutionary action. Scholars—the products of new graduate programs in history, political science, and literature—joined popular writers in the 1880s. The volume of scholarship increased exponentially thereafter. In the wake of the growing civil rights, labor, women's rights, and other reform movements, so did the number of Southern life accounts.

Students of these matters have brought to bear contrasting views about life writing, its examination, and its uses. Consider four Southern historians who became influential in the latter half of the 20th century, thus more than 60 years after the first scholars of the South began to write. Although nearly a quarter of a century apart, the elder—C. Vann Woodward and Eugene Genovese—came to share recognition, over the third of a century in which they both published books, as arguably the most important historians of the 19th-century South. The other two scholars were much closer in age, having been born within a couple of years of each other during the Second World War. Elizabeth Fox-Genovese began to collaborate with her husband, Eugene Genovese, in the late 1960s and became a noted historian of the planter class and of black and white Southern women and their writings. She also earned a reputation as a controversial interlocutor in feminist discourses. Sheldon Hackney went on from his studies with Vann Woodward to be a university president and then chairman of the National Endowment for the Humanities—serving under his friend, President Bill Clinton—before returning to full-time teaching and writing.

These four repeatedly used biography in their scholarship and wrote memoirs, but they did so with different attitudes and to divergent ends. The spectra of attitudes and ends are suggested in part by the papers that they left and in part by their published writings. Genovese destroyed or intentionally did not keep many of his papers. Still, he left research files and a draft manuscript book at his death. Portions of his outgoing correspondence, as well as copies of some letters to him, can be found in the papers of such contemporaries as Woodward. There are as well some amusing letters by him in his wife's papers. Except perhaps in university presidential records and the papers of Christopher Lasch, memoranda and other communications by Genovese apparently are not yet available in the University Archives and the Rare Books and Special Collections Department of the University of Rochester, where he chaired the History Department. They do show up in the records of the Organization of American Historians, which he served as president.[6]

Woodward in his turn led several scholarly organizations in the course of his career and kept voluminous papers. Yet he did not generate many university administrative records, as he resisted appointments that would have taken him from his writing. He also apparently excised certain, more personal materials, reticent as he was about private emotions and troubles. Fox-Genovese, by contrast, left extraordinarily rich, personal—even intimate—documentation. There also are numerous collections relating to the Institute for Women's Studies that she created at Emory University, although the online finding aid does not suggest a significant presence by her in them. Hackney's administrative papers necessarily are scattered among the institutions he led, and his personal papers are not yet available.

The memoirs that these four wrote add dimension, but not clarity, to their views of life writing. Genovese's candid and affectionate account of his wife and their life together clearly is about more than the cooking they learned to share, the baseball they watched avidly, and the children they regretted not having. In a sense, it is critically about their shift from Marxism to Roman Catholicism in the face of their persistent and principled animus against liberalism.[7] Despite (or, perhaps, because of) her extended and incisive historical treatment of autobiography as a genre and her training as a Freudian psychoanalyst, Fox-Genovese only published a couple of article-length autobiographical pieces, these on her conversion to Roman Catholicism. Elsewhere, the occasional aside about her life is all that appeared in print before her death. Since then, her selected religious meditations have been edited and published, and her biographer is drawing on her earlier journals.[8] Woodward in his turn reflected in a collection of invited lectures on the changes in the writing of Southern history over his lifetime. In doing so, he assessed the influence of, and debates with, his principal theses. These contentions included the centrality of race, class conflict, and discontinuities in Southern history.[9]

Hackney wrote about the politics of the cultural wars that he endured in the confirmation process as nominee for the post of chairman of the National Endowment for the Humanities. Later, as his daughter was dying of pancreatic cancer, he shared many wrenching e-mail letters detailing the process over sixteen months. These became the basis of a book. Yet even in the case of these deeply personal notes that helped bind and inform the support community around Virginia Hackney, he was not really writing a conventional life narrative.[10] Although it may be true that "a growing number of historians have also become autobiographers," he and the three other Southernists considered here were more intent on using episodes in their lives to reflect on subjects and people important to them. Except Fox-Genovese, they all sought as well to address their critics.[11]

Whether ethical or aesthetic, this common sense of the limits and purposes of the academic memoir contrasts with the very different approaches that the four scholars took to the treatment of the lives of their historical subjects. Each found lives telling and used them to examine issues and dynamics important to their historical studies. Yet, despite their shared interest in ideology, these historians chose widely varying subjects. They differed not so much in chronology and place as in focus and rationale.

Woodward's first book was his Watson biography. This study of the Georgia Populist leader's ultimate failure as a political reformer concluded with the resulting frustration that Watson felt and how he lashed out against African Americans, Jews, and the Roman Catholic Church. Woodward won his Pulitzer Prize, though, for his edition, and the attendant framing and analysis, of the Civil War diaries of Mary Boykin Chesnut. Chesnut was the daughter and wife of elite South Carolina planters. Famously, too, she was an intriguing combination of sharp observation, style, and wit, as well as what Woodward termed "heretical" opinions on slavery and women. Recorded at the political and social epicenter of the Confederacy, where her husband was an aide to President Jefferson Davis, her wartime life and reflections make vivid the new nation's rise and fall.[12]

Many of Genovese's essays also sprang from consideration of particular Southern writers (or writers on the South) and their views. Despite his attention to slaves and slavery, most of the authors on whom Genovese wrote essays were white men. A number came out of, and addressed, the antebellum Southern master class. They were generally not belletrists, but ministers, lawyers, politicians, and writers of treatises. Others, some of them literary, were self-declared conservative heirs of that era and world. Still others were scholars who intervened trenchantly in the study of slavery or Southern plantations, thought, and society.[13]

Fox-Genovese treated individual writers and their works as well. Indeed, her predisposition was strongly biographical. Her dissertation and first book considered a group of French economic reformers and their thought before the French Revolution. Later, her subjects were more likely to be belletrists or diarists, most often white or black Southern women, who wrote between the 1830s and the last quarter of the 20th century. She also used conversations with contemporary women informants to shape rhetorically her books on feminism.[14] Together with her husband, she developed as well composite portraits of the antebellum Southern master class when fleshing out the worldview of the great majority of that class who did not publish.[15]

Initially Hackney was more prosopographical in his approach. Following his first book on Populists and progressives in Alabama, however, he increasingly turned to individual liberal figures important to him over his lifetime.

Not surprisingly, given his administrative roles, this was primarily in essays, many gathered in his 2005 collection, *Magnolias Without Moonlight: The American South from Regional Confederacy to National Integration*. In these pieces he ranged from his mentor Vann Woodward to his fellow Alabamian and one-time uncle-in-law, Hugo Black, the former Ku Klux Klansman who became an influential and long-serving U.S. Supreme Court Justice.[16]

The agendas shaping these investigations have ranged widely as well. Reform-minded, the young Woodward sought to understand the failure of Populism's promise. While feeding his sense of irony and appreciation of artful writing, Chesnut offered him the chance late in life to examine the collapse of slavery and the subsequent emergence of the world that produced the post-Reconstruction race and class struggles that had occupied his scholarship for half a century. In the intervening years, Woodward increasingly came to be seen, not as a radical any longer, but as an ever-more conservative old liberal and scion of progressivism. Yet, even when he shared the radical label with Genovese in the early 1960s, he was clearly a different sort.[17]

Genovese never saw the world through liberal-tinted spectacles—spectacles he refused to wear. Neither did he consider the struggles that he studied to be defined by discontinuities between the colonial and antebellum or the antebellum and postbellum South. Historical materialism, through the creation of a modern slave regime, may have resulted in the South's development as a society and culture distinct from the North, where industrial capitalism was increasingly the shaping force. Yet slavery's end did not mean the South's disappearance. Instead, Genovese argued for continuities that emerged out of the antebellum clash between capitalism and slavery. This clash of worldviews continued, he insisted, past slavery's end. That was why he focused not only on Southern proponents of slavery, but also on Southern critics of capitalism, including a few who wrote in the 20th century. Yet, he did not consider Tom Watson and his ilk, despite *their* critiques of capitalism.[18]

As a Harvard graduate student, Fox-Genovese began her own investigation of the pre-conditions for capitalism's and modern slavery's development, though in France. Yet, within a dozen years she shifted to the study of women in the Southern past. In particular, she considered the marginalized who too often had no recognized historical voice or presence. She also focused on especially articulate, as well as elite, women; they left the compelling writings and rich records that invited layered analysis. To these preoccupations she added engagement with the challenges facing women, and the role of second wave feminism, in contemporary America. In doing so, she did not lose her focus on the influence of class and race and the consequences of power inequalities in social relations and thought. This was because she wanted to understand women in history, not women apart sharing elements of a feminine culture of their own.[19]

Hackney's approach has been different. Committed to liberal reform, like Woodward, he has persistently asked how and why Southern reformers emerged and with what consequences. He has done so while at the same time exploring the characteristics of Southern society and culture that continue to make life in the region distinctive. Finally, he has reflected on ways of understanding the South and reform there. He began by distinguishing between the reform impulses moving first Populists and then progressives in Alabama. Since, he has focused on those who came later and represented strains of liberalism and the struggles for civil rights.

Obviously, more has shaped these choices than "elective affinities," as Johann Wolfgang von Goethe called them, borrowing a concept from 18th-century chemistry. He used the phrase as the title of his third novel, sometimes translated instead as *Kindred by Choice*. A classic German *novelle*, this 1809 story explores the tension between marital choice and natural attraction. The chemical reference suggests that there is equivalence between, on the one hand, selective responses to emotional attraction and, on the other hand, the interaction of certain chemicals under particular conditions.[20] To choose is not the same as to be attracted: witness Woodward's selection of Watson as a subject despite his profound dislike of the man. Yet choice does not explain adequately why and how historians write on the subjects they select. Elements of their engagement are determined instead by when and where they write and to what purposes.

Two periods of change in Southern life writing illustrate this point. One is the second third of the 19th century. It was then that the meaning and nature of revolutionary patriotism became a subject of contention and dueling life-telling. The other period unfolded as the Confederate model of patriotism and white solidarity began to be replaced in the South by preoccupations with social conflict and change. Reformers such as Tom Watson resisted capitalism's growing sway. Populists insisted, too, that they were preserving abiding agrarian values. Progressives instead wanted to ameliorate capitalism's influence by improving working and living conditions. Others saw themselves fighting on behalf of minority or women's rights. These last often hoped for fundamental economic, social, and cultural change.

Ever since, these divergent strands of reform and conflict have engaged scholars. They have used studies of reformers to access and assess the issues that galvanized the reformers. Woodward and Hackney represent different generations in that study. For his part, Genovese sought to look behind the reformers to the forces shaping their world and the hegemonic culture that they at once resisted and participated in. Fox-Genovese added to that preoccupation her acute attention to neglected historical actors, especially women. In this she was following Genovese's powerful recovery of slave voices in his *Roll, Jordan, Roll* and other books. The distances among these writers on Southern lives are considerable even in the face of the sympathies binding Woodward and Hackney or Genovese and Fox-Genovese. Yet the understandings separating these four historians and the life writers of a century-and-a-half earlier are much larger. One way to help put in perspective later 20th-century biographical scholarship is to consider in more detail the changes in motives and preoccupations informing Southern life writing in the interval.

THE TRANSFORMATION OF PATRIOTISM

Members of America's Revolutionary generation wrote memoirs or otherwise shared reminiscences of the War for Independence in growing profusion over the first quarter of the 19th century. The same years saw a swelling hagiographic library treating the lives and characters of Revolutionary leaders. No one contributed more influentially or inventively than Mason Locke "Parson" Weems. He famously was the author, in 1800, of a mythically hued biography of George Washington. In the so-called fifth edition of 1806, he had the recently deceased president confess that, when a boy, he had cut down a cherry tree. Behind the story was the classical understanding that history in general and biography in particular should teach morality—in this case, truthfulness. The further inference was that patriotism was an ethical commitment, and patriots were—or should be—virtuous. If creative license were necessary to bring home the moral, so be it.[21]

Not all writers of patriotic lives shared Weems's preoccupation. Timothy Flint continued the tradition of inventive life telling but to different purposes. True, his accounts of escapes and fights in his 1833 biography of Daniel Boone seem to have gone beyond the record: he even had Boone swing Tarzan-like on a vine. Yet, in Flint's version, Boone served to highlight additional qualities besides those of patriotic virtue. A Revolutionary hero, he also ranked as a quintessential American because of his standing as frontiersman extraordinaire. More, Flint insisted, Boone was a harbinger of civilization's westward spread. His life, then, was about the country's promise and future and not just America's heroic birth and character.[22]

The melding of patriotism, Americanism, and progress continued apace. These intertwined preoccupations defined the priorities of a New York-centered circle of writers who became self-identified as Young America after the fashion of romantic European nationalist organizations. Edgar Allan Poe, Nathaniel Hawthorne, and Herman Melville, as well as George Bancroft, James Fenimore Cooper, and William Gilmore Simms were some of the authors recruited by John L. O'Sullivan and Evert Augustus Duyckinck to publish in Young America journals and book series. Mostly Democratic, the group espoused manifest destiny and nationalist revolutions in addition to what an Alabama writer of the day, Alexander B. Meek, called "Americanism in Literature." Generally pro-slavery, their publications nevertheless occasionally featured Whigs and abolitionists such as John Greenleaf Whittier.[23]

That fissure in the unifying presuppositions and commitments of the movement foreshadowed a growing conflict. As abolitionism acquired public resonance, the definitions of patriotism, Americanism, and progress shifted in the North to include opposition to slavery and, eventually, condemnation of slaveholders among the founding fathers. A forceful statement of the shift was that of a former slave, Frederick Douglass. Seventy-six years after the Declaration of Independence, he plaintively asked of a white anti-slavery audience: "What, to the American slave, is your 4th of July?" The answer: "a day that reveals to him [the slave], more than all other days in the year, the gross injustice and cruelty to which he is the constant victim." Douglass acknowledged that the signers of the Declaration were brave and also great. Yet he held that "the rich inheritance of justice, liberty, prosperity and independence" was an affront because not equally shared.[24]

Many Northerners and most white Southerners did not agree even in 1852. Five years later the U.S. Supreme Court held, in its infamous *Dred Scott* decision, that African Americans could not be citizens of the United States. Rather than settle the matter, the determination fueled accelerating

battles in a spreading cultural war. Among them were the increasingly sharp
conflicts over the changing meaning of patriotism and patriotic virtues. A
principal site of these was in biographies of Revolutionary-era figures. The
fact was highlighted in an attack in the U.S. Senate. In an 1856 speech on
slavery in Bloody Kansas, delivered on May 19 and 20, Charles Sumner took
his dismissal of Southern patriotism during the Revolution to the Senate floor.
There, on May 22, Congressman Preston Brooks of South Carolina caned
him at his desk. This was just after the close of business. The senator had been
preparing copies of his speech for the mails.[25]

In scathing tone, the speech drew on the massive study of *The American
Loyalists* by New Englander Lorenzo Sabine. When Sabine initially published
his *Biographical Sketches of Adherents to the British Crown in the War of the
Revolution* in the *North American Review*, many Northerners were unhappy at
what they regarded as an unnecessary and inappropriate darkening of patriotic
memories. Yet after the appearance of the resulting book in 1847, the work
became fodder for political one-upmanship. Sabine's "Preliminary Historical
Essay," backed by his sketches, was the authority for Sumner's contention
that South Carolina had been home to so many loyalists in the Revolution
that New Englanders had had to prosecute the patriot cause there. In short,
Sumner contended, New Englanders had been and still were true patriots,
unlike the Carolinians.[26]

Nine years before, U.S. Senator Daniel Webster, in his perpetual presidential campaign, managed to laud his fellow New Englanders without
overtly damning the Carolinians. This was in speeches shortly after the Sabine
volume appeared. He delivered them to the New England Society and the
Bar of Charleston. Addressing those audiences, he focused on the patriotic
fervor that led many New Englanders to come to South Carolina during the
Revolution. As he proudly agreed, there they fought and died together with
their Southern compatriots, uniting their country through the mingling of
their spilt blood.[27]

Presumably having read the full local press accounts, William Gilmore
Simms, the sometime Charleston member of the Young America circle, was
indignant at Webster's (and, later, Sabine's) claims. New Englanders, he insisted,
had not marched to the aid of their fellow countrymen in large numbers. He
may never have made the point to Webster, who died in 1852, but he wrote
Sabine in 1856 to correct him. The South, Simms noted, was where most of

the fighting in the war occurred; yet most New England soldiers were home patriots, only serving in their region. Moreover, it was local South Carolina paramilitary forces that kept alive the patriot cause, again and again saving the Continental Army, which was under the command of New England generals.[28]

Simms also averred that Sabine's errors had had awful consequences. The New Englander's unsupported assertions about the conduct of Carolinians in the Revolution had fueled the intemperate accusations that led to the entirely justified caning of Charles Sumner. It had been insufferable that the Carolinians, who had sacrificed more in the Revolution than any other population, should have been maligned so—and by someone with such poisonous, abolitionist views. After all, the loyalists in the state, under color of fighting on behalf of the Crown, had come from as far as Florida and New York to maraud and pillage. Yet, in the face of their bloody predations, the complete defeat of the Continental Army in the state, and the British seizure of all of South Carolina's fortifications, the patriot paramilitary forces of Francis Marion, Thomas Sumter, Andrew Pickens, and others fought on, giving Congress time to raise another army—an army that the paramilitary forces rescued repeatedly as well.

No Southerner was more qualified than Simms to speak to the history of the Revolution in South Carolina. Since his boyhood in Charleston, he had avidly read on the subject. He also had explored area battlefields and other war-related sites. Inspiring him were his grandmother's tales of his great-grandfather's and grandfather's service and his own conversations with veterans. Long after the last soldier was buried, he still sought information from locals. Even in the midst of the Civil War he was writing to potential informants.[29]

Simms's first separate publication, which appeared in 1825, when he was 19, was *Monody, on the Death of General Charles Cotesworth Pinckney*. The recently deceased Revolutionary hero, delegate to the U.S. Constitutional Convention, and two-time Federalist presidential candidate from Charleston, had been a prisoner of war in British Florida with Simms's great-grandfather—this after the fall of Charleston in 1780. Simms's neo-classical poetic celebration of the patriot praised both the struggle for freedom of oppressed peoples and the exemplary hero, "in this case, the model citizen and lawyer, soldier and statesman, noted for his service to his people and place."[30]

Over the next 30 years, Simms wrote seven Revolutionary romances—prose epics in the manner of Sir Walter Scott—set in South Carolina. He also wrote or edited a dozen biographies—several of them book-length—of Revolutionary generals who served in or came from the South. Measured by sales, perhaps his most successful Revolution-related work was his 1844 biography of Francis Marion, the Swamp Fox, who also was a figure in a number of his romances. His research for the volume was the fruit of more than two decades. In the interval, however, his reasons for writing had begun to change.[31]

When planning the first of his Revolutionary romances ten years after Pinckney's death, Simms focused on asserting South Carolina's role in the making of the nation. This commitment flowed naturally from his stand as a Unionist. Over the previous several years, he had resisted South Carolina's efforts to nullify the federal tariff unilaterally and for his pains had been mobbed and seen his newspaper fail. The experience taught him that "the excesses of patriotism, when attaining power, have been but too frequently the product of a tyranny more dangerous in its exercise, and more lasting in its effects, than the despotism which it was invoked to overthrow." By concentrating in his romance series on "That atrocious and reckless warfare between the whigs and the tories, which had deluged the fair plains of Carolina with native blood," he in effect was urging the unity that the peace after the war eventually accomplished, if only provisionally. He also was showing what South Carolinians had had to overcome on behalf of their future country.[32]

Hoping to teach his children (one of them in boarding school in New England), as well as other young South Carolinians, about this legacy, Simms published *The History of South Carolina* in Charleston in 1840. It focused on the Revolution. He extended his audience for the topic with his Marion biography, published in New York. It was gratifying that in response the country further elevated the Swamp Fox as a national hero. This was especially so, as Parson Weems's earlier Marion biography was a less substantial and less historically sound work, one that had frustrated his chief informant, an officer who had served under Marion.

Yet Northern opinion was changing at an accelerating rate. Simms rhetorically asked a July 4, 1844, audience in Aiken, South Carolina: "Do they [the people of the North] not hourly encroach upon our rights, insult our pride and denounce our institutions?" It infuriated him, too, that Southerners inadvertently fed this growing Northern denigration of the South's ardor in the Revolution. In 1845–46 he attacked (initially, unknowingly) Ann Pamela Cunningham, daughter of a one-time law partner of John C. Calhoun, for her treatment of her loyalist ancestors in South Carolina. He did so first in a review of a volume to which she had anonymously contributed biographies of these men and then in his own biographical sketches of Bloody Bill Cunningham and others. He also found himself excoriating Maryland novelist John Pendleton Kennedy's fictional portrayals of the British occupation of South Carolina. Continuing his counter-offensive, in 1853 he gathered several essays under the title *South-Carolina in the Revolutionary War: Being a Reply to Certain Misrepresentations and Mistakes of Recent Writers, in Relation to the Course and Conduct of This State*. Then, in the fall of 1856, he took the campaign north, on a lecture tour. His passion repelled rather than converted his initially packed audiences, and he cut the tour short.[33]

This brief tactical history of the antebellum deployment of Southern Revolutionaries hides a different and equally portentous shift. Early writers on Revolutionary warriors framed the conflict as a matter of political and moral principle. The rights of freeborn Englishmen had been trampled upon and were reclaimed through the Revolution. Simms presented a different case in his July 4, 1844, oration and elsewhere. The War for Independence "was a revolt of the native mind of the country." "The educated and wealthy classes" sought to emancipate themselves when they felt able to stand on their own feet. They judged that "the domestic genius [was] eager for employment . . . and restive under the foreign domination." Therefore, despite the indifference or hostility of the lower classes, they led the colonies out of the Empire, propelled by the British refusal to acknowledge their right to self-governance and full citizenship.[34]

Simms considered this example of leadership paradigmatic. He modeled his behavior accordingly. In the summer of 1847, therefore, he decided to join the vanguard of the future Southern revolution. It was then that he started urging, not just predicting the possibility of, secession. His argument was ethnogenesis: Americans had become a people, although incompletely, and white Southerners were becoming one in their turn. Once again, moreover, "the educated and wealthy classes" should lead.[35]

Timothy Flint had cast Daniel Boone as not just a representative American but the epitome of aspects of his country and people. Simms began to see his Revolutionary and other regional heroes as representative and epitomic Southerners. What he intentionally did not do was prettify them. Already in 1836, he insisted, in the face of criticism of the bloodiness and crudeness of some of his fictional characters, that his "object usually [was] to adhere, as closely as possible, to the features and the attributes of real life." Fifteen years later he was marrying social realism to his romance formula and having his chief protagonists overcome deep flaws in themselves in order to succeed. He also lauded Elizabeth Ellet's recovery of social history in her compendium of biographical sketches of *The Women of the American Revolution*. In his view, the home, the farm, and daily life were at the heart of a people's history, although war was "the greatest element of civilization," making peoples, men, and manners.[36]

By identifying Southerners as a rising people and also identifying them historically with their homes and farms, Simms was laying part of the conceptual framework for the Southern History that Vann Woodward, Gene Genovese, Betsey Fox-Genovese, and Sheldon Hackney came to write a century later. His South was not theirs, of course, but his Southerners made Southern identity matter. When Woodward wrote about the difference between the two Souths, he was emphasizing how far from the Old South was the New. When Genovese and Fox-Genovese wrote about the cultural and ideological continuities binding Southerners of different eras, they were suggesting that origins and identity—community values and commitment— matter. Material conditions and worldviews change at different rates. That is how societies stick together through upheaval.

After the Civil War, Simms made a similar argument. In a speech shortly before his death in 1870, he told the Ladies Horticultural Society in Charleston that the past was a bulwark against Yankee influences. He urged the importance of the values of that past for the future health of Southern society and culture, which otherwise would be overwhelmed by soul-stealing capitalism. He did not contend, however, that the past was in any sense ideal. Rather, he insisted that it had fostered cultural values that developed in conscious opposition to materialism and that could protect Southerners from national excesses into the future. The true patriot would adhere to those ideals in the face of the country's addiction to alien and alienating influences.[37]

THE REORIENTATION OF SOUTHERN BIOGRAPHY

In his further writing on the Revolution, during and after the Civil War, Simms moved from social toward psychological realism. The broader movement in the South, however, was toward eulogy. As after the Revolution, the overwhelming inclination in life writing was to remember and honor the dead and those who survived. Given their cause, these men were heroic by definition. No eulogist was more classically eloquent than Charlestonian William Henry Trescot, America's first diplomatic historian and Acting United States Secretary of State in 1860. Before the war, it was he, not John C. Calhoun, who truly was, in Richard Hofstadter's phrase, "the Marx of the master class." When writing to influence as well as memorialize men after the Civil War, he continued his analysis of the interplay of class and race, as well as the other contestations shaping interest politics. His vision was not that of the Lost Cause school that, through the eulogistic impulse, transformed the Southern past into a collective, mythic memory of once halcyon and then heroic days.[38]

The Lost Cause ideology distorted life writing in other ways. It focused attention on the Civil War generation, while scanting earlier ones. It also focused on certain populations, while scanting others. In reality, therefore, the Southern Historical Society, founded in 1868–69, should have been called the Confederate Historical Society. The 52 volumes of its *Papers*, begun in 1876, dealt almost entirely with wartime experiences and memories.[39]

Excluded from those pages were the roughly 50 percent of Southerners who did not support the Confederate cause. Among them were the overwhelming majority of the more than four million African Americans in the region and also the smaller majority of the more than 2.5 million whites in the Border States. In addition, there were diehard unionists and anti-Confederates among whites in every Confederate state. Despite their cumulative numbers, these populations were progressively eliminated from public memory in the wake of the retaking of state governments by former Confederates. This erasure meant that they were not part of the history that most whites acknowledged. Retrospectively, they became nonpersons—people without pasts that mattered.[40]

Another example of the Lost Cause's power of distortion is *The Library of Southern Literature*, completed in 1909 under the editorship of many of the then leading Southern men of letters and other prominent cultural figures. It provided biographies and selected writings of 274 individual authors and orators in its first 13 volumes. Of the 261 for whom even approximate dates were given, less than a third—85—were colonial, Revolutionary, or antebellum figures. Yet they represented the first 250 years of Southern letters. Ninety-six—35 percent—were from the Civil War generation, and 80 (29 percent) were born too late to fight. Together, they represented authorship in the last three-quarters of a century, overlapping with the previous generation in the earlier years. None was Native American, African American, or drawn from Spanish or French chapters in the South's history. None had fought for the Union during the Civil War. The Lost Cause myth had no room for such. Women were given some space, but not much.[41]

The Library was radically different from the one Simms proposed during the Civil War. That was to have supplied biographies on, and selected writings of, individual noted writers—one volume per author. Together, these collections would have emphasized political thought, from the mid-19th century back to the colonial era. Too few Southerners, Simms believed, knew this heritage. He wanted to arm his countrymen with the intellectual antecedents and arguments for Southern independence.[42]

The Lost Cause myth assumed those antecedents and arguments rather than highlighted them. Its rationale and function were different. The hegemonic force of this exclusionary, eulogistic culture was powerful. Largely the domain of Democrats, it was a political instrument: it not only told which lives mattered, but how. Like the patriot hagiographies after the Revolution, too, it emphasized the instructional and community value of life writings rather than any divisions and discontents that biographies could reveal.[43]

Several factors caused a shift away from the writing of former Confederates' lives, as earlier they caused a shift in the writing of patriots' lives. One was simply generational change. Veterans wrote about the Civil War and warriors. After the war, their wives and sisters also contributed to such compendia as *Our Women in the War*. Of necessity, however, their children could only write of the war either through the reports of others and from research in written documents or from a child's memories and perspective. They had neither the authority of the experience nor the range of recall of their elders.[44]

No more did the children and grandchildren of the Revolution. Yes, Simms sat at his grandmother's feet, listening to her reminiscences, and Ellet gleaned enough to compile *The Women of the American Revolution* at about the same time as Sabine wrote his lives of American loyalists, two-thirds of a century after the end of the conflict. Yet the outpouring of life writing by the Revolutionaries themselves had been decades earlier. It was different in the 1880s and '90s—indeed, into the 1910s. Then veterans still commanded the field. Their children could not compete.

There were additional reasons for the next generation to look beyond the war for biographical subjects and approaches. In contrast to the patriotic harmonies used by Lost Cause writers, what many children of the war encountered and knew instead were dissonances. Perhaps the majority chose, as best they could, not to hear the discords, but others could not help it. As Tom Watson learned firsthand, there was terrible sadness in the home lives of wounded and broken veterans. For many, like Watson's father, the war's consequences constricted life rather than ennobled it. The shame of lost status and capacity to care for one's family undermined manhood and honor, so self-identity and self-worth. Because immiseration was the lot of a much higher percentage of the population after the Civil War than after the Revolution, this was an issue that had much greater social and cultural impact in Reconstruction than it had had in the years around the ratification of the U.S. Constitution. Watson, like many other children of the 1860s and '70s, grew up with it.[45]

The defeat and despair were not just personal; they were region-wide. Rather than emulating their Revolutionary ancestors, as secessionists claimed, the Confederates had failed them. Noble victors, such as the patriots in the War for Independence, were easier to celebrate than their defeated heirs. These latter could be honored but not given laurels. Those who wanted to use life writing to inform a better future, therefore, went beyond eulogizing fallen or former Confederates and reminiscing about the war. Three brief examples serve—one progressive, one Populist, and one African American. The futures they envisioned or assumed were radically different from one another. Yet, having been born in the dozen years between 1856 and 1868, the three were all of the same generation. Two were trained as scholars—the first generation to study the South with such educations—and worked as academics. One was a lawyer, politician, and journalist. All wrote enormously and influentially.

The progressive was William Peterfield Trent, scion of one of the First Families of Virginia. Born in 1862—too late to "recollect ever seeing a slave"—he attended the University of Virginia at the same time as Woodrow Wilson, the future U.S. president, and then the Johns Hopkins University, where Wilson had finished and was teaching. Trent wrote on and taught both American history and literature and English literature, first at the University of the South and then at Columbia University. Three of his many volumes treated Southerners—an 1892 life of Simms, the 1897 *Southern Statesmen of the Old Regime: Washington, Jefferson, Randolph, Calhoun, Stephens, Toombs, and Jefferson Davis* (dedicated to Trent's friend Theodore Roosevelt), and an

1899 life of Robert E. Lee. He also published a 1905 anthology of Southern writers. Then and later he championed Edgar Allan Poe, George Washington Cable, and other authors with a modernist appeal.[46]

Trent wrote "with the full consciousness that unless [he] reached certain conclusions it would be unacceptable to a majority of the people . . . to whom [he was] united by ties of friendship." Yet he "disdained to pander to a provincial sentimentalism that shivers at honest and fair criticism of any man or cause that may have become a shibboleth." Although he welcomed correction, he was "certainly not to be turned from [his opinions] by unstinted personal abuse," coming from "hypersensitive portions of the Southern people." The abuse after publication of his *William Gilmore Simms* was intense, but not for his *Robert E. Lee*, written, as it was, with "a steadfast determination to see him as he is, . . . a supremely great and good man." More readers might have bridled had they followed the logic of Trent's further conclusion, that Lee's "fame should not be limited by the characteristic conceptions of patriotism." It was not the hero's devotion to the South, but his character that ennobled him.[47]

Trent gave high marks for character and courage to his Southern statesmen, too, but that did not stop his criticism of them. Davis "was a failure not so much through his own lack of ability to govern as through the inherent weakness of the cause he represented." "The Southern Confederacy was bound to fail, because it had been founded precisely as Alexander H. Stephens had claimed, upon slavery as its cornerstone." The Southern politicians betrayed the planter, luring him on rather than telling him "that it was slavery that kept his roads bad, that gave him wretched 'Oldfield' schools, that prevented his cities from growing, that kept immigrants from public lands." What distinguished Jefferson and Washington from those, who later propounded slavery as a positive good, was that they "perceived that the slave basis of [Southern] society . . . was rotten to the core." After them, the South's course was a "constant downward slope." Southerners failed to keep "abreast of the thought of the world" and so did not understand that "the relation of master and slave," based on the premise that "might makes right," had become "abhorrent to civilization and progress."[48]

Slavery also hobbled Southern culture, in Trent's view. His *William Gilmore Simms*, the first substantive, scholarly study, damned the romancer with faint praise. Impatient with the lingering influence of the overturned order of the old South, Trent argued that Simms was unable to rise to his literary potential in the environment of antebellum Charleston and South Carolina. Giving color to the judgment was the fact that Simms himself often said as much. Moreover, Trent, with his modernist sensibility, was scathing about both the romance tradition and what he judged to be Simms's failure in it. Henry F. May summarized this cultural critique by Trent and others almost seventy years later: "the South, unable to look clearly at slavery in the midst of a Christian and democratic tradition, had developed an inveterate taste for shallow fantasy."[49]

Trent included Simms's Southern readership in his scorn. As he subsequently explained, "On feudality and slavery had been erected an aristocracy which had naturally developed the chief traits of this form of government,— bravery, pride, and conservatism." Yet, happily, "out of the ashes of the Old South, a new and better South [had] arisen. . . ." Southerners were adding "to their inherited virtues and powers" new ones, as they moved "forward with civilization."[50]

That was not how the New South looked to some from Thomson, Georgia. From there the past had virtues the present did not. Populist Tom Watson regarded Robert Toombs and Alexander Stephens as local heroes—and had done so from boyhood. Nevertheless, at first blush, it might seem that he still could agree with Trent at least about Jefferson. Trent's appreciation was glowing: "Manhood suffrage, the rule of the majority, perfect freedom of thought and action, peace rather than war, and devotion to science and the useful arts,—these are the leading ideas that Jefferson inculcated, and they are the leading ideas that guide the American citizen to-day." Trent continued, however: "We no longer have Jefferson's fear of tyranny before our eyes, and we have outgrown his prejudice against manufactures, but we are still in the main his disciples." The first sentence explains how progressives, including Woodrow Wilson, could consider themselves Jeffersonians. The second makes clear that they were not the same kind as Watson and the Populists.[51]

Far from having outgrown Jefferson's prejudice and fear, Watson saw in Jefferson a bulwark against capitalism and tyranny. As the masthead of the weekly *People's Party Paper* proclaimed in 1894: this newspaper, edited by Watson, was and ever would be "a fearless advocate of the Jeffersonian Theory of Popular Government" and, therefore, opposed "to the bitter end [to] the Hamiltonian Doctrines of Class Rule, Moneyed Aristocracy, National Banks, High Tariffs, Standing Armies and formidable Navies—all of which go together as a system of oppressing the people." What inoculated Watson against these interests was an agrarianism that he identified with Jefferson, as well as with his antebellum boyhood. As Woodward explained in 1938, "Throughout the triumphant rise of the New South, in which he was to fight his battles, his face remained fixed upon his vision of agrarian bliss." The vision was of "that old Southern homestead," which "was a little kingdom, a complete social and industrial organism, almost wholly sufficient unto itself."[52]

Sharecropping, tenant farming, industrialization, and urbanization all were undermining the idyll. What the Civil War had not destroyed, money and its rapacious pursuit were accomplishing. Thus Watson's anger against Federalist interpretations of Jefferson in the longer version of his biography of the third president of the United States.[53] Thus, too, in the same place Watson's attack in a footnote on Woodrow Wilson, the scholar: Wilson inexcusably neglected the South's early stand against Britain in the Revolution and thereby fueled a Northeastern bias against his people's past and potential. Thus, finally, Watson's admiration for the administrative ability of the subject of another of his biographies, Napoleon. The Emperor had gotten things done, not been consumed by politics. As a result, France had the Code Napoleon and its vaunted system of education.[54]

In the fight for such systematic betterment of the circumstances of the farmers and other "little people" for whom he advocated, Watson used the pen as a sword. He did so not just in the newspapers and magazines he edited and to which he contributed, but also in the lives he authored. Given this agenda, it is not surprising that he never got around to writing the biography of Robert E. Lee for which he was offered a contract. Lee's cause was lost, but not Watson's—not so long as he continued to fight. His beloved South had failed in its bid for independence, but there would be no surrender in the pursuit of independence and equality for those who adhered to the agrarian ethic and Populist program.[55]

W. E. B. Du Bois, in similar fashion, pursued independence and equality for African Americans and other people of color. Although not a Southerner, he studied at Fisk University in Nashville. Then, taking his doctorate in History at Harvard (the first received by an African American), he cumulatively taught at Atlanta University for almost a quarter of a century. In between his two stints there, he spent nearly another quarter of a century editing *The Crisis: A Record of the Darker Races,* the magazine of the National Association for the Advancement of Colored People, the organization he had worked to establish in 1909. Like Frederick Douglass, Harriet Jacobs, and Booker T. Washington, Du Bois insistently deployed chapters from his life to illustrate and make vivid the conditions of African Americans.[56]

The slave narrative genre that Douglass and Jacobs used was formative as well in the different versions of Washington's life narrative, set mostly after emancipation. Although several generations removed from slavery himself, Du Bois nevertheless drew on this historically resonant genre to frame episodes in his life story. In the chapter on the death of his son in *The Souls of Black Folk* (1903), he observed: "thus, in the Land of the Color-Line, I saw, as it fell across my baby, the shadow of the Veil." The reference to the veil picks up a metaphor from the first chapter of this pioneering sociological study of racism's consequences for the post-Emancipation African American: "In those sombre forests of his striving his own soul rose before him, and he saw himself,—darkly as through a veil." The meditation on the death of Du Bois's son concludes: "He knew no color-line . . . and the Veil, though it shadowed him, had not yet darkened half his sun . . ., and in his little world walked souls alone uncolored and unclothed."[57]

This use of autobiography, and also poetry, in the midst of a sociological study is not so startling if one considers the genre-bending writings of Johann Gottfried Herder, Johann Wolfgang von Goethe, and others that Du Bois read when a graduate student at the University of Berlin and later. Neither is the appropriation of the biography of the Reverend Alexander Crummell in the following chapter. There, Du Bois took Crummell through four stages of temptation. First came hatred of whites and the condition of blacks, then despair for blacks and himself. Next came doubt of himself and his mission on behalf of blacks. That was followed by humiliation at the hands of racist individuals and a racist world. Having thus gone through fire and water, Crummell, Du Bois judged, had achieved wisdom, hope, and peace. After all, Du Bois observed, "The nineteenth was the first century of human sympathy,—the age when half wonderingly we began to descry in others that transfigured spark of divinity which we call Myself. . . ."[58]

Yet lynchings—for instance, of Sam Hose in 1899—and the Atlanta race riots of 1906 only strengthened Du Bois's conviction that racism had to be confronted directly and forcefully. He made the point publicly in two ways in 1909. One was through a biography of John Brown, the abolitionist leader in Bloody Kansas in 1856 and in the raid on Harper's Ferry national armory and arsenal in (West) Virginia in 1859. Declaring that "John Brown began the war that ended American slavery," Du Bois attacked what struck him as a critical misunderstanding. It stemmed from a coincidence: having been executed after the raid and the subsequent trial, "John Brown suffered martyrdom" in the same year "that first published the *Origin of Species*."[59]

Du Bois argued against the conclusion that *Origin* supported the conviction that "there is essential and inevitable inequality among men and races of men." Not so—at least not in a critical respect. "Freedom of development and equality of opportunity is the demand of Darwinism," he insisted, "and this calls for the abolition of the hard and fast lines between races, just as it calls for the breaking down of barriers between classes." The NAACP, which he helped establish the same year as his Brown biography appeared, had that as its objective. On the subject of class, he sounded not unlike Tom Watson, but the Populists did not pursue interracial alliances with the same racial objective.[60]

Although abhorring the commitment to slavery by antebellum Southern political leaders, urgent for progressive change, and admiring of George Washington Cable's stories about the complexities of Creole New Orleans race relations, Trent also had a radically more limited sense of equality across class and color lines than did Du Bois. In a piece published in 1901, he wrote: "It is true that in the South there is a socio-political question concerning the suffrage, but this, we trust, is being settled." Guiding his own thinking was James Hyslop's *Democracy*. It advocated "differentiating the franchise" between the general population, possessing "personal rights," and those with "political rights."[61]

Emphasizing the color line, too, was the fact that Trent, but not Du Bois nor, indeed, any other African American, joined Watson in contributing to a second South-focused, multi-volume work launched in 1909: *The South in the Building of the Nation*. The guiding principles of the enterprise were two: to call attention to the South's contributions to the country's history and development and to provide biographical "sketches . . . written from a sympathetic point of view." This latter was because "Heretofore the biographical estimates of Southerners in the works of reference have been, in general, unfriendly, contemptuous, or inadequate." Given these constraints, Trent wrote on Poe, not Simms—also on Caroline Gilman, Sidney Lanier, John Smith, and others—but not on African Americans.[62]

Unwritten Lives

Late in 1909, Woodward turned a year old. Twenty-nine years later, just before his 30th birthday, he published his Watson biography. During the intervening years, the Southern historical view had been dominated by *The South in the Building of the Nation* and the *Library of Southern Literature*. Given the Pulitzer Prize that Margaret Mitchell had won recently for her 1936 novel *Gone with the Wind*, this is hardly surprising. The Lost Cause ethos became even more potently present with the release of the movie version of the novel in 1939. Yet, in fact, a significant shift in preoccupations in Southern history had begun in the two decades before Woodward's first birthday. By this shift, Trent, Watson, and Du Bois, with others, had started to constrict the scope of the Lost Cause's reach and power. Among their chief weapons was life writing—a lesson Woodward learned well.

The shift was from lives defined by Confederate patriotism toward lives that highlighted what was wrong and what was right in the South's development and potential before and after the Civil War. Although Trent, Watson, and Du Bois did not agree in their preoccupations and analyses, they did concur on the necessity of looking beyond the Civil War and its immediate causes and consequences. With time, that understanding would claim progressively more attention and the war less. In between, however, the students of the early professors of Southern history—whether William A. Dunning or Ulrich B. Phillips or William E. Dodd—kept the eyes of the generation that taught Woodward mostly on the South for which the Confederacy was the proud emblem and memory.

Yet what the juxtaposition of the Souths of Trent, Watson, Du Bois, and their biographical subjects showed the young scholar of 1938 was how contested—not unified—the region was, both early and late. Woodward made that contestation, at once economic and political, classist and racist, central to his Watson biography and also to the work that followed. Genovese in his turn focused on the contestations implicit in and contained by the dynamics between enslaved and slave owners, between a slave society and capitalism, and between classes within the white South and beyond. Fox-Genovese in her turn argued that class and race mattered more than gender in Southern women's lives, while reflecting on the complex relations that gender influenced. Hackney eventually moved in his work from the era of Watson to that of his mentor, Woodward, and Justice Black. The phase of the civil rights struggle which Du Bois helped formulate and lead became a chapter in a longer struggle for human rights in the South.

The lives written and life writings edited with these preoccupations in mind differed dramatically. Woodward's Mary Boykin Chesnut was not Fox-Genovese's. His railed against slavery and black concubinage. Hers embraced the privileges and worldview of her class. Both are rooted in the record, as is Chesnut, the early modernist writer depicted by Michael O'Brien.[63]

Trent's Calhoun failed because his premise was that slavery is a positive good. Yet to Genovese, this was the logic that emerged out of the South's anti-capitalist socioeconomic system and the hegemonic culture ruling it. From this perspective, what was illogical was the free labor system that was developing along with industrialization in the North and Britain. Rather than reprehend slavery, as had Jefferson, the next generations of white Southern thinkers, the ones about whom Genovese and Fox-Genovese wrote most, used such new intellectual tools as sociology to urge unfree labor as the answer to the immiseration produced by capitalism. Again, the record cannot be the arbiter. It is the viewpoint of the life writer that determines the conclusion.

That unsurprising point begs a question. How does one rewrite a life? Du Bois addressed it at the outset of his *John Brown*: "the only excuse for another life of John Brown is an opportunity to lay new emphasis . . ., and to treat these facts from a different point of view." His novel perspective was "that of the little known but vastly important inner development of Negro America." In short, the life was a vehicle, not the point. This was no less true for Watson's Jefferson or Trent's Simms or Woodward's Watson.[64]

According to Eugen Rosenstock-Huessy, "It's much easier to describe a man just for his consciousness and for his actions." Indeed, Rosenstock-Huessy argued "that biography is a great problem. It destroys history." Telling a life is not the same as analyzing an historical issue. For Plutarch, biography, unlike history, had a moral purpose. David Blight insists that memory and historical analysis possess different kinds of authority and meaning. Yet "nobody nowadays," according to Arnaldo Momigliano, "is likely to doubt that biography is some kind of history."[65]

The fusion of the two approaches and genres—the biographical and the historical—that emerged about the same time in antiquity means that there are always issues of balance and priority. Harnessed to conflicts and causes, life writings of the sort historians often produce and use end up presenting their subjects in terms of those consuming involvements. History trumps the life, because the life is used as an avenue to the history. Consequently, Woodward scanted Watson after the failure of Populism. Writing initially for serial publication in one of William Randolph Hearst's journals, Watson, a sometime Hearst political ally, brushed impatiently past much of Jefferson's life while picking fights with other interpreters. Du Bois elevated Crummell as an icon, ostensibly ignoring their differences—especially those reflected in Crummell's late writings. By the same token, in Du Bois's hands John Brown served as an agent of emancipation, not as the case study in the psycho-dynamics of political extremism which Du Bois acknowledged was there. Genovese's and Fox-Genovese's theorists of slavery in the abstract are logical thinkers, however misguided and self-deluded—not the anxious, attitudinal, and reactionary figures seen by other scholars. Hackney's Woodward continues to carry the banner of social justice.

Clearly, in theory, no last words are ever written. The current crop of Jefferson studies, for instance, overwhelms the already copious libraries on which Trent and Watson drew. Later writers on John Brown have not been troubled by Du Bois's concern that the subject is already well known. Crummell and Du Bois are now in conversation in ways that they never were when the two men were alive and met on the campus of Wilberforce University.[66] Watson's life continues to intrigue and perplex beyond the artfully argued conclusions of Woodward 75 years ago.

Where to go? One of Du Bois's professors at the University of Berlin was the philosopher and sociologist Wilhelm Dilthey. His son-in-law, Georg Misch, wrote the monumental seven-volume *History of Autobiography* from antiquity through the middle ages. It followed Misch's one-time colleague Friedrich Leo's *Greek-Roman Biography in its Literary Form*, a work admired by Rosenstock-Huessy. Where Leo was concerned with the consequences of literary form, Misch was following the suggestion of Dilthey that he study the rise of individuality through autobiography. Goethe a century earlier had expressed the same interest in "the ways in which the individual's sense of personality has developed."[67]

Du Bois put the question differently: how has racism collectively and individually shaped African Americans' (also abolitionists') sense of personality? For Southern historians more generally, the relationship of diverse Southern environments and personality has become an abiding question. When Trent contended that Washington and Jefferson belonged to the nation, not the South, he was suggesting that the regionalization of Southern identity and influence came later. It followed the development of the argument that slavery is a positive good. This position alienated Southerners from the universalist principles articulated by Jefferson and represented by Washington.

Simms wrote as the shift was taking place, and patriotism became a divided legacy. The fight over Revolutionary inheritances, like the later fights for progressive, Populist, minority, and gender agendas, not only divided Southerners but cast their future in radically different terms. Across these divisions, however, the conviction remained that the past mattered to the future. Woodward, Genovese, Fox-Genovese, and Hackney agreed. The question therefore became—not who owns history? nor even whose history?—but rather: why share lives? In retrospect, it is not surprising that the demands of patriot hegemony could not contain the conflicting identities, ideologies, and interests that they masked or suppressed. The dialectic between individuals' pasts and collective futures is complex. That is why Southern lives remain difficult to tell and at the same time important to recount.[68]

Notes

1   Records of the St. George Tucker Society's first dozen years are in the Southern Historical Collection (SHC) at the University of North Carolina at Chapel Hill (UNC). Hackney and I were the co-conveners of the Watson-Woodward conference.

2   Woodward made the observation to me more than once. At the time I directed the SHC and the Center for the Study of the American South, also at UNC.

3   A classic meditation on the influence of Shakespeare on Richard III's reputation is Josephine Tey [Elizabeth MacKintosh], *The Daughter of Time* (London: Macmillan & Co., 1951). In a *Washington Post* column (March 12, 2003), Jonathan Yardley quotes another Tey novel on Richard III, *Miss Pym Disposes*: "'Richard III' . . . is a criminal libel on a fine man, a blatant piece of political propaganda, and an extremely silly play." There is a Richard III Society dedicated to rescuing the king's reputation.

4   C. Vann Woodward, *Tom Watson: Agrarian Rebel* (New York: Macmillan, 1938). Woodward invited me to visit him in New Haven to discuss the proposed conference and at the end of the day concluded: "I hate the son-of-a-bitch too much" to proceed.

5   See Peter C. Mancall, *Hakluyt's Promise: An Elizabethan's Obsession for an English America* (New Haven: Yale University Press, 2010); J. A. Leo Lemay, *The American Dream of Captain John Smith* (Charlottesville: University Press of Virginia, 1991); Kenneth A. Lockridge, *The Diary, and Life, of William Byrd II* (Chapel Hill: University of North Carolina Press, 1987).

6   In his paper at the February 21–23, 2013, Southern Intellectual History Circle meeting,

Michael O'Brien discussed letters to Woodward from Genovese in Woodward's papers at Yale. Douglas Ambrose has the electronic file of the book manuscript, which I saw in earlier paper form in late 2011. Deborah Symonds, Fox-Genovese's biographer, has mentioned several letters from Genovese in the Fox-Genovese papers in SHC.

7   Eugene D. Genovese, *Miss Betsey: A Memoir of Marriage* (Wilmington: ISI Books, 2009).

8   "The Rise of Bourgeois Individualism and Autobiography: Selections from the Introduction to *The Autobiography of Du Pont de Nemours*," is in Elizabeth Fox-Genovese, *Unbought Grace: An Elizabeth Fox-Genovese Reader*, ed. Rebecca Fox and Robert L. Paquette (Columbia: University of South Carolina Press, 2012), vol. 5 in *History & Women, Culture & Faith: Selected Writings of Elizabeth Fox-Genovese*, gen. ed. David Moltke-Hansen. "Caught in the Web of Grace," "A Conversion Story," and "Selected Spiritual Writings of Elizabeth Fox-Genovese" are in Elizabeth Fox-Genovese, *Explorations and Commitments: Religion, Faith, and Culture*, ed. Ann Hartle and Sheila O'Connor-Ambrose (Columbia: University of South Carolina Press, 2012); the volume is the fourth in *History & Women, Culture & Faith*.

9   C. Vann Woodward, *Thinking Back: The Perils of Writing History* (Baton Rouge: Louisiana State University Press, 1986).

10 Sheldon Hackney, *The Politics of Presidential Appointment: A Memoir of the Culture War* (Montgomery: New South, 2002); Sheldon Hackney, *Following Virginia, 1958–2007* (Raleigh: Lulu, 2009).

11 Jeremy D. Popkin, *History, Historians, and Autobiography* (Chicago: University of Chicago Press, 2005), 12.

12 Mary Chesnut, *Mary Chesnut's Civil War*, ed. C. Vann Woodward (New Haven: Yale University Press, 1981).

13 In *In Red and Black: Marxian Explorations in Southern and Afro-American History* (Knoxville: University of Tennessee Press, 1971), Genovese critiqued and interacted with a range of scholars of slavery and the South, from Ulrich B. Phillips to C. Vann Woodward. The second half of *The World the Slaveholders Made: Two Essays in Interpretation* (New York: Pantheon Books, 1969) focuses on the views of George Fitzhugh. In *The Political Economy of Slavery: Studies in the Economy and Society of the Slave South* (New York: Pantheon Books, 1965), Genovese first sought to rehabilitate Phillips. *The Southern Front: History and Politics in the Culture War* (Columbia: University of Missouri Press, 1995) includes essays on figures ranging from Confederate cavalier James Johnston Pettigrew to Martin Luther King Jr.

14 See the following by Elizabeth Fox-Genovese: *The Origins of Physiocracy: Economic Revolution and Social Order in Eighteenth-Century France* (Ithaca: Cornell University Press, 1976); *Within the Plantation Household: Black and White Women of the Old South* (Chapel Hill: University of North Carolina Press, 1988); *Feminism without Illusions: A Critique of Individualism* (Chapel Hill: University of North Carolina Press, 1991); *"Feminism Is Not the Story of My Life": How Today's Feminist Elite Has Lost Touch with the Real Concerns of Women* (New York: Nan A. Talese, 1996); *Women Past and Present*, ed. Deborah A. Symonds (Columbia: University of South Carolina Press, 2011), vol. 1 in *History & Women, Culture & Faith*; *Ghosts and Memories White and Black Southern Women's Lives and Writings*, ed. Kibibi Mack-Shelton and Christina Bieber-Lake (Columbia: University of South Carolina Press, 2011), vol. 2 in *History & Women, Culture and Faith*.

15   Fox-Genovese and Genovese earlier gave lectures and contributed essays published separately to this end, but the major works are the three volumes on the mind of the master class: *The Mind of the Master Class: History and Faith in the Southern Slaveholders' Worldview* (New York: Cambridge University Press, 2005); *Slavery in White and Black: Class and Race in the Southern Slaveholders' New World Order* (New York: Cambridge University Press, 2008); and *Fatal Self-Deception: Slaveholding Paternalism in the Old South* (New York: Cambridge University Press, 2011).

16   Sheldon Hackney, *Populism to Progressivism in Alabama* (Princeton: Princeton University Press, 1969), and *Magnolias without Moonlight: The American South from Regional Confederacy to National Integration* (New Brunswick: Transaction Publishers, 2005).

17   Woodward and Genovese both contributed, for instance, to a forum on the "Legacy of Slavery and Roots of Black Nationalism" in *Studies on the Left* 6.6 (1966). In his review of Woodward's *The Burden of Southern History* in the September 11, 1969, *New York Review of Books*, Genovese commented: "Woodward combines a strong Populism with liberal political views." Sheldon Hackney's characterization of his mentor is "C. Vann Woodward, Dissenter," *Historically Speaking* 10.1 (2009), 31–34.

18   Michael O'Brien, *Placing the South* (Jackson: University Press of Mississippi, 2007), 136, argues, mostly correctly, that Genovese saw a sharp discontinuity in 1865 and, too summarily, that he did not concern himself much with the aftermath. Genovese's *The Southern Tradition: The Achievement and Limitations of an American Conservatism* (Cambridge: Harvard University Press, 1994) insists that the Southern conservative worldview linked John Randolph and John C. Calhoun, as well as Calhoun and such 20th-century figures as Allen Tate, Lewis Simpson, and Robert Penn Warren. See also John B. Boles and Bethany L. Johnson, eds., Origins of the New South *Fifty Years Later: The Continuing Influence of a Historical Classic* (Baton Rouge: Louisiana State University Press, 2003), and John Herbert Roper, *C. Vann Woodward, Southerner* (Athens: University of Georgia Press, 1987).

19   The argument about women in history is made, *inter alia*, in Fox-Genovese's "Placing Women's History in History" in her *Women Past and Present* and in "The Personal Is Not Political Enough" in her *Intersections: History, Culture, Ideology*, ed. David Moltke-Hansen (Columbia: University of South Carolina Press, 2011), vol. 3 of *History & Women, Culture & Faith*.

20   Johann Wolfgang von Goethe, *Elective Affinities*, trans. R. J. Hollingdale (1809; London: Penguin Books, 1971).

21   Mason L. Weems, *The Life of Washington*, ed. Peter S. Onuf (Cambridge: Belknap Press, 1962).

22   Timothy Flint, *Biographical Memoir of Daniel Boone: The First Settler of Kentucky* (1833; New York: Cosimo, 2010). See Michael Lofaro, *Daniel Boone: An American Life* (Lexington: University Press of Kentucky, 2003), 181, 199.

23   David Moltke-Hansen, "Southern Literary Horizons in Young America: Imaginative Development of a Regional Geography," *Studies in the Literary Imagination* 42.1 (2009): 1–31, and Critical Introduction, William Gilmore Simms, *Views and Reviews in American Literature, History and Fiction*. Series 1 and 2 (1845 [1846–47]; Columbia: University of South Carolina Press, 2013). Simms's review of Meeks's Americanism oration before the University of Georgia is the first essay in this collection, 1–19. On Young America,

see also Edward Widmer, *Young America: The Flowering of Democracy in New York City* (New York: Oxford University Press, 2000), and Yonaton Eyal, *The Young America Movement and the Transformation of the Democratic Party, 1828–1861* (New York: Cambridge University Press, 2007).

24 Frederick Douglass, *Oration, Delivered in Corinth Hall, Rochester . . . July 5th, 1852* (Rochester: Lee, Mann & Co., 1852), 20, 10–11, 15.

25 Recent treatments of the caning are Williamjames Hull Hoeffer, *The Caning of Charles Sumner: Honor, Idealism, and the Origins of the Civil War* (Baltimore: Johns Hopkins University Press, 2010), and Stephan Puleo, *The Caning: The Assault That Drove America to Civil War* (Yardley: Westholme Publishing, 2012). Some may doubt Puelo's conclusion that the caning made war inevitable.

26 Lorenzo Sabine, *The American Loyalists: Or, Biographical Sketches of Adherents to the British Crown in the War of the Revolution; Alphabetically Arranged; with a Preliminary Historical Essay* (Boston: C. C. Little and J. Brown, 1847).

27 William Way, *History of the New England Society of Charleston, South Carolina for One Hundred Years, 1819-1919* (Charleston: the Society, 1920), 188-210; Daniel Webster, *The Works of Daniel Webster*. Vol. 2, ed. Edward Everett (Boston: Little, Brown and Co., 1853), 378-88.

28 Simms's letters to Sabine are in the newly supplemented William Gilmore Simms, *The Letters of William Gilmore Simms*. 6 vols., ed. Mary C. Simms Oliphant *et al.* (Columbia: University of South Carolina Press, 1952-2012), 6: 328-37. See Todd Hagstette, "Private vs. Public Honor in Wartime South Carolina," in *William Gilmore Simms's Unfinished Civil War: Consequences for a Southern Man of Letters*, ed. David Moltke-Hansen (Columbia: University of South Carolina Press, 2013), 52-58.

29 David Moltke-Hansen, "Critical Introduction: The Revolutionary Romances," xxiii-li, serves to introduce seven of these Simms romances in the University of South Carolina Press edition, released in fall 2013–14; included, in chronological order by date of original publication, are *The Partisan, Mellichampe, The Scout [The Kinsmen], Katherine Walton, The Forayers, Eutaw,* and *Joscelyn,* as well as *Woodcraft,* introduced by James E. Kibler and already published (2012). Simms completed *Joscelyn* after the Civil War.

30 James B. Meriwether, "The Significance of Simms's First Long Poem," *Simms Review* 17.1–2 (2009), 19.

31 Steven D. Smith, "Imagining the Swamp Fox: William Gilmore Simms and the National Memory of Francis Marion," in *William Gilmore Simms's Unfinished Civil War*, 32–47. Simms also edited, substantially revising, a life of Nathanael Greene, the New England general who contested Cornwallis's British troops' march out of South Carolina toward Yorktown in Virginia. In addition, he was co-author, with Rufus W. Griswold and Duncan Ingraham, of the two volumes of biographical sketches, *Washington and the Generals of the American Revolution* (Philadelphia: Carey & Hart, 1847). Other sketches by Simms appeared in journals he edited.

32 William Gilmore Simms, *Mellichampe: A Legend of the Santee*, 2 vols. (New York: Harper & Brothers, 1836), 1: v; Jon L. Wakelyn, *The Politics of a Literary Man: William Gilmore Simms* (Westport: Greenwood Press, 1973), 19–50; William Gilmore Simms, *The Kinsmen: or The Black Riders of Congaree*. 2 vols. (Philadelphia: Lea and Blanchard, 1841), 1:17.

33   William Gilmore Simms, *The Sources of American Independence* (Aiken: [The Town]
     Council, 1844), 2–4; William Gilmore Simms, "The Civil Warfare in the Carolinas and
     Georgia, during the Revolution," *Southern Literary Messenger* 12.5–7 (1846): 257–65,
     321–36, 385–400; David Moltke-Hansen, "Why History Mattered: The Background
     of Ann Pamela Cunningham's Interest in the Preservation of Mount Vernon," *Furman
     Studies* n.s. 26 (Dec. 1980): 34–42; William Gilmore Simms, *South-Carolina in the
     Revolutionary War: Being a Reply to Certain Misrepresentations and Mistakes of Recent
     Writers, in Relation to the Course and Conduct of This State* (Charleston: Walker and
     Evans, 1853).

34   Simms, *The Sources of American Independence*, 16–17.

35   David Moltke-Hansen, "The Fictive Transformation of American Nationalism after Sir
     Walter Scott," *Historically Speaking* 10.3 (2009): 24–27.

36   Simms, *Mellichampe*, 1: x–xii, and "Ellet's 'Women of the Revolution'," in *William Gilmore
     Simms's Selected Reviews on Literature and Civilization*, ed. James E. Kibler and David
     Moltke-Hansen (Columbia: University of South Carolina Press, 2014, forthcoming);
     Simms, *Letters*, 2: 322.

37   William Gilmore Simms, *The Sense of the Beautiful. An Address* (Charleston: Charleston
     Country Agricultural and Horticultural Association, 1870); Sara Georgini, "The Angel
     and the Animal," in *William Gilmore Simms's Unfinished Civil War*, 212–23; John D.
     Miller, "The Sense of Things to Come: Redefining Gender and Promoting the Lost Cause
     in *The Sense of the Beautiful*," in *William Gilmore Simms's Unfinished Civil War*, 224–38.

38   Michael O'Brien, *Conjectures of Order: Intellectual Life and the American South, 1810–1860*,
     2 vols. (Chapel Hill: University of North Carolina Press, 2004), 2: 1178–81; David
     Moltke-Hansen, "William Henry Trescot," in *American Historians, 1607–1865*, ed.
     Clyde N. Wilson, Dictionary of American Biography, vol. 30 (Detroit: Gale Publishing,
     1984), 311–13. Gaines M. Foster, *Ghosts of the Confederacy: Defeat, the Lost Cause, and
     the Emergence of the New South, 1865–1913* (New York: Oxford University Press, 1987),
     sees people mourning and factions contesting the Civil War's meaning early, a surge and
     consolidation of the Lost Cause between 1883 and 1898, and then a shift away from the
     Confederate tradition under the influence of academic historians and the reconciliation
     of the North and South illustrated by Southern participation in the Spanish American
     War and then, fifteen years later, in the anniversary of the battle of Gettysburg. David
     Blight, *Race and Reunion: The Civil War in American Memory* (Cambridge: Harvard
     University Press, 2001), devotes considerable attention to "the reminiscence industry."
     Sarah E. Gardner, *Blood & Irony: Southern White Women's Narratives of the Civil War,
     1861–1937* (Chapel Hill: University of North Carolina Press, 2004), emphasizes how
     Confederate women helped shape the Lost Cause and transmit it before their children
     started to consider issues of Southern womanhood by the turn of the century.

39   With its headquarters in Richmond, the Society gave the preponderance of its attention
     to the war in the East.

40   William W. Freehling, *The South vs. The South: How Anti-Confederate Southerners Shaped
     the Course of the War* (New York: Oxford University Press, 2001). Drew Gilpin Faust,
     "Alters of Sacrifice: Confederate Women and Narratives of War," *Journal of American
     History* 76.4 (1990): 1200–28, argues that by late in the war many Confederate women
     were also resisting the Confederate war effort.

41 Edwin Anderson Alderman and Joel Chandler Harris, eds. in chief, *The Library of Southern Literature*, 16 vols. (Atlanta: Martin and Hoyt Co., 1909).

42 David Moltke-Hansen, "When History Failed: William Gilmore Simms's Artistic Negotiation of the Civil War's Consequences," in *William Gilmore Simms's Unfinished Civil War*, 12–13.

43 Gary Gallagher and Alan T. Nolan, eds., *The Myth of the Lost Cause and Civil War History* (Bloomington: Indiana University Press, 2000).

44 *"Our Women in the War": The Lives They Lived; the Deaths They Died* (Charleston: News and Courier Book Presses, 1885). Gardner, *Blood & Irony*, 6, observes that "the myth of the Lost Cause did not persist in its original rendition but emerged from, flowed into, and continually revised [the] emerging collective memory of the war as Southerners rebuilt and reassured their position in the world." On generational change, see David Herbert Donald, "A Generation of Defeat," in *From the Old South to the New: Essays on the Transitional South*, ed. Walter J. Fraser Jr. and Winfred B. Moore Jr. (Westport: Greenwood Press, 1981), 3–20.

45 Woodward, *Tom Watson*, 10–43. Drew Gilpin Faust, *Mothers of Invention: Women of the Slaveholding South in the American Civil War* (Chapel Hill: University of North Carolina Press, 1996), concludes that elite white women supported the restoration of a patriarchal order after the war in the face of veterans' debilitations and social upheaval. LeeAnn Whites, *The Civil War as a Crisis in Gender: Augusta, Georgia, 1860–1890* (Athens: University of Georgia Press, 1995), arrives at broadly the same conclusion when considering Tom Watson's neighborhood. James Marten, *Sing Not War: The Lives of Union and Confederate Veterans in Gilded Age America* (Chapel Hill: University of North Carolina Press, 2011), considers the degrees of successful and failed reintegration into society and also the degrees of successful and failed personal coping with the war's physical, psychological, and social impact by veterans.

46 Wendell H. Stephenson, "William P. Trent as a Historian of the South," *Journal of Southern History* 15.2 (1949), 152–77. Trent's books on Southerners are *William Gilmore Simms* (Boston: Houghton Mifflin, 1892); *Southern Statesmen of the Old Regime: Washington, Jefferson, Randolph, Calhoun, Stephens, Toombs, and Jefferson Davis* (Boston: Thomas Y. Crowell, 1897); and *Robert E. Lee* (Boston: Small, May & Co., 1899). His anthology is titled *Southern Writers: Selections in Prose and Verse* (New York: Macmillan, 1905).

47 Trent, *Southern Statesmen*, 259, ix–x; Stephenson, "William P. Trent," 163–65; John McCardell, "Trent's *Simms*: The Making of a Biography," in *A Master's Due: Essays in Honor of David Herbert Donald*, ed. William J. Cooper Jr., Michael Holt, and John McCardell (Baton Rouge: Louisiana State University Press, 1985), 179–203. Trent, *Robert E. Lee*, x.

48 Trent, *Southern Statesmen*, 262, 292, 176–77, 181, 257.

49 McCardell, "Trent's *Simms*"; Henry F. May, *The End of American Innocence: A Study of the First Years of Our Time, 1912–1917* (New York: Alfred A. Knopf, 1959), 84.

50 Trent, *Southern Statesmen*, 176; Trent, *William Gilmore Simms*, 289–90.

51 Trent, *Southern Statesmen*, 83.

52 *People's Party Paper* 3.40 (June 22, 1894), 4; Woodward, *Tom Watson*, 5; Thomas E. Watson, *Bethany: A Story of the Old South* (New York: D. Appleton & Co., 1904), 12.

53 Watson's earlier *Thomas Jefferson* (Boston: Small, Maynard & Co., 1900) appeared in

the same Beacon Biographies series as Trent's *Robert E. Lee*.

54 Thomas E. Watson, *The Life and Times of Thomas Jefferson* (New York: D. Appleton and Co., 1903), 330, 85–6; Thomas E. Watson, *Napoleon; a Sketch of His Life, Character, Struggles, and Achievements* (New York: Macmillan, 1902).

55 In his *The Life and Speeches of Thomas E. Watson* (Thomson: The Jeffersonian Publishing Co., 1911), 50–51, Watson praised Lee as an embodiment of "the old" values of the South. See Jerald Bryan, *Henry Grady or Tom Watson? The Rhetorical Struggle for the New South, 1880–1890* (Macon: Mercer University Press, 1994), 75, 91. Although Watson planned to write the biography of Lee, he never signed the contract.

56 On the slave narrative genre, see, for instance, William L. Andrews, *To Tell a Free Story: The First Century of Afro-American Autobiography, 1760–1865* (Urbana: University of Illinois Press, 1988). Du Bois's deployments and revisions of his self-narratives is a theme of David Levring Lewis, *W. E. B. Du Bois: Biography of a Race, 1868–1919* (New York: Henry Holt and Co., 1993).

57 W. E. B. Du Bois, *The Souls of Black Folk: Essays and Sketches* (Chicago: A. A. McClurg & Co., 1903), 150, 8, 152.

58 Ingeborg Solbrig, "Herder and the 'Harlem Renaissance' of Black Culture in America: The Case of *Neger-Idyllen*," in *Herder Today: Contributions from the International Herder Conference, Nov. 5–8, 1987, Stanford, California*, ed. Kurt Mueller-Vollmer (Berlin: de Gruyter, 1990), 402–14; Du Bois, *The Souls of Black Folk*, 157.

59 Edwin T. Arnold, *What Virtue There Is in Fire: Cultural Memory and the Lynching of Sam Hose* (Athens: University of Georgia Press, 2009), 171–72. One of the most recent of the many books on the 1906 Atlanta race riot that treats Du Bois's reaction in some detail is David Fort Godshalk, *Veiled Visions: The 1906 Atlanta Race Riot and the Reshaping of American Race Relations* (Chapel Hill: The University of North Carolina Press, 2005). W. E. B. Du Bois, *John Brown* (Philadelphia: G. W. Jacobs & Co., 1909), 353, 375.

60 Du Bois, *John Brown*, 375, 395.

61 William P. Trent, *War and Civilization* (Boston: Thomas Y. Crowell, 1901), 45; James H. Hyslop, *Democracy: A Study of Government* (New York: Charles Scribner's Sons, 1899), 212–14.

62 J. A. C. Chandler *et al.*, *The South in the Building of the Nation: A History of the Southern States Designed to Record the South's Part in the Making of the American Nation, to Portray the Character and Genius, to Chronicle the Achievements and Progress and to Illustrate the Life and Traditions of the Southern People,* 13 vols. (Richmond: Southern Historical Publishing Society, 1909–13), 11: vii.

63 Fox-Genovese recurred to Chesnut often in *Within the Plantation Household*. See Michael O'Brien, "The Flight Down the Middle Walk: Mary Chesnut and the Forms of Observance," in *Haunted Bodies: Gender and Southern Texts*, ed. Anne Goodwyn Jones and Susan V. Donaldson (Charlottesville: University Press of Virginia, 1997), 109–31.

64 Du Bois, *John Brown*, 7.

65 Eugen Rosenstock-Huessy, Lectures, vol. 20, transcript, 33; David Blight, *American Oracle: The Civil War in the Civil Rights Era* (Cambridge: Belknap Press, 2011). Arnaldo Momigliano, *The Development of Greek Biography* (1971; Cambridge: Harvard University Press, 1993), 6.

66 For example, three 2012–13 books, in the series that Mark Smith and I edit, Cambridge (University Press) Studies on the American South, significantly treat Jefferson: Christopher Michael Curtis, *Jefferson's Freeholders and the Politics of Ownership in the Old Dominion*, Brian Steele's *Thomas Jefferson and American Nationhood*, and Ari Helo's *Thomas Jefferson's Ethics and the Politics of Human Progress: The Morality of a Slaveholder*. Recent books treating John Brown's impact in innovative ways include Franny Nudelman, *John Brown's Body: Slavery, Violence, and the Culture of War* (Chapel Hill: University of North Carolina Press, 2004), and David S. Reynolds, *John Brown, Abolitionist: The Man Who Killed Slavery, Sparked the Civil War, and Seeded Civil Rights* (New York: Alfred A. Knopf, 2005). Recent treatments of the complex relations of the thought of Crummell and Du Bois include Laurie Maffly-Kipp, *Setting Down the Sacred Past: African-American Race Histories* (Cambridge: Belknap, 2010), and Robert Gooding-Williams, *In the Shadow of Du Bois: Afro-Modern Political Thought in America* (Cambridge: Harvard University Press, 2011).

67 Only the first two volumes of Misch's massive work have been translated: *A History of Autobiography in Antiquity*. Parts 1 and 2, trans. E. W. Dickes (London: Routledge and Keagan Paul, 1950). Leo's study has not been translated into English. The quote is from Misch, 1: 3. See Popkin, *History, Historians, and Autobiography*, 17–19.

68 John Inscoe, *Writing the South through the Self: Explorations in Southern Autobiography* (Athens: University of Georgia Press, 2011), examines some of these complexities of the dynamics of place and the self in the 20th century, using self-writing.

10

A Southern Radical and His Songs

Lee Hays, the Almanacs, and the Weavers

Charles Joyner

It was November of 1940, and New York gave a cold reception to the young man from the South. Lee Hays had recently arrived from Arkansas with a bag of songs, and he hoped to publish a songbook for the labor movement, only to learn that a young fellow named Pete Seeger was trying to do the same thing. The two arranged to meet. They would not be hard to spot: Lee was 25, large and disheveled, while Pete was 22, lanky and looking a bit like the long-necked banjo he carried. The two young men struck up what would be a lifetime friendship. Seeger told me, "Lee and I hit it off immediately." Lee leaned toward Pete, "How about teaming up? I know some songs, and you know that banjo." Pete recalled, "I couldn't sing with the banjo; I had to either play the banjo or sing, but couldn't do both." Either way, teaming up seemed a good idea. In another month Lee, Pete, and Lee's roommate Millard Lampell had acquired a repertoire, a residence in a large loft on 13th Street near the Bowery, and even a name—the Almanac Singers.[1]

Lee Hays was born in 1915 in Little Rock, Arkansas, the son of a Methodist minister. Growing up in a series of rural parsonages, he learned to sing the folksongs and the old rural hymns of the South. He marveled when his father baptized people with a jug of water from the Jordan River after he came back from a trip to the Holy Land. But he rebelled against his father when he caught him refilling the jug. After his father's death Lee finished secondary school in the preparatory academy of Emory Junior College in Oxford, Georgia. During the Great Depression he saw the despair of white and black Southerners who plowed their worn-out fields and lost their worn-out farms to the drought and the mortgage companies. He saw the misery of black and white Southerners who had no farms to plow or to lose, who lived on cornbread and beans in rickety no-good sharecropper shacks. He saw their shared fear and poverty; and he believed the only way out was for them to get together to fight for honest pay and fair treatment, for freedom and justice and brotherhood. But he also saw that whenever blacks and whites got together they were called Reds. So long as the idle few stole so much of the world's wealth from the hard-working many, Lee felt he could not stand aside without shame.[2]

During those years Lee came under the influence of radical preacher Claude Williams, son of a Tennessee sharecropper. He wrote that Williams was "a fighting Presbyterian" who "tried to take the Bible seriously." Williams preached a "Faith to Free the People" in the pulpit and on the picket line: "I have taken my stand with Jesus of Nazareth," he declared. "If I believe in Him, I cannot believe in race prejudice or class antagonism and exploitation." He asked, "Do you really believe the Bible? Then for Heaven's sake, let's do what the Bible tells us to do." He preached that "if we all did that, we'd have no Jim Crow, no hate." Williams used all the methods he knew—"movies, pamphlets, books, tent meetings, cake suppers"—to bring the message of Christian democracy to the people. He made his church "a community center for coal miners, and young people and Negroes." For such active faith he was ostracized, jailed, terrorized, and expelled from his pulpit. As Lee recalled decades later, "I got to be his chief helper." Under Williams's influence, Lee briefly studied for the ministry at Missouri's College of the Ozarks in 1934–35. He was licensed to preach, baptize, marry, and bury; and with his rumbling bass and his expansive proportions, he cut an imposing figure in the pulpit as he preached social justice like his mentor.[3]

But Lee soon decided the pulpit was not for him, and he moved on to Highlander Folk School. Highlander, founded in 1932 by Myles Horton and Don West near Monteagle, Tennessee, embodied their belief in the power of education to help Southerners take control of their own lives and solve their own problems. At Highlander, Lee came to understand the deep links between the folk music he loved and the effort to achieve economic, political, and racial justice. Through the guidance of Zilphia Horton (Myles's wife and Lee's old friend from Arkansas) he learned how songfests and homemade plays could help Highlander train more effective union leaders and how music, drama, and dance might be applied to organize a union or conduct a strike.[4]

When Claude Williams became director of Commonwealth College in rural Arkansas in 1937, he invited his 22-year-old protégé to teach "Worker's Dramatics." Commonwealth called itself a "labor college," providing leadership training for the labor movement and promoting a workers' culture through lectures, literary magazines, theater programs, and adult education courses. The buildings at Commonwealth were unfinished, with only wood stoves to relieve the freezing Arkansas winters; and all students and faculty were expected to put in four hours a day in the cannery or garden to support the school.[5]

Lee thrived at Commonwealth College. He began to write labor lyrics to traditional tunes, often religious tunes, creating cadences that tapped into hallowed time-honored images of the hand of the Lord delivering His children from the house of bondage in such songs as "We Shall Not Be Moved," "Join the Union," and "Union Train." His Southern roots, his booming church-house bass voice, and his talents as a song leader were helpful; but he also scouted the countryside for traditional singers and songs. One of the great performers Lee found was Emma Dusenbury, a blind singer who lived in a log cabin. When she sang at the college, large groups turned out to hear her. They "cherished the old lady. She was part of their history," he wrote. "She told the young farmers about the covered wagon days, about plowing with wooden plows behind oxen or, in bad times, cows. She told the young girls how to spin and how to make counterpanes for their wedding beds." Dusenbury sat downstage, leaning forward over the footlights, and sang from her enormous repertoire of songs and ballads. After she was recorded by the Library of Congress, she became recognized as one of America's great traditional artists. Her singing helped forge a bond between the college and Arkansas farmers. Even if they didn't respond to Commonwealth's labor plays, they found many of the movement's ideas palatable when expressed in the songs of their own culture.[6]

When Williams learned of the Southern Tenant Farmers' Union's effort to organize small farmers to resist eviction, he offered Commonwealth's active support. The STFU, begun by H. L. Mitchell and Clay East in the summer of 1934 with eleven white and seven black farmers, "had no idea of establishing an interracial union," Mitchell later recalled; but "it was the middle of the Depression and it was damn hard. . . . None of us had ever belonged to a union and we didn't know anything about it." But, as STFU organizer J. R.

Butler noted, "the plantation element in that part of the country absolutely did not want them 'niggers' organized, and they didn't hesitate to say it in just those words. The whites were niggers, too. There was no difference, and some of 'em was beginning to see that there was no difference." "The government was paying farmers to plow up every third row of cotton that year," he said, "and the tenant farmers should have gotten half of that money. The landowners were keeping most of it, though." He admitted that "we adopted, without really knowing what we were doing, the idea of nonviolence. We appealed for what was right, not on a racial basis, but entirely on an economic basis." By 1937 the STFU claimed a membership of about 35,000. "I called myself a Socialist back then and I didn't make any bones about it," Mitchell added, summing up the Union's achievement by saying, "We created a new way for our members to view each other and themselves."[7]

Lee joined the Southern Tenant Farmers' Union, signing up members and making up songs in the union's biracial organizing efforts in the winter of 1936. He met people black and white whose lives were marked by hard work and hard times. He learned straight from the lungs of hungry farmers about dried-up crops that brought nothing at the market and ragged and hungry kids with nobody to take care of them. John Handcox, an African American organizer for the STFU, wrote that the planters were ordering union members off the land. "They didn't wait for some of them to git—they threw them off. It was a cold winter. The hungry people had no place to go. Whey they held union meetings the laws clubbed them 'til they lay like dead." Men or women, some union members were jailed and others were killed. Lee began to write narrative songs with lyrics echoing their stories of bending their backs and dragging their sacks, of the beatings and sluggings and cheatings and killings they faced trying to organize the Southern Tenant Farmers' Union. When Lee heard black members sing their old spirituals at union meetings, he recognized that their repetitions of lines made ideal structures for group singing, so he set his lyrics to traditional Southern hymns and folksongs. To help overcome the legacy of racism that left both black and white farmers vulnerable, he wrote "black and white together, we shall not be moved / black and white together, we shall not be moved / just like a tree standing by the water, we shall not be moved." Singing such songs, the striking farmers refused to be intimidated. They chose "We Shall Not Be Moved" to be the official anthem of their union.[8]

Although two of the STFU founders, Mitchell and East, were socialists, they imposed no ideology on the union. By 1937, however, a rift developed over a letter outlining plans for a Communist takeover of the STFU that Mitchell claimed to have discovered in Williams's coat pocket. Williams denied that he had ever been "a card-carrying, dues-paying member of the communist party" but conceded he had "worked closely with people I knew to be communist." The STFU expelled Williams and severed its ties with Commonwealth College. His friend Don West blamed Mitchell for the estrangement. He said, "Claude and I were close personal friends for, my gosh, half a lifetime." According to him, "Mitchell red-baited Claude," and so did Mitchell's associate Howard Kester. The controversy over Williams's role cost Commonwealth much of its financial support. He tried to mend fences but was unable to keep the college afloat, and it closed in 1940.[9]

So LEE HAYS HAD come to New York after a baptism-by-total-immersion in radical politics during a critical era in Southern history. Pete Seeger's background was quite different. His father was a distinguished musicologist, his mother a classical violinist and teacher, and his stepmother a prominent modernist composer. Even so, Pete had little interest in music until his father took him to Bascom Lamar Lunsford's Folk Song and Dance Festival in Asheville, North Carolina, to hear real folk music in its native setting. There he "fell in love with the old-fashioned five-string banjo, rippling out a rhythm to one fascinating song after another," propelled by the nimble fingers of a young woman named Samantha Bumgarner. He was also enchanted by the lyrics of the ancient ballads. They were "frank, straightforward, honest," with "all the meat of human life in them." They sang of "heroes, outlaws, murderers, fools." They did not shrink from being "tragic instead of just sentimental." And he was captivated by the tunes, "time-tested by generations of singers."[10]

Lee, Pete, and Millard Lampell comprised the original Almanac Singers, but soon they were joined by Woody Guthrie and Bess Lomax. Not only did Lee bring to the Almanac Singers a background in pro-labor and anti-racism activism that was authentically Southern, his rumbling, resonant bass became the foundation of the rural harmonies that made the Almanacs' songs sound like rural hymns. "Lee was a better song leader than I," Pete recalled, "and I learned a lot from him." Lee had something to say, and he knew how to say it in a way people could understand. His down-home storytelling and sly

Southern wit enabled him to endow traditional songs with new lyrics specific enough to be topical, but universal enough to last. Pete called Lee "the best wordsmith" he'd ever known. Bess described him as "a beautiful bass singer with a great Southern repertoire and a great stage presence. Lee was witty and totally engaging; when he waved his great arms at you, it was impossible not to sing with him."[11]

Pete "was just starting out," Bess recalled. He sang in tune, but his voice was "not very strong." And "he practiced so much it could drive a person crazy." She described Mill Lampell as "a slick and sassy lyricist (by far the quickest and cleverest of us all in that department), young and handsome, with a long train of girlfriends."[12] Woody Guthrie was a Dust Bowl Okie who could play anything with strings on it and make a song on any subject. A man acquainted with freight trains and jail houses, his "persona and brilliance and total devotion to getting the world to listen to him" was matched by "none of the rest of us," Bess wrote. Fresh from Bryn Mawr, she was the daughter of the renowned folksong collector John A. Lomax, and the sister of Alan Lomax of the Archive of American Folk Song in Washington.[13]

On Sunday afternoons the Almanacs hosted gatherings to raise the rent money. According to Bess, "Lee Hays suggested we call these amorphous affairs 'hootenannies,' and they helped us keep going fiscally and professionally." Pete recalled that they charged 35 cents to get in, and they sang all afternoon. Lee sang along with other members of New York's Southern radical musical subculture, such as the Louisiana-born Huddie Ledbetter, who had first been recorded in 1933 at Angola Prison in Louisiana by John A. Lomax and his son Alan, then 18 years old, for the Library of Congress. Ledbetter had a unique high sweet voice and an enormous repertoire of work songs, love songs, ballads, and blues. Such songs as "Take This Hammer," "Rock Island Line," and "Goodnight, Irene" were almost unknown before his recordings. He called himself the "King of the 12-string guitar players," but he was dubbed "Leadbelly" by the other inmates.[14]

Lee also came to know Aunt Molly Jackson and her family from the coal fields of Harlan County, Kentucky, singing their own labor lyrics to traditional mountain tunes. Her raw, vehement renditions were full of fire and incipient violence. Her brother Jim Garland, a coal miner, union organizer, singer and songwriter, wrote the songs "I Don't Want Your Millions, Mister," and "The Ballad of Harry Simms." And her half-sister, Sarah Ogan Gunning, made songs about "the One Big Union that has got to come." Woody Guthrie said they were "deadlier and stronger than rifle bullets, and have cut a wider swath than a machine gun." Two other Oklahomans would soon become Almanac Singers themselves: Sis Cunningham, a talented accordion player and song leader, like Lee a veteran of Commonwealth College. She was described by Mill Lampell as "a square-jawed woman who played the accordion and had a singing voice sharp as the wind whipping across the flatland," while her husband Gordon Friesen was a "big-shouldered and callused" former Mennonite raised on a "hard-scrabble Dust Bowl farm." Woody's friend Cisco Houston and the Hawes Brothers—Peter and Butch—became what Bess called "sort of in-and-out members of the Almanacs."[15]

Lee became especially close to another wandering preacher's son: the South Carolina-born Josh White. A year younger than Lee, Josh was expected by his family to live up to his biblical namesake. By the age of seven he had learned to be eyes for the blind. Over the next decade he led more than sixty blind men, many of them itinerant musicians, and practiced their guitar licks while they slept. By the time he was 18, he had become a virtuoso; and his mother was offered $100 to let him make recordings in New York City. She agreed on condition that he only record religious songs. He recorded spirituals under the name "The Singing Christian," but after two long days in the recording studio, he had exhausted his sacred repertoire. So he recorded blues—under the name of "Pinewood Tom" to avoid trouble at home. Josh had earned $4 a week leading blind men; recording paid him $100 a week He honed his talents as a musician, learning to deepen the mood by infusing dynamics, drama, and shifting rhythms into the interplay between his voice and his guitar. Josh became an occasional member of the Almanacs performing notably on their recording of Lee's union version of the spiritual "Get Thee Behind Me, Satan."[16]

The hoots were often joined as well by Bess Lomax's brother Alan. In his mid-twenties, he was already a famous folksong collector with an unabridged repertoire built up in the course of recording hundreds of living traditional singers. He was captivated by the Almanacs' repertoire of traditional songs, their rural instruments and harmonies, and especially the new lyrics they wrote for old tunes. He shared Lee's interest in the deeper meanings inherent in folk music and in the social and political context out of which they emerged and evolved. Alan's wide contacts and his position as "Assistant-in-Charge" at the Archive of American Folk Song in the Library of Congress made him a crucial catalyst in introducing American folk music to a mass audience.[17]

THE POLITICAL CONTEXT IS crucial to understanding Lee Hays, his friends, and the songs they created. I asked Seeger in 2002 if he thought the political context could now be discussed more frankly. He told me, "I think the time has come for complete candor." His next sentence began somewhat equivocally: "I don't think Lee was ever actually a Communist Party member," he said. Then he added three words—"as I was"—that gave his statement more credibility. He said that Lee applied for membership "three or four times," but the Party considered him too undisciplined," too "unreliable." Pete had joined the Young Communist League when he was a student at Harvard and had become a Party member about the time he met Lee. Whether Lee was a Party member or not, the Almanacs supported the Party more than the Party supported them. Despite their performing in countless political rallies and benefits for left-wing causes, the reaction they got from the Party was indifference, even sometimes hostility.[18]

The Almanac Singers began to develop a following with their satirical political commentary, usually set to traditional folk tunes. Woody scrawled a letter to Alan Lomax reporting on the Almanacs' activities, "Been singing around at some few peace rallies, women's teas, union meetings, and so forth." Bess wrote that they "never wore costumes or other distinguishing marker" but simply performed "in the clothes we had on." Nor did they use intricate arrangements. Pete explained that "we want the folks who listen to be able to pick up the songs easily." The *Daily Worker* dubbed them "the Peace Army" and said their songs came "from the heart of the American people."[19]

The Almanacs met Theodore Dreiser when they sang at a meeting of the League of American Writers in the spring of 1941. As Lee recalled it, "Dreiser embarrassed the hell out of the Almanacs when he jumped up after a song and gave me a hug and a kiss on the cheek in front of the crowd, and declared that 'If we had six teams like these boys we could save America.'" Lee thought it might "take a few more than six."[20]

The *Sunday Worker* favorably reviewed the Almanac Singers' album *Songs for John Doe*, singling out one of their songs for quotation: "Remember when the AAA / Killed a million hogs a day / Instead of hogs it's men today / Plow the fourth one under." The reviewer considered the album "very suitable for performance before large bodies of people—peace rallies, union meetings, and other gatherings. Simple songs of peace, they should be brought into every town and hamlet in this country."[21]

Songs for John Doe was also reviewed in the *Atlantic Monthly* by Carl Joachim Friedrich, a German-born Harvard professor of government. He denounced the Almanac Singers and their recordings as "poison in our system." The recordings were "distributed under the innocuous appeal: 'Sing out for peace,'" he wrote. "Yet they are strictly subversive and illegal." Friedrich asserted the singers were "either Communist or Nazi financed" and warned that "you can never handle situations of this kind democratically by mere suppression."[22]

Hays denied that the Almanacs were controlled by the Communist Party, despite some efforts by the Party to do so. Their intellectual independence often irked Party activists. For instance, the Almanacs looked forward to performing Lee's anti-racist song "Jim Crow" at the American Youth Congress in Washington in 1941: "Lincoln set the Negro free. / Why is he still in slavery? / Why is he still in slavery? / Jim Crow!" A Party official ordered them to alter the last line from "Jim Crow" to "Jim Crow Gotta Go!" Lee refused to sacrifice his artistic integrity just to parrot the Party's slogan of the week. In another song that year, "No Discrimination," Hays praised President Roosevelt's Fair Employment Practices Committee, which the Party had attacked as "too bourgeois" in 1941 and as "too militant" in 1942. The difficulty of keeping up with frequent shifts in the Party line prompted Woody to write a satire on the problem: "I learned a song to sing / To the entire population, / But I ain't a-doing a thing tonight / On account of the new situation." Pete subtly parodied the Party's ineffectual attempts at thought control: "A nice man" came several times "to give the Almanacs a little instruction." He would ask them "'What do you think of the news of the week?' We'd give our interpretation. He'd say, 'Well, have you thought of this?' Oh, no, we didn't think of that. 'Well, you should. Marx pointed out the class basis of things.'" But for the most part the Almanacs and the Party ignored or distrusted each other.[23]

LEE AND HIS FRIENDS lived and worked *communally*, within a little-c communist milieu. They shared domestic responsibilities and held their income in common. Recalling what he called "Almanac Times," Lee noted wryly that "Left-wing cultural groups have been mighty handy with manifestoes," but he doubted any group's "production so equaled its *theory* of production" as the

Almanac Singers. Even their *songs* were the product of communal composition. They realized that "if the Almanacs wanted to work full time at the task of writing songs to save America, they had to live cooperatively—share and share alike—setting aside individual ambitions for fame and fortune. One go-getter with his eye on the main chance could have spoiled the game for all."[24]

Hays believed the Almanacs should "tap that root of the people's own culture—to mine out a particular vein." And their songs conveyed the plight of poor blacks in the black belts of the South, poor whites in Appalachian coal fields and dust-bowl farms far more effectively than articles in the *Daily Worker* or the *New Masses*. He believed "the Almanacs came closer to the mother lode than any other group before or since, because they were closer to the people, and from the people drew their wisdom and strength."[25]

Lee persuaded the group, at least for a while, that "cooperative effort produced songs on a higher creative level than solo writing." He encouraged what they called "Almanac anonymity," so that no individual "might claim credit for a song unless he had written it *in toto,* which seldom happened." What mattered was the song itself, *what* was written rather than *who* wrote it. "There was a critique in tossing verses back and forth which was much more than a mere trial and error, or 'thinking out loud' method. It was truly a matter of the sum being more than the total of the parts. A qualitative change took place which transcended individual abilities."[26]

The Almanacs' repertoire and style were rooted in what Bess called "the best of traditional Southern music, both black and white, just the kind of thing that Alan and my father had been recording." Such sounds were new and fresh to New York audiences. The various Almanacs spent "hours and hours daily in front of the record player absorbing into their bones the intonations and nuances of great folk musicians." Listening one afternoon, Lee and Mill were inspired to write new union verses to the "Talking Blues" first recorded by the South Carolinian Chris Bouchillon. Within a few hours they had it almost completed. "The only trouble was we couldn't see how to end it," Pete said. "A couple of weeks later, mulling it over, I realized there was no solution except in the old slogan, 'Stick together.' So, ignoring the rhyme, I slung on the last two stanzas, and we had a song." Pete performed it with the Almanac Singers as "Talking Union." Alan Lomax, Bess recalled, was convinced the Almanacs had figured out "how to bring country music to the city and doing a whale of a job with it."[27]

Communal composition, however, eventually provoked discord. In their desire to create songs with a purpose, they developed an appetite for self-examination, holding forth in incessant discussions of how to compose their repertoire. Lee and Woody of course stressed having lived the songs they wrote. Lee felt it was "impossible for anyone to write a worthwhile song about something outside his or her personal experience." Woody agreed: "Anybody can set down and think up a lot of pretty things and all but that don't count no more than a sneeze in a cyclone." As an example, he said, "You can't write a good song about a dust storm unless you been in one."[28]

On the other hand, Woody complained that the Almanacs were not serious enough in their politics. They "let their work drop from a high political level, almost to a low, gossiping personal basis." But Lee angrily resisted the notion that *all* their songs should be political. It would be "a dull life indeed," he retorted, "if workers didn't know anything but labor songs. One of the things workers have fought for was to have TV's and radios so they could have the culture of the country and the whole world."[29]

They also clashed over communal composition. Lee usually did his best work in collaboration, while Woody worked best when the spirit moved him. He regarded Lee's notion that cooperative efforts produced better songs as nonsense. "I like talk and speeches about songs," he said, but "too much broth spoils the cook." Woody could be "cooperative and creative at times," according to the composer Earl Robinson, who occasionally participated in their discussions, but "depending on how he felt at the moment, he could be impossible to work with."[30]

The other Almanacs, especially Mill Lampell, became increasingly annoyed with Woody's proletarian pretensions. Although Woody had adopted a hayseed image as a hillbilly singer and homespun philosopher on a California radio station, he was neither unlettered nor proletarian. Privately Woody admitted as much to Lomax: "I wasn't in the class that John Steinbeck called 'the Okies' because my dad to start with was worth about thirty-five or forty thousand dollars, and he had everything hunky-dory. Then he started having a little bad luck." One day Mill had as much as he could take of Woody's relentless lecturing on artistic authenticity and challenged him. Woody shot back, "Leastways I don't write songs about stuff I don't know the first doggone thing about. *You* never done it, and *you* never lived it." Mill pointed out that "you were never on the *Reuben James*, either."[31]

Woody was also given to virtuoso tantrums. He belittled Bess for singing "House of the Rising Sun" when she had never been "within ten country miles of a cathouse." He called her "a pampered, middle-class, college-educated daddy's pet who didn't know what real work meant." Woody's attack elicited an unexpected outburst from the normally mild-mannered Gordon Friesen, who had grown up in a big family on a small farm. "Woody, what on earth are you talking about?" You are "an intellectual, a poet," he said. "You never did a day's work in your life."[32]

Communal living can be stressful even in the best of times, and for the Almanac Singers, insolvent musicians struggling to reconcile their musical aspirations and their politics with one another, the early 1940s may have seemed more like the worst of times. Life at Almanac House was increasingly strained. Woody complained that the place was "hard to get into, hard to pay rent on, and hard to get out of." Bess complained that Pete was too puritanical. "He didn't approve of liquor, cigarettes, coffee, even sex."[33] Pete complained that Lee was "cantankerous." Lee complained of Pete's "arrogant modesty." They all complained about what they considered Lee's malingering. He constantly missed performances, saying he was too sick to sing. None believed his claim to have tuberculosis, but there was not enough money between them for a doctor to confirm or discredit his self-diagnosis. Once, as they left Lee reclining on a couch while they were off to a performance, Pete pulled his recorder from his pocket and played "Taps." Eventually Lee was expelled from the Almanacs. Later he was diagnosed with diabetes; it would cost him both legs.[34]

THE ALMANACS HAD DIFFICULTY keeping up with the Party's sudden lurches from one position to another. They were dutifully anti-war following the Hitler-Stalin Pact; but after Germany attacked the Soviet Union "our whole politics took a terrible shift," Lee said, from "the Yanks *ain't* coming" to "the Yanks *are* coming" Leadbelly's friend Junius Scales—a 20-year-old Communist organizer from North Carolina who was in New York for a honeymoon and a Party conference—recollected that "for months the war had been denounced as imperialist. The new Party line was that the entire character of the war had changed, that with the entry of the Soviet Union it had become an anti-Fascist war, and that everything should be done to defeat Fascism." The Almanac Singers were relieved; but, as Lee noted, "It sure knocked hell out of our repertoire."[35]

Public anti-Communism joined with Party apathy to impede the Almanacs'
efforts to make a living. They could only get small bookings on what they
called the "subway circuit"—five dollars here and ten dollars there, with subway
rides between. Prospects were poor in '41, but the question was mooted in
the summer of '42 when Pete received his draft notice. He was "almost glad,"
he wrote in his journal, "to get out of the Almanacs before they fell apart."
While Private Seeger was shipping out to the South Pacific, Woody and Cisco
signed up for the war effort, sailing the Atlantic in the Merchant Marine.
The *Daily Worker* reported in January 1943 that the Almanac Singers were no
more, "but everybody who ever was an Almanac is still going strong, each in
his own way, each keeping the tradition of folk-singing in America alive."[36]

After the war, Lee, Pete, Woody, Mill Lampell, Alan Lomax, and others
organized People's Songs to spread their music to as many people as possible.
Pete was elected president and Lee vice president. In the very first issue of
People's Songs Bulletin, Lee proclaimed that "the people are on the march and
must have songs to sing." In theory, of course, whatever "the people" sang
was "people's music." In practice, the people of People's Songs favored songs
with a political message set to folk tunes, like the ones Lee and Woody were
writing. "The only kind of music that I know how to sing is folk music," Lee
acknowledged, adding that "the music I most enjoy singing, and sing best,
is the music that I learned from Negro singers." All that really counted, Lee
noted, "was that we were singing. It was a drawing together of inner strengths,
and what mattered was that each offered his voice to the others, and his own
strength." In the Cold War atmosphere, however, much of the country was
marching to the right, and many of their friends were seeking less risky careers
by cleansing their songs of radical commentary. Still hopeful, Lee wrote the
lyrics and Pete the music for the 1948 presidential campaign of Progressive
Party candidate Henry Wallace. But Wallace lost, and by March 1949 the
political and financial problems of People's Songs forced it to cease.[37]

On the Saturday before Labor Day 1949, several thousand people assembled
in a large field near Peekskill—a summer resort about 40 miles north of New
York City—for an outdoor concert featuring Paul Robeson and Seeger. Robeson's outspoken and well-publicized opinions aroused the hostility of more
than a dozen right-wing groups calling themselves veterans' organizations.
They threatened to disrupt the concert, but Robeson had vowed to "take my
voice wherever there are those who want to hear the melody of freedom."

The applause was overwhelming when Robeson sang his revised ending to "Old Man River": "I get weary / and sick of tryin', / I must keep fightin' / Until I'm dyin' / But Old Man River / he just keeps rollin' along." Pete sang a new song he and Lee had written a few months earlier, reaffirming both for themselves and for their audience their defiance of efforts to shut them up. They had premiered the song at a benefit concert for the 11 Communist leaders then on trial in New York City. Lee's lyrics were so controversial that no commercial music publisher had been willing to publish it: "If I had a hammer, I'd hammer in the morning / I'd hammer in the evening—all over this land. / I'd hammer out danger! I'd hammer out a warning! / I'd hammer out love between all of my brothers / All over this land." The song reaffirmed the commitment of Lee and Pete and their audience to such dangerous ideals as justice, freedom, and brotherly love.[38]

The concert seemed to have gone well, but when it was over the exiting audience had to run a gauntlet through what Lee called "a tunnel lined on both sides with the enemy. And rocks, boards, bottles." He said the "police slowed down vehicles so the hoodlums could get better aim." Mothers and fathers "shielded their children with their bodies," and he described "the people in the buses singing, Woody leading, 'I'm worried now but I won't be worried long.' Our battle song, 'We shall not be moved!'" And then "I'll sing out danger! I'll sing out warning! I'll sing out love. . . ." Peekskill was the first riot of the Cold War. There were no arrests.[39]

LEE AND PETE WERE determined not to give up on the fight they believed must be waged for justice, freedom, and love. They discussed "forming a more organized singing group." Lee thought it should be "like the old Almanacs, but with discipline." Woody had called the Almanacs "the only group that rehearses on the stage." Soon Fred Hellerman, "a gifted guitarist who could sing either high or low," and Ronnie Gilbert, an "exciting contralto," joined their voices with "my split tenor and Lee's big gospel bass," Pete wrote, referring to his own flights into the falsetto range. They were delighted to find that their blend gave "a big solid warmth to the songs of Leadbelly and to many songs which had seemed ineffectual with one voice." As they rehearsed, Pete's fingers added slight rhythmic and harmonic adjustments to his accompaniment that helped bring the songs to life. They decided to call themselves the Weavers. Lee said they would weave themselves into the warp and woof of American music. "I'll do the woofing, and the others will continue being warped."[40]

In November 1949 the Weavers' prospects seemed negligible. Many of their friends found the stoning and shattered glass at Peekskill eerily similar to *Kristallnacht* eleven years earlier in Nazi Germany, and few among their audience were eager to gather in public. Lee and Pete—so optimistic when they founded People's Songs—were uneasy with the Party's new militant temper and sectarian infighting. Its membership was plunging, and Pete became one of the dropouts. The Weavers considered disbanding, but Pete persuaded them that they needed new audiences. As a "last desperate gasp," he said, "we decided to do the unthinkable: get a job in a nightclub." They got a two-week booking at New York's Village Vanguard during Christmas of 1950. They were paid $200 a week with free hamburgers, soon revised to $250 a week without hamburgers.[41]

The Weavers stayed at the Village Vanguard for six months. There they met Gordon Jenkins, a man who would change their lives. Music director for Decca Records, he came to hear them one night, and then returned "for something like 40 nights running," Lee recalled. "For forty nights he sat there listening to our music, which is how we got our commercial start." He took them up to Decca's New York Studios, where they auditioned for Dave Kapp. Kapp was dubious. "Take that Tzena song," he said, referring to their performance of an Israeli soldiers' tune. "That obviously has to be rewritten in English and Tzena has to come out as a girl's name. But you have to decide in which direction you want to go, whether you want to be *good* or *commercial*. Think it over and let me know." According to Lee, Jenkins "told Kapp that he was going to sign us up himself and record us, which I think was the clincher."[42]

On May 4, 1950, they made their first record, with "Tzena" on side A and Leadbelly's "Goodnight, Irene" on the other. Gordon had dutifully rewritten "Tzena" in English, so that Tzena became a girl's name. But he doubted that Kapp would accept "Irene." While the song had a memorable chorus, he feared that such downbeat lines as "jump in the river and drown" and "take morphine and die" might consign it to the wastebasket. But after he sanitized it a bit, Kapp let it go through. The record rose up the charts so fast that by June, disc jockeys didn't know which side they were expected to play. "As it turned out," Lee wrote, "'Tzena' was number one for weeks and weeks and then "Goodnight, Irene" turned around and became one and 'Tzena' became number two, both on the same record, much to the dismay of Decca because if they had put out two records they would have had twice as much income."[43]

Within weeks, the Weavers were stars. By late September *Time* magazine reported that "both sides of the record were on the hit parade for the eleventh time" with "Irene" in first place and "Tzena" in fourth. By October "Irene" was playing on radios and juke boxes across America at the rate of 1,400 times a minute. By November it was number one in Britain as well, selling altogether more than a million-and-a-half copies. Paul Cohen, head of Decca's country and western operation, told Lee that the Weavers had "hit the top of both popular lists and C and W lists. That's amazing—it's never been done before." Unlike Kapp, Cohen was as much cheerleader as executive, later becoming president of the Country Music Association. "Goodnight, Irene" was soon covered by Frank Sinatra, Jo Stafford, and Dennis Day in popular music, Red Foley and Ernest Tubb in country music, and Paul Gayten on the R&B charts.[44]

With Gordon Jenkins producing, the Weavers recorded hit after hit. According to Lee, "when he arranged our songs for recording, he never required us to change one note of the way we sang it in night clubs or in public. He packaged it with a lot of violins before and after and during. But the thing that came out was the song intact." For example, Pete had picked up an interesting song on a record from South Africa by Solomon Linda. It was a vocal solo by Pete without words—just vocalizing. The title—"Mubube"—was written on the record in Zulu. Pete played the record over and over, finally pronouncing it "Wimoweh." Gordon didn't record it right away. He worried that dealers—especially for the juke-box trade—typically listened to the first few seconds of the record and made their decisions to accept or reject on the spot. "After puzzling over the problem," Lee recalled, Jenkins "wrote a magnificent orchestral arrangement on most of the first half of the record. Then he bridged with a lovely piano break which he did with one finger, that being one of the things he was noted for, one-fingered piano. And then he turned us loose to begin singing and the whole thing achieved a kind of unity which was unexpected and most successful."[45]

In the meantime, the Weavers moved from the Village Vanguard to Manhattan's Blue Angel nightclub for four more months. By the end of September, *Time* reported, they were scheduled to move into Broadway's Strand Theater for $2,250 a week. Lee's satirical wit "spiced every performance," according to Pete. One of his best stories involved a preacher who claimed that music was an invention of the devil. "Preacher," Hays asks, "how can you not like music? Music is the language of the soul: it expresses the inexpressible, satisfies the insatiable." The preacher opines, "I don't care if it unscrews the inscrutable, it's sinful, and I'm against it." A Reno nightclub provided another example: Lee tells Pete that a poet friend of his claims "everything in the world is grist for the writer's mill." Pete looks around the room with mock incredulity. "Grist?" he asks. "Yeah," Lee replies, "but where do you start shoveling when it's up to your neck?"[46]

THE WEAVERS SUDDEN RISE into the pop music limelight was dazzling. In the summer of 1950 they were offered a weekly television show, but a few days later the right-wing journal *Counterattack* published a tract titled *Red Channels: The Report of Communist Influence in Radio and Television*. It named 151 actors, writers, musicians, broadcast journalists, and others as participants in what they called "the spread of Communist influence in the entertainment industry." To be listed in *Red Channels* was to be blacklisted in the motion picture, television, and radio industries. By the end of the week the Weavers' television contract was withdrawn. Then, in February 1952 a hired informant named Harvey Matusow testified under oath before the House Committee on Un-American Activities that he knew the Weavers "and they are Communists."[47]

Lee and Pete were called before the House Un-American Activities Committee. On August 16, 1955, Lee invoked the Fifth Amendment privilege against self-incrimination and was excused. Pete took a riskier course two days later. Implicitly invoking the First Amendment, he simply stated, "I am not going to answer any questions as to my associations, my philosophical or religious beliefs or my political beliefs, or how I voted in any election or any of these private affairs. I think these are very improper questions for any American to be asked, especially under such compulsion as this." He insisted that "in my whole life I have never done anything of any conspiratorial nature" and he deeply resented the implication "that I am any less of an American than anybody else. I love my country very deeply, sir." He said "I have sung for Americans of every political persuasion, and I have never refused to sing for anybody because I disagreed with their political opinion." He believed his songs "cut across and find perhaps a unifying thing, basic humanity." The Committee cited him for Contempt of Congress. As 1952 wore on fewer and fewer venues were willing to book the Weavers. By 1953 they took what Lee called a "sabbatical." He said that it "turned into a Mondical and a Tuesdi-cal" as well. Pete was tried and convicted in March 1961 and sentenced to a year and a day in federal prison. A year later a court of appeals dismissed the case on a technicality, mooting the Constitutional question. In 1955 Matu-sow would admit lying under oath and be sentenced to nearly four years in prison for perjury. But there would be no reversals for those who lost their jobs because of his lies.[48]

Despite *Red Channels* and Harvey Matusow, the Weavers' string of best-selling records continued. Between 1950 and 1952 they had nine more hits on the *Billboard* pop music charts, including "On Top of Old Smoky," "Wimoweh," Leadbelly's "Kisses Sweeter than Wine," and Woody's "So Long, It's Been Good to Know You."[49] As Pete put it, the Weavers had performed "on vaudeville stages and in some high-priced saloons," and they had seen "the glorious and the seamy sides of the commercial music business." They staged a comeback on Christmas Eve of 1955 with a well-received concert at Carnegie Hall, accompanied only by their own musical instruments and making their own political commentary. "This concert was received so well," wrote Pete, "that the Weavers were in business again." They liked making "freer choices about where and how we wanted to sing; and audiences responded to the informal give-and-take which we ourselves enjoyed."[50]

LEE HAYS EXEMPLIFIED WHAT Robert Korstad calls "a distinctive Southern wing" of the Popular Front. The suffering of the Great Depression and the New Deal's efforts for recovery and reform helped at least many white Southerners put their economic interests ahead of inherited racial assumptions. Lee's fusion of traditional Southern hymns and folk songs with progressive political ide-als gave them deeper theological and ideological resonance and helped build the labor movement in the South. He brought his Southern experience with him to New York and shared his knowledge and his talents. As part of the Almanac Singers and the Weavers, he was part of an exciting upsurge of grass-roots cultural activity in the 1930s and 1940s that has come to be called the cultural front. Acknowledging its origins in the Communist Party's Popular Front, and conceding the influence of the Party on the left turn in America's art, music, and literature in the period, this "Second American Renaissance" was prompted less by Party efforts or control than by the Great Depression and the Second World War.[51]

Lee and his friends could have sought purely private pleasure and gain, but the more clearly they recognized the worst in their society, the more obvious was the need to cherish what was best. More perhaps than any other artistic effort, their passion for folk music confirmed and carried forward the spirit of the cultural front. They launched the growing popularity of folk music from the '40s into the 60s, but their enthusiasm for folk music was neither shared nor supported by the official Party leaders. "The Communist Party didn't know what to do with folk music," recalled Irwin Silber, a party functionary but a folk music supporter. "Although a number of us in the leadership of People's Songs and People's Artists were members of the Communist Party, the Party itself played almost no role in determining policies and activities." Lee simply became indifferent. "When it came to shifts and turns in the Party line, I didn't pay any attention to them," he said. "I knew what I thought was right, and I wasn't gonna lose sleep over it."[52]

Lee and his friends paid a price for their politics. They had their full share—perhaps more than their share—of blind faith, illusions and disillusionment with a cause they came to repudiate. In the early morning hours of February 25, 1956, at the 20th Party Congress, Soviet Prime Minister Nikita Khrushchev delivered a devastating denunciation of what he called Joseph Stalin's "repression and physical annihilation, not only against actual enemies, but also against individuals who had not committed any crimes against the party or the Soviet Government." It came to be called the "Secret Speech," but it did not remain secret very long. American communists were stunned. Rumors of purges and gulags were not new, but most had considered them anticommunist lies. It was almost unbearable to learn, as Junius Scales expressed it, that "Stalin—my revered symbol of the infallibility of Communism, the builder of socialism in one country, the rock of Stalingrad, the wise, kindly man with the keen sense of humor at whose death I had wept just three years before—Stalin had been a murderous, power-hungry monster."[53]

The youthful passions and convictions that had led Lee and his friends into a lifetime of commitment now lay shattered, although some managed to repress their doubts and stifle their uncertainties for years. After decades of ambiguity, in 2007 Pete Seeger displayed an almost Calvinistic sense of conscience in "False from True," ruefully recalling "when I found tarnish on some of my brightest dreams" and "when some folks I knew and trusted turned out not quite what they seemed." His song ends with a confession of his need "to start the job of separating *false* from *true*." And he explicitly condemns Stalin in his "Big Joe Blues": "I'm singing about old Joe, cruel Joe. / He ruled with an iron hand. / He put an end to the dreams / Of so many in every land. / He had a chance to make / A brand new start for the human race. / Instead he set it back / Right in the same nasty place. / I got the Big Joe Blues. / (Keep your mouth shut or you will die fast.) / I got the Big Joe Blues. / (Do this job, no questions asked.) / I got the Big Joe Blues."[54] Lee's poet friend Walter Lowenfels wrote, "Remember us / Not for the stupid things we've done and can't forget . . . / Nor all the sad chronicles that we leave behind, / But that we loved as much as anyone ever did . . . / The dream of changing the world to something new . . . / Our greatest joy was in opening the way for you." Certainly their ideals sometimes misled them, but their dream of making a better world cannot be rejected as altogether worthless. [55]

The Khrushchev revelations and the brutal Soviet invasion of Hungary were a last straw for even many of the truest believers. Lee and his friends were less true believers than skeptical idealists. They agonized over the inherent tension between their rival commitments to the ideals of the people—a source of unity—and to the rights of individuals to determine their own destinies—a source of division. On a personal level they felt keenly the tension between their own need for individual self-expression and for belonging to a community. They believed that the soul of America was to be found in the *people*, in the fluency of their speech, and in the joy of their music. Whatever America's faults, there was something intrinsically good about the country. The people's ideals and the people's songs provided a path to a happier and safer world. The Weavers added a new introduction to the old spiritual "When the Saints Go Marching In" and began their concerts with it: "We are traveling in the footsteps / of those who've gone before / and we'll all be reunited / on a new and sunlit shore."[56]

HISTORICALLY THERE HAVE BEEN gaps between ideals and reality in all ideologies; and in the name of their ideals men and women have committed many heroic acts, many stupid blunders, and many vicious atrocities. But the ideals that led Lee Hays *into* the communist milieu were the very same ideals that motivated and sustained him and that animated his best songs. In other times and other places, perhaps he might have found other allies. But in the American South of the 1930s, those who found the poverty and racism around them intolerable had few options. In North Carolina, Junius Scales noted that at the time the Communist Party was "the only organization that was foursquare for economic justice for blacks" and the only one saying that "people should live together in peace and brotherhood." The "Communists were putting themselves on the line and getting beaten to death," he added, "and they were the most courageous people I knew." Looking back late in his life, he said in an interview, "With all the wrong turns and missteps I made, those ideals of human brotherhood that led me *into* the Communist Party and *out* of the Communist Party are the same ones that I will advocate as long as I live."

Lee Hays could have sought fame and fortune for himself, but he was not even comfortable with such fame and fortune as he achieved. He chose to use his talents not to enrich himself but through his music to enrich the lives and hopes and dreams of people around the world. His songs were created out of his commitment to those ideals. If they were the source of his greatest commercial failures, they also inspired his greatest artistic achievements.[57]

• • •

For conversations over the past half-century that, in their varying ways, have helped me to understand better the ideologies and ideals explored in this essay, I am profoundly grateful to John Dos Passos, Granville Hicks, Pete Seeger, Eugene Genovese, Junius Scales, William McKee Evans, and Robert Korstad.

NOTES

1 Pete Seeger, telephone interview with Charles Joyner, June 3, 2002, hereinafter Seeger interview (first quote); Lee Hays and Pete Seeger, quoted in David King Dunaway, *How Can I Keep from Singing: Pete Seeger* (New York, 1981), 76 (second and third quotes). See also Doris Willens, *Lonesome Traveler: The Life of Lee Hays* (Lincoln, Neb., 1988), 65–67, and Dunaway, *How Can I Keep from Singing,* 76–81. The folksinger Oscar Brand, who had personally experienced Lee Hays's leaning, described it as "very impressive." See his *The Ballad Mongers: Rise of the Modern Folk Song* (New York, 1962), 107.

2 Seeger interview; Willens, *Lonesome Traveler,* 3–4, 9–17.

3 Hays, "The Singing Preacher," in Lee Hays Papers, Ralph Rinzler Folklife Archive and Collection, Smithsonian Institution, Washington, D.C. (hereinafter cited as LHP) first four quotes; Claude Williams, quoted in John Egerton, *Speak Now Against the Day: the Generation Before the Civil Rights Movement in the South* (Chapel Hill, 1994), 158 (fifth quote); Hays, "Singing Preacher," seventh and eighth quotes; Hays, quoted in Jim Capaldi, "Wasn't That a Time! A Conversation with Lee Hays," *Sing Out!* 28 (September–October, 1980), 3–4 (ninth quote); See also Willens, *Lonesome Traveler,* 30–31; Mark Naison,

"Claude and Joyce Williams: Pilgrims of Justice," *Southern Exposure*, 1 No. 3–4 (Winter, 1974), 38–50.

4   Highlander Folk School Collection, Tennessee State Library and Archives, Nashville, Tennessee; Willens; *Lonesome Traveler,* 37–40. See also Jacquelyn Hall and Ray Flaherty, interview with Don West, Southern Oral History Collection, Wilson Library, University of North Carolina, Chapel Hill, interview E 16; *Highlander Folk School: The FBI Files* , vol. 1 (Washington: Federal Bureau of Investigation, 2009), available online at ault. fbi.gov/Highlander%20Folk%20School. See also Robbie Lieberman, *My Song Is My Weapon: People's Songs, American Communism, and the Politics of Culture, 1930–50* (Urbana: University of Illinois Press, 1989, 45–46; Hulan Glyn Thomas, "The Highlander Folk School: The Depression Years, *Tennessee Historical Quarterly*, 23 (December, 1964), 358–71; Thomas Bledsoe, *Or We'll All Hang Separately: The Highlander Idea* (Boston, 1969); Frank Adams, with Myles Horton, *Unearthing Seeds of Fire: The Idea of Highlander* (Winston-Salem, 1975); John M. Glen, *Highlander: No Ordinary School, 1932–1962* (Lexington, Ken., 1988); Aimee I. Horton, *The Highlander Folk School: A History of Its Major Programs, 1932–1961* (New York, 1989); Frank Adams, *James A. Dumbroski: An American Heretic* (Knoxville, 1992); Myles Horton, with Herbert Kohl and Judith Kohl, *The Long Haul: An Autobiography,* rev. ed. (New York, 1997); Dale Evans, ed., *The Myles Horton Reader: Education for Social Change* (Knoxville, 2003); Jeff Biggers and George Brosi, eds., *No Lonesome Road: Selected Prose and Poetry by Don West* (Urbana, 2004).

5   Willens, *Lonesome Traveler*, 50–51. See also Agnes "Sis" Cunningham and Gordon Friesen, *Red Dust and Broadsides*, ed. Ronald D. Cohen (Urbana: University of Illinois Press, 1999), 112–13, 327–29; Ronald D. Cohen, *Rainbow Quest: The Folk Music Revival and American Society, 1940–1970* (Amherst: University of Massachusetts Press, 2002), 20, 22, 23, 28; Michael Denning, *The Cultural Front: The Laboring of American Culture in the Twentieth Century*, the Haymarket Series (New York: Verso,1998), 72. See also Willens, *Lonesome Traveler*, 49–59; Agnes "Sis" Cunningham and Gordon Friesen, *Red Dust and Broadsides*, ed. Ronald D. Cohen (Amherst, 1999), 112–34; Egerton, *Speak Now Against the Day*, 155–8, 172; Josh Dunson, *Freedom in the Air* (New York, 1965), 24–26; Raymond and Charlotte Koch, *Educational Commune: The Story of Commonwealth College* (New York, 1972); and William H. Cobb, *Radical Education in the Rural South: Commonwealth College, 1922–1940* (Detroit, 2000). Neighbors and deputy sheriffs complained of nude swimming and cohabitation among the students. Furthermore, "their militant actions in fostering and leading and agitating dissensions by strikes," a legislative panel concluded, "are extremely radical and close to the border line." And worst of all, a student was reported to have returned home from Commonwealth "a believer in complete racial equality, social, political, and economical." See "Foreword to the Legislative Investigation of Commonwealth College," Appendix IV to William H. Cobb, "Commonwealth College: A History," MA thesis, University of Arkansas, 1963, 254–5.

6   Hays, "Let the Will Be Done" LHP. The Northerners at Commonwealth "made no bones about their displeasure" at Dusenbury's "high, cracked, rhythmless voice." Hays, "Emma Dusenberry," in LHP; Hays, in Capaldi, "A Conversation with Lee Hays," 3. Alan Lomax noted that she held in her head more than two hundred ballads and folk songs. See his "Preface: *Our Singing Country*," in Ronald D. Cohen, ed., *Alan Lomax: Selected Writings, 1934–1997* (New York, 2003), 61. Hays spells her name *Dusenberry,* but the earliest

collectors to record her—the folklorist Vance Randolph, the poet John Gould Fletcher, and the composer and conductor Laurence Powell—spelled it *Dusenbury*, as does Vance's biographer Robert B. Cochran, who told me his "strongest evidence" was the obituary notice in the *Mena Evening Star*, her hometown newspaper Thursday, May 10, 1941). Cochran to Joyner, April 30, 2010. See also his "Emma Hays Dusenbury (1862–1941)," in *Encyclopedia of Arkansas History and Culture* http://www.encyclopediaofarkansas. net; and his "'All the Songs in the World': The Story of Emma Dusenbury," *Arkansas Historical Quarterly*, 44, 1 (Spring, 1985), 3–15; William K. McNeill, introduction to *Ozark Folksongs Collected and Edited by Vance Randolph* (Columbia: University of Missouri Press, 1980), 14–15; Ben F. Johnson, *Fierce Solitude: A Life of John Gould Fletcher* (Fayetteville: University of Arkansas Press, 1994), 216.

7   7. Hays, "Post-humous [sic] Memoirs," LHP; H.L. Mitchell, quoted in William Thomas, "Sharecroppers' Union Celebrates 48th Anniversary of 'Revolution,'" Memphis *Commercial Appeal*, March 28, 1982, D16 (first and second quotes); J. R. Butler, quoted in Sue Thrasher and Leah Wise, "The Southern Tenant Farmers' Union," *Southern Exposure* 1, No. 2 (Winter 1974), 15 (third quote); Mitchell, quoted in "They Tried to Aid Tenants," Valdosta *Daily Times*, April 19, 1972, 9 (fourth quote); Mitchell, quoted in Thomas BeVier, "The '30s Were the Start," Memphis *Commercial Appeal*, March 3, 1972 (fifth quote); Mitchell, quoted in BeVier, "The '30s Were the Start," 1972 (sixth quote); Mitchell, quoted in Little Rock *Arkansas Advocate*, June 1972, 5 (seventh quote). On the struggles of the Southern Tenant Farmers' Union, see Donald H. Grubbs, *Cry from the Cotton: The Southern Tenant Farmers' Union and the New Deal* 2d ed. (Fayetteville, Ark., 2000); Elizabeth Anne Payne, "The Lady Was a Sharecropper: Myrtle Lawrence and the Southern Tenant Farmers' Union," *Southern Cultures*, 4, No. 2 (Summer 1998), 5–27; M. Langley Biegert, "Legacy of Resistance: Uncovering the History of Collective Action by Black Agricultural Workers in Central East Arkansas from the 1860s to the 1930s," *Journal of Social History*, 32 (1998), 73–99; Martin, *Howard Kester*, 89–99; 104–108; Alexander Yard, "'They Don't Regard My Rights At All': Arkansas Farm Workers, Economic Modernization, and the Southern Tenant Farmers' Union," *Arkansas Historical Quarterly*, 47 (1988), 210–29; H. L. Mitchell, *Roll the Union On: A Pictorial History of the Southern Tenant Farmers' Union* (New York, 1987), his *Mean Things Happening in This Land: The Life and Times of H. L. Mitchell, Co-Founder of the Southern Tenant Farmers' Union* (Montclair, N.J., 1979), and his "The Founding and Early History of the Southern Tenant Farmers' Union," *Arkansas Historical Quarterly*, 33 (1973), 342–69; Thrasher and Wise, "The Southern Tenant Farmers' Union," *Southern Exposure* 1, No. 2 (Winter 1974), 5–32; Jerold S. Auerbach, "Southern Tenant Farmers: Socialist Critics of the New Deal," *Labor History*, 7 (1966), 3–18; M. S. Venkataramani, "Norman Thomas, Arkansas Sharecroppers, and the Roosevelt Agricultural Policies, 1933–1937," *Mississippi Valley Historical Review*, 47 (1960), 225–46; and Howard Kester, *Revolt among the Sharecroppers* (New York, 1936).

8   Hays, "The 'Post-humous' Memoirs," LHP; Seeger interview; John Handcox, quoted in William Thomas, "Farmer's Memory Sings 'Raggedy' Tune," Memphis *Commercial Appeal*, April 17, 1982, B1. In response he wrote a song entitled "Raggedy," because "it was written for rough, tough, raggedy times," he added. See John Handcox, "Raggedy, Raggedy Are We," in Woody Guthrie and Pete Seeger, eds., *Hard Hitting Songs for Hard-Hit People*, comp. Alan Lomax (New York, 1967), 260. A poetic example of how

Lee's creative efforts were inspired both by plight of the people and by the structures of their folk music is his "Times Are Gettin' Hard," in Irwin Silber, ed., *Lift Every Voice: The Second People's Songbook* (New York, 1953), 50. His version of "We Shall Not Be Moved" appears uncredited in Pete Seeger and Bob Reiser [eds.], *Carry It On: A History in Song and Picture of America's Working Men and Women* (New York, 1985), 141–42.

9   Don West, interview with Jacquelyn Hall and Ray Flaherty, Southern Oral History Collection, Wilson Library, University of North Carolina, Chapel Hill, interview E 16, 21–22; (22) West was a co-founder of Highlander Folk School with Myles Horton and James Dumbrowski. He had known Williams since they were students at Vanderbilt. See also Robert F. Martin's biography of Mitchell's friend Howard "Buck" Kester, a member of the socialist faction, *Howard Kester and the Struggle for Social Justice in the South, 1904–77* (Charlottesville, 1991), 107–8. Whether or not the actual document came from Williams's pocket, its second paragraph states the following: "Since the reorganization of the school in August 1937, when a Party member became director of the school [Commonwealth], there has been on the campus complete political unity. . . . Students who are not members when they arrive almost invariably become members either here or immediately after they leave." Paragraph six notes that "a situation has now arisen which offers us an extraordinary opportunity to move into the most important organization in the agricultural South: the STFU. H.L. Mitchell, secretary of the STFU, who has been consistently opposed to the International with which that union is affiliated, to the Party, and to Commonwealth, is on a leave of absence from his office. . . . We believe it would place us in a position to capture the union for our line at the next convention. This is an opportunity for establishing a real party base in the STFU." The document summarizes in the final paragraph that "Commonwealth is possibly the Party's most strategic position from which to work at this time in the South, where the danger of Fascism is greatest." Copy of Document Discovered by J. R. Butler, Appendix VI to Cobb, "Commonwealth College: A History," 259, 261.

10   Archie Green, "Charles Louis Seeger (1886–1979)," *Journal of American Folklore* 92 (Oct.–Dec, 1979), 393–94) (391–99); Dunaway, *How Can I Keep from Singing*, 49. The Seeger quotes are in his *Incompleat Folksinger*, 13.

11   Seeger, interview; Bess Lomax Hawes, *Sing It Pretty: A Memoir* (Urbana: University of Illinois Press, 2008), 39–40. "Back in the days of the Almanac Singers," Pete wrote, "Lee Hays taught me what fun it was to improvise a bass part of some old hymn or spiritual. . . . Your tried-and-true bass does not envy the singer of the melody, or the tenor, or anyone else. He knows he is the rock foundation of the musical edifice, the firm support of all that glorious superstructure. And do not think, either, that he is restricted rigidly to a few limited notes. It is true that at certain crucial points he must give out with one basic note and none other. But between these points he is free to roam, to develop what is known as a 'bass line.'" See Pete Seeger, *The Incompleat Folksinger* (New York, 1972), 359. The Almanac Singers may be heard on the following CDs: *The Almanac Singers: Their Complete General Recordings*, MCA 1149; *Songs of Protest*, Prism Leisure PLATCD 704; and *Talking Union*, Naxos 8.120567.

12   Hawes, *Sing It Pretty,*39 (first quote), 40 (second and third quotes); Seeger interview; Willens, *Lonesome Traveler*, 65–67; Klein, *Woody Guthrie*, 190; Richard Reuss, "Woody Guthrie and the Folk Tradition," *Journal of American Folklore*, 83 (1970), 21–32; Dunaway, *How Can I Keep from Singing,* 79–106; Joe Klein, *Woody Guthrie: A Life* (New

York, 1980), 188–239; 243–46, 255; Will Kauffman, *Woody Guthrie, American Radical* (Urbana: University of Illinois Press, 20–21.

13 Hawes, *Sing It Pretty,* 40.

14 Hawes, *Sing It Pretty*, 41; Seeger, *Incompleat Folksinger*, 17; Huddie Ledbetter, quoted in Lomax, *Selected Writings*, 51; Charles K. Wolfe and Kip Lornell, The Life And Legend Of Leadbelly (New York: HarperCollins, 1992) ; Although Lead Belly (two words) is considered by some the proper spelling for Ledbetter's nickname, there is a picture of him and his wife Martha in Moe Asch and Alan Lomax, *The Leadbelly Songbook* (New York: Oak Publications, 1962. The inscription, in Ledbetter's own hand, reads "Lisen folks this Leadbelly [one word] talking to you How do you do" [sic, absence of punctuation in original].

15 Shelly Romalis, *Pistol Packin' Mama: Aunt Molly Jackson and the Politics of Folksong* (Urbana, 1999), 112–13, 147, 153–54; Jim Garland, *Welcome the Traveler Home: Jim Garland's Story of the Kentucky Mountains,* ed. Julia S. Ardery (Lexington, Ky., University of Kentucky Press,1983); Sarah Ogan Gunning, "My Name Is Sarah Ogan Gunning," *Sing Out!* 25 (July–August 1976), 15–17); Woody Guthrie, "The Story of Sara Ogan," in *Hard-Hitting Songs,* 154 ; Millard Lampell, "Home Before Morning," Unpublished manuscript, quoted in Cunningham and Friesen, *Red Dust and Broadsides*, 339, n 28; Hawes, *Sing It Pretty*, 42.

16 Elijah Wald, *Josh White: Society Blues* (Amherst: University of Massachusetts Press, 2000),

17 John Szwed, *Alan Lomax: The Man Who Recorded the World* (New York: Viking, 2010), 183–84; Ronald D. Cohen, ed., *Alan Lomax, Assistant in Charge: The Library of Congress Letters* (Jackson: University Press of Mississippi, 2011).

18 Seeger interview.

19 Woody Guthrie to Alan Lomax, n.d. [early 1941], in Woody Guthrie Mss. Coll., Box 1, Folder A, Correspondence, 1940–1950, A20, Archive of American Folk Song, Library of Congress (hereinafter cited as WGM; Hawes , *Sing It Pretty,* 40 (first quote); "Pete Bowers" [Seeger's Party Name] quoted in *Daily Worker*, May 15, 1941 (second quote); *Daily Worker*, May 15, 1941 (third quote); *Daily Worker*, March 24, 1941 (fourth quote).

20 Hays, untitled column, *People's Songs Bulletin*, Dec 1948. There was a news story on the incident in the *Daily Worker*, March 24, 1941.

21 *Sunday Worker*, May 18, 1941.

22 Carl Joachim Friedrich, "The Poison in Our System," *Atlantic Monthly*, 167–72 (June 1941), 661–72. It was reprinted as a pamphlet by the "Council for Democracy" in New York.

23 Hays, "The Cisco Tapes," quoted in Koppelman, *Sing Out Warning*, 23–24; Lieberman, *My Song Is My Weapon*, 7; Guthrie, "The New Situation," quoted in Richard A. Reuss, "American Folklore and Left-Wing Politics: 1927–1957," PhD dissertation, Indiana University, 1971, 229; Seeger, quoted in Kauffman, *Woody Guthrie*, 72. See also Lieberman, *My Song Is My Weapon,* 56. Hays had encountered the Party's combination of indifference and hostility in his Commonwealth College days. Some at the labor school found it quite difficult. Charlotte "Chucky" Moskowitz, Commonwealth's executive-secretary, vented her frustration to her novelist friend and fellow-Party member Jack Conroy: "Most of us down here consider ourselves pretty good communists, you know, but we can't work with the party." Jack Conroy Papers, 1924–1991, The Newberry Library, Chicago, Illinois.

24   Hays, Untitled column in *People's Songs Bulletin*, November, 1948, LHP.

25   Hays, "The Singing Preacher," LHP.

26   Hays, Untitled Column in *People's Songs Bulletin*, September 1948, LHP.

27   Hawes, *Sing It Pretty*, 40–41; Hawes, "When We Were Joyful," written for the program book of the Smithsonian Institution's annual Festival of American Folklife, 1997; Hawes, *Sing It Pretty*, 41. See http://www.folklife.si.edu/97fest/joyful.htm. Hear it on the Almanac Singers CD *Talking Union*, Naxos 8.120567.

28   Lee Hays, quoted in Cunningham and Friesen, *Red Dust and Broadsides*, 283 (first quote); Woody Guthrie to Alan Lomax, April 1941, in Correspondence, 1940–1950, Guthrie Manuscript Collection, Archive of American Folk Songs, Library of Congress. (second quote); Woody Guthrie, quoted in Cunningham and Friesen, *Red Dust and Broadsides*, 283; (third quote).

29   Woody Guthrie, notes on back of the lyrics to his "In Washington," Woody Guthrie Papers, Smithsonian Institution, hereinafter identified as WGP; Lee Hays, quoted in Capaldi, "Wasn't That a Time!" 6–7.

30   Woody Guthrie, handwritten notes on "My Union County Girl," WGP; Earl Robinson with Eric Gordon, *Ballad of an American: the Autobiography of Earl Robinson* (Lanham, Md: Scarecrow Press, 1998, 142.

31   Woody Guthrie, on a recording of songs and conversation with Alan Lomax, recorded in Washington March 1940, *Woody Guthrie: the Library of Congress Recordings*, (Rounder B0000002QZ, Disc 1, Track 5; Millard Lampell, "Home Before Morning," unpublished manuscript in Ronald Cohen Collection, Gary, Indiana, 224, quoted in Kaufmann, *Woody Guthrie*, 89. See also Bill C. Malone, review of Ed Robbin, *Woody Guthrie and Me: An Intimate Reminiscence* (Berkeley: Lancaster-Miller, 1979), and Joe Klein, *Woody Guthrie: A Life* (New York: Knopf, 1980), in *American Music*, 3 (1985), 485–86. The *Reuben James* was an American ship sunk in the Atlantic by a German U-boat a few weeks before Pearl Harbor. It was the subject of one of Woody's best songs.

32   Lampell, "Home Before Morning," 224, 236; Gordon Friesen, in Cunningham and Friesen, *Red Dust and Broadsides*, 339, n 28. Hear Woody's own recording of "The House of the Rising Sun" with the Almanac Singers on Pete Seeger and Woody Guthrie, *House of the Rising Sun*, Delta Music Company.UK, B001NV1DQA.

33   Woody Guthrie to Alan Lomax, Correspondence 1940–1950, GMP; Bess Lomax Hawes, quoted in Dunaway, *How Can I Keep from Singing*, 96.; Seeger interview.

34   Seeger interview; Seeger, *Incompleat Folksinger*, 17 (second and third quotes); Willens, *Lonesome Traveler*, 230–32, 65–75. For the Almanac years, see also Alan Lomax, "Music in Your Own Back Yard," *The American Girl*, October, 1940, in Cohen, ed., *Alan Lomax*, 53, 61; Richard Reuss, "Woody Guthrie and the Folk Tradition," *Journal of American Folklore*, 83 (1970), 21–32; Dunaway, *How Can I Keep from Singing*, 79–106; Joe Klein, *Woody Guthrie: A Life* (New York, 1980), 188–239; 243–46, 255; Charles Wolfe and Kip Lornell, *The Life and Legend of Leadbelly* (New York, 1992); Frederic Ramsey, Jr., "Leadbelly's Legacy," in *Saturday Review Reader* (New York, 1951), 122–23; Elijah Wald, *Josh White: Society Blues* (New York, 2002). 75–79; Shelly Romalis, *Pistol Packin' Mama: Aunt Molly Jackson and the Politics of Folksong* (Urbana, 1999), 112–13, 147, 153–54; Jim Garland, *Welcome the Traveler Home: Jim Garland's Story of the Kentucky Mountains*, ed. Julia S. Ardery (Lexington, Ky., 1983); Sarah Ogan Gunning, "My Name Is Sarah

Ogan Gunning," *Sing Out!* 25 (July–August 1976), 15–17; Cunningham and Friesen, *Red Dust and Broadsides,* 112–34, 208–15.

35 Hays, quoted in Jim Capaldi, "Wasn't That a Time! A Conversation with Lee Hays," *Sing Out!* 28 (September–October 1980), 5 (first and third quotes); Junius Irving Scales and Richard Nickson, *Cause at Heart: A Former Communist Remembers* (Athens, Ga., 1987) 123–24 (second quote).

36 Pete Seeger, quoted in Dunaway, *How Can I Keep from Singing,* 105; *Daily Worker,* January 8, 1943, 7.

37 Hays, in *People's Songs Bulletin,* 1 (February 1946), 1 (first quote); *Ibid.,* 1 (October 1946), 4 (second quote); 2 (February–March 1947), 15 (third quote).

38 Paul Robeson, quoted in Lieberman, *My Song Is My Weapon,* 140; "The Hammer Song," quoted in Silber, ed., *Lift Every Voice,* 84.

39 Hays, "Simon McKeever at Peekskill," LHP. See also Howard Fast's account in his *Being Red: a Memoir* (Boston: Houghton-Mifflin, 1990), 226–239.

40 Seeger, *Incompleat Folksinger,* 22 (first quote), Hays, quoted in Brand, *Ballad Mongers,* 107 (second quote); Guthrie, quoted in Seeger, *Incompleat Folksinger,* 22 (third quote); Seeger, *Incompleat Folksinger,* 22 (fourth, fifth, sixth, and seventh quotes); Hays, quoted in Brand, *Ballad Mongers,* 109 (eighth quote). On the Weavers' career, see also Willens; 118–19, 135–50, 152–53, 184–85, 196–98; Dunaway, *How Can I Keep from Singing?* 137–57; Klein, *Woody Guthrie,* 371–74.

41 Seeger interview; Seeger, *Incompleat Folksinger,* 22.

42 Hays, "'Post-humous Memoirs," LHP, in Koppelman, *Sing Out Warning,* 103–04.

43 *Ibid*; *Time* magazine, reporting "Irene's" commercial success, dubbed Leadbelly (the magazine spelled it *Lead Belly*) "the murderous old minstrel." *Time,* August 14, 1950. Lee was told that Julius and Ethel Rosenberg, convicted as Communist spies, had asked to hear the Weavers' "Goodnight Irene" on their way to the electric chair. Dunaway 156–57.

44 *Time,* September 25, 1950 (first quote); Wolfe and Lornell, *Life and Legend of Leadbelly,* 204; Seeger, *Incompleat Folksinger,* 22 (third quote). Paul Cohen, quoted in Brand, *Ballad Mongers,* 115. Richard A. Peterson, *Creating Country Music: Fabricating Authenticity* (Chicago, University of Chicago Press. 1997), 192.

45 In his "'Post-humous Memoirs," Hays recalled warmly his life-long friendship with Gordon Jenkins and his pleasure in the Decca Recording Sessions. Hays, "'Post-humous Memoirs," LHP, in Koppelman, *Sing Out Warning,* 111 (first quote), 107, 111 (second quote).

46 Seeger, *How Can I Keep from Singing,* 23 (first quote), (second quote) 272. The poet friend was Walter Lowenfels, who is described by Seeger as "the nimble-witted poet who coauthored with Lee Hays some good songs, such as 'Lonesome Traveler,' 'Wasn't That a Time,' and 'Lousy Dime.'"

47 *Red Channels: The Report of Communist Influence in Radio and Television* (New York: Counterattack, 1950); 130; Harvey Matusow, *False Witness* (New York, 1955), 51. Robert M. Lichtman and Ronald D. Cohen, in their *Deadly Farce: Harvey Matusow and the Informer System in the McCarthy Era (Urbana: University of Illinois Press, 2002)* devastatingly document—with FBI records, court transcripts, private papers, and in-

terviews—how the Justice Department and such prominent anti-communists as Roy Cohn colluded to create an institutional inquisition promoting a political environment hostile to dissent. See also Ellen Schrecker, *The Age of McCarthyism: A Brief History with Documents*. New York: Palgrave, 2002;

48   Hearings Before The Committee on Un-American Activities, House of Representatives, Eighty-Fourth Congress, First Session, Part VI, Testimony of Lee Hays, August 16, 1955, 2470–84; *Ibid*, Part VII, Testimony of Peter Seeger August 18, 1955; 2447–59, especially 2449 (first two quotes) and 2452 (second and third quotes). See also Eric Bentley and Frank Rich, *Thirty Years of Treason: Excerpts from Hearings Before the House Committee on Un-American Activities 1938–1968* (New York: Viking, 1971), and the overviews in Willens, *Lonesome Traveller*,149–52; and Dunaway, *How Can I Keep from Singing*, 164–82

49   Seeger, *Incompleat Folksinger*, 22 and 46; Willens, *Lonesome Traveller*. 142–50; Dunaway, *How Can I Keep from Singing*,150–51; Peterson, *Creating Country Music*, 198.

50   Seeger, *Incompleat Folksinger*, 22 (first quote); 23–24 (second quote); 461(third quote); Jim Capaldi, "Weavers Reunion," *Folk Scene*, March–April, 1981. The recording was *The Weavers at Carnegie Hall*, Audio CD, Vanguard B000000EFX .

51   Robert Korstad, *Civil Rights Unionism: Tobacco Workers and the Struggle for Democracy in the Mid-Twentieth Century South* (Chapel Hill: University of North Carolina Press, 2003), 5; Korstad describes this Southern Front" as something more than the "short-lived product of Party policy." It was a "loose coalition of labor unionists, civil rights activists, and Southern New Dealers that saw a strong labor movement and the re-enfranchisement of the Southern poor as the keys to reforming the South." 8. See also Lieberman, *My Song Is My Weapon*, 49. Michael Denning, *The Cultural Front: The Laboring of American Culture in the Twentieth Century*, the Haymarket Series (New York: Verso, 1998).

52   JoAnne C. Reuss, interview with Irwin Silber, quoted in Richard A. Reuss, with JoAnne C. Reuss, *American Folk Music and Left-Wing Politics, 1927–1957* (Lanham, Md,: Scarecrow Press, 2000), 206–7; Hays, quoted in Jim Capaldi, "Wasn't That a Time! A Conversation with Lee Hays," *Sing Out!* 28 (September–October, 1980), 4.

53   Nikita Khrushchev, "On the Cult of Personality and Its Consequences" speech delivered to the 20th congress of the Communist party of the USSR in Moscow, February 25 1956, full text published in *The Guardian*, April 26, 2007; Scales, *Cause at Heart*, 302.

54   Seeger, "False from True," *At 89*, Appleseed CD; Seeger, "Big Joe's Blues Blues," quoted in Nicholas Wapshott, "Seeger turns on Uncle Joe Observations on Folk Music," *New Statesman*, September 27, 2007.

55   Walter Lowenfels, "Tomorrow's Children," Stormking Music, 1964; "Seeger Turns on Uncle Joe," *New Statesman*, September 27, 2007.

56   *The Weavers at Carnegie Hall*, December 24, 1955, Vanguard VMD 73101.

57   Scales, quoted in Oliver Maxson, "History Haunts Ex-Communist," Middletown, N.Y. *Sunday Record*, March 24, 1996, 3; Scales, quoted in Matt Robinson, "Junius Irving Scales, 1920–2002," *Indy Week* (Cary, Chapel Hill, Durham, Raleigh, N.C.), August 2002; Scales, interviewed by Mickey Friedman, in his *A Red Family: Junius, Gladys, & Barbara Scales* (Urbana: University of Illinois Press, 2009), 151.

Lessons Along the Color Line

Radicals, New Dealers, and Tom Watson: Agrarian Rebel

PATRICIA SULLIVAN

T he publication of *Tom Watson: Agrarian Rebel* in March of 1938 was a pivotal event in the life and career of C. Vann Woodward. The manuscript, which was his dissertation, was published by a major New York publisher less than a year after he earned his PhD. The book announced the arrival of a young scholar who would eventually be counted among the preeminent historians of his generation.[1]

Like few historical works, *Tom Watson* spoke to a particular moment, elevating its significance beyond the academic world and the career of a budding scholar. In resurrecting the promise of the Populist movement, the book recovered a past that seemed to mirror the challenges and opportunities that came to the fore during the peak years of the New Deal, with the rise of vibrant movements for labor rights and political democracy in the South. Race, as it had been during the tumultuous political struggles of the late 19th century, once again emerged as a critical element in efforts to advance economic and political democracy in the South. Alabama labor activist Robert F. "Rob" Hall wrote in a review essay, "Seldom has the publication of an important book appeared at a more timely moment."[2]

The book reflected Woodward's development and experience, particularly his youthful engagement with the problems of poverty, labor, and the vexing issue of race. He came to Tom Watson through a circuitous route, one guided in part by his immersion in the writers of the Southern literary Renaissance of the 1920s, the ruminations of New South critic H. L. Mencken, and the penetrating essays of W. E. B. Du Bois. As a young man, Woodward was "deeply moved" by Du Bois's *The Souls of Black Folk,* the seminal work which aimed, in the words of Du Bois, to show readers "the strange meaning of being black in the dawning of the 20th century."[3] A restless and curious spirit that set him traveling in Europe and to the Soviet Union at the age of 19 also found him bending the color line in Georgia and moving with ease into interracial spaces in New York.

After graduating from Emory University in 1930 during the depths of the Depression, Woodward's greatest ambition was to read widely, travel, and write. There were "new voices in the land and new forces astir in the South" Woodward later recalled; no better time, he said, "to be spending one's youth." He kept thoughts of a career at bay. Wary of the constraints of academic life, he accepted a scholarship to Columbia to take a master's degree in the social sciences because it allowed him to spend a year in New York City. During his time in New York, he socialized with young luminaries of the Harlem Renaissance and performed as the only white cast member in a production of *Underground,* a play based on *Uncle Tom's Cabin* and staged by the Harlem Experimental Theatre. He sought out W. E. B. Du Bois at the office of *The Crisis,* the NAACP's monthly magazine, to discuss his interest in writing his master's thesis on Du Bois. The conversation stalled, Woodward later surmised, "after he heard that Deep South accent of mine." Du Bois nonetheless remained an important influence on Woodward and his work.[4]

Woodward eventually wrote a thesis on J. Thomas Heflin, the U.S. Senator from Alabama who helped lead the retreat from Reconstruction and erect the South's racial caste system. The thesis turned out "remarkably well," Woodward confided to a friend, and bore the seeds of future work. The pull of the South, along with accumulated debt, brought Woodward home to Georgia in the late summer of 1932, after several months traveling through Germany, France, and the Soviet Union. There was a year of teaching English at Georgia Tech and political work around the defense of Angelo Herndon, a young black labor organizer arrested and convicted under a Reconstruction-era anti insurrection law.[5] Most formative, perhaps, was a summer job with the Works Progress Administration, investigating impoverishment in rural Georgia. Exposure to hunger and human desperation on a massive scale shocked Woodward and elevated his interest in understanding the roots of the poverty and injustice that riddled the South.[6]

During this time Woodward began to work on Tom Watson as part of a collective biography of Southern demagogues, building from his master's thesis. The subject, he later wrote, offered what he then "perceived as an unparalleled opportunity to expose all that was worst in Southern life and politics."[7] Watson's story drew him into the complexities of the man and his times, bringing the Populist upheaval of the 1890s front and center, and introducing Woodward to a dimension of the Southern past that had been largely neglected or minimized by histories of the post-Civil War South. Historians and publicists of the "New South" school had celebrated industrial development and white racial unity, mythologized the virtues of the Old South, and promoted the lessons of Reconstruction as a tragic era, demonstrating the perils of black political participation.

Tom Watson, "born of a slaveholding family of planters in the upper part of the Georgia black belt in 1856," experienced the material loss wrought by the Civil War and Emancipation and the tumult of the Reconstruction era during his youth. Watson's political coming of age, however, was shaped by the rise of an industrial capital class in Georgia that asserted political and economic dominance in the state, while preaching the doctrine of white supremacy. In 1880, Watson emerged as a leader in the burgeoning rebellion of small farmers united in opposition to the rule of business and banking interests. He went on to become a major figure in the Farmer's Alliance which united more than a million farmers from the South through the Midwest; black farmers organized separately into the Colored Farmers Alliance. With the founding of the People's or "Populist" Party in 1891, Watson led the effort to organize the common economic interests of blacks and whites into a powerful political movement, in defiance of the region's new racial order.[8] Violence, terror, and fraud met the Populist challenge of the 1890s, methods similar to those used to crush the political alliances of the Reconstruction era. Following defeat and perceived betrayals, and reflecting his darker moods and a core racism, Watson ended his days as a virulent white supremacist. Through Watson's story, Woodward exposed "the fallacies, omissions, and long silences that characterized the New South school," as the conflicts and tragedy of Southern life and history emerged.[9]

Woodward's interest in Watson was rewarded when Georgia Doremus Watson, Watson's granddaughter and literary executor, granted him access to the massive collection of papers recently archived at the University of North Carolina, making him the first researcher to plumb those depths.[10] After working for a year from his parents' home in Georgia, Woodward accepted a scholarship to graduate school at the University of North Carolina as a way to support the writing of the book. He arrived in Chapel Hill with four chapters completed, traveled the torturous road of course work and examinations, and finally completed a 600-page manuscript in the spring of 1937. At the end of the summer, Macmillan offered him a book contract.[11]

A month prior to the book's publication in March 1938, Woodward published an article drawn from the book in the *Journal of Southern History*. "Tom Watson and the Negro in Agrarian Politics" turned attention to what would be a major focus of interest among young Southern activists who faced racial barriers that had grown deeper since the Populist moment four decades earlier. In the article, which charted the extremes Watson traveled from his advocacy of interracial politics and his alliance with key black figures in the Populist movement to becoming one of the most outspoken white supremacists during his later years, Woodward paused to underscore the significance of the cross-racial alliance that emerged in the early 1890s. "Never before or since," he wrote in 1938, "have the two races in the South come so close together politically. The Negroes, it should be emphasized, continued their support for Populism in the face of as much or more intimidation and violence than they encountered from the Democrats during Reconstruction." Woodward addressed questions about the sincerity of Watson's appeals to blacks—questions that attended "the sincerity of any appeal to the Negro vote"—and the nature of his motives, concluding that such speculation should not distract from the significance of the effort. He thought it relevant that W. E. B. Du Bois, "a Negro leader not given to uncritical enthusiasm for Southern politicians, was sufficiently convinced of the sincerity of Watson to regard the failure of his movement as a calamity for the Negro race."[12]

Woodward promptly sent an off-print of the article to Du Bois. It was "written in a spirit that I hope you will approve," he told Du Bois, "whether you can agree with my conclusion or not." He acknowledged his indebtedness to Du Bois "for the insight" he gained from *Black Reconstruction in America*, published three years earlier. Subtitled "An Essay toward a History of the Part which Black Folks Played in the Attempt to Reconstruct Democracy in America, 1860–1880," *Black Reconstruction* recovered the role of freed black men and women in the political life of the South in the years immediately following the Civil War and the brief flourishing of a biracial democracy in the region. It was the first major scholarly treatment of African Americans in the Reconstruction era, challenging the dominant school of thought characterizing Reconstruction as a tragic era and describing blacks as unfit for full citizenship. Woodward expressed a desire to visit with Du Bois in Atlanta to discuss his future research plans.[13]

Tom Watson arrived during the high tide of New Deal-era reform. The publication of the book in the spring of 1938 coincided with the release of the *Report on the Economic Conditions of the South* by the Franklin Delano Roosevelt administration and rising labor activism and protest, which worked in tandem to shake the foundations of the so-called Solid South. In announcing the report, Roosevelt described the region as the "Nation's Number One Economic Problem." Congress of Industrial Organizations (CIO) organizers fanned out across the South to aid and enlist black and white workers in the union movement in the face of widespread violence and repression. Sharecroppers and tenant farmers in the Arkansas Delta had formed the interracial Southern Tenant Farmers Union in 1934 and won some gains but remained the target of planter-led vigilante attacks. At the same time, NAACP activists were chipping away at voter restrictions in the courts. For Woodward and a new generation of Southerners engaged in these struggles, *Tom Watson* recovered a history of democratic activism that had been suppressed and forgotten, offering a glimpse of what might be possible as well as a cautionary tale.[14]

Rob Hall wrote Woodward in May 1938, anxious to begin a discussion about the book and its relevance to his work in Birmingham, Alabama. Hall was secretary of the southern office of the Communist Party in Birmingham. He had been at Columbia when Woodward was there and led a student strike Woodward had taken part in, a connection Woodward reminded him of in the course of their correspondence that spring. Two years older than Woodward, Hall's experiences growing up in the Deep South had generated questions and concerns similar to those that marked Woodward's formative years. While working as a reporter for the *Mobile Register* fresh out of high school, he covered several stories relating to the lives of African Americans in that city and became an advocate for black voting rights. He attended the University of Alabama, but left after a year and took a job with a Southern railroad company. Four years of extensive travel through the South exposed Hall to rural conditions and the desperate plight of farmers. His concerns about rural poverty led him to Columbia University in 1929 to study agrarian economics with Rexford Tugwell.

During his time in New York, Hall became active in the student movement, led a delegation to Harlan County, Kentucky, to aid striking miners, and was a founding member of the Communist-affiliated National Student League. The Party's strong stand on racial equality was part of its attraction to him, he later recalled. Tugwell became a leading member of FDR's "Brain Trust" and offered Hall a job in the Roosevelt administration, which Hall declined. After graduating from Columbia he organized farmworkers in the Midwest before returning to Alabama in 1934, becoming district organizer and secretary for the Communist Party. Central to Hall's work were efforts to help organize sharecroppers and industrial workers, promote voter registration, and support political activism, with attention to the unique struggles of African Americans under the Jim Crow system.[15]

For Hall, *Tom Watson* was a powerful revelation. He viewed himself and his allies as "inheritors of the best traditions of the Tom Watsons" of the past and found that the history Woodward had recovered spoke directly to the possibilities facing the South. "The rise of the Populist movement," Hall wrote in his review of the book for *The New South,* "demonstrates that the Southern people can be shown their class interests and that unity with the Negro people for these interests is not simply a utopian dream." In speculating on the failure of the Populists, Hall suggested that a major factor was that the movement had not gone far enough to address "the basic inequalities of the Negro people." The Populists' fight for "Negro rights" was "mainly for the right of Negroes to vote Populist." He felt guardedly hopeful that the rise of a "strong and powerful labor movement" added a new element capable of supporting common cause and political action across race lines.[16]

Woodward's book invited a fuller consideration of the kinds of challenges they faced, one that Hall pursued in an extended correspondence into the fall. In his first letter to Woodward, Hall asked Woodward "why did Populism fail?" Hall offered his own insights, expanding on the discussion he began in his review, noting that while Watson and others had made gestures to African Americans they failed to realize that the demands of black people for civil rights must be "a keystone to the fight." He noted that his experience with the CIO in Birmingham provided further evidence—a situation whereby blacks were permitted to join on equal terms, but the union made no consistent fight against lynching, for the right to vote, and other issues of concern to blacks. While thousands signed up for the steelworkers' union, few blacks attended the meetings or paid dues—"a serious consequence if not corrected." Hall allowed that he had been so engrossed in these "lessons of Populism," he had not seriously considered the "problem of Tom Watson as an individual," a point Woodward apparently raised in their correspondence.[17]

Based on Hall's letters, it is evident that the two discussed the differences between the Souths of 1900 and 1930, exchanged an article on Southern regionalism, and shared opinions about H. C. Nixon's *Forty Acres and Steel Mules*. During this time, Hall made efforts to convince a mass-distribution paperback publisher to bring *Tom Watson* out in a 50-cent or $1 edition, to help gain a wider readership than it would attract at the more prohibitive $3.75 cost, but with no success. Late in July, Hall reported on a massive meeting of black and white unemployed that provided hopeful signs of broadening political activism. A crowd of 300 had been anticipated; 4,500 turned out, necessitating an open-air meeting. Demands for higher WPA wages were accompanied by calls for the abolition of the poll tax and voting rights for Negroes—which won general applause. With "a number of progressive Democrats, New Deal office holders" present along with the labor crowd, Hall held out hope for "the real Democratic Front to come."[18]

Arthur "Tex" Goldschmidt, one of the prominent young Southerners working in the Roosevelt administration and a lead author of FDR's *Report on the Economic Conditions of the South,* was equally enthusiastic about *Tom Watson*. Raised and educated in Texas, followed by undergraduate study at Columbia University, he was surprised to realize that such a pivotal moment in the South's past had not been part of his education. "I was carrying that book all over the place because it was a terrific revelation to me personally," he recalled. Goldschmidt, who had helped organize the Works Progress Administration, was a close associate of Claude Pepper, the liberal New Deal Senator from Florida. The two were collaborating on an article about the South when Goldschmidt urged him to read the book on Watson. "When I saw him a week later he said it was a terrific book with some wonderful quotes we should use on the South and on black and white cooperation. We ought to be showing people he had these ideas way back then," Goldschmidt recounted. "And I said, you haven't finished the book, have you. Let's discuss it then. And we never discussed it in terms of using Watson's quotes. [But] the first half of the book is terrific in terms of black and white cooperation."[19]

During the summer and fall of 1938, various organizing efforts across the South found a political outlet in FDR's efforts to help liberalize and democratize Southern politics. In the wake of the *Report on the Economic Conditions of the South*, Roosevelt intervened in several key primary elections to support candidates who challenged three powerful and staunchly anti-labor Southern Democrats who were leading opponents of the New Deal: Senator Walter George of Georgia, South Carolina's Senator "Cotton" Ed Smith, and Virginia Congressman Howard W. Smith. In a bold speech in Gainesville, Georgia, Roosevelt charged George with supporting a low-wage, feudalistic economic system in opposition to an expanded program of New Deal reform. FDR anticipated that Georgians would choose representatives "whose minds are cast in the 1938 mold and not the 1898 mold," referencing the time when reactionary politics triumphed in the South. The widespread disfranchisement of blacks and whites implemented during that time, however, kept many of the New Deal's beneficiaries from the ballot box, and Roosevelt's opponents comfortably triumphed on primary day.[20]

In response to FDR's efforts, his Southern supporters convened a conference in Birmingham over Thanksgiving weekend dedicated to organizing the varied constituents of the New Deal—labor, African Americans, liberals, and others—into an active and effective political force for change. Woodward wrote Rob Hall that he was hoping to get to Birmingham for the meeting, but "just now it looks doubtful." There is no evidence that he attended. But Hall was among the 1,200 black and white attendees who came together to address the issues of the report and develop a plan for political action, in what was the founding meeting of the Southern Conference for Human Welfare (SCHW). Arthur Raper described it as "one of the most exaggerated expressions of change in the South. . . . Here was a revival, a bush-shaking, something that just jumped up." Harking back to the unfulfilled promise of the Populist moment, CIO organizer Lucy Randolph Mason observed: "The South cannot be saved by middle class liberals alone—they must make common cause with labor, the disposed of the land, and the Negro . . . This is the basis for progress in democracy, economic justice, and social values in the South."[21]

While the conference endorsed several provisions that reflected the concerns of a burgeoning civil rights movement, including federal anti-lynching legislation and equal salaries for black and white teachers, organizers did not intend to focus attention on the contentious issue of racial segregation. The group met on a non-segregated basis in Birmingham's municipal auditorium; such meetings had been held there before. Police commissioner Eugene "Bull" Connor, however, decided to enforce a municipal ordinance requiring segregation. Rather than let the meeting be shut down, participants decided to comply in this instance, but conference leaders pledged that they would never again meet in a venue where segregation could be enforced. Whites moved to one side of the auditorium, blacks to the other. Returning to the hall after the group had separated, First Lady Eleanor Roosevelt sat with the black attendees. When instructed by a police offer to move, she placed her chair in the middle of the aisle. Rob Hall recalled: "That was a glorious moment."[22]

While conference organizers accommodated segregation policy in Birmingham, the agreement that there would be no segregation at future meetings earned the SCHW a tag as a "racial equality" organization—a characterization that it grew into. The SCHW's policy marked an important departure from the customary caution of white Southern liberals who shrank from any overt challenge to the caste system, and, as a consequence, many prominent liberals avoided further association with the group. The Southern Conference appealed to civil rights groups and organized labor, and expanded the possibilities for interracial alliances in the political realm. Beyond supporting the emergence of a loose coalition of Southern black and white activists, the SCHW worked within a national framework to build support for federal legislation to secure the enforcement and protection of voting rights in the South.

Tex Goldschmidt, a founding member of the SCHW, sought out Woodward in the aftermath of the Birmingham meeting. In December 1939, when Woodward was in Washington for the annual meeting of the American Historical Association, Goldschmidt arranged for him to meet with several fellow Southern New Dealers, including Virginia Durr. A native Alabamian, Durr had been transformed by her experiences of the Depression and the New Deal and had emerged as a leader of the SCHW's voting rights efforts. Durr's initial meeting with Woodward blossomed into a warm and lifelong friendship, and she wasted no time in recruiting him to aid in her work.[23]

The SCHW's first major effort sought the rolling back of the disfranchisement measures that were the hallmarks of the battles waged from the 1890s through the turn of the century. The poll tax had become a potent symbol of the undemocratic political structure that supported some of the most powerful anti-labor members of Congress. As a measure that affected poor whites as well as blacks, the fight for its repeal created an arena for interracial cooperation and action. Under the direction of Virginia Durr and Joseph Gelders, the SCHW's Committee on Civil Rights—which subsequently became the National Committee to Abolish the Poll Tax (NCAPT)— initiated the nearly three-decade long campaign to extend federal protection of voting rights in the South. Durr built a broad coalition that included major labor unions, the NAACP, the League of Women Voters, student activists, and other progressive groups. By the fall of 1939, she and Gelders, with the help of Eleanor Roosevelt, had recruited Congressman Lee Geyers and Senator Claude Pepper to introduce legislation to eliminate the poll tax in federal elections. Durr enlisted Woodward as an expert to testify on behalf of the legislation.[24]

On April 3, 1940, Woodward testified before a subcommittee of the House Committee on the Judiciary. Woodward provided a stark review of the state of voting in the eight poll-tax states—where the average voter turnout was 19.9 percent compared to 68.9 percent in non-poll-tax states. These Southern states ranked among the poorest 14 states in the Union, making the tax on voting most onerous to those least able to pay. Woodward traced the roots of this disfranchisement measure to the "reaction against the agrarian movement in the 1890s—the populist movement"—a disfranchisement movement led by commercial and industrial interests, in effect eliminating a class as a political force in government. He warned that "the argument of white supremacy and Negro domination" would be used to try and defeat anti-poll tax legislation, as it will be "against every other element of reform" in the South. But in 1940, it seemed that the convergence of forces stimulated by the New Deal, the labor movement, and emerging civil rights movement might overcome the barriers raised in reaction to the Populist surge nearly fifty years earlier. As Virginia Durr wrote Woodward, "I have an invincible belief that if the right people ever get together something is bound to happen."[25]

The Geyer-Pepper bill initiated the first full-scale congressional debate of federal protection of voting rights in the South in 50 years. Southern Democrats led the opposition to the legislation, as a violation of state sovereignty and a thinly veiled effort to enfranchise black voters. Yet, Southern legislators such as Luther Patrick from Birmingham and Estes Kefauver of Tennessee were among the leading supporters in the struggle for anti-poll tax legislation. Patrick described the poll tax as the tool of "reactionary political and economic interests." In October 1942, the bill passed the House by a robust margin of 254 to 84 votes. With few exceptions, Southern senators lined up to oppose the bill, warning, in the words of Mississippi's Theodore Bilbo, that any federal tampering with voter qualifications would open the "floodgates," leaving the South no way "of preventing the Negroes from voting." South-erners filibustered the bill and blocked successive efforts on Capitol Hill. As the poll tax bill stalled on Capitol Hill, the NAACP mounted a final and successful legal challenge to the whites-only Democratic primary, the most effective method of black disfranchisement in the South.[26]

Forces of change and reaction heightened during World War II. Black demands for full inclusion in the war effort resulted in the establishment of the Fair Employment Practices Committee and made civil rights an issue of national consequence. In the wake of the U.S. Supreme Court's 1944 *Smith v. Allwright* decision striking down the all-white primary, black voter regis-tration increased dramatically. Blacks became, in Virginia Durr's words, "the generating force" in the movement to liberalize Southern politics. In the im-mediate postwar years, a loose coalition of groups including the CIO-Political Action Committee (CIO-PAC), the NAACP, SCHW state committees, and the Southern Negro Youth Congress supported local efforts throughout the region to promote voter education, registration, and turnout. These efforts culminated in the 1946 primary season, the first open primary in the South since the Court's ruling opened the Democratic primary to black voters.

Contests throughout the South demonstrated the shifting currents of Southern politics as expanded grassroots political activism pushed against the color line with mixed results. In Georgia, the CIO and other groups targeted the rabidly racist and anti-labor Eugene Talmadge for defeat in the gubernato-rial primary. The citizens of Georgia, wrote CIO-Political Action Committee organizer Dan Powell, were "politicized as not since the days of Watson and the Populist movement." Black voter registration in Georgia climbed from 20,000 to 135,000 and the black vote gave Talmadge's opponent, James Carmichael, the margin of victory in the popular vote. But through an aggressive campaign that relied on fraud, violence, and race-baiting, Talmadge supporters won the county unit vote by two to one. In neighboring Alabama, the landslide victory of James E. Folsom, the candidate who had the support of labor and black voters, encouraged the belief that democratic change was possible in the postwar South. Rosa Parks, then an officer in the Montgomery NAACP branch, voting for the first time, cast her vote for Folsom.[27]

Reports from Texas by CIO-PAC organizer Palmer Weber turned attention to the fragile nature of biracial political coalitions in the South. In a desperate effort to hold onto white voters, Homer Rainey, the liberal former president of the University of Texas and CIO-favored candidate for governor, advocated separate polling booths for blacks and whites. CIO organizers, Weber reported, put little effort into the voter registration push. They were, Weber wrote, like "hogs at a trough." Meanwhile, black organizers and NAACP leaders around the state outdid themselves, mounting a comprehensive effort to turn out the black vote on primary day and, in Weber's words, showing "tremendous *espirit de corps.*"[28]

Leading Democrat and labor officials viewed the Southern primaries as evidence that the hoped-for realignment of the Democratic Party in the South was within reach. The boost in black voter registration, which tripled in the aftermath of the white primary decision, was a potent liberalizing force, especially when working in tandem with a receptive coalition of liberal and labor groups. Jack Kroll, head of the CIO-PAC, predicted that "the cry 'nigger' employed to divide the liberal forces in the South was losing its old magic."[29] At the same time, Southerners wed to the region's economic and political arrangements used the specter of a resurgent black electorate to stir racial fears and revive white solidarity as a unifying force in Southern politics. The contending forces competed against the backdrop of postwar developments, particularly the start of the Cold War, that further weakened the broadly cast Democratic front which had supported racial equality and anti-segregation as fundamental to the reforms they sought. In the end, 1946 turned out to be the high-water mark of the bold experiment in biracial politics.

Numerous scholars have considered why this season of biracial politics was so quickly eclipsed. Some have claimed that anti-communism was the primary factor in aborting biracial unionism which, they argue, would have served as the foundation for a new political order.[30] Yet such an analysis overestimates the extent to which biracial unionism had gained the support of white workers for a program that included blacks on the basis of equality, and it underestimates the hard work of cross-race organizing in the Jim Crow South. In a concession to regional folkways, Highlander Folk School, the progressive workers education school in Tennessee, limited its residency program to white workers until 1944, largely due to the reluctance of CIO

unions to sponsor interracial sessions for fear doing so would undermine efforts to organize white workers. Highlander opened its residency program to
black workers in 1944 and would become a staging ground for the civil rights
movement of the 1950s and '60s. As black pressures for change increased
during World War II, however, many traditional Southern liberals became
apologists for the segregation system. Journalist Ralph McGill declared in
1942 that "anyone with an ounce of common sense must see . . . that the
separation of the races must be maintained in the South."[31]

The capacity of Southern politicians and demagogues to mobilize white
resistance to any compromise with the mandates of Jim Crow, aided by fraud
and violence, remained a major controlling factor. Indeed, the politics and
language of massive resistance associated with the reaction to the 1954 *Brown*
ruling were fully on display in the backlash that met *Smith v. Allwright* and
the growth in black voter participation a decade earlier. The embrace of anti-
communism by liberal Democrats and leading labor unions in the postwar
period weakened support for progressive efforts in the South. The failure of
biracial coalitions to secure a foothold in the region, however, reflected the
power of racial segregation to structure the experience and imagination of
white Southerners, diminishing possibilities for the democratization and
transformation of Southern politics at a promising moment.

In considering the demise of the biracial movement that emerged in
the South during the 1930s–1940s, anti-communism functioned as one
of the elements that reinforced the culture, practice, and ideology of white
supremacy. Many of the violent attacks on the civil rights activism of the
New Deal–World War II era preceded and were independent of Cold War-
era repression. The widespread suppression of black voting rights efforts and
related challenges to the Jim Crow system in the South targeted individuals
and communities struggling for political empowerment in ways reminiscent
of the Reconstruction era and the late 19th century. Some examples: the
massive attack on voting registration drives in Greenville, South Carolina,
in 1939; the abduction and murder of NAACP voting rights activist Elbert
Williams in Brownsville, Tennessee, in 1941; and state-sponsored fraud and
assaults targeting thousands who attempted to vote in Mississippi and Georgia,
many of whom were veterans, during 1946 primary elections. An important
episode anticipated a pivotal 1960s moment when in 1944 the black-led
South Carolina Progressive Democratic Party challenged the seating of the

state's all-white delegation to the Democratic National Convention (and went on to register 50,000 black voters in the state). But through the combined effects of police harassment, attacks on local leaders, and widespread fraud, the Progressive Democratic Party had lost its edge by the late 1940s. Indeed, history bears out the words of W. E. B. Du Bois, "everything tends to break along the color line."[32]

Unlike earlier times, however, a movement rooted in black communities and institutions in the South survived the backlash and racially charged politics of the post-World War II era, to steadily chip away at the foundations of Jim Crow and voter disfranchisement. It provided the foundation for the civil rights movement that would transform the South and the nation in fundamental ways.

REFLECTIONS BY ROB HALL and C. Vann Woodward on developments in the South and the nation in the aftermath of the New Deal era pull the thread forward. In the decades following the publication of *Tom Watson,* Hall, who had left the Communist Party in 1955, wrote a few letters to Woodward continuing the discussion that began in the late 1930s. In 1956, he wrote in response to the publication of *The Strange Career of Jim Crow,* which was based on a series of lectures Woodward had given at the University of Virginia after the *Brown* ruling. Hall reminded Woodward of their earlier correspondence, recalling that "at the time you predicted—as against my bouncing optimism—that our country was in for a period of Metternichean reaction" and conceded that Woodward "had the better of that argument." But looking forward, in the aftermath of the Supreme Court ruling that dismantled the legal underpinning of segregation, Hall saw "a glorious sunset ahead." He was hopeful that "humanity, even in our poor benighted South, will achieve its Great Day."[33]

Ten years later, Woodward looked back on a remarkable decade of protest, activism and far-reaching legislative change that followed in the wake of *Brown* and asked, "What Happened to the Civil Rights Movement?" His essay offered a penetrating exploration of the cumulative toll of America's racial past. Writing less than two years after the Selma march and the passage of the Voting Rights Act, Woodward allowed that the sound of these events "still ring in our ears" yet in November 1966, they "seemed at the same time so remote, so improbable." It was over. "We no longer live in the same moral, political, and intellectual climate that we have accustomed ourselves to in the period recently ended." He cautioned that this was not a temporary pause or interruption in a "continuous movement" for to entertain such a thought was "to miss the historic integrity and distinctiveness of the recent period." It was, he wrote, ". . a period of restitution, an effort to fulfill promises a century old, the redemption of a historic commitment." Notably, "the struggle for fulfillment took place largely in the South, the proper historic (and properly remote) setting for reconstructions."[34]

Woodward identified 1966 as the critical year, a time when a new set of forces converged to produce a turn toward reaction and retrenchment. The evidence was written in congressional debates, changing political rhetoric, shifts in policy at the federal level, and a rightward turn in the November elections. There were cracks in the interracial coalition that had grown up around the civil rights movement. The call to Black Power jarred some. Many formerly engaged were distracted by other concerns, such as the war in Vietnam. But it ran deeper. "A great stillness descended upon quarters long known for outspoken opinions," Woodward observed, and "from the rest of the country came mainly silence or consent."[35] In a letter written to a close friend in the fall of 1966, Woodward asked, "Is it really as bad as it looks? Or is that possible? Or is it some nightmare about the ghost of Tom Watson?"[36]

In assessing the seemingly abrupt ascendancy of a politics of backlash, Woodward considered various explanations, from the life cycle of revolutions to the claims that Black Power and urban riots were largely to blame for the demise of the movement. He dismissed them as insufficient. Woodward reflected on how the movement had exposed the entrenched nature of the color line, which expanded its reach during the peak decades of black migration to the urban North and was visible in the slums, housing discrimination, unemployment, and deteriorating and segregated schools that characterized racial conditions in Northern cities. These problems were "tough and harsh and brutally raw" and "not amenable to romantic crusades and the evangelical approach." When the movement "moved" north, Woodward wrote, "the great withdrawal" set in.[37]

The civil rights movement of the 1950s and 1960s succeeded in dismantling the legal structure of segregation and removing the barriers to voter participation that were erected partly in response to the Populist upsurge of the 1880s and 1890s. The nation's racial landscape had changed dramatically in the intervening decades. Yet as Woodward's essay observed, the power and reach of racial segregation and its progeny continued to be a defining force in American life and politics. Writing to Woodward in 1988, Rob Hall expressed similar sentiments. "Racism endures in our country . . . dormant, almost invisible, and yet in danger of violent eruption," he wrote. It was, he allowed, "your old nemesis Jim Crow [that] remains the main enemy. The barriers which prevent people from knowing each other close up nurture prejudice and racism. I hope the next generation will solve it or at least make some big gains."[38]

The history of black and white political alliances in the South—from Reconstruction, through the Populist movement of the late 19th century, and the labor and civil rights struggles of the New Deal–World War II era—invites continuing study and exploration. While each era offers insight on the ways of the color line at a particular historical moment, collectively they raise broader questions regarding how race has structured human relations, political culture, and the process of social change in the South and the nation at large.

Tom Watson, Woodward observed, was "a book for the times and of the times."[39] Since its publication nearly 80 years ago, a rich outpouring of scholarship has expanded upon and challenged Woodward's interpretation of Tom Watson and the Populist movement. However, as a text of the Depression-New Deal era, *Tom Watson* has a unique place in Southern History. For Southern activists of Woodward's generation, it recovered a past that was foundational to their struggles in the 1930s. The promise and ultimate tragedy of the Populist movement informed their efforts to disrupt racial barriers and revive the possibilities for economic and political democracy in the region. Confronting the complex and enduring power of race, past and present, they worked to forge a new path forward.

NOTES

1   C. Vann Woodward, *Tom Watson: Agrarian Rebel* (New York: Macmillan, 1938).

2   R. F. Hall, "What Tom Watson Taught the South: Lessons from the Populist Movement," *The New South,* June 1938, 13.

3   C. Vann Woodward, *Thinking Back: The Perils of Writing History* (Baton Rouge: LSU Press, 1986, 85–86).

4   Ibid.; CVW to Glenn Rainey, Sept. 17, 1931, ca. April 1932 in Michael O'Brien, ed. *The Letters of C. Vann Woodward* (New Haven: Yale University Press, 2013).

5   Woodward's experience with the leading Communists working on the Herndon case left him wary of the tactics and motives of Party operatives, but he remained open to Southern activists who were Party members. Woodward aided Communist Party organizer Don West in organizing support for striking textile workers in Burlington, NC in 1934.

6   Woodward, *Thinking Back,* 10–12.

7   Ibid., 33.

8   C. Vann Woodward, "Tom Watson and the Negro in Agrarian Politics," *The Journal of Southern History* (1938), 14; Woodward, *Tom Watson: Agrarian Rebel,* 1–5, 12–16, 56–74, 174–79.

9   Woodward, *Thinking Back,* 29.

10 CVW to Georgia Doremus Watson, Oct. 3, 1933; CVW to Glenn Rainey, Oct. 3, 1933, in O'Brien, *Letters.*

11 CVW to Glenn Rainey, Sept 11, 1937, O'Brien, *Letters.*

12 Woodward, "Tom Watson and the Negro in Agrarian Politics," 21.

13 CVW to W. E. B. Du Bois, April 3, 1938. Du Bois acknowledged receipt of the article, which he had not yet had a chance to read but welcomed as "a subject that greatly needed investigation." He added that he would be glad to see Woodward "any time you are in Atlanta." Du Bois to CVW, April 8, 1938. W. E. B. Du Bois Papers,

14 Patricia Sullivan, *Days of Hope: Race and Democracy in the New Deal Era* (Chapel Hill: UNC Press, 1996) 63–67, Woodward considered going to his native Arkansas in the summer of 1936 to aid the STFU. CVW to Glenn Rainey, July 2, 1936, O'Brien, Letters.

15 Robert F. Hall, "Those Southern Liberals," review of Morton Sosna's *In Search of the Silent South: Southern Liberals and the Race Issue* (New York: Columbia University Press, 1979) in *Dissent,* Fall 1979, 490–91; Robin Kelley, *Hammer and Hoe: Alabama Communists during the Great Depression* (Chapel Hill: UNC Press, 1990), 125–26; Hall to CVW, June 4, 1938; Peter Hall, e-mail to Patricia Sullivan, June 14, 2013.

16 Rob Hall, "What Tom Watson Taught the South: Lessons from the Populist Movement," *The New South,* June 1938, 12–13. *The New South,* a journal published by the Communist Party, aimed to appeal to Southern liberals and progressives. It ran articles on politics, voting, the work of Southern liberals, and occasionally included pieces on Southern history. See Kelley, *Hammer and Hoe,* 133.

17 Rob Hall to CVW, May 21, 1938; June 4, 1938. C. Vann Woodward Collection, Yale University Library, Box 1. Only one letter from Woodward to Hall during this period is included in Woodward's papers. Hall's papers, archived at the New York State Archive, include correspondence from Woodward during the 1980s.

18 Rob Hall to CVW, July 23, 1938, July 30, 1938; Hall to CVW, July 30, 1938; Hall to CVW, Oct. 31, 1938; CVW to Rob Hall, Nov. 9, 1938, CVW Papers; Kelley, *Hammer and Hoe,* 156. Hall contacted Modern Age Books. The publisher responded: "although what you say about its popularity in the South is quite true, the sales generally for this particular title could hardly justify Modern Age edition. We have to count on a 25,000 immediate sale." Louis Birk to Mary Craik Speed, Aug. 25, 1938.

19 Sullivan interview with Tex Goldschmidt, July 4, 1991.

20 Sullivan, *Days of Hope,* 61–66.

21 CVW to Hall, Nov. 9, 1938; Hall to CVW, Nov. 14, 1938; Lucy Randolph Mason to Eleanor Roosevelt, July 28, 1938, Eleanor Roosevelt Papers, Franklin D. Roosevelt Library; Sullivan *Days of Hope,* 98–100.

22 Sullivan interview with Rob Hall, Oct. 22, 1991; Sullivan, *Days of Hope,* 98–100.

23 Virginia Durr to CVW, Jan. 26, 1940, CVW Papers, Box 1.

24 Sullivan, *Days of Hope,* 113–16.

25 C.Vann Woodward, Testimony before the subcommittee of the House Judiciary Committee, April 3, 1940, *Congressional Record* (December 1941), 309–311; Durr to CVW, January 26, 1940, CVW Papers, Box 1.

26 U.S. Congress, Senate, "Elimination of the Poll Tax in Election of Federal Officials," H.R. 1024,"77th Cong., 2d. sess., 20, 21, 23 Nov. 1942; *Congressional Record,* 88: 9029–31, 9048–49, 9063–64.

27 Dan Powell, "PAC Field Report" Feb. 1947, copy in author's possession; Ira DeA. Reid, "The White Primary," July 1946, Grace Towns Hamilton Papers, Trevor Arnett Library, Atlanta, Georgia, 15-B-3; George Sims, *The Little Man's Big Friend: James E. Folsom in Alabama Politics,* 1946–1958 (Tuscaloosa: University of Alabama Press, 1986), 27–37; Jeanne Theoharis, *The Rebellious Life of Rosa Parks* (Boston: Beacon Press, 2013), 21–22.

28 Dan Powell, "PAC Field Report" Feb. 1947, copy in author's possession; Ira DeA. Reid, "The White Primary," July 1946, Grace Towns Hamilton Papers, Trevor Arnett Library, Atlanta, Georgia, 15-B-3; George Sims, *The Little Man's Big Friend: James E. Folsom in Alabama Politics, 1946–1958* (Tuscaloosa: University of Alabama Press, 1986), 27–37; Palmer Weber, report on Homer Rainey campaign, Aug. 1946, copy in author's possession.

29 Jack Kroll, "The PAC Today," *Nation* 163 (1946), 510–11; transcript of Jack Kroll speech, The Daily Worker, Oct. 20, 1946; Luther Porter Jackson, "Race and Suffrage in the South since 1940," New South, June–July, 1948, 1–26.

30 Arguably, currently the most widely cited distillation of this argument is Jacquelyn Dowd Hall, "The Long Civil Rights Movement and the Politics and Uses of the Past, *Journal of American History* (March 2006), 1233–63. One of the earliest articles advancing this thesis: Robert Korstad and Nelson Lichenstein, "Opportunities Found and Lost: Labor, Radicals and the Early Civil Rights Movement," *Journal of American History* (Dec. 1988) 786–811.

31 John M. Glenn, *Highlander: No Ordinary School, 1932–1962* (Lexington: University of Kentucky Press, 1988) 97–98; John Kneebone, *Southern Liberal Journalists and the Issue of Race* (Chapel Hill: University of North Carolina Press, 1985), 201.

32 Ralph Bunche, *Political Status of the Negro,* 319–22; 421–24; Edwin Hoffman, "The

Genesis of the Modern Movement for Civil Rights in South Carolina," in *The Negro in Depression and War: Prelude to Revolution, 1930–45,* ed. By Bernard Sternsher (Chicago: Quadrangle Books, 1969), 210–11; Patricia Sullivan, *Lift Every Voice: The NAACP and the Making of the Civil Rights Movement* (New York: the New Press, 2009), 237–44; 317–20; John Dittmer, *Local People,* 1–3; Stephen Tuck, *Beyond Atlanta,* 62–69; Du Bois quote: W. E. B. Du Bois to Joel Spingarn, Oct. 28, 1914, Joel E. Spingarn Papers, Beinecke Rare Book and Manuscript Library, Yale University, Box 1.

33   Rob Hall to CVW, July 27, 1956; Rob Hall to CVW, Feb 25, 1986; Sullivan interview with Rob Hall.

34   C. Vann Woodward, "What Happened to the Civil Rights Movement," *Harpers,* Jan. 1967, 171–72, 176–77.

35   Ibid., 173–76.

36   CVW to Glenn Rainey, Oct. 4, 1966, O'Brien, *Letters.*

37   Ibid., 173, 176, 177.

38   Rob Hall to CVW, Oct. 29, 1988.

39   Woodward, *Thinking Back,* 42.

12

'The Goddamn Boss'

Cecil B. Moore, Philadelphia, and the Reshaping of Black Urban Politics

THOMAS SUGRUE

When Sheldon Hackney arrived in Philadelphia in 1981 to take the helm of the University of Pennsylvania, he found himself in a city that many called "up South," the northernmost Southern city, a place that had a long history of racial conflict, inequities, and struggle against it. Philadelphia was no Montgomery or New Orleans. It had a venerable tradition of antislavery activism and racial reform, an extraordinary black civic life that had been chronicled by W. E. B. Du Bois—who had a short affiliation with Penn in the late 1890s—and a black bourgeoisie without rival. But when it came to race relations, Philadelphia was no city of brotherly love. Its history was punctuated by anti-black riots, unofficial but pervasive Jim Crow in its movie theaters, swimming pools, and schools, and deep-rooted discrimination in housing markets and workplaces. By the middle of the 20th century, Philadelphia ranked among the most racially segregated cities in the United States. Philadelphia was one of the most important sites for a civil rights struggle that proved every bit as important as its Southern counterparts in reshaping racial politics in modern America.[1]

Over the course of nearly two decades, Sheldon and I had many lively discussions, mostly in Philadelphia, about our shared interests in the history of America in the 1960s, political biography, the civil rights movement, and the city that we both chose as our adopted homes. It is in that spirit that I have written a political biography of a key figure in Philadelphia's civil rights struggle between the 1950s and the 1970s, whose career embodied the tensions and contradictions, the openings and the closures, the triumphs and failures of the unfinished struggle for racial equality in the North.[2]

By the mid-20th century, North Philadelphia had seen better days. Blocks of red-brick rowhouses lined up in a grim vista, the monotony broken by the plywood covering shattered windows. A sinew of rail lines wove through the neighborhood, passing by decaying factory buildings and rubble-strewn lots. This was the heart of black Philadelphia. Beginning in the 1920s, black migrants from the South had begun moving into the neighborhood, as waves of whites picked up and moved out. On the west was Brewerytown, once a German enclave. Further north was Strawberry Mansion, named for the incongruous colonial country house that stood amidst a sea of Victorian and early 20th-century homes in what had been an enclave for upwardly mobile Jews. And down around the old Shibe Park, in its last days as the city's streetcar stadium, a shabby "little Ireland" had been supplanted by an even shabbier black neighborhood. Many of the larger residences, like the grand Victorians along Diamond Street, had been subdivided into boarding homes and apartments. Fleeing whites often hung on to their properties, collecting rent while deferring maintenance, getting every last dollar out of their investments as the surrounding buildings began to suffer from demolition by neglect.[3]

It was another world, down around Columbia Avenue and North Broad Street, black Philadelphia's downtown. Along Columbia Avenue—"Jump Street"—clusters of men threw dice and socialized in front of neighborhood stores. Churches, from the Gothic towers built as a sign of immigrant piety, to former synagogues turned evangelical churches, were everywhere. Just as ubiquitous were the little neighborhood "stop and go" stores that sold six-packs and two-quart bottles of beer. Barber shops and beauty salons, which proliferated, served as community centers, where getting the latest gossip or line on a job was every bit as important as a conk or pompadour. At night the streets bustled with crowds, for blues, entertainment, and vice. Down Broad Street was another cluster of institutions central to black Philadelphia, including the Uptown Theater and the Blue Horizon boxing gym.

North Philadelphia was a tough neighborhood by the early 1950s. White policemen and journalists nicknamed it "the Jungle," barely concealing their racial disdain for the area's poor residents. If you were in trouble with the law, as many area residents were, chances were good that you would end up in the office of criminal defense attorney Cecil B. Moore. His quarters were cluttered, cramped, and, like the building that housed them, in need of a good updating. Moore didn't have high-end clients, and he had no need to impress them with expensive furniture and costly books. If they needed to be impressed, Moore's baritone voice and his firm handshake and his reputation as a man of the people would do it.

In every respect except personality and style, Moore could have been a typical scion of Philadelphia's famed black bourgeoisie. The only child of a doctor and grandson of a prominent minister, he was born in 1915 in Fork Hollow Yukon, a small coal-mining town in West Virginia. Everyone in town knew Doctor Moore. Cecil grew up in relative privilege, in a part of the South not known for racial violence—even if it was not much of a place for an ambitious young man like Moore. Moore looked back romantically on his days in coal country. "We didn't have any discrimination problems." On an occasion when he was called a "nigger," a "damn good fight ensued." But Moore recalled that in his blue-collar town of Italians, Hungarians, Slavs, and Poles, "most of my little gang was all-white."[4]

If he didn't want to follow in his father's footsteps—he never had much aptitude for science—his best bet was to become a minister like his grandfather. But Moore was not a praying man. Smart and on the make, he went to Bluefield State College. After a short stint selling insurance in the South, he joined the Marines and fought—in a segregated unit—in the Pacific Theater during World War II. Of all of the armed services, the Marines were particularly notorious for their resistance to blacks. Nearly 20,000 blacks enlisted in the Marines, the vast majority of whom were confined to mess units, cooking and serving food, or to ammunition and depot companies, which hauled and distributed heavy cargo. But by 1944, a shortage of manpower led military officials to commit black troops to the battlefront. Moore found himself at the front lines of one of the war's bloodiest battles. "During combat operations," he recalled, "all those damn color lines broke down anyway." In June 1944, Moore led a raid on a Japanese garrison on the occupied island of Saipan. It was one of the proudest moments in an all-segregated military. Marine Corps Commandant Arthur Vandegrift reported that "the Negro Marines are no longer on trial. They are Marines period."[5]

Despite its ingrained culture of hostility to blacks, Moore served in the

Marines until 1951, spending his last four years at Fort Mifflin in Philadelphia. At night, he earned a law degree at Temple University—with tuition paid by the GI Bill—and worked as a whiskey salesman to support his family.

IN 1953, MOORE STARTED his own law practice in Philadelphia. Charismatic and willing to let clients pay what they could when they could, Moore quickly drummed up as much business as he could handle. He hardly ever turned down a case. Getting paid was a dubious proposition at best. "Monetary-wise," he complained about his practice, "it ain't worth shit." Though he was fond of crisply tailored suits and fine cigars, Moore otherwise lived a fairly ascetic life. He preferred military-style haircuts, which were cheap. His office was spartan. And he handled most of the routine office business himself.[6]

Like those of most inner-city lawyers, Moore's docket was depressing. Every day, he patiently heard the stories of men who got into fistfights—or worse, knife fights and shootouts—after a night of drunken reverie. He listened to the sad tales of clients who lost their jobs and could not afford to pay their rent or bills. He mediated domestic disputes. He also took civil rights cases, including that of a black family, among the first in the blue-collar Brewerytown neighborhood, whose white neighbor protested their arrival by taking an axe to their front door. But of all of his cases, one type made Moore's blood boil. He grew visibly tense and angry when young men told him about being shaken down and beaten by the police.[7]

Most of Moore's clients lived in an all-black world. Their only encounters with whites were with the neighborhood shop owners, absentee landlords, and the city's overwhelmingly white police force that patrolled in North Philadelphia more like an occupying force. If you were in the wrong place at the wrong time, or if you had an attitude—as many of Moore's clients did—you could be near certain of a beating. Over the course of the 1950s, Philadelphia's police force came under siege for corruption and violence, including charges of taking payoffs from West Philadelphia bar owners. Down in Center City, police officers played cat and mouse with gay bars and bohemian coffee houses, taking payments to "look the other way" and then rushing in to make mass arrests for deviance or delinquency. Up in Moore's neighborhood, the police were even less restrained.[8]

Moore handled many police-related complaints. In 1952, fresh out of law school, he represented black West Philadelphians who complained that new police captain Frank Rizzo (the future police chief and mayor) had brutalized blacks. A rising star in the city's police force, Rizzo zealously busted illegal speakeasies and numbers-running operations. He led club-wielding cops who broke down doors, shattered windows, and made arrests. The police targeted the "rent parties" that many black Philadelphians held—complete with admission tickets—to supplement their incomes. But they also pounded down the doors of fraternal organizations—private clubs like Elks Lodges—that were so central to the social life of respectable black Philadelphians. Isaiah Groppens, speaking for the Irvin Lodge of the Elks, accused the police of discrimination and bitterly asked, "Why don't you raid the Union League?" one of Philadelphia's most exclusive white clubs. "They drink there too." Rizzo pursued his targets relentlessly, for as he once told an interviewer, "the way to treat criminals is 'Spaco il cappo' (break their heads)." Moore later accused Rizzo of using "storm trooper tactics" in West Philadelphia. It wasn't clear whether Moore's confrontational tactics made for effective representation, but as two of his rivals, A. Leon Higginbotham and William Coleman recalled, "people think he's a great lawyer because he really gave that goddamn white judge hell."[9]

MOORE FOUND A CAUSE in his crusade against police brutality, but he clearly had larger political ambitions. In the 1950s, Moore was one of a dying breed, a black Republican. Beginning in the New Deal, urban blacks defected en masse from the party of Lincoln to the party of FDR. But that shift was uneven. West Virginia, Moore's home state, remained a bastion of black Republicanism longer than most places, and Philadelphia was the one major northeastern city whose Republican machine had survived the New Deal. When Moore arrived in 1947, Philadelphia's Republicans were on the ropes, challenged by a new generation of Democratic reformers. Even so, many Philadelphia blacks clung to the GOP because of the benefits of patronage and because of their use of "balance of power" tactics to win concessions from both parties. So long as the black vote was up-for-grabs in a state whose electorate was closely divided on party lines, both Democrats and Republicans had it in their interest to respond to black demands. Still, by the early 1950s, nearly two-thirds of black Philadelphians had become Democrats.[10]

Nonetheless, Moore hung on to his Republican affiliation. He served as a GOP ward leader and in 1956 was a delegate to the Republican National

Convention and made his first run for political office, challenging Philadelphia's first black member of Congress, Democrat Robert N. C. Nix. The same year, he coordinated a group of black Republicans to support renegade New York congressman Adam Clayton Powell Jr., who had bucked his party to endorse Dwight Eisenhower for the presidency. Moore also launched a vitriolic attack on NAACP Executive Director Roy Wilkins for his "vacillatory, conciliatory state of mind" when he endorsed the "watered down" 1957 Civil Rights Act.

But by the early 1960s Moore had moved away from the Republican Party. At the local level, Republican power was fast waning. The local GOP had less to offer to politicians like Moore, especially in terms of patronage. And winning elections as a Republican had become nearly impossible. The Party itself was in flux. Its Eisenhower/Rockefeller wing—including Pennsylvania leaders like William Scranton—supported gradualist civil rights measures. But at the national level, GOP leaders were starting to move rightward. Moore could not abide the GOP's increasingly vocal right-wing faction, led by Arizona Senator Barry Goldwater; Moore denounced him as a tool of the segregationists.[11]

Moore's political ambition, his record of face-offs with the police, and his contempt for black Philadelphia's old guard added up to a powerful formula for success in a city where blacks were growing increasingly impatient. In 1959, Moore set his sights on Philadelphia's respectable but hidebound NAACP chapter. During the 1950s, the local NAACP had steadily shrunk in size. Fractured by the purge of some its most vocal, blue-collar members during the Red Scare, Philadelphia's chapter lost most of its grassroots support. Those who remained were black and white moderates, who directed most of their energies toward fundraising for the Southern civil rights effort. It was ripe for a takeover.[12]

Jockeying for power in the local NAACP was another black lawyer, the formidable A. Leon Higginbotham. The son of a laborer and a domestic servant, Higginbotham went to liberal Antioch College—a white-dominated institution well-known for its hospitality to black students—and graduated with honors from Yale Law School. Higginbotham clerked for prominent Philadelphia judge Curtis Bok (whose son Derek, later Harvard University president and crusader for affirmative action in higher education, had recently married Gunnar Myrdal's daughter Sissela). Higginbotham then served briefly as an assistant district attorney before starting a private practice in civil and appellate law. In 1959, only 30 years old, Higginbotham won the presidency of the NAACP chapter on a reformist platform. He pushed the local chapter in a more militant direction, but in 1962 he resigned to take an appointment to the Federal Trade Commission. The following year, President John F. Kennedy nominated him to the federal bench—one of several prominent black jurists elevated in the early 1960s—and he was confirmed in 1964.[13]

INTO THE VOID LEFT by Higginbotham came Moore. In 1962, Moore ran again as an insurgent for the presidency of Philadelphia's chapter of the NAACP and won. What Moore would do at the helm remained to be seen. At his inauguration, he came out fighting against the status quo. "We are serving notice that no longer will the plantation system of white men appointing our leaders exist in Philadelphia," raged Moore. "We expect to be consulted on all community issues which affect our people." He would be satisfied with nothing short of Negro "self determination."[14] Some moderate civil rights leaders worried that under Moore, the "NAACP will move out of the camp of the integrationists, where it was a leader, to some unknown hitching post in militancy."[15] Part brilliant organizer, part charlatan, Moore represented a new generation of grassroots activists, who spoke a populist rhetoric and who deployed protest tactics that many of the city's older civil rights leaders thought were dangerous and counterproductive.

Moore took his militant message to the press, angrily denouncing whites, peppering his speeches with anti-Semitic slurs, and demanding immediate action on civil rights. Above all, Moore rejected integrationism. He was deeply suspicious of the motivations of whites, especially white liberals. In a version of the dozens, the black game of pushing slurs to their outer limits, he claimed that the "white man is so low, he'd sell his grandmother to make some money." Moore showed little restraint in criticizing whites and grew angrier by the year.

A rebel against his bourgeois roots, Moore chafed at well-to-do black folks, "the 20 percent or so who don't want to be Negroes." Moore's animus was as much personal as political. As North Philadelphia grew rougher and poorer, Moore stayed in his aging rowhouse at 17th and Jefferson, just a few blocks from Jump Street. He was committed to living and working with the folks that he affectionately called his "barbeque, porkchops, collard green eating people." Walking down 17th Street toward Moore's house meant dodging an obstacle course of overflowing garbage cans, broken beer bottles, and crumpled blowing newspapers and sandwich wrappings. Residents of the neighborhood regularly complained about poor service from the city sanitation department. Most blacks with a little money or job security tried to move out, following the receding tide of the city's waning white population.

By the early 1960s, Philadelphia's small but visible cadre of black lawyers, doctors, and "race" businessmen were moving to the leafy neighborhoods of northwest Philadelphia, particularly in Mount Airy, a place that the black-owned *Philadelphia Tribune* described as "like the countryside of England." Along Pelham Road and Lincoln Drive, curving streets lined with large stone homes built as part of one of America's first planned communities, they found a comfortable base. Raymond Pace Alexander, a leading black lawyer (who had graduated second in his class at Harvard Law School) and his wife, Sadie Mossell Alexander (the first black woman to receive a PhD in economics from the University of Pennsylvania), moved into a rambling Tudor revival house on Westview Street, one of the most beautiful blocks in the city. (In a particularly ironic twist, Moore purchased the Alexanders' former North Philadelphia house.) In a nearby stone manse lived Robert C. Nix, Philadelphia's first black congressman. Even if the homes were "hand-me-downs" from whites moving to the newly fashionable suburbs, they were not the rat-infested crumbling houses, chopped up into apartments, that lined the streets of Moore's neighborhood. That Mount Airy was one of the city's few racially-mixed neighborhoods reaffirmed the racial liberalism and the respectability of Nix, Alexander, and their elite black neighbors.[16]

Of this world, Moore was contemptuous. Philadelphia Commission on Human Relations members Sadie Alexander and Christopher Edley Sr. were "little Uncle Toms" and "occasional Negroes." Appealing to popular resentment of the city's large black bourgeoisie, Moore lashed out at Alexander as an "Aunt Dinah" and a "Judas who has accepted her 20 pieces of silver." Philadelphia's black elite responded with disdain. Fifteen of Philadelphia's most prominent blacks—including the Alexanders and Nix—signed a public letter which accused Moore of "acting like a man bereft of reason." Moore was prone to "bombast, silly threats and other ineffective tactics which are more consistent with the program of the black Muslims" than the NAACP. Moore's tactics, they argued, would "forfeit [the NAACP's] respectability and status and destroy it as an effective instrumentality for racial advancement." In a pointed rejoinder, Moore chastised them for launching their critique from "their lofty perch midway between the integration they long for and the segregation from which they have profited."[17]

"I run a grassroots group," Moore contended in a rebuke to the "old guard" who had run the NAACP in the 1950s, "not a cocktail-party, tea-sipping, fashion-show attending group of exhibitionists." Moore's street-wise demeanor brought him considerable support in poor and working-class neighborhoods. One fervent Moore supporter from North Philadelphia frankly acknowledged that the NAACP president was "an arrogant foul mouth radical" but praised Moore for his interest in the "rank and file negro," an approach "much needed . . . among a restless people." It was precisely Moore's brashness that won the support of blacks whose grievances remained unaddressed after World War II and who were alienated from the cautious racial liberalism of the 1950s. "His method," argued one prominent minister, was "to get in touch with the people who are not being reached too effectively by the moral, religious leadership."[18]

Moore brought NAACP soliciting to where it had never been before. Rather than recruiting in the churches and synagogues of the city, Moore went right to "his" people. In 1964, Philadelphia's NAACP began a membership outreach campaign in 400 bars and taprooms in black Philadelphia. "The NAACP must serve the entire community and we warmly welcome the support of the bars and taprooms in our community." Moore's fearless challenges to white authorities did not go unappreciated among ordinary blacks. When police busted a party in a Philadelphia housing project in 1964, one angry young man shouted, "Wait till Cecil Moore gets a hold of you guys."[19]

"I AM RUTHLESS," CECIL Moore bragged to *New York Times* reporter Joseph Lelyveld. If the civil rights activists of the 1950s were restrained and cautious, Moore was anything but.[20] Moore began his tenure as NAACP president with a battle. When Ford Foundation officials announced a community development program for black Philadelphia in January, Moore immediately criticized Ford for selecting a white lawyer to direct the program. Demanding "self-determination," Moore threatened to boycott Ford dealerships. The Ford Foundation stuck with its appointment, but the battle whetted Moore's appetite.[21]

In the spring of 1963, he found a new cause—one that would make him a household name in Philadelphia—breaking down "Jim Crow" in the construction industry. CORE activists had targeted the construction industry and blocked the streets in front of Mayor James Tate's modest North Philadelphia rowhouse in April. But in mid-May, Moore attempted to bump CORE out of the picture and take over the protests himself. He spearheaded protests at two construction sites during the last two weeks of May—a new city office building being built in Center City and a new school being built in North Philadelphia's mostly black Strawberry Mansion neighborhood. The protests were theatrical and, like a growing number of Northern protests, teetered tensely between nonviolence and violence. At the school site, protestors included housewives and briefcase-toting black lawyers, the embodiment of black respectability. A group of youthful protestors—inverting the symbolism of the police-dog attacks on protestors in Birmingham—joined the picket with "fierce-looking mastiffs. Also joining the picket line were members of the fledging Revolutionary Action Movement (RAM), including Max Stanford, a young man whom Moore had hired as a community organizer. RAM, however, threatened to outflank Moore; he had removed RAM members from a City Hall picket line for displaying inflammatory signs and distanced himself and the NAACP from RAM when Stanford and a colleague were arrested for battling with the police at the school site. By 1964, RAM had fully broken with Moore; in a cartoon, RAM's magazine *Black America* labeled "Slick Cecil" a "sell out" and a puppet of Philadelphia's white leadership. Moore might have been a radical by the standards of Philadelphia's black bourgeoisie, but by the mid-1960s, black power militants found even his brand of incendiary politics a little too polite.[22]

In the aftermath of the victories at city construction sites, Moore launched attacks on employment discrimination by companies ranging from national corporations to neighborhood jewelry stores. Scattershot, he threatened and cajoled discriminatory employers. Those who did not capitulate faced pickets. He sent blistering telegrams to Railway Express Trucking, to the U.S. Army Electronics Material Agency, and to Greyhound Bus Company. Moore and NAACP activists picketed Shapiro's Shoe Store in West Philadelphia for its lack of black salespeople, and they denounced the Philadelphia post office, where sixty percent of workers were black, as the "30th Street Plantation." The local NAACP adopted the rhetoric of "direct action" from CORE and began to deploy the tactic of civil disobedience. In December 1964, Moore and dozens of local activists were arrested after blocking traffic in front of the Philadelphia Bus Depot to protest the lack of black drivers on Trailways buses.[23]

If Moore was moving toward a rejection of nonviolence, he still had his limits. During the summer of 1964, Philadelphia erupted in a riot, one of several conflagrations in the North that summer. In June, when a minister was killed by a bulldozer at a school desegregation protest in Cleveland, police and protestors clashed in the streets. In mid-July, a week of looting and arson swept through the Harlem and Bedford-Stuyvesant neighborhoods in New York after a 15-year old boy in Harlem was shot by an off-duty police officer. In late July, two days of unrest shook Rochester, New York, after an altercation between police and youths at a street dance, in the aftermath of weeks of protests against discrimination at Kodak corporate headquarters. Rochester calmed only after Governor Nelson Rockefeller deployed the National Guard. Smaller riots had broken out in early August—all provoked by police incidents—in Dixmoor, Illinois, and in Jersey City, Patterson, and Elizabeth, New Jersey.

In Philadelphia, a confrontation with the police also sparked one of the most severe uprisings that summer. On the steamy evening of August 28, police attempted to arrest a black woman whose car had stalled at the corner of Columbia Avenue and 22nd Street. A crowd gathered, catcalling the police. Officer Robert Wells, on the scene, reported that "about 8 or 10 'whinos' with rags around their heads" came out of a bar at the corner and began throwing bricks. They were joined by young men hurling bottles and other objects from nearby rooftops. Shaykh Muhammad, also known as Abyssinia Hayes, a renegade Black Muslim, began spreading the rumor that the police had killed the woman—whom he claimed was pregnant—while in custody. Crowds of young men began running down Columbia Avenue, breaking windows, looting stores, and engaging in pitched battles with the police. "It was like being in a war," recounted a witness. (Muhammad was later arrested on charges that he had stockpiled weapons and Molotov cocktails at his headquarters, Muhammad's African-Asian Cultural Center, also on Columbia Avenue.)[24]

Moore lived only a few blocks from the epicenter of the riot. As dozens of police cars and hundreds of police officers swarmed, Moore headed out to the streets. He pleaded with rioters to "talk out their grievances instead of resorting to violence," and persuaded a few to follow him to nearby Fairmount Park where they could cool off. He worked the crowds, fearlessly approaching looters and asking them to cooperate with the police. On the morning of August 29, Moore swept Muhammad up into the NAACP sound truck, conscripting him—unwillingly—to join the appeal for calm in the streets. With them was none other than Odessa Bradford, the woman whose arrest had sparked the conflagration the pervious night. "Here she is," Moore shouted through his loudspeaker. "She's very much alive. She's not dead. She's not pregnant. She's not even hurt." Skipping a meeting with city officials and church leaders on the second day of the riot, Moore went to a concert at the Uptown Theater and told the youthful audience that "nobody wins in a riot except the bondman, the lawyers, and the doctors."

Because of his reputation for militancy, Moore got a better hearing than most civil rights leaders. The sight of black elected officials climbing onto a car trunk or commandeering a bullhorn to put down protests would become commonplace in the long hot summers of the 1960s. But the call to quietude usually fell on deaf ears. When Raymond Pace Alexander tried to calm rioters on Columbia Avenue, they ignored him. "I'll confess that I received no response," he lamented. Moore, on the other hand, worked the crowds tirelessly, pleading for calm. Eventually, 1,300 police descended on the riot-torn neighborhood, temporarily banned liquor sales, and set a curfew in a 410-square-block section of North Philadelphia. After two and half days of rioting, two people were dead, 339 were injured, and 308 were arrested.[25]

Moore took a middle-ground approach to the riots. Mainstream black leaders like Alexander worried about the impact of the riots on the public image of blacks. "In my day, every home was a Christian home," Alexander lamented. "We had no riots then. I feel very much as if our race has been diminished." U.S. Representative Robert N. C. Nix blamed the uprising on "a bunch of hoodlums and bums. They are not representative of Negroes in this community." Prominent black minister Leon Sullivan concurred, calling for "law and order." Moore countered that whites were not embarrassed by the Mafia, so "I'm not going to be embarrassed by hoodlums." Looking back in retrospect, Moore blamed the uprising on "a long history of police mistreatment." The "perpetual exploitation of the Negro," he argued, "was one of the big causes of the riots. Nothing has changed."[26]

MOORE RATCHETED UP THE NAACP's campaign of "direct action" in 1965. His new target was "the wall of Jericho," a biblical metaphor for the ten-foot high stone wall that surrounded the campus of Girard College in North Philadelphia. The college's neoclassical white marble buildings, reminscient of Greek temples, were designed by Thomas U. Walter, the architect of the national capitol, at the bequest of Stephan Girard, the wealthiest man in America when he died in 1831. For most of its first 120 years, Girard College operated as a school—under the terms of Girard's will—for "poor white male orphans."[27] As the surrounding neighborhood became a magnet for blacks beginning in the 1940s, the fortified school became an even more powerful symbol of exclusion. Beginning in 1953, civil rights activists targeted Girard College for desegregation. Lawyer Raymond Pace Alexander oversaw a legal case against the Girard Estate that made a byzantine 14-year trip through the judiciary system, eventually landing twice in the U.S. Supreme Court. Despite being rebuffed in the courts, Alexander clung to his position that litigation was the only appropriate strategy for opening the doors of Girard College to blacks.[28]

Impatient with the glacial pace of the legal case, Moore stepped up protests at Girard College beginning in May 1965. The goal was nothing short of breaking down the invisible walls of racial discrimination that had kept blacks out of the school for more than a century. Alexander worried that the protests would be counterproductive, causing "great unrest and wide fear of damage to the fine and healthy relations between the races in Philadelphia."[29] Through mid-December, picketers stood vigil at the Girard College gates, sometimes numbering in the handful, sometimes in the thousands. Keeping the path clear were police officers in riot helmets, poised to break heads if necessary. Their commander was Moore's sometime nemesis, Frank Rizzo.[30]

The Girard College protests attracted the attention of Martin Luther King Jr. After a string of victories in the South and with the passage of the Civil Rights Act of 1964 and Voting Rights Act of 1965, the Southern Christian Leadership Conference began to look northward. Many civil rights activists shared James Bevel's worry that President Johnson had "signed the civil rights movement out of existence." In late July 1965, King planned a trip to Philadelphia, scouting for a location to expand the Southern movement to the North. Philadelphia had all of the ingredients: one of the oldest and largest black communities in the North, a venerable tradition of interracial activism dating back to the Quaker abolitionists of the early 19th century, and an active local civil rights movement. Girard College was a textbook case of entrenched racial privilege—a discriminatory institution, guarded by club-wielding police who kept nonviolent protestors at bay. As a stage for the next phase of struggle, it seemed ideal. What King had not bargained for was an icy reception by Cecil Moore. Of all of Philadelphia's civil rights leaders, Moore was the most turf-conscious. He had engaged in an ongoing battle with CORE over who would lead the city's construction site and Trailways bus protests, and denounced CORE's James Farmer as an "Uncle Tom" who presided over "90 percent insincere, frustrated beatnik white intellectuals and Negroes whose sole purpose is to call attention to themselves." When Jesse Gray, a tenant organizer from Harlem, came to Philadelphia hoping to organize a citywide rent strike, Moore chased him out of town. And when other "so-called civil rights groups" threatened to mediate the Girard College case, Moore threatened to boycott any negotiations. Moore's critics were scathing. Philip Savage, a Philadelphia CORE activist, called Moore "dictatorial—[he] wants to rule and dominate everything, even God."[31]

To Moore, King was an outside agitator, hoping to take credit for a movement that was not his own. Moore was not alone in his suspicion of King's motives. By the mid-1960s, many Southern activists grew increasingly critical of King for his hit-and-run approach to protesting. Some members of the Student Non-Violent Coordinating Committee started referring to King as "De Lawd," for his autocratic, ministerial style. Their criticism filtered northward. New York's prickly Adam Clayton Powell Jr. warned that it would be "unwise" to come to Harlem without broad-based community support there. Moore was just as wary as his mentor. Philadelphia activists had targeted Girard College for decades. They were on the brink of victory—so why should King get any credit for that? Always sensitive to disrespect, Moore was angry that SCLC had announced King's trip to Philadelphia without consulting him first. Why should King take the limelight away from Moore?[32]

Two men could not have had more different political and personal styles. King was critical of the white establishment, but always respectful of whites who seemed to be making a good-faith effort to change the racial status quo. In public settings, King maintained a stentorian presence. He was first and foremost a preacher. Moore, on the other hand, seldom quoted the Bible, scorned moralistic churchgoers, and peppered his speeches and interviews with slang and profanity. Perhaps their most important divergence, on the issue of nonviolence as a protest strategy, became clear at the Girard College protests.

Moore and the Philadelphia NAACP had embraced a strategy of "direct action," borrowing a concept that had its origins in CORE and its application of Gandhian nonviolence to American-style protest. By the late 1950s, King and the SCLC had popularized the Indian leader's protest strategies and some referred to King himself as the American Gandhi. But throughout the early 1960s, particularly in the North, a growing number of black activists embraced an alternative rhetoric of "self defense." By 1965, Moore himself was moving away from the embrace of nonviolent strategy. He welcomed members of the Morroccans, "one of the largest, toughest, and best organized gangs" in Philadelphia, whom he hoped would "keep the pressure on" at Girard College. Moore also played on city officials' deep fear that the protests would spark another riot.[33] He was not averse to using force if necessary, or using the threat of force as a way to create tension and instability.

The protests at Girard were about much more than the desegregation of the school. Increasingly, Moore and protestors turned their anger toward the Philadelphia police department. Under the glare of floodlights erected by the police department at the Girard College gate, nighttime protests grew tense. In mid-May, protestors taunted the police, singing to the tune of "Jingle Bells": "Shotgun shells, shotgun shells, freedom all the way. Oh what fun it is to blow the blue suit man away." On the evening of June 24, five weeks before King's proposed visit, Moore provoked a confrontation with the police on Girard Avenue. About one hundred protestors, most of them young men, attempted to scale the college walls, charged at the police, threw bricks and stones, and engaged in a pitched battle on the street. Police commander Frank Rizzo ordered police motorcyclists to ride into the crowd. In the ensuing chaos, several protestors were injured. While nonviolent protests continued at Girard College, the bloodshed of the 24th was a signal of Moore's rejection of the principles of direct action.[34]

When King announced a trip to Philadelphia on July 31, Moore was outraged. He denounced King as a "divisive force" solely motivated by a desire "for headlines and money." King, he argued, clung to the "imported Gandhi philosophy of nonviolence," which "would not be accepted in Philadelphia where we believe in self-help and self-defense." Only after lengthy negotiations with King's Philadelphia supporters and SCLC leadership did Moore give his reluctant blessing to King's Philadelphia visit. For his part, King was duly deferential to Moore. "We are here not to establish a movement," King apologized, "but to support the one that is already here." SCLC leaders promised to return the proceeds from King's fundraisers to Philadelphia, and Moore was mollified. The two activists appeared together at a joint press conference and, later, at a 5,000-person rally outside Girard College. But King, chastened by his experience in Philadelphia, turned his sights on other Northern cities, eventually choosing Chicago for SCLC's symbolic move northward.[35]

By 1965, MOORE WAS coming under criticism on many fronts. White-dominated liberal groups had distanced themselves almost from his first day at the helm of the NAACP. When he announced that he did not know a single Jewish civil rights activist "who wasn't a goddam phony," he faced intense criticism from labor, religious, and liberal political organizations. Editors of the *Jewish Exponent* denounced his language. Liberal labor leaders, long supportive of the NAACP, lashed out at him for his insensitivity. Philadelphia's Mayor James Tate called him a "yellow general who hides behind the lines," and compared him to Hitler and Mussolini.[36]

Moore's brash style also alienated many of the local NAACP's longstanding members. Every time he criticized whites or lashed out against "Uncle Toms," Gloster Current, the director of branches, was flooded with angry letters. Many liberal Philadelphians, black and white, began withholding their contributions to the local chapter. In late 1963 and 1964 alone, the Philadelphia branch lost 10,000 members. The Philadelphia chapter went into deficit and in 1965 donated a mere $50 to the NAACP Legal Defense Fund.[37] Many longtime members of the NAACP sent their checks to the national office, repudiating their affiliation to the Philadelphia chapter. Others angrily resigned. The national office faced a crisis. How could they neutralize Moore without alienating his local grassroots supporters and further discrediting the NAACP? Sensitive to the criticism of the NAACP as an "accommodationist" organization, Roy Wilkins was loathe to come down hard against Moore. During the Girard College protests, he even joined Moore on the picket line, "much to the dismay of many Moore antagonists."[38]

In 1965, Henry Nichols, a prominent local minister, the first black member of the Philadelphia Board of Education, and a longtime NAACP member, ran against Moore, charging that he ran a "one-man show." Moore's critics charged him with fiscal improprieties and launched an investigation of his practices, Moore was exonerated, not surprisingly, given his nonchalance about wealth; he may have been impolitic, but he was not corrupt. Despite Nichols's backing among NAACP stalwarts, Moore won handily, in large part because so many Moore critics had left the Philadelphia branch. Moore crowed, "I am still the goddamn boss!"[39] As a way out of their bind, NAACP officials announced a plan in 1966 to break the Philadelphia chapter into five separate chapters, each with its own president. This would be a temporary expedient. They hoped that an angry Moore would resign from the organization and that the Philadelphia chapter could be reconstituted with a less inflammatory leader at the helm. Moore launched an unsuccessful lawsuit against the NAACP and refused to resign. Finally, he was ousted from the NAACP on the pretext that he was using his office to run an insurgent congressional campaign against Democratic incumbent Robert Nix.[40]

For Moore, expulsion from the NAACP liberated him to take an even more militant position. As more cities erupted in violence in the mid-1960s, Moore began to use the threat of violence as a powerful bargaining chip. In Philadelphia, as throughout the country, politicians and civic leaders created programs that they hoped would serve as "riot insurance." They feared that if they did not meet the increasingly militant demands of black activists—at least symbolically—the cities would continue to burn. Whites trembled at the prospect of retributory violence. Although most of the rioting had been confined to black neighborhoods, they feared, in the famous words of Julius Lester, "look out, whitey, black power's gonna get yo mama." Ever the strategist, Moore played on white fears. "The only way they [white folks] are going to learn anything is if we keep them in that fear." He threatened white store owners in black neighborhoods. At a rally on South Street in June 1967, Moore boasted: "We ain't fighting each other no more, so we are going to fight the enemy, we are gonna get some of these thieving merchants that give you all that bad meat, the short weights, and the high prices, or get one of these errand boys that work for some of these crackers." To black audiences, he celebrated "the right of self-defense." Adapting the persona of a street tough, he told a West Philadelphia audience that "I got a switchblade and I learned how to cut before I did anything else. Will you cut with me?" Moore himself had no record of violence. But whether or not he actually carried a knife, he established some street credibility and contributed to a sense, felt by both blacks and whites, that he was the harbinger of violent revolution.[41]

MOORE GREW INCREASINGLY VITRIOLIC, stepping up his now infamous criticism of black moderates and Jews. In 1966, he protested outside the National Urban

League annual meeting, denouncing it as a gathering of "Uncle Toms."[42] As the black power movement grew, he adopted its language and ramped up his angry rhetoric. At several rallies in the summer of 1967, he was greeted with chants of "Kill the Toms, Kill the Toms." Moore also expressed anti-Semitic sentiments with even less restraint. In a 1967 lawsuit against the Philadelphia public schools, he castigated Jewish attorney David Berger, who represented the Board of Education. "You're playing footsie with racial bigots. You and the rest of the Jews get out of my business."[43] At a rally in black South Philadelphia, Moore railed against Jewish merchants on South Street, a tawdry strip of clothing stores and junk shops that catered to a predominantly black clientele. "We're going to put them all out of business," he shouted. "Four blocks away from you that Jew on South Street . . . he's been making 100 percent profit and taking advantage of your ignorance." Jewish merchants "steal from us and send $2 million to Israel and won't even give [us] $100." As Moore grew more strident, members of the liberal Fellowship Commission denounced his "appeals to violence" and "appeals to blind hatred."[44]

By the late 1960s, Moore had fashioned his own idiosyncratic version of black power. In an ill-fated attempt to set a national agenda for the fledgling movement, he joined in a black power "summit" held by Adam Clayton Powell Jr. in 1966. Although Powell had a tumultuous relationship with black activists of nearly every stripe, he remained a firm supporter of Moore and appointed him to chair a panel to set "action guidelines" for black power activists. Powell's version of black power never had much traction, but Moore attempted to build a coalition of black separatists back on his home turf.[45] Celebrating "unity" at a South Philadelphia rally, Moore noted that "we got the Black Muslims, the Black Unity Movement, and we got my brand of the NAACP, not the absentee brand." But although Moore shared sympathies with the Nation of Islam, he found their strictures too confining. "They're against eating pork," he joked, "and I ain't going to give up my sowbelly." Moore was also suspicious of the newfound Afrocentrism that swept through the black city during the late 1960s. Dismissing romantic views of African "savages," he mockingly told a friend, "I ain't going to climb trees no more." Moore's ever-abrasive politics earned him some detractors among black nationalists. In 1967, Moore's longtime nemesis, the Revolutionary Action Movement, which had one of its largest chapters in Philadelphia, denounced Moore for "selling out" and "trick[ing] his people into thinking he is 'for real.'"[46] But if Moore rejected the Afro style, he shared much in common with the rising black power movement.

At the vanguard of a new abrasive style of politics, Moore flouted the respectability and disdained the moralism that had characterized the activism of the previous generation. He rejected the ideal of racial integration and embraced the rhetoric of black separatism and self-determination. It would be up to blacks themselves, militant and uncompromising, to win the struggle against inequality and injustice. Whites and their moderate black "Uncle Tom" supporters could be counted on for one thing: to perpetuate the racist status quo. It would take Moore and his "field hands" to rise up against the white "plantation owners" and their obsequious black "house Negroes." By the late 1960s, Moore embraced a form of racial separatism, even if he never wholly embraced the nationalism that drove so many black radicals in the late 1960s. Distrustful of whites, he embraced the notion of black-owned, black-controlled, and black-patronized stores.

If many black Philadelphians applauded Moore for his brash challenges to the status quo, they remained largely unwilling to hand him political power. Building on his notoriety, Moore launched a campaign for mayor in 1967. Running as an outsider in a hotly contested race between two white candidates, incumbent Mayor James Tate and district attorney and future senator Arlen Specter, Moore's quest for City Hall was quixotic at best. Tate was reelected by a narrow margin—attributable to his strong support among black voters. Moore lost overwhelmingly. Even in the North Philadelphia wards where Moore was well-known and widely admired, he barely picked up five percent of the ballots cast.[47]

BY THE EARLY 1970S, the terrain of Philadelphia's politics had changed dramatically—and Moore's career followed. In 1971, Philadelphia voters elected Frank Rizzo as mayor. To many white Philadelphians, who were alienated by the growing assertiveness of black activists, upset by the city's economic woes, and threatened by racial transition (Philadelphia's population was over 30 percent black by 1970), Rizzo promised law and order. He had served as police chief during the long hot summers from 1965 to 1969 and many credited him (without justification) for preventing rioting. Rizzo was in his own way as theatrical as Moore, once leaving a formal dinner to put down a disturbance in South Philadelphia, with his nightstick in his cummerbund.

As mayor, Rizzo strengthened Philadelphia's machine, significantly increasing spending on costly public works projects and raising city workers' wages, leading to a fiscal crisis in the early 1970s. At the same time, Rizzo began to drift from the Democratic Party (though he would not leave it until the 1980s), befriending Richard Nixon and embracing his "silent majority" politics.

Rizzo's rise gave urgency to Philadelphia's new generation of black politicians. Some, like future mayor Wilson Goode, collaborated with the city's liberal reformers, but some of the most visible, like Moore, adopted a flamboyant politics of street theater. Among those influenced by Moore were brothers Milton and John Street, who organized street vendors, protested against Rizzo, and began to lay the groundwork for their own political careers. (Milton would serve a troubled term in the state house of representatives, join the state Republican caucus, and end up a professional gadfly; Street would serve on Philadelphia's city council, become its powerful president, and get elected to two terms as mayor at the turn of the 21st century.) Their lesson from Moore was as much stylistic as substantive: they were media-savvy and outspoken and used protest politics to launch their careers. Moore himself finally made a successful run for city council from North Philadelphia's fifth district in 1975. He served one term, plagued by deteriorating health, and died in 1979. John Street succeeded Moore, but over the next 20 years refashioned his own image as a dealmaker rather than a protestor.[48]

Moore's career—his eternal striving to be *the* spokesman for black Philadelphia—also embodied a tension at the heart of urban black politics. From Marcus Garvey to Al Sharpton, black politics has been shaped and limited by a search for a single race spokesman. Moore tried, ultimately unsuccessfully, to make himself into the single most important black leader in a city that was remarkably heterogeneous. Rather than playing to the handful of the city's black elites, whose claim to power was their access to the city's white power structure, Moore cast himself as a man of the people. Whenever he faced political competition, whether it be from Congressman Robert Nix, black society lawyer Raymond Alexander, CORE chair Louis Smith, Muslim militant Shaykh Muhammad, or the Reverend Martin Luther King Jr., Moore attempted to marginalize his critics.

Even if Moore did not achieve the political success that he so desired, he represented a real shift in civil rights politics—from the quiet, respectable tactics of the 1950s liberals to the more militant tactics of the 1960s, from the nearly anonymous, behind-the-scenes politics of black moderates to the flamboyant, personality-driven politics that would become increasingly important in black America. And finally, in an era when the news media covered black politics to an extent unimaginable in the 1940s or 1950s, Moore could grab the headlines, ensuring that however representative or unrepresentative his views were, they got more than their fair share of a hearing in the public forum. His legacy—and the legacy of countless unstudied Cecil B. Moores throughout the North and South—was his transitional place in the unfolding history of black urban politics from protest to power, from outsider to insider.

Notes

1 Matthew Countryman, *Up South: Civil Rights and Black Power in Philadelphia* (Philadelphia, 2005). For other important studies of Philadelphia, see James Wolfinger, *Philadelphia Divided: Race and Politics in the City of Brotherly Love* (Chapel Hill, 2007); Lisa Levenstein, *A Movement without Marches: African American Women and the Politics of Poverty in Postwar Philadelphia* (Chapel Hill, 2009).

2 Useful but dated studies of Moore include Paul Lermack, "Cecil B. Moore and the Philadelphia Branch of the National Association for the Advancement of Colored People: The Politics of Negro Pressure Group Organization," in Miriam Ershkowitz and Joseph Zikmund, eds., *Black Politics in Philadelphia* (New York, 1973), 145–160 and the hagiography, *Cecil's City: A History of Blacks in Philadelphia, 1638–1979* (New York: Carlton Press, 1990). More recently, Moore has been treated at some length by Countryman, *Up South*, 120–79.

3 Bruce Kuklick, *To Every Thing a Season: Shibe Park and Urban Philadelphia, 1909–1976* (Princeton, 1993); Philadelphia; "Bitterness and Heartbreak are Bedfellows of Residents of North Philly Ghetto," *Philadelphia Tribune*, October 3, 1967; "Inspections Jobs Made Tough By Absentee Landlords," *Philadelphia Tribune*, October 17, 1967.

4 Gaeton Fonzi, "Cecil Storms In," *Greater Philadelphia Magazine* (July 1963), 48; "In Memoriam, Cecil Bassett Moore, Esq.," Saturday, February 17, 1979, Clippings File, 003–127, Schomburg Center, New York Public Library; see generally, Joe W. Trotter, *Coal, Class, and Color.*

5 Fonzi, "Cecil Storms In," 49; "New Navy Policy," *Crisis*, May 1942, 166; John W. Davis, "The Negro in the United States Navy, Marine Corps, and Coast Guard," *Journal of Negro Education* 12 (1943), 347–49; David Kennedy, *Freedom from Fear*, 816–17; Bernard Nalty, *Strength for the Fight: A History of Black Americans in the Military* (New York, 1986), 199–201.

6 The Marines continued to turn away black recruits and restrict blacks to certain jobs after the war, see, for example, "Along the NAACP Battlefront," *Crisis*, April 1946, 121.

7 *Philadelphia Tribune*, July 16, 1957; Fonzi, "Cecil Storms In," 50.

8 Marc Stein, *City of Sisterly and Brotherly Loves: Lesbian and Gay Philadelphia, 1945–1972* (Chicago, 2000); Nicole Maurantonio, "Crisis, Race, and Journalistic Authority in

Postwar Philadelphia," PhD dissertation, University of Pennsylvania, 2008.

9 *Pittsburgh Courier*, September 15, 1953; Sal Palantonio, *Frank Rizzo: The Last Man in Big City America* (Philadelphia, 1993), 51, 53; Kenneth A. Mack, *Representing the Race: The Creation of the Civil Rights Lawyer* (Cambridge, Mass., 2012), 249.

10 Clemmie L. Harris, Jr., "Race, Leadership, and the Local Machine: The Origins of the Struggle for Political Recognition and the Politics of Community Control in Black Philadelphia, 1915–1968," PhD Dissertation, University of Pennsylvania, 2013.

11 *Amsterdam News*, Nov. 17, 1956, Lermack, "Cecil B. Moore," 147; *Philadelphia Tribune*, August 27, 1957. Moore maintained an ongoing relationship with Powell throughout the 1960s, including working with Powell on a black power agenda and leading a national group of supporters of Powell when he faced expulsion from the House of Representatives. See *New York Times*, September 4, 18, 1966.

12 "Support These Candidates Because They Believe as You Believe--That the Philadelphia Branch NAACP Should Be--Independent--Efficiently Run--Maintain A Constructive Program," NAACP Papers, Library of Congress, Group II, Box C136, Folder: Philadelphia, 1959.

13 On Bok: *New York Times*, May 8, 1955; On A. Leon Higginbotham, *New York Times*, September 27, 1962); Mack, *Representing the Race*, 258.

14 *Pennsylvania Guardian*, 1/25.63; "Moore Strengthens Control," *Pennsylvania Guardian*, February 8, 1963; Palantonio, *Rizzo*, 72.

15 "Burress First Casualty of Leadership Change," *Guardian*, February 8, 1963.

16 "Slums Spell Death, Destruction and Despair," *Philadelphia Tribune*, October 19, 1967; "Negro Home Ownership in Philadelphia," *Philadelphia Tribune*, November 21, 1967.

17 Press Release, PNAACP, January 23, 1963, Subject: NAACP's Position on PCCA's Project," in NAACP Papers, Group III, Box C137. Fonzi, "Cecil Storms In."

18 *New York Times*, September 2, 1964; "Pennsylvania: 'The Goddam Boss'," *Time*, September 11, 1964.

19 James R. Moses to Roy Wilkins, [received] September 16, 1964, NAACP, Group III, Box C137, Folder: Philadelphia, July–Sept. 1964; *New York Times Sunday Magazine*, August 2, 1964.

20 *New York Times*, September 2, 1964

21 *Philadelphia Bulletin*, January 22, 1963; "Moore Strengthens Control Over Phila NAACP," *Pennsylvania Guardian*, February 8, 1963.

22 Thomas J. Sugrue, "Affirmative Action from Below: Civil Rights, the Building Trades, and the Politics of Racial Equality in the North, 1945–1969" *Journal of American History* 91 (2004), 145–73; Max Stanford curriculum vita, July 1974, Revolutionary Action Movement Papers (hereafter RAM), Reel 1; Max Stanford, FBI File, Memo dated 9/25/64, RAM, Reel 3; Max Stanford, MA Thesis draft, sent to John Bracey and Ernie Allen for Comment (May 1979), chapter 4, 10, RAM, Reel 3; cartoon, *Black America* (Nov–Dec. 1963), 3.

23 Press Release, n.d. [July 23, 1963], Subject: 30th Street Post Office and Robert C. Nix, NAACP, Group III, Box C137; Press Release, July 30, 1963, Subject: NAACP and Bus Company Reach Agreement, ibid., Press Release, Sept. 19, 1963, Subject: US Army Electronics Material Agency, ibid.; Press Release, n.d. [received, August 26, 1964],

Subject: Shapiro's Children's Shoe Store, ibid.; News Release, n.d. [received 7/8/64], ibid.; *New York Times*, December 17, 1963.

24 Report of the National Advisory Commission on Civil Disorders (New York, 1968), 36–37; *Philadelphia Bulletin*, August 29, 1964; August 30, 1964

25 *Philadelphia Bulletin*, August 29, 30, 31, 1964; New York Times, September 1, 2, 1964; Taylor Branch, *Pillar of Fire*, 499–500.

26 *New York Times*, August 29, 1964; September 2, 1964, November 7, 1964; Lenora E. Berson, *Case Study of a Riot: The Philadelphia Story* (Philadelphia, 1966); *Philadelphia Bulletin*, August 30, 1964; Nicole Maurantonio, "Standing By: Police Paralysis, Race, and the 1964 Philadelphia Riot," *Journalism History* 38 (2012), 110–121.

27 Cheesman Herrick, A History of Girard College (Philadelphia, 1927), 377; *New York Times*, January 17, 1965.

28 Bulletin, 8/11/53; Commonwealth v. Board of Directors of City Trusts of the City of Philadelphia 350 U.S. 230 (1957); *Philadelphia Inquirer* May 21, 1968; Mack, *Representing the Race*, 252.

29 *Philadelphia Inquirer*, May 10, 1965; *Philadelphia Bulletin*, May 23, 1965

30 For an overview of the Girard College protests, see *Philadelphia Tribune*, May 3, 1969; and generally Countryman, *Up South*, 168–78.

31 *Philadelphia Inquirer,* December 31, 1964; *Philadelphia Bulletin*, January 6, 1965, *Philadelphia Independent*, January 16, 1965; *Philadelphia Tribune*, July 6, 1965, *New York Times* August 15, 1965; conversation with Philip Savage, February 2, 1965, August Meier Papers, Schomburg Center, New York Public Library, Box 57, folder 5.

32 *New York Times*, August 15, 1965

33 *Philadelphia Tribune*, May 15, 1965

34 *New York Times*, May 14, 1965; *Philadelphia Tribune*, May 8, May 15, June 22, 1965.

35 Garrow, *Bearing the Cross: Martin Luther King, Jr. and the Southern Christian Leadership Conference* (New York, 1986), 435–36; Palantonio, *Rizzo*, 76–77; *Philadelphia Bulletin*, July 30, 1965; *New York Times*, August 4, 1965; *Philadelphia Tribune*, August 7, 1965.

36 Criticism of Moore's anti-Semitism dated to his first days as head of the Philadelphia branch of the NAACP. See "Moore Demands, Does He Deliver," *Pennsylvania Guardian*, November 15, 1963; *Philadelphia Bulletin*, May 11, 1965; *Philadelphia Inquirer*, July 9, 1965.

37 Gloster Current to Cecil B. Moore, September 9, 1964, NAACP, Group III, Box C137; *Philadelphia Bulletin*, Oct. 24, 1965; Lermack, "Cecil B. Moore," 157.

38 "63-Day March Arouses Silent Voice: Tempers Flared, Nerves Frayed," *Baltimore Afro-American*, July 24, 1965.

39 *Philadelphia Independent*, January 16, 1965; *Philadelphia Tribune*, January. 9, 16, 19, Feb. 13, 1965.

40 "Cecil Moore Takes a Look at 'His City,'" *Pennsylvania Guardian*, June 7, 1963; "Cecil Storms In."

41 Excerpts from Speeches Made at Cecil B. Moore Rallies, Fellowship Commission Papers, Temple Urban Archives, Box 58, Folder 16.

42 *Philadelphia Bulletin*, August 1, 1966.

43   *New York Times*, December 10, 1967.

44   Excerpts from Speeches, Fellowship Commission Papers Fellowship Commission, "Report to the Community" (Sept–October 1967).

45   *New York Times*, September 4 1966.

46   "Cecil Storms," 52; Stanford claimed that he worked as a community organizer under Moore's supervision. See Max Stanford, "Curriculum Vita," July 1974, in RAM Papers, Reel 1; "WANTED DEAD OR ALIVE PUBLIC ENEMY," n.d. in RAM Papers, Reel 12, Frame 134.

47   "Mayor Tate Owes His Victory to Negro Vote," *Philadelphia Tribune*, November 11, 1967.

48   Andrew Feffer, "The Land Belongs to the People: Reframing Urban Protest in Post-Civil Rights Philadelphia," in Van Gosse and Richard Moser, eds., *The World the 60s Made: Politics and Culture in Recent America* (Philadelphia, 2003), 80–81; 83–86; Countryman, *Up South*, 320–22; on black urban politics in the period more generally Thomas J. Sugrue, *Sweet Land of Liberty: The Forgotten Struggle for Civil Rights in the North* (New York, 2008), chapter 14.

13

From Racial Liberalism
to Racial Literacy

Brown v. Board of Education *and the Interest-Divergence Dilemma*

Lani Guinier

O n its approaching 60th anniversary, *Brown v. Board of Education* no longer enjoys the unbridled admiration it once earned from academic commentators. Early on, the conventional wisdom was that the courageous social engineers from the National Association for the Advancement of Colored People Legal Defense and Educational Fund, whose inventive lawyering brought the case to fruition, had caused a social revolution. Legal academics and lawyers still widely acclaim the *Brown* decision as one of the most important Supreme Court cases in the 20th century, if not since the founding of our constitutional republic. *Brown*'s exalted status in the constitutional canon is unimpeachable, yet over time its legacy has become complicated and ambiguous.[1]

The fact is that almost six decades later, many of the social, political, and economic problems that the legally trained social engineers thought the Court had addressed through *Brown* are still deeply embedded in our society. Blacks lag behind whites in multiple measures of educational achievement, and within the black community, boys are falling further behind than girls. In addition, the will to support public education from kindergarten through 12th grade appears to be eroding despite growing awareness of education's importance in a knowledge-based society. In the Boston metropolitan area in 2003, poor people of color were at least three times more likely than poor whites to live in severely distressed, racially stratified urban neighborhoods.

Whereas poor, working-class, and middle-income whites often lived together in economically stable suburban communities, black families with incomes above $50,000 were twice as likely as white households earning less than $20,000 to live in neighborhoods with high rates of crime and concentrations of poverty. Even in the so-called liberal North, race still segregates more than class. Gerald N. Rosenberg, emphasizing the limited roles courts can generally play, bluntly summed up his view of *Brown*'s legacy: "The Court ordered an end to segregation and segregation was not ended." If *Brown* was a decision about integration rather than constitutional principle, Mark Tushnet observed in 1994, it was a failure.[2]

Even as constitutional principle, the Court's analysis and the formal equality rule it yielded became more troubling in the intervening years. Presented with psychological evidence that separating black children from whites "solely because of their race generates a feeling of inferiority as to their status in the community that may affect their hearts and minds in a way unlikely ever to be undone," Chief Justice Earl Warren led the Court to declare segregation unconstitutional. *Brown*'s holding became the gold standard for defining the terms of formal equality: treating individuals differently based on the color of their skin was constitutionally wrong. However, once the Court's membership changed in the 1970s, advocates of color blindness used *Brown*'s formal equality principle to equate race-conscious government decisions that seek to develop an integrated society with the evils of de jure segregation. The new social engineers on the right adapted the Warren court's rhetoric to create a late 20th-century constitutional principle that forbids government actors to remediate societal discrimination. They changed *Brown* from a clarion call to an excuse not to act.[3]

The academy has produced a host of explanations for the discontinuity between *Brown*'s early promise and its present reality. Some scholars have challenged the Warren court's motives; others have criticized its reasoning; still others have found fault with its method of implementation. For example, focusing on motivation, Derrick A. Bell Jr. questioned the case's power to promote social justice because it was shaped, not by the intentional coalescing of a transforming social movement that reached across boundaries of race and economic class, but by the calculated convergence of interests between Northern liberals, Southern moderates, and blacks. The resulting alliance was temporary, lacked deep populist roots, and built on a tradition of treating black rights as expendable. For throughout United States history, Bell contended, the rights of blacks have regularly been sacrificed to preserve the greater interests of the whole society.[4]

In an influential article published in 1980 in the *Harvard Law Review,* Professor Bell concluded that the *Brown* decision represented the *interest convergence* between blacks and middle- and upper-class whites:

> [The] principle of "interest convergence" provides: The interest of blacks in achieving racial equality will be accommodated only when it converges with the interests of whites. However, the fourteenth amendment, standing alone, will not authorize a judicial remedy providing effective racial equality for blacks where the remedy sought threatens the superior societal status of middle and upper-class whites. . . . Racial remedies may instead be the outward manifestations of unspoken and perhaps subconscious judicial conclusions that the remedies, if granted, will secure, advance, or at least not harm societal interests deemed important by middle and upper-class whites.[5]

In the post-World War II period the alignment of interests of a biracial elite shifted to accommodate legal challenges to Jim Crow, Bell argued. The Court gave its imprimatur to the desegregation of public schools to add legitimacy to the U.S. struggle against Communism; to reassure blacks that precepts of equality heralded in World War II would be applied at home (and thus to quiet the resentment and anger of black veterans who returned from the war only to be denied equality); and to eliminate an important barrier to the industrialization of the South and the transition from a plantation to a modern economy. Consistent with Bell's interest-convergence thesis, Philip Elman, special assistant to the attorney general, filed a brief on behalf of the United States in which he framed the problem of racial discrimination "in the context of the present world struggle between freedom and tyranny."[6]

The ideals of racial liberalism helped fashion the legal strategy of the biracial elite. Racial liberalism emphasized the corrosive effect of individual prejudice and the importance of interracial contact in promoting tolerance. Racial liberals stressed the damaging effects of segregation on black personality development to secure legal victory as well as white middle-class sympathy. The attorneys in *Brown* and their liberal allies invited the justices to consider the effects of racial discrimination without fear of disrupting society as a whole. The Court responded by seeking to mollify Southern whites even as it declared the end to the de jure separate but equal system. Yet, to the extent that *Brown* reflected the alliance of some blacks and some upper-class whites unthreatened by desegregation, it left out crucial constituencies for change, including Southern black educators and poor rural blacks.[7]

Reservations also abound about the Court's reasoning, which was influenced by the litigation tactics of *Brown*'s advocates and allies. The lawyers wanted to dismantle segregation so that all black children would have access to resources presumptively enjoyed by all white children. The lawyers chose to achieve their goal by encouraging the Court to assume the role of protecting black children from the intangible effects of stigma and self-hate. This intangible damage thesis seemed to offer the best possible means of directly dismantling Jim Crow (de jure, formal inequality) and *indirectly* dismantling its effects. Unfortunately, in this court-centered universe, the tactic of desegregation became the ultimate goal, rather than the means to secure educational equity. The upshot of the inversion of means and end was to redefine equality, not as a fair and just distribution of resources, but as the absence of formal, legal barriers that separated the races.

Advocates for the NAACP made a conscious choice to abandon cases that demanded that states equalize the facilities, staff, and budgets of separate white and black schools to focus the Court's attention on segregation itself. As part of their litigation strategy, they appended studies by social scientists to their brief in *Brown*. The plaintiffs' attorneys successfully mobilized social scientists to support the fight against segregation, presenting racism as pathological because of the "toll it took on the black psyche." In a magisterial study, Daryl Michael Scott faulted the Court's dependence on psychological damage imagery to demonstrate the intangible costs of segregation. Segregation's evils had social and economic, not just psychological, ramifications. Even more, as others have pointed out, the psychology of segregation did not affect blacks alone; it convinced working-class whites that their interests lay in white solidarity rather than collective cross-racial mobilization around economic interests. Writing in 1935, W. E. B. Du Bois described the "public and psychological wage" paid to white workers, who came to depend upon their status and privileges as whites to compensate for low pay and harsh working conditions.[8]

The Court's reasoning suffered once it considered the caste system of Jim Crow narrowly, as a function of individual prejudice. The Court's minimalist analysis had legal, sociological, and psychological consequences. In legal terms, the focus on prejudice alone cast a long doctrinal shadow, allowing subsequent courts to limit constitutional relief to remedying acts of *intentional* discrimination by local entities or individuals. Absent evidence that local officials or state actors intentionally manipulated school boundaries *because of racial animus, Brown*'s principled conclusion ultimately excused inaction in the face of a gradual return to racially segregated schools that are unquestionably separate *and* unequal. The sociological ramifications—that de facto separation became invisible—were predictable, given the Court's lopsided psychological framing. The Court's measure of segregation's psychological costs counted its apparent effect on black children without grappling with the way segregation also shaped the personality development of whites. This analytic asymmetry influenced the reaction of blue-collar whites and arguably re-stigmatized blacks. The decision modified but did not eliminate "the property interest in whiteness" that Du Bois earlier observed and that came to define the Court's equal protection jurisprudence. As Cheryl I. Harris has written, "*Brown I*'s dialectical contradiction was that it dismantled an old form of whiteness as property while simultaneously permitting its reemergence in a more subtle form" by failing to redress "inequalities in resources, power, and, ultimately, educational opportunity."[9]

Other scholars deplore the Court's remedial approach as overly deferential to Southern whites; some also criticize integration efforts as benefiting very few poor blacks. What blacks won was not freedom, but tokenism. A cadre of middle-class blacks has enjoyed the privileges of upward mobility, but for the mass of blacks (and poor and working-class whites), educational opportunities remain beyond reach.[10]

A few scholars have sought to demonstrate that a bench-based, lawyer-crafted social justice initiative was ill equipped to address complex social problems. *Brown* actually had little effect on educational opportunity, Michael J. Klarman has argued, serving instead to reenergize white racial consciousness, while providing little in the way of integrated or improved educational facilities. Without executive and legislative branch leadership, the courts could not bring about the dynamic social change envisioned by the *Brown* lawyers. The federal judge John Minor Wisdom, renowned for his landmark decisions ordering desegregation in the wake of the Supreme Court's ruling in *Brown,* was candid about the lack of judicially inspired progress in the face of fierce white backlash. Like Wisdom, Rosenberg concluded that "the courts acting alone have failed." It was not until nonviolent and courageous civil rights activists were violently brutalized on national television that blacks won their "freedom" from state-sanctioned oppression. But they won through legislative action, which was after all the more democratic and sustaining force for change.[11]

Beyond the academic debates, many black activists struggle to reconcile their early optimism and contemporary hopelessness. A sense of lost opportunity has sparked increasing cynicism among some. There is an eerie nostalgia for the feeling of community that was destroyed post-*Brown.* As Adam Fairclough has noted, school integration has long divided the black community. For a surprising number of blacks, the question is not whether we mistook integration for the promised land. Confusion, even skepticism, reigns in some quarters over whether the promised land can exist in a United States that has yet to come to terms with the way slavery and the racialized compromises it produced shaped our original understanding of the nation as a republic.[12]

Racism—meaning the maintenance of, and acquiescence in, racialized hierarchies governing resource distribution—has not functioned simply through evil or irrational prejudice; it has been an artifact of geographic, political, and economic interests. In the United States racism was foundational, indeed constitutional. Mainstream historians are now busy tracing the constitutional legacy of the three-fifths clause that gave Southern states, and most often Southern plantation owners, disproportionate electoral clout at the national level. For roughly 50 of our country's first 72 years, the presidency was won by Southern slave owners. Indeed, before and after the Civil War the social alliances between Northern and Southern elites encouraged both to suppress the ideological dissonance of a country "of free men" that "worshipped liberty while profiting from slavery" and "left the public arena to men of propertied independence." Such histories remind us that the Northern "lords of the loom" and the Southern "lords of the lash" were complicit in the maintenance of slavery and its aftermath. As David Brion Davis has explained, the South may have lost the Civil War battles, but it won the ideological civil war, propagating white acceptance nationwide of both "Negro inferiority" and white supremacy for most of the 19th and 20th centuries.[13]

Under those circumstances, it is an open question whether any legal analysis, even one grounded in more rigorous social science research or employing a more balanced assessment of segregation's causes and effects, could have accomplished the goals of the *Brown* attorneys or could now accomplish the massive tasks that still await us: to extirpate a complex system of relationships that have tortured this country from its earliest beginnings and then to refashion a new social and economic order in its place. Formal legal equality granted through the courts could never guarantee economic, political, and social opportunity for the mass of blacks, for whom civil rights alone were not the measure of success. Their struggle was for "jobs and freedom" and encompassed many of the principles of self-government and property ownership that animated the early American revolutionaries.[14]

While Bell focused on interest *convergences* to explain the limited reach of the Court's initiative in *Brown,* geographic, racial, and class-based interest *divergences* were also at work ordering social, regional, and class conflict between Northern and Southern elites; between white elites and poor whites, North and South; between poor blacks and poor whites, whose concern was not unequal treatment, but the maldistribution of resources and opportunity; and between poor and middle-class blacks, who arguably benefited most. When *Brown* is read in light of these divisions, it is clear that the task confronting those who took on Jim Crow would prevent even the most ambitious policy-minded experts from challenging white supremacy as it reemerged in new garb. The social engineers in *Brown* identified state-sponsored segregation as the visible manifestation of American racism. This understandable preoccupation with de jure segregation disabled the plaintiffs' attorneys and their liberal allies from comprehending Jim Crow as the visible manifestation of a larger, constantly mutating racialized hierarchy. That hierarchy was racialized both by elites to consolidate their power and privilege and by poor whites to palliate their own debased circumstances.

Brown's legacy is clouded at least in part because post-World War II racial liberalism influenced the legal engineers to treat the symptoms of racism, not the disease. Their strategy was to eliminate desegregation, which they assumed would strike a fatal blow to racialized hierarchies. The lawyers' assumption and its corollary remedial emphasis were limited by the nature of their allies, who wanted to do good without sacrificing any of their own privileges, believing integration was possible without significant resource redistribution. The legal engineers failed to anticipate the downsides of a singular preoccupation with desegregation because their analysis essentialized all white children, without identifying the regulatory role race and class played within the white community. The lawyers and their allies went to court to enforce a right without consciously considering the remedy, which ended up re-stigmatizing blacks, reinforcing white working-class fear of economic downward mobility, and reserving for a privileged few the resources they needed to learn. Finally, while dismantling Jim Crow was a noble imperative, the lawyers did not realize that the disease Jim Crow betokened could and did easily reappear in a new guise. Racism was not ended by the defeat of Jim Crow, even in school systems that achieved unitary status. As Judge Robert Carter, one of the NAACP LDEF lawyers in *Brown,* has since written, "Both Northern and Southern white liberals and blacks looked upon racial segregation by law as *the primary* race relations evil in this country. It was not until *Brown I* was decided that blacks were able to understand that the fundamental vice was not legally enforced *racial segregation* itself; that this was a mere by-product, a symptom of the greater and more pernicious disease—white supremacy."[15]

Even when race is no longer explicitly coded by appearance or ancestry, the allocation of seats in a classroom, the use of buses to transport schoolchildren, or the hue of the dolls with which those children play, race is, and was, about the distribution of power. Race in the United States is a by-product of economic conflict that has been converted into a tool of division and distraction. It is not just an outgrowth of hatred or ill will. Racism has had psychological, sociological, and economic consequences that created the separate spheres inhabited by blacks and whites in 1954 but extended well beyond them.

To address the full range of racialized inequities in this country, racial justice advocates need to move beyond the early tenets of racial liberalism to treat the disease and not just its symptoms. A first step would be to make legible racism's ever-shifting yet ever-present structure. The oppressive conditions that most blacks still confront must not be ignored, but the continuing puzzle is how to address the complex ways race adapts its syntax to mask class and code geography. Racism is a structural phenomenon that fabricates interdependent yet paradoxical relationships between race, class, and geography—what I am calling *the interest-divergence dilemma.* It is the interest-divergence dilemma that requires a new racial literacy, meaning the capacity to decipher the durable racial grammar that structures racialized hierarchies and frames the narrative of our republic. To understand why *Brown v. Board of Education* has not lived up to its promise, I propose a paradigm shift from racial liberalism to racial literacy.

Racial Liberalism and the Interest-Divergence Dilemma

Post-World War II racial liberalism rejected scientific racism and discredited its postulate of inherent black inferiority. At the same time, racial liberalism positioned the peculiarly American race "problem" as a psychological and interpersonal challenge rather than a structural problem rooted in our economic and political system. Segregation was a "symptom of some psychological maladjustment" among those who imposed it; it was also a source of psychological maladjustment among those who were subjected to it. Reeling from the horrors of fascism abroad, fearing the specter of totalitarian domination, and facing continued pressure to fight racial inequities at home, proponents of greater tolerance suggested that racism was irrational and would surrender to logic and interpersonal contact. Equality before the law, through the persistent pursuit of civil rights, was the goal. That goal would be realized through racial integration. And that goal, in its singular and universalistic truth, would provide the ultimate reconciliation. The defining elements of postwar racial liberalism were its pragmatic devotion to a single strategy, its individualized and static view of American racism, and its focus on top-down social reform.[16]

The coalition promoting racial liberalism took hold only after Northern elites began to align their interests with black emancipation rather than with the interests of their putative Southern counterparts who used legal segregation to preserve upper-class power. In the shadow of the Cold War, international pressure and elite-dominated racial liberalism gave the civil rights quest moral and strategic heft; but it also reconfigured civil rights advocacy. According to some scholars, the alliance between middle-class blacks and white moderates filled the void as labor influence eroded in the late 1940s due to anticommunist assaults, the slow pace of reform through administrative changes, and union leaders' unresponsiveness to the specific needs of black union members. The result was a more conservative civil rights movement. Martha Biondi has argued that anticommunism propelled desegregation efforts while displacing grass-roots movements that had focused on building economic coalitions across lines of race.[17]

In the struggle between grass-roots insurgency emphasizing both political and economic issues and top-down elite control of a social agenda based on a single principle, the elites prevailed. Relying on psychological evidence of the intangible damage segregation does to black personality development, the strategic shift to challenge Jim Crow enabled many white allies to maintain their social and economic advantages without giving up the moral high ground. While anti-communist fervor helped fuel the willingness of national elites to take on segregation, it also channeled dissent from the status quo into status-based legal challenges that focused on formal equality through the elimination of de jure segregation.[18]

Scholars such as Biondi have suggested that biracial activism around common economic interests existed prior to, and was displaced by, *Brown,* while others find minimal evidence of such coalitions. The real surprise, the latter have argued, has been the antipathy to the civil rights movement that Northern working- and lower-middle-class whites displayed. Guided by the assumption that closer contact with whites would assure dignity and citizenship rights for blacks, the "new integrationist orthodoxy" failed to connect its version of the psychology of blacks with an equally probing analysis of the psychology of whites. The bargain struck by Northern elites—that desegregation would restore credibility to the United States during the Cold War and provide social stability as it eased the dissonance experienced by black veterans returning from World War II—disregarded the substantial investment poor whites had in their superior social status vis-à-vis blacks.[19]

North and South, many working-class and poor whites had acquired an investment in white racial privilege even before the decision in *Brown.* Not surprisingly, remedies involving desegregation evoked virulent hostility among such whites, who were the people initially targeted by those remedies. After the Supreme Court's decision in *Milliken v. Bradley,* which held that only districts found to have intentionally discriminated could be subject to a school desegregation plan, they became the group of whites most affected by desegregation in both North and South, as wealthier whites fled inner cities for surrounding suburbs. Even the most committed proponents of racial integration of the schools acknowledge that it is poor rather than rich whites who have experienced dislocation in the transition to integrated schools. As

Bell has recognized, poor whites and blacks have much in common, yet poor whites "feared a loss of control over their public schools," a loss "intensified by the sense that they had been betrayed."[20]

Racial liberalism identified a thin slice of the problem, while the multiple interest divergences that defined the country in 1954 continued to incubate. The conflicts were transformed but not overcome. Indeed, in the petri dish of racial liberalism, those conflicts were allowed to fester. Ironically, the change the racial liberals wrought was not always the change they sought. A preliminary, and mostly tentative, review of the historical literature suggests that the *Brown* Court's doctrine that "separate but equal is inherently unequal" had unanticipated consequences. It intensified divergences between Northern elites and Southern whites, solidified the false interest convergence between Southern white elites and Southern poor whites, ignored the interest divergences between poor and middle-class blacks, and exacerbated the interest divergences between poor and working-class whites and blacks.

Interest Divergence: Racialized Geography and the Psychology of White Solidarity

Unlike the Jim Crow system it challenged, *Brown*'s asymmetric focus on the psychological damage segregation did to blacks gave the psychological benefits segregation conferred on whites short shrift. In the ideology of racial liberalism, the class and geographic interests of rural and poor Southern whites—and of working-class Northern whites—also receded from view. That inattention had two consequences. First, many poor and working-class whites saw themselves as victims. Second, they saw desegregation as downward economic mobility. To poor whites, compulsory association with blacks brought no added value and endangered the sense of autonomy and community they did have. *Brown*'s racial liberalism did not offer poor whites even an elementary framework for understanding what they might gain as a result of integration. Neither the opinion nor the subsequent legal strategy to implement *Brown* made clear that segregation had offered elites an important means of exercising social control over poor and working-class whites as well as a means of dominating or disadvantaging blacks.[21]

Little attention was paid to the disparities between the educational resources of poor and working-class whites and those of more affluent whites, who had access to better education through private school or geographic mobility. Although whites in the aggregate enjoyed educational resources that far exceeded those available to blacks, poor whites, especially in rural communities in the South, were often educational orphans. Levels of schooling declined with falling income more precipitously in the South than in other parts of the country. In 1940 nearly three-quarters of the wealthiest 17-year-olds in the South, but less than one-sixth of the poorest, had completed at least 11 years of schooling. There were also rural-urban disparities. According to the 1950 census, among Southerners in their late twenties, the state-by-state percentages of functional illiterates (defined as people with less than five years of schooling) for whites on farms overlapped with those for blacks in cities. In most Southern states, more than half of urban whites in their late twenties had completed high school, but less than a quarter of whites of the same age living on farms had done so. The majority of Southern whites, considering older and younger people and farm, village, and city dwellers, were semiliterates (defined as those with less than 12 years of schooling) who shared disadvantages with blacks, while an affluent white minority completed elementary and high school, standing far apart from the rest of the whites and from virtually all blacks.[22]

Ideologically committed to an integrationist orthodoxy, racial liberalism initially failed to contemplate a mechanism for acknowledging the psychological paradox of poor whites or their need for greater material resources and other tangible benefits. As a result, poor whites experienced desegregation, in Bell's terminology, as a net "loss." That sense of loss was exploited by demagogic politicians, who have successfully used racial rhetoric to code American politics to this day and who continue to solidify the original bargain between poor and wealthy Southern whites. Regional differences remain pronounced, as evidenced in the "red" and "blue" states that defined media maps of the presidential elections of the 21st century to date. And yet regional differences are less evident when race and class are disaggregated.[23]

In the South, for example, integration was successfully portrayed as downward mobility through compulsory association with blacks. The dramatic events accompanying the integration of Central High School in Little Rock, Arkansas, illustrate the dynamic. In 1957 there were three high schools serving Little Rock: the new all-white Hall High School, the all-black Horace Mann High School, and Central. Central had been the only white high school in Little Rock, but in summer 1957, Hall opened in the western and more affluent portion of the city. Middle- and upper-middle-class white students transferred to the new high school just before the school year began. This meant that once the senior class at Central graduated in 1958, Central would lose its "citywide character." The school board had approved a plan to integrate Central in 1955. It was scheduled to take effect in fall 1957, at the very time when affluent whites were exiting to attend the new school. Horace Mann would remain all-black; Hall would be all-white. Only Central would experience integration, albeit with nine carefully chosen black students. Despite the academic credentials and middle-class appearance of the black trailblazers, those white students who remained at Central perceived a twisted symmetry: poor blacks and rich whites would remain in the isolated, racially homogeneous environments of Horace Mann and Hall high schools, while working-class whites became the guinea pigs in the integration experiment at Central. In their minds, the "symmetry" was not coincidental; school superintendent Virgil Blossom had "sold" his desegregation plan to the leadership in Little Rock by reassuring them that their children could attend the new Hall High School, "a high school segregated by both class and race." As Elizabeth Huckaby, who was then assistant principal of Central High School, recalled, "Except for a hundred of our seniors who had elected to stay at Central for their final year, we would have no more boys and girls from [the northwest] section of Little Rock where the finest houses were being built, where the families of the most successful businessmen were moving, where the country clubs are."[24]

The exodus of white elites from Central High School threatened working-class dreams of upward mobility and put working-class students' virtual membership in the "dominant class" at risk. The sociologist Beth Roy subsequently interviewed some white students who were then at Central. Even thirty years later, her interviewees criticized the disruption desegregation brought into their lives: "I became very disenchanted with the whole thing. I just kept thinking, This is my senior year, and this is not what I was looking forward to. This is just unfair." Another, searching for a way to explain her hatred for one of the black students who entered Central in 1957, exclaimed, "She walked the halls as if she belonged there." To working-class whites, integration, timed to coincide with the flight of the city's elite, was a stigmatizing force that interfered with their ability to pursue the American dream. Thus they resisted it.[25]

Goaded on by the racial demagoguery of local politicians, such whites came to view the potential economic consequences of desegregation in psychological terms. Politicians preyed on their sense of betrayal and unfair sacrifice, deliberately organizing the conversation about desegregation around a white racial consciousness. Although working-class whites initially saw this "experiment in interracial education" in class terms, a racially polarized contest was easily manufactured using antebellum conceptions of race and class that had crystallized under segregation. Lacking a vocabulary of either class or structure, Roy's working-class white informants were still fluent in the language of racial scapegoating some thirty years later. Disappointed with their own economic and social status, they blamed blacks. Cause and effect were reduced to race.[26]

Although poor and working-class whites were among the most visible protesters, they acted with the tacit approval of the more affluent whites in their communities. According to some accounts, Southern elites, with the exception of a few moderates, remained defiant post-*Brown,* often encouraging massive resistance in the South. For example, during the 1940s white elites in Birmingham, Alabama, had played the race card to defuse opposition to the poll tax, which disenfranchised poor whites as well as blacks. Poor whites, more than half of whom did not vote, acquiesced in the downplaying of their economic and political interests in favor of a vigorous defense of white supremacy. Post-*Brown* the Birmingham elites ensured their continued dominance by undermining any class identity among poor and working-class whites. Aided by the same fear of Communism that may have led the Court to rule unanimously in *Brown,* ambitious Southern politicians quickly perceived the benefits to be derived from racial demagoguery. It had long been in the interests of the white upper class, whether planters or industrialists, to "make all whites think in racial or sectional ways—indeed, in any terms *except* class." As "the only class fully conscious of its power and purpose," the Birmingham "industrialists, and the lawyers and politicians who served them," continued, after *Brown* as before, to deploy a white racial consciousness as an instrument of social control.[27]

Upper-class whites in the South, however, were not monolithic; some scholars have argued that the *Brown* decision radically altered elite treatment of race issues as the focus of white moderates shifted from labor reforms to eliminating de jure segregation. Resistance within the South was more muted in those metropolitan areas where local leadership had fewer incentives to mine a white racial consciousness in order to maintain political power. Michael J. Klarman, for example, argues that affluent city residents who were cocooned within racially and economically segregated housing patterns were less likely to lead resistance. Wealthier whites "retained the option of exiting the public school system altogether either by educating their children privately or by fleeing to the (generally white) suburbs."[28]

Politicization of the experience of desegregation as loss existed in the North, not just the South, and affected blue-collar workers, not just poor whites. In a study of white neighborhood associations in Detroit in the 1950s, Thomas J. Sugrue found that government programs that subsidized white home ownership or defined political boundaries to determine access to education were taken for granted and remained largely invisible. Government programs designed to give blacks a hand up were highly visible and resented. Blue-collar whites in Detroit measured their success by their ability to control their distance from blacks as a group. Failure meant being forced to share community, schools, or economic status with blacks.[29]

Arnold Hirsch's study of public housing in Chicago and Sugrue's account of homeowner associations in Detroit suggest that maintaining racially homogeneous neighborhood enclaves was central to white working-class identity in the North. Aspirations to upward mobility, bonds of family and community, and the "white racial identity premised on American individualism" depended on maintaining residential distance from blacks. Although it was often the more affluent and educated blacks who sought to move into white neighborhoods, all their prospective white neighbors could see was a deluge of poor black people crowded together in crime-ridden neighborhoods. Working-class whites interpreted the poverty they associated with blacks in two ways. First, the "wretched conditions" in predominantly black communities "were the fault of irresponsible blacks." Second, those neighborhoods served as a "grim prophesy" of what theirs would become if they welcomed upwardly mobile black pioneers. They equated racial integration with crime and violence.[30]

Many white working-class people perceived the American dream as assuring them a right to a racially homogeneous community. While it appeared that race trumped class, it was equally true that class was defined by race and urban-suburban geography. Sugrue's study demonstrates the post-New Deal political realignment of blue-collar workers in Detroit with their corporate bosses living in Grosse Pointe, an exclusive suburb. No longer did they direct their rage at the economic or social conditions that kept them off balance. Politicians and real estate brokers were able to reorient populist rage to target civil rights organizations and their upper-class white allies. It was those groups who threatened to destroy racial homogeneity within the blue-collar home-owners' community and thus to undermine a precondition for achieving the American dream, especially in uncertain economic times.[31]

The stories told by Hirsch about housing desegregation in Chicago and Sugrue about working-class white resistance, abetted by government policies and private real estate brokers, to social or residential intermingling with blacks in Detroit suggest the key role played by politicians and self-interested business people who resorted to a racially coded rhetoric to manipulate or divert attention from economic conditions. On the one hand, the approaches to desegregation instituted by political and judicial actors represented burden shifting. Although a few middle- and upper-class whites exercised constraint and exhorted moderation, many took advantage of their power artificially to shift the burden from themselves. The method used in Little Rock was also employed in other cities: the establishment in upper-class neighborhoods of new schools that would remain segregated. The formation of new towns and cities based on racial geography had the same effect. Because *Brown* did not change the funding structure of public education and did not reduce geographic segregation by class (and consequently race), it left the costs of integration to already underfunded schools in poor white areas. Those schools were often geographically closest to the poor black areas, and their students often experienced great anxiety about their own educational abili-ties and future opportunities. In addition, because small and medium-sized cities and therefore school districts were often dominated by a single racial group, preexisting race-based borders hindered *Brown's* capacity to provide meaningful integration.[32]

On the other hand, some costs of integration under the *Brown* framework fell "naturally" on poor and working-class whites. Explicit burden shifting was often unnecessary. Class geography, untouched by *Brown,* would have sheltered upper-class whites from the "burden" of integration even without subsequent selfish or racist manipulations, as Richard Thompson Ford, for example, has argued.[33]

Whether the geographic boundaries were natural or political, poor whites felt stigmatized by black demands for first-class citizenship. Watching the dismantling of their psychological position of relative privilege, they were left without an alternative understanding of their actual condition relative to more affluent members of the society. According to Sugrue, racial liberalism succumbed to "simmering white discontent," constrained by "the politics of race and neighborhood." For many white workers from Little Rock to Detroit, the explanation has been simple. With the aid of the federal government, blacks absconded with the American dream.[34]

Witness Beth Roy's working-class white informants in Little Rock, who collectively assigned their own failures to blacks. Whites who succeeded believed they did so because of individual merit; they earned their success. By contrast, in the stories reported to Roy, if they failed, it was because black people "stole" the American dream. Working-class whites did not get into the colleges of their choice, did not get the jobs they needed, or were the victims of crime because blacks benefited from affirmative action, lived on welfare, or chose to hustle rather than perform honorable work. The stories of Little Rock, Detroit, and Chicago suggest that it was middle-class and often suburban whites who were subsidized in large measure by government programs for homeownership and highways and who tended to monopolize access to the best educational resources, the good jobs, and the safe streets. Yet poor and working-class whites accepted the terms of racial solidarity rather than confront the fundamental need to organize collectively and across racial lines to obtain similar benefits.[35]

Their fears inflamed by economic insecurity as constructed by the individualism of the American dream, many whites turned to race as an explanation and an identity. According to Jennifer L. Hochschild, the American dream is an inclusive, optimistic, and high-minded myth that "evokes" "unsullied newness, infinite possibility, [and] limitless resources." The dream has universal elements of sharing opportunity broadly: Everybody should have the chance to succeed as measured by income, a good job, and economic security. The opportunity for everyone to succeed is an inclusive fantasy, but that opportunity is presumptively obtained through one's individual effort. Those who succeed are those who exert strenuous effort so that their talents prevail; they work hard, take risks, and imagine a better future for themselves and their children. Virtue leads to success; success is evidence of virtue. Therefore, those who fail to climb up the ladder of success must be without talent or without discipline. The losers are not only miserable failures; they also lack character unless they assume personal responsibility for their flaws.[36]

While it is easy to see success as a sign of merit rather than luck, few people willingly accept an equally self-referential explanation of failure. Race arguably fills the gap, providing a believable account of all that went wrong. Race functions as a pragmatic explanation for the fact that few working-class and poor whites achieve their version of the American dream. The choice of race as the explanatory covariant is neither irrational nor aberrant, given the otherwise highly individualized structure of this metanarrative. In the words of Du Bois, the psychological wage of whiteness put "an indelible black face to failure." Once blackness becomes the face of failure, race then influences and constrains social, economic, and political opportunities among and between blacks and whites and among and between blacks and other people of color.[37]

In a somewhat incongruous fashion, race is the variable explaining failure for both whites and blacks. Blacks think racial discrimination inhibits their chances to participate in the American dream; whites think reverse discrimination is the culpable party. For many blacks, success and failure are both understood in more collective terms. Indeed, contemporary sociological and psychological research suggests that an understanding of failure as a product of systemic rather than personal deficiencies is a healthy psychological response, at least insofar as it may lead to collective action to change one's circumstances.[38]

INTEREST DIVERGENCE: STIGMATIZING RACE

Brown helped change the quality of life for many blacks. It educated the country about the changing meaning of the United States Constitution and allowed blacks to claim the Constitution as theirs despite the tragic role race had played in its earliest formulation. It overruled *Plessy v. Ferguson,* the constitutional straitjacket in which the Court had put itself in 1896. It represented the triumph of racial liberalism over scientific racism and other theories of inherent black inferiority. It also served for most of the second half of the 20th century as the "principal ideological inspiration" to those who sought racial justice through the courts, according to Jack Greenberg, Thurgood Marshall's successor as head of the NAACP LDEF and one of the lawyers who argued a companion case to *Brown.*[39]

Yet as Marshall's colleague Robert Carter concluded, *Brown* promised more than it could give. *Brown's* analysis was limited by its singular focus on the harm segregation caused the personality development of black children. Predicated on experiments purportedly showcasing blacks' lack of self-esteem, the opinion reinforced the stigma long associated with blacks, even as it attributed the stigma to segregation rather than biology. Subsequent cases added insult to injury as the Court began to label the legal claim as arising from differential treatment rather than demeaning treatment within a racialized hierarchy.[40]

Significantly, the Court's analysis was framed as requiring racial desegregation to end damage to black psyches. The district court judge and later the Supreme Court adopted almost verbatim testimony by the psychologist Louisa Holt in the Kansas case that segregation, especially when sanctioned by law, had a detrimental effect on "the personality development of the Negro child." One of the lawyers in *Brown* found in her testimony, which he attributed to a "God-given eloquence," "the seeds of ultimate victory." Linking responsibility for educational disadvantage to black self-loathing and connecting that to a psychological abstraction did little, however, to disrupt the powerfully negative views of blacks in the popular imagination. As Charles R. Lawrence III has written, many whites do not believe that racial discrimination is the principal cause of black inequality. The explanation lies instead in some version of black inferiority. "Few will express this belief openly. It is no longer consistent with American ideology to speak in terms of inherent racial traits. But the myth of racial inferiority remains embedded in the fabric of our culture."[41]

Basing its opinion on the psychological research of the time, the Court misunderstood the source of self-esteem for many blacks and unwittingly contributed to the divergence of interests along class and geographic lines within and without the black community. These outcomes can be traced, in part, to the flawed studies on which plaintiffs relied to prove that physically equal but segregated facilities had a negative psychological impact on all black children. The most famous of the psychological studies cited by the Court was the doll experiment of Kenneth Clark and Mamie Clark. The Clark study aggregated findings of Northern and Southern black children, light-skinned and dark-skinned black children, and middle-class and poor black children to conclude that segregation caused feelings of inferiority among all blacks. Black children in the more integrated North had more frequently preferred the white dolls than black children in the South. Many Northern black children also verbalized unease when prompted to consider their physical similarity to the brown dolls, yet Kenneth Clark concluded that Northern black children were actually psychologically healthier. A historian has summarized Clark's argument: The reaction of the Northern children showed their "discomfort with the complicated and harsh reality of racial mores rather than resignation," whereas racial segregation and isolation had caused Southern black children to accept their inferior social status as normal. "Such an acceptance," Clark reported, "is not symptomatic of a healthy personality." Clark argued that the racial identification of the Southern children, almost 80 percent of whom identified themselves in some way with the brown dolls, was tainted because of the terms they used to verbalize their choices. The Southern black children described the black dolls as "pretty," "nice," or "good" but accompanied their choices with statements such as, "This one. It's a nigger. I'm a nigger."[42]

Clark's message was that group self-hatred among blacks begins at an early age, involves the rejection of brown skin color by black children, and becomes embedded in the personality of blacks as a result of the "damage inherent in racial segregation." These conclusions may have had some merit, but none was entirely consistent with his research. According to Daryl Scott, Clark's conclusions (unlike his data) also contradicted other contemporary studies that suggested that black children with *greater contact with whites* experienced the most psychological distress. While many blacks hailed the Court decision, especially for its vast symbolic value, the opinion's emphasis on the psychological damage segregation does to blacks camouflaged the ways *de*segregation "hurt" some blacks, while segregation motivated others to excel, a possibility Holt had conceded. For some black children, segregated schools provided a sanctuary from psychological conflict. More recently, psychological literature has also suggested that those blacks who are the most invested in achieving academically within the larger society are often more vulnerable to what Claude Steele and others term stereotype threat, the situational threat of being negatively stereotyped. Unlike Clark's "self-fulfilling prophecy" that black students internalize and then fulfill negative stereotypes and low expectations for achievement, stereotype threat is context-dependent rather than intrinsic. Moreover, social psychologists have found that in some circumstances the ability to maintain a sense of self-worth in a hostile environment may actually enhance self-esteem. The key point is that data on self-esteem differences between black kids and white kids were not well developed then; even today "there's not much evidence of chronic psychological damage done to blacks' self-esteem as a result of segregation" per se.[43]

A desegregation solution based on concerns about psychological stigma did not necessarily have the desired effect of providing meaningful educational and economic opportunity even for those middle-class blacks whom compulsory segregation had denied a first-class education. For example, desegregation meant that some black teachers, the backbone of the black middle class at the time, lost their jobs. And the mentoring provided to high-achieving middle-class black students at some all-black elite public high schools, such as Dunbar High School in Washington, D.C., was neither replaced nor reproduced in more integrated environments. Within integrated schools, the interaction with white students was often limited literally and figuratively by tracking, skepticism about blacks' intellectual ability by their teachers and white classmates, and the loss not only of black mentors but also of a sense of community in which the adults were invested in the students' achievement.[44]

In addition, the prejudice-centered approach set in motion forces that have cemented the connection between public education and damaged goods in a way that disadvantaged poor blacks in particular. Much of Derrick Bell's scholarship and that of others presents evidence that poor blacks were abandoned by middle-class blacks who now had the opportunity to choose educational situations consistent with their class interests. Similarly, Carter, an NAACP LDEF lawyer in *Brown,* later concluded that "to focus on integration alone is a luxury only the black middle-class can afford. They have the means to desert the public schools if dissatisfied." Poor blacks suffered as urban public schools became the primary locus of integration; the change fomented an unhealthy battleground of racial tensions. Race became synonymous with poor blacks, and public education itself became stigmatized as it became more and more closely associated with racialized poverty.[45]

The focus on educational quality soon abated, as administrators, teachers, and students became political figures or political pawns rather than learners; educational funds were diverted to conflict avoidance and resolution and education budgets manipulated to promote political goals about race policy. Although *Brown* heralded the crucial role that public education plays in a democracy and gave eloquent voice to the importance of an educated citizenry to society as a whole, its legal analysis forestalled political interest convergences to the detriment of poor people of all colors: black, brown, and white, urban and rural. The Court's analysis became the basis for a doctrinal distinction between race and class that lifted unequal resource distribution out of the constitutional canon.[46] What appeared to be "eloquence from God" in the testimony of a witness at the trial court in Kansas that compulsory segregation damages children's ability to learn soon became manifest in a different prophecy: that black children simply cannot or do not wish to learn. Legally compelled segregation became socially acceptable separation; separation became stigma; stigma became association with blacks who still occupied and defined separate, albeit public, education. Integration was reduced to diversity, a benefit to be enjoyed by a critical mass, but not by the masses.

Sadly, it was the appellees in *Brown* whose prognostications came closest to describing current realities. In his oral argument before the Supreme Court in the companion case of *Davis v. County School Board,* Attorney General Lindsay Almond of Virginia argued that integration would "destroy the public school system as we know it today" because the "people would not vote bond issues through their resentment to it." Colgate Darden, then president of the University of Virginia and a former governor of Virginia, testified that desegregation would "impair the opportunities for both races" because goodwill toward the public school system would be "badly impaired," which would lead to a "sizable falling off of the funds required for public education." Indeed, urban and rural public schools became stigmatized as the dumping ground for those with nowhere else to go.[47]

The ambiguity of *Brown*'s legacy is as much a consequence of interest divergence as of the temporary alliance between Northern elites and civil rights advocates to promote social reform through biracial top-down cooperation grounded in the values of racial liberalism. The Court relied on incomplete data regarding the damage segregation did to the self-esteem of blacks while it underestimated the potentially negative impact of *de*segregation on the self-esteem of some blacks and perhaps inadvertently reinforced the identification of blackness with inferiority and stigma in the minds of whites. There was also a divergence of interests inside the black community between poor and middle-class blacks arising from the practical consequences of *Brown* (including the loss of community and the exodus of middle-class blacks from urban public schools). That the divergences were relegated to the background was partly a result of the prejudice-centered orthodoxy of racial liberalism. That the divergences remain mostly intact may also have been a function of the elevated and preeminent role of legal analysis in fashioning a social change strategy. The Court, acting alone, was not in a position to explore the triangulation of interests along race, class, and geographic lines.

Racial Literacy and the Interest-Divergence Dilemma

The apparent interest convergence between Northern liberals and Southern blacks ultimately perpetuated a more durable divergence of interests within and between the black and white communities. The ideals of racial liberalism produced a legal icon but did little to disrupt the historic pattern in which race was used to manufacture dissensus, complicating relationships within and outside communities of color. That dissensus was not produced by race, but by social and economic conflict that was simultaneously revealed and concealed by race. Post-*Brown*, the ability to use race to code and cloak diverging interests sustained racial hierarchies—a phenomenon that tainted our founding arrangements and remains at our ideological core.

Through the creation and maintenance of racialized hierarchies, the plight of poor blacks and poor whites was mostly ignored; similarly, under the shibboleth of equal opportunity, urban and rural communities were abandoned as the maldistribution of material resources persisted undisturbed. Just as significant, the psychological bribe that segregation offered working-class and poor whites was not examined or countered even as white racial solidarity assumed crucial importance in the decision's aftermath. Indeed, the focus on race as a source of one-way psychological stigma had deleterious consequences for the public school system. Public education became a battlefield rather than a constructive gravitational force within many communities. Race was used to pathologize blacks rather than to reveal how economic and social privilege hid behind racial fault lines. Ultimately, the class interests of those who could afford to invest personally in their children's education triumphed.

The first step in understanding these diverging interests is to make them legible. A racially literate analysis seeks to do just that by deciphering the dynamic interplay among race, class, and geography. In contrast to racial liberalism, racial literacy reads race as epiphenomenal. Those most advantaged by the status quo have historically manipulated race to order social, economic, and political relations to their benefit. Then and now, race is used to manufacture both convergences and divergences of interest that track class and geographic divisions. The racialized hierarchies that result reinforce divergences of interest among and between groups with varying social status and privilege, which the ideology of white supremacy converts into rationales for the status quo. Racism normalizes these racialized hierarchies; it diverts attention from the unequal distribution of resources and power they perpetuate. Using race as a decoy offers short-term psychological advantages to poor and working-class whites, but it also masks how much poor whites have in common with poor blacks and other people of color.[48]

Racial liberalism triumphed in *Brown* by presenting racism as a departure from the fundamentally sound liberal project of American individualism, equality of opportunity, and upward mobility. But racial liberalism's individualistic and prejudice-centered view of formal equality failed to anticipate multiple interest divergences, helped fuel a white backlash, and doomed both integration and the redistribution of resources. Racial literacy, in contrast, requires us to rethink race as an instrument of social, geographic, and economic control of both whites and blacks. Racial literacy offers a more dynamic framework for understanding American racism.

There are many differences between what I call racial literacy and racial liberalism, but for the purposes of this essay three stand out. First, racial literacy is contextual rather than universal. It does not assume that either the problem or the solution is one-size-fits-all. Nor does it assume that the answer is made evident by thoughtful consideration or expert judgment alone. Racial literacy depends upon the engagement between action and thought, between experimentation and feedback, between bottom-up and top-down initiatives. It is about learning rather than knowing. Racial literacy is an interactive process in which race functions as a tool of diagnosis, feedback, and assessment. Second, racial literacy emphasizes the relationship between race and power. Racial literacy reads race in its psychological, interpersonal, and structural dimensions. It acknowledges the importance of individual agency but refuses to lose sight of institutional and environmental forces that both shape and reflect that agency. It sees little to celebrate when formal equality is claimed within a racialized hierarchy. Although legally enforced separation was identified as a dignitary harm and the issue being litigated ridiculed as a matter of "racial prestige" by John W. Davis, attorney for South Carolina in the *Brown* case, it soon became distorted into an issue of mere separation rather than subjugation. Indeed, it is precisely as a legal abstraction that we are now being asked to honor equality. But things seldom are equal, as W. E. B. Du Bois pointed out in 1935 as he weighed the benefits of segregated and integrated education for blacks. He concluded that blacks needed education for their minds, not just integration of their bodies: "Other things being equal, the mixed school is the broader, more natural basis for the education of all youth. It gives wider contacts; it inspires greater self-confidence; and suppresses the inferiority complex. But other things seldom are equal, and in that case, Sympathy, Knowledge, and the Truth, outweigh all that the mixed school can offer."[49]

Third, while racial literacy never loses sight of race, it does not focus exclusively on race. It constantly interrogates the dynamic relationship among race, class, geography, gender, and other explanatory variables. It sees the danger of basing a strategy for monumental social change on assumptions about individual prejudice and individual victims. It considers the way psychological interests can mask political and economic interests for poor and working-class whites. It analyzes the psychological economy of white racial solidarity for poor and working-class whites and blacks, independent of manipulations by "the industrialists and the lawyers and politicians who served them." Racial literacy suggests that racialized hierarchies mirror the distribution of power and resources in the society more generally. In other words, problems that converge around blacks are often visible signs of broader societal dysfunction. Real interest convergences among poor and working-class blacks and whites are possible, but only when complex issues are analyzed and acted upon with their structural, not just their legal or their asymmetric psychological, underpinnings in mind. This means moving beyond a simple justice paradigm that is based on formal equality, while contemplating what it will take to create a moral consensus about the role of government and the place of the public itself.[50]

One of the original architects of the *Brown* strategy apparently understood the importance of further interrogating the interest divergences that promote a purely formal, legal equality within a system where social and economic inequalities persist. Charles Hamilton Houston, the former vice-dean at Howard Law School, director-counsel of the NAACP LDEF, and the consummate social engineer, declared six years before the case was decided:

> There come times when it is possible to forecast the results of a contest, of a battle, of a lawsuit all before the final event has taken place. So far as our struggle for civil rights is concerned, the struggle for civil rights is won. What I am more concerned about is that the Negro shall not be content simply with demanding an equal share in the existing system. It seems to

me that his historical challenge is to make sure that the system which shall survive in the United States of America shall be a system which guarantees justice and freedom for everyone.[51]

Conclusion

Race is a powerful explanatory variable in the story of our country, which has been used to explain failure in part by associating failure with black people. Racial literacy suggests that legal equality granted through the courts will not extirpate the distinctive, racialized asymmetries from the DNA of the American dream. The courts can be and often have been a critically important ally, but neither the judiciary nor lawyers acting alone possess the surgical skill required to alter the genetic material of our organizing narrative. Nor is the attainment of civil rights by itself an adequate measure of success, in part because the problem is not just race but race as conjugated by class, geography, and the organizing narrative of upward mobility.

Through its invocation of the language of prejudice, the Court in *Brown* converted the structural phenomenon of racism into a problem of individual psychological dysfunction that whites and blacks are equally capable of exhibiting. In the 1950s prejudice was understood as an aberration in individuals who disregard relevant information, rely on stereotypes, and act thoughtlessly. Prejudice was a function of ignorance. Educated people, it was assumed, are not prejudiced. Yet many who acquiesce in racialized hierarchy derive tangible benefits from such a hierarchy. They are acting rationally, not irrationally, when they ignore the ways hierarchy systematically disadvantages groups of individuals and privileges others consistent with socially and culturally constructed definitions of race that predictably order and rank.

In legal terms, *Brown*'s rule of "equality by proclamation" linked segregation to prejudice and reinforced the individuating of both the cause of action and the remedy. By defining racism as prejudice and prejudice as creating individual psychological damage, the Court's opinion paved the way for others to reinterpret *Brown* as a case mandating formal equality and nothing more. Subsequent courts have tended to limit the equal protection clause of the 14th Amendment by a symmetrical, perpetrator-oriented focus on color blindness. If the problem is that separate is inherently unequal, then equality is simply presumed when the separation is eliminated. Any remaining inequality is the fault of black people themselves.[52]

In the end, *Brown*'s racial liberalism had little to offer poor and working-class whites to counter the psychological benefits of white racial solidarity. Jim Crow was a caste system that oppressed all blacks, regardless of class and geographic lines, but the psychology of Jim Crow allowed white elites to limit the educational and economic opportunities of poor and working-class whites. Working-class whites were also complicit, as they perceived their own advancement as dependent on their ability to separate and distinguish themselves from blacks as a group. It is the conflation of psychological benefits with economic and political self-interest that crafts the popularly accepted fiction that failure is not only measured by race but also *explained* by it.

Brown's effect on public education, for example, showed why it is critical to link race and class without losing sight of race and in ways that invite the people most directly affected to speak for themselves. *Brown* relied on the lawyers' and the justices' understanding of the key role played by public education in a democracy. Yet it unwittingly nationalized the Southern white racial consciousness, which downplayed the collective interest in a vigorous public in favor of the social interest of one class in private, individual choice. Nevertheless, it is important to remember that, although the trisection of interests along race, class, and regional lines haunted *Brown* from the beginning, the stark lines of divergence emerge more clearly in retrospect, viewed from the perspective of significant social progress that was inconceivable in 1954.

To be sure, the NAACP lawyers were audacious social engineers. Their ingenious litigation strategy bolstered insurgent efforts to dismantle de jure segregation. But for all their brilliance, the lawyers in *Brown* were unable to kindle a populist revolution in which the people, not just the lawyers, come to understand the crippling effects of race and racism on our entire social, economic, and political order. Race matters not just for blacks, in other words, but for every citizen of the United States. Because of its foundational role in the making of this country's history and myths, race, in conjunction with class and geography, invariably shapes educational, economic, and political opportunities for all of us.

My proposed paradigm shift to racial literacy is more a thought experiment than a judicial brief. We need to learn to use the courts as a tool rather than a panacea to overcome the structured dissension race has cemented in our popular consciousness as well as in our lived experience. If we can become more literate about the role racism continues to play in structuring and narrating economic and political opportunity, we may be better able to combine legal and legislative advocacy that enlists support among people of all colors, whites as well as blacks. It may be that the time has come for "a new policy compass," as Derrick Bell wrote, "to assert petitions for racial justice in forms that whites will realize serve their interests as well as those of blacks." But however petitions for racial justice are framed, they need to avoid confusing tactics with goals, forever freezing a formalistic theory of racial equality into the Constitution, which can then be used to undermine opportunities for progressive innovation in the future.[53]

If there is only one lesson to be learned from *Brown,* it is that all Americans need to go back to school. The courts acting alone cannot move us to overcome, and the federal government has not assumed leadership in this arena since the 1960s. At the beginning of the twenty-first century, a racially literate mobilization of people within and across lines of race, class, and geography might finally be what it takes to redeem the optimistic assessment of those early academic commentators. Of course, a racially literate analysis, meaning the ability to read race in conjunction with both contemporary institutional and democratic hierarchies and their historical antecedents, may not resolve the interest-divergence dilemma. Nor should it. But at least it may help us understand why *Brown* feels less satisfying 60 years later.

ACKNOWLEDGMENTS

The phrase "interest-divergence dilemma" in the title of this essay modifies and elaborates on the "interest-*convergence* dilemma" proposed by Professor Derrick Bell.

I thank Stephanie Camp, Kevin Gaines, Danielle Gray, Evelyn Brooks Higginbotham, Ken Mack, Joanne Meyerowitz, Frank Michelman, Martha Minow, Gerald Torres, and David Wilkins for enormously helpful comments on earlier drafts. Jay Cox, Jenee Desmond, Amos Jones, and Nathan Kitchens provided excellent research assistance. Susan Armeny, Lori Creed, Jenee Desmond, Amos Jones, and Samuel Spital provided very useful editorial and substantive feedback.

Notes

1 On the importance of the *Brown* decision, see Jack Greenberg, *Crusaders in the Courts: How a Dedicated Band of Lawyers Fought for the Civil Rights Revolution* (New York, 1994), 197; James T. Patterson, Brown v. Board of Education: *A Civil Rights Milestone and Its Troubled Legacy* (New York, 2001), xxvii–xxviii; Jordan Steiker, "American Icon: Does It Matter What the Court Said in *Brown*?," *Texas Law Review,* 81 (Nov. 2002), 305; Martin Guggenheim, "Symposium: Translating Insights into Policy: Maximizing Strategies for Pressuring Adults to Do Right by Children," *Arizona Law Review,* 45 (Fall 2000), 779; David A. Strauss, "Interdisciplinary Approach: Afterword: The Role of a Bill of Rights," *University of Chicago Law Review,* 59 (Winter 1992), 547; and Jack M. Balkin, ed., *What* Brown v. Board of Education *Should Have Said: The Nation's Top Legal Experts Rewrite America's Landmark Civil Rights Decision* (New York, 2001), 3. See also Ronald S. Sullivan Jr., "Multiple Ironies: *Brown* at 50," *Howard Law Journal,* 47 (Fall 2003), 29.

2 Nancy McArdle, "Beyond Poverty: Race and Concentrated-Poverty Neighborhoods in Metro Boston," Dec. 2003, *The Civil Rights Project, Harvard University* <http://www.civilrightsproject.harvard.edu/research/metro/ poverty_boston.php> (Jan. 22, 2004). For figures on declining levels of school-age children enrolled in Boston public schools by race and as total percentages of the population, see "Lessons for the Boston Schools," *Boston Globe,* March 14, 2004, A1. After ten years of court-ordered desegregation, barely 1% of black children in the eleven Southern states attended school with whites, according to Gerald N. Rosenberg, *The Hollow Hope: Can Courts Bring About Social Change?* (Chicago, 1991), 52. See also Adam Fairclough, *Better Day Coming: Blacks and Equality, 1890–2000* (New York, 2001), 329; Patterson, Brown v. Board of Education, 202–4, 211–12, 229, 231; and Lani Guinier, "Admissions Rituals as Political Acts: Guardians at the Gates of Our Democratic Ideals," *Harvard Law Review,* 117 (Nov. 2003), 113, 118–19nn24–27. Mark Tushnet, "The Significance of *Brown v. Board of Education,*" *Virginia Law Review,* 80 (Feb. 1994), 175.

3 *Brown v. Board of Education,* 347 U.S. 483, 494 (1954). Decisions that rejected race-conscious governmental policies and/or required a showing of prior intentional discrimination to justify a limited racial classification as a remedy include *Regents of the University of California v. Bakke,* 438 U.S. 265 (1978); *City of Mobile v. Bolden,* 446 U.S. 55 (1980); *Wygant v. Jackson Board of Education,* 476 U.S. 267, 274 (1986) (plurality opinion); and *Richmond v. J. A. Croson Co.,* 488 U.S. 469, 496 (1989). The Court held that a school desegregation plan must be limited to districts with an actual history of racial discrimination in *Milliken v. Bradley,* 418 U.S. 717, 744–45 (1974).

4 Derrick A. Bell Jr., "*Brown v. Board of Education* and the Interest-Convergence Dilemma," *Harvard Law Review,* 93 (Jan. 1980), 518–33.

5 *Ibid.,* 523.

6 For the interest-convergence principle framed broadly, see Derrick A. Bell, *Race, Racism, and American Law* (Boston, 1980). On desegregation and the Cold War, see Greenberg, *Crusaders in the Courts,* 164–65; Mary L. Dudziak, "Desegregation as a Cold War Imperative," *Stanford Law Review,* 41 (Nov. 1988), 61–120; and Mary L. Dudziak, *Cold War Civil Rights: Race and the Image of American Democracy* (Princeton, 2000). On the arousal of civil rights consciousness among blacks during World War II, see, for example, Earl Lewis, *In Their Own Interests: Race, Class, and Power in Twentieth-Century Norfolk,*

Virginia (Berkeley, 1991), 173–76; Martin Sosna, *In Search of the Silent South: Southern Liberals and the Race Issue* (New York, 1977); and Michael J. Klarman, "*Brown,* Racial Change, and the Civil Rights Movement," *Virginia Law Review,* 80 (Feb. 1994), 17–18. On desegregation and Southern industrialization, see *ibid.,* 56. The brief on behalf of the United States is quoted in Yale Kamisar, "The School Desegregation Cases in Retrospect: Some Reflections on Causes and Effects," in *Argument: The Oral Argument before the Supreme Court in* Brown v. Board of Education of Topeka, *1952–55,* ed. Leon Friedman (New York, 1969), xiv. On Special Assistant to the Attorney General Philip Elman, see Robert J. Cottrol, Raymond T. Diamond, and Leland B. Ware, Brown v. Board of Education: *Caste, Culture, and the Constitution* (Lawrence, 2003), 161–62. On the embarrassment to foreign visitors who were mistaken for American blacks, see Brief for the United States as Amicus Curiae at 4–5, *Brown v. Board of Education,* 347 U.S. 483 (1954) (No. 1). 2003), 161–62. On the embarrassment to foreign visitors who were mistaken for American blacks, see Brief for the United States as Amicus Curiae at 4–5, *Brown v. Board of Education,* 347 U.S. 483 (1954) (No. 1).

7   The Court itself refocused on segregation per se: "Here, unlike *Sweatt v. Painter,* there are findings below that the Negro and white schools involved have been equalized, or are being equalized, with respect to buildings, curricula, qualifications and salaries of teachers, and other 'tangible' factors. Our decision, therefore, cannot turn on merely a comparison of these tangible factors in the Negro and white schools involved in each of the cases. We must look instead to the effect of segregation itself on public education." *Brown v. Board of Education,* 347 U.S. at 492. On racial liberalism, see Daryl Michael Scott, *Contempt and Pity: Social Policy and the Image of the Damaged Black Psyche, 1880–1996* (Chapel Hill, 1997), xiii. On constituencies *Brown* ignored, see David S. Cecelski, *Along Freedom Road: Hyde County, North Carolina, and the Fate of Black Schools in the South* (Chapel Hill, 1994), 8, 12. According to the National Association for the Advancement of Colored People (NAACP) lawyer Constance Baker Motley, many black teachers became major foes of school desegregation after *Brown.* See Adam Fairclough, *Teaching Equality: Black Schools in the Age of Jim Crow* (Athens, Ga., 2001), 62–65, esp. n. 46. See also Martha Biondi, *To Stand and Fight: The Struggle for Civil Rights in Postwar New York City* (Cambridge, Mass., 2003), 164–65, 170–71, 180–85.

8   The social scientist survey on the psychological effects of segregation submitted to the Supreme Court as an appendix in *Brown* is cited in Kenneth B. Clark, *Prejudice and Your Child* (Boston, 1955), 39–41. Scott, *Contempt and Pity,* xii–xiv, 125–26, 138; W. E. B. Du Bois, *Black Reconstruction in America, 1860–1880* (New York, 1935), 700.

9   For an example of the judiciary's perception of racism as a matter of prejudice, see Justice Anthony M. Kennedy's concurrence in *Board of Trustees of the University of Alabama v. Garrett,* 531 U.S. 356, 374–75 (2001). On the development of a specific intent theory of equal protection, see John Charles Boger, "Willful Colorblindness: The New Racial Piety and the Resegregation of Public Schools," *North Carolina Law Review,* 78 (Sept. 2000), 1794. *Washington v. Davis,* 426 U.S. 229 (1976); *Mobile v. Bolden,* 446 U.S. 55 (1980). On the cost of segregation to black schoolchildren and ultimately their communities, one source noted "the contrasts in support of white and Negro schools are appalling . . . the median expenditure per standard classroom unit in schools for white children is $1,160 as compared with $476 for Negro children." See Brief of the American Federation of Teachers as Amicus Curiae at 9, *Brown v. Board of Education,* 347 U.S.

483 (1954) (No. 1). Derrick A. Bell, "Bell, J., Dissenting," in *What* Brown v. Board of Education *Should Have Said,* ed. Balkin, 185–200. Stephen E. Gottleib, "*Brown v. Board of Education* and the Application of American Tradition to Racial Division," *Suffolk University Law Review,* 34 (2001), 282–83. See also George Lipsitz, *The Possessive Investment in Whiteness: How White People Profit from Identity Politics* (Philadelphia, 1998), 34. But contrast Fairclough, *Teaching Equality,* 66. Cheryl I. Harris, "Whiteness as Property," *Harvard Law Review,* 106 (June 1993), 1714.

10   On the Court's deference to Southern whites, see Harris, "Whiteness as Property," 1753n9. For criticism of integration efforts, see Derrick A. Bell Jr., "Serving Two Masters: Integration Ideals and Client Interests in School Desegregation Litigation," *Yale Law Journal,* 85 (March 1976), 470–516. For a critique of Bell's view that it was midde-class blacks who sought integration, see Tomiko Brown-Nagin, "Race as Identity Caricature: A Local Legal History Lesson in the Salience of Intraracial Conflict," *University of Pennsylvania Law Review,* 151 (June 2003), 1913–76. On tokenism, consider that as recently as 2002, in a flagship state school that was the subject of a precedent on which *Brown* relied, nearly 90% of the undergraduate classes "with five to twenty-four students had no or only one African American to contribute their experiences or perspectives to a class discussion." Office of Admissions, University of Texas at Austin, "Diversity Levels of Undergraduate Classes at the University of Texas at Austin, 1996–2002," Nov. 20, 2003 <http://www.utexas.edu/student/admissions/research/ClassroomDiversity96-03 .pdf> (Feb. 3, 2004). Cf. *Sweatt v. Painter,* 339 U.S. 629 (1950).

11   Michael J. Klarman, "How *Brown* Changed Race Relations: The Backlash Thesis," *Journal of American History,* 81 (June 1994), 81–118; Klarman, "*Brown,* Racial Change, and the Civil Rights Movement," 7–150. Some commentators have suggested Klarman may have exaggerated the possibilities of Northern and Southern biracial cooperation or treated the role of litigation without sufficient nuance. See, for example, David Garrow, "Hopelessly Hollow History: Revisionist Devaluing of *Brown v. Board of Education,*" *Virginia Law Review,* 80 (Feb. 1994), 151. Robert Korstad and Nelson Lichtenstein, "Opportunities Found and Lost: Labor, Radicals, and the Early Civil Rights Movement," *Journal of American History,* 75 (Dec. 1988), 787. On the role of courts in implementing desegregation, see *U.S. v. Jefferson County Board of Education,* 372 F. 2d 836, 847 (1966); Rosenberg, *Hollow Hope,* 52.

12   Cecelski, *Along Freedom Road,* 8, 10, 12, 15, 34, 36. Cf. Fairclough, *Better Day Coming,* 148, 219, 221–23; and Fairclough, *Teaching Equality,* 62–65. Patterson, Brown v. Board of Education, xxvi–xxix, 201–5. See also Bell, "Serving Two Masters," 470–516.

13   For a definition of racism, see Lani Guinier and Gerald Torres, *The Miner's Canary: Enlisting Race, Resisting Power, Transforming Democracy* (Cambridge, Mass., 2002), 302. On the role of racial hierarchy in American history, see, for example, David Brion Davis, "Free at Last: The Enduring Legacy of the South's Civil War Victory," *New York Times,* Aug. 26, 2001, sec. 4, 1; Garry Wills, "The Negro President," *New York Review of Books,* Nov. 6, 2003, 45, 48–49; Gordon S. Wood, "Slaves in the Family," *New York Times,* Dec. 14, 2003, sec. 7, 10; and Lipsitz, *Possessive Investment in Whiteness,* 18. Eric Foner, *The Story of American Freedom* (New York, 1998), 31–32; Henry Wiencek, "Yale and the Price of Slavery," *New York Times,* Aug. 18, 2001, A15; Davis, "Free at Last," 1.

14   Biondi, *To Stand and Fight,* 183; Foner, *Story of American Freedom,* 21.

15   On racism as the "dominant interpretative framework" for understanding and securing social stability in the United States, see Bell, "Bell, J., Dissenting," 185, 187–190. See also Lipsitz, *Possessive Investment in Whiteness*, 2, 19. On the difficult relationship between the legal rights in *Brown* and potential remedies, see Jack M. Balkin, "*Brown v. Board of Education*—A Critical Introduction," in *What* Brown v. Board of Education *Should Have Said*, ed. Balkin, 64–71. Robert Carter, "A Reassessment of *Brown v. Board*," in *Shades of* Brown: *New Perspectives on School Desegregation*, ed. Derrick A. Bell (New York, 1980), 23. See also Kenneth B. Clark, "The Social Scientists, the *Brown* Decision, and Contemporary Confusion," in *Argument*, ed. Friedman, xl. Lewis, *In Their Own Interests*, 199–200.

16   While color blindness was also a goal, most racial liberals were willing to endorse a temporary period of race consciousness. On racial liberalism, see Scott, *Contempt and Pity*, xiii.

17   On the creation of a more conservative civil rights movement, compare Biondi, *To Stand and Fight*, 171, 182–83; Lewis, *In Their Own Interests*, 144–46, 165; and Korstad and Lichtenstein, "Opportunities Found and Lost," 800–801, 804–5.

18   Biondi, *To Stand and Fight*, 171; Scott, *Contempt and Pity*, 184; Lewis, *In Their Own Interests*, 148, 165, 199–202.

19   On the new integrationist orthodoxy, see Biondi, *To Stand and Fight*, 182–83. On the extent of biracial activism and the antipathy of Northern working-class whites toward coalition building, compare Klarman, "*Brown*, Racial Change, and the Civil Rights Movement," 102–3; Thomas J. Sugrue, "Crabgrass-Roots Politics: Race, Rights, and the Reaction against Liberalism in the Urban North, 1940–1964," *Journal of American History*, 82 (Sept. 1995), 551–78; and Arnold R. Hirsch, "Massive Resistance in the Urban North: Trumbull Park, Chicago, 1953–1966," *ibid.*, 522–50. On social scientists' underestimates of the effect of racism on blacks and whites in North and South, see Clark, "Social Scientists, the *Brown* Decision, and Contemporary Confusion," xl–xlv, xlix.

20   *Milliken v. Bradley*, 418 U.S. 717 (1974). On desegregation and white flight, see Paul Gewirtz, "Remedies and Resistance," *Yale Law Journal*, 92 (March 1983), 628–65; Jeffrey A. Raffel, *The Politics of School Desegregation: The Metropolitan Remedy in Delaware* (Philadelphia, 1980), 177; and Finis Welch and Audrey Light, *New Evidence on School Desegregation* (Washington, 1987), 74. For the debate on whether white flight was a response to school desegregation, see Gary Orfield, *Must We Bus? Segregated Schools and National Policy* (Washington, 1978); Gary Orfield and David Thronson, "Dismantling Desegregation: Uncertain Gains, Unexpected Costs," *Emory Law Journal*, 42 (Summer 1993), 759–90; and Charles T. Clotfelter, "Are Whites Still Fleeing? Racial Patterns and Enrollment Shifts in Urban Public Schools, 1987–1996," *Journal of Policy Analysis and Management*, 20 (Spring 2001), 199–221. See also James S. Coleman, Sara D. Kelly, and John A. Moore, *Trends in School Segregation, 1968–73* (Washington, 1975), 53–80; and David J. Armor, *Forced Justice: School Desegregation and the Law* (New York, 1995), 174–93. On poor whites weathering the transition to integrated schools, see Gary Orfield, "Metropolitan School Desegregation: Impacts on Metropolitan Society," *Minnesota Law Review*, 80 (April 1996), 831. Bell, "*Brown v. Board of Education* and the Interest-Convergence Dilemma," 525. See also Linda Hamilton Kreiger, "The Content of Our Categories: A Cognitive Bias Approach to

Discrimination and Equal Employment Opportunity," *Stanford Law Review,* 47 (July 1995), 1240.

21 Beth Roy, *Bitters in the Honey: Tales of Hope and Disappointment across Divides of Race and Time* (Fayetteville, 1999), 318; Pete Daniel, *Lost Revolutions: The South in the 1950s* (Chapel Hill, 2000), 270. Many whites believed that if race relations changed, they could only lose social status and power. See Robert J. Norrell, *Reaping the Whirlwind: The Civil Rights Movement in Tuskegee* (New York, 1985), 107.

22 C. Arnold Anderson, "Social Class Differentials in the Schooling of Youth within the Regions and Community-Size Groups of the United States," *Social Forces,* 25 (May 1947), 440, 436; C. Arnold Anderson, "Inequalities in Schooling in the South," *American Journal of Sociology,* 60 (May 1955), 553, 549, 557. See also Allison Davis, "Socio-Economic Influences upon Children's Learning," in *Proceedings of the Midcentury White House Conference on Children and Youth,* ed. Edward A. Richards (Raleigh, 1951), 7; Robert L. Marion, *Rural Education in the Southern United States* (Austin, 1979); and Rashi Fein, "Educational Patterns in Southern Migration," *Southern Economic Journal,* 32 (July 1965, part II), 106–24.

23 Bell, "*Brown v. Board of Education* and the Interest-Convergence Dilemma," 525; Armor, *Forced Justice,* 174–93, 206–7. See also Charles E. Kimble, "Factors Affecting Adults' Attitudes toward School Desegregation," *Journal of Social Psychology,* 110 (April 1980), 216. On regional differences based on race, see, for example, Thomas Byrne Edsall with Mary D. Edsall, *Chain Reaction: The Impact of Race, Rights, and Taxes on American Politics* (New York, 1991). On maps that color code the electorate, with red for Republican states and blue for Democratic states, see Robert David Sullivan, "Beyond Red and Blue," *Commonwealth Magazine* <http://www.massinc. org/commonwealth/new_map_exclusive/beyond_red_blue.html> (Feb. 3, 2004); and Tom Zeller, "One State, Two State, Red State, Blue State," *New York Times,* Feb. 8, 2004, 16.

24 Daniel, *Lost Revolutions,* 251; Elizabeth Huckaby, *Crisis at Central High: Little Rock, 1957–58* (Baton Rouge, 1980), 1–13. The Central High School integration plan had originally called for the desegregation of grades ten through twelve with 300 black students. Over time, the number was scaled back to 25. See Greenberg, *Crusaders in the Courts,* 228–29. On the twisted symmetry of the integration process, see Daniel, *Lost Revolutions,* 254–55; and David R. Goldfield, *Black, White, and Southern: Race Relations and Southern Culture, 1940 to the Present* (Baton Rouge, 1990), esp. 108. Huckaby, *Crisis at Central High,* 2. In 1960, the per capita income in the geographic region associated with Central High was $3,826; in the region associated with Hall High it was $8,012. See Donald Bogue, "Census Tract Data, 1960: Elizabeth Mullen Bogue File" (University of Chicago, Community and Family Study Center, 1975), computer file, Inter-University Consortium of Political and Social Research (ICPSR) version <http://www.icpsr.umich.edu:8080/ICPSR-STUDY/02932.xml> (Feb. 3, 2004).

25 Daniel, *Lost Revolutions,* 257; Roy, *Bitters in the Honey,* 179, 206, 338, 343–44.

26 On the role of Gov. Orval Faubus and others in manufacturing the conflagration and violence that attended the desegregation of Central High in Little Rock, see Greenberg, *Crusaders in the Courts,* 228–43. Goldfield, *Black, White, and Southern,* 108.

27 Robert J. Norrell, "Labor at the Ballot Box: Alabama Politics from the New Deal to the Dixiecrat Movement," *Journal of Southern History,* 57 (May 1991), 201, 234, 227, 233. On antebellum conceptions of race and class and political use of white supremacy, see

W. J. Cash, *The Mind of the South* (1941; New York, 1991), 38–39, 109–10. See also Norrell, *Reaping the Whirlwind,* 92–102.

28   Norrell, "Labor at the Ballot Box," 227. Some scholars argue that in several Southern states, the postwar political elite was dominated by progressives who campaigned successfully for the interests of poor blacks and whites. After *Brown,* Southern elites who were not threatened economically seemed to acquiesce in racial progress, as in Little Rock. See Goldfield, *Black, White, and Southern,* 48, 108; and Klarman, "*Brown,* Racial Change, and the Civil Rights Movement," 85–90, 102–3. On urbanization in the South, the way an influx of Northern whites affected Southern racial reform efforts, and the gradual weakening of Jim Crow's hold on the region, see *ibid.,* 52–65, 67–71; and Daniel, *Lost Revolutions,* 282. Klarman, "*Brown,* Racial Change, and the Civil Rights Movement," 64–65.

29   On how Northern white working-class residents came to expect racially segregated neighborhoods, largely because of New Deal policies, and how the stage was set for the "backlash" long before the racial liberalism of the 1950s and 1960s, see Thomas J. Sugrue, *The Origins of the Urban Crisis: Race and Inequality in Postwar Detroit* (Princeton, 1996); and Hirsch, "Massive Resistance in the Urban North," 522–50. See also Charles R. Lawrence III, "The Id, the Ego, and Equal Protection: Reckoning with Unconscious Racism," *Stanford Law Review,* 39 (Jan. 1987), 342. Lipsitz, *Possessive Investment in Whiteness,* 18.

30   Hirsch, "Massive Resistance in the Urban North"; Sugrue, "Crabgrass-Roots Politics," esp. 561, 560.

31   On the alignment of working-class whites with upper-class whites to resist civil rights, see Roy, *Bitters in the Honey,* 46–48, 132–33, 148–66, 179–84; and Sugrue, "Crabgrass-Roots Politics." See also Hirsch, "Massive Resistance in the Urban North."

32   Hirsch, "Massive Resistance in the Urban North"; Sugrue, "Crabgrass-Roots Politics." A comparison of the desegregation methods in Wilmington, Delaware, and the more evasive ones used in Dallas, Texas, illustrates how upper-class whites used political and social power to tailor the implementation of desegregation to limit their burden. Compare Raffel, *Politics of School Desegregation,* 13, 20, 110–11, 210; and Glenn M. Linden, *Desegregating Schools in Dallas: Four Decades in the Federal Courts* (Dallas, 1995), 24. On racial segregation in the formation of new towns, see Nancy Burns, *The Formation of American Local Governments: Private Values in Public Institutions* (New York, 1994), 35–36.

33   Burns, *Formation of American Local Governments,* 112; Richard Thompson Ford, "The Boundaries of Race: Political Geography in Legal Analysis," *Harvard Law Review,* 107 (June 1994), 1847–57.

34   Sugrue, "Crabgrass-Roots Politics," 570, 578; Roy, *Bitters in the Honey,* 326, 338.

35   On working-class whites' racializing of failure, see Roy, *Bitters in the Honey,* 324–25, 338–44; Sugrue, "Crabgrass-Roots Politics," 551–78; and Sugrue, *Origins of the Urban Crisis,* 213–14.

36   Jennifer L. Hochschild, *Facing Up to the American Dream: Race, Class, and the Soul of the Nation* (Princeton, 1995), 15.

37   See Guinier and Torres, *Miner's Canary,* 102–4, 224–29. David Levering Lewis, "'The Souls of Black Folk,' a Century Hence," *Crisis* (March–April 2003), 18.

38 See Guinier and Torres, *Miner's Canary*, 74–86.

39 *Plessy v. Ferguson*, 163 U.S. 537 (1896). Jack Greenberg made the statement in a 1974 speech delivered to the New York City Bar Association. See Gerald N. Rosenberg, "*Brown* Is Dead! Long Live *Brown*!: The Endless Attempt to Canonize a Case," *Virginia Law Review*, 80 (Feb. 1994), 171n32.

40 Robert Carter quoted in Kamisar, "School Desegregation Cases in Retrospect," xxv. In recent cases challenging affirmative action, the Court's analysis often sees race merely as phenotypic difference, fails to recognize the asymmetrical ways in which race functions in American society, and allows whites to claim reverse discrimination. See Guinier and Torres, *Miner's Canary*, 32–66.

41 Greenberg, *Crusaders in the Courts*, 130–32. Cf. Brief for the United States as Amicus Curiae at 3, *Brown v. Board of Education* (No. 1). Lawrence, "Id, the Ego, and Equal Protection," 322, 374–75, esp. 375. Scott, *Contempt and Pity*, 71–91; Charles R. Lawrence III, "If He Hollers Let Him Go: Regulating Racist Speech on Campus," *Duke Law Journal* (June 1990), 439–40, 466.

42 Initially hailed for bringing a measure of reality into the legal proceedings, the evidence cited in *Brown*'s famous footnote 11 was primarily (though not exclusively) from one social science—psychology. In the years after *Brown*, it was the doll studies that gained cultural salience. The Court also cited a sociologist and an economist: E. Franklin Frazier, *The Negro in the United States* (New York, 1949); Gunnar Myrdal, *An American Dilemma: The Negro Problem and Modern Democracy* (2 vols., New York, 1944). The other citations in footnote 11 of *Brown*, which described the psychological effects of segregation, included Max Deutscher and Isidor Chein, "The Psychological Effects of Enforced Segregation: A Survey of Social Science Opinion," *Journal of Psychology*, 26 (1948), 259–87; and Isidor Chein, "What Are the Psychological Effects of Segregation under Conditions of Equal Facilities?," *International Journal of Opinion and Attitude Research*, 3 (Summer 1949), 229–34. For the doll studies, see, for example, Midcentury White House Conference on Children and Youth, "The Effects of Prejudice and Discrimination," in *Personality in the Making: The Fact-Finding Report of the Midcentury White House Conference on Children and Youth*, ed. Helen Lelan Witmer and Ruth Kotinsky (New York, 1952), 135–58, esp. 142; and Clark, *Prejudice and Your Child*, 19–20, 22–24. On the methodological problems of these studies, see Scott, *Contempt and Pity*, 93–136. On the children examined in the doll studies and Kenneth Clark's conclusions about them, see a historian's account: Ben Keppel, "Kenneth B. Clark in the Patterns of American Culture," *American Psychologist*, 57 (Jan. 2002), 29–37, esp. 32.

43 Clark, *Prejudice and Your Child*, 50. Scott, *Contempt and Pity*, 124. On contemporary testing situations that trigger vulnerability to negative stereotypes, see Claude M. Steele, "Thin Ice: 'Stereotype Threat' and Black College Students," *Atlantic Monthly*, 284 (Aug. 1999) <http://www.theatlantic.com/issues/99aug/9908stereotype2.htm>, part 2, para. 2 (April 2, 2004). On how stigmatization may strengthen self-esteem, see Jennifer Crocker and Brenda Major, "Social Stigma and Self-Esteem: The Self-Protective Properties of Stigma," *Psychological Review*, 96 (Oct. 1989), 608–30. On the lack of evidence that segregation by itself damaged self-esteem, see Geoffrey Cohen to Lani Guinier, e-mail, Dec. 4, 2003 (in Lani Guinier's possession). See also David Glenn, "Minority Students with Complex Beliefs about Ethnic Identity Are Found to Do Better in School," *Chronicle of Higher Education*, [online version], June 2, 2003, now available at <http://sitemaker.

umich.edu/daphna.oyserman/files/ chronicle_of_ higher_education.htm> (March 2, 2004); and D. Oyserman, M. Kemmelmeier, S. Fryberg, H. Brosh, and T. Hart-Johnson, "Racial-Ethnic Self-Schemas," *Social Psychology Quarterly,* 66 (Dec. 2003), 333–47.

44 On black teachers' losing their jobs due to integration, see Cecelski, *Along Freedom Road,* 8. On the loss of outstanding black high schools, see Derrick Bell, *Silent Covenants: Brown v. Board of Education and the Unfulfilled Hopes for Racial Reform* (New York, 2004), 124–25.

45 Bell, "Serving Two Masters," 470–516; Brown-Nagin, "Race as Identity Caricature," 1913–76. See also Coleman, Kelly, and Moore, *Trends in School Segregation,* 53–80; Armor, *Forced Justice,* 174–93; Lewis, *In Their Own Interests,* 199–202; and Sugrue, *Origins of the Urban Crisis,* 268. On efforts by middle-class blacks to separate themselves from poorer blacks, see Grace Carroll, *Environmental Stress and African Americans: The Other Side of the Moon* (Westport, 1998), 9; Orfield and Thronson, "Dismantling Desegregation," 774; Lisa W. Foderaro, "A Suburb That's Segregated by Money More than Race," *New York Times,* Nov. 24, 2003, A22. Class differences within the black community also influenced who led in challenging segregation. See Goldfield, *Black, White, and Southern,* 90–91. But cf. Klarman, "*Brown,* Racial Change, and the Civil Rights Movement," 56–62. On "racial outsiders" who have sought the privileges of whiteness, see Lipsitz, *Possessive Investment in Whiteness,* 3. See also Patterson, Brown v. Board of Education, 42–44, 200–201; and Cecelski, *Along Freedom Road,* 34. Carter, "Reassessment of *Brown v. Board,*" 28.

46 The Court rejected the possibility that the 14th Amendment implicated distributional considerations, striking down a judicial attempt to mandate equalization of resources, stating that "at least where wealth is involved, the equal protection clause of the Fourteenth Amendment does not require absolute equality or precisely equal advantages." See *San Antonio Independent School District v. Rodriguez,* 411 U.S. 1, 24 (1973). Dissenting, Justice Thurgood Marshall lamented the Court's refusal to consider how much governmental action itself had caused the wealth classifications. *Ibid.,* 123–24.

47 *Davis v. County School Board,* 103 F. Supp. 337 (E.D. Va. 1952). For Lindsay Almond's statements, see "Oral Argument," in *Removing a Badge of Slavery: The Record of* Brown v. Board of Education, ed. Mark Whitman (Princeton, 1993), 157. For Colgate Darden's testimony, see "Colgate Darden," *ibid.,* 83, 84.

48 I define racial literacy at greater length in Guinier, "Admissions Rituals as Political Acts," 201–12. See also Guinier and Torres, *Miner's Canary,* 29–31.

49 John W. Davis quoted in "1953 Argument," in *Argument,* ed. Friedman, 216. W. E. B. Du Bois, "Does the Negro Need Separate Schools?," *Journal of Negro Education,* 4 (July 1935), 335.

50 Norrell, *Reaping the Whirlwind,* esp. 57.

51 Charles Hamilton Houston (1949) quoted in *The Road to* Brown, dir. Mykola Kulish (California Newsreel, 1990).

52 Emphasis on formal equality gave birth to the (Warren E.) Burger and (William H.) Rehnquist courts' legal doctrine interpreting the Constitution narrowly, limiting relief to proven acts of intentional discrimination. See, for example, *Washington v. Davis,* 426 U.S. 229 (1976); and *City of Mobile v. Bolden,* 446 U.S. 55 (1980). Even when the Court finds diversity to be a compelling governmental interest, it diverts concern and

resources away from the real barriers to educational opportunity, according to Derrick Bell, "Diversity's Distractions," *Columbia Law Review,* 103 (Oct. 2003), 1622–33.

53 Derrick A. Bell, "Comments from the Contributors," in *What* Brown v. Board of Education *Should Have Said,* ed. Balkin, 206. Bell, *Silent Covenants,* 119–20; W. E. B. Du Bois, *Dusk of Dawn: An Essay toward an Autobiography of a Race Concept* (New York, 1940), 303.

14

The Montgomery Bus Boycott and American Politics

Raymond Arsenault

During the first three months of the Montgomery bus boycott, the members of the Montgomery Improvement Association (MIA) spent little time thinking about the broad political implications of their actions. To the MIA, a fledgling organization that had no expectation of changing the world, politics—at least the politics that mattered—was a local affair. While the Reverend Martin Luther King Jr. and others were well aware that more than local bus desegregation was at stake, their primary concern was sustaining the boycott, not developing a strategy that would influence public policy at the national level. Faced with an oppressive system of racial control, the boycotters simply patched together a religiously-based social movement that promised to change the distribution of power in the city of Montgomery. Although their mass meetings frequently invoked the expansive rhetoric of democratic politics—calling upon such hallowed words as *freedom, liberty,* and *justice*—they paid little attention to the dictates of political theory or partisan loyalty. And yet, long before the boycott was over, a number of observers both inside and outside of the MIA sensed that the protest in Montgomery would have profound political consequences.

This judgment proved to be correct, and in the years since the boycott the conclusion that black Montgomerians radically altered the nature and scope of citizen-based political activism in the United States has become almost axiomatic among interpreters of the civil rights movement. By demonstrating the transformative power of nonviolent direct action, the boycotters gave the nation an object lesson in sociopolitical philosophy. Indeed, by experiencing the existential truth of personal empowerment, they helped to redefine the rights and responsibilities of American citizenship. Despite its modest begin-nings, the boycott initiated the direct-action phase of the modern civil rights struggle, setting the stage for the sit-ins and Freedom Rides of the early 1960s. Collectively, these nonviolent campaigns changed American politics forever, initiating a new era of grassroots citizen action. During the 1960s and 1970s, group after group followed the civil rights activists' lead, proving again and again that ordinary citizens can change the world, or at least a significant part of it—with or without the collaboration of political elites.[1]

The political legacy of the Montgomery movement makes it doubly ironic that the American political establishment all but ignored the boycott in 1956. In the early weeks of what appeared to be a minor local struggle, this attitude was understandable. But the neglect persisted long after the mass indictment of boycott leaders in late February 1956 made the Montgomery crisis an object of national and international interest. Even in March and April, when the boycotters and their allies around the world cried out for justice, there was a deafening silence in Washington. Mired in the traditional paradigm of partisan politics, the leaders of both major parties were slow to grasp the significance of what was happening in Montgomery.

During the mid-1950s, the notions that black Americans could sustain a successful mass movement and that economic boycotts and other acts of nonviolent resistance could actually transform American race relations were simply beyond the imagination of mainstream politicians. Such radical ideas were limited to a small intellectual and religious subculture that had no access to the national political arena. Many politicians undoubtedly remembered A. Philip Randolph's threatened "March on Washington" that had forced President Franklin Roosevelt to establish the Committee on Fair Employ-ment Practices (FEPC) in 1941. And a few may have recalled the Congress of Racial Equality's April 1947 "Journey of Reconciliation," a series of inter-racial bus and train rides through the upper South. But in the 15 years since the original FEPC controversy such tactics had been confined to the politics of the Third World[2]. Everyone, of course, knew about Gandhi's victory over British colonialism in India, but the exotic quality of the Subcontinent and the eccentric behavior of the sandal-clad Mahatma reinforced the assumption that nonviolent resistance and Satyagraha ("truth force") had no relevance to American politics.

Even among the few politicians who recognized the applicability of Gandhianism to the United States, there were grave doubts about the wisdom of encouraging such tactics. Although most American politicians had welcomed the success of nonviolent resistance in India during the late 1940s, by the mid-1950s many had begun to question the benefits of self-liberation. To Democrats and Republicans alike, several disturbing developments—most notably, the bloody civil war between Moslems and Hindus that accompanied independence and Prime Minister Nehru's recent enthusiasm for Third World nonalignment—had demonstrated the perils of self-liberation. Gandhian protest, it seemed, was uncontrollable and potentially dangerous. Despite its undeniable moral power, no one knew exactly where it would lead. Thus, to encourage black leaders to follow Gandhi's lead was to risk anarchy and massive civil disorder.[3]

The troubling legacy of Gandhianism, coupled with the specter of assertive black protesters, was enough to scare off most politicians. But in the Montgomery protest there was the added factor of economic coercion, which to some observers was tantamount to blackmail. In a nation that prided itself on political consensus and economic opportunity, the word "boycott" sounded needlessly confrontational. Indeed, to some it smacked of anticapitalist radicalism. There was also the widespread fear that a successful black boycott would inevitably lead to economic countermeasures by white segregationists. Viewed from this perspective, the boycott was an engine of disaster that would propel the South into a downward spiral of economic ruin and civil unrest. Following the mass indictment of late February 1956, these fears and reservations were partially mitigated by the growing realization that religious leaders were directing the boycott and by the suspicion that there was more dignity and restraint among the boycotters than among their white segregationist opponents. But even then, most national politicians were reluctant to become involved in a superheated controversy that showed no sign of cooling off. For political leaders who were already having enough trouble dealing with the legal ambiguities and moral pressures of school desegregation, adjusting to the tactics of direct resistance and economic boycott was, to say the least, an unpleasant prospect. In the unsettled atmosphere of the mid-1950s, publicly endorsing a mass movement was problematic even for politicians who were deeply committed to the cause of civil rights. As we shall see later in this essay, when the twin storms of black protest and white resistance swept out of the

Deep South during the winter and spring of 1956, national politicians of all persuasions ducked for cover.[4]

THE UNPRECEDENTED NATURE OF the boycott led to indecision and inaction in national politics. But there was no such paralysis among the state and local politicians of the Deep South. With few exceptions, their response to the protest in Montgomery was swift and uncomplicated. In the time-honored tradition of Southern sectionalism, they rushed to the defense of white supremacy. Still smarting from the *Brown* decision, they were not about to turn the other cheek when a group of misguided racial "inferiors" challenged the sanctity of Jim Crow transportation. Throughout the Deep South, condemnation of the boycott became a daily ritual for many local and state politicians. In legislative chambers and on courthouse steps across the region, politicians fulminated against the impudent, meddling agitators of the MIA. The standard charges against the boycotters were repeated over and over: Negro "goon squads" were preventing "good Negroes" from riding the buses; the bus boycott was the entering wedge of a social revolution masterminded by the NAACP; it was clearly the work of "outside agitators," part of a Communist plot to destroy the "Southern way of life"; and so on.

In the border South the segregationist response to the boycott was intermittent and unorganized, but in the Deep South the growing power of the White Citizens' Councils ensured an unrelenting stream of white supremacist invective. From Louisiana, where State Senator William Rainach held sway, to South Carolina, where Governor George Bell Timmerman Jr. and State Senator L. Marion Gressette took the lead, politicians associated with the White Citizens' Councils led a coordinated attack on the boycott. At rally after rally, Citizens' Council politicians called for an economic counterattack that would bring the boycotters and other uncooperative Negroes to their knees. "I shudder to think," Georgia Attorney General Eugene Cook remarked on several occasions, "when the masses of my state begin to move in self-defense." Once described as "a small man with a big voice," Cook regarded the bus boycott as the natural outcome of the "mulatto decision" issued by the Supreme Court in May 1954. Encouraged by Georgia's ultraconservative governor Marvin Griffin, Cook became a regular on the Citizens' Council circuit during the winter and spring of 1956 and was probably the most vocal opponent of the MIA outside the state of Alabama.[5]

In Alabama itself, the most persistent political critic of the boycott, other than Mayor W. A. "Tacky" Gayle and the embattled members of the Montgomery City Commission, was Senator Sam Engelhardt of Macon County. The owner of a 6,500-acre cotton plantation near Tuskegee, Engelhardt was a leading figure in the militantly segregationist American States Rights Association and the executive secretary of the Association of Citizens' Councils of Alabama. In late February, he praised the mass indictment of boycott leaders, assuring the white masses that "the Citizens' Council is 100 per cent behind the grand jury and its officials." And, in early March, he introduced a bill that empowered railroads and bus lines to draw up and enforce "reasonable rules for the seating of passengers." Not surprisingly, Engelhardt made it clear that his definition of "reasonable rules" did not include integrated seating.[6]

Under Engelhardt's leadership, the Alabama legislature produced a barrage of white supremacist legislation during the winter and spring of 1956. One resolution, which received the unanimous approval of the state senate, asked Congress to establish a federal program to disperse "Negroes among the several Northern and Western states, the areas where Negroes are wanted and can be assimilated." A second resolution, also approved unanimously, urged the United States Supreme Court to "modify" its recent anti-segregation decisions in view of the fact that "it is well established that said decrees are not enforceable in all the states at this time." In a similar vein, Senator Gerald Bradford of Clarke County sponsored an amendment to the state constitution that would allow "city governing bodies to lease or sell . . . property to private operators to get around the U.S. Supreme Court decisions on segregation." The legislature also approved several laws aimed at the NAACP, including one that empowered the legislature to investigate "subversive organizations." And, to the dismay of the few remaining moderates in state politics, it even passed a law that prohibited whites and blacks from sitting together at public gatherings or from playing with or against each other in sporting events; the ban on interracial sports included "any game of cards, dice, dominoes, checkers, baseball, softball, basketball, track" as well as all activities "in swimming pools, lakes or ponds, or on any beaches."[7]

The only Alabama politician who showed any inclination to swim against the segregationist tide was Governor James E. Folsom. Known as "the little man's big friend," the 6'8" Folsom was a folksy populist who had earned a reputation as a racial moderate since his election to the governorship in

1946. Elected to a second term in 1954, he became a leading critic of the White Citizens' Councils and a committed gradualist on the issue of school desegregation. Publicly, Folsom maintained a strict neutrality toward the bus boycott, distancing the state government from the controversy. But privately he did what he could to facilitate desegregation. During the crucial second month of the boycott, he held at least three secret meetings with the leaders of the MIA. Arranged by Winston Craig, the governor's black chauffeur, these confidential meetings gave Folsom an understanding of the boycott strikingly different from that any other white leader. Most importantly, his conversations with Martin Luther King seemed to inspire genuine sympathy for the boycotters' cause. At one meeting, Folsom reportedly encouraged MIA leaders to broaden their demands. "Segregation don't make no sense no way," he told them in a moment of surprising candor, "What you ought to do is try to get segregation completely abolished. The Supreme Court has already spoken about it. Why go after a few crumbs when you can have the whole loaf." Folsom later denied that he ever made such a statement, but he did admit that he had counseled King to study the teachings of Gandhi. Some years earlier, Folsom had been given a book on Gandhi's life, and he recommended it to King. "Whatever you do, if you haven't read that book, you go read it," he urged, "Whatever you do, don't fight back. They'll put you in jail or whatever, but don't you fight back."[8]

Folsom's unexpected behind-the-scenes support was encouraging to boycott leaders, but any hope that he would publicly endorse the boycott all but disappeared during the Autherine Lucy crisis in early February. Just as the controversy surrounding Lucy's attempt to enroll at the University of Alabama came to a head, Folsom seemed to have a failure of nerve. During the fateful weekend of February 3–5, when a minor riot erupted at the campus in Tuscaloosa, Folsom was away on a fishing (and drinking) trip in Florida. On several occasions he had pledged that state law enforcement officials would do whatever was necessary to uphold the rule of law and prevent violence. But the governor's forces were nowhere in sight when angry segregationists stormed the campus. After his return from Florida, he tried to justify his inaction. But nearly everyone recognized that he had lost control of the situation. Whatever chance he had of stemming the tide of white supremacist reaction was slipping away. Faced with an increasingly hostile legislature, which did not appreciate his criticism of the White Citizens' Council or his characterization of a nullification resolution as "just a bunch of hogwash," the once popular governor had few political allies and little public support.[9] On February 24, three days after the mass indictment, Folsom made a daring but futile attempt to neutralize the growing political power of Engelhardt and the "Citizens' Council crowd."

Amid great fanfare, he summoned the leaders of the state press to Montgomery to help him form a "biracial commission which will seek to settle racial disputes." Speaking to an overflow crowd in the House chamber, Folsom called upon the "molders of public opinion" to help resolve "the differences that have arisen between the two races." "The racial difference is one of the most fundamental of all human nature, outside of reproduction," he conceded, "and there is race tension all over the world wherever different races reside together. But there is no hard and fast rule to solve these problems except through a Christian approach." The governor's statement drew polite applause, but several of the most militant segregationists in the audience were openly skeptical. When asked to respond to the proposal, Jack Brock, the publisher of the *Alabama Labor News*, pronounced it "a fine gesture" but went on to warn the governor that "we will fight at every turn if the Negro race seeks to mongrelize the white race of the South." Some of the politicians in the crowd were equally wary. When Albert Boutwell, a powerful senator from Jefferson County, reminded the governor that the Northern press and other "outside influences" were to blame for the state's problems, Folsom returned to the podium to reassure the audience that he had no intention of abandoning segregation:

> Anybody with any sense knows that Negro children and white children are not going to school together in Alabama anytime in the near future . . . In fact, not in a long time. . . . Alabama has had the best relation of any state in the nation until recently and this was due to Tuskegee Institute. At Tuskegee they teach education and understanding before action. My intention is to create a biracial commission composed of outstanding leadership of both races. Not the wild and woolly element of the colored race, and not the extremists of the white race. The average Negro fears the leadership in his own race more than he fears the white man, and the white man fears his own leadership more than he fears the Negro. We shouldn't have fear among the two races.

Later in the day Folsom met with a committee of editors and publishers, which immediately drew up a plan for a 25-member commission. The plan required the governor to appoint one white and one black member from each of the state's nine congressional districts, plus seven members from the state at-large.[10]

Despite some initial enthusiasm and widespread press support, the proposed biracial commission never got off the ground. White Citizens' Council leaders and other white supremacists attacked the proposal, claiming it was part of a plot to weaken segregation, and the legislature repeatedly rebuffed Folsom's efforts to obtain the legislative authorization needed to make the commission a reality. Although black leaders showed some interest in the proposal, public support in the white community was lacking. As one white segregationist reminded the governor, in a letter to the editor of the *Montgomery Advertiser*, "Alabama does not need a biracial committee to speak its piece on segregation. Even a branchheader knows that." As the commission proposal faded from view, Folsom turned to other strategies. On March 12, he issued a public statement imploring Mayor Gayle and the leaders of the MIA to put aside their differences "so that life can return to normal in our Capital City." For the first time, he admitted that he had met privately with Gayle on three separate occasions and that he had held three similar meetings with boycott leaders. He had been patient and discreet, but now it was time "to settle this dispute" once and for all.[11]

Folsom's impatience drew a few headlines in the state press, but neither Gayle nor the MIA paid much attention to his plea. By mid-March, Folsom's political base had deteriorated to the point where he could be safely ignored. At that point, Asa Carter, the executive secretary of the North Alabama Citizens' Council, was already circulating a petition calling for the governor's impeachment. The charges cited in the petition contained few specifics, but according to Carter, Folsom's lack of leadership in the fight to preserve segregation was grounds enough for impeachment. A few legislators were tempted by Carter's suggestion, but most saw no need to humiliate a man who was already dead politically. Although the impeachment movement soon fizzled, Folsom's corpse-like status was confirmed when he ran for national Democratic committeeman later in the spring. During the campaign, Folsom tried to shore up his political position by appealing to moderate segregationists. While reaffirming his belief that "the white and Negro children of Alabama are not going to be forced to go to the same public schools as long as I am governor," he ridiculed the "mobocracy" of the White Citizens' Councils. "You can call the Supreme Court justices s.o.b.'s if you want to," he warned, "but that doesn't relieve Southern officials sworn to uphold the Constitution of their responsibility." This was a strategy that might have worked a year or two earlier, but in the spring of 1956 the white voters of Alabama were in no mood for moderation. In the May 1 Democratic primary, Folsom finished a distant second to Representative Charles McKay, an ultraconservative from Talladega, who billed himself as "Alabama's Fighting Champion for Segregation." The vote was 232,751 to 79,644, with Folsom winning a majority in only three of the state's 67 counties.[12]

FOLSOM'S PRECIPITOUS DECLINE SERVED as a warning to other Southern moderates. The surprising calm of the immediate post-*Brown* era had given way to emotionalism, defiance, and the politics of massive resistance. By early 1956, most white Southerners, whatever their previous feelings, were no longer interested in appeals to reason or legalistic platitudes. "Interposition" and "nullification" had become the watchwords of Southern politics, and the rhetoric of compromise had become a sure ticket to political oblivion. The regional roster of self-proclaimed moderates still included a dozen or more influential politicians—most notably Governors LeRoy Collins of Florida, Frank Clement of Tennessee, and Orval Faubus of Arkansas; Senators Albert Gore and Estes Kefauver of Tennessee, J. William Fulbright of Arkansas, Ralph Yarborough of Texas, and John Sparkman and Lister Hill of Alabama; and Congressmen Brooks Hays of Arkansas, Frank E. Smith of Mississippi, Wright Patman of Texas, and Carl Elliott of Alabama. But, individually and collectively, their influence was on the wane—especially when it came to matters of race. Pressured by demagogic colleagues and angry constituents, the moderates' longstanding commitment to "gradualism" was shading into a politics of avoidance and indefinite delay. Four of the moderate senators and congressmen noted above—Gore, Kefauver, Hays, and Patman—bravely refused to sign the March 1956 "Dixie Manifesto," which pledged continued Southern resistance to the *Brown* decision. But the rest, realizing that their political careers were on the line, quietly acquiesced.

On the subject of the boycott, the Southern moderates maintained a collective silence. Most probably harbored some sympathy for the boycotters in

1956, and virtually all later claimed to admire Martin Luther King and the nonviolent movement he helped to create. But during the boycott itself—and for several years thereafter—not one of these men publicly endorsed the boycott or said anything that might encourage direct resistance to segregation. In the halls of Congress, in Southern statehouses, and out on the stump, the Southern moderate voice was mute. To their credit, the moderates—with the exception of Faubus—refused to join the expanding chorus of white supremacist extremism. But the fact that cowering silence was all that they could manage was a sad commentary on a tradition that had promised to lead the South out of the darkness. A Roper public opinion poll conducted in April 1956 indicated that more than a quarter of the white South approved of the boycott's goals, yet there was no one to speak for this minority in Washington. From start to finish, Southern political commentary on the boycott was uniformly negative.[13]

AT THE NATIONAL LEVEL, the most vocal critic of the boycott was Senator James O. Eastland of Mississippi. A throwback to the pyrotechnic tradition of James K. "The White Chief" Vardaman and Theodore "The Man" Bilbo—the white supremacist demagogues who solidified Mississippi's well-deserved reputation for racial backwardness—Eastland had been an outspoken advocate of Jim Crow politics since his election to the Senate in 1948. Always on the outer edge of racial extremism, Eastland was, in the words of liberal Arkansas journalist Harry Ashmore, a "thin-lipped and hating" man. An inveterate Cold Warrior and the chairman of the Senate's Internal Security Subcommittee, he presided over a series of anti-Communist investigations that often tried to link political subversion and racial heterodoxy. According to Eastland, the *Brown* decision proved that the United States Supreme Court had been "indoctrinated and brain-washed by Left-wing pressure groups." The theme of alleged integrationist subversion received full exposition when Eastland addressed the first statewide meeting of the Mississippi Association of Citizens' Councils in early December 1955. After warning the all-white crowd that "We must take the offense," he attacked racial integration as a "monstrous crime . . . dictated by political pressure groups bent upon the destruction of the American system of government and the mongrelization of the white race." The groups pressing for desegregation, according to the Senator, ranged "from the blood red of the Communist Party to the almost equally red of the National Council of

Churches of Christ in the U.S.A." "The drive for racial amalgation," he added, "is both illegal and immoral, and those who would mix little children of both races are following an illegal, immoral, and sinful doctrine."[14]

The senator's deepest fears revolved around school desegregation, but his vigilant defense of segregation extended to all breaches of racial etiquette, however small. To Eastland, any attempt to force an adjustment of the racial status quo—including something as minor as a change in bus seating arrangements—represented a threat to the entire Jim Crow system. Thus, he could not sit idly by while the MIA challenged the power and wisdom of white Montgomerians. As a leading advocate of the Citizens' Councils' economic pressure tactics, he was incensed by the boycotters' attempt to turn the tables on white segregationists. His interest in Alabama was heightened by the militant opposition to Autherine Lucy's admission to the state university, which he viewed as a watershed event, and by the Alabama legislature's consideration of an interposition resolution, which he heartily endorsed. Thus, when Sam Engelhardt invited him to be the featured speaker at a "monster" Citizens' Council rally in Montgomery on February 10, he was delighted.

With Eastland on the program, the organizers had no trouble filling the 15,000-seat state agricultural coliseum. But the senator's actual performance fell far short of their expectations. Although he excited the crowd, which included the entire Montgomery city commission, with a brief diatribe against the MIA and the NAACP, most of his speech was a dry exposition of the constitutional doctrine of interposition. This was disappointing to much of the crowd, which had expected an old-fashioned, hammer-and-tongs depiction of the evils of integration. Sensing the audience's restlessness, Eastland offered a few ad lib comments on outside agitators and cut six pages from his prepared text. But it was too late to rekindle the crowd's enthusiasm. By the time he left the podium a significant portion of the audience had already drifted out of the stadium. To some extent, the sense of disappointment was mutual. If the crowd went away with less than it came for, Eastland got more than he bargained for. The tone of the meeting was simply too close to that of a Klan rally. As rabid as he was, Eastland was still a United States senator; while he shared the crowd's anger, he was not sure he wanted to be associated with some of the literature that was circulating through the stadium. One handbill, entitled "A Preview of the Declaration of Segregation" parodied the preamble to the United States Constitution:

When in the course of human events it becomes necessary to abolish the Negro race, proper methods should be used, among these are guns, bows and arrows, sling shots and knives. We hold these truths to be self-evident: that all whites are created equal with certain rights, among these are life, liberty, and the pursuit of dead niggers. In every stage of the bus boycott, we have been oppressed and degraded because of the juicy, unbearably stinking niggers. Their conduct should be dwelt upon because behind them they have an ancestral background of pygmies, head hunters, and snot suckers. My friends, it is time we woke up to these black devils. I tell you they are a group of two-legged agitators who persist in walking up and down our streets protruding their black lips. If we don't stop them African flesh-eaters, we will soon wake up and find Rev. King in the White House.[15]

Reprinted in the *Chicago Defender* and other black newspapers, this particular piece of racist propaganda affected Eastland's image for the remainder of his career. To the senator's dismay, his appearance at the infamous Montgomery rally undercut his periodic attempts to portray himself as a reasoned defender of liberty and states' rights. It also may have taught him a lesson. In the aftermath of the Montgomery rally, he became more selective in his choice of speaking engagements. Although he continued to speak out against the bus boycott and other racial heresies, he did not return to Montgomery for several years.

EASTLAND'S AGGRESSIVE OPPOSITION TO the boycott, though standard fare on the Deep South stump, was unrepresentative of the region's national leadership. Even the most bellicose white supremacists—men like Senators Strom Thurmond of South Carolina, Herman Talmadge of Georgia, and Harry Flood Byrd of Virginia—said very little about the boycott in the halls of Congress. Although the vast majority of the South's representatives in Washington undoubtedly opposed the boycott, public invective was kept to a minimum—and with good reason. Aggressive race-baiting was politically profitable in the South, where thumping the Yankees and the NAACP was an easy game. But it was a different story in Washington. At the national level the fate of the segregationist cause depended on the continued support of Northern moderates and conservatives, politicians who responded more favorably to a reasoned defense of tradition than to the old-style Dixie demagoguery. In the decade following World War II, even the most extreme segregationists in Washington learned to cloak their racist appeals with the language of moderation. In many cases this meant that they either toned down their rhetoric or kept their real views to themselves, at least while they were in the nation's capital.[16]

Changing proprieties complicated all aspects of the political defense of segregation, but Southern politicians found it especially difficult to deal with the situation in Montgomery. Despite a virtual consensus that the bus boycott was an ill-advised attack on the "Southern way of life," for a variety of reasons most segregationist politicians in Washington chose to remain silent on the matter. For many the simple justice of the boycotters' demands was disarming. Although segregationists generally portrayed the Jim Crow system as an immutable and all-encompassing system of social order, privately many must have realized that keeping blacks in the back of the bus was less important than maintaining segregated schools. Following the logic of what Gunnar Myrdal called the "rank order of discrimination," Southern politicians were preoccupied with the school desegregation issue, which provoked fear of interracial dating and miscegenation. In the early weeks of the boycott, prior to the mass indictment of late February, this approach seemed reasonable, since no one at that point expected the Montgomery bus controversy to amount to much. Who had time to worry about a fleeting protest in Montgomery when the wall of school segregation was about to be breached? This preoccupation with the school issue was critical, because by the time they recognized the significance of the bus boycott it was too late. To the segregationists' dismay, the national media had already conceded the high moral ground to the boycotters. Most importantly, as an international cause heavily invested with moral and religious symbolism, the boycott made a poor target for segregationists in search of political capital. If Southern politicians were going to win the Northern moderates to their side, they were not going to do it by attacking ministers and old ladies walking to work. The segregationists of Montgomery were already committed to this self-defeating strategy, but regional leaders were understandably reluctant to follow suit.[17]

A somewhat different calculus prevailed among Northern Democrats, but the result was the same. With few exceptions, they simply ignored the unexpected events in Montgomery. Even though their racial attitudes tended to be far more liberal than the views of their Southern counterparts, Northern

Democratic leaders were generally wary of civil rights agitation. While they were willing to endorse civil rights in the abstract, any real movement towards racial equality made them extremely nervous. Most publicly endorsed the *Brown* decision, but few were in a hurry to see it enforced. The range of opinion among Northern Democratic leaders was obviously broad, from conservatives who still accepted the conventional wisdom that Southern blacks regarded racial separation as natural and reasonable, to genuine liberals who knew better. But nearly everyone agreed that pressing for immediate desegregation was out of the question. Whatever their views, Northern Democrats plotted a middle course that involved a minimum of political risk.

The political whipsaw of regional and racial politics was most apparent when Democratic Party leaders tried to dance around the school desegregation issue. But a similar ambivalence characterized their response to the bus boycott. Indeed, in the case of the boycott their ambivalence was heightened by a perceived disjunction of means and ends. On the one hand, most Northern Democrats considered the boycotters' substantive demands to be eminently reasonable. Racially integrated transportation was an accepted fact of life in the North, where only 24 percent of the white respondents in an April 1956 Roper poll favored "separate sections for Negroes in streetcars and buses."[18] On the other hand, many Democratic leaders were reluctant to endorse a form of protest that might lead to civil disorder, or that might make the United States look bad in the eyes of the world. While their sense of fair play produced genuine sympathy for the aims of the Montgomery protest, their commitment to Cold War politics told them to keep the boycott at arm's length. Faced with this dilemma, most chose to remain silent, at least during the early stages of the boycott. During the summer and fall of 1956, when it was clear that aggressive segregationists posed a greater threat to the nation's image abroad than nonviolent black pedestrians, some of the Party's more liberal leaders offered the boycotters a few words of encouragement. But even then there was no rush to embrace the boycotters' cause.[19]

THE NORTHERN DEMOCRATS' FAILURE to speak out on behalf of the boycotters stemmed from a variety of sources, some ideological and some political. However, many were simply following the lead of Adlai Stevenson of Illinois, who was widely regarded as the frontrunner for the 1956 Democratic presidential nomination even though he had already lost one bid for the White House. As governor of Illinois from 1948 to 1952, Stevenson compiled an impressive civil rights record, desegregating the state parks system and the Illinois National Guard, leading the fight for a state FEPC, and protecting black citizens following an anti-desegregation riot in Cicero in 1951. However, since his 1952 defeat, he had grown increasingly cautious in his dealings with the civil rights issue—and with good reason. Even though he had tried to downplay civil rights during the 1952 campaign, his support for the FEPC and the desegregation of the military had given him a clear advantage over General Eisenhower among black voters. To the dismay of black leaders, the general was strongly opposed to the FEPC; moreover, many blacks were troubled by his inconclusive response to President Harry Truman's charges that he had actively opposed military desegregation in the late 1940s. By the end of the campaign Stevenson had earned the endorsement, albeit lukewarm, of most of the black press, and on election day he won three-fourths of the black vote, a slightly higher percentage than Truman had won in 1948. In at least two states—Louisiana and South Carolina—black support represented the margin of victory for the Stevenson ticket. Nevertheless, Stevenson's overall showing was poor, especially among white voters in the South. Even with Senator John Sparkman of Alabama as his running mate, he lost seven border and upper South states—Delaware, Maryland, Missouri, Florida, Tennessee, Texas, and Virginia—and barely held on to the rest of the region.[20]

For Stevenson and the rest of the Democratic leadership, the political lesson of the 1952 campaign was clear: if Stevenson was to have any hope of defeating Eisenhower in 1956, he would have to mend his political fences south of the Mason-Dixon line. Following the *Brown* decisions of 1954 and 1955, catering to the Democratic Party's Southern wing became more complicated but no less essential. Coupled with the Dixiecrat movement of 1948 and Eisenhower's strong showing in 1952, the rise of massive resistance had dispelled the mystique of the Solid South. As long as there was a realistic threat of a second Dixiecrat revolt, Northern Democrats like Stevenson had little room to maneuver. Thus, despite the widespread suspicion that Stevenson was personally liberal on matters of race, few observers expected him to stick his neck out on the civil rights issue.

Whatever his private feelings, Stevenson's avowed strategy was "to keep civil rights out of the presidential campaign in 1956." And for the most part he was successful. During the winter and spring of 1956, he said as little as possible about the desegregation crisis in the South. And what he did say left many of the blacks and white liberals who had voted for him in 1952 disappointed and confused. After Stevenson delivered a particularly disappointing speech in Los Angeles in early February—he told a predominantly black audience that he would not use federal troops to enforce the *Brown* decision and that he was determined to "proceed gradually, not upsetting habits or traditions that are older than the Republic"—Roy Wilkins concluded that his former ally had "all but capitulated to the go-slow boys." Wilkins eventually became so disgusted with Stevenson's defense of gradualism and states rights that he threw his support to Eisenhower, and at one point his criticism of the Democratic standard-bearer was so severe that former First Lady Eleanor Roosevelt, a close friend of Stevenson's, threatened to resign from the national board of the NAACP.[21]

Through it all, Stevenson said next to nothing about the bus boycott in Montgomery. Despite repeated promptings from reporters, he refused to take sides. Like everyone else, he condemned the bombing of black homes, but as for the rest of it he hoped the locals could work out their problems without outside interference. In late February, following the mass indictment of boycott leaders, he temporarily abandoned his hands-off recommendation, admonishing President Eisenhower for failing to act as a mediator in the crisis. But even then he refused to endorse the boycott or to say anything that might be construed as a deviation from gradualism. Hiding behind the shibboleths of tradition and moderation, he made sure that his Southern flank was covered. If he felt in his heart that the boycotters' cause was just, he kept it to himself.[22]

Convinced that a renewed Dixiecrat revolt would doom the Party's bid to recapture the White House, national Democratic leaders cooperated with Stevenson's strategy of noninvolvement in the Alabama civil rights crisis. In the upper echelons of the Party, almost no one broke ranks. Aside from Eleanor Roosevelt, only two nationally prominent Democrats—Representatives Adam Clayton Powell Jr. and Charles Diggs Jr.—championed the boycotters' cause. Both were black.

For Powell, the flamboyant congressman from Harlem, the connection with a religiously inspired mass movement was a natural. The son of a legendary black preacher, he had succeeded his father as pastor of the Abyssinian Baptist Church in 1937, at the age of 29. With a membership of more than 10,000,

Abyssinian was the largest Protestant congregation in the United States in the mid-1950s. The Abyssinian congregation provided Powell with a powerful political base, which catapulted him onto the New York city council in 1941, making him the first black councilman in the city's history. Elected to Congress in 1944, he quickly gained a reputation as a political maverick and a mercurial personality. Despite repeated charges of financial fraud and a series of romantic escapades and international junkets which earned him the title of "playboy pastor," he became the nation's most powerful black politician. Much of this power was wasted on self-indulgent diversions, but when Powell decided to focus on an issue he could be a formidable advocate. More than any other member of Congress, he pressed the Truman and Eisenhower administrations to expand the federal government's commitment to civil rights. Dissatisfied with the pace of desegregation and critical of both major parties, he targeted discrimination at military installations and veterans' hospitals, and in April 1955 he led a movement to attach an anti-segregation rider (later known as the Powell Amendment) to the Eisenhower administration's school construction bill. A month later he offered an amendment to the National Reserve Training Program Bill that banned "enlistments in, and transfers to" segregated National Guard units. Neither amendment became law, but his willingness to work with the leadership of the NAACP and his strenuous efforts to force the Eisenhower administration to honor its professed commitment to racial equality greatly enhanced his stature as a civil rights leader.[23]

The introduction of the Powell Amendment, which would have prohibited the use of federal funds for the construction of segregated schools, reflected Powell's conviction that economic leverage was an important weapon in the struggle for civil rights. Following in the footsteps of his father, who led a "Don't buy where you can't work" movement in Harlem in the 1930s, he had been a leading advocate of strikes and boycotts throughout his political career. During the summer and fall of 1955, he repeatedly urged Southern blacks to consider the tactic of economic boycott and offered "to lead a boycott of communities which refuse to integrate." Such urgings received a lot of play in the black press and may even have had some influence on the decision to boycott the buses in Montgomery. In November, less than a month before the arrest of Rosa Parks, Powell discussed the boycott issue while in Montgomery to participate in a voter registration drive. At one point in his speech he turned his attention to the plight of the black community in nearby Selma, where the White Citizens' Councils were using economic pressure to forestall school desegregation. According to Powell, the best response to this kind of pressure was to fight fire with fire, to refuse to patronize pro-segregation businesses. A few days later he repeated this advice during a stirring speech at the 16th Street Baptist Church in Birmingham. There was not "a single business in Birmingham," he told the crowd, "that Negroes couldn't put out of business if they stopped buying from it."[24]

During the first two months of the bus boycott, Powell limited his involvement to a few words of encouragement. But following the mass indictment of late February, he stepped forward as the self-appointed national spokesperson for the Montgomery Improvement Association. On February 24, three days after the indictment, he called for a "National Deliverance Day of Prayer" and a one-hour work stoppage for all black workers and school children. To bring attention to the boycotters' plight, March 28 would be set aside as a day of prayer and righteous solidarity. Hinting that this one-day protest might grow into a "national Mahatma Gandhi-type movement," with "prolonged national work stoppages and mass fastings by the nation's Negroes," Powell served notice that he and other black leaders would not rest until equal justice came to Montgomery. The original plan, conceived by two of Powell's political lieutenants, Dr. George Cannon and New York City Councilman McDougall, called for a simple day of prayer. But during a televised news conference, the impulsive Powell could not resist adding the call for a national work stoppage. After a weekend of consultation with Cannon, McDougall, and others, Powell changed his mind and publicly stated that "we are interested in prayer only." But the implied threat in his original statement reverberated in the Southern press for weeks.[25]

Powell's announcement got everyone's attention, including the leaders of the boycott, who had no prior knowledge of his plans. Not surprisingly, this arrogation of responsibility troubled some MIA leaders, who regarded his involvement as a mixed blessing. While they appreciated the moral support and the financial resources that his public statements helped to generate, they were never quite sure what he was going to do next. Although Powell was in periodic contact with boycott leaders, he clearly had his own agenda; moreover, he was a Northerner who had only a vague sense of what the boycotters were up against. In fact, during his visit to Montgomery the previous fall he had demonstrated just how little he knew about the realities of Southern life.

Invited to participate in Operation 5000—a voter registration drive dedicated to enrolling 5,000 additional black voters in Montgomery County—Powell turned his visit into a tragicomic sideshow that all but destroyed the political career of Governor Folsom.

Folsom's undoing began innocently enough. While Powell's plane was en route to Montgomery's Maxwell Field on November 3, Folsom's chauffeur, Winston Craig, informed his boss that a group of angry Klansmen was planning to picket the airport. Hoping to avoid an ugly incident, Folsom ordered Craig to whisk Powell away from the scene in the governor's limousine. The diversion worked, and within minutes of his arrival an amazed Powell was sitting in an easy chair drinking scotch with the governor. After exchanging pleasantries, the two men launched into a surprisingly amicable discussion of the prospects for change in Alabama race relations. Craig then drove the congressman to a speaking engagement at Alabama State Teachers College. Seeing the governor's limousine at a black voter registration drive was undoubtedly a shock for the black Montgomerians attending the rally, but what came next was truly amazing. Before delivering his prepared remarks, Powell publicly thanked Folsom for his gracious hospitality. Straining to keep a straight face, he told the crowd that the governor had offered him a scotch and soda, plus some encouraging words on the prospects for racial equality. "Integration in Alabama is not only inevitable," Folsom had told him, it "is already here." All of this was shocking enough, but Powell went on to imply that Folsom had given his blessing to the struggle for civil rights. The next day, before flying back to New York, he told the same story to a group of white news reporters. The resulting press coverage sent shock waves across the state. Leaders of the White Citizens' Councils and other militant segregationists called for the governor's impeachment, and even political moderates wondered out loud about his sanity.

In response, Folsom desperately tried to explain his way out of the situation. At first, he insisted that there had been no breach of racial etiquette. He had sent the limousine to the airport because it was the only car driven by a black chauffeur; he had entertained Powell in an official receiving room and not in the private quarters of the governor's mansion; following Southern custom, Powell had entered the mansion through the back door and had spent more time with Winston Craig than with him; the statement that he had offered Powell a drink of scotch was a lie; and so on. He also emphatically denied that he had endorsed racial integration or that he had admitted that integration was already a reality in Alabama. All he had said was that integration was taking place in other parts of the nation. When none of this worked, he switched to an alternate explanation for his behavior: he had met with Powell as a matter of protocol—"I have always made it a practice to extend the hospitality of the State to visiting governors, congressmen, and senators. Their title deserves that courtesy regardless of . . . what race they might be."—and because he wanted to convince Powell that filing a lawsuit on behalf of desegregation was counterproductive and futile in Alabama. In the end, none of these explanations had much effect, leaving Folsom to conclude that "Adam Clayton Powell is one son of a bitch I wish I'd never seen." By speaking out as he did, Powell signed Folsom's political death warrant—a development that seriously weakened the forces of moderation in Alabama politics.[26]

Despite this damaging indiscretion and other self-serving antics, Powell proved useful to the boycotters on several occasions. In March, he got the Eisenhower administration's attention—something the boycotters themselves had not been able to do—by following through with his National Deliverance Day of Prayer. On the designated day, Wednesday, March 28, more than 1,000 churches across the nation held prayer vigils and other observances honoring the courage and determination of the bus boycotters. In several Northern cities the response was well beyond the organizers' expectations. In Chicago alone, an estimated 28,000 people attended prayer meetings, mostly in black Baptist churches. In Boston, 800 sympathizers, many of whom were white, jammed into the historic Old North Church to hear Episcopal Bishop Herman B. Nash call for greater racial tolerance everywhere. "The guilty are not only 'they'," he proclaimed, "but also 'we.'" In New York City, Congressman Powell himself spoke to an interracial audience of 3,500 at the Manhattan Center and later to an overflow crowd of 500 in the ballroom of the Hotel New Yorker. He was joined by boycott leader E. D. Nixon, who told the crowd: "We are tired of riding the buses . . . whether we are going to live to see the next day, or whether we are going to go to jail, we are not going to ride the buses!" Prayer meetings in several cities featured speeches by boycott leaders, including the Reverend Ralph Abernathy, who spoke to a crowd of 10,000 in Los Angeles, and the Reverend Ralph Waldo Hilson, the pastor of Montgomery's St. John's AME Church, who led an emotional gathering at Yale University's Woolsey Hall.

Despite the religious tone of the observances, several labor unions co-sponsored prayer day activities, and in at least two states the day of prayer received official governmental endorsement. In Massachusetts the state legislature suspended its activities for an hour to express its "sympathy" with the boycott, and in California Governor Goodwin J. Knight proclaimed a statewide day of prayer. Of course, not all individuals in positions of authority were so supportive. In Chino, California, nine black employees of the Pacific Airmotive Corporation were fired when they left their jobs for an hour of prayer. And in Bayonne, New Jersey, civilian employees at the Naval Supply Depot were forced to hold their prayer meeting at a local YMCA after Navy officials, concerned about the "political implications" of Deliverance Day, barred them from the Depot's chapel. This official recalcitrance was discouraging, but the rarity of such episodes only served to confirm that the plight of the boycotters had captured the imagination of a large number of Americans. To Powell, and to the boycotters themselves, the overall results of Deliverance Day could hardly have been more encouraging. In addition to its financial impact—the total amount of contributions collected at Deliverance Day observances probably exceeded $100,000—Deliverance Day reinforced the image of the boycott as a nonviolent, religious movement and reminded everyone in Montgomery, boycotters and segregationists alike, that the outside world was watching. Most important, when thousands of ordinary Americans, many of whom had no previous involvement in the struggle for civil rights, stopped to pray for "deliverance from the evils of race prejudice," the process of building a national civil rights movement took a small but significant step forward.[27]

Both before and during the Deliverance Day celebration, Powell hinted that March 28 was only the beginning, that he was prepared to lead a series of Gandhi-like prayer meetings. But, as was so often the case in his career, he failed to follow through. In fact, once the publicity surrounding Deliverance Day died down, he seemed to lose interest in what was happening in Montgomery. Preoccupied with personal affairs and the presidential election, which he hoped to influence as the self-appointed boss of the black vote, Powell had little involvement in the boycott from early April on. Although he was a featured speaker at a massive May 24 rally at Madison Square Garden, his blatant attempt to steal the limelight from Martin Luther King Jr. and Autherine Lucy infuriated A. Philip Randolph, Bayard Rustin, and other rally organizers. Although at least half of the 16,000 people in the hall were members of Powell's Abyssinian congregation, he arrived conspicuously late with a carefully staged interruption of another speaker's remarks. As one of his biographers described the scene:

> . . . the Garden lights clicked off. Slight tremors, a nervousness, ran through the crowd. All of a sudden a spotlight came on and zoomed to the back of the Garden, to land on a tall figure standing alone: Adam Powell. The Garden erupted; his Abyssinians erupted. And he stood there, still; then he began walking, cutting a swath right down the middle of the Garden, the spotlight trailing every step of the way. Chants exploded: "We want Adam," "We want Adam." Adam Clayton Powell, in the flesh, wanted King and Rustin and the others to remember: his New York City, his Garden.[28]

The speech that followed was a stemwinder—and a first-class filibuster. Stirred by the enthusiasm of his Abyssinian parishioners and others caught up in the emotion of his words, Powell went on and on, eventually prompting Bayard Rustin to send a note to the lectern reminding the long-winded congressman that they had to leave the hall by 10:30 and that Eleanor Roosevelt had yet to speak. Unmoved, Powell chided the organizers for spoiling the moment:

> I have a note here handed me by Bayard Rustin, anyone know who he is? And he says we have to be out of here by ten-thirty. Has this Bayard Rustin never heard about freedom? The only reason we would have to leave here is because we would have to pay more money to stay. Everybody in here who is in favor of paying for our freedom raise your hands. You must pay for freedom. And if we want to stay here until noon tomorrow we will stay, and we will speak to this nation, and we will let them know that we will pay for our freedom. But Mr. Randolph, you need not worry, Abyssinian Baptist Church will pick up the check!

Predictably, Powell later reneged on his promise, leaving Randolph and the organizing committee to pay the $6,000 surcharge.[29]

THE ONLY OTHER NATIONAL politician to embrace the boycotters' cause as his own was Charles C. Diggs Jr., a 33-year-old black Congressman from Detroit. A first-term Democrat from a predominantly black district, Diggs was a political neophyte trying to make the transition from entrepreneurship to congressional politics. The son of a politically prominent black businessman—his father served several terms in the Michigan state senate—he was the vice president of the House of Diggs, Inc., a small empire of family businesses that included Michigan's largest funeral home and a popular Detroit radio station. In Detroit, he and his father were living symbols of the black community's economic clout, so no one was surprised when he became a vocal supporter of the bus boycott. He enthusiastically endorsed Powell's call for a National Deliverance Day of Prayer and even suggested that the day could be used to spur black voter registration. On March 28, "Negroes who are eligible should go to their respective city halls, in those communities where they are permitted, and register to vote," Diggs insisted, "In those communities where they are not permitted to vote, they should be urged to take time to fill out an application for membership with the NAACP, or if they are already members, they should contribute at least one dollar to a special fund to help finance the fight against these latest uprisings." From mid-February on, he worked closely with the NAACP and the local Baptist ministers' conference in their joint effort to raise funds for the MIA. By early March, his radio station was broadcasting daily appeals for contributions to an MIA defense fund, and on March 17 he announced that he and his attorney, Basil Browne, were flying to Montgomery to deliver $5,000 in contributions and to attend the trial of the Reverend Martin Luther King, who had been selected to be the first of the boycotters tried as a result of the mass indictment.[30]

As the only prominent politician to attend the King trial, Diggs drew considerable attention from the national and international press, particularly after a minor incident involving Basil Browne's seating arrangements momentarily disrupted the first day of the trial. When the light-skinned Browne tried to take a seat next to his employer, the bailiff directed him to the whites-only section of the courtroom. Once Diggs identified his attorney as a Negro, Browne was allowed to sit in the black section. But the episode added a touch of irony to an already bizarre proceeding. Diggs remained in Montgomery for several days, meeting with MIA leaders and generally enjoying his newfound notoriety. All of this was more than a little upsetting to local segregationists, many of whom had difficulty fathoming the concept of a black congressman. Although he was soft-spoken and polite, his words were only slightly more palatable than the bombast of Adam Clayton

Powell. "We're not trying to shove anything down anyone's throat," he told a *Montgomery Advertiser* reporter, "But segregation is an evil which must be ended. We have some segregation in the North, but two wrongs don't make the South right." As long as the evil of segregation persisted in Montgomery, Diggs vowed, he would continue to speak out against it—a promise that he did his best to honor after returning to Detroit.[31]

POWELL AND DIGGS WERE obviously eager to identify with the movement in Montgomery, but this was not the case with William Dawson, the third black member of Congress. Throughout the boycott, Dawson shunned any association with the MIA. A powerful politician who had represented the southside of Chicago in Congress since 1945, Dawson was in a position to help the boycotters politically as well as financially. But he showed no inclination to do so. When Martin Luther King and Ralph Abernathy visited Chicago in April 1956, Dawson's name was conspicuously absent from the list of welcoming dignitaries. As a tough-minded conservative with close ties to Mayor Richard Daley, he had little interest in civil rights agitation, especially when it involved people who lived 700 miles from Chicago. Not everyone connected with the Daley machine shared Dawson's disdain for the boycott. State Senator Fred J. Smith, an influential black Democrat who had represented Chicago's Third District since 1942, was an enthusiastic supporter. "Fair minded men and women everywhere are with you," he wrote Ralph Abernathy in early March 1956, "for none can deny that the cause for which you fight is a Just cause." But in the world of Chicago politics Dawson's attitude was closer to the norm than Smith's.[32]

THE BOYCOTTERS NEVER EXPECTED much from Stevenson and the Democrats. But they had somewhat higher expectations of the Eisenhower administration. Relying on the federal government was not part of the MIA's strategy, at least in the early going, and no one expected the president to go out of his way to identify with the boycotters' cause. Indeed, even Eisenhower's strongest supporters in the black community acknowledged that the native Texan was something less than a crusading civil rights advocate. However, once the bus boycott became a cause, many blacks anticipated a measure of moral and legal support from an administration that had officially endorsed the gradual desegregation of American life.

Despite lingering doubts about the president's personal commitment to racial equality, most blacks believed that the nation had made significant progress in the area of civil rights during the Eisenhower administration's first three years in power. The *Brown* decision had occurred on the Republicans' watch, thanks in part to the president's appointment of Chief Justice Earl Warren; President Eisenhower had appointed more black officials than any previous president; the Justice Department, under Attorney General Herbert Brownell, and the President's Committee on Government Contracts, led by Vice President Richard Nixon, had made a vigorous effort to end discrimination in public accommodations and employment within the District of Columbia; and the administration had extended the desegregation of the military, most notably in base schools and Navy shipyards. Critics of the administration's record pointed out the obvious: that Eisenhower's commitment to enforce the *Brown* decision was still in doubt; that the president and his advisors had stymied congressional efforts to reinstate the FEPC; that he had failed to issue an unqualified endorsement of school desegregation, fair employment practices, or civil rights in general; and that he had been conspicuously silent on the dangers of massive resistance and white supremacist violence. But for most black Americans these disappointments were overshadowed by the administration's record of accomplishment. Although most of them had voted for Stevenson in 1952, in the immediate post-*Brown* era they were reluctant to give up on an administration that, despite a mixed record, held more promise in the field of civil rights than any previous administration.[33]

In the year following *Brown*, Eisenhower drew high praise from several civil rights leaders, including Walter White, the executive director of the NAACP. Nevertheless, by the summer of 1955 it was becoming increasingly apparent that the administration had failed to keep pace with the rising expectations of the post-*Brown* era. Indeed, by the time the boycott began in December, many civil rights advocates had grown apprehensive about the administration's plans and were no longer willing to give the president the benefit of the doubt. The president's vague interpretation of the *Brown* II dictum "with all deliberate speed" and his failure to speak out against the White Citizens' Councils were unsettling. But for many blacks the most alarming development was the administration's silence following the "wolf-whistle" murder of 14-year-old Emmett Till in Money, Mississippi, in August 1955. Ignoring the public outrage over the murderers' acquittal, the administration made no effort to reassure black Americans that the federal government would protect them from racist terrorism. As Roy Wilkins complained to Val Washington, the black director of minorities for the Republican National Committee, if the administration "had made a move and been rebuffed it could have collected some kudos for effort. But it said nothing and did nothing."[34]

Black Americans were still waiting for an expression of concern when the president suffered a serious heart attack on September 24. For the next three months, Eisenhower was out of the loop, but during his absence black leaders continued to press the administration for a forthright statement or action that would relieve the anxieties unleashed by the Till case. In early November, black leaders were encouraged by the Justice Department's refusal to endorse the extradition of the Reverend J. A. Delaine from New York City to Clarendon County, South Carolina. Delaine, the legendary black activist who sponsored the Clarendon County school desegregation suit in 1948, had fled to New York after the local sheriff accused him of firing at a passing car from his parsonage. According to Delaine, the sheriff was part of a Ku Klux Klan group that had threatened to kill him and his wife, a charge that eventually convinced New York Governor Averill Harriman to deny South Carolina's extradition request. The Eisenhower administration also received praise for the November 26 Interstate Commerce Commission decision that endorsed the desegregation of interstate travel on trains and buses, and in public waiting rooms. Nevertheless, the continued silence on the Till case, coupled with the slow pace of school desegregation, kept most black Americans in a state of unease about the administration's intentions.[35]

The degree of unease would have been even greater if blacks had been privy to the inner workings of the administration. Throughout the fall and early winter of 1955, while President Eisenhower recuperated in Colorado and Pennsylvania, the widespread fear that Vice President Nixon was positioning himself for the 1956 presidential nomination triggered a fierce power struggle within the administration. This struggle, which pitted Nixon against a faction led by Secretary of State John Foster Dulles, was more personal than ideological, but it often spilled over into policy issues. On the issue of civil rights the alignment was hopelessly confusing, which undoubtedly contributed to the administration's near paralysis on racial matters during the final weeks of 1955. Nixon, the "conservative" candidate of the Republican Right, was actually moderate to liberal on the race issue, while his "moderate" opponents, with the exception of press secretary James Hagerty, were staunchly conservative when it came to civil rights. None of the administration's cabinet-level officials was a consistent advocate of civil rights, but several cabinet members, including Attorney General Herbert Brownell, were generally favorable to gradual desegregation. Of course, even those who had strong feelings about desegregation were determined to protect the administration's moderate image. To moderates and conservatives alike, civil rights was above all else a political issue, to be handled sensitively and dispassionately. In the political calculus of Eisenhower Republicanism, there was no allowance for moral fervor on either side of the segregation question, and certainly no sentimental risk-taking on behalf of minorities.[36]

DESPITE THIS SUPERFICIAL CONSENSUS, a few voices within the administration were calling for a more passionate commitment to civil rights. The most influential racial liberal in the administration was Maxwell Rabb, a Boston-born Jewish lawyer and former campaign aide to Senator Henry Cabot Lodge Jr. Although Rabb's duties as secretary of the cabinet took up most of his time, he also served as the administration's unofficial adviser on minority affairs. He was the chief liaison between the cabinet and the administration's black appointees, and, other than Brownell, he was the only high-ranking official to keep close tabs on what was happening in the South. Unfortunately, he had no direct experience with race relations in the Deep South. Moreover, his approach to civil rights was narrowly legalistic, a limitation that would have important consequences when the administration addressed the racial crisis in Alabama. Even Rabb was careful to couch his civil rights advocacy in politically palatable terms; when he did stray from the moderate path, it was usually in response to a plea from one of the administration's two-dozen black officials.[37]

Rabb's role was critical, because none of the black appointees held a high-level position with direct access to the president. When they were dissatisfied with the administration's civil rights policies, their only recourse was to funnel suggestions through Rabb's office. Despite Rabb's good intentions, this system proved to be cumbersome, and in the end black officials had few opportunities to influence the president and his cabinet. Although Republican leaders claimed otherwise, this isolation was largely a matter of design. Several black officials held diplomatic posts and were far removed from the scene of domestic policymaking, but even those holding domestic appointments in Washington were isolated from the channels of power. As historian Robert Burk has noted, "the nature of the positions given to blacks in the executive branch clearly reflected the belief of high-ranking officials that the value of black government employees lay in their presence as symbols of national racial democracy rather than in their usefulness as policy makers."[38]

Only three black officials were able to break through this wall of enforced silence on a regular basis: E. Frederic Morrow, a special projects administrator on the White House staff; J. Ernest Wilkins, an assistant secretary of Labor; and Val Washington, the director of minorities for the Republican National Committee. Of these, Morrow was the most persistent and the most influential, though by the end of the Eisenhower years he was also the most frustrated. The son of a prominent Methodist minister and the grandson of North Carolina slaves, Morrow grew up in a middle-class household in Hackensack, New Jersey, where he attended integrated schools. A 1930 graduate of Bowdoin College, where he was one of only two black students, Morrow worked as a writer for the Urban League publication *Opportunity* in the mid-1930s. He later spent several years as a field secretary and fundraiser for the NAACP. During World War II, he successfully challenged a discriminatory ruling that had barred him from the Army's Officers' Candidate School, and after the war he earned a law degree at Rutgers University. In 1950 he took a position as a public affairs executive for the Columbia Broadcasting System, but in August 1952 he left CBS to become a Republican campaign consultant.

During the 1952 campaign, Morrow was promised a White House staff position, but after the election he was shunted off to the Department of Commerce where he served as an adviser on business affairs. In the summer of 1955, he moved over to the White House staff, "the first Negro ever to be named to a presidential staff in an executive capacity." Orchestrated by chief of staff Sherman Adams, a rock-ribbed conservative who had little interest in civil rights, Morrow's appointment was a calculated attempt to shore up the administration's image among black voters. Predictably, during his tenure as a White House staffer Morrow suffered a series of slights and humiliations. Adams, though personally cordial, restricted Morrow's official role to ceremonial functions, resisting his frustrated aide's entreaties for a full-fledged adviser's position.[39]

Morrow's quiet demeanor and solid respectability made him a logical choice to represent the administration's low-key commitment to civil rights. As a self-styled black moderate and a lifelong Republican, he could be trusted to uphold the Party's commitment to gradualism and political circumspection. For the most part, Morrow fulfilled the role set out for him. However, both his moderation and his faith in the Grand Old Party would be sorely tested during his first year in the west wing of the White House. He could not understand why administration officials were afraid to speak out on the Till case, or why the president's staff was so timid in its dealings with the loud-mouthed segregationists of the Deep South. No one had ever accused him of being a rabble-rouser, but as 1955 drew to a close he felt he had to do something to shake his superiors' passivity.

On November 29, two days before the arrest of Rosa Parks, Morrow sent a lengthy memorandum to Rabb describing the "climate of fear and terrorism" created by the Till murder and the spread of the White Citizens' Councils. "There are visible indications that we are on the verge of a dangerous racial conflagration in the Southern section of the country," Morrow wrote, "The warning signs in the South are all too clear: the harrassed Negro is sullen, bitter, and talking strongly of retaliation whenever future situations dictate. . . . My mail has been heavy and angry, and wherever I go, people have expressed disappointment that no word has come from the White House deploring this situation." Morrow urged Rabb to convene a White House conference where senior administration officials such as Vice President Nixon and Sherman Adams could discuss the situation with "a dozen of the prominent Negro leaders in the country."[40]

Morrow also sent a copy of the memorandum to Roy Wilkins, who confirmed his alarming assessment of racial tensions. "The situation is fully as dangerous as you indicate," Wilkins wrote to Morrow on December 2, ". . . I might add that from a number of sources (some of which are not radical or irresponsible) the NAACP is being criticized for being 'too legal.' We are being told that the other side is stopping at nothing, while we proceed according to legal technicalities. Believe me, there is considerable support from hitherto fairly conservative areas of opinion for what may be termed a 'strike back' action, whether it is legal or not, or whether it is productive of anything except blind retaliation."[41]

Few members of the Eisenhower administration shared Morrow's sense of alarm, but there was a growing realization that the administration needed to revamp its image, if not its actual policies, on civil rights. Foremost among the would-be reformers was Attorney General Herbert Brownell, who presented a series of recommendations at a December 2 cabinet meeting. With Vice President Nixon presiding—the president was still recuperating in Colorado—cabinet members engaged in an unusually frank discussion of the political implications of civil rights advocacy. Brownell's proposals for a bipartisan commission to investigate interracial violence in the South and the creation of a civil rights division within the Department of Justice received strong support from Vice President Nixon, but several conservative cabinet members, including Secretary of State John Foster Dulles, spoke out in opposition. Dulles, while lamenting the Till episode and other acts of white supremacist violence, saw no need for aggressive federal intervention in the South. Even Nixon's support for Brownell's proposals was couched exclusively in political terms; the moral outrage which Morrow hoped would propel the administration into a new era of civil rights activism was nowhere in evidence. To Morrow, the Republican Party's chance of winning a significant number of electoral votes in the 1956 presidential election was so poor that the administration might as well eschew political considerations and take a bold and principled stand on behalf of civil rights. But none of the party's top leaders agreed with him; no one else was willing to write off the white South just yet.[42]

Morrow tried to redirect the administration's attention to the black vote, to encourage the Republican Party to recapture its "noble beginning under Lincoln." But he was unable to counter the widespread suspicion within the administration that black voters would continue to vote for the Democratic Party no matter what the Republicans accomplished in the field of civil rights. At a December 7 luncheon, Sherman Adams, who was angry about a recent Gallup Poll that "showed the Democrats still running far ahead in the matter of Negro political support," sarcastically asked Morrow what miracles the Party would have to perform "in order to win the Negro vote."

In mid-December, Morrow responded with a lengthy memorandum. Despite what the Eisenhower administration had done on their behalf, Morrow explained, many blacks retained a strong sense of loyalty to the party that had come to their aid during the Great Depression. "It is the area of economics, job opportunities, etc.," he told Adams, "that have more interest to the Negro race than anything that will be or has been done in the field of civil rights." Nevertheless, the present crisis in the South had given the Republicans a golden opportunity to weaken the Democrats' hold over the black vote, an opportunity that to date the Republicans had squandered:

> In the past year, the Negro has been extremely concerned about the plight of his kinfolk in the Deep South, and particularly in Mississippi. Almost every Negro north of the Mason-Dixon line has relatives in the South, and whatever happens to them is reflected in the northern Negro's attitude toward those in power for what he feels is their failure to protect his defenseless kinfolk in the Deep South. The failure of any prominent member of the Administration to speak out against, and deplore, the present condition of terrorism and economic sanction against the Negroes in Mississippi is causing deep concern among Negro leaders in the country today. They feel that despite the magnificent record of the Eisenhower Administration, it has completely abandoned the Negro in the South and left him to the mercy of state governments that have manifested their intention to violate all laws, human and divine, as long as it results in "keeping the Negro in his place."[43]

Morrow's memorandum made no mention of the two-week old bus boycott in Montgomery; nor did the boycott come up during a special "civil rights" meeting held in Maxwell Rabb's office on December 19. At this unprecedented meeting, which included many of the administration's top black appointees—Morrow, Val Washington, J. Ernest Wilkins, Samuel Pierce, Joe Douglas, and Scovelle Richardson—a frustrated Rabb lamented his inability to convince the president's top advisors that a forthright statement reiterating the administration's commitment to civil rights was essential. Rabb felt that he was losing his struggle against the powerful White House insiders who were "utterly conservative on the matter of race," those who were unconvinced "that the Administration should do any more than it has done on this explosive topic."[44]

During the next two weeks, the racial conservatives who were counseling silence on civil rights issues continued to have the upper hand. But there was a glimmer of hope for civil rights advocates on January 5, when the president's State of the Union address not only affirmed the administration's commitment to civil rights but also acknowledged "that in some localities allegations persist that Negro citizens are being deprived of their right to vote and are likewise being subjected to unwarranted economic pressures." To the dismay of many white Southerners, Eisenhower went on to "recommend that the substance of these charges be thoroughly examined by a Bipartisan Commission created by the Congress." This was bold rhetoric for a man who had gone five months without uttering a public comment on civil rights, and many civil rights leaders continued to question the president's sincerity. But at least the long silence had been broken.[45]

BY LATE JANUARY, EISENHOWER was back in harness, meeting with his staff and holding weekly press conferences, but those who hoped that the returning president would now speak out forcefully on behalf of civil rights were soon disappointed. Indeed, those who had attributed the administration's recent lack of interest in civil rights to the president's absence were in for a rude shock. Despite the deepening crisis in Alabama and Mississippi, Eisenhower made little effort to reassure black Southerners that their basic rights would be protected, and whenever possible he dodged reporters' questions on the issue. On the rare occasions when he did address the desegregation issue, his responses were not what most civil rights advocates, including some members of his own administration, wanted to hear. For example, at the January 25 press conference, he ignored the advice of press secretary Hagerty and came out foursquare against the Powell Amendment to the school construction bill.[46] Two weeks later, at the February 8 press conference, civil rights leaders suffered another disappointment when he made no mention of the recent bombings in Montgomery and managed a less than inspiring response when asked about the University of Alabama's refusal to admit Autherine Lucy. Although the Justice Department was "already looking into" the situation, he saw no need for the federal government to intervene on Lucy's behalf:

> . . . while there has been an outbreak that all of us deplore, when there is
> a defiance of law, still the chancellor and the trustees, the local authorities,
> the student body and all the rest of them have not yet had an opportunity,
> I should think, to settle this thing as it ought to be settled. And I would
> certainly hope that we could avoid any interference with anybody else as
> long as that State, from its governor on down, will do its best to straighten
> it out.[47]

Following the February 8 press conference, Eisenhower retreated into three weeks of silence on civil rights. The White Citizens' Councils rally in Montgomery on February 10, the continued threats against Autherine Lucy, even the mass indictment of the boycott leaders on February 21 and the subsequent reaction by the press—nothing seemed to shake the administration's hands-off policy. Following the indictments, the White House was flooded with letters and telegrams expressing concern for the boycotters, but even this failed to move the president. "Is it proper to divide buses, the front for the white people and the rear for the colored people?" an 11-year-old girl from Passaic, New Jersey, plaintively asked the president in a handwritten note. "If children can understand the right and wrong of it, why can't adults? I respectfully urge you to use your high office to do something about correcting such abuses so that there will no longer be any racial discrimination." A civil service worker from White Plains, New York, expressed similar sentiments: "I don't think it is fair to make the Negroes sit in the back of busses . . . So what if their skin is brown? We should all treat each other like brothers. Please try to do something about the people who dislike the Negroes." In all likelihood, few, if any, of these messages ever reached Eisenhower's desk. But it probably didn't matter: during the week of the mass indictment, the president was busy playing golf with Jock Whitney at a segregated country club in Thomasville, Georgia. One message that did get through was a February 24 telegram from Congressman Adam Clayton Powell Jr., who implored the president to intervene on the indicted boycotters' behalf. But within hours presidential aide Bryce Harlow informed Powell that the Justice Department could find no basis for federal intervention.[48]

POWELL AND OTHER CIVIL rights advocates were dismayed by Eisenhower's apparent apathy and insensitivity. Only later did they discover that the administration's public passivity was somewhat misleading. From early February on, there was an increasing amount of behind-the-scenes federal activity, though it was not always the kind that civil rights advocates desired. Most notably, several special agents from the Mobile office of the Federal Bureau of Investigation were on the scene in Montgomery, quietly monitoring the activities of the MIA, the NAACP, and the White Citizens' Councils. The agents sent daily reports to FBI Director J. Edgar Hoover, who regarded Montgomery as a potential powder keg of interracial violence. One report, dated March 13, claimed that "the NAACP at Montgomery has proposed violence in connection with the bus boycott," and cited evidence that black enforcers had been ordered to "beat hell out of any Negroes riding a bus." And several others suggested that handgun sales were skyrocketing in Alabama, particularly among blacks. Later reports revealed that local gun and ammunition sales were almost flat, dispelling the rumor that Alabama blacks were arming for a race war. But Hoover and his agents remained skeptical of the boycotters' commitment to nonviolence. Assertive blacks had always made Hoover nervous, and nothing that he read in the dispatches from Montgomery made him feel otherwise. A firm believer in black inferiority, he had no confidence in the MIA's ability to keep the situation under control.[49]

From the beginning, Hoover was convinced that the boycotters were playing into the hands of Communist agitators who were secretly fanning the flames of racial discord. Accordingly, he ordered his agents to maintain close surveillance of any "outside agitators" or other known subversives, and predictably the agents found just enough "suspicious" activity to feed their boss's obsession. When Bayard Rustin, William Worthy, and several other "unsavory" characters arrived in Montgomery, the director's worst fears seemed to be confirmed. On March 3, one local informer told Special Agent Hallford that he had "heard persistent rumors that 'the Communists' are 'moving in on Montgomery' to take part in possible racial disturbances." There were also alarming reports that a correspondent for the *Daily Worker* was lurking around the boycott's leadership and that agents of the Socialist Workers' Party were busily recruiting Montgomery blacks. Much of this was relayed to the assistant chief of staff for Army Intelligence, and to the White House via Assistant Attorney General William Tompkins. These secondary FBI reports were pivotal in shaping the administration's understanding of the boycott, because, other than the military personnel at Maxwell and Gunter Air Force bases, the FBI represented the only significant federal presence in Montgomery. If J. Edgar Hoover and his agents in Alabama insisted that a dangerous mixture of militant blacks, angry whites, and subversive Reds posed a serious threat to civic order and national security, who in Washington could say otherwise?[50]

Fortunately for the boycotters, there was at least one Washington official who managed to look beyond the FBI's unsympathetic depiction of black protest. As director of the National Selective Service System, General Lewis

B. Hershey was a reluctant participant in the controversy surrounding the draft status of MIA attorney Fred Gray. Although the Indiana-born soldier was something less than a champion of civil rights, he resented Montgomery Circuit Solicitor W. F. Thetford's attempt to use the selective service system as a segregationist bludgeon. On February 5, at Thetford's request, the Montgomery draft board had revoked Gray's ministerial draft deferment; reclassifying him as 1-A, the board ordered him to report for duty. As a part-time minister ordained by the Church of Christ, Gray had received a 4-D deferment in 1954. But when his church hired a full-time minister in January 1956, the all-white draft board had all the pretext it needed, at least as far as state and local officials were concerned. According to Alabama's state selective service director James W. Jones, the decision to review Gray's draft status had nothing to do with his legal activities on behalf of the MIA and the NAACP. But General Hershey was not so sure. After Gray lost his appeal at the state level, Hershey refused to order an immediate induction and allowed Gray's federal level appeal to drag on into the summer. In August, the presidential appeals board rejected Gray's appeal, but to the surprise of many the president overruled the board's decision. Eisenhower's decision, which some observers attributed to Hershey's influence, infuriated Alabama segregationists, triggering a mass resignation from local draft boards across the state. Future governor George C. Wallace, who handled draft appeals as a circuit judge, also resigned in protest, prompting Senators Lister Hill and John Sparkman to call for a congressional investigation of the Gray case.[51]

For the boycotters, Hershey's refusal to cooperate with Alabama draft officials was the first hint of federal support. It was a modest gesture, which civil rights leaders did not know quite how to interpret, but it was a start. Perhaps the patient few who had given the Eisenhower administration the benefit of the doubt were correct after all; perhaps the silent president was doing all he could behind the scenes. In the tense period following the mass indictment, not all black leaders accepted this hopeful logic. And even those who did generally had few illusions about the president's commitment to civil rights; instead they pinned their hopes on the ability of Maxwell Rabb, Fred Morrow, and Val Washington to convince the president and the cabinet that civil rights advocacy was not only morally and legally sound but also good politics.

MORROW WAS THE KEY. Indeed, many civil rights leaders, including Roy

Wilkins, regarded the soft-spoken White House aide as their last best hope. As the highest-ranking black official in the administration, he was in the best position to inform the president about the realities of African American life. Morrow himself accepted this responsibility, even though he more than anyone knew the limitations of his designated role in the White House.

Like his white colleagues, Morrow was slow to recognize the significance of the Montgomery protest. As a lawyer and as an eminently respectable member of the Northeastern black bourgeoisie, he had limited experience with the power and emotion of black Christianity in the Deep South; and he knew even less about the strategy of nonviolent resistance. Nevertheless, having served as an NAACP field secretary in the 1930s, he knew enough about black America to realize that the mass indictment of ministers and other boycott leaders had created a volatile situation that required the administration's immediate attention. Thus, in late February he sprang into action.[52]

On February 24, Morrow traveled to New York to meet with Fred Friendly, the producer of *See It Now*, the popular but controversial CBS television series hosted by Edward R. Murrow.

Friendly wanted to do a show "depicting the highlights of the current racial tension in the South," but he was having difficulty convincing the network's top executives to approve the project. Conservative Republicans had complained bitterly about the muckraking "liberal" slant of several earlier *See It Now* broadcasts, including a memorable a show on the Red-baiting tactics of Senator Joseph McCarthy of Wisconsin and a documentary that cast a negative light on the Eisenhower administration's agricultural policies. Secretary of Agriculture Ezra Taft Benson's angry reaction to Murrow's treatment of the farm issue had left some CBS executives so gun-shy that they wanted the administration's blessing before going ahead with another potentially controversial project. Friendly planned to devote considerable attention to the bus boycott and had already dispatched a crew of photographers and interviewers to Montgomery.

According to his own account of the meeting, Morrow applauded the decision to focus on Montgomery: "I pointed out to Mr. Friendly that despite all the risks involved, I felt he and Mr. Murrow would be performing a great public and patriotic service if they could see fit to do this documentary. He promised to give it every consideration and said that if they do not do it currently, they would certainly do it later in the fall. I certainly hope something comes of this, because the country and the world are sorely in need of the unvarnished truth!" As it turned out, this endorsement was not enough to allay the fears of CBS's decision-makers, including Ed Murrow. Despite his reputation as a courageous journalist, the North Carolina native "was known to have an aversion to mass movements, nonviolent or not"; he had never shared Friendly's enthusiasm for a documentary on Montgomery. When the network finally aired a *See It Now* documentary on the civil rights struggle, in January 1957, the show presented a narrowly focused look at the legal battle for school desegregation in Clinton, Tennessee.[53]

CBS's decision to downplay the importance of the boycott mirrored Republican policy. Administration officials, from the president on down, were extremely reluctant to call attention to the mass movement in Montgomery, even after it became front-page news. They felt much more comfortable dealing with legal and legislative matters, exerting a measure of control over what was happening in federal courthouses and congressional committee rooms. And they probably would have gone on in this way indefinitely if the unfolding events in Alabama and the national political situation had not forced them to acknowledge what was happening in the streets.

Even Morrow, the one administration official who appreciated the significance of the boycott, was a little uneasy about the implications of mass protest. Following his Friday meeting at CBS, he remained in New York for the weekend. Thus, when Adam Clayton Powell announced on Saturday that he was planning a "National Deliverance Day of Prayer," Morrow was already on the scene. On Sunday, acting on his own initiative, he held a marathon, five-hour meeting with the Harlem-based committee that was organizing the affair. By his own account, Morrow welcomed the committee's desire "to give moral assistance to the Negroes in the Deep South in their present crisis," but he was less enthusiastic about the idea of a national work stoppage, which some members of the committee were pushing. At the end of the meeting, he was convinced that Powell and the committee would heed his advice and "that this national observance will now be principally one of prayer and not any other kind of controlled or uncontrolled demonstration."[54]

When Morrow returned to Washington, on Monday the 27th, he sent a memorandum to Sherman Adams describing the ad hoc negotiations with the Powell committee and the seriousness of the situation in Alabama. Noting the rising tide of anger among blacks who were tired of waiting for the administration to "do something about these intolerable conditions," he counseled Adams to urge the president to speak out on behalf of the indicted black leaders in Montgomery. "It is true the President has deplored what was happening at the University of Alabama," Morrow reminded Adams, "but the situation in Montgomery climaxed by the wholesale arrests of Negro leaders is one that has developed a new keg of racial dynamite to be exploded at any moment." Indeed, the "explosive condition" of Alabama had reached the point where even a strong statement by the president would fail to satisfy some black leaders. According to Morrow, the administration also needed an official representative on the scene, someone who could "have conferences with the Negro leaders in the Montgomery situation," who could reassure the black community in Montgomery "that the Administration is doing, and has done, everything constitutionally possible to prevent disorder and deprivation of civil rights." Not surprisingly, Morrow offered himself as the best choice for this delicate undertaking:

> I am well-known by many of the leaders in the South who are involved in this controversy. They trust me and my judgment. . . . I should like to counsel them to use wisdom and forbearance in their present actions, and that under no circumstances should they be led along the wrong path by politicians who intimate that they can get better assistance and more consideration from some other party. All these conferences would be unofficial, and off the record, and I would not promise anything, but my presence would give these leaders the assurance of our interest and the feeling that we are not completely indifferent to the plight that besets them.[55]

Morrow was well aware that Adams was generally unsympathetic to the cause of civil rights. But he also knew that Adams was a shrewd politician who might accept a reasonable plan of action if he were convinced that continued inaction would hurt the Republican Party politically. To miss this opportunity, Morrow warned, was to leave the field to the Democrats and to play into the hands of the "flamboyant opportunist," Adam Clayton Powell.[56]

If Adams had any doubts about the political salience of the civil rights struggle in Alabama, they were dispelled on the evening of February 27, when Adlai Stevenson implored President Eisenhower to convene a meeting of Southern black and white leaders to discuss the growing racial tensions in the South. Several leading Northern Democrats, including Adam Clayton Powell, endorsed the proposal. At this point in the campaign, it was obvious that Stevenson needed to do something dramatic to cut into Eisenhower's lead; thus, even some Party leaders who were wary of the civil rights issue applauded his newfound aggressiveness. Powell, of course, supported Stevenson's proposal but was determined not to be upstaged. Later in the week, the Harlem congressman, having already labeled the mass indictment "another ghastly victory for communism," beseeched the president to declare Montgomery off-limits to all military personnel stationed at Maxwell and Gunter Air Force bases.

The clear implication that Eisenhower had been derelict in his handling of the racial crisis in the Deep South and that his inaction had damaged the nation's reputation around the world got nearly everyone's attention, but there was widespread disagreement within the administration over how to respond to Stevenson's proposal for an interracial conference. Morrow, who had long advocated just such a conference, went to see White House advisers Howard Pyle and Maxwell Rabb, hoping to get some assurance that the president would finally act upon his proposal. Instead, he received a polite brush-off from Pyle and a thorough "tongue lashing" from Rabb for failing to appreciate the administration's growing impatience with ungrateful Negroes. According to Morrow, Rabb felt that despite what the administration had done in civil rights, Negroes had not demonstrated any kind of gratitude, and that most of the responsible officials in the White House had become completely disgusted with the whole matter. He said that there was a feeling that Negroes were being too aggressive in their demands; that an ugliness and surliness in manner was beginning to show through. He felt that the leaders' demands were intemperate ones and had driven most of the liberals to cover. He said that Negroes had made no effort to carry along with them the white friends they had gained, and that what they were insisting on at the present time so far exceeded what reasonable white people would grant that he was afraid these white friends were becoming few and far between.[57]

Rabb's diatribe, coming from one of the administration's most liberal voices, was deeply discouraging to Morrow. But he was not about to give up. Joined by Val Washington, the outspoken director of minority affairs for the Republican National Committee, he continued to press for an interracial conference and a public statement by the president affirming the rule of law and the sanctity of civil rights in Alabama. Morrow and Washington were hopeful that Eisenhower would address the civil rights issue at a scheduled press conference on February 29, but the president's long-awaited announcement that he would run for a second term took up most of the conference, precluding a lengthy discussion of other issues. However, he did make one brief, telling comment on civil rights. When William V. Shannon of the *New York Post* asked a question about the legality of Southern resistance to school desegregation, Eisenhower had a clear opening to discuss the situation in Alabama. Yet all he could muster was a few words about the Supreme Court's commitment to gradualism.[58]

IN THE WEEK FOLLOWING the press conference, the threat of violence in Tuscaloosa increased dramatically. Despite the Justice Department's refusal to get involved, a federal court had ordered Autherine Lucy's reinstatement at the University of Alabama, effective Monday morning, March 6. Convinced that it was "just a question of time before there will be a bloody outbreak," Morrow met with Rabb on March 1 to map out the administration's response to the expected "mob violence." When Rabb seemed confused about what was happening in Tuscaloosa, Morrow urged him to call Roy Wilkins in New York. Wilkins, who had just been informed that University of Alabama officials had defied the court order by permanently expelling Autherine Lucy, offered a somber progress report but reiterated the NAACP's determination to continue the fight. With this development, Morrow was more convinced than ever that the administration needed someone on the scene and that it had to do something soon to let the beleaguered blacks of Alabama know that the federal government was on their side.[59]

Tired of waiting for his superiors to act, Morrow made a symbolic gesture of his own on March 2. After reading that The Guardsmen, a prominent black social club in New York, had appropriated more than $10,000 "for a week's cruise to Bermuda," the normally cautious Morrow fired off an angry telegram to Major Robinson, the organizer of the junket:

> It is incredible to me that at this critical period in the Negro's fight
> for first-class citizenship in this country, with every self-respecting person
> being called upon to make financial sacrifices to see the fight through, that
> a group of young, talented, and apparently financially responsible Negroes

could contemplate a social jaunt out of the country costing thousands of dollars—the only rewards for such a trip being intangible ones. It must be disheartening, indeed, to our brothers in Montgomery, Alabama, who have placed everything, including life itself, on the altar of sacrifice, in order to achieve human dignity and respect, that they must cry for funds to assist them in this monumental effort to be free. Added to a day of prayer for our salvation, we might also have a day of self denial, when we give up the cost of selfish, foolish, and unnecessary indulgences, and turn the funds over to those agencies and institutions who are fighting for our right to walk this land with heads high and bodies secure. Is there a Daniel in the crowd?

In response, Major Robinson and several other Guardsmen counseled the White House aide to mind his own business. The press eventually picked up on the story, and in a series of speeches later in the month Morrow repeated his claim that "this is hardly the time for a flagrant display of spending on the part of responsible colored people." To some, Morrow's outrage seemed strangely selective and a bit contrived, but to others, including the publisher of the *Pittsburgh Courier*, it was an encouraging sign that at least one member of the administration was willing to endorse the boycott publicly.[60]

Morrow, of course, wanted to do much more. He was still waiting for a response from Sherman Adams, still hopeful that he would be sent to Alabama. On March 3, the day after he initiated the Guardsmen flap, his hopes soared when Adams summoned him to a special Saturday meeting to discuss the racial situation in the South. But, to his dismay, there would be no trip to Montgomery or Tuscaloosa. Despite an obvious nervousness about rising racial tensions, Adams had no intention of dispatching any administration official to Alabama. Although he appreciated the suggestion, Adams was convinced that direct involvement in the Alabama crisis "would be politically and personally dangerous" for Morrow. The public and even many high-ranking members of the administration, he told Morrow, had no idea of what was actually going on behind the scenes. As White House chief of staff, Adams was privy to FBI reports that documented the involvement of Red agitators and provocateurs. "The Communist influence in the situation was tremendous," according to Adams, "and he was certain that none of the responsible Negroes involved realized the extent of this." Indeed, "the matter was so serious that it would be discussed in a Cabinet meeting and in the Security Council" later in the week. Since national security was at stake, J. Edgar Hoover himself had been asked to brief the cabinet on the Alabama situation.[61]

The briefing, presented on March 9, was vintage Hoover. With Attorney General Brownell's proposal for a civil rights bill hanging in the balance, the pugnacious director presented a 24-page report that profiled a dangerous combination of civil rights agitation, massive resistance, and Communist infiltration. Less than a page dealt with Montgomery, but in a telling paragraph Hoover quoted approvingly from the grand jury's mass indictment: ". . . if we continue on our present course . . . violence is inevitable. The leaders of both races are urged to take a long and thoughtful look into the future." Alabama was on the verge of mass violence, and, according to Hoover, the NAACP and the White Citizens' Councils were equally responsible for the explosive situation. Although neither organization advocated violence, their disagreement over segregation was being manipulated by Communist agents who were on the scene fomenting strife and disorder. At one point, Hoover exhibited a poster-size diagram entitled "Communist Party Tactics Affecting Racial Tension." On the left side of the diagram a menacing arrow labeled "propaganda" connected a series of boxes representing a range of crises from the "Emmett Louis Till Case" to the "Montgomery, Alabama City Bus Boycott." Other than a passing reference to the "disgraceful incident at the University of Alabama," he displayed little sympathy for the cause of civil rights, and his sensational revelations were full of factual errors and half-truths, especially when he discussed the situation in Montgomery. But no one in the room, including the president and the attorney general, knew enough to challenge the director's grim portrait of subversion and impending violence.

Following Hoover's riveting performance, Brownell did what he could to repair the damage, outlining the case for a bolder endorsement of civil rights by the administration. But the conservative wing of the cabinet—led by Ezra Taft Benson, the secretary of Agriculture, and Marion Folsom, the secretary of Health, Education, and Welfare—would have none of it. Hoover's alarming report had confirmed their worst fears: to associate the administration with civil rights agitation, even in the form of moderate legislation, was to risk the taint of extremism. At the end of the meeting, Eisenhower gave Brownell permission to proceed cautiously with the drafting of civil rights legislation, but the chance that the administration would assume an active role on behalf of beleaguered Southern blacks—the role that black leaders had been pressing for—was clearly slipping away. Autherine Lucy, the NAACP, and black Montgomerians would have to fend for themselves.[62]

IN THE WAKE OF the Hoover briefing, the Eisenhower administration's public stance on civil rights continued to drift. When segregationist congressmen threatened to block Eisenhower's future judicial appointments and when more than a hundred Southern congressmen, including all but three of the region's senators, signed the "Dixie Manifesto," pledging their defiance of the *Brown* decision, the president's reaction was a masterpiece of equivocation. Responding to a question from Edward P. Morgan of ABC News, during a March 14 press conference, Eisenhower upheld the authority of the Supreme Court but refused to condemn Southern obstructionists:

> If ever there was a time when we must be patient without being complacent, when we must be understanding of other people's deep emotions, as well as our own, this is it. Extremists on neither side are going to help this situation. . . .We are not talking here about coercing, using force to, in a general way; we are simply going to uphold the Constitution of the United States, see that the progress made as ordered by them is carried out. Now let us remember this one thing, and it is very important: The people who have this deep emotional reaction on the other side were not acting over these past three generations in defiance of law. They were acting in compliance with the law as interpreted by the Supreme Court of the United States under the decision of 1896. Now, that has been completely reversed, and it is going to take time for them to adjust their thinking and their progress to that. But I have never yet given up my belief that the American people, faced with a great problem like this, will approach it intelligently and with patience and with understanding, and we will get somewhere; and I do deplore any great extreme action on either side.[63]

Just what Eisenhower meant by "extreme action" is unclear, but there can be little doubt that he would have included the boycotters among the ranks of extremists. To this point he had made no public statements on the boycott, but on March 21 he finally broke his long silence on the matter. At a press conference dominated by questions about Southern resistance to desegregation, Robert Spivack asked the president how he felt "about Negroes being brought to trial for refusing to ride the Montgomery buses." Eisenhower's brief, legalistic response confirmed what many black leaders had suspected: the president had no understanding of the emotional significance of the boycott, and no inkling of the moral outrage that the mass indictments had provoked. Without a hint of irony, he told the crowd of reporters: "Well, you are asking me, I think, to be more of a lawyer than I certainly am. But, as I understand it, there is a state law about boycotts, and it is under that kind of thing that these people are being brought to trial."

Before Spivack could interject a follow-up question, the president, obviously uncomfortable with the reference to Montgomery, abruptly shifted to an innocuous rehashing of his position on school desegregation:

> I think that the statement I made last week on this whole subject represents . . . all the views that I now have to make; and I do believe that it is incumbent on all the South to show some progress. That is what the Supreme Court asked for. And they turned it over to local district courts. I believe that we should not stagnate, but again I plead for understanding, for really sympathetic consideration of a problem that is far larger, both in its emotional and even in its physical aspects than most of us realize.[64]

The contradiction between these two statements was revealing. As far as the Montgomery indictments were concerned, it was simply a question of enforcing state law, but for the white opponents of school desegregation the law had to be tempered to accommodate practical realities and a deeply-held attachment to regional customs. Martin Luther King's conviction on March 22, the day after the press conference, gave the president a second chance to question the advisability of using an obscure 35-year-old law to intimidate the leaders of a peaceful protest. But the controversial conviction drew no comment from the White House.

Eisenhower's inaction and insensitivity disappointed the boycotters and their allies. But no one who knew the president well or who was privy to the inner workings of the administration was surprised by his disengagement. Despite the Republican Party's avowed commitment to the basic concept of civil rights, a presidential statement endorsing the boycott was never a realistic possibility. From the very beginning, Eisenhower had a jaundiced view of the Montgomery protest. Relying on a string of unsympathetic FBI reports and the alarmist projections of J. Edgar Hoover, he misjudged the nature and significance of the boycott. Misinterpreting a legitimate struggle for simple justice as a contrived and subversive Cold War crisis, he viewed the boycott as a political liability and a national embarrassment. If Eisenhower's understanding of the MIA had been grounded in reasonably accurate information—if he had dispatched Fred Morrow or Val Washington to Montgomery to see what was going on—he might have developed more sympathy for the boycotters' plight. But one suspects that no amount of information would have remedied Eisenhower's congenitally low-key approach to civil rights or his fundamental distrust of mass action. For an ex-military man who was more interested in social order than social change, the boycott raised issues that were either too troubling or too complicated to sort out. Of course, the same criticism could be made of most of Eisenhower's aides and advisers, regardless of military background. As Fred Morrow later commented, reflecting on the disappointing civil rights record of his former colleagues, "Civil rights in the Eisenhower administration was handled like a bad dream, or like something that's not very nice."[65]

EISENHOWER'S BAD DREAM COULD have turned into a nightmare for the MIA. But it didn't. In fact, in one of the boycott's many ironies, the popular president unintentionally did more to advance the boycotters' cause than any other politician. By appointing Earl Warren chief justice of the United States Supreme Court—a choice he later came to regret—Eisenhower inadvertently accelerated a process of judicial change that greatly enhanced the MIA's chances of successfully challenging de jure segregation. When the Warren Court struck down *Plessy v. Ferguson* in the *Brown* decision of May 1954, more than legality changed. A new spirit of hope and determination reverberated throughout the African American community, even in places like Montgomery where the probability of enforcing the *Brown* decision was low. The "with all deliberate speed" dictum of the second *Brown* decision left a lot of questions unanswered, and the scope and pace of court-ordered desegregation were still in doubt at the time of the boycott. But such uncertainties did not change the fact that for the first time in their lives civil rights advocates could be reasonably confident that at least one branch of the federal government was on their side. Despite a measure of recalcitrance, the lower federal courts appeared to be following the Supreme Court's lead. Moreover, they had begun to extend the *Brown* doctrine to public accommodations and transportation. In July 1955, a three-judge panel of the U.S. Fourth Circuit Court of Appeals had concurred with the NAACP position in the South Carolina bus desegregation case known as *Flemming v. South Carolina Electric and Gas Company*. When the boycotters filed their own bus desegregation suit in early February 1956, the Supreme Court had yet to rule on South Carolina Electric's appeal. But Fred Gray, Thurgood Marshall, and other NAACP attorneys were optimistic that the circuit court's ruling would be sustained.[66]

MIA leaders were less confident about the fate of their own case, at least at the circuit court level. The three-judge panel selected to hear *Browder v. Gayle* included: veteran U.S. Fifth Circuit Judge Richard Rives Sr., a native Montgomerian with a moderate to liberal record on civil rights; District Judge Seybourn Lynne, a Bourbon paternalist from Birmingham who was a lost cause as far as the boycotters were concerned; and District Judge Frank M. Johnson Jr., a recent Republican appointee from Winston County, a hill country area northwest of Birmingham. Most observers expected the two Democrats, Rives and Lynne, to cancel each other out, leaving Johnson to cast the deciding vote. MIA leaders, aware of Johnson's reputation for political independence, were hopeful that he would prove to be another Earl Warren. But they were less than certain about the steely-eyed judge's attitude toward desegregation.

The same could be said of the man who appointed him. Eisenhower apparently knew very little beforehand about Johnson other than that he was a United States attorney and a lifelong Republican who had led the Alabama Veterans for Eisenhower during the 1952 campaign. The two men met only once, in 1953, just prior to Johnson's appointment as United States Attorney for the Northern Alabama district. According to Johnson, the 15-minute meeting, which took place in the Oval Office, was "very affable." But, to his surprise, there was no discussion of race or civil rights. The president simply wanted him to pledge that he would bring a "high level" of integrity to federal law enforcement. Johnson fulfilled this pledge, both as a United States attorney and as a federal judge—sometimes to the chagrin of his superiors. In *Browder v. Gayle* and elsewhere, his highly principled pro-civil rights rulings disappointed racial conservatives both inside and outside the administration. Fortunately, there would be no such disappointments for the boycotters, who came to regard the Johnson appointment as an unexpected gift from the inchoate politics of Eisenhower Republicanism.[67]

Notes

1   See Richard H. King, *Civil Rights and the Idea of Freedom* (New York: Oxford University Press, 1992); Louis E. Lomax, *The Negro Revolt* (New York: Harper and Row, 1962); Sara M. Evans and Harry C. Boyte, *Free Spaces: The Sources of Democratic Change in America* (New York: Harper and Row, 1986); and Harry C. Boyte, *Commenwealth: A Return to Citizen Politics* (New York: The Free Press, 1989). On the sit-ins and Freedom Rides, see Jeffrey A. Turner, *Sitting In and Speaking Out: Student Movements in the American South, 1960–1970* (Athens: University of Georgia Press, 2010); and Raymond Arsenault, *Freedom Riders: 1961 and the Struggle for Racial Justice* (New York: Oxford University Press, 2006).

2   See Paula F. Pfeffer, *A. Philip Randolph, Pioneer of the Civil Rights Movement* (Baton Rouge: Louisiana State University Press, 1990), 45–132; Jervis Anderson, *A. Philip Randolph: A Biographical Portrait* (New York: Harcourt Brace Jovanovich, 1972), 241–261; August Meier and Elliott Rudwick, *CORE: A Study in the Civil Rights Movement* (Urbana: University of Illinois Press, 1975), 3–71. On the Journey of Reconciliation, see Arsenault, *Freedom Riders*, 11–55.

3   See Larry Collins and Dominique Lapierre, *Freedom at Midnight* (New York: Simon and Schuster, 1975); Erik H. Erikson, *Gandhi's Truth: On the Origins of Militant Nonviolence* (New York: W. W. Norton, 1969); Louis Fischer, *The Life of Mahatma Gandhi* (London: Jonathan Cape, 1951); Judith M. Brown, *Gandhi: Prisoner of Hope* (New Haven: Yale University Press, 1989); Stanley Wolpert, *Gandhi's Passion: The Life and Legacy of Mahatma Gandhi* (New York: Oxford University Press, 2001); and Joseph Kip Kosek, "Richard Gregg, Mohandas Gandhi, and the Strategy of Nonviolence," *Journal of American History* 91 (March 2005): 1233–1250.

4   "1860 Without Guns," ; "Two-Way Squeeze; White Citizens Councils," *Nation* 181 (December 24, 1955): 546; Meier and Rudwick, *CORE*, 87. According to Meier and Rudwick, "Boycotts, which avoided direct confrontation with the oppressive whites, seemed far more feasible in the deep South than CORE-style sit-ins."

5   Alfred Maund, "Monster Rally at Montgomery," *Nation* (February 11, 1956); Neil R. McMillen, *The Citizens' Council: Organized Resistance to the Second Reconstruction, 1954–1964* (Urbana: University of Illinois Press, 1971), 9, 35–36, 41–58, 61–62, 65, 85, 117, 313; Numan V. Bartley, *The Rise of Massive Resistance: Race and Politics in the South During the 1950s* (Baton Rouge: Louisiana State University Press, 1969), 83–149; John Bartlow Martin, *The Deep South Says "Never"* (New York: Ballantine Books, 1957). My analysis of the Southern political reaction to the boycott relies on a broad survey of Southern newspapers during the fifteen months from December 1955 to February 1957. Newspapers consulted include *Montgomery Advertiser, Montgomery States Rights Advocate, Montgomery Alabama Journal, Mobile Register, Birmingham News, Dothan Eagle,* Little Rock *Arkansas Gazette,* Little Rock *Arkansas Democrat, Tallahassee Democrat, Jacksonville Florida Times-Union, Miami Herald,* St. Petersburg *Evening Independent,* St. Petersburg *Times, Tampa Tribune, Atlanta Constitution, Augusta Chronicle, Savannah Morning News, Savannah Tribune, Louisville Courier Journal, New Orleans Times-Picayune, Baton Rouge State Times, Baltimore Sun, Jackson Clarion, Meridian Star, Charlotte Observer, Durham Morning Herald, Raleigh News and Observer, Charleston Evening Post, Charleston News and Courier, Columbia State, Chattanooga Daily Times, Nashville Banner, Memphis Commercial Appeal,* and *Richmond Times Dispatch.*

6   *Montgomery Advertiser*, February 24, 1956; *Montgomery Alabama Journal*, March 7, 1956;
     Bartley, *The Rise of Massive Resistance*, 56, 87–90, 127, 281; Martin, *The Deep South Says
     "Never,"* 105–14. McMillen, *The Citizens' Council*, 45–57, 316; For a detailed analysis of
     the origins of massive resistance in Alabama, see J. Tyra Harris, "Alabama Reaction to the
     Brown Decision, 1954–1956: A Case Study of Early Massive Resistance" (PhD thesis,
     Middle Tennessee State University, 1978). See also Clive Webb, ed., *Massive Resistance:
     Southern Opposition to the Second Reconstruction* (New York: Oxford University Press,
     2005); Clive Webb, *Rabble Rousers: The American Far Right in the Civil Rights Era* (Athens:
     University of Georgia Press, 2010); and Frye Gaillard, *Cradle of Freedom: Alabama and
     the Movement That Changed America* (Tuscaloosa: University of Alabama Press, 2004),
     17–44. For a fascinating survey of black insurgency and white supremacist resistance in
     three Alabama cities, see J. Mills Thornton III, *Dividing Lines: Municipal Politics and the
     Struggle for Civil Rights in Montgomery, Birmingham, and Selma* (Tuscaloosa: University
     of Alabama Press, 2002).

7   *Montgomery Advertiser*, March 6, 10, 1956; *Montgomery Alabama Journal*, March 7,
     1956. See also William Bundy, "Alabama Legislature Seen in Action on Racist Bills,"
     The Militant, March 12, 1956, 1–2, a fascinating eyewitness account by a correspondent
     representing the Socialist Workers Party.

8   George E. Sims, *The Little Man's Big Friend: James E. Folsom in Alabama Politics, 1946–
     1958* (Tuscaloosa: University of Alabama Press, 1985), 177–78; Carl Grafton and Anne
     Permaloff, *Big Mules and Branchheads: James E. Folsom and Political Power in Alabama*
     (Athens: University of Georgia Press, 1985), 193–4. For an analysis of Folsom's early
     career and his first term as governor, see William D. Barnard, *Dixiecrats and Democrats:
     Alabama Politics, 1942–1950* (Tuscaloosa: University of Alabama Press, 1974). See
     Thomas J. Gilliam, "The Second Folsom Administration: The Destruction of Alabama
     Liberalism, 1954–1958," (PhD thesis, Auburn University, 1975) for a detailed narra-
     tive of Folsom's second administration. The only other Alabama politician to register
     any public opposition to the segregationist status quo during the mid-1950s was State
     Representative Charles Nice of Birmingham, who cast a lone nay vote on most pro-white
     supremacist, pro-segregation bills during the 1956 term.

9   Sims, *The Little Man's Big Friend*, 178–88; Grafton and Permaloff, *Big Mules and Branch-
     heads*, 196–8; *Montgomery Alabama Journal*, February 3–March 1, 1956; *Montgomery
     Advertiser*, February 1956; Bartley, *The Rise of Massive Resistance,* 279–286. See also
     Gilliam, "The Second Folsom Administration," passim; and Harris, "Alabama Reaction
     to the *Brown* Decision, 1954–1956," passim.

10   *Montgomery Advertiser*, February 25, 1956; *Montgomery Alabama Journal*, February 25,
     1956; Sims, *The Little Man's Big Friend,* 184–5; Gilliam, "The Second Folsom Admin-
     istration," 327–33; Bartley, *The Rise of Massive Resistance,* 284–5.

11   *Montgomery Alabama Journal*, March 13, 1956; *Montgomery Advertiser*, February 28,
     1956; Sims, *The Little Man's Big Friend,* 184–5; Grafton and Permaloff, *Big Mules and
     Branchheads,* 198–201.

12   *Montgomery Alabama Journal*, March 13, 1956; *Montgomery Advertiser*, May 1–2, 1956;
     Birmingham News, March 15, April 1, May 2, 8, 1956; Grafton and Permaloff, *Big Mules
     and Branchheads,* 200; Sims, *The Little Man's Big Friend,* 186; Bartley, *The Rise of Massive
     Resistance*, 284–5.

13   Bartley, *The Rise of Massive Resistance*, 23–7, 56–7, 108–49; Martin A. Dyckman, Florid-

ian of His Century: The Courage of Governor LeRoy Collins (Gainesville: University Press of Florida, 2006). Tom R. Wagy, *Governor LeRoy Collins of Florida: Spokesman of the New South* (Tuscaloosa: University of Alabama Press, 1985); Carl Elliott and Michael D'Orso, *The Cost of Courage: The Journey of an American Congressman* (Garden City: Doubleday, 1992); Brooks Hays, *Politics is My Parish: An Autobiography* (Baton Rouge: Louisiana State University Press, 1981); Frank E. Smith, *Congressman from Mississippi* (New York: Capricorn Books, 1967); Frank E. Smith, *Look Away from Dixie* (Baton Rouge: Louisiana State University Press, 1965); For a discussion of the Southern "liberal" tradition, see Morton Sosna, *In Search of the Silent South: Southern Liberals and the Race Issue* (New York: Columbia University Press, 1977).

14   Bartley, *The Rise of Massive Resistance*, 35–36, 67, 106, 117–125, 136, 166, 171, 186–188; Harry S. Ashmore, *An Epitaph for Dixie* (New York: Norton,1958), 103–104; Harry S. Ashmore, *Hearts and Minds: The Anatomy of Racism from Roosevelt to Reagan* (New York: McGraw-Hill, 1982), 225, 256; "The Citizens' Council," *Time* 66 (December 12, 1955): 24–25; Interview with Frank Wilkinson (Raymond Arsenault), March 23, 1993. For a discussion of Eastland's career as an anti-Communist, see Chris Myers Asch, *The Senator and the Sharecropper: The Freedom Struggles of James O, Eastland and Fannie Lou Hamer* (New York: New Press, 2008), 113–121, 134–156; Jeff Woods, *Black Struggle, Red Scare: Segregation and Anti-Communism in the South, 1948–1968* (Baton Rouge: Louisiana State University Press, 2004), 42–47, 151–153, 208–212, 231–233; Patricia Sullivan, *Freedom Writer: Virginia Foster Durr, Letters from the Civil Rights Years* (New York: Routledge, 2003), 30–31, 65–74; Hollinger F. Barnard, ed., *Outside the Magic Circle: The Autobiography of Virginia Foster Durr* (New York: Simon and Schuster, 1987), 171–172, 205, 207, 254–263, 266, 269–272, 321; John A. Salmond, *The Conscience of a Lawyer: Clifford J. Durr and American Civil Liberties, 1899–1975* (Tuscaloosa: University of Alabama Press, 1990), 160–6. For information on Mississippi's rich tradition of racial demagoguery, see Albert D. Kirwan, *Revolt of the Rednecks: Mississippi Politics, 1876–1925* (Lexington: University of Kentucky Press, 1951); William F. Holmes, *The White Chief: James Kimble Vardaman* (Baton Rouge: Louisiana State University Press, 1970); A. Wigfall Green, *The Man Bilbo* (Baton Rouge: Louisiana State University Press, 1963); William Alexander Percy, *Lanterns on the Levee: Recollections of a Planter's Son* (New York: Alfred A. Knopf, 1941); Chester M. Morgan, *Redneck Liberal: Theodore G. Bilbo and the New Deal* (Baton Rouge: Louisiana State University Press, 1985); Neil R. McMillen, *Dark Journey: Black Mississippians in the Age of Jim Crow* (Urbana: University of Illinois Press, 1989); and James C. Cobb, *The Most Southern Place on Earth: The Mississippi Delta and the Roots of Regional Identity* (New York: Oxford University Press, 1992).

15   Maund, "Monster Rally at Montgomery," *Chicago Defender*, March 17, 1956; Bartley, *The Rise of Massive Resistance*, 106; *Montgomery Advertiser*, February 11, 1956.

16   *Congressional Record*,1956 ; Herman E. Talmadge, with Mark Royden Winchell, *Talmadge, A Political Legacy, A Politician's Life: A Memoir* (Atlanta: Peachtree Publishers, 1987); Nadine Cohodas, *Strom Thurmond and the Politics of Southern Change* (New York: Simon and Schuster, 1993); Jack Bass and Marilyn W. Wright, *Ol' Strom: An Unauthorized Biography of Strom Thurmond* (Columbia: University of South Carolina Press, 2003); Joseph Crespino, *Strom Thurmond's America* (New York: Hill and Wang, 2012); Robert Sherrill, *Gothic Politics in the Deep South* (New York: Grossman, 1968), 37–73; Bartley, *The Rise of Massive Resistance*, 3–46; Numan Bartley, *The New South 1945–1980* (Baton

Rouge: Louisiana State University Press, 1995), 1–103; John Egerton, *Speak Now Against the Day: The Generation Before the Civil Rights Movement in the South* (New York: Knopf, 1994), 3–12, 345–432.

17   Gunnar Myrdal, *An American Dilemma: The Negro Problem and American Democracy* (New York: Harper and Brothers, 1944), 60–67. For public opinion data that substantiate Myrdal's thesis, see Howard Schuman, Charlotte Steeh, and Lawrence Bobo, *Racial Attitudes in America: Trends and Interpretations* (Cambridge: Harvard University Press, 1985).

18   National Opinion Research Center Survey #386 (April 1956), Question 33, data on file at the Roper Public Opinion Research Center, Williamstown, Massachusetts; Andrew M. Greeley and Paul B. Sheatsley, "Attitudes Toward Racial Integration," *Scientific American* 225 #6 (December 1971), 13–14. For a fuller discussion of Northern attitudes, see Raymond Arsenault, "Rocking the Cradle of the Confederacy: The Montgomery Bus Boycott and White Public Opinion," paper presented at the annual meeting of the Organization of American Historians, Atlanta, Georgia, April 9, 1977.

19   See the coverage of, and absence of outright public endorsements of, the boycott in the editorial and commentary pages of the newspapers cited in n. 5. See also the growing despair in 1956 over the lack of political support for the boycott, as reflected in the *Chicago Defender, Pittsburgh Courier, Baltimore Afro-American*, and other black newspapers. On the press coverage of the bus boycott, see Gene Roberts and Hank Klibanoff, *The Race Beat: The Press, the Civil Rights Struggle, and the Awakening of a Nation* (New York: Alfred A. Knopf, 2006), 119–42. On the general conservatism of white Northern Democrats during the 1950s, see Gary W. Reichard, "Democrats, Civil Rights, and Electoral Strategies in the 1950s," *Congress and the Presidency* 13 (Spring 1986), 59–60. For a broader view of attitudes towards civil rights during the first decade of the Cold War, see Thomas Borstelmann, *The Cold War and the Color Line: American Race Relations in the Global Arena* (Cambridge: Harvard University Press, 2001), 1–134.

20   Herbert J. Muller, *Adlai Stevenson: A Study in Values* (London: Hamish Hamilton, 1968), 49, 73, 101, 181–183; John Bartlow Martin, *Adlai Stevenson of Illinois* (Garden City: Doubleday, 1976), 30, 158, 325, 330, 336–337, 381, 409, 482, 507–508, 517–518, 540, 551–552, 590–591, 607, 631, 643, 652, 656–657, 680, 689–691, 720–721, 729, 735–736, 760, 768–769; Porter McKeever, *Adlai Stevenson: His Life and Legacy* (New York: William Morrow, 1989), 120, 168, 221–223, 364; Robert Frederick Burk, *The Eisenhower Administration and Black Civil Rights* (Knoxville: University of Tennessee Press, 1984), 15–18, 20, 92; Herbert S. Parmet, *Eisenhower and the American Crusades* (New York: Macmillan, 1972), 80; Roy Wilkins, with Tom Mathews, *Standing Fast: The Autobiography of Roy Wilkins* (New York: The Viking Press, 1982), 212.

21   Wilkins, *Standing Fast*, 231–233; Muller, *Adlai Stevenson: A Study in Values*, 177, 181–3; McKeever, *Adlai Stevenson: His Life and Legacy*, 221, 364, 374; John Bartlow Martin, *Adlai Stevenson and the World* (Garden City: Doubleday, 1977); Parmet, *Eisenhower and the American Crusades*, 417, 436, 438, 443–444. On the Dixiecrat faction of the Democratic Party, see Kari Frederickson, *The Dixiecrat Revolt and the End of the Solid South, 1932–1968* (Chapel Hill: University of North Carolina Press, 2001); William C. Berman, *The Politics of Civil Rights in the Truman Administration* (Columbus: Ohio State University Press, 1970); Robert A. Garson, *The Democratic Party and the Politics of Sectionalism, 1941–1948* (Baton Rouge: Louisiana State University Press, 1974); Bart-

ley, *The Rise of Massive Resistance;* Barnard, *Dixiecrats and Democrats: Alabama Politics, 1942–1950;* Dewey W. Grantham, *The Life and Death of the Solid South* (Lexington: University of Kentucky Press, 1988), 119–148; Alexander P. Lamis, *The Two-Party South* (New York: Oxford University Press, 1984), 3–19; and Cohodas, *Strom Thurmond and the Politics of Southern Change.*

22 *New York Times,* February 1–29, 1956; E. Frederic Morrow, *Black Man in the White House: A Diary of the Eisenhower Years by the Administrative Officer for Special Projects, The White House, 1955–1961* (New York: Coward-McCann, 1963), 45–48; *Chicago Defender,* February 11, 18, 25, 1956; Wilkins, *Standing Fast,* 231–233.

23 Adam Clayton Powell, Jr., *Adam by Adam: The Autobiography of Adam Clayton Powell, Jr.* (New York: The Dial Press, 1971); Charles V. Hamilton, *Adam Clayton Powell, Jr.: The Political Biography of an American Dilemma* (New York: Atheneum, 1991); Will Haygood, *King of the Cats: The Life and Times of Adam Clayton Powell, Jr.* (New York: Houghton Mifflin, 1993); Thomas Kessner, "Raffish and Righteous," *New York Times Book Review,* February 21, 1993, 11–12; Irwin Ross, "Adam Clayton Powell, Jr.," *Washington Afro-American,* April 17, 1956, 1, 4 (magazine section); Burk, The Eisenhower Administration and Black Civil Rights, 30–31, 35–42, 112, 145–149, 158–159.

24 Hamilton, *Adam Clayton Powell, Jr.: The Political Biography of an American Dilemma,* 90–107; *Chicago Defender,* November 19, 1955.

25 E. Frederic Morrow Diary Transcript, February 27, 1956, Box 1, Folder 1, E. Frederic Morrow Papers, Dwight David Eisenhower Library, Abilene, Kansas; *Montgomery Alabama Journal,* February 25, 1956; *New York Times,* February 25–29, 1956; *Washington Post and Times Herald,* February 29, 1956; *Buffalo Courier Express,* February 27, 1956; Ross,"Adam Clayton Powell, Jr.," *Washington Afro-American,* April 26, 1956, 1.

26 Sims, *The Little Man's Big Friend,* 175–177, 186, 190, 203, 220; Grafton and Permaloff, *Big Mules and Branchheads,* 194–201; Bartley, *The Rise of Massive Resistance,* 283; *Montgomery Advertiser,* November 4–5, 1955, March 21, 1956, June 8, 1958; *Nashville Tennessean,* November 4, 1955 The account of the Folsom-Powell meeting in Haygood, *King of the Cats,* 205–206, is unreliable and factually incorrect.

27 *Washington Afro-American,* April 3, 1956.

28 Haygood, *King of the Cats,* 212–214.

29 Ibid.

30 Marjorie Dent Candee, ed., *Current Biography Yearbook 1957* (New York: H. W. Wilson, 1957), 144–146; "A New Congressman with an Interest in Negro History," *Negro History Bulletin* 18 (April 1955): 149, 162–163; "Negroes Stage a Progressive Show," *Business Week* (July 14, 1956): 55–56; Michael Barone, Grant Ujifusa, and Douglas Matthews, eds., *The Almanac of American Politics 1980* (New York: E. P. Dutton, 1979), 442–443; *Chicago Defender,* March 17, 1956; *Detroit Michigan Chronicle,* March 10, 1956; SAC, Detroit to FBI Director J. Edgar Hoover, March 8, 1956, and FBI Director J. Edgar Hoover to Assistant Attorney General William F. Tompkins, March 14, 1956, in "Racial Situation—Montgomery, Alabama," Federal Bureau of Investigation HQ File 100–135–61, Document 81; Typescript of "Resolutions Approved by the Baptist Ministers Conference of Detroit and Vicinity, February 28, 1956," Box 91, Folder XII-5, Martin Luther King, Jr. Papers, Boston University, Boston, Massachusetts; and "Panorama of Progress" (June 30–July 4, 1956) program, Box 80, Folder X-51, King Papers, Boston University.

31   *Montgomery Advertiser*, March 19–20, 1956; *Chicago Defender*, March 17, 1956. The relationship between Powell and Diggs is discussed in Hamilton, *Adam Clayton Powell, Jr.: The Political Biography of an American Dilemma*, 281, 284, 290, 464, 468, 480; and Haygood, *King of the Cats*, 195, 237–8, 328–9.

32   *Chicago Defender*, April 7, 14, 21, 1956; Taylor Branch, *Parting the Waters: America in the King Years, 1954–63* (New York: Simon and Schuster, 1988), 342–3; Alan B. Anderson and George W. Pickering, *Confronting the Color Line: The Broken Promise of the Civil Rights Movement in Chicago* (Athens: University of Georgia Press, 1986), 52–3, 77, 132, 323, 348; Frank Wilkinson Interview; Fred J. Smith to Reverend Ralph Abernathy, March 5, 1956, Box 64, Folder VIII 26, King Papers; Lamont Yeakey, "The Montgomery, Alabama Bus Boycott, 1955–56," (PhD Thesis, Purdue University, 1978), 607. For an early biographical sketch of Dawson, see Anna Rothe, ed., *Current Biography: Who's News and Why, 1945* (New York: H. W. Wilson, 1946), 143–5.

33   Burk, *The Eisenhower Administration and Black Civil Rights*, 23–173; Borstelmann, *The Cold War and the Color Line*, 90–101; Parmet, *Eisenhower and the American Crusades*, 436–441; Stephen E. Ambrose, *Eisenhower: The President* (New York: Simon and Schuster, 1984), 124–7, 142–3, 189–92; Hamilton, *Adam Clayton Powell, Jr.: The Political Biography of an American Dilemma*, 199–223; Richard Kluger, *Simple Justice: The History of Brown v. Board of Education and Black America's Struggle for Equality* (New York: Alfred A. Knopf, 1976), 665, 726–7, 753–4, 774.

34   Parmet, *Eisenhower and the American Crusades*, 437, 440; Valoreus Washington to Sherman Adams, January 4, 1956, Official File 138-A-6, Eisenhower Library; *New York Times*, September 8, 18, 26, October 3, November 14, 1955; "Death in Mississippi," *Commonweal* 62 (September 23, 1955): 603–604; "Race and the Future," *Commonweal* 63 (November 25, 1955): 190; William Bradford Huie, "The Shocking Story of Approved Killing in Mississippi," *Look* 20 (January 24, 1956): 46–8, 50; William Bradford Huie, *Wolf Whistle and Other Stories* (New York: Signet, 1959). For a detailed analysis of the Till case, see Stephen J. Whitfield, *A Death in the Delta: The Story of Emmett Till* (New York: The Free Press, 1988).

35   *New York Times*, June 30, July 15–16, October 19, 21, 27, November 4, 26–28, December 2, 29, 1955; Kluger, *Simple Justice*, 3–4, 9–25, 295, 303, 329, 525; Parmet, *Eisenhower and the American Crusades*, 411–26; Ambrose, *Eisenhower the President*, 270–86.

36   Burk, *The Eisenhower Administration and Black Civil Rights*, 85; Parmet, *Eisenhower and the American Crusades*, 411–26; Ambrose, *Eisenhower the President*, 270–86. See also J. W. Anderson, *Eisenhower, Brownell, and the Congress: The Tangled Origins of the Civil Rights Bill of 1956–1957* (Tuscaloosa: University of Alabama Press, 1964).

37   Maxwell Rabb Interview (Steven Lawson), October 6, 1970, Columbia University Oral History Project; Burk, *The Eisenhower Administration and Black Civil Rights*, 30, 35, 61–2, 70–1, 79–80. 93, 97–8, 115, 142, 145, 149–150, 155, 161–5.

38   Burk, *The Eisenhower Administration and Black Civil Rights*, 70; "Negroes Appointed to Top Positions in the Eisenhower Administration," January 14, 1954, Official File, Box 731, Folder 142-A, Eisenhower Library.

39   Burk, *The Eisenhower Administration and Black Civil Rights*, 54, 69–70, 77–88, 155, 208; E. Frederic Morrow, *Way Down South Up North* (Philadelphia: United Church Press, 1973); Morrow, *Black Man in the White House*; E. Frederic Morrow Diary Transcript,

Box 1, E. Frederic Morrow Papers, Eisenhower Library.

40   E. Frederic Morrow to Maxwell Rabb, November 29, 1955, Box 10, Morrow Records, Eisenhower Library; Burk, *The Eisenhower Administration and Black Civil Rights*, 208.

41   Roy Wilkins to E. Frederic Morrow, December 2, 1955, Box 10, Morrow Records, Eisenhower Library.

42   Parmet, *Eisenhower and the American Crusades*, 444–5; Burk, *The Eisenhower Administration and Black Civil Rights*, 208–9; Sherman Adams, *Firsthand Report* (New York: Harper and Brothers, 1961), 336.

43   E. Frederic Morrow to Sherman Adams, December 16, 1955, Box 10, Morrow Records, Eisenhower Library; Morrow, *Black Man in the White House*, 27–9; Burk, *The Eisenhower Administration and Black Civil Rights*, 155.

44   Morrow, *Black Man in the White House*, 29–31.

45   *Public Papers of the Presidents of the United States: Dwight D. Eisenhower, 1956* (Washington: Government Printing Office, 1958), 25; Burk, *The Eisenhower Administration and Black Civil Rights*, 157.

46   *Public Papers of the Presidents of the United States: Dwight D. Eisenhower, 1956*, 32–38, 160–71, 182–96.

47   Ibid., 233–4.

48   See "Montgomery, Alabama Bus Boycott by Negroes," Box 2140, Alpha File, Eisenhower Library; Harriet Bayansky to Dwight David Eisenhower, February 29, 1956, in ibid.; Frank Levine to Dwight David Eisenhower, February 29, 1956, in ibid.; "Pre-Press Conference Briefing, Feb. 29, 1956," February 1956 Miscellaneous (1) Folder, Box 13, Dwight David Eisenhower Diaries (Whitman File), Eisenhower Library; Bryce Harlow to Adam Clayton Powell, Jr., February 25, 1956, Box 732, Official File, Eisenhower Library; Burk, *The Eisenhower Administration and Black Civil Rights*, 159–160.

49   See the voluminous correspondence in "Racial Situation–Montgomery, Alabama," Federal Bureau of Investigation HQ File 100-135-61, Birmingham Public Library, Birmingham, Alabama; see especially SAC, Mobile to Director, March 13, 1956 (100-135-61-Documents 73 and 74); Frank Wilkinson Interview. Hoover's racism and the endemic racial prejudice in the FBI are discussed in David J. Garrow, *The FBI and Martin Luther King, Jr.: From "Solo" to Memphis* (New York: W. W. Norton, 1981); Kenneth O'Reilly, *"Racial Matters": The FBI's Secret File on Black America, 1960–1972* (New York: The Free Press, 1989), especially Chapter 1; Jack Levine, "Racism in the FBI," *Liberator 2* (November-December 1962): 10; and David Wise, "The Campaign to Destroy Martin Luther King," *New York Review of Books* 23 (November 11, 1976): 38–42.

50   "Racial Situation-Montgomery, Alabama," FBI HQ File 100-135-61; see especially SAC, Mobile to Director, March 3, 1956 (100-135-61-Document 61); Director Hoover to Assistant Chief of Staff, Intelligence, Department of the Army, March 23 and 26, 1956 (100-135-61-Documents 87 and 95); SAC, Mobile to Director, March 23, 1956 (100-135-61-Document 91); Frank Wilkinson Interview. For a discussion of Hoover's propensity to link the civil rights movement with Communist subversion, see Garrow, *The FBI and Martin Luther King, Jr.*, 21–100; and O'Reilly, *"Racial Matters": The FBI's Secret File on Black America*, 1960–1972, 125–155. See also Burton Hersh, *Bobby and J. Edgar: The Historic Face-Off Between the Kennedys and J. Edgar Hoover That Transformed America* (New York: Carroll and Graf, 2007), 93, 115, 334-45, 381-6.

51   "Biographical Sketch of Attorney Fred D. Gray," April 19, 1956, NAACP Papers, Library of Congress; Fred D. Gray, Interview by J. Mills Thornton III, October 17, 1978; *Montgomery Alabama Journal*, February 23, March 2, 1956; "Racial Situation–Montgomery, Alabama," FBI HQ File 100-135-61; "The President Should Act," Editorial, *Washington Afro-American*, August 14, 1956; Fred D. Gray, *Bus Ride to Justice: The Life and Works of Fred Gray* (Montgomery: NewSouth Books, 2002), 76–78; Branch, *Parting the Waters*, 168, 192. For a sketch of Hershey's background, see Anna Rothe, ed.,*Current Biography: Who's News and Why, 1951* (New York: H. W. Wilson, 1951), 270–272. Hershey's experience with the South dated back to 1922, when he attended Field Artillery School at Fort Sill, Oklahoma. From 1927 to 1931, he was stationed at Fort Bliss, Texas. For most of the remainder of his career, he lived in the greater Washington, D.C., area.

52   Morrow, *Black Man in the White House*, 42–58; *Washington Afro-American*, February 21, 28, 1956; *Chicago Defender*, February 18, 25, 1956; Branch, *Parting the Waters*, 180–1. For a different view of Morrow's role, see Hamilton, *Adam Clayton Powell, Jr.: The Political Biography of an American Dilemma*, 264. According to Hamilton, "There is little evidence that Powell or most other Negro leaders—politicians or civil rights activists—viewed Morrow as an influential insider. And therefore his role was seldom if ever part of serious political calculations in dealing with the White House. In the spring and summer of 1956, with the approaching Presidential election, that certainly was the case."

53   E. Frederic Morrow Diary Transcript, February 27, 1956, E. Frederic Morrow Papers, Box 1, Folder 1, Eisenhower Library; Morrow, *Black Man in the White House*, 45; A. M. Sperber, *Murrow: His Life and Times* (New York: Freundlich Books, 1986), 524–5; William Peter, "What You Can't See on TV," *Redbook* (July 27, 1957). Entitled *Clinton and the Law: A Study of Desegregation*, the documentary was broadcast nationwide on CBS on January 6, 1957.

54   E. Frederic Morrow to Sherman Adams, February 27, 1956, Folder 142-A, Box 731, Official File, Eisenhower Library; Hamilton, *Adam Clayton Powell, Jr.*, 263; E. Frederic Morrow Diary Transcript, February 27, 1956, Box 1, Folder 1, E. Frederic Morrow Papers, Eisenhower Library. The members of the Harlem committee included Dr. George Cannon, New York City Councilman McDougall, Dr. Arthur Logan, Professor John Davis of the City College of New York, the noted sculptor Charles Alston, and George Gregory, the deputy civil service commissioner of New York City.

55   E. Frederic Morrow to Sherman Adams, February 27, 1956; Hamilton, *Adam Clayton Powell, Jr.: The Political Biography of an American Dilemma*, 263.

56   E. Frederic Morrow to Sherman Adams, February 27, 1956; Hamilton, *Adam Clayton Powell, Jr.: The Political Biography of an American Dilemma*, 259–264.

57   Morrow, *Black Man in the White House*, 45–8; *New York Times*, February 27–March 4, 1956; Bryce Harlow to Adam Clayton Powell, Jr., February 25, 1956; Burk, *The Eisenhower Administration and Black Civil Rights*, 159–60; Branch, *Parting the Waters*, 180–1; Hamilton, *Adam Clayton Powell, Jr.: The Political Biography of an American Dilemma*, 262–4.

58   Morrow, *Black Man in the White House*, 48–51; "Excerpts From the President's Press Conferences," (January 25–March 21, 1956), Folder 142-A, Box 731, Official File, Eisenhower Library; *Public Papers of the Presidents of the United States: Dwight D. Eisenhower, 1956*, 269–70; Parmet, *Eisenhower and the American Crusades*, 442.

59   Morrow, *Black Man in the White House,* 49–51.

60   E. Frederic Morrow to Major Robinson, March 2, 1956, Box 10; E. Frederic Morrow Diary Transcript, March 16, 1956, Folder 1, Box 1, E. Frederic Morrow Records, Eisenhower Library; Morrow, *Black Man in the White House,* 56–7.

61   Morrow, *Black Man in the White House,* 51–3; Branch, *Parting the Waters,* 181; Hamilton, *Adam Clayton Powell, Jr.,: The Political Biography of an American Dilemma,* 263–4.

62   "Racial Tension and Civil Rights," March 1, 1956, Box 6, Whitman File, Cabinet Series, Eisenhower Library; Branch, *Parting the Waters,* 181–2; Burk, *The Eisenhower Administration and Black Civil Rights,* 160–1.

63   "Excerpts From the President's Press Conferences" (January 25–March 21, 1956), 4–5; *Public Papers of the Presidents of the United States: Dwight D. Eisenhower, 1956,* 303–305.

64   "Excerpts From the President's Press Conferences" (January 5–March 21, 1956), 5–6; *Public Papers of the Presidents of the United States: Dwight D. Eisenhower, 1956,* 335–6; Ambrose, *Eisenhower the President,* 307; Parmet, *Eisenhower and the American Crusades,* 442; Burk, *The Eisenhower Administration and Black Civil Rights,* 160.

65   Burk, *The Eisenhower Administration and Black Civil Rights,* 263.

66   Catherine A. Barnes, *Journey from Jim Crow: The Desegregation of Southern Transit* (New York: Columbia University Press, 1983), 117–21; Jack Bass, *Unlikely Heroes: The Dramatic Story of the Southern Justices of the Fifth Circuit Who Translated the Supreme Court's Brown Decision into a Revolution for Equality* (New York: Simon and Schuster, 1981); Kluger, *Simple Justice,* 665.

67   Bass, *Unlikely Heroes,* 19, 56–77; Jack Bass, *Taming the Storm: The Life and Times of Judge Frank, M. Johnson, Jr., and the South's Fight Over Civil Rights* (New York: Doubleday, 1993), 3–172; Robert Jerome Glennon, "The Role of Law in the Civil Rights Movement: The Montgomery Bus Boycott, 1955–1957," *Law and History Review* 9 (Spring 1991), 59–112. For assessments of Judge Johnson's civil rights-related rulings, see Tinsley Yarbrough, *Judge Frank Johnson and Human Rights in Alabama,* (Tuscaloosa: University of Alabama Press, 1981); Frank Sikora, *The Judge: The Life and Opinions of Alabama's Frank M. Johnson, Jr.* (Montgomery: NewSouth Books, 2007); and Robert F. Kennedy, Jr., *Judge Frank M. Johnson, Jr.: A Biography* (New York: G. P. Putnam's Sons, 1978).

15

The Double Death of Martin Luther King Jr.

Paul M. Gaston

The last time I met Martin Luther King Jr. was in March of 1963. On a previous occasion, at a conference in Nashville, I had asked him if he would like to come to my university to speak. He was enthusiastic and when a student civil rights group sent a formal invitation, he readily accepted. After his speech before a packed auditorium and a reception following, my wife and I, joined by a student, strolled about the university grounds with King. We all heard a loud report. I assumed it was a car back-firing (which it was). A white person like me might make that assumption. Wesley Harris, the student, could not. He pinned Dr. King to the wall of the building we were passing. Many years later I asked Wes about that moment. This is what he told me:

> It was without thought; it was instinct. Out of what I would describe as the Southern experience of a black person, in that era. That we had seen so many of our leaders jailed and beaten and dragged through the streets, so a person of King's stature is priceless. So any possible threat of danger or whatever, you would need to protect him. I shall never forget that night.

Back in King's motel room, getting on toward midnight, Dr. King spoke gently to Wes, Mary, and me about what had happened. Then, still in the calm and caring voice we had come to know, he told us that, yes, one of these days (and probably soon) he would be shot and killed. We left the room humbled and anxious. None of us was ever in his presence again. Five years after our evening with him, in April 1968, his prediction came true. Standing on the balcony of the Lorraine Motel in Memphis, he was shot and killed. Despite the subsequent conviction of James Earl Ray, several writers, most importantly Mark Lane, have questioned Ray's sole culpability. In Lane's writings, the responsibility lies with King's longtime enemy, the Federal Bureau of Investigation.[1] Disagreements continue.

King's murder unleashed a flood of reaction, much of it violent. The loss of such a major world figure set off, among other things, attempts to define his legacy and the meaning of that legacy for the ongoing struggle for racial justice. King himself, in his many statements about what he believed to be the ultimate aims of the civil rights movement, had supplied much fodder for the debates that followed.

Five months after our 1963 meeting, King was in Washington to lead a march for jobs and freedom. His "I Have a Dream" speech, the highlight of the occasion, began with a prediction that the day would "go down in history as the greatest demonstration for freedom in the history of our nation." For many Americans, white as well as black, so it did. Ironically, however, that speech would soon be distorted and manipulated. It has been used to turn the civil rights movement into yet another example of the unique and dramatic story of American democracy. His dream, he said, was "deeply rooted in the American dream." And so the civil rights movement, as it swept away segregation and disfranchisement, came to be described as presumed proof of America's unique democracy, its self-corrective power to right the nation's wrongs.

Since the moment of his death, King's image has been manipulated to turn back radical social change and to underwrite reactionary political and economic policies. At memorial ceremonies all over the country immediately following his death, he was lauded as the 20th century's greatest black liberation leader. Some of the white speakers may have praised him for leading the war against Jim Crow, but their favored theme was his philosophy and practice of nonviolence. In the violent year of 1968, however, that philosophy and practice was manipulated to become a weapon to douse flames burning in American cities and to turn back the angry protests of brick-throwing black Americans. King's nonviolence, at the moment of his death, meant repression of the ongoing, now often violent, black freedom movement.

Following his death, he moved quickly to the role of martyred hero. There is no record, however, of anyone hoisting James Agee's flag of warning, telling what it meant to praise famous men: "Every fury on earth has been absorbed in time, as art, or as religion, or as authority in one form or another. The deadliest blow the enemy of the human soul can strike is to do fury honor. Swift, Blake, Beethoven, Christ, Joyce, Kafka, name me a one who has not been thus castrated. Official acceptance is the one unmistakable symptom that salvation is beaten again, and is the one surest sign of fatal understanding, and is the kiss of Judas."[2]

The absorption of King's fury, begun so pointedly at the moment of his death, has deepened ever since. Long before a national holiday was established in his honor, most official celebrations of his civil rights leadership routinely began with selections from his "I Have a Dream" speech that climaxed the 1963 March on Washington. His dream, he said, was "deeply rooted in the American dream." Incessant repetition of this phrase gave birth to the myth of King the reformer who wanted nothing more for his people than to win admission to a fundamentally sound society, one whose values, ideals, and economic order were flawed only by its practice of racial exclusion. Racism, according to this myth, was an independent variable that could be excised without disturbing the basic architecture of the society in which it flourished or altering the nature of its dream. Thus was the fury of America's most charismatic and influential warrior against racism tamed and the nation's image of itself as fair, just, and superior vindicated.

It was this image of the nonviolent warrior who was nonetheless a great champion of his country and its values who was celebrated when the national holiday bill was proposed and established. Ronald Reagan, on whose watch the deed was done, was a reluctant supporter of the inevitable, but he predictably turned it to his advantage by praising King as a good man who believed in brotherhood and harmony. "Such a carefully cropped portrait," as Robert Weisbrot wrote of Reagan's manipulative characterization, "enables the nation to create a comforting icon."[3] That has been the familiar presidential line ever since, as witness even Bill Clinton's opening question when he began King holiday speeches with: "Remember what Martin Luther King said?" And then his answer: "My dream is deeply rooted in the American dream."[4]

It has not been enough for the King myth to serve as an authoritative endorsement of the American social order. Pundits and politicians of the right, lavishly supported by an ever-increasing number of so-called think tanks, have fixed on and distorted fragments of the dream speech, pressing it into service as a weapon against affirmative action and other Johnson-era efforts to right social wrongs. George Will, the intellectual voice of conservatism, concedes the existence of continuing poverty and disadvantage, but explains them as the "terrible price" blacks have been made to pay "for the apostasy of today's civil rights leaders from the original premise of the civil rights movement." That premise, he declares, was that "race must not be a source of advantage or disadvantage."[5]

Rush Limbaugh, the strident spokesman of the far right, declares that "the vision that Dr. Martin Luther King Jr. had for a color-blind society has been perverted by modern liberalism."[6] Ward Connerly (the Sacramento business-man and University of California regent) and Newt Gingrich, blasting what they call "the failure of racial preferences," conjure up King's "heartfelt voice" wishing for an end to judging people by skin color.[7] Linda Chavez, promi-nent crusader against affirmative action, came to my university a few years ago where I heard her admonish us to cease judging applicants for admission "based on the color of their skin" (which we did not do). Dr. King, she told us, would be opposed because our policy "smacks of the kind of racism that has long plagued this nation." She and a legion of others have given life to what George Orwell, in his novel *1984*, called Newspeak, the use of words in ambiguous and contradictory ways, telling lies by appearing to tell the truth.

The "content of their character rather than the color of their skin" excerpt from the "dream" speech has become the incantation of choice for much of the nation, including virtually everyone on the right. It drapes the King mantle over the most unlikely partisans of the civil rights movement and uses the most famous voice of that movement to condemn policies to which it gave birth: Ward Connerly launched, on King's birthday, a personal crusade to win votes for the California anti-affirmative action referendum with the announcement that King "personifies the quest for a color-blind society." Understanding of the King legacy should help the nation "resume the journey" he started and stop the terrible "drift from the ideal of a color-blind society." The drift, as conservative Arch Puddington put it, widened into a powerful rush "to the diversity training and the like." No champion of King pledging fealty to civil rights history could possibly support such things."[8]

KING'S DREAM SPEECH, THE primary text of those who would cast him as an ally of the contemporary right wing, has a memorable passage about a promissory check returned for insufficient funds, and his other speeches and actions are full of ideas for many forms of what are now called "race-based" policies to begin the long process of undoing the effects of the "race-based" policies of the previous three centuries. In the final three years of his life he greatly expanded on these themes. It was time to move beyond the reformist tactics of the previous decade. Having cleared away the debris of Jim Crow it was easier to see the fundamental tasks yet to be accomplished.

"We must recognize," he said, "that we can't solve our problems now until there is a radical redistribution of economic and political power." Among other things, this would require facing the truth that "the dominant ideology" of America was not "freedom and equality" with racism "just an occasional departure from the norm." Racism was woven into the fabric of the country, intimately linked to capitalism and militarism. They were all "tied together," he said, "and you really can't get rid of one without getting rid of the others." What was required was "a radical restructuring of the architecture of American society."[9]

That phrase—"a radical restructuring of the architecture of American society"—was not uttered in the dream speech of 1963. The time was not right for it. The Jim Crow shackles had to be smashed first. But the phrase carries the essential message and embodies the enduring legacy of Martin Luther King Jr.—and it is a message virtually airbrushed from history. His radical critique was drowned out from the beginning by angry White House rejections (reflecting LBJ's resentment of King's opposition to the Vietnam war), white fear of the Black Power movement, escalating riots in Northern cities, and liberal integrationists' continuing loyalty to their reformist principles of contained social change. Little time passed before the King who would remake the structure of American society was absent from schoolbooks, anniversary celebrations, and political oratory. Julian Bond had it right when he wrote that "we do not honor the critic of capitalism, or the pacifist who declared all wars evil, or the man of God who argued that a nation that chose guns over butter would starve its people and kill itself. We do not honor the man who linked apartheid in South Africa and Alabama. We honor an antiseptic hero." William Buckley, the dean of conservative pundits, who quoted these words, pronounced Bond to be "absolutely correct." King's "kindergarten socialism," as Buckley called it, had no place in America.[10]

King's radical prescription for remaking America extended beyond economic, political, and foreign policy to embrace a call for a "revolution in values," specifically a rejection of marketplace mentality and its obsessive fealty to the profit motive. Testifying before a Senate committee, he stated that "the values of the marketplace supersede the goals of social justice. We narrowly define economic cost and ignore social costs. We rely on the unseen hand of economic growth to do the work of social justice. The theme of 'efficiency' overwhelms the need for equity."[11]

CELEBRATIONS OF KING'S LIFE and leadership continue, on his birthday and on the anniversaries of his 1968 death and his 1963 dream speech. They tend to focus, however, on his philosophy of nonviolence and his ability to mobilize men, women, and children to mount protests that would result in laws striking down segregation and making real the right to vote. Largely missing from these celebrations are the words of his last three years of life, especially his call for the reconstruction of the "architecture of American society." As if in approval of this dismissal of the deeper legacy he has bequeathed to his country, the monument recently constructed in the nation's capital does not include, among his many phrases, a call for the reconstruction he advocated.

NOTES

1   See Mark Lane and Dick Gregory, *Code Name "Zorro": The Murder of Martin Luther King, Jr.* (Englewood Cliffs, NJ: Prentice Hall, 1977).

2   James Agee, *Let Us Now Praise Famous Men* (New York: Houghton Mifflin, 1941), 15.

3   Robert Weisbrot, "Celebrating Dr. King's Birthday: A Legacy of Confrontation and Conciliation," *New Republic,* January 30, 1984.

4   Bill Clinton, "Remarks Honoring Martin Luther King, Jr.," *Weekly Compilation of Presidential Documents,* January 23, 1995.

5   George F. Will, *The Leading Wind: Politics, the Culture, and Other News, 1990–1994* (New York, Viking, 1994), 143.

6   Rush H. Limbaugh III, *See: I Told You So* (New York: Pocket Books, 1993), 244.

7   Newt Gingrich and Ward Connerly, "Face the Failure of Racial Preferences," *New York Times,* June 15, 1997.

8   Arch Puddington, "What to do about Affirmative Action," *Commentary,* June 1995.

9   "Federal Role in Urban Affairs": *Hearing before the Subcommittee on Executive Operations, U.S. Senate, 89th Cong,.,* pt. 14: 2981.

10   William F. Buckley, "The Other Dr. King," *National Review,* May 20, 1993, 20.

11   *Hearings before the Subcommittee on Executive Reorganization,* pt. 14: 2969.

16

Birmingham, 1978

A Photographic Homage to Sheldon Hackney

WILLIAM R. FERRIS

Sheldon Hackney has shaped the American academy in profoundly important ways. As a Southerner, born in Alabama, he was a student, professor, and administrator at four major universities during his academic career. Hackney's PhD in history at Yale under the tutelage of C. Vann Woodward positioned him as a leading thinker and writer of the American South. Teaching and administrative positions at Princeton University led to his appointment as president of Tulane University and, later, the University of Pennsylvania. Hackney was then tapped by President Bill Clinton to chair the National Endowment for the Humanities.

While teaching at Yale in the seventies, I became friends with Jessica Mitford, an old friend of Hackney's in-laws, Clifford and Virginia Durr of Montgomery. Mitford told me she received a call from Hackney's future mother-in-law. Virginia's daughter Lucy was coming home for the holidays and announced she was bringing "a right nice young man." That man was Sheldon Hackney, and thus were bonded two powerful Southern families.

It was my pleasure to meet Sheldon Hackney several times during his distinguished career. We spent an evening together in the president's box of the New Orleans Superdome watching Tulane play football and talking about shared interests related to the Crescent City and the South.

Several years later we met at the National Endowment for the Humanities in Washington when I received the National Humanities Medal from President Clinton. Hackney's warmth and love for learning were reflected in conversations we shared in his office, home, and the White House.

In 1997, I was chosen to succeed Hackney as chairman of the NEH. I called and asked him what the job involved. He replied, with a touch of humor, "It is very simple. You serve Congress, the White House, and the American People."

Sheldon Hackney has written eloquently about the inherent contradictions that Southerners—black and white—confront in their history. The South and its people bring a unique perspective to the American experience. Their strong sense of the past, their attachment to place, and their gift for storytelling bond Southerners to the region and to the nation.

Hackney understands that life is filled with profound contradictions. Leadership must be built with this vision in mind. At every step in his life, Sheldon Hackney has strengthened the institutions with which he worked, while never forgetting his Alabama roots and the complex ways in which the South has shaped his life.

In honor of Sheldon Hackney's Alabama roots, these photographs are offered as an homage to his life and to his distinguished academic career. The photographs were taken during a single day in Sheldon's hometown of Birmingham in 1978. They capture scenes in and around the Redmont Hotel, at 2101 Fifth Avenue North.

12

17

Minority Representation
in Alabama

The Pivotal Case of Dillard v. Crenshaw County

PEYTON MCCRARY

When the Voting Rights Act was adopted in 1965, only one in five African American adults were registered to vote in Alabama and only a handful of blacks held public office—all in jurisdictions where members of their race were a substantial majority of the registered voters. Fifteen years later a majority of Alabama blacks were registered to vote as a result of enforcement of the Act but still very few African Americans held public office—and those were almost entirely elected from majority-black single-member districts or majority-black jurisdictions. By 1990, however, African Americans had succeeded in electing their candidate of choice to office in Alabama local governing bodies at a rate approximating their percentage of the voting age population, virtually all from majority-minority single-member districts or predominantly black jurisdictions. This extraordinary degree of minority representation was due primarily to successful lawsuits brought pursuant to Section 2 of the Act after it was amended in 1982 to allow challenges to discriminatory election practices without proving that they were adopted or maintained with a racially discriminatory intent.[1]

Despite the fact that it was unnecessary to prove that a challenged election law had a discriminatory purpose, evidence of discriminatory intent continued to play a key role in some Section 2 cases in Alabama. In terms of its impact on minority representation the most notable was *Dillard v. Crenshaw County*, which consolidated challenges to the at-large election of commissioners in nine Alabama counties where no black had ever been elected. Triggered by Judge Myron Thompson's 1986 decision enjoining further use of at-large elections in the defendant counties, within two years *Dillard* produced the extraordinary result that 176 Alabama counties, municipalities, and school boards agreed to switch from at-large elections to ward plans or limited or cumulative voting plans, which invariably resulted in the election of black-preferred candidates to local office.[2] The story of that litigation and its impact on minority representation in Alabama provides the focus of this study.

Vote-Dilution & Reconstruction Amendments, 1966–82

In 1966, as African Americans were beginning to vote in large numbers as a result of the Voting Rights Act, the Democratic executive committee of Barbour County, Alabama (white supremacist Governor George Wallace's home county), switched from electing its members by single-member districts to electing them county-wide. Veteran Alabama civil rights lawyer Fred Gray challenged this change in what proved to be the first racial vote-dilution lawsuit, *Smith v. Paris*.[3] Black voters already constituted a majority of the registered voters in some Barbour districts (called "beats" in Alabama) but were still a minority in the county at large. The clear effect of the change, as demonstrated in the 1966 elections, was that minority voting strength would be diluted by the bloc votes of the white majority in a county-wide election.[4] Frank M. Johnson Jr., the chief district judge in the Middle District of Alabama, who played a role in most of the important civil rights decisions in the state for a quarter-century, ruled that the change was motivated by an unconstitutional racial purpose and thus violated the 14th and 15th Amendments.[5]

For the next decade and a half the federal courts decided all challenges to at-large elections and other dilutive election procedures pursuant to the Reconstruction Amendments, rather than Section 2 of the Voting Rights Act. In 1973, applying the Equal Protection Clause of the 14th Amendment, the Supreme Court for the first time struck down the use of at-large elections—in this case the multi-member districts in which members of the Texas state house of representatives were elected in Dallas and Bexar counties—in *White v. Regester*.[6] Based on what it called "the totality of the circumstances"—a history of racial discrimination, continuing disparity in registration and voting rates, the use of numbered place and runoff requirements (which enhance the discriminatory potential of at-large elections), and a lack of responsiveness to minority voters by elected officials—the Court found that minority voters in these two counties had "less opportunity than did other residents . . . to participate in the electoral processes and to elect candidates of their choice."[7] Although in later decisions the Supreme Court interpreted *White* as incorporating an intent requirement, the 1973 majority opinion did not, in fact, address whether proof of discriminatory intent was required under the totality of circumstances test. For years thereafter, beginning with *Zimmer v. McKeithen*, the Fifth Circuit Court of Appeals treated the test as requiring proof of either purpose or effect, but not both.[8]

Under this approach, plaintiffs in vote dilution cases were often able to win by documenting a history of racial segregation and discrimination in the jurisdiction and by showing that, due to racially polarized voting, the election system operated such that minority voters did not have a reasonable opportunity to elect representatives of their choice.[9] The lower courts understood how to apply the standard which Judge Irving Goldberg of the Fifth Circuit later characterized as "a jurisprudence produced by ten years of struggle and compromise between judges of varying political and jurisprudential backgrounds."[10]

In 1980, however, the Supreme Court ruled in *City of Mobile v. Bolden*, a challenge to the city's use of at-large elections, that under the 14th Amendment, as well as under Section 2 of the Voting Rights Act, plaintiffs must prove not only that an election practice has a discriminatory effect due to racially polarized voting but also that it was adopted or maintained for the purpose of diluting minority voting strength.[11] The Court remanded the case, and a companion suit challenging at-large school board elections in Mobile County, for a new trial on the intent question. The plaintiffs prevailed in both cases under the intent standard, after demonstrating that a racial purpose lay behind shifts to at-large elections in 1876 and 1911; however, those victories came at great cost in both time and money.[12]

In the view of many observers, the Supreme Court's decision in *Mobile* was inconsistent with the intent of Congress when it adopted and expanded the Voting Rights Act in 1965, 1970, and 1975. A substantial bipartisan majority in both houses voted to revise Section 2 in 1982 to outlaw election methods that result in diluting minority voting strength, without requiring proof of discriminatory intent.[13] In creating a new statutory means of attacking minority vote dilution, Congress cited the "totality of circumstances"

test of *White* and *Zimmer* as the evidentiary standard for applying Section 2.
Vote-dilution cases previously decided under the 14th Amendment would
henceforth be tried under the new statutory results test.[14]

CONTINUING RELEVANCE OF INTENT EVIDENCE IN SECTION 2 CASES

Section 2 of the Voting Rights Act, as amended in 1982, had two
prongs—plaintiffs could prevail under the new results test but also, as before,
by proving intentional discrimination.[15] The lawyers who had successfully
litigated the Mobile cases under the intent standard, James U. Blacksher,
Larry Menefee, and Edward Still, continued to mine Alabama's rich history
of racial discrimination that included the intentional adoption of racially discriminatory election laws. Expert testimony by historians played a key role in
these cases.[16] For example, in a case filed as a 14th Amendment challenge on
behalf of African American citizens of Jefferson and Montgomery counties,
Still successfully challenged the "petty crimes" provision of the 1901 Alabama
constitution, which itemized various misdemeanors (believed by the provision's sponsors to be more often committed by blacks) that would disqualify
individuals from the right to vote. Citing evidence of explicit racial purpose
from the 1901 convention debates, expert historians for both plaintiffs (J.
Morgan Kousser) and the state (J. Mills Thornton) agreed that the provision
was designed to disfranchise blacks. The state's defense, rejected unanimously
by the Supreme Court, was that the provision was also intended to prevent
many poor whites from voting.[17]

In *Harris v. Graddick,* African American plaintiffs represented by Blacksher,
Menefee, and Still successfully challenged the underrepresentation of blacks
among poll officials in the state. Judge Myron Thompson initially granted
a preliminary injunction, based on the Section 2 results test, requiring state
and local officials to appoint African American poll officials in each county in
reasonable relation to the black percentage of the county's population.[18] After
a full trial on the merits, the court made this requirement permanent, relying
in part on detailed evidence of intentional discrimination in the adoption of
an 1893 election law devised by legislator A. D. Sayre and still in the 1980s
a key part of the method of appointing poll officials. Sayre's bill included use
of an Australian ballot with no straight-ticket option, a five-minute limit on
attempting to vote, and limiting election assistance to the poll officials—appointed by the governor, all were white Democrats, when virtually all blacks

in Alabama voted Republican. According to a contemporary news account, "Sayre, the author of the bill, made a plain and straightforward explanation of the bill and its purposes, and called upon every member of the house who felt that he wanted to preserve white supremacy, without the necessity of resorting to the fraudulent practices now so generally charged to be in vogue, to vote with him for the passage of the bill, which he felt would largely remove the negro [sic] from politics."[19]

The *Harris* litigation made it easier for African Americans to cast their votes without hindrance, but as long as they faced at-large election systems with a numbered place requirement, they could still find themselves unable to elect candidates of their choice. Of course, minority plaintiffs could attack at-large elections on a county by county, city by city basis, and had often done so.[20] In the mid-1980s, however, Blacksher, Menefee, and Still devised a way of attacking the state's at-large elections more systematically, seeking to consolidate lawsuits in the nine counties still using at-large elections where no blacks had been elected. Their rationale for consolidation was that the state of Alabama had long used at-large elections and numbered place requirements to dilute black voting strength. On this basis Thompson, a graduate of Yale Law School and the first African American appointed to the federal district court in Montgomery, in 1980, agreed to consolidate all nine cases in his court in *Dillard v. Crenshaw County*.[21]

THE HISTORICAL PATTERN OF AT-LARGE ELECTIONS IN ALABAMA

At a preliminary injunction hearing in the spring of 1986, the plaintiffs' expert historian testified about intentionally discriminatory election laws, beginning with the post-Reconstruction period.[22] As a result of the 15th Amendment, African Americans could still vote in Alabama in the 1880s and 1890s, and thus they still had the potential for winning elections in some of the black-majority plantation counties. To prevent that, the legislature passed a series of laws that eliminated elections for county commissioner altogether in certain specified counties—the governor was to appoint the local governing body—a step Thompson characterized as "widely understood to have been designed to prevent the election of black county commissioners."[23] The rise of the Populist movement in the 1890s threatened the possibility of an alliance of blacks and disgruntled white farmers, triggering the passage of the Sayre election law—at issue in *Harris*—which resulted in a drop of 22 percent in

black turnout between 1892 and 1894, remaining below 50 percent thereafter.[24] The Populist threat also occasioned a shift from single-member districts
to at-large elections for county commissioners in a number of counties.[25]

Thompson noted that the 1901 constitutional convention substantially
disfranchised African Americans through the adoption of a literacy test and
other devices, so that "all but approximately 4,000 of the nearly 182,000
black persons had been removed from the rolls of eligible voters."[26] As a result
counties felt free to adopt single-member districts, a trend that continued for
the next four decades.[27] Because state officials believed that black voting was
no longer a threat, the Alabama legislature also adopted a municipal election
code that provided the option of single-member districts for most cities in
the state.[28]

Like other Southern states in the early 20th century Alabama adopted
party primary laws that permitted the dominant Democratic Party to restrict
participation in the primary to white persons. Thus even blacks who could
surmount the state's registration barriers could not vote in the Democratic
primary, the only election that mattered. When in 1944 the Supreme Court
struck down the use of all-white primaries, African Americans sought to register
and vote in much larger numbers in the Democratic primary. In response
the state passed a series of laws requiring black persons seeking to register "to
satisfy different and more stringent standards and tests than white persons,"
observed Thompson.[29] In addition many counties shifted from single-member
districts back to at-large elections.[30]

Most Alabama municipalities elected council members at large and it was
still possible for voters to cast their votes for fewer than the number of seats
up for election, a practice often termed "single-shot" or "bullet" voting, thus
increasing the mathematical weight of their votes for preferred candidates in
determining the outcome. Sam Engelhardt was a state representative from
predominantly black Macon County, where the presence of Tuskegee Institute
and a black veterans' hospital led to an unusually large number of black registered voters, mostly in the county seat, Tuskegee. As Thompson characterized
the legislator's later career, "Engelhardt was the founder of the racist White
Citizens Council Movement of the 1950's" and was also "the author of the
infamous, racially inspired Tuskegee gerrymander stuck down by the federal
courts" in *Gomillion v. Lightfoot*.[31] In 1951 Engelhardt sponsored a law prohibiting the use of single-shot voting for all municipal elections in the state.

In Thompson's view the racial purpose of the law was no secret. Engelhardt's father-in-law, State Senator J. Miller Bonner, explained to reporters that the legislature passed the anti-single-shot measure because "there are some who fear that the colored voters might be able to elect one of their own to the city council by 'single shot' voting." Thompson added that for "the same racial reasons the ban on single-shot voting was extended in the late 1950's to cover at-large primary elections for county commissioners."[32]

THE 1961 NUMBERED PLACE LAW

In 1961 the Alabama legislature replaced the anti-single-shot laws with a comprehensive statute (Act 221) requiring that all at-large elections in the state apply a numbered place system; candidates would have to qualify for Place Number 1, Place Number 2, etc., so that all seats on local governing bodies, both houses of the state legislature, and all judicial posts would be filled by head-to-head contests—rather than a traditional "first-past-the post" at-large system.[33] A numbered place requirement makes it impossible to use single-shot voting. As Thompson saw it, "the numbered place laws had the same effect on black voting strength in at-large elections as the laws banning single-shot voting, and there can be no doubt that they sprang from the same motivation."[34] He characterized the 1961 numbered place requirement as the "discriminatory centerpiece of the new at-large system."[35]

On what evidence did Thompson base this conclusion? As with most state legislatures of the period, there was nothing comparable to federal legislative history documents—no detailed committee reports, no transcripts of floor debates—only a bare-bones legislative journal recording actions on each bill and recording roll-call votes. Nor were newspaper accounts of legislative proceedings—normally a key part of a historian's testimony about the intent of a state law—very informative about the legislative history of what became Act 221 of 1961. The focus of newspaper coverage during this session was the contentious debates over congressional redistricting—Alabama lost one seat in Congress due to relative population loss and adopted an idiosyncratic "9–8 Plan" to be implemented in the 1962 elections. Congressional candidates ran in each of the nine old districts in the Democratic primary but then competed for eight seats in the general election.[36] Instead, the key evidence came from the transcript of the meeting of the Alabama State Democratic Committee, which was charged under Alabama law with determining how

to implement such laws as Act 221 in the only election that mattered at the
time, the Democratic primary.[37]

Sam Engelhardt, by then Governor John Patterson's highway director, was
also Patterson's choice to chair the state executive committee in 1959. Despite
his record of pushing racially discriminatory voting laws through the legislature
and heading the state's White Citizens' Council, Engelhardt was actually the
more moderate candidate, opposed by the leader of the "state's rights" faction within the party, attorney Frank Mizell of Montgomery. Patterson had
won the governorship in 1958 by campaigning as more committed to white
supremacy than his opponent, George Wallace, but he nevertheless wanted to
keep the state party loyal to the national Democratic Party, and did not want
Mizell and the "anti-loyalist" forces to control the state executive committee.[38]

With Engelhardt in the chair, Mizell presented a detailed proposal setting forth the rules under which the 1962 Democratic primary was to be
conducted, including the unusual provisions necessary to implement the 9–8
Plan for congressional redistricting. Each of the nine former congressional
districts was to hold a district primary, after which the nine district winners
would compete in a statewide congressional election, with the top eight vote-
getters representing the party against the weak Republican Party in the general
election.[39] Paragraph 17 of the Mizell proposal called for the implementation
of Act 221—the numbered place law—in most future elections, but not the
1962 congressional elections, where the 9–8 Plan was to apply. In the general
election for the eight congressional seats, however, Section 18 required the
use of the full-slate (anti-single shot) rule.[40]

Opponents from small counties—who saw the numbered place requirement as giving an advantage to counties with larger populations in contests
for the state executive committee—as well as those with only small black
populations moved to table the proposal.[41] Mizell defended the numbered
place law with a remarkable speech—a speech which Thompson quoted at
length—explaining to the state committee members why the legislature had
adopted Act 221.

> [W]e have increasing Federal pressure to . . . register negroes en masse,
> regardless of the fact that many of them ordinarily cannot qualify because
> of their criminal records, or criminal attitudes, because of the fact that
> they are illiterate and cannot understand or pass literacy tests, but those

qualifications are things that don't worry the people from Washington, the army of people who are here in Montgomery County harassing our Board of Registrars, harassing the Registrars throughout most of the State of Alabama . . . and in one county where there were very few darkies registered, there has probably increased 4 or 5 hundred percent already, and . . . it has occurred to a great many people, including the Legislature of Alabama, that to protect the white people of Alabama, that there should be numbered places.[42]

Passage of the proposal, Mizell emphasized, meant that "this committee would be following the purpose and intent of the legislature." The state executive committee then adopted the numbered place requirement for the 1962 Democratic primary by a voice vote.[43]

APPLYING THE LEGAL STANDARD

The analytical framework within which judges were—and are still—required to assess whether a decision is racially discriminatory in intent was set forth by the Supreme Court in a 1977 decision regarding allegations of intentional discrimination in housing policy in Arlington Heights, Illinois. Because direct evidence regarding the purpose of a decision is rare, courts ordinarily have to rely on circumstantial evidence. Under the Arlington Heights approach, judges are told to consider the historical background of a decision, the specific sequence of events leading to the decision, and the views of decision-makers on racial issues generally.[44] The Supreme Court emphasized, moreover, that a racial purpose will ordinarily not be the "sole" purpose: "Legislation is frequently multipurposed; the removal of even a 'subordinate' purpose may shift altogether the consensus of legislative judgment supporting the statute."[45]

Clearly the historical background described in the preceding pages reveals a consistent pattern of discriminatory intent. When African Americans were still able to vote in the post-Reconstruction period, white Democratic officials either used at-large elections or—where blacks were in the majority—eliminated elections altogether in favor of gubernatorial appointment of county commissions. After disfranchisement of most blacks, many counties or cities shifted to single-member district elections, but when African Americans once again became a significant portion of the electorate counties once again adopted at-large elections. The state legislature, moreover, enhanced the discriminatory potential of at-large elections by means of statewide anti-single shot or numbered place laws. These laws reflected a state policy imposed on local governing bodies without respect to the preferences of either local officials or their constituents.

Election laws do not exist in a vacuum, of course. Placing this pattern of discriminatory election laws in a more general context, Thompson identified other state laws that explicitly discriminated against blacks—segregating them in all walks of life—until outlawed by federal court decisions. "As children black persons were required to go to segregated schools . . . play in segregated parks . . . and use segregated recreational facilities."[46] As they grew up, Thompson continued, "black persons faced continued discrimination in education . . . and were also discriminated against in state employment . . . and even in their private lives."[47] African Americans were also victims of discrimination "on both sides of the legal system," being routinely excluded from juries and "kept in segregated quarters in the state's jails and prisons."[48] As Thompson wryly observed, "no matter what form of public transportation they chose, black persons were subjected to segregation."[49]

The key direct evidence was, of course, the actions of the State Democratic Executive Committee, responding to committee member Frank Mizell's racially explicit explanation of the purpose of the statewide numbered place requirement. Even without this direct evidence, however, the circumstantial evidence may have been more than enough to satisfy the Arlington Heights standard. Defendant counties pointed out that they had adopted at-large elections at different times and the plaintiffs had not undertaken to investigate each of those separate adoptions. The plaintiffs contended, however, and Thompson agreed, that in adopting the numbered place requirement in 1961—a requirement that was still in place in 1986—"the state reshaped at-large systems into more secure mechanisms for discrimination" and the evidence made clear that "this reshaping of the systems was completely intentional."[50]

Once a court determines that intentional discrimination has played a significant role in the adoption of an election practice, there remains the question of assessing the degree to which the decision has produced a racially discriminatory effect. As Thompson pointed out, this presents a different problem than the standard effects test under Section 2.[51] A case brought under the results test created by the 1982 revision of Section 2 requires expert statistical analysis of the degree of racially polarized voting in the jurisdiction, evidence that minority-preferred candidates are usually defeated as a result of bloc voting by majority whites, and examination of the factors identified by Congress as necessary to prove that the "totality of the circumstances" in the case weigh in favor of the plaintiffs.[52] Where the court has concluded that the election practice is infected by intentional discrimination, however, the effects test "is less stringent and may be met by any evidence that the challenged action is having significant adverse impact on black persons today."[53]

At the preliminary injunction hearing the plaintiffs presented a fact witness, field director Jerome Gray of the Alabama Democratic Conference—the major black political organization in the state—whose undisputed testimony was that no black candidates had ever been elected under the at-large systems in any of the county commissions at issue in the litigation.[54] That was sufficient evidence that the intentionally discriminatory system of at-large elections— enhanced by numbered place and majority-vote requirements—continued to have a racially discriminatory effect, and thus violated Section 2 of the Voting Rights Act.

THE CONTINUING HISTORY OF THE *Dillard* LITIGATION

One month after Judge Myron Thompson enjoined further use of at-large elections in the affected counties, the Supreme Court handed down the landmark decision in a North Carolina redistricting case, *Thornburg v. Gingles*, affirming the ruling of the lower courts striking down the use of multi-member districts and setting forth the standard by which future courts should enforce the Section 2 results test. Under this standard plaintiffs must first meet three preconditions by proving: 1) that a single-member districting plan can be drawn with a black-majority district; 2) that minority voters form a cohesive voting bloc; and 3) that white voters usually vote as a bloc and thus prevent the election of any minority-preferred candidates. If these preconditions are met, plaintiffs then must provide evidence to satisfy the "totality of circumstances" test set forth in the 1982 Senate Report.[55] Because it was widely understood that plaintiffs can usually meet the *Gingles* standard, jurisdictions throughout the South with at-large elections saw this as "the handwriting on the wall" and agreed to settle Section 2 lawsuits.[56] In Alabama the combination of *Dillard* and *Gingles* was overwhelming. Most of the 183 defendants in *Dillard* settled with the African American plaintiffs and agreed to adopt fair single-member district plans or, in a few cases, limited voting or cumulative voting plans.[57]

Some jurisdictions ended up in court, however. For example, Calhoun, Lawrence, and Pickens counties proposed to settle the case by adopting district election plans but retaining at-large chairpersons. The plaintiffs in those counties rejected the at-large chair proposals on the grounds that these mixed plans would not provide a complete remedy to the Section 2 violation; Thompson agreed and instead ordered the implementation of the plaintiffs' proposed districting plans.[58] Calhoun County appealed this decision but the 11th Circuit, in an opinion written by Judge Frank M. Johnson Jr., affirmed the district court opinion, quoting the 1982 Senate Report's instruction that courts enforcing Section 2 should "fashion the relief so that it completely remedies the prior dilution of minority voting strength."[59]

In another case the settlement talks between the African American plaintiffs and the school board in Baldwin County—16 percent black—broke down over the nature of the remedial districting plan and the case went to trial in early 1988, complete with statistical analysis of the degree of racially polarized voting.[60] In settlement talks the school board had agreed to elect its five members from single-member districts but none of its proposed districts had a black voting-age majority. The plaintiffs countered with a seven-member plan which had one black-majority district. As the school board saw it, the proposed black-majority district was "unacceptable because it is too elongated and curvaceous and thus fails to meet the requirement of 'compactness.'"[61] Thompson rejected that claim. "By compactness," he emphasized, the Supreme Court was not referring to an "aesthetic norm" but to a "practical" or "functional" concept. "A district would not be sufficiently compact if it was so spread out that there was no sense of community, that is, if its members and its representative could not effectively and efficiently stay in touch with each other."[62] Combining the findings in regard to the *Gingles* preconditions, the Senate factors, and the intent underlying the state's use of at-large elections and numbered place requirements, Thompson ruled that the school board's at-large election system failed "both the intent and results tests" and ordered the school board to implement the plaintiffs' plan in time for the next election.[63]

Each of the *Dillard* settlements had to be submitted for preclearance by the Department of Justice, as well as satisfy the requirements of the trial court. The interaction of Section 2 litigation and the preclearance requirement often worked to the advantage of the *Dillard* plaintiffs. A particularly important example of the advantage afforded by Section 5 review is the deterrence of municipal annexations that would have minimized the effectiveness of the settlement plans. One of the *Dillard* defendants was the city of Valley, incorporated in 1980 for the purpose of creating a school system separate from the schools of Chambers County. The city boundaries were irregularly shaped, in part because they "excluded significant areas of black population concentration."[64] The plaintiffs challenged the city's refusal to annex several nearby black neighborhoods, and Thompson stayed the city's 1988 elections pending resolution of the issue; the city then agreed to annex the black neighborhoods. Before the single-member districts went into effect for the 1992 elections, however, Valley tried to annex another 243 persons, only two of whom were black. The Department of Justice refused to preclear the annexation until the issue between the parties was resolved. In the end the city council adopted a seven single-member district plan with two majority-black districts and the settlement was finalized.[65]

CONCLUSION

By 1990 enforcement of the Voting Rights Act had transformed Alabama politics to a degree unimaginable in 1965. African Americans were not only voting with little actual hindrance but also at rates often approaching white participation rates. Blacks were also increasingly serving as poll officials, thanks to Thompson's court order in the *Harris* litigation. Minority representation in the state legislature and in local governing bodies was approaching proportionality as well, primarily as a result of successful litigation in the 1980s under Section 2 that eliminated at-large elections in favor of court-ordered single-member district plans.[66] The Section 5 preclearance requirement was less important in Alabama than in some other states because only voting changes require preclearance and Alabama systematically required at-large elections and numbered place requirements before the Section 5 coverage date, November 1, 1964.[67] The history of that systematic effort to deny minority representation, however, proved to be the key to eliminating the at-large system, with its numbered place requirement, by winning the pivotal multi-jurisdictional case, *Dillard v. Crenshaw County*.

Notes

1   Peyton McCrary, Jerome A. Gray, Edward Still, and Huey Perry, "Alabama," in Chandler Davidson and Bernard Grofman (eds.), *Quiet Revolution in the South: The Impact of the Voting Rights Act, 1965-1990* (Princeton: Princeton University Press, 1994), 38–66, 397–409.

2   640 F. Supp. 1347 (M.D. Ala. 1986). The injunction only affected five of the defendant counties. Crenshaw, Escambia, and Lee counties settled with the plaintiffs before the court's decision. Ibid., 1352. The intent claim against Pickens County was barred by the legal principle of *res judicata*—the intent claim in a prior challenge to the county's at-large elections had been unsuccessful, but not the Section 2 results claim. Ibid., 1352, 1363–66. In all there were 183 defendant jurisdictions, but for various reasons only 176 consent decrees. *Dillard v. Baldwin County Board of Education*, 686 F. Supp. 1459, 1461–62 (M.D. Ala. 1988), summarizes the history of this complex litigation to that date and enumerates the court-approved settlements. Aspects of the case are still in the courts more than a quarter century after the 1986 preliminary injunction. According to a recent study, Judge Myron Thompson's decision in this case resulted in "by far the biggest advance in equal access for black voters" of any case in the state's recent history. James Blacksher, et. al., "Voting Rights in Alabama, 1982–2006," 17 *Review of Law & Social Justice* 249, 259 (2008).

3   *Smith v. Paris*, 257 F. Supp. 901 (M.D. Ala. 1966). An earlier instance in which the use of multi-member districts was found to be racially discriminatory was in the Alabama reapportionment case *Reynolds v. Sims*, on remand as *Sims v. Baggett*, 247 F. Supp. 96, 107–09 (M.D. Ala. 1965).

4   *Smith v. Paris*, 257 F. Supp. 901, 904 (M.D. Ala. 1966), modified and aff'd 386 F.2d 979 (5th Cir. 1967). For a fuller account, see McCrary, et.al., "Alabama," 39–41, 399–400.

5   The party committee's defense was that they shifted to at-large elections because their old districts violated the one person, one vote principle. Dismissing this claim as "nothing more than a sham," Judge Frank M. Johnson Jr. pointed out that the committee could simply have reapportioned its districts. 257 F. Supp. 901, 905 (M.D. Ala. 1966). The change was, wrote Johnson, "born of an effort to frustrate and discriminate against Negroes in the exercise of their right to vote, in violation of the Fifteenth Amendment." 257 F. Supp. at 904 (M.D.Ala. 1966).

6   *White v. Regester*, 412 U.S. 755, 766, 769 (1973.

7   412 U.S. 755, 766, 769 (1973).

8   *Zimmer v. McKeithen*, 485 F.2d 1297 (5th Cir. 1973)(en banc), aff'd sub nom. *East Carroll Parish School Bd. v. Marshall*, 424 U.S. 636 (1976).

9   *Zimmer v. McKeithen*, 485 F.2d 1297 (5th Cir. 1973). James U. Blacksher and Larry Menefee, "From Reynolds v. Sims to City of Mobile v. Bolden: Have the White Suburbs Commandeered the Fifteenth Amendment?" 34 *Hastings L.J.* 1, 18–26 (1982). Steve Bickerstaff, "Reapportionment by the State Legislatures: A Guide for the 1980's," 34 *Sw. L. J.* 635, 646–49 (1980); Katherine I. Butler, "Constitutional and Statutory Challenges to Election Structures: Dilution and the Value of the Right to Vote," 42 *La. L. Rev.* 863, 883–90 (1982); Timothy G. O'Rourke, "Constitutional and Statutory Challenges to Local At-Large Elections." 17 *Univ.Richmond L. Rev.* 39, 51–57, 78–81 (Fall 1982). Peyton McCrary, "Racially Polarized Voting in the South: Quantitative Evidence

from the Courtroom," *Social Science History*, 14 (1990), 510–14, explains the statistical procedures used in these cases to measure the degree of racial bloc voting.

10   *Jones v. City of Lubbock*, 640 F.2d 777 (5th Cir. 1981).

11   *City of Mobile v. Bolden*, 446 U.S. 55 (1980). Although supported by only a plurality, Justice Potter Stewart's opinion was the prevailing view on the Court. Not only did the opinion require proof of intent but it appeared to require a more difficult standard for inferring racial purpose through circumstantial evidence. The Fifth Circuit Court of Appeals had anticipated the intent requirement in *Nevett v. Sides*, 571 F.2d 209 (5th Cir. 1978), *Bolden v. City of Mobile*, 571 F.2d 238 (5th Cir. 1978), *Blacks United for Lasting Leadership v. City of Shreveport*, 571 F.2d 248 (5th Cir. 1978), and *Thomasville Branch of NAACP v. Thomas County*, 571 F.2d 257 (5th Cir. 1978). See O'Rourke, "Constitutional and Statutory Challenges," 56–57.

12   *Bolden v. City of Mobile*, 542 F. Supp. 1050 (S.D. Ala. 1982); *Brown v. Board of School Commissioners of Mobile County*, 542 F. Supp. 1078 (S.D. Ala. 1982). Peyton McCrary, "History in the Courts: The Significance of *City of Mobile v. Bolden*," in Davidson (ed.), *Minority Vote Dilution*, 47–63, summarizes the testimony in both cases (and the cost).

13   Frank R. Parker, "The 'Results' Test of Section 2 of the Voting Rights Act: Abandoning the Intent Standard," 69 *Va. L. Rev.* 715 (1983); Thomas M. Boyd and Stephen J. Markman, "The 1982 Amendments to the Voting Rights Act: A Legislative History," 40 *Wash. & Lee L. Rev.* 1347 (1983); and Armand Derfner, "Vote Dilution and the Voting Rights Act Amendments of 1982," in Chandler Davidson (ed.), *Minority Vote Dilution* (Washington: Howard University Press, 1984), 145–63. Abigail Thernstrom, who favors an intent standard, argues that Congress was misguided in adopting a results test. Thernstrom, *Whose Votes Count? Affirmative Action and Minority Voting Rights* (Cambridge: Harvard University Press, 1987), 79–136.

14   McDonald, "The Quiet Revolution in Minority Voting Rights," 1265; Blacksher and Menefee, "From *Reynolds v. Sims* to *City of Mobile v. Bolden*," 31–32.

15   *Dillard v. Crenshaw County*, 640 F. Supp. 1347, 1353 (M.D. Ala. 1986), citing the governing appeals court decision, *McMillan v. Escambia County, Fla.*, 748 F.2d 1037, 1046 (11th Cir. 1984).

16   The approach taken by the federal courts in assessing the intent of a decision under challenge under the 14th Amendment—set forth in *Village of Arlington Heights v. Metropolitan Housing Corp.*, 429 U.S. 252, 265–66 (1977)—is also the approach taken in Section 2 cases and is consistent with the methods traditionally employed by historians in assessing circumstantial evidence of intent. See Peyton McCrary and J. Gerald Hebert, "Keeping the Courts Honest: The Role of Historians as Expert Witnesses in Southern Voting Rights Cases," 16 *Southern University L. Rev.* 101, 105–06 (Spring 1989); Peyton McCrary, "Discriminatory Intent: The Continuing Relevance of 'Purpose' Evidence in Vote-Dilution Lawsuits, 28 *Howard L.J.* 463 (1985).

17   *Underwood v. Hunter*, 730 F.2d 614 (11th Cir. 1984), aff'd 471 U.S. 222 (1985).

18   *Harris v. Graddick*, 593 F. Supp. 128 (M.D. Ala. 1984). As a result, the state agreed to appoint substantial numbers of black poll officials, to establish a training program for all poll officials, and to undertake an outreach program targeting young black adults. McCrary, et.al., "Alabama," 53, 407; *Harris v. Graddick*, 615 F. Supp. 239 (M.D. Ala. 1985).

19   *Harris v. Siegelman*, 695 F. Supp. 517, 522 (M.D. Ala. 1988), quoting a contemporary news account from the *Mobile Register*, Feb. 14, 1893. I testified as an expert in this case, as did sociologist Chandler Davidson. The Sayre election law's discriminatory purpose was widely understood, as Thompson recognized in relying on David Bagwell, "The 'Magical Process': The Sayre Election Law of 1893," *Alabama Review*, 25 (April 1972), 83–104; Malcolm C. McMillan, *Constitutional Development in Alabama, 1798–1901: A Study in Politics, the Negro, and Sectionalism* (Chapel Hill: University of North Carolina Press, 1955), 223; and J. Morgan Kousser, *The Shaping of Southern Politics: Suffrage Restriction and the Establishment of the One-Party South, 1880–1910* (New Haven: Yale University Press, 1974), 133–38. See 695 F. Supp. 517, 522–23 (M.D. Ala. 1988).

20   See for example *Hendrix v. McKinney*, 460 F. Supp. 626 (M.D. Ala. 1978); *Clark and United States v. Marengo County Commission*, 469 F. Supp. 1150 (S.D. Ala. 1979), rev'd 731 F. 2d 1546 (11th Cir. 1984), cert. denied, 469 U.S. 976 (1984), on remand, 643 F. Supp. 232 (S.D. Ala. 1986), aff'd, 811 F. 2d 609 (11th Cir. 1987)(liability) and 811 F.2d 610 (11th Cir. 1987)(remedy); *United States v. Dallas County Commission*, 548 F. Supp. 875 (S.D. Ala. 1982), rev'd 739 F.2d 1529 (11th Cir. 1984), on remand, 636 F. Supp. 704 (S.D. Ala. 1986)(liability), 661 F. Supp. 955 (S.D. Ala. 1987)(remedy), rev'd 850 F.2d 1433 (11th Cir. 1988).

21   *Dillard v. Crenshaw County*, 640 F. Supp. 1347, 1368–71 (M.D. Ala. 1986).

22   In the interest of full disclosure, I was the expert witness presenting this testimony: see *Dillard v. Crenshaw County*, 640 F. Supp. 1347, 1356 (M.D. Ala. 1986).

23   640 F. Supp. 1347, 1358 (M.D. Ala. 1986). See McMillan, *Constitutional Development in Alabama*, 222.

24   640 F. Supp. 1347, 1358 (M.D. Ala. 1986), citing *Bolden v. City of Mobile*, 542 F. Supp. 1050, 1062 (S.D. Ala. 1982).

25   640 F. Supp. 1347, 1358 (M.D. Ala. 1986). The court's assessment of changes in the method of electing county commissioners, both in the 1890s and subsequently, relied on Plaintiffs' Exhibit 187, a database of session laws dating from 1865 through 1984, prepared by graduate assistants under my supervision.

26   Ibid., citing *Bolden v. City of Mobile*, 542 F. Supp. at 1063 & n. 10.

27   Ibid., relying on Plaintiffs' Exhibit 187.

28   Ibid., 1358 (citing *Bolden v. City of Mobile*, 542 F. Supp. at 1063 & n. 10).

29   Ibid., 1359, citing *Davis v. Schnell*, 81 F. Supp. 872 (M.D. Ala. 1949), aff'd 336 U.S. 93; *United States v. Penton*, 212 F. Supp. 193 (M.D. Ala. 1962); and *United States v. Parker*, 236 F. Supp. 511 (M.D. Ala. 1964).

30   Ibid., relying on Plaintiffs' Exhibit 187 and the testimony of the plaintiffs' expert historian. Thompson illustrated the racial purpose underlying this pattern with a specific example taken from a news article in which a state senator from Barbour County, George Wallace's home county, explained that the purpose of his bill switching the method of electing county commissioners in Barbour County to at-large elections was "to lessen the impact of any bloc vote in any district." As Thompson noted, "the term 'bloc vote' was commonly used at that time as a code to refer to the black vote."

31   Ibid., 1357 (citing *Gomillion v. Lightfoot*, 364 U.S. 339 (1960)).

32   Ibid. As the federal courts had noted in the 1970's, anti-single-shot laws disadvantage

minority voters "because it may force them to vote for nonminority candidates, thus depreciating the relative position of minority candidates." Ibid., 1356 (quoting *Nevett v. Sides*, 571 F.2d 209, 217 n. 10 (5th Cir. 1978), cert. denied, 446 U.S. 951 (1980)).

33 "First-past-the-post" is a term of art referring to a system in which—if five persons are to be elected at large—the top five vote-getters win.

34 Ibid., 1357.

35 Ibid., 1356.

36 Anne Permaloff and Carl Grafton, *Political Power in Alabama: The More Things Change* . . . (Athens: University of Georgia Press, 1995), 121–39; Permaloff and Grafton, "The Chop-up Bill and the Big Mule Alliance," *Alabama Review*, XLIII (October 1999), 243–269. Newspaper focus during the session also included the unsuccessful effort to redistrict the Alabama legislature. That failure, in turn, led urban plaintiffs from Birmingham, Montgomery, and Mobile to mount a successful challenge the malapportioned legislative districts in federal court. Richard C. Cortner, *The Reapportionment Cases* (Knoxville: University of Tennessee Press, 1970), 163–68. The case was *Sims v. Frink*, 208 F. Supp. 431 (M.D. Ala. 1962), aff'd, *Reynolds v. Sims*, 377 U.S. 533 (1964).

37 Proceedings of the State Democratic Executive Committee of Alabama, January 20, 1962, SDEC Papers, Alabama Department of Archives and History, Montgomery, Alabama.

38 Permaloff and Grafton, *Political Power in Alabama*, 112–13. Mizell was also a serious candidate for lieutenant governor in 1962. Ibid., 159–60.

39 Proceedings, 4–22. See Permaloff and Grafton, "The Chop-Up Bill," 266.

40 Proceedings, 9, 11.

41 Ibid., 13, 15.

42 Ibid., 13.

43 The motion to table the numbered place section failed by a significant margin, and the committee then adopted the motion by a voice vote. Ibid., 13–15, 18–20.

44 *Village of Arlington Heights v. Metropolitan Housing Corp.*, 429 U.S. 252, 265–66 (1977). The opinion was written by Justice Lewis Powell, a relatively conservative Virginian nominated by President Richard Nixon.

45 Ibid., 429 U.S. at 265, quoted in *Dillard v. Crenshaw County*, 640 F. Supp. 1347, 1355 (M.D. Ala. 1986).

46 Citing *Lee v. Macon County Bd. of Ed.*, 231 F. Supp. 743 (M.D. Ala. 1964) (three-judge court) (segregated schools); *Gilmore v. City of Montgomery*, 176 F. Supp. 776 (M.D. Ala. 1959), modified, 277 F.2d 364 (5th Cir. 1960) (segregated parks); and *Smith v. Y.M.C.A.*, 316 F. Supp. 899 (M.D. Ala. 1970), aff'd as modified, 462 F.2d 634 (5th Cir. 1972) (segregated recreational facilities).

47 Citing *United States v. Alabama*, 628 F. Supp. 1137 (N.D. Ala. 1985) (educational discrimination); *Paradise v. Prescott*, 585 F. Supp. 72 (M.D. Ala. 1983), aff'd, 767 F.2d 1514 (11th Cir. 1985) (discrimination in promotion of state troopers); *NAACP v. Allen*, 340 F. Supp. 703 (M.D. Ala. 1972), aff'd, 493 F.2d 614 (5th Cir. 1974) (discrimination in hiring of state troopers); *United States v. Frazer*, 317 F. Supp. 1079 (M.D. Ala. 1970) (employment discrimination against blacks by four departments of state government); *Marable v. Alabama Mental Health Board*, 297 F. Supp. 291 (M.D. Ala. 1969) (discrimination against black mental health workers); and *United States v. Brittain*, 319 F. Supp.

1058 (N.D. Ala. 1970) (anti-miscegenation laws).

48   Citing *Black v. Curb*, 464 F.2d 165 (5th Cit. 1772) (exclusion from juries), and *Washington v. Lee*, 263 F. Supp. 327 (M.D. Ala. 1966) (three-judge court), aff'd, 390 U.S. 333 (1967) (segregated jails).

49   Citing *United States v. City of Montgomery*, 201 F. Supp. 590 (M.D. Ala. 1962) (segregated municipal airport); *Lewis v. Greyhound Corp.*, 199 F. Supp. 210 (M.D. Ala. 1961) (segregated bus terminals); and *Browder v. Gayle*, 142 F. Supp. 707 (M.D. Ala. 1956) (three-judge court), aff'd mem., 352 U.S. 903 (1956) (segregated city buses).

50   *Dillard v. Crenshaw County*, 640 F. Supp. 1347, 1357 (M.D. Ala. 1986).

51   Ibid., 1354n.

52   S. Rep. No. 97–417 (1982), 28–30, 33–34. *Thornburg v. Gingles*, 478 U.S. 30 (1986), established the standard of proof still controlling court decisions applying the Section 2 results test in vote dilution cases.

53   *Dillard v. Crenshaw County*, 640 F. Supp. 1347, 1354n (M.D. Ala. 1986), emphasis added. Thompson specifically relied for this proposition on the unanimous Supreme Court decision in *Hunter v. Underwood*, 471 U.S. 222 (1985).

54   640 F. Supp. 1347, 1353, 1360 (M.D. Ala. 1964).

55   *Thornburg v. Gingles*, 478 U.S. 30 (1986).

56   Chandler Davidson, "The Recent Evolution of Voting Rights Law Affecting Racial and Language Minorities," in Davidson and Grofman (eds.), *Quiet Revolution in the South*, 35; Davidson and Grofman, "The Voting Rights Act and the Second Reconstruction," ibid., 385.

57   Blacksher, et.al., "Voting Rights in Alabama," 264–65 (adding that *Gingles* "provided the political cover Alabama's elected officials might have needed to justify to their majority-white constituencies not to continue defending racially discriminatory election systems when they were challenged in court.")

58   *Dillard v. Crenshaw County*, 649 F. Supp. 289 (M.D. Ala. 1986). The plaintiffs also objected to the particular district boundaries in these plans, and the court agreed that the "new redistricting plans themselves violate Section 2 under the results test." Ibid., 296.

59   *Dillard v. Crenshaw County*, 831 F.2d 246, 250 (11th Cir. 1987) (emphasis added by the court).

60   *Dillard v. Baldwin County Board of Education*, 686 F. Supp. 1459 (M.D. Ala. 1988). Political scientist Gordon Henderson, a veteran expert witness, provided the statistical evidence.

61   *Dillard v. Baldwin County Board of Education*, 686 F. Supp. 1459, 1462, 1465 (M.D. Ala. 1988).

62   Ibid., 1465–66.

63   Ibid., 1470. The Baldwin County Commission tried a different tack—proposing as a settlement a "pure" at-large system, abandoning the numbered place and majority vote requirements and increasing the number of commissioners from three to five. *Dillard v. Baldwin County Commission*, 694 F. Supp. 836, 838 (M.D. Ala. 1988). Thompson ruled, however, that the commission's proposed plan would not completely remedy the violation—in fact it continued to violate Section 2—and required the county commis-

sion to use the same seven-district plan as the school board (thus facilitating effective administration of elections). Ibid, 840, 844–45.

64   Blacksher, et.al., "Voting Rights in Alabama," 257.

65   Ibid. The city of Foley in Baldwin County had also pursued a selective annexation policy, prompting Section 5 objections by the Department of Justice to city's proposal to annex predominantly white areas while denying annexation efforts by black neighborhoods. The city agreed to annex the black as well as white areas as part of a consent decree in *Dillard. Dillard v. City of Foley*, 926 F. Supp. 1053, 1058 (M.D. Ala. 1996).

66   McCrary, et.al., "Alabama," 54–66. Although the Department of Justice successfully litigated a few cases in the plantation counties, most of the cases were in fact brought by private attorneys who were native Alabamians. Ibid., 49–50, 404–05. A few jurisdictions settling Section 2 lawsuits preferred a limited voting or cumulative voting plan, rather than district elections. A few voluntarily switched to district elections, beginning with the college town of Auburn in 1972 and the capitol city of Montgomery in 1973. Ibid., 48–49, 404.

67   Ibid., 39. Virtually all the shifts to district elections that resulted from Section 5 objections came about as a means of obtaining preclearance of municipal annexations. Ibid., 55, 408, and Table 2.8 (61–64).

18

Strange Career and the Need for a Second Reconstruction of the History of Race Relations[1]

J. MORGAN KOUSSER

I. Ambitions

From the beginning, C. Vann Woodward wanted to change the world by uncovering the truth. The remarkably ambitious goals of his doctoral dissertation, which eventually became *Tom Watson*, were not just to spotlight Southern rebels—proving that the South had never been solid, that it had a usable radical past, that the apparently timeless Southern consensus had been shattered before—but also to find out what had gone wrong, why his heroes had lost, what they had faced, and how they were flawed, so that readers could learn their lessons and perhaps avoid sharing their fates.[2] The same public purposes, many of the same themes, the same faith—not that the truth will make you free; he was never blinded by that illusion; but the negative version of the platitude, that without the truth, we can never be free or equal—also pervade *Reunion and Reaction*, *Origins of the New South*, and especially *The Strange Career of Jim Crow*.

These days, historians have filed the book away, misunderstood its aims, forgotten or denied its alternatives. Thus, Woodward's first biographer, John Herbert Roper, haughtily dismissed *Strange Career* as "most fatally flawed," a book that "ignored racism by studying only legal formalism," one whose implications for policy in the 1950s and '60s made it "most obviously dated in later years," a work, therefore, whose "genius . . . was orchestration"—merely good timing.[3] In an article commemorating the 50th anniversary of the book's publication in the *Boston Globe*, Stephen Kantrowitz remarked that "I'm not sure how important the book is for contemporary scholarship. The scholarship on Jim Crow has mutated into something quite different." And Mark Smith patronized it as merely ornamental, remarking that "if *Strange Career's* arguments gradually lose historiographical purchase, at least it'll keep alive an art form I sometimes worry is in danger of evaporating."[4]

But *Strange Career* was no more a quaint decoration than it was merely a reinterpretation of history or just an effort to inspire public policy. The book's revisionism attracted enormous attention and provoked, for a long while, considerable research, research that is no longer stylish, though it is not yet finished.[5] Yet there was another, larger, less apparent purpose of the work that has been only very partially fulfilled—the creation of a new field, the history of race relations, as *Origins* created the new field of the history of the post-Reconstruction South.[6]

This paper sketches broad trends in the history of American race relations in works published since 1955, as well as general trends in actual race relations since that year, in an attempt to understand what forces have shaped those two trends and to propose a Woodwardian reorientation of the field. After *Strange Career*, race relations history wandered for a time down a too-narrow path. More recently, it has unfortunately veered off course, concentrating on racial identity, rather than racial interaction;[7] on violence, rather than vital statistics;[8] on personal, rather than public politics.[9] Too many historians, in this field and others, have succumbed to the *fin-de-siècle* temptations of romanticism and intellectual despair, awarding everyone agency and denying anyone domination,[10] and doubting the possibility of knowledge, while seemingly smug in the assurance that they alone possess the truth.[11] In contrast to Woodward's emphasis on conflict and the possibility of change, many historians, often professed devotees of the political left, have ignored or dismissed distinctions between historical actors, promulgating an image of consensus in race relations that can only hamper effective action against discrimination.[12] Placing themselves outside the fray, historians in general, except those on the political right,[13] have largely retreated from efforts to change the minds that shape the institutional rules of racial interaction. Some have voiced a despair about human nature so profound, and a conviction of the irrationality and unpredictability of human beings so deep as to paralyze efforts at racial or any other type of reform.[14] Woodward initiated the field of comparative reconstruction. It is now time for a second reconstruction of the field of race relations history.

II. Propositions

Begun in research for the NAACP-LDF for *Brown v. Board of Education*, the short, but influential *Strange Career* was composed on the cusp of change from the legally segregated to the legally desegregated South. Woodward's guarded optimism about the future of race relations after *Brown* rested on four propositions—first, that institutions, not culture, had shaped Southern race relations; second, that slavery and segregation were not equivalent, and that, more particularly, segregation had not immediately replaced slavery as a "natural" form of racial control or interaction; third, that the extreme domination of one race over the other was not inevitable, that there were "forgotten alternatives" to segregation and disfranchisement in the post-1877 South; and finally—a proposition so fundamental as to remain unnoticed, perhaps even to Woodward, but which has emerged against the background of more recent static cultural treatments of the subject[15]—that race relations, like any other aspect of human relationships, could change and vary.

Strict, virtually uniform segregation was, Woodward asserted, the result of state and local laws that regularized and policed previously untidy, frequently mixed, and in scattered instances, nearly egalitarian, if furtive, relations between people of different races. Whereas party competition, especially, Woodward thought, between Populists and Democrats, tended to preserve black rights and status, white Democratic desires to end both partisan opposition and any shreds of racial equality prevailed only through law.

As the civil rights movement intensified and then retrenched in the 20 years after *Brown*, and as national administrations moved from tepid support of black civil rights under Dwight Eisenhower, to enthusiastic co-optation under Lyndon Johnson, to politicized backlash under Richard Nixon, *Strange Career* went through three editions that mirrored the times.[16] Even more than in the first edition, the later versions emphasized changes that might lurch forward or backward and the profound difficulty of sustaining policies that benefitted minorities. At the time of the earlier classic, Gunnar Myrdal's *An American Dilemma*, it had seemed to many people of good will that all America needed to solve its race problem was for whites to recognize the inconsistency between racial discrimination and the egalitarian American Creed.[17]

But by 1974 it was clear to Woodward and nearly everyone else that ideological consistency was at best only a first step. There is an Olympian despair about the third and last revised edition of *Strange Career*, as the decade after the passage of the two major national civil rights laws brought a seeming abandonment on the part of both blacks and whites of the nonviolent methods that inspired the movement for the laws and the integrationist ideals that both the movement and the laws embodied. Victory over segregation was no sooner declared than it was reversed. By the time of *Milliken v. Bradley*, the 1974 case that ended the possibility of metropolitan desegregation in the North,[18] the federal courts and executive branch, which had wielded the chief tools to unravel racial inequality, had apparently become the engines of its reinforcement.

Yet ironically, the uneven decline of discrimination during the generation after the first edition of *Strange Career*, so depressing to Woodward and those who shared his hopes, had subtly supported his position. The abrupt demise of segregation in public accommodations (restaurants, buses, hotels and motels, etc.)[19] after the passage of the 1964 Civil Rights Act should have convinced everyone that the core of Woodward's argument about the dependence of segregation on law had been validated, and the surge in African American voter registration after the passage of the 1965 Voting Rights Act should have added more evidence.[20] The fact that school, housing, and employment discrimination took longer to diminish[21] should have undermined cultural explanations of discrimination, which argued that discrimination is all of a piece, independent of governmental action. Events after the 1955 first edition of *Strange Career*, in other words, should have been seen to offer broad support for its findings, for they proved once again that no system of race relations—not slavery, not segregation, not integration—is "natural," and that each has sub-systems (e.g., political, social, economic) that do not necessarily develop in sync with each other. All systems and sub-systems depend on institutional rules and capabilities; all vary and change. Ultimately, all are about power. Race relations, the events of the 1950s, '60s, and '70s demonstrated, are politically constructed.

III. Evaluations

But historians ignored the lessons of the present—unfortunately, in my view[22]—in assessing what became known as "the Woodward thesis."[23] The first scholars to test it examined small, isolated, largely static examples, rather than making large, explicitly comparative studies of change, though larger historical studies began to appear in the 1980s,[24] and this approach still lives, especially in the work of Rebecca J. Scott, Anthony Marx, and Richard Valelly.[25] The initial articles and monographs typically focused on a single state and looked for evidence of the extent of segregation before the passage of state Jim Crow laws.[26] That evidence was scattered, instead of systematic; what constituted a "test" was difficult to agree upon; and whether segregation should be considered an inflexibly intertwined social system or a practice that might differ in various social, political, and economic realms, was not resolved, and in many cases, not even acknowledged.

First, consider the evidence. If one found few newspaper stories or letters or diary entries or court cases on railroad or streetcar or hotel segregation during the 1870s and '80s in a Southern state, did that mean that integration had been un*think*able, or that it had been un*remarkable*; that segregation had been un*challenged*, or that it had not *needed* to be challenged? How was one to know whether African Americans had ridden in the smoking cars of trains because they were forced there, or because they could not afford first-class tickets? How was it possible, on such evidence, to gauge what was usual and what was unusual? Was there a difference between the extent of segregation as indexed by each of the three statistical measures of central tendency—the mean (the arithmetic average), the median (the number in the middle of a set of ordered numbers), and the mode (the most common number)? If such concepts seem impossibly precise in summarizing such a vague state of evidence, does that in itself not suggest caution in blanket assertions about the general tendencies of social relations?

And what if it was easier to be precise about the degree of discrimination in one area of race relations than another? In particular, although it might be impossible on current evidence to determine just how segregated trains or hotels or other public accommodations were before the imposition of explicit segregation laws, it has become quite possible since the development of "ecological regression" in the 1950s to recover voting turnout rates and racial voting patterns for candidates and parties in Southern elections from the 1860s on. If the Jim Crow Thesis includes suffrage restriction, which Woodward certainly believed, and if the evidence from statistical studies of

Southern voting in the post-Reconstruction South is both much more solid than that about public accommodations and more clearly supportive of a later date for the perfection of the system of discrimination and an institutional means for accomplishing that perfection, which it certainly is, then ought we not to conclude that the Jim Crow Thesis is alive and well?[27]

Second, reflect on the tests. Should Woodward be read as claiming that the *typical* experience of African Americans until the late 19th century was integrated, or only that their experience of segregation was much less *uniform* than it later became? Thus, Charles E. Wynes adopted both interpretations, concluding that "the most distinguishing factor in the complexity of social relations between the races [in Virginia], was that of inconsistency. From 1870–1900, there was no generally accepted code of racial mores. It is perhaps true that in a majority of the cases where a Negro presumed to demand equal treatment—in hotels, restaurants, theatres, and bars, and even on the railroads—he was more likely to meet rejection than acceptance."[28] The most influential challenge to Woodward's position was by Joel Williamson on the entirely atypical—more heavily black, more dependent on cotton, with the weakest tradition of democratic political competition—state of South Carolina. Williamson read Woodward's thesis as an assertion about average experiences in what Williamson paints as a society that was nearly static in the 19th century, making his rejection of the Woodward thesis virtually automatic.[29] Others, most notably John William Graves, in his marvelous book on the understudied state of Arkansas, read the thesis as an assertion about variation and found that the evidence supported it.[30]

Third, is the Jim Crow Thesis about specific social behavior or general culture or even more vaguely, about thought or feeling? Woodward was admittedly not altogether clear about this, but Williamson was: "The real color line," he declared, "lived in the minds of individuals of each race, and it had achieved full growth even before freedom for the Negro was born. Physical separation merely symbolized and reinforced mental separation."[31] This forthright statement encapsulates the view of what might be called the "Berkeley School of the history of race relations," encompassing Williamson, who received his PhD thesis at Berkeley, and Leon Litwack and Lawrence Levine, both of whom long taught at that branch of the University of California. In this cultural-intellectual view, all whites felt "separated" from African Americans, and this fact mattered much more than the form of behavior in which the mental separation was manifest—slavery, segregation, or even integration. Echoing Williamson, Litwack titled his major work on black history *Trouble in **Mind***[32] (my emphasis). Although evidence about racial thought or feeling can be measured at least somewhat systematically even before attitude surveys began,[33] Williamson, Litwack, and others made no attempt to do so.

The Berkeley school emphasized violence and discounted any cross-racial alliances. Where Woodward had memorably recounted the gathering of hundreds of Georgia Populists to protect a black Populist minister, the Reverend Seb Doyle, during Tom Watson's 1892 campaign for Congress,[34] Williamson spotlighted mobs of white Southern men, displaced from their roles as breadwinners by the depression of the 1890s, seeking to reestablish control over their restive wives by lynching alleged black rapists. Their actions were completely irrational and utterly unpredictable: "Anytime, anyplace, white people in large crowds might suddenly fall into a frenzy and lynch a black person."[35] What would falsify such a contention—a demonstration of the instrumental employment of violence, such as Woodward's example of Democratic attempts to stop a black preacher from speaking in favor of a white Populist, or perhaps the observation that interracial lynching, however horrible, was much less prevalent than other forms of violence or crime, and that patterns in it could be discerned?[36] Somewhat less excitedly, Leon Litwack emphasized the "terror, intimidation, and violence" that whites employed to "doom Reconstruction" and the "violence and the fear of violence" that "helped to shape black lives and personalities" from then through the Great Migration to the North during World War I, and he completely discounted any instances of white political "collaboration" with blacks, whether under the banner of Populism or Republicanism.[37] But Reconstruction-era African Americans had an amazing ability to overcome violence,[38] and partisan politics in which blacks played major roles continued to be vigorous until laws and constitutional amendments brought it to an end after 1890.[39]

Although eschewing explicit references to social psychology or sociology, the Berkeley School often reduced race relations to some assertedly more fundamental conflict, usually sexual or perhaps sexual-economic, for which evidence was purely rhetorical, if it existed at all. Wielding only quotations from novelist Thomas Nelson Page and unenfranchised feminist radical Rebecca Latimer Felton, Litwack asserted that the motive for the disfranchisement of black voters was sexual: "To bar the black man from the polling place was to bar him from the bedroom. If blacks voted with whites as equals, they would insist on living and sleeping with whites as equals, and no white Southerner could contemplate such degradation. . . . The issue was not black political power," he concluded[40] without examining the plentiful evidence that the issue was, indeed, black and white oppositional power.[41] Relying primarily on his own untestable intuitions, Williamson postulated even more grandiosely that "the Negro was a scapegoat in the turn-of-the-century South, that whites were having difficulty coping with a burgeoning industrial-commercial-political order as it impacted upon a social-psychological-sexual order earlier generated, and that in that crisis they used the Negro in constructing an illusion that they were indeed managing their lives in important ways."[42] What skein of social facts, paired with what all-powerful social psychological theory, would be necessary to validate such assertions? Compared to such cultural mystification, the Jim Crow Thesis was a model of clarity and testability.

Fourth, how are different spheres of social relations connected, and how should contradictory trends in the different spheres weigh for and against the Jim Crow Thesis? Was school segregation, apparently almost universal in the South after emancipation, except in New Orleans, evidence for the pervasiveness of segregation, or, because segregation was less strictly adhered to in other spheres, was school segregation actually evidence that separation required legal enforcement? Were black churches, so comforting to Southern whites as evidence that "they" wanted to be with "their own kind," instead supportive of the connection between systems of racial interaction and power? That is, in spheres of activity in which blacks could attain power only in segregated institutions, such as churches, they preferred segregation; whereas, in institutions where they could enjoy power only by mixing with whites, such as legislatures, they preferred integration—the common denominator, more compelling than social preferences, being the search for power. Focusing on schools and churches, Williamson depicted segregation as "the Negro's answer to discrimination," though he also noted that the black political leadership insisted on integrated public accommodations by law. He apparently did not consider these two judgments contradictory.[43]

How did the Jim Crow Thesis apply to the political sphere, in which blacks remained active participants long after schools and churches, and some railroads and streetcars were segregated? How did disfranchisement, which was not a "horizontal," but a "vertical" division, more like exclusion than it was like segregation, fit into the assessment of *Strange Career*? What was the implication of the fact that poor white suffrage was restricted, as well? What of the economic sphere, where only in large cities could there be a semblance of a separate black economy? In small towns and rural areas of the South, whites were much more economically powerful than blacks, but the two races were interdependent and incompletely segregated. In Southern cities, small neighborhood clusters of racial concentrations only became concentrated into large racial housing blocs after the 1890s, and they were often enforced by explicitly racial zoning restrictions. Should one count the early minimal segregation as evidence of racial preferences for separation or the delayed appearance of "colored towns" and racial zoning ordinances evidence for the Jim Crow Thesis?[44]

The rural and urban contrast in the economy is part of what might be termed the principal paradox of segregation: social segregation was more characteristic of "modern" than of "traditional" sectors of society, of urban, rather than rural areas, and thus, during the antebellum period, of the North, rather than of the South.[45] Scholars have often drawn misleading implications from the modernity of segregation. One possible conclusion is that segregation was natural and did not need laws to establish it. But the conclusion is wrong because the observation is incomplete. The first state to take comprehensive action against legal segregation—i.e., to repeal laws against racial intermarriage, to end railroad segregation, and to mandate school integration—was the most modern antebellum commonwealth, Massachusetts.[46] By 1890, all of the ex-free states with any appreciable number of African Americans except Indiana had followed the Bay State's example by repealing their "black laws" and passing public accommodations and school integration laws.[47]

Although the correlation between modernization and segregation was negative in the 19th and much of the 20th century North (the more modern the society, the less segregated), it seems to have been positive in most of the 19th century South, as well as in South Africa.[48] What are the implications of this fact? First, segregation is merely one form of racial discrimination, and often not the harshest. Slavery and poorly paid agricultural wage labor usually required constant monitoring and strict authoritarian control. Second, there is only a tenuous connection between segregation, slavery, or any other system of discrimination, on the one hand, and, on the other hand, an undifferentiated racism of ideas, either informal or highly theorized. The harshest and most fervent and frequent expressions of racism came from those whites who lived with the largest proportion of African Americans, but segregation, as well as anti-segregation movements, were products of the usually whiter, more cosmopolitan cities, where less benighted racial attitudes were much more common.[49] Perhaps demonstrations of the intricate connections between segregation and socioeconomic modernization will finally convince historians to accept what social psychologists have been demonstrating since the 1930s—that the connections between racial attitudes and behavior are weak.[50] Historians should cease to treat evidence of cultural attitudes about race relations as a perfect proxy or unproblematic cause of discriminatory behavior.

Third, the view of Southern segregation as primarily an urban phenomenon adds support to Woodward's position, for Southern cities, again with the exception of New Orleans, grew large only in the late 19th century. Laws were more necessary to enforce social norms in cities than in rural and small-town societies. Outside of cities, informal enforcement mechanisms, from forms of torture to less dramatic expressions of disapproval, were usually sufficient to maintain a racial hierarchy.

IV. Emendations

The Jim Crow Thesis stimulated not only efforts to affirm or deny it, but also attempts to amend or add to it. Following suggestions by Joel Williamson, Howard Rabinowitz viewed segregation as a positive step forward for African Americans, an alternative both to slavery and to total exclusion from such institutions as public schools,[51] though not as desirable as the full integration that Radical Republicans preferred and that seven Southern legislatures endorsed, at least for public accommodations, during Reconstruction. Interpreting Woodward as speaking primarily about public accommodations, Rabinowitz granted that there was noticeable integration in at least second-class railway cars before the passage of Jim Crow laws and that blacks continued to vote and hold office until legal disfranchisement, but he contended that in almost all other areas of Southern life in the Reconstruction and post-Reconstruction eras, especially schools, segregation was the predominant pattern. On even less evidence, he speculated that segregation and disfranchisement were not as total and rigid after the passage of the nominally strict laws as Woodward had assumed.[52]

The Rabinowitz Exclusion Thesis suffers from many of the problems already outlined. It treats all areas of behavior as highly correlated, while admitting that some were exceptions. It has no explicit index of practice in any area, and, unlike the Jim Crow Thesis, which only needs a few examples to demonstrate a lack of uniformity, the Rabinowitz Thesis must demonstrate some central tendency, which would seem to require measurement. It does not fit politics at all, for in this sphere integration is the only mode of participation, and exclusion comes not only at the beginning, in the antebellum period and the Black Codes, but also at the end, in disfranchisement. It applies primarily to cities, for segregation was impossible in rural areas and even small towns. Yet the South was overwhelmingly rural from 1865 to 1900, areas containing 4,000 or more people constituting only 13.5 percent of the population of the South Central states and 19.6 percent of that of the South Atlantic states in 1900.[53]

But Rabinowitz's was not the only important amendment. Curiously for an Arkansan, Woodward had asserted, without any very systematic recital of evidence, that "the newer states [i.e., those further west, which had come into the Union later] were inclined to resort to Jim Crow laws earlier than the older commonwealths of the seaboard, and there is evidence that segregation and discrimination became more generally practiced before they became law."[54] John William Graves, however, suggested that if the sub-regional observation is true, it represents a genuine Woodwardian irony, the earlier passage of Jim Crow laws in the "newer states" representing a backlash against a more fluid race relations there, as compared with the more settled pattern of discrimination in the eastern commonwealths. At least in Arkansas, African Americans, Graves concluded, "may have received more humane treatment and enjoyed more real opportunity" because society was "less structured" and "social relationships were less constrained by inherited mores, at least in their rapidly developing cities and towns."[55]

But there are other possible and interesting extensions of the Jim Crow Thesis, especially if it is considered more broadly as one concerned with the connections between institutions and patterns of race relations in many periods. Reversing Woodward's time frame—he argued from 19th-century history that the pattern of race relations in the 20th century could change; I will argue from trends in the 20th and 21st centuries that patterns of race relations in the 19th need to be reexamined—may prove productive.

V. Fluctuations

Trends in the world outside the academy have always affected the way race-relations history is written, and they should, because the recent past may provide sufficiently different conditions as to throw light on previous events. When Woodward gave the lectures that became *Strange Career*, the Southern system of segregation and discrimination seemed completely intertwined, tightly bound. Extreme pessimists believed that it had always been that way and always would be. Extreme optimists believed that if one string were loosened, the whole fabric would quickly unravel. They were both wrong. Some sections of weaving were denser than others—and they were not the ones that many people thought.

That since 1954 segregation and discrimination have ebbed and flowed in quite different rhythms in different areas of social, political, and economic life, as well as in different regions and demographic areas (cities, suburbs), suggests three major observations. I will initially assert these observations, then provide skeletal evidence for and discussion of them: First, the tight matrix of segregation and discrimination in the first half of the 20th century in the South was unusual, not typical. Discrimination in societies is more often uneven, fractured, disorganized. It is the unusually connected structure that made the Jim Crow Era distinctive and that needs to be accounted for, and pure prejudice will not suffice as an explanation. Prejudice guides rather than drives discrimination. It is the steering wheel, not the engine. Second, some of the other common explanations for the existence, growth, or persistence of discrimination should not be maintained, in light of recent American experiences. In particular, the post-*Brown* era casts doubt on the importance of sexual or psychosocial causes of discrimination. Third, the pattern of variations and trends, and broad, tentative explanations of those fluctuations suggest a framework for analyzing changes in race relations.

How have post-*Brown* race relations varied in different facets of society? After an intense, but comparatively short struggle bracketed by the Montgomery bus boycott and the 1964 Civil Rights Act, segregation in public accommodations (restaurants, hotels, theaters, and the like)—the symbolic heart of Jim Crow—completely collapsed.[56] By 1965, integrated groups could eat at restaurants and stay in motels in the deepest parts of the Deep South without attracting overt hostility. In the summer of 1965, the U.S. Commis-

sion on Civil Rights, where I was interning, held a very integrated conference
on implementation of the 1964 Civil Rights Act in Demopolis, in the heart
of Black Belt Alabama, incidentally putting Section 2 of that Act into active
practice in the surrounding area without the least sign of an incident. As
someone who had grown up in the segregated South, I was amazed at the
instant integration of traditional Southern hospitality.

Black political rights and power followed a different course. Political segregation ended abruptly, in a sense, with the abolition of the white primary
in 1944, but it took innumerable registration drives and largely unsuccessful
political campaigns, two civil rights laws and the Voting Rights Act of 1965,
and numerous court challenges, before the first African American members
of Congress were elected from the 20th-century South, in 1972. The judicial
backlash of *Beer v. U.S.* and *Mobile v. Bolden*, in 1976 and 1980, respectively,[57]
was partially reversed in the renewed Voting Rights Act of 1982, but minority political rights suffered a series of grave defeats beginning with *Shaw v.
Reno* in 1993.[58] The hostility of a 5–4 Supreme Court majority climaxed in
the Court's 2013 declaration that the coverage scheme for the requirement
that some state and local jurisdictions "pre-clear" changes in their election
laws before putting them into effect was so unfair to the white South as to
deny an implicit constitutional principle of "equal [state] sovereignty."[59]
The majority believed that what George Wallace would have termed "states'
rights" outweighed the explicitly stated principle of equal protection of the
law, guaranteed to individuals by the 14th and 15th amendments, regardless
of the individuals' race.

"Deliberate speed" in the desegregation of schools was very slow, indeed,
until Health, Education, and Welfare Department directives in 1967 and the
Supreme Court's "root and branch" *Green v. New Kent County* decision in
1968.[60] The 1971 *Swann* case in Charlotte increased the pace of desegregation,
but in 1974, *Milliken v. Bradley* slowed it markedly by adopting a judicial ban
on requiring integration across school district lines.[61] In 2007, the same 5–4
majority on the Supreme Court that later protected state and local power to
dilute the votes of racial minorities struck down state and local power to take
any action to integrate public schools.[62]

Housing discrimination, more widespread than public accommodations
restrictions before *Brown*, has been linked since then with the integration
of schools. Despite numerous state and a few national laws against housing

bias, it continues strong, anchored in the self-interest of Anglos who fear that having "too many" minorities in a neighborhood will signal deterioration, eroding their investments.[63]

Job discrimination has been easier to attack and monitor, at least in large organizations, especially public ones, and factories and offices seem much more integrated than homes or schools despite the fact that members of different races working side by side in conditions of relative equality would seem most threatening to the social and economic status of the groups initially on top. Affirmative action laws have worked just as a reader of *Strange Career* would have predicted.[64]

Although Southern racists who played the sex card so long and so loudly would be as amazed as they would be appalled, anti-racial-intermarriage laws were the easiest to overthrow, dissolving in the *Loving* case of 1967, with remarkably little protest and not a shred of the predicted cultural terror.[65]

One new, or rather, expanded form of discrimination has arisen, the incarceration, primarily through arrests for possession of narcotics, of as many as a quarter of young black men, blighting their subsequent employment opportunities, reducing the black vote through felon disfranchisement laws, and, because of its severe disruption of the black nuclear family and interruption of African American wealth accumulation, damaging the prospects of subsequent generations.[66]

These different facets of the Jim Crow system have unraveled at different rates and to different extents, I suggest, because race relations are not segregated from other interests and values, and because they are affected by different, sometimes changing institutional constraints. Two schematic figures may serve to emphasize the forces outside of what we normally consider race relations, the institutional barriers to or drivers of racial equality, and the possibility that changes in the forces, as well as the institutions, may bring about racial change.

Figure 1 portrays the system of public accommodations segregation laws and the forces that maintained and then disrupted that system. On the left of the diagram are two forces, the ideology of white supremacy and its relevant economic manifestation, the willingness of whites to pay more for segregated trains, restaurants, hotels than they would have had to if the consumer bases of those accommodations were larger, by allowing African Americans to partake of them. In fact, whites managed to shift most of these costs to blacks by

Figure 1: Forces and Institutional Barriers

Preventing Public Accommodations Integration

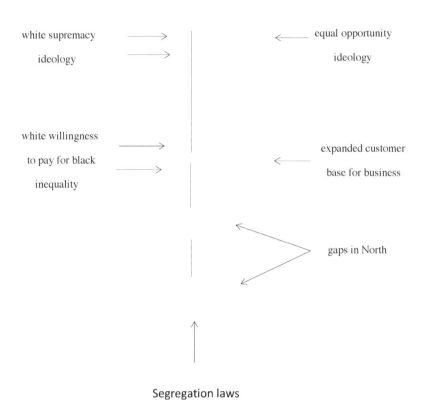

Segregation laws

providing blacks with only inferior facilities, such as second-class train cars, inferior hotels, etc. On the right of the diagram are forces pushing for more equality, Myrdal's "American Creed" of equal opportunity and the desire of businesspersons for the higher revenues that more customers would bring. There are two arrows pointing from each of the factors on the left, because during the era of Jim Crow, they were stronger than the factors on the right. As segregation became more expensive to maintain, especially when African Americans boycotted downtown stores during the sit-ins, and as the civil rights movement so skillfully drew attention to the American Creed, the forces on

Figure 2: Institutions, Values, and Interests in Black Voting Rights

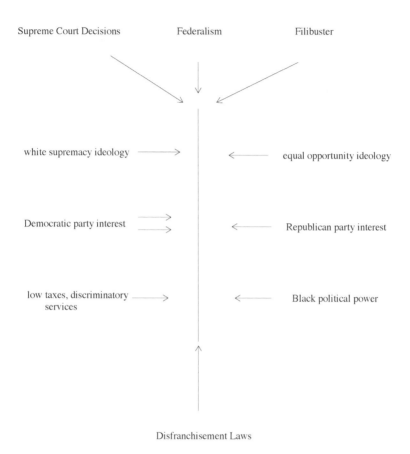

the left eroded, and those on the right strengthened. When the segregation laws, which had almost all been repealed in the North in the 19th century, were overturned by the national courts, a force from outside the South, and integrated public accommodations were mandated, the forces of white supremacist ideology were no longer enough to maintain segregation, and whites' behavior, especially that of owners of businesses, shifted very rapidly.

Figure 2 schematizes the system that disfranchised and eventually re-enfranchised African Americans in the South. Again, the white supremacist and equal opportunity ideologies confronted each other, and nationally, at least for voting, they seem to have been approximately balanced throughout the period from 1870 on. What determined the fate of disfranchisement measures, it seems to me, was not so much racial attitudes *per se* as the shifting interests of the Democratic and Republican parties, both in the South and in the nation, and three institutional constraints: Supreme Court opinions, the filibuster in the U.S. Senate, and the federal system that restrained national government power over state voting regulations. Once African Americans were enfranchised in the South in 1867, Democrats could not secure national victory if Southern blacks voted without restraint and those votes were counted as cast. Consequently, no Democrat in the U.S. Congress cast a single vote for any 19th-century civil rights measure after the 13th amendment, and Northern Democrats became the pivotal defenders of Southern electoral violence and disfranchisement.[67] Republican party interest in Southern black votes, very high during Reconstruction, moderated particularly after the party's Northern sweep in the 1894 elections. The interests of Southern whites, particularly elite Southern whites, in not paying the taxes that would have been required to finance equal public services for African Americans added policy content to prejudice, and from the 1880s or '90s until the 1950s and '60s, it outweighed the countervailing push among blacks for expanded services and the higher taxes required to finance them.

But what Figure 2 most emphasizes is the importance of the three institutional factors in facilitating and later reversing suffrage restrictions. First, the Supreme Court's opinions in the *Reese* and *Cruikshank* cases in 1876 hamstrung the 1870–71 national Supervisory Laws,[68] and its 1898 and 1903 opinions in *Williams v. Mississippi* and *Giles v. Harris* made it much more difficult to attack Southern state constitutional suffrage restrictions.[69] In bookend fashion, a later Supreme Court's decisions outlawed the white primary and facilitated attacks on state restrictions, as well as validating the national Voting Rights Act.[70] Of these decisions, only the last, *South Carolina v. Katzenbach*, represented a strong surge of national opinion; on the others, opinion was deeply (1876) or shallowly (1898, 1903, 1944) divided. The Supreme Court is not a transparent conductor of some unified national public opinion; whatever they pretend, the justices make policy. Second, the Senate filibuster killed the 1875 Elections Bill ("the Force Bill"), the 1890 Lodge Elections Bill (also called "the Force Bill"), and numerous anti-poll tax and anti-lynching bills through the 1940s. Only a shift toward civil rights by the extraordinarily gifted and opportunistic legislative leader, Lyndon Johnson, and a residual warmth toward civil rights in the leadership of the Republican party beat civil rights filibusters in 1957, 1960, and 1964. A landslide Democratic election in 1964 passed the first effective national voting rights law in 94 years.[71] Had the filibuster not been available as a tool, the forces promoting and maintaining black disfranchisement could not have prevailed, and even if they had, the forces pushing for franchise equality would have had much more incentive to make it a national issue sooner than the 1960s, because they would have had a much less difficult obstacle to overcome. Third, the last of the institutions that shaped the nation's civil rights policies, federalism (the division of governmental powers between national and state governments), preserved most power over electoral rules to the states. Courts often deferred to the states, even after the passage of the 14th and 15th amendments, and the density of state and local electoral regulations made it easy for those governments to engage in subtle discrimination and difficult for national authorities or federal judges to fashion tools to protect minority rights, even when they desired to intervene. Without state semi-autonomy, uncommon in other countries, the white South could not, by itself, have disfranchised blacks or maintained a white electoral monopoly for so long and, on the other hand, Northern African Americans and their white allies could not have comprised an increasingly large and insistent voting bloc that pressed successfully for national voting rights laws in the 1950s and '60s. Federalism both enabled black disfranchisement and helped prepare the way to unravel it.

As five members of the Supreme Court today invoke federalist principles to reverse the direction of voting rights law, and as Senate Republicans make unprecedented use of the filibuster to block legislation and executive and judicial nominations that they oppose, the history of the way these institutions have been used to contract and then expand minority voting rights should be of increased interest to the historical profession and the public.

Similar schematic figures could be proposed for other policies or areas of concern. They would feature different values and interests—class, economic, gender, or religious, for example; they would involve different institutions; and they might model different outcomes, or at least similar outcomes at different times. The point of the schemas is to remind us that race relations is never an autonomous sphere, that it always overlaps with other human concerns, and that institutions, which may inherently or originally have little to do with racial matters, may very directly shape racial policy.

The historiography of the Jim Crow Thesis may be faulted for engaging largely in pure descriptions of racial practices, unsystematically measured; for a concentration solely on racial and even gender attitudes as causes of racially oriented behavior; for a refusal to take the possibility of less discriminatory policies seriously; and, most of all, for a failure to examine the influence and workings of institutions in shaping racial policy. These intellectual mistakes should be avoided in any reconsideration of the Jim Crow Thesis, which is timely, as we seem to be transitioning to yet another era of race relations, moving backward, toward more racial segregation and more restrictions on minority voting rights. What differentiated the Jim Crow Era, what made discrimination in sphere after sphere solidify after 1890 and move synchronously for so long was the disfranchisement of African Americans by law, a disfranchisement made possible only by the three institutional levers spotlighted in Figure 2. The larger analysis presented above also suggests the benefits of extending to the study of other systems of race relations the themes that Woodward introduced.

VI. Deviations

But historians have largely abjured such investigations and the methods and theories of the social sciences that are necessary to carry them out, or even to understand the studies that social scientists do perform, and historians' divergence from the path Woodward began to lay out has impeded any desires they might have had to affect public policy, directly or indirectly. The cultural turn in history and the disillusionment with politics and even the notion of truth that followed the disasters of 1968 (Paris, Prague, Mexico City, Chicago, and the assassinations of Martin Luther King Jr. and Robert Kennedy)[72] helped to replace the history of race relations with two varieties of identity history: what might be called minority-agency history and whiteness studies.

Although studies of the history of nonwhite groups in America have many virtues, they often suffer from an inability or unwillingness to weigh the importance of their topics to larger national themes. In rescuing their subjects from anonymity, scholars sometimes give way to the desire to make every person, every action, every topic profoundly influential—janitors as potent as judges, attending meetings as effective as passing laws, signing petitions as crucial to overthrowing slavery as lecturing to thousands.[73] Just as important, minority history tends to insulate its subjects, even to segregate them, as though a black economics, politics, or society could exist in America without being profoundly affected by the dominant white society or without having their own considerable effects on white groups.[74] While the separate study of African Americans, Native Americans, Latinos, and Asian Americans will continue to make significant contributions, it is time that it paid more attention to the older topic of interactions among these groups and between these groups and Anglos, and it is well to remind ourselves again that to grant everyone agency is to deny anyone real power, which is profoundly unrealistic and, more important, unproductive for the larger, continuing struggle for equality.

If agency history is sometimes "feel-good" history, whiteness studies is "feel-bad" history, Ulrich B. Phillips's "central theme" writ national, but spun differently, to induce guilt, instead of to celebrate triumph—consciousness-raising for the skin-privileged.[75] It ignores systematic change and variation, ignores generations of social scientific studies of assimilation and group formation and divergence, ignores class, religious, and persistent ethnic divisions that often had large effects on the way nonwhites and various white subgroups interacted, whether they were able to cooperate directly or indirectly, whether intraracial divisions allowed minorities room for maneuver.[76] Timeless and homogenized, too vague to test and too cultural to care, whiteness studies cannot contribute to the central task of the history of race—to bring about racial equality.

To supplement minority-identity history, historians should take up more large-scale, comparative analyses of the rises and falls of ethnically discriminatory laws and practices of every sort, the explanations for those patterns, and the relationships between those patterns and other patterns of discrimination. To give just two examples: Why did different Southern states adopt Jim Crow railroad and streetcar segregation laws at different times? And how different were the patterns of the adoption of laws facilitating and constraining discrimination in jobs and property acquisition by race and by gender? What do such patterns imply for larger questions of changes in racial and gender relations? Fortunately, one virtue of federalism is that it provides us with a natural laboratory for assessing such questions. Statisticians have provided the tools, tools historians have yet to discover but which they need, for there is much productive work to be done.[77]

VII. Dedication

Today, as much as 75 years ago when Woodward began his historical career, the world needs changing, and just as much as then, historians' work can help foster desirable—or undesirable—change. Indeed, in areas of history that affect or potentially affect public policy, we can be sure that versions of history will be employed, often the biased history of policy gladiators, whether professional historians, trained in the healthy critical give and take that sharpens the discipline, choose to enter the arena or not. Professional reticence will not mean that history isn't used, only that it will be used badly. When Chief Justice John Roberts announced in *Parents Involved* that "the way to stop discrimination on the basis of race is to stop discriminating on the basis of race,"[78] he may have been merely restating a "colorblind" ideological statement as a catch-phrase. But he could also be taken to have offered an empirical, potentially testable generalization: Is the reason that racial discrimination in education and other areas of social life has declined since the 1950s that government began to ignore race in framing regulations? To put it more generally, does legally explicit discrimination *between* persons because of race or ethnicity always and inevitably lead to discrimination *against* members of disadvantaged minority groups? Or, in the *Shelby County* voting rights case, Chief Justice Roberts condemned the coverage scheme that required certain jurisdictions, particularly those in the Deep South, to submit changes in election laws for preclearance as "a formula based on 40-year-old facts having no logical relation to the present day."[79] He did not, however, consider whether the formula had an empirical relation to present-day discrimination. Historians might have much important research to contribute to the examination of the questions raised by the chief justice's unevidenced assertions, as they have done so usefully in contributing *amicus curiae* briefs to the Supreme Court in gay rights and gun control cases and as they have attempted to do in recent voting rights cases.[80]

Of course, the principal means of communication for historians are articles and monographs and courses. And there is plenty of work for historians to do not only in reexamining the original intent of ordinances, statutes, and constitutional provisions, charting the development of and attacks on minority rights, commenting and testifying, but also in deepening public and student understanding of the context and background in which the events took place. The fulfillment of such public duties—the reconstruction of the civic purpose of the profession—should be publicly recognized and encouraged by the history profession, instead of, as at present, ignored or, as it was by several of Woodward's critics, derided.[81]

Woodward inspired, marched in Montgomery, testified in Congress, all without compromising his commitment to the highest standards of scholarship. That his scholarship had effects at the highest levels of power and in ways he could not have initially foreseen may be illustrated by a simple anecdote. When Woodward and I testified on June 24, 1981, before the House Judiciary Committee Subcommittee on Civil and Constitutional Rights in favor of renewing and strengthening the Voting Rights Act, the presiding officer much of the time was a freshman congressman from Chicago named Harold Washington. That afternoon, I was sitting in the audience listening to further testimony by eminent voting rights lawyers when Representative Washington took a long walk from behind the dais to sit down next to me and ask whether Professor Woodward was still around. After I explained that Woodward had returned to New Haven to care for his wife, who was ill, Washington, two years from becoming Chicago's first and only black mayor, remarked how honored he had been to listen to Woodward, whose *Strange Career of Jim Crow*, he said, he had read in college and been inspired by ever since. Those of us who wish to honor C. Vann Woodward's legacy have much to do. We might start by rededicating ourselves to his principles.

NOTES

1   An earlier version of this paper was given at a session on "The Continuing Career of Jim Crow," chaired by Sheldon Hackney, at the Southern Historical Association convention in 2005. I want to thank Vernon Burton for his many helpful comments.

2   C. Vann Woodward, *Thinking Back: The Perils of Writing History* (Baton Rouge: LSU Press, 1986), 29–42; John Herbert Roper, *C. Vann Woodward, Southerner* (Athens: University of Georgia Press, 1987), 75–79.

3   Roper, *C. Vann Woodward: A Southern Historian and His Critics* (Athens, Georgia and London: University of Georgia Press, 1997), 29; Roper, *C. Vann Woodward, Southerner*, 194–95, 198. Ironically, Roper, a student of Joel Williamson, one of the chief critics of *Strange Career*, reads *Strange Career* as, in effect, prefiguring Williamson's interpretation of Southern race relations. *C. Vann Woodward, Southerner*, 188–92. According to Roper, Woodward saw segregation laws and the upsurge of lynching in the 1890s as an irrational expression of lower-class white frustration with the economic depression of the decade, which caused them to scapegoat African Americans, dragging formerly paternalistic aristocrats behind them in the Jim Crow movement. But this is inconsistent with Woodward's notion of a post-1890s "soured Populism," his careful differentiation between members of the Populist party *per se* and Democrats like Ben Tillman and James K. Vardaman, who used racist tactics to combat opponents of the Democratic party, and his indictment of "progressives," not 1890s Populists, as the authors of disfranchisement. In his testimony before a subcommittee of the House Judiciary Committee on the renewal of the Voting Rights Act in 1981, for instance, Woodward remarked that "I think one of the great and pathetic ironies of our history is that the most reactionary period of racial legislation got tied with the name of 'progressivism.' That was the period when the great bulk of the discriminatory laws about voting and civl rights were put on the books . . ." *Hearings Before the Subcommittee on Civil and Constitutional Rights of the Committee on the Judiciary, House of Representatives, Ninety-seventh Congress, First Session on Extension of the Voting Rights Act* (Washington: U.S. Government Printing Office, 1982), 2024.

4   Clay Risen, "Strange Career," *Boston Globe*, July 17, 2005.

5   Two convenient introductions to a portion of Woodward's "Jim Crow Thesis" are Joel Williamson, ed., *The Origins of Segregation* (Lexington, Massachusetts: D.C. Heath and Co., 1968) and John David Smith, ed., *When Did Southern Segregation Begin?* (Boston and New York: Bedford/St. Martin's, 2002).

6   This aim is most fully on view in Woodward's essay "The Strange Career of a Historical Controversy," in his *American Counterpoint: Slavery and Racism in the North-South Dialogue* (Boston: Little, Brown, 1971), 234–60.

7   E.g., Elizabeth Rauh Bethel, *The Roots of African-American Identity: Memory and History in Free Antebellum Communities* (New York: St. Martin's Press, 1997); Eddie S. Glaude, Jr., *Exodus! Relgion, Race, and Nation in Early Nineteenth Century Black America* (Chicago: University of Chicago Press, 2000).

8   Steven Hahn, *A Nation Under Our Feet: Black Political Struggles in the Rural South from Slavery to the Great Migration* (Cambridge: Harvard University Press, 2003), 8 spoke of "the paramilitary character of Southern politics . . ."

9   Eschewing synthesis as reductionist and a focus on "the limitations Southerners endured" as itself limited, Edward L. Ayers's *The Promise of the New South: Life After Reconstruc-*

tion (New York: Oxford University Press, 1992), viii-ix emphasized "a more active and intimate history"of the period in Southern history that its predecessor, Woodward's *Origins*, had not considered "promising."

10 Thus, Lawrence W. Levine, contended that "the most important intellectual breakthrough by historians in the past two decades" was their revised view of "the folk . . . as actors in their own right who, to a larger extent than we previously imagined, were able to build a culture, create alternatives, affect the situation they found themselves in, and influence the people they found themselves among." Levine, "The Unpredictable Past: Reflections on Recent American Historiography," *American Historical Review*, 94 (1989), 673. He applied assertions about informal political power to slavery in "Clio, Canons, and Culture," *Journal of American History* 80 (1993), 864: "Blacks during and after slavery were engaged in the most serious game of politics and exerted power of many kinds—especially cultural power, the importance of which we are just now beginning to appreciate." Hahn, *A Nation Under Our Feet*, 2–3, was concerned to a large extent with "how unfranchised and disfranchised people might conduct politics," and he considered slavery constructed around "the fictions of domination and submission." The intensity of the struggles of African Americans and women for the abolition of slavery and for their own enfranchisement and the all-out efforts of slaveholders and white and male supremacists to deny both groups equality suggest that historical actors put less stock in cultural power and more in institutionalized power than these historians later suggested.

11 See Kousser, "The New Postmodern Southern Political History," *Georgia Historical Quarterly*, 87 (2003), 427–48.

12 The echoes of Ulrich B. Phillips's "central theme of Southern history" in Joel Williamson's *The Crucible of Race: Black-White Relations in the American South Since Emancipation* (New York: Oxford University Press, 1984), 247–48, are deafening: "Behind it all, in politics as well as in everything else, it was white unanimity against blackness, molded rigid in a white culture monolithic, total, and tight, that put the black man either down or out." Indeed, Williamson, 317–18, says that Phillips's chief flaw was that he believed whites had to struggle to maintain white supremacy. Of course, Williamson condemned the alleged white consensus, while Phillips approved it.

13 Most prominently, Stephan Thernstrom and Abigail Thernstrom, *America in Black and White: One Nation, Indivisible: Race in Modern America* (New York: Simon and Schuster, 1997); Abigail Thernstrom, *Voting Rights—And Wrongs: The Elusive Quest for Racially Fair Elections* (Washington: AEI Press, 2009).

14 Williamson, *The Crucible of Race*, 321: ". . . all people are liable to be mistaken in their perceptions, and to do horrible things in consequence." Levine's essay and book title, "The Unpredictable Past," cloaks intellectual despair in cleverness. If one cannot analyze the past, when we have a pretty good idea how things came out, how can one possibly analyze the present sufficiently to frame a course of reformative action?

15 Williamson, *Crucible of Race*; David R. Roediger, *The Wages of Whiteness: Race and the Making of the American Working Class* (London: Verso, 1991); Matthew Frye Jacobson, *Whiteness of a Different Color: European Immigrants and the Alchemy of Race* (Cambridge: Harvard University Press, 1998). For critiques of whiteness studies, see Eric Arnesen, "Whiteness and the Historians' Imagination," *International Labor and working-Class History*, 60 (2001), 3–32; Peter Kolchin, "Whiteness Studies: The New History of Race in America," *Journal of American History*, 89 (2002), 154–73.

16 Woodward's next paragraph after discussing the passage of the Voting Rights Act in the Third Revised Edition begins: "For a very brief interval the optimists had things their way." (Woodward 1974, 186)

17 Myrdal, *An American Dilemma: The Negro Problem and American Democracy* (New York: Harper & Row, 1944), lxxi.

18 418 U.S. 717.

19 These trends will be discussed at somewhat greater length later in this essay.

20 Gavin Wright, *Sharing the Prize: The Economics of the Civil Rights Revolution in the American South* (Cambridge, Mass.: Harvard University Press, 2013), 188.

21 Wright, *Sharing the Prize*, 105–82.

22 While distorting the analysis of past events in order to justify policies or points of view in the present represents bias, reexamining explanations of past events in light of more recent events may be just another form of comparative history, deepening and/or calling into question analyses of the past. In this instance, the quite different, uneven trajectories of discrimination in different areas of social, political, and economic life, as well as the stark regional and urban-rural differences in those trajectories, casts significant doubt on the causal sufficiency of cultural explanations of earlier patterns of discrimination.

23 As a hypothesis, it could be clarified, tested, amended, extended, or rejected, and it attracted the attention of scholars who sought to perform any of these actions. By contrast, in the postmodern idiom, which Woodward did not find attractive, an "interpretation" can only be catalogued and added to other, incommensurable, compatible, irrefutable points of view about the past. The controversy over the Jim Crow Thesis was itself productive of much historical knowledge and learning, and it might serve as a paradigm about how historical scholarship ought to develop.

24 The foremost of these comparative studies agreed broadly with Woodward's approach, though it summarily, without detailed discussion, concluded that post-Reconstruction race relations were less open than Woodward suggested. Discrimination "depends comparatively little on individual attitudes and much more on the racism that is ingrained in institutions. . . . Segregation is created and enforced by power. It is a political phenomenon." John W. Cell, *The Highest Stage of White Supremacy: The Origins of Segregation in South Africa and the American South* (New York: Cambridge University Press, 1982), 8, 17 for the quotations and 82–102 for the more specific evaluation.

25 Rebecca J. Scott, *Degrees of Freedom: Louisiana and Cuba After Slavery* (Cambridge, Mass.: Harvard University Press, 2005); Anthony W. Marx, *Making Race and Nation: A Comparison of South Africa, the United States, and Brazil* (New York: Cambridge University Press, 1998); Richard M. Valelly, *The Two Reconstructions: The Struggle for Black Enfranchisement* (Chicago: University of Chicago Press, 2004).

26 The best, which actually preceded the publication of *Strange Career*, was George Brown Tindall's nuanced *South Carolina Negroes, 1877–1900* (Columbia: University of South Carolina Press, 1952), 291–302, which carefully traced the development of segregation over time and distinguished between different areas of social and political life.

27 See Kousser, *The Shaping of Southern Politics: Suffrage Restriction and the Establishment of the One-Party South, 1880–1910* (New Haven: Yale University Press, 1974).

28 Wynes, *Race Relations in Virginia, 1870-1902* (Charlottesville: University of Virginia

Press, 1961), 68–83, excerpted in Williamson, *Origins of Segregation*, 20–31, quotes at 20–21. Note the careful and tentative nature of Wynes's judgment: "perhaps . . . more likely . . ." Strangely, Williamson glosses this excerpt as "challeng[ing] the extent of fluidity in race relations" that Woodward had highlighted in *Strange Career*. Williamson, *Origins of Segregation*, 20.

29   Williamson, *After Slavery: The Negro in South Carolina During Reconstruction, 1861–1877* (Chapel Hill: University of North Carolina Press, 1965), 274–99.

30   Graves, *Town and Country: Race Relations in an Urban-Rural Context, Arkansas, 1865–1905* (Fayetteville and London: University of Arkansas Press, 1990). Similarly, see Joseph H. Cartwright, *The Triumph of Jim Crow: Tennessee Race Relations in the 1880s* (Knoxville: University of Tennessee Press, 1976).

31   *After Slavery*, 298. Or as he put it in *The Crucible of Race*, 318, "Race, in brief, is a problem of the mind. . . ."

32   *Trouble in Mind: Black Southerners in the Age of Jim Crow* (New York: Alfred A. Knopf, 1998).

33   See, for example, Kousser, "'The Supremacy of Equal Rights': The Struggle Against Racial Discrimination in Antebellum Massachusetts and the Foundations of the Fourteenth Amendment," *Northwestern University Law Review* 82 (1988), 970–72.

34   Woodward, *Tom Watson, Agrarian Rebel* (New York: Macmillan, 1938), 239–40.

35   Williamson, "Wounds, Not Scars: Lynching, the National Conscience, and the American Historian," *Journal of American History*, 83 (1997), 1228.

36   Stewart E. Tolnay and E. M. Beck, *A Festival of Violence: An Analysis of Southern Lynchings, 1882–1930* (Champaign: University of Illinois Press, 1995).

37   Litwack, *Trouble in Mind*, xiii, xvi, 221–22.

38   Kousser, *Colorblind Injustice: Minority Voting Rights and the Undoing of the Second Reconstruction* (Chapel Hill: University of North Carolina Press, 1999), 23–24.

39   Kousser, *Shaping of Southern Politics*.

40   Litwack, *Trouble in Mind*, 221.

41   Kousser, *Shaping of Southern Politics*, especially 238–46.

42   Williamson, *The Crucible of Race*, 318. Some years later, the economic edge of the scapegoat thesis was sliced off, leaving only gender: ". . . the real war, the essence of the conflict, concerned gender, not race, and . . . lynching and even disfranchisement, segregation, and proscription had more to do with relations between white men and white women than with relations between blacks and whites. . . ." Williamson, "Wounds, Not Scars," 1253.

43   *After Slavery*, 278–79.

44   For a discussion and references to many other metropolitan studies, see Thomas W. Hanchett, *Sorting Out the New South City: Race, Class, and Urban Development in Charlotte, 1875–1975* (Chapel Hill: University of North Carolina Press, 1998), 116–144.

45   A convenient short introduction is in the selections by Richard C. Wade and Leon Litwack in Williamson, ed., *Origins of Segregation*, 81-95.

46   Kousser, "'Supremacy of Equal Rights."

47   Kousser, "'The Onward March of Right Principles': State Legislative Actions on Racial

Discrimination in Schools in Nineteenth-Century America," *Historical Methods*, 35 (2002), 177–204.

48   Cell, *Highest Stage of White Supremacy*.

49   Although there were no direct, comprehensive measures of racial attitudes before the 1940s, V.O. Key's *Southern Politics in State and Nation* (New York: Vintage Books, 1949), 5, famously found the that in the first half of the 20th century, voters in the "Black Belt," the counties over about half black, had "the deepest and most immediate concern about the maintenance of white supremacy," and more direct survey evidence gathered more recently confirms that the relationship between racial environment and white racial attitudes in the South continues strong. For a summary, see James M. Glaser, "Back to the Black Belt: Racial Environment and White Racial Attitudes in the South," *Journal of Politics*, 56 (1994), 21–41.

50   Social psychological research on attitudes about groups increasingly relies on implicit, rather than explicit measures of attitudes and finds correlations between implicit and explicit measures themselves, and between either and behavior rather complex. See, for a recent review, Gerd Bohner and Nina Dickel, "Attitudes and Attitude Change," *Annual Review of Psychology*, 62 (2011), 391–417. The most important implication for historical research on race-related behavior is that it may well differ from explicit, seemingly-related statements.

51   Rabinowitz, *Race, Ethnicity, and Urbanization: Selected Essays by Howard N. Rabinowitz* (Columbia: University of Missouri Press, 1994), which contains a complete bibliography of the controversy over *Strange Career*, up to that point, 26–28.

52   *Race, Ethnicity, and Urbanization*, 28–31.

53   *Twelfth Census, 1900* (Washington: Government Printing Office, 1901), lxxxvi.

54   Woodward, *Strange Career*, 41

55   Graves, *Town and Country*, 228. The unsettled nature of race relations in frontier societies is a recurrent theme from William Faulkner's *Absolom, Absolom!* (New York: Random House, 1936), one of Woodward's favorite books, to Ira Berlin's *Many Thousands Gone: The First Two Centuries of Slavery in North America* (Cambridge: Harvard University Press, 1998).

56   Richard Cortner, *Civil Rights and Public Accommodations: The Heart of Atlanta and Mc-Clung Cases* (Lawrence: University Press of Kansas, 2001), 6, 29, 64; Benjamin Muse, *The American Negro Revolution* (Bloomington: Indiana University Press, 1968), 75, 156–57. I of course do not deny the extensive efforts against segregation in public accommodations in the 19th century and earlier in the 20th. Integrationists certainly had many successes at the state and local levels. But they did not for a long time manage national successes. There was a considerable break between the 1875 Civil Rights Act and that of 1964.

57   *Beer*, 425 U.S. 130 (1976), held that changes in election laws could only be denied "pre-clearance" under Section 5 of the Voting Rights Act if they made minorities worse off than under the previous law, not merely if the laws had a discriminatory effect. *Bolden*, 446 U.S. 55 (1980), ruled that election laws could be declared illegal under Section 2 of the Voting Rights Act only if it was proven that they had a discriminatory intent, not merely when a discriminatory effect was shown.

58   509 U.S. 630 (1993). *Shaw* held that whites had standing to challenge a "racial gerry-mander" in favor of minorities even if they could not prove that the districting scheme

injured them. On this and related legal cases, see generally, Kousser, *Colorblind Injustice*; Kousser, "The Strange, Ironic Career of Section Five of the Voting Rights Act," *Texas Law Review*, 86 (2008), 667–775.

59 *Shelby County v. Holder*, 133 S.Ct. 2612 (2013).

60 *Green* outlawed "freedom of choice" plans that had been used to delay desegregation, ruling that racial discrimination had to be "eliminated root and branch." 391 U.S. 430, at 438 (1968).

61 The best introduction is a series of books by Gary Orfield, some with coauthors: *The Reconstruction of Southern Education: The Schools and the 1964 Civil Rights Act* (New York: John Wiley and Sons, 1969); *Must We Bus? Segregated Schools and National Policy* (Washington: Brookings Institution, 1978); *The Closing Door: Conservative Policy and Black Opportunity* (Chicago: Univeersity of Chicago Press, 1991); *Dismantling Desegregation: The Quiet Reversal of Brown v. Board of Education* (New York: New Press, 1996); *School Resegregation: Must the South Turn Back?* (Chapel Hill: University of North Carolina Press, 2005); *Lessons in Integration: Realizing the Promise of Racial Diversity in American Schools* (Charlottesville: University of Virginia Press, 2007).

62 *Parents Involved in Cmty. Sch. v. Seattle Sch. Dist. No. 1*, 551 U.S. 701 (2007).

63 Douglas Massey and Nancy Denton, *American Apartheid: Segregation and the Making of the Underclass* (Cambridge: Harvard University Press, 1993); and for a more current overview, Vincent J. Roscigno, Diana L. Karafin, and Griff Tester, "The Complexities and Processes of Racial Housing Discrimination," *Social Problems*, 56 (2009), 49–69.

64 The best sources are many papers by economist James Heckman, many with coauthors, including "The Impact of the Economy and the State on the Economic Status of Blacks: A Study of South Carolina," in David Galenson, ed., *Markets and Institutions* (New York: Cambridge University Press, 1989), 321–43; "Determining the Impact of Federal Antidiscrimination Policy on the Economic Status of Blacks: A Study of South Carolina," *American Economic Review* (1989), 138–77; "Affirmative Action and Black Employment," *Proceedings of the Industrial Relations Research Association*, 41 (1989), 320–29; "The Central Role of the South in Accounting for the Economic Progress of Black Americans," *Papers and Proceedings of the American Economic Association* (1990),; "Racial Disparity and Employment Discrimination Law: An Economic Perspective," *Yale Law and Policy Review* (1990), 276–98; "Continuous vs. Episodic Change: The Impact of Affirmative Action and Civil Rights Policy on the Economic Status of Blacks," *Journal of Economic Literature* (1991), 1603–43.

65 388 U.S. 1 (1967). See Peter Wallenstein, *Tell the Court I Love My Wife: Race, Marriage, and Law—An American History* (New York: Palgrave Macmillan, 2002). By 2012, only about 10% of the American public thought that increased racial intermarriage had been bad for American society, and 17.1% of black newlyweds married someone of a different race. See Wendy Wang, "The Rise of Intermarriage: Rates, Characteristics Vary by Race and Gender," Pew Research, Feb. 16, 2012, available at <http://www.pewsocialtrends.org/2012/02/16/the-rise-of-intermarriage/2/#chapter-1-overview>.

66 Michelle Alexander, *The New Jim Crow: Mass Incarceration in the Age of Colorblindness* (New York: The New Press, 2011)

67 Kousser, *Colorblind Injustice,* 39.

68 See my review of Robert M. Goldman, *Reconstruction and Black Suffrage: Losing*

the Vote in Reese and Cruikshank, <http://www2.h-net.msu.edu/reviews/showrev.cqi?path=179141046324369>. *Cruickshank,* 92 U.S. 542 (1876), required that the government charge and prove that the seventy or so African Americans who died in the "Colfax Massacre" were murdered because of their race. *Reese,* 92 U.S. 214 (1876) ruled that the discriminatory use of a voting requirement was not illegal because the Section 3 of 1870 Enforcement Act did not repeat an earlier statement in the law that the discrimination had to be by race.

69   See R. Volney Riser, *Defying Disfranchisement: Black Voting Rights Activism in the Jim Crow South, 1890–1908* (Baton Rouge: Louisiana State University Press, 2010). *Williams,* 170 U.S. 213 (1898) held that it was not enough to show that the Mississippi constitution of 1890 was intended to disfranchise blacks, unless it was proven to have that effect. *Giles,* 189 U.S. 475 (1903), held that a proof of both the discriminatory intent and effect of the 1901 Alabama constitution was not enough; disfranchisement was a "political question," not subject to judicial interference.

70   See Steven F. Lawson, *Black Ballots: Voting Rights in the South, 1944–1969* (New York: Columbia University Press, 1976).

71   Lawson, *Black Ballots.*

72   Joyce O. Appleby, *Knowledge and Postmodernism in Historical Perspective* (New York: Routledge, 1996).

73   E.g., Robin D.G. Kelley, "'We Are Not What We Seem': Rethinking Black Working Class Opposition in the Jim Crow South," *Journal of American History,* 80 (1993), 75–112; Tera Hunter, *To 'Joy My Freedom': Southern Black Women's Lives and Labors After the Civil War* (New York: Cambridge University Press, 1997); Elsa Barkley Brown, "'Negotiating and Transforming the Public Sphere: African American Political Life in the Transition from Slavery to Freedom," in Dailey *et al., Jumpin' Jim Crow,* 28–66; C. Peter Ripley, Roy E. Finkenbine, Michael F. Hembree, and Donald Yacovone, eds., *Witness for Freedom: African American Voices on Race, Slavery, and Emancipation* (Chapel Hill: University of North Carolina Press, 1993). For a gentle critique of such studies, see Barbara J. Fields, "Origins of the New South and the Negro Question," *Journal of Southern History,* 67 (2001), 811–26.

74   E.g., Robin D.G. Kelley, *Race Rebels: Culture, Politics, and the Black Working Class* (New York: Free Press, 1996).

75   In its focus on the Northern white working class and immigrants who settled primarily in the North, whiteness studies might be considered the Yankee counterpart of Williamson's Southern-focused *Crucible of Race,* discussed earlier.

76   See, e.g., Roediger, *Wages of Whiteness;* Jacobson, *Whiteness of a Different Color;* Michelle Brattain, *The Politics of Whiteness: Race, Workers, and Culture in the Modern South* (Athens: University of Georgia Press, 2004); Grace Elizabeth Hale, *Making Whiteness: The Culture of Segregation in the South, 1890–1940* (New York: Pantheon Books, 1998); George Lipsitz, *The Possessive Investment in Whiteness: How White People Profit from Identity Politics* (Philadelphia: Temple University Press, 1998); Ruth Frankenberg, *White Women, Race Matters: The Social Construction of Whiteness* (Minneapolis: University of Minnesota Press, 1993).

77   See Kousser, "'Onward March of Right Principles;'"Janet M. Box-Steffensmeier and Bradford S. Jones, *Event History Modeling: A Guide for Social Scientists* (New York:

Cambridge University Press, 2004); Anthony Y. Chen, *The Fifth Freedom: Jobs, Politics, and Civil Rights in the United States, 1941–1972* (Princeton: Princeton University Press, 2009).

78 *Parents Involved in Community Schools*, 748, is briefly discussed in Section IV, above.

79 *Shelby County v. Holder*, 133 S.Ct. 2612 (2013), slip opinion at 21–22.

80 See "Brief of the Organization of American Historians and the American Studies Association as Amici Curiae in Support of Respondents," *Hollingsworth v. Perry*, 130 S.Ct. 2432 (2013); <http://38.106.4.56/Modules/ShowDocument.aspx?documentID=1196>; "Brief of Amici Curiae Jack N. Rakove, Saul Cornell, David T. Konig, William J. Novak, Lois G. Schwoerer et al., in Support of Petitioner," *District of Columbia v. Heller*, 554 U.S. 579 (2008), <http://www.scotusblog.com/wp-content/uploads/2008/01/07-290_amicus_historians.pdf>; "Brief Amici Curiae of Historians and Other Scholars in Support of Petitioners," *Crawford v. Marion County*, 553 U.S. 181 (2008), <http://moritzlaw.osu.edu/electionlaw/litigation/documents/Rokita-BriefamicuscuriaeofHistorians.pdf>; "Brief of Historians and Social Scientists as Amici Curiae in Support of Respondents," *Shelby County v. Holder*, <http://sblog.s3.amazonaws.com/wp-content/uploads/2013/02/12-96bsacHistoriansSocialScientists.pdf >

81 According to Kevin Mattson, "History Lesson: Those who don't know history are doomed to distort it—and our political discourse," *Democracy* (Winter, 2006), 79–87 <http://www.democracyjournal.org/article.php?ID=6506> , "To be 'presentist,' to care about what the public is thinking and worried about and to try to shed historical light on such concerns, is [for historians] to perform career suicide." (81) By contrast, Mattson's model in the article of what a historian should do is Woodward's *Strange Career*.

19

C. Vann Woodward

The Outsider as Insider

SHELDON HACKNEY

O n December 17, 1999, C. Vann Woodward died at his home in
Hamden, Connecticut, 91 years, half a continent, and a cultural
millennium away from his birth on November 13, 1908, in Vann-
dale, Arkansas. His journey is a fascinating American success story, as well as a
universal tale of love and loss. It is also a narrative that is intimately intertwined
with the national epic of the rise and fall of New Deal liberalism. The lessons
of Woodward's intellectual life are powerfully instructive with regard to how
to be a scholar's scholar and a committed activist at the same time. His career
also paralleled the ongoing transmutation of New Deal liberalism into some
form of post-modern progressivism. It all has to do with human values—
American values—and how they are deployed on the battleground of history.

Anyone examining Woodward's life is likely to be intrigued by a number
of difficult-to-explain inconsistencies. Why would a man raised in comfortable circumstances in a conservative, perhaps backward, region become an
activist on behalf of the excluded and oppressed? How can one explain the
fact that one so genteel in dress and manner became embroiled in so many
public controversies? Why was the ultimate establishment insider such a visible advocate for remaking the existing order? How could such a private man
relish conflict in the public arena?

Woodward's personality was hardly a predictor of his political position.
He was quiet, not dramatic, and even a bit shy. In conversation, he was essentially a counterpuncher, full of fascinating information and observations,
but hardly a dominating personality. His sense of humor was active but wry.

Irony was a favorite mode of intellectual analysis. He dressed conservatively, looking very "Ivy League" in his hounds-tooth sport coat and tie even before he arrived at Yale in 1961, and even after Ivy League faculty in the 1960s ceased dressing in an Ivy League way.

It would help to know when and why Woodward became a dissenter. Woodward himself was puzzled about this. He could produce no memory of a Saul-on-the-road-to-Damascus conversion experience. When asked that probing question by an interviewer during his retirement years, Woodward replied that he thought it must have been when he went to Emory University for the final two years of college. There he got to know and admire Will Alexander, the head of the Commission on Interracial Cooperation (forerunner of the Southern Regional Council) that had been founded in 1919 to improve race relations and to ease the oppressive effects of segregation, though not to end segregation itself.

Woodward's Atlanta experience was thoroughly progressive, but his life as a dissenter had its origins much earlier. Woodward recalled to another interviewer during his retirement that on his first day in school at the age of six in Wynne, Arkansas, he expressed his resentment about being there by sitting on his desk with his feet in the chair and his back to the teacher. The teacher wisely ignored the incipient rebellion, which was eventually abandoned. To his interviewer, Woodward self-mockingly insisted that the incident was full of Freudian significance, a reference to the fact that his father was principal of that school.[1] This may be the first instance of Woodward's life-long enactment of his chosen role of insider as outsider.

On other occasions, Woodward produced memories with more obvious meanings. As he told his former student, Jim Green, in 1983: "I do remember a Klansman who came in robes to make a gift to the church in the course of a service. It made a profound impression. There was a lynching incident I didn't see, but I saw the mob gathering. I do remember these incidents very strongly; they affected my attitude. I was an adolescent in rebellion, and part of my rebellion was against the church, my father's religion."[2]

It is difficult to understand Vann Woodward's life without noticing a few of the not-so-obvious dilemmas of his growing up. He was born into a very respectable white Southern family. His maternal grandfather, John Mager Vann, was one of those planters-turned-businessmen whose land was worked after the Civil War by tenant farmers—ex-slaves—who were also customers of the landowner's country store. Such agrarian capitalists were to be among the leading characters in *Origins of the New South, 1877–1913*, the masterpiece that reoriented Southern history and put Woodward at the top of his profession at the age of forty-three.

WOODWARD SPENT HIS PRE-SCHOOL years in Vanndale, in the northeastern quadrant of the state, across the Mississippi River from Memphis. The town of his birth took its name, as did Woodward himself, from his great-grandfather, a pioneer planter with 26 slaves and 600 acres of land, who moved his country store to a location on the new railroad line in 1857. Neighbors followed, and Vanndale emerged. Though not aristocracy, being a Vann in Vanndale provided comfortable social status.

Jack Woodward was a school principal in nearby Wynne. Soon, however, he got the job of school superintendant in Arkadelphia, Arkansas, in the foothills of the Ouachita Mountains in the southwestern quadrant of the state. He moved the family there in 1916, and his son, Vann, completed grades three and four there. Vann's mother, Bess, had dropped out of Galloway College to get married She always wanted to be a Latin teacher, so she eventually finished her college degree in Atlanta after her two children were out of the house. In Arkadelphia, Vann and Ida, brother and sister, therefore had the privilege and the problem of going to school while being raised by teachers. That mixed blessing became more mixed when Jack moved the family in 1918 to Morrilton, in the central part of the state, near the Arkansas River, where he became the superintendent in a larger school system. Vann finished grammar school and high school there.

Woodward chafed under the teasing he got from his fellow students because his father was the ultimate authority in their lives, another irritant in the father-son relationship.[3] This was a case of the ultimate insider being also an outsider, an ambiguous position in relation to his schoolmates. That ambiguity was probably deepened by the fact that Woodward was a good student, even a bookish one, in a culture that celebrated physical virtues. He was also the editor of the school newspaper, implying a solid position in the social hierarchy of the school.

Even with this standing, Woodward went out for the high school football team, playing center, an unglamorous position that required minimum skills and maximum fortitude. He was "one of the boys" to the extent possible under the circumstances. It is hard not to understand this athletic adventure on the part of someone who never enjoyed athletics as the desperate attempt of an outsider to become an insider. As he said with emphasis later, he was not the star of the team.[4]

In such late-life interviews, Woodward observed that he was in rebellion against his father. Interestingly enough, that rebellion took the form of pursuit of the values professed by his Methodist father to extents far beyond the father's conformist public posture. As Erik Erikson observed of Martin Luther, he rebelled against his father's plans for the son's business career by becoming a priest, of which the Catholic father could not disapprove.[5] It was a way of conforming and not conforming at the same time.

It was this ambiguous position as son of the superintendent, while also a non-star athlete and a "brain," that left Vann free to see the injustices of Southern society. He was already at odds with the common beliefs of white Southerners. No conversion was needed. He even remembered in the late 20th century the Elaine Riots in the fall of 1919, just after World War I, when he was only 11.[6] With the aid of the Progressive Farmers and Household Union of America, black tenant farmers organized to demand fair payment for their shares. The white community came together and violently crushed the unionization effort. Five whites lost their lives, and more than a hundred blacks were killed. Jack Woodward served on a gubernatorial commission to investigate the violence and to determine what had happened and who was at fault. No whites were punished.

As Woodward told Jim Green in 1986, "After all, rebellions take many forms, and I was very much a reader, and I came into contact with critical ideas. I remember the first movement I was part of was the opposition to the U.S. Marine intervention in Nicaragua in the 1920s when Sandino was rising." That military action occurred in the spring of 1926 when Woodward was graduating from high school and on the way to college. He wrote a strong editorial in the high school newspaper in opposition to the Marine intervention.

One of the most powerful influences on the young scholar was his uncle Comer Woodward, an ordained and fervent Methodist minister and successful college professor. He had done his PhD in Sociology at the University of Chicago and then joined the faculty of Southern Methodist University in Dallas. Uncle Comer was a frequent guest in the home of his brother and sister-in-law, so Vann saw and heard him in conversation about the issues of the day. He noted that Uncle Comer was aggressive in his condemnation of racial injustice, not only lynching but the sort of everyday injustices of the Jim Crow system whose history Woodward examined and undermined in 1955 in *The Strange Career of Jim Crow*. Woodward's father was not a racist in the way white Southerners would then have defined the term, but he was not eager to take action against segregation and the cruelties it bred. That bothered his son, though in late life Vann expressed his understanding that his father, the school superintendent, could not act or speak against the racial system. To do so would not only have cost him his job; it would have risked his life and that of his family.[7]

Being a member of an elite family in a backward region may have had something to do with the many contradictions in Woodward's life. He championed the oppressed, but he dressed and behaved in a punctilious bourgeois manner. He became a sophisticated world citizen, and a cosmopolitan intellectual, but he remained devoted to the history of the South. Throughout his career, he studied and identified with the South, but after 1961 he did not live there. When Woodward graduated from high school in 1926, he enrolled in Henderson-Brown College in Arkadelphia. It was an extremely small Methodist school that Comer and Jack Woodward were trying to save from being consolidated with two other struggling Methodist colleges. Vann was an editorial writer on the student newspaper, a position that gave him a taste of public controversy. He rose to be an assistant editor as a sophomore. His intellectual extracurricular life included the Garland Literary Society, of which he became the recording secretary in his sophomore year, when he was also the first president of the International Relations Club and Treasurer of the Sophomore Class. Given his later renown as a humdrum public speaker, it is particularly interesting that he was a member of the debating team that won the Arkansas state championship by defeating Hendrix College.

Uncle Comer changed everything. He left SMU to become a dean at Emory. Before long he arranged for his brother to be named dean of the associated junior college in Oxford, Georgia. Vann transferred to Emory for his junior and senior years. There, it is not surprising that he was not the sort of campus politico that he had been at Henderson. He had individualistic friends who shared his progressive values. He observed segregation in its urban brutality. He even attended a ball at a black college with a black woman student he had gotten to know. He also took a summer job on a Dutch freighter and then spent several weeks in the Netherlands, France, and the Soviet Union.

After graduating in 1930, he took a second trip to Europe, revisiting France and the Soviet Union and traveling into Germany. He then coached writing for a year at Georgia Tech, before spending the academic year 1931–32 at Columbia University studying for a master's degree in political science, though his major activity was exploring Harlem, where he even had a bit part in a play. Returning to Atlanta, he earned a living teaching at Georgia Tech again, while he snooped about for a writing project of his own. He even became chairman of the Defense Committee for Angelo Herndon, a black communist who had been tried, convicted, and sentenced to death under a pre-Civil War anti-insurrection law. Eventually, he was given a scholarship to the PhD program in History at the University of North Carolina in Chapel Hill. He was already at work on his biography of Tom Watson, the Populist radical of the 1890s who flipped after the demise of Populism to become the radical segregationist, right-wing governor of Georgia.

When Woodward submitted his dissertation to his faculty committee in 1937, he mailed a copy to the New York publishing house, Macmillan. It appeared the next year as *Tom Watson, Agrarian Rebel*. Well-received, it attracted the notice of the historians in charge of the LSU Press series on the history of the South. Woodward was signed up to research and write the volume on the South between Reconstruction and World War I.

Meanwhile, Woodward met and married Glenn MacLeod, who had attended Columbia University graduate school but was then working as a textile union organizer in North Carolina. He also became friends with John Hope Franklin, the black scholar who broke all sorts of racial barriers. Together they plotted to integrate the Southern Historical Association convention program in 1948, when Woodward was chair of the program committee, and more dramatically in 1952 when Woodward was president. Franklin and Woodward also each provided historical research and analysis for Thurgood Marshall and his team of lawyers that was working on the set of segregation cases that resulted in the 1954 *Brown* decision. The South was in for a struggle, but it would never again be the same.

When Woodward returned to civilian life in 1946 after wartime service as an officer in the Navy, he joined the faculty at Johns Hopkins University.

He moved to Yale in 1961, from which position, during the transformative decade of the 1960s, he served as a major intellectual leader while the country went through the turmoil of the civil rights movement, the black power movement, the anti-war movement, the women's rights movement, and various other social change movements.

In 1955, Woodward had delivered a series of lectures at the University of Virginia, published as *The Strange Career of Jim* Crow, which drew on history to expose the relatively recent "invention" of the Southern caste system. The lectures revealed Woodward's hope for an integrated society. A decade later, at the end of the march from Selma to Montgomery in 1965, Martin Luther King Jr. looked out at the huge crowd in front of his podium on the steps of the Alabama Capitol and saw his friend, Vann Woodward. He called the crowd's attention to the author of *The Strange Career of Jim Crow*, a book that he described as "the historical Bible of the civil rights movement."

A year later, Stokely Carmichael, who had succeeded John Lewis as head of the Student Non-Violent Coordinating Committee, announced the new slogan and policy of Black Power. This was on the mass march through Mississippi in June 1966, the dramatic continuation of the "march against fear" by James Meredith that had been interrupted by a white farmer who had leaped out of the bushes and shot the lonely hero, wounding him and ending his march. Black Power became the aggressive motto and goal of SNCC, reorienting the civil rights movement, as whites were ushered out. When Woodward was asked to endorse the SNCC Faculty Fund, he replied with civility that he could not endorse Black Power because he was devoted to the philosophy and organizations of his friends such as Martin Luther King.

WHEN WOODWARD STOOD AT the podium on December 28, 1969, in Washington, D.C., to deliver his presidential address to the assembled membership of the American Historical Association, he was at the height of his career. Earlier in that same year he had completed his year of service as the president of the Organization of American Historians with a speech, "Clio with Soul," on the importance of African American history, an importance so great that the task could not be left only to black historians. Woodward had served as president of the Southern Historical Association in 1952 in the early stage of his remarkable career. This trifecta is evidence of his standing as perhaps the most admired American historian of the second half of the 20th century, a public intellectual with a broad readership and abundant influence within the historical profession and in the life of the country more generally.

The irony of this moment in the life of the master ironist is that it was also the low point. His only son, Peter, a promising graduate student at Princeton University, had died of cancer in the summer of 1969. His close friend Richard Hofstadter was terminally ill. His wife, Glenn, was in a deep depression over their son's death, a depression from which she never fully recovered. Furthermore, the 2,000 historians who sat before him, ten times the usual number at this session of the annual meeting, were excited not so much by the prospect of hearing Woodward's discussion of "The Future of the Past" as by the likelihood of fireworks to follow. After speaking, Woodward was to convene the business meeting which was to consider not only some bland administrative measures for the most comprehensive professional association for historians in the United States, but also a resolution putting the AHA on record as being opposed to the war in Vietnam.

Another irony of this moment in Woodward's life is that he was fervently anti-war, but he was just as fervently against having the AHA take a political position. That was not its purpose, and to act politically would abuse the rights of members who were not anti-war but who belonged to the AHA because of its services to the profession of history. Indeed, in his address, after describing how the historical profession had enjoyed a boom in popularity in the two decades following the end of World War II, a boom that had begun to be reversed in the Sixties with the rise of the "Now" generation, Woodward warned that "a fatal betrayal of the craft would be to permit the profession of history to become inextricably entangled with the future of the past, the purposeful past of the rationalizers, the justifiers, and the propagandists."[8] Members, of course, could express opinions and take positions, but the organization should remain open to ideas of every variety. If it took a political stance, those who disagreed would feel misrepresented and less welcome. On matters related to teaching and research, the AHA should speak and act in furtherance of its mission to promote and improve teaching and research. As an organization, it should leave politics alone. After much drama, the anti-war resolution failed to pass.

THOUGH THIS WAS A turning point in Woodward's career, he did not disappear from the scene. The rise of the Black Power movement, and the revolutionary tendencies of the New Left, did not carry Woodward along with them. He spent the 1970s as a major player in several dramatic conflicts at Yale and in New Haven in which he seemed to be an opponent of the tactics of the Left. For example, he did not go out of his way to support Staughton Lynd for promotion to tenure in the History Department after Lynd visited North Vietnam as a gesture against the war in Vietnam. Lynd left Yale a year before his non-tenured appointment was to end.

Woodward served as chair of a committee on free speech appointed by President Kingman Brewster, after Brewster had made headlines by saying that it might be impossible for a black man to get a fair trial in New Haven, and after leftist students disrupted the public speech of an infamous conservative. That committee produced a report in defense of free speech on Yale's campus that has become a Yale classic. Brewster took the report to the Yale Corporation where it was confirmed in spring 1975 as Yale policy. Woodward also resigned in protest from the advisory committee to Herbert Aptheker for his edited volumes of the W. E. B. Du Bois papers. Shortly thereafter, Woodward unsuccessfully led the opposition to Aptheker's appointment as a visiting professor at Yale. After retiring as Sterling Professor of History at Yale University at the end of the academic year 1976–77, he remained active as a scholar and public figure until his death in 1999. Indeed, he was awarded the Pulitzer Prize in 1982 for his editing of *Mary Chesnut's Civil War*.

A measure of his continuing status is the symposium at Rice University in February 2001 on the fiftieth anniversary of the publication of *Origins of the New South*, the book that remains the starting point for scholars studying the late 19th- and early 20th-century South. The papers from that symposium were rushed into print in the *Journal of Southern History* in November of that same year.

His activism also persisted, and he never gave up on his old causes.[9] He provided scholarly support for John Doar's investigations for the House Judiciary Committee looking into the possible impeachment of Richard Nixon in 1974. He testified in favor of the extension of the Voting Rights Act in 1981. He testified with Sean Wilentz and Arthur Schlesinger Jr. in 1998 against the pending impeachment of William Jefferson Clinton.

Woodward did not sour. He applied consistent principles, but the threat to those principles changed over time. As the left indulged in what Woodward came to judge as excesses of action and rhetoric that cost it public support, he did not talk about the shift as merely a matter of pragmatic calculation. Revolutionary rhetoric and black nationalism were offenses against his strongly held liberal principles, especially to his devotion to free speech, academic freedom, and intellectual integrity, as well as to his life-long commitment to racial integration.

Notes

1   The existing biography of Woodward is: John Herbert Roper, *C. Vann Woodward, Southerner* (Athens: The University of Geogia Press, 1987).

2   James Green, "Past and Present in Southern History: An Interview with C. Vann Woodward," *Radical History Review* 36 (1986), 83.

3   John Herbert Roper, interview with C. Vann Woodward, June 20, 1983. Roper Papers, Southern Historical Collection, University of North Carolina, Chapel Hill.

4   Ibid.

5   Erik Erikson, *Young Man Luther: A Study in Psychoanalysis and History* (New York: The Norton Library, W. W. Norton , 1958).

6   John Egerton, interview with CVW, xxxx, Southern Oral History Project.

7   James Green, "Past and Present in Southern History," 83.

8   C. Vann Woodward, *The Future of the Past* (New York: Oxford University Press, 1989), 23. See also, John Herbert Roper (ed.), *C. Vann Woodward: A Southern Historian and His Critics*, Athens: The University of Georgia Press, 1997.

9   See my article, "C. Vann Woodward, Dissenter," *Historically Speaking*, Vol. X, No. 1 (January 2009), 31-34.

Select Bibliography of
Sheldon Hackney's Writings

Books

Populism To Progressivism in Alabama. Princeton: Princeton University Press, 1969.

Populism: The Critical Issues. ed. Boston: Little, Brown and Co., 1971.

Understanding the American Experience: Recent Interpretations. 2 vols., ed. With James M. Banner, Jr. and Barton J. Bernstein. San Diego: Harcourt Brace Jovanovich, Inc., 1973.

Partners in the Research Enterprise: University-Corporate Relations in Science and Technology. prologue and co-editor, Philadelphia: University of Pennsylvania Press, 1983.

One America Indivisible: A National Conversation on Pluralism and Identity. Washington: Government Printing Office for the National Endowment for the Humanities, 1997.

The Politics of Presidential Appointment: A Memoir of the Culture War. Montgomery: NewSouth Books, 2002.

Magnolias Without Moonlight. New Brunswick: Transaction Publishers, 2005.

Following Virginia, 1958–2007. Raleigh: Lulu, 2009.

Journal Articles And Book Chapters

"Southern Violence," *American Historical Review*. LXXIV (February 1969): 906–925.

"Power To The Computers: A Revolution in History?" *AFIPS, Proceedings of the 1970 Spring Joint Computer Conference.*

"Origins of the New South in Retrospect," *Journal of Southern History*, 38 (May 1972): 191–216.

"The South as a Counterculture," *The American Scholar*, Vol. 42, No. 2, (Spring 1973): 283–293.

Introduction, Gerald Gaither, *Blacks and the Populist Revolt*. Tuscaloosa: University of Alabama Press, 1977.

"System for the Twenty-First Century," *Universities and Community Schools* (Univ. of Pennsylvania), 4 (Fall–Winter 1994): 9–11.

"The American Identity," *The Public Historian*, Vol. 19, No. 1, (Winter 1997): "Education for the Pursuit of Happiness," *Proceedings of the American Revolutionary Colleges Conference on the Liberal Arts and Education for Citizenship in the Twenty-First Century* (March 26–27, 1998), Dickinson College, Carlisle, Pennsylvania, 72–77.

"Higher Education as a Medium of Culture," *American Behavioral Scientist*, Vol. 42, No. 6, (March 1999): 987–97.

"Little Rock and the Promise of America," in Elizabeth Jacaway and C. Fred Williams (eds.), *Understanding the Little Rock Crisis: An Exercise in Remembrance and Reconciliation*. Fayettville: University of Arkansas Press, 1999, 23–28.

"Culture and Democracy in America," in Alexander Bearn (ed.), *Useful Knowledge: The American Philosophical Society Millennium Program* (Philadelphia: The American Philosophical Society, 1999), 283–294. (A paper read April 24, 1999).

"In Memoriam: C. Vann Woodward (1908–1999)," *OAH Newsletter* (February 2000): 1, 10.

"C. Vann Woodward, 1908–1999: In Memoriam," *The Journal of Southern History* (May 2000): 207–214.

"The Contradictory South," *Southern Cultures* 7 (Winter 2001): 64–80.

"C. Vann Woodward," *Proceedings of the American Philosophical Society: Biographical Memoirs*, Vol. 145, No. 2, (June 2001): 234–240.

"Woodward, C(omer) Vann," *Scribners Encyclopedia of American Lives* (New York: Charles Scribner's Sons, 2002), Vol. 5. (1997–1999) 631–633.

"Remarks on the 200th Anniversary of the Accession of John Marshall as Chief Justice," *Journal of Supreme Court History*, Vol. 27, No. 3 ( ): 219–221.

"The Ambivalent South," in *Warm Ashes*, edited by Wilfred B. Moore. Columbia: University of South Carolina Press, 2003.

"Origins of the New South in Retrospect Thirty Years Later," in John B. Boles and Bethany L. Johnson (eds.), *Origins of the New South Fifty Years Later: The Continuing Influence of a Historical Classic*. Baton Rouge: Louisiana State University Press, 2003, 25–58.

"Identity Politics, Southern Style," in Anthony Dunbar (ed.), *Where We Stand*. Montgomery: NewSouth Books, 2004, 181–196.

"C. Vann Woodward, Dissenter," *Historically Speaking*, Vol. X, No. 1 (January 2009): 31–34.

"Shades of Freedom in America," Jose V. Ciprut (ed.), *Freedom: Restatements and Rephrasings*. Cambridge: The MIT Press, 2008, 253–272.

"C. Vann Woodward: The Outsider as Insider," in Raymond Arsenault and Orville Vernon Burton, eds., *Dixie Redux: Essays in Honor of Sheldon Hackney*. Montgomery: NewSouth Books, 2013.

"Social Justice, the Church, and the Counterculture, 1963–1979," in David R. Contosta (ed.), *This Far by Faith: Tradition and Change in the Episcopal Diocese of Pennsylvania*. University Park: The Pennsylvania State University Press, 2012), 298–334.

NEWSPAPER AND EDUCATION ARTICLES

"Policing Is Not For Colleges," *The Philadelphia Inquirer*, Op-ed page, August 9, 1984.

"Student Financial Aid for Public service," *The Philadelphia Inquirer*, Op-ed page, November 14, 1985.

"Angling for Red Herrings in Academe," The Christian Science Monitor, December 9, 1985.

"College Shouldn't Be Just For The Rich," *The Philadelphia Inquirer*, February 9, 1986.

Is My Armor Straight? A Year In The Life Of A College President, Richard Berendzen, Adler and Adler, 1986. Review in *The Philadelphia Inquirer*, June 15, 1987.

"Skyrocketing Tuition: Why College Is So Expensive," *Educational Records*, American Council on Education, Spring/Summer 1986.

"Colleges Must Not Cut Quality To Curb Costs," *USA Today*, guest editorial, March 3, 1987.

"Cutting Student Aid Would Be Unfair," *The Washington Post*, guest editorial, May 17, 1987.

"Idealism Is Alive On Campus And Can Be Lifelong," *The Philadelphia Inquirer*, Op-ed page, April 8, 1989.

"The Helms Amendment Imperils The Basis Of Intellectual Freedom," *The Chronicle of Higher Education*, September 6, 1989.

"Perspectives on Literacy," *YMCA Souvenir Journal*, October 1990.

"Dealing With Campus Rape," *Higher Education and National Affairs*, American Council on Education, Vol. 40, No. 4, February 25, 1991.

"Campuses Aren't Besieged By Politically Correct Storm Troopers," *The Philadelphia Inquirer*, Op-ed page, October 3, 1991.

"Don't Relegate Education To The Marketplace," (with Marvin Lazerson) *The Philadelphia Inquirer*, Op-ed page, July 12, 1992.

"Organizing A National Conversation," *The Chronicle of Higher Education*, April 20, 1994. .

"At Century's End, What Kind of Nation Are We?" *Birmingham News*, May 23, 1999 (Commencement Address, University of Alabama).

"Amerikaner Sein Dagegen Sehr: Was Die US-Amerikanische Einwanderung Lehrt: Wunsch Und Wirklichkeit Liegen Oft Weit Auseinander," *Die Welt*, September 6, 2000. Op-ed page.

Contributors

RAYMOND ARSENAULT is the John Hope Franklin Professor of Southern History and chair of the Department of History and Politics at the University of South Florida, St. Petersburg. He is the author of several prize-winning books and essays, including "The End of the Long Hot Summer: The Air Conditioner and Southern Culture," *Journal of Southern History* (1984), *The Wild Ass of the Ozarks: Jeff Davis and the Social Bases of Southern Politics, Freedom Riders: 1961 and the Struggle for Racial Justice,* and *The Sound of Freedom: Marian Anderson, the Lincoln Memorial, and the Concert That Awakened America.* The 2011 PBS *American Experience* documentary, *Freedom Riders,* based on his book, won three Emmys and a George Peabody Award.

ORVILLE VERNON BURTON is Creativity Professor of the Humanities; Professor of History, Sociology, and Computer Science; and director of the Clemson CyberInstitute at Clemson University. From 1974 to 2008, he taught at the University of Illinois where he is emeritus University Distinguished Teacher/Scholar, University Scholar, Professor of History, African American Studies and Sociology, and from 2008 to 2010, he was the Burroughs Distinguished Professor of Southern History and Culture at Coastal Carolina University. His many books include *In My Father's House Are Many Mansions: Family and Community in Edgefield, South Carolina,* and the award-winning *The Age of Lincoln.* In 2004, he received the American Historical Association's Eugene Asher Distinguished Teaching Prize, and in 2011–12 he served as president of the Southern Historical Association.

DREW GILPIN FAUST is President of Harvard University, where she is also the Lincoln Professor of History. The former dean of the Radcliffe Institute and a member of the History and American Civilization faculties at the University of Pennsylvania for 25 years, she is the author of *The Creation of Confederate Nationalism: Ideology and Identity in the Civil War South, Mothers of Invention: Women of the Slaveholding South in the Civil* War, which won the Francis Parkman Prize in 1997, and *This Republic of Suffering: Death and the Civil War*, which won the Bancroft Prize in 2009. In 1999–2000, she served as president of the Southern Historical Association.

WILLIAM R. FERRIS is the Joel L. Williamson Eminent Professor of History and senior associate director of the Center for the Study of the American South at the University of North Carolina, Chapel Hill. He is also an adjunct instructor in Folklore at UNC. From 1997 to 2001, he served as chairman of the National Endowment for the Humanities. He has produced more than a dozen documentary films, and he co-edited (with Charles Reagan Wilson) the monumental *Encyclopedia of Southern Culture*. He is also the author of *Blues from the Delta, Local Color, Images of the South: Visits with Eudora Welty and Walker Evans*, and *Give My Poor Heart Ease: Voices of the Mississippi Blues*.

PAUL M. GASTON is Professor of History Emeritus at the University of Virginia, where he taught from 1957 until his retirement in 1997. He is the author of *The New South Creed*, which won the 1970 Lillian Smith Book Award, *Women of Fair Hope, Man and Mission: E. B. Gaston and the Origins of the Fairhope Single Tax Colony,* and *Coming of Age in Utopia: The Odyssey of an Idea*. In 1978 he received the Bethune-Roosevelt Award for contributions to racial understanding, in 2008 the NAACP Legendary Activist Award, and in 2013 the Martin Luther King Jr. Award from the city of Charlottesville. He is a Life Fellow and former president of the Southern Regional Council.

LANI GUINIER is the Bennett Boskey Professor of Law at Harvard University. From 1988 to 1998, she taught at the law school of the University of Pennsylvania, where she got to know both Sheldon and Lucy Hackney. Prior to joining the Penn faculty, from 1981 to 1988 she was assistant counsel at the NAACP Legal Defense and Educational Fund. She is the author of *The Tyranny of the Majority: Fundamental Fairness in Representative Democracy; Lift Every Voice: Turning a Civil Rights Setback into a New Vision of Social Justice; Becoming Gentlemen: Women, Law School and Institutional Change* (with Michelle Fine and Jane Balin); and *The Miner's Canary: Enlisting Race,*

Resisting Power, Transforming Democracy (with Gerald Torres).

STEVEN HAHN is the Roy F. and Jeanette P. Nichols Professor of American History at the University of Pennsylvania. He taught previously at the University of California, San Diego, and Northwestern University. He is the author of *The Roots of Southern Populism: Yeoman Farmers and the Transformation of Georgia's Upper Piedmont, 1850–1899, The Political Worlds of Slavery and Freedom,* and *A Nation Under Our Feet: Black Political Struggles in the Rural South from Slavery to the Great Migration,* which was awarded the Pulitzer Prize in History, the Bancroft Prize, and the Merle Curti Prize in Social History in 2004.

CHARLES JOYNER is Burroughs Distinguished Professor Emeritus of Southern History and Culture at Coastal Carolina University. He also taught at the University of Alabama and was visiting professor at the University of South Carolina; the University of Mississippi; the University of California, Berkeley; and the University of Sydney, Australia. He was an Associate of the Du Bois Institute for African and African American Research at Harvard University. Among his books are *Down by the Riverside: A South Carolina Slave Community,* which was named winner of the National University Press Book Award by the Eugene M. Kayden Fund, and *Shared Traditions: Southern History and Folk Culture.* In 2004–05 he served as president of the Southern Historical Association.

RANDALL L. KENNEDY is the Michael R. Klein Professor of Law at Harvard University. He is the author of *Race, Crime, and the Law, Nigger: The Strange Career of a Troublesome Word, Interracial Intimacies: Sex, Marriage, Identity and Adoption, Sellout: The Politics of Racial Betrayal,* and *Persistence of the Color Line: Racial Politics and the Obama Presidency.* A leading public commentator on racial and legal issues, he is a frequent contributor to the *New York Times, American Prospect,* and *The New Republic.*

J. MORGAN KOUSSER is William R. Kenan Jr. Professor of History and Social Science at the California Institute of Technology. He is the author of *The Shaping of Southern Politics: Suffrage Restriction and the Establishment of the One-Party South,* and *Colorblind Injustice: Minority Voting Rights and the*

Undoing of the Second Reconstruction, which won the Lillian Smith Prize and the Ralph M. Bunche Prize of the American Political Science Association. He was the editor of the journal *Historical Methods* 2000–2013. He has also served as an expert witness in 33 state or federal voting rights or school desegregation cases.

PEYTON MCCRARY is a historian in the Civil Rights Division of the U.S. Department of Justice, where he has worked since 1990, specializing in voting rights cases. He is also a Professorial Lecturer in Law at the George Washington University Law School, and from 1996 to 1999, he was the Eugene Lang Visiting Professor at Swarthmore College. He taught previously at the University of Minnesota, Vanderbilt University, and the University of South Alabama. He is the author of *Abraham Lincoln and Reconstruction: The Louisiana Experiment.*

STEPHANIE MCCURRY is the Christopher H. Browne Distinguished Professor of History at the University of Pennsylvania. She taught previously at the University of California, San Diego, and Northwestern University. She is the author of *Masters of Small Worlds: Yeoman Households and the Political Culture of the Antebellum South Carolina Low Country*, which was awarded the John Hope Franklin Prize by the American Studies Association and the Charles S. Sydnor Prize by the Southern Historical Association, and *Confederate Reckoning: Power and Politics in the Civil War South*, which won the Frederick Douglass Prize and was a finalist for the Pulitzer Prize in History in 2011.

JAMES M. MCPHERSON is the George Henry Davis '86 Professor of American History Emeritus at Princeton University. The nation's preeminent Civil War historian, he is the author of *The Struggle for Equality, The Abolitionist Legacy, Ordeal by Fire: The Civil War and Reconstruction, Crossroads of Freedom: Antietam, The Battle That Changed the Course of the Civil War, For Cause and Comrades: Why Men Fought in the Civil War*, which won the Abraham Lincoln Prize in 1998, *Tried by War: Abraham Lincoln as Commander in Chief*, which won the Abraham Lincoln Prize in 2009, and *The Battle Cry of Freedom*, which won the Pulitzer Prize in History in 1989.

DAVID MOLTKE-HANSEN, who lives in Asheville, North Carolina, is an independent scholar and the former president of the Historical Society of Pennsylvania. He is also the former director of both the Southern Historical Collection at the University of North Carolina, Chapel Hill, and Special Collections at the South Carolina Historical Society and the Simms Initiatives of the University of South Carolina. He is editor of *Art in the Lives of South Carolinians, Intellectual Life in Antebellum Charleston* (with Michael O'Brien), *Women & History, Culture & Faith* (five volumes of Elizabeth Fox-Genovese's selected, uncollected writings), and *William Gilmore Simms's Unfinished Civil War.* He and Mark Smith edit Cambridge Studies on the American South.

MICHAEL O'BRIEN is Professor of American Intellectual History at the University of Cambridge and a Fellow of the British Academy. He is the author of, among other works, *Conjectures of Order: Intellectual Life in the American South, 1810–1860* (2 vols.), which won several awards, including the Bancroft Prize; he has twice been a Nominated Finalist for the Pulitzer Prize. His most recent book is an edition of *The Letters of C. Vann Woodward* (2013).

THOMAS SUGRUE is the David Boies Professor of History and Sociology and Director of the Penn Social Science and Policy Forum at the University of Pennsylvania. He is the author of *The Origins of the Urban Crisis,* which was awarded several prizes including the 1998 Bancroft Prize; *Sweet Land of Liberty: The Forgotten Struggle for Civil Rights in the North;* and *Not Even Past: Barack Obama and the Burden of Race.* With Michael Kazin, Marco Canaday, and Glenda Gilmore, he is co-editor of the book series "Politics and Culture in Modern America" published by the University of Pennsylvania Press.

PATRICIA SULLIVAN is Professor of History at the University of South Carolina and a Fellow of the W. E. B. Du Bois Institute at Harvard University, where since 1997 she and Waldo Martin have conducted an NEH summer seminar on "Teaching the Civil Rights Movement." She is the author of *Days of Hope: Race and Democracy in the New Deal Era,* and *Lift Every Voice: The NAACP and the Making of the Civil Rights Movement.* She is also the editor of *Freedom Writer: Virginia Foster Durr, Letters from the Civil Rights Years,* and with Waldo Martin, the two-volume encyclopedia *Civil Rights in the United States.*

J. MILLS THORNTON III is Professor of History Emeritus at the University of Michigan. In 2007–08, he was the Pitt Professor of American History and Institutions at the University of Cambridge. He is the author of *Politics and Power in a Slave Society: Alabama, 1800–1860*, which was awarded several prizes including the 1978 John H. Dunning Prize, and *Dividing Lines: Municipal Politics and the Struggle for Civil Rights in Montgomery, Birmingham, and Selma*, which won the Organization of American Historians' Liberty Legacy Foundation Award in 2002.

Index